THE LAW OF HUMAN RIGHTS
SECOND ANNUAL UPDATING SUPPLEMENT

THE LAW OF HUMAN RIGHTS

SECOND ANNUAL UPDATING SUPPLEMENT

by

RICHARD CLAYTON, QC

Barrister, 39 Essex Street, London
Visiting Fellow, Centre for Public Law, University of Cambridge

HUGH TOMLINSON, QC

Barrister, Matrix Chambers, London

Contributing Editors

NIAZI FETTO, *Barrister, 2 Temple Gardens*
AKASH NAWBATT, *Barrister, Devereux Chambers*
VINA SHUKLA, *Barrister, 4 Stone Buildings*
DANIEL SQUIRES, *Barrister, Matrix Chambers*

Contributors

NICOLA GREANEY, *Barrister, 39 Essex Street*
SUZANNE MCKIE, *Barrister, Devereux Chambers*
GORDON NARDELL, *Barrister, 39 Essex Street*
VIKRAM SACHDEVA, *Barrister, 39 Essex Street*
KATHERINE SCOTT, *Barrister, 39 Essex Street*
MATTHEW SELIGMAN, *Barrister, 39 Essex Street*

OXFORD

UNIVERSITY PRESS

OXFORD

UNIVERSITY PRESS

Great Clarendon Street, Oxford OX2 6DP

Oxford University Press is a department of the University of Oxford.
It furthers the University's objective of excellence in research, scholarship,
and education by publishing worldwide in

Oxford New York

Auckland Bangkok Buenos Aires Cape Town Chennai
Dar es Salaam Delhi Hong Kong Istanbul Karachi Kolkata
Kuala Lumpur Madrid Melbourne Mexico City Mumbai Nairobi
São Paulo Shanghai Taipei Tokyo Toronto

Oxford is a registered trade mark of Oxford University Press
in the UK and in certain other countries

Published in the United States
by Oxford University Press Inc., New York

First published 2001
Second annual updating supplement published 2003

Crown copyright material is reproduced under Class Licence Number
C01P0000148 with the permission of the Controller of HMSO
and the Queen's Printer for Scotland

British Library Cataloguing in Publication Data

Data available

Library of Congress Cataloging in Publication Data

Data available

Second Updating Supplement 0-19-925431-1
Main Work and Second Updating Supplement 0-19-925822-8

1 3 5 7 9 10 8 6 4 2

Typeset in Garamond by
Cambrian Typesetters, Frimley, Surrey

Printed in Great Britain
on acid-free paper by
Biddles Ltd, Guildford and King's Lynn

CONTENTS

v

IV REMEDIES AND PROCEDURES

APPENDICES

INTRODUCTION

The Law of Human Rights was published in September 2000, less than a week before the Human Rights Act 1998 came into full force. The first two years of the Act's existence have not been altogether easy. They began quietly, with little sign of the constitutional revolution predicted by its exponents. Despite the occasional outburst of criticism from the press and politicians,[1] the Act continues to receive a generally positive reception. Although the Act has now been relied on in several hundred cases, in many of these the human rights arguments did not play a central role.

The Act has been decisive in a small number of cases[2] but its principal significance is more long term. It has provided a template for developments in many different fields. The 'tentacles' of the Act have reached into some unexpected places:[3] from the Commercial Court to the Chancery Division. The House of Lords has recognised the need, in Lord Slynn's metaphor, to be prepared to cull sacred jurisprudential cows.[4] The language of the law has begun to undergo a subtle but decisive change. The vocabulary of the common law has begun to absorb that of human rights, the 'reasonable man' has begun to give way to the requirement of 'proportionality'.[5]

In this Introduction we shall briefly discuss some of the important decisions concerning the Act during the first two years of its operation. We will also deal with developments in Strasbourg. The Introduction concludes with a comment on the organization of this Supplement to the Main Work.

Statutory construction under the Human Rights Act

One of the most important but uncertain questions under the Act is the impact of section 3 which requires the court to construe legislation 'so far as possible'

---

[1] Most notably in relation to the position of asylum seekers which recently led the Prime Minister to suggest that it might be necessary to withdraw from the Convention.

[2] The extent to which the Human Rights Act has affected the outcome of cases is inevitably controversial; see, eg, the analysis in E M Salgado and C O'Brien, 'Table of Cases Under the Human Rights Act' [2001] EHRLR 181; [2001] EHRLR 376; [2002] EHRLR 80; [2002] EHRLR 239 and 245; [2002] EHRLR 364; [2002] EHRLR 493 and 502.

[3] In the words of David Steel J in *Mousaka Inc v Golden Seagull Maritime* [2002] 1 WLR 395.

[4] *R v Lambert* [2001] 3 WLR 206, 210.

[5] See, eg, *London Regional Transport v The Mayor of London* [2003] EMLR 3, para 55, *per* Sedley LJ.

compatibly with Convention rights. The principles to be applied have been extensively analysed in a number of decisions of the House of Lords.[6]

This new approach to construction will radically alter the meaning of statutes. For example, in *R v Offen*[7] the Court of Appeal interpreted the power[8] to impose an automatic life sentence following a conviction for a second serious offence in accordance with section 3 of the Human Rights Act and adopted a broad interpretation of the phrase 'exceptional circumstances'. Such an approach did not contravene the prohibition on inhuman and degrading treatment.[9]

In *Cachia v Faluyi*[10] the Court of Appeal held that a provision of the Fatal Accidents Act 1976 barring a second action 'in respect of the same subject matter of complaints' had to be construed, in the light of Article 6, as not applying where the first writ had been issued but not served. Brooke LJ commented that the case was 'a very good example of the way in which the enactment of the Human Rights Act now enables English judges to do justice in a way which was not previously open to us'.[11]

The limits of a section 3 construction were examined by the House of Lords in *Re S (Care Order: Implementation of Care Plan)*.[12] Not only will section 3 be defeated by express words but the use of section 3 will also be impermissible where, by necessary implication, it conflicts with a cardinal feature of the legislation under consideration.

There have been a number of occasions where the courts have found that section 3 was insufficient to render a statutory provision compatible with Convention rights. As a result, the courts have exercised their powers to make 'declarations of incompatibility' under section 4 of the Act. In *R (H) v Mental Health Review Tribunal*[13] certain provisions of the Mental Health Act 1983 were declared to be incompatible with Article 5[14] and have been the subject of a remedial order under section 10 of the Act. In *Wilson v First County Trust (No 2)*[15] the bar to the enforcement of improperly executed consumer credit agreements under the Consumer Credit Act 1974 was declared incompatible with Article 1 of the First

---

[6] See *R v A (No 2)* [2002] 1 AC 45, *per* Lord Steyn at 1062, 1064, paras 44, 45 and *R v Lambert* [2001] 3 WLR 206, *per* Lord Hope at 233, 235; and *In Re S (Care Order: Implementation of Care Plan)* [2002] 2 AC 291, *per* Lord Nicholls at paras 40, 41 (see, further, Supplement, para 4.28).

[7] [2001] 1 WLR 253.

[8] Formerly the Criminal (Sentences) Act 1997, s 2, and now the Powers of the Criminal Courts (Sentencing) Act 2000, s 109.

[9] See Supplement, para 8.71A.

[10] [2002] 1 WLR 1966.

[11] Ibid, para 21; see Supplement, para 11.306.

[12] [2002] 2 AC 291; see Supplement, para 4.28.

[13] [2001] 3 WLR 512.

[14] See Supplement, para 10.182.

[15] [2002] QB 74.

Protocol.[16] In *R (International Transport Roth) v Secretary of State for the Home Department*[17] the Court of Appeal held that the statutory scheme which penalized carriers of illegal immigrants into the UK under the Immigration and Asylum Act breached Article 6 and made a declaration of incompatibility. In *Hooper v Secretary of State for Work and Pension*[18] Moses J took the view that sections 36 to 38 of the Social Security Contributions Act was discriminatory against widowers and therefore with Article 14, read together with Article 1 of the First Protocol, and made a declaration of incompatibility. In *Wilkinson v Inland Revenue Commissioners*[19] he made another declaration holding that section 262 of the Income and Corporations Taxes Act discriminated against widowers. In *R (Anderson) v Secretary of State for the Home Department*[20] the House of Lords made a declaration of incompatibility after holding that the setting of a tariff for a mandatory life prisoner by the Home Secretary breached Article 6.

Changes to the common law

The courts have, in general, refused 'to rest on the laurels of earlier judicial statements, albeit of high authority, that the English common law already conforms'[21] with the Convention. The Human Rights Act has led to substantive changes in the common law in several areas:

- the removal of the liability for 'unintentional defamation' by lookalike photographs as being inconsistent with Article 10 (*O'Shea v MGN*); and[22]
- the removal of the liability of the owner of former rectorial glebe land to pay the cost of chancel repairs as being inconsistent with Article 1 of the First Protocol and Article 14 (*Aston Cantlow v Wallbank*).[23]

As was widely predicted[24] the right to respect for private life under Article 8 has encouraged development of the common law. In *Douglas v Hello!*[25] the Court of Appeal set aside an interlocutory injunction restraining *Hello!* magazine from publishing celebrity wedding pictures the exclusive rights to which had been sold to its rival *OK!* The Court of Appeal was not prepared to recognise a new tort of privacy, preferring to consider the claim as an arguable breach of confidence.[26] Although Sedley LJ expressed the view that 'we have reached a point at

---

[16] See Supplement, para 4.47.
[17] [2002] 3 WLR 344.
[18] [2002] UKHRR 785.
[19] (2002) STC 347.
[20] [2002] 3 WLR 1800.
[21] *Berezovsky v Forbes* [2001] EMLR 1030.
[22] [2001] EMLR 943 (Morland J); see Supplement, para 15.252.
[23] [2002] Ch 51; see Supplement, para 18.99.
[24] See, eg, Main Work, paras 12.165ff.
[25] [2001] QB 967.
[26] Ibid, *per* Brooke LJ at para 96 and Keene LJ at para 166.

which it can be said with confidence that the law recognizes and will appropriately protect a right of personal privacy',[27] he said that the right was 'grounded' in the equitable doctrine of breach of confidence. Sedley LJ took the view that 'the law no longer needs to construct an artificial relationship of confidentiality between intruder and victim'; instead, the right to privacy could be substituted for this element of the tort.[28] (The trial of this action is taking place at the time of writing.)

In *Venables v News Group Newspapers Ltd*[29] the children who had murdered the infant James Bulger were granted injunctions against the whole world to prevent the publication of information which might lead to their identification. Dame Elizabeth Butler-Sloss P considered such relief constituted an 'extension of the law of confidence' which was warranted by the 'exceptional circumstances' of the case. In particular, the court was concerned that as a result of the widespread hatred of the applicants and the many threats to their lives, the publication of information which might lead to their identification posed a real risk to the rights of the applicants under Articles 2 and 3 of the Convention. The judge said that she was 'uncertain' whether it would be appropriate to grant injunctions to restrict the press in this case if only Article 8 were likely to be breached.[30]

It nevertheless remains unclear whether the Act will lead to the development of a new tort of privacy. The Court of Appeal has provided guidelines to be applied where injunctions are sought against the media to protect rights to privacy.[31] At present the case law indicates a number of different approaches are being taken.[32] The issue is likely to be clarified over the next twelve months.

The criminal law

It was widely predicted that the Human Rights Act would modify the criminal law in many respects. A large number of claims have been brought but most have been unsuccessful. There have been important decisions on the following points:

- that an alleged breach of Convention rights by the trial court could not be relied upon as a ground of appeal in respect of a conviction which took place before the Act came into force;[33]

---

[27] Ibid, para 110.
[28] Ibid, para 126; see Supplement, para 12.201.
[29] [2001] Fam 430.
[30] See Supplement, para 12.201.
[31] *A v B plc* [2002] 3 WLR 542.
[32] See Supplement, para 12.06.
[33] *R v Lambert* [2001] 3 WLR 206. The point is a controversial one though the House of Lords nevertheless declined to overrule the decision in *R v Kansal (No 2)* [2001] 3 WLR 1562; see Supplement, para 3.75A.

- that the criteria for determining fairness under Article 6 are the same criteria that would be applied when considering an application for exclusion of evidence under section 78 of the Police and Criminal Evidence Act 1984;[34]
- that there would, in general, only be a breach of the 'reasonable time' requirement in Article 6(1) if the accused can show prejudice;[35]
- that the right not to incriminate oneself is not an absolute right and must be balanced against other clear and proper public objectives such as the regulation of road traffic offences;[36]
- that the approach of the English courts to the admission of evidence of undercover officers is consistent with the accused's right to a fair trial;[37]
- that applications for a confiscation order[38] are not subject to Article 6(2) or, if they are, that Article 6(2) is complied with;[39]
- that the refusal of the DPP to give an undertaking not to prosecute a husband for assisting the suicide of his severely disabled wife did not breach Convention rights;[40]
- that breaches of the Official Secrets Act were compatible with Article 10;[41] and
- that it was not in breach of Article 8 for the police to maintain on file DNA and fingerprint samples from individuals who were not convicted of criminal offences.[42]

The most important developments have been in relation to evidence. In *R v A (No 2)*[43] the House of Lords held that the test of admissibility of evidence of previous sexual relations between an accused and a complainant under section 41(3)(c) of the Youth Justice and Criminal Evidence Act 1999 was whether the evidence (and questioning in relation to it) was so relevant to the issue of consent that to exclude it would endanger the fairness of the trial under Article 6 of the Convention. If that test was satisfied, the evidence should not be excluded.[44]

In *R v Lambert*[45] the House of Lords held that the presumptions in sections 5(4) and 28 of the Misuse of Drugs Act 1971 placing a legal burden on the accused were incompatible with Article 6(2). It was pointed out that the imposition of a legal burden meant that the accused must be convicted even if he persuaded the jury that it was as likely to be true as not that he did not know that packages in his

---

[34] *R v Looseley* [2001] 1 WLR 2060.
[35] *A-G's Reference (No 2 of 2001)* [2001] 1 WLR 1869.
[36] *Brown v Stott* [2001] 2 WLR 817.
[37] *A-G's Reference (No 3 of 1999)* [2001] 2 WLR 56.
[38] *Her Majesty's Advocate v McIntosh* [2001] 3 WLR 107.
[39] *R v Benjafield* [2001] 3 WLR 75.
[40] *R (Pretty) v DPP* [2002] 1 AC 800.
[41] *R v Shayler* [2002] 2 WLR 754.
[42] *R (Marper) v Chief Constable of South Yorkshire* [2002] 1 WLR 3223.
[43] [2001] 2 WLR 1546.
[44] See Supplement, para 4.28.
[45] [2001] 3 WLR 206.

possession contained drugs. As a result, the transfer of the legal burden of proof did not satisfy the principle of proportionality. The House of Lords applied section 3 of the Human Rights Act to interpret sections 5(4) and 28 as placing only an evidential burden on the accused.

The compulsory production of documents or other material which have an existence independent of the will of the suspect or accused person is not an infringement of the right to silence and the right not to incriminate oneself.[46]

The impact on public law

Claimants in judicial review cases frequently raise points under the Human Rights Act.[47] The greatest areas of impact are probably in mental health and prisoner cases.

The Court of Appeal made a declaration of incompatibility in *R (H) v Mental Health Review Tribunal*.[48] It decided the system for listing hearings before the Mental Health Review Tribunal breached Article 5(4);[49] but had rather more difficulty in reconciling the requirements of Article 5 with the problems experienced by health authorities when providing community care to patients following their discharge under the Mental Health Act.[50]

Prisoners have achieved some successes in bringing human rights claims. The House of Lords decided in *R (Anderson) v Secretary of State for the Home Department*[51] that the Home Secretary breached Article 6 by setting the tariff for mandatory life prisoners but went on to decide in *R (Lichniak) v Secretary of State for the Home Department*[52] that mandatory life sentences themselves were not unlawful under Articles 3 and 5. In *R (Giles) v Secretary of State for the Home Department*[53] the Court of Appeal held that Article 5(4) did not apply to determinate sentences and took the view that Article 6 rights do not extend to prison disciplinary adjudications[54] or to Parole Board decisions to recall prisoners on licence.[55]

---

[46] *R v Kearns* [2002] EWCA Crim 748; *A-G's Reference (No 7 of 2000)* [2002] 2 Cr App R 286.

[47] There are no overall figures for assessing the number of cases which have raised arguments under the Act. However, the *Practice Statement (Administrative Court: Annual Statement)* [2002] 1 All ER 633 states that they were raised in 19% of the 5,298 cases received.

[48] [2001] 3 WLR 512.

[49] *R (C) v Mental Health Review Tribunal* [2002] 1 WLR 176.

[50] *R v Camden and Islington Health Authority, ex p K* [2001] 3 WLR 553; *R (C) v Secretary of State for the Home Department* [2002] 3 WLR 967.

[51] [2002] 3 WLR 1800.

[52] [2002] 4 All ER 1122.

[53] [2002] 3 All ER 1123.

[54] *R (Al-Hasan) v Secretary of State for the Home Department* [2002] 1 WLR 545.

[55] *R (Giles) v Secretary of State for the Home Department, The Times*, 21 November 2002.

By comparison, challenges in planning cases have not flourished. The House of Lords rejected the root-and-branch attack on the Secretary of State's lack of independence in making policy decisions in *R (Alconbury) v Secretary of State for the Environment*.[56] In that case the House of Lords took the view that planning decisions which breached Article 6 did not require a full rehearing on the merits. The fundamental question was whether there is sufficient judicial control; and this will depend on the nature of the decision in question. In *R (Adlard) v Secretary of State for the Environment*[57] the Court of Appeal held that the rights of third-party objectors were not breached by a failure to give them a public hearing or any form of oral hearing. On the other hand, decisions to grant injunctions for breaches of planning control must comply with the Article 8 rights of those who are affected.[58]

One particularly controversial issue has been the application of Article 6 to public law rights. Following the House of Lords decision in *Alconbury*, the courts have struggled to establish a coherent set of principles to determine when judicial review will be sufficient to satisfy Article 6 where the decision-maker must decide disputes of primary facts.[59] This debate has led in turn to the Court of Appeal looking at the statutory scheme as a whole to see if questions of judgment, discretion and policy predominate over findings of fact.[60]

Impact on family law

The Human Rights Act has had some effect on family law. In *Clibbery v Alan*[61] the Court of Appeal considered the conflict between the Article 10 rights of a party who wished to publicize Family Division proceedings concerning property which had taken place in private and the Article 8 rights of the other party who wished the proceedings to remain confidential. The Court of Appeal adopted the approach of Munby J who held that a blanket prohibition on disclosure was not 'necessary in a democratic society', there was no 'pressing social need' for such a rule and it would not be proportionate to the legitimate aim of protecting Article 8 rights.

The 'judgment summons' procedure in use in the Family Division was not compatible with Article 6.[62] A new procedure for such applications has now been laid down.[63]

---

[56] [2001] 2 WLR 1389.
[57] [2002] 1 WLR 2525.
[58] *Porter v South Bucks DC* [2002] 1 WLR 1359.
[59] See Supplement, para 11.304A.
[60] See *Rona Begum v Tower Hamlets London Borough Council* [2002] 1 WLR 2491; *R (Adlard) v Secretary of State for the Environment* [2002] 2 WLR 2515.
[61] [2002] 2 WLR 1511; see Supplement, para 15.245.
[62] *Mubarak v Mubarak* [2001] 1 FLR 698.
[63] *Practice Direction (Committal Applications)* [2001] 2 All ER 704; see Supplement, para 318A.

Developing Convention principles

Perhaps the most notable achievement of the two years of the Act has been the initial formulation of some of the principles of a domestic human rights jurisprudence. One of the most controversial issues that has arisen concerns the proportionality principle.[64] Initially, the Court of Appeal took an approach which bore strong similarities to *Wednesbury*.[65] However, in *R v Home Secretary, ex p Daly*[66] and *R v A (No 2)*[67] the House of Lords took a stricter approach and held that proportionality required the court to examine:

- whether the legislative objective is sufficiently important to justify limiting the fundamental right;
- whether the measures designed to meet the legislative objective are rationally connected to it; and
- whether the means used to impair the freedom are no more than is necessary to accomplish that objective.

The Court of Appeal has subsequently refined the criteria further in *R (Samaroo) v Home Secretary*.[68] Nevertheless, the approach of the courts to proportionality has been patchy and unpredictable and the courts continue to apply a highly deferential standard of review in some cases.[69]

Another difficult area has been identifying what bodies are public authorities for the purpose of the Act. The two leading decisions of the Court of Appeal[70] have not provided a clear set of criteria for identifying public authorities and appear to take a rather more restrictive view than was envisaged by the promoters of the Act.

The Strasbourg cases

The caseload of the Court of Human Rights continues to increase at a substantial rate. In 2002 there were 28,255 applications registered (as opposed to 13,858 in 2001 and 10,482 in 2000). A total of 985 applications were registered from the United Kingdom (there were 626 in 2000 and 474 in 2001). Between 2 May 2000 and 10 February 2003 the United Kingdom was found to be in violation of Convention rights in 69 judgments of the Court.

---

[64] See Supplement, para 6.81A.

[65] See *R (Mahmood) v Secretary of State for the Home Department* [2001] 1 WLR 840; *R (Isiko) v Secretary of State for the Home Department* [2001] HRLR 295.

[66] [2001] 2 AC 532.

[67] [2002] 1 AC 45.

[68] [2001] UKHRR 1150.

[69] *R (Farrakan) v Secretary of State for the Home Department* [2002] QB 1391; *International Transport Roth v Secretary of State for the Home Department* [2002] 3 WLR 344. Cf *R (Prolife Alliance) v BBC* [2002] 2 All ER 756; see Supplement, para 6.81A.

[70] *Poplar Housing Community Association v Donoghue* [2002] QB 48; *R (Heather) v Leonard Cheshire Foundation* [2002] 2 All ER 936 (see Supplement, para 5.27).

During 2002 the Court of Human Rights gave judgments on the merits in 844 admissible cases (the figure for 2001 was 888). These covered an extremely wide range of topics. The Court's jurisdiction now extends to the whole of Eastern Europe and has had to engage with a new range of problems arising out of the fall of communism, including matters such as the effect of Article 7 on the criminal prosecution of the former leaders of East Germany[71] and the Article 8 justification for the keeping of Romanian secret police records.[72] The notable cases of the past two years include:

- *Jordan v United Kingdom*[73] where the Court laid down a number of requirements which must be fulfilled to ensure an effective investigation to protect the right to life.
- *Keenan v United Kingdom*[74] where the Court rejected a claim that the positive obligation to protect the right to life was breached when a mentally ill patient committed suicide in prison.
- *Cyprus v Turkey*[75] in which the Court considered a large number of complaints arising out of the Turkish military intervention and found breaches of, amongst others, Articles 3, 8, 14 and Article 1 of the First Protocol.
- *Z v United Kingdom*[76] in which the Court departed from its own decision in *Osman* and held that the inability of the applicants to sue the local authority flowed not from an immunity but from the applicable principles governing the substantive right of action in domestic law.
- *Ferrazzini v Italy*[77] in which a Grand Chamber held by a majority of 11 to six that Article 6(1) should not be extended to cover disputes as to the lawfulness of the decisions of the tax authorities.
- *Maaouli v France*[78] in which a Grand Chamber held that a decision regarding the entry, stay or deportation of aliens did not involve a breach under Article 6 of the applicant's 'civil rights or obligations' or a 'criminal charge'.
- *Chapman v United Kingdom*[79] in which the Court decided that planning enforcement proceedings against the occupation of caravans by gypsies did not contravene Article 8.
- *Vgt Verein gegen Tierfabriken v Switzerland*[80] where the Court held that a ban on television advertising by a controversial group promoting animal welfare could not be justified under Article 10.

---

[71] *Streletz, Kessler and Krenz v Germany* (Judgment of 22 March 2001).
[72] *Rotaru v Romania* (2000) 8 BHRC 449.
[73] (2001) 11 BHRC 1; see Supplement, para 7.38.
[74] (2001) 11 BHRC 319; see Supplement, para 7.41.
[75] (2001) 11 BHRC 45; see Supplement, para 8.28A.
[76] (2001) 10 BHRC 384; see Supplement, para 11.175.
[77] (2002) 34 EHRR 1086; see Supplement, para 11.172.
[78] (2000) 10 BHRC 205; see Supplement, para 11.173.
[79] (2001) 11 BHRC 48; see Supplement, para 12.146.
[80] (2001) 10 BHRC 473; see Supplement, para 15.61.

- *Refah Partisi v Turkey*[81] in which the Court held (by a majority of four to three) that a ban on the pro-Islamic Welfare Party in Turkey (which had commanded a substantial proportion of the popular vote) was not a breach of Article 11.
- *Wilson v United Kingdom*[82] where the Court held that inducements to employees to relinquish their trade union membership breached Article 11.
- *Willis v United Kingdom*[83] in which the Court held that an entitlement to a widow's payment and a widowed mother's allowance were possessions within the meaning of Article 1 of the First Protocol.
- *Pretty v United Kingdom*[84] in which the Court rejected complaints that the refusal of the DPP to give an undertaking not to prosecute the applicant for assisting in the suicide of his profoundly disabled wife breached the Convention. However, the Court declined to follow the approach of the House of Lords[85] and held that Article 8 extended to the right to pursue activities which were personally harmful.
- *Hatton v United Kingdom*[86] in which the Court decided that the noise from night flights at Heathrow breached Article 8. The case was referred to the Grand Chamber[87] and judgment is awaited.
- *Ezeh and Connor v United Kingdom*[88] where the Court decided that prison disciplinary hearings were within the scope of Article 6. The case is now to be referred to the Grand Chamber.
- *Stafford v United Kingdom*[89] where the Grand Chamber reassessed the application of the Convention to the mandatory life sentence for murder in the United Kingdom and held that Article 5(4) required continued detention beyond the tariff period to be reviewed by an independent body.
- *Goodwin v United Kingdom*[90] where the Grand Chamber once again departed from previous cases and held that the United Kingdom's failure legally to recognize a gender reassignment breached Article 8.

Organization of the Supplement

The developments that have taken place since October 2000 have inevitably required changes in the way the Supplement has been organized.

---

[81] (2002) 35 EHRR 56; see Supplement, para 16.80.
[82] (2002) 35 EHRR 523; see Supplement, para 16.83.
[83] (2002) 35 EHRR 21; see Supplement, para 18.36.
[84] (2002) 12 BHRC 149; see Supplement, para 12.84.
[85] *R (Pretty) v DPP* [2002] 1 AC 800.
[86] (2002) 34 EHRR 1; see Supplement, para 12.99.
[87] The importance of the hearing before the Grand Chamber was recognized by making it the first subject of a live webcast on the Court's website.
[88] (2002) 35 EHRR 691; see Supplement, para 11.179.
[89] (2002) 35 EHRR 32; see Supplement, para 10.167.
[90] (2002) 35 EHRR 447; see Supplement, para 12.93.

The crucial modifications are in relation to the Convention Rights, Part III of *The Law of Human Rights*. Chapters 7 to 20 of the book have an identical format and are divided into four parts with appendices on international human rights cases. The general developments in English law are discussed in Part B which is now titled 'The Right in English Law' and the domestic Human Rights cases are examined in Part D, 'The Impact of the Human Rights Act'. Where domestic human rights cases contain extensive analysis of Strasbourg principles they are also considered under Part C, 'The Law of the European Convention'.

The law in the Supplement is stated as at 1 December 2002 although we have been able to note some later developments in the Addendum below. We would wish to express our thanks to our Contributing Editors, Contributors and to the many friends and colleagues who have drawn our attention to cases and with whom we have discussed many of the points dealt with in the pages that follow. Any errors and omissions, of course, remain our responsibility.

Richard Clayton QC   Hugh Tomlinson QC
39 Essex Street   Matrix Chambers
                                                15 February 2003

Addendum

The speed of development of the law in this area is such that a number of new cases have been decided since the text of this Supplement was completed. We draw attention, in particular, to the following:

- In *Anufrijeva v Southwark London Borough Council* (4 December 2002, Newman J) the claimants were asylum seekers who had been housed by the respondent local authority in unsuitable accommodation. Their claim for damages under section 8 of the Act was refused because, it was held, an error of judgment, inefficiency or maladministration would rarely give rise to a breach of a positive obligation under the Convention. The infringement would have to amount to a flagrant and deliberate failure to act in the face of obvious and gross circumstances affecting Article 8 rights. On the facts the claim did not engage Article 8.
- In *Shaw (Inspector of Taxes) v Vicky Construction* [2002] STC 1544 a subcontractor complained that the refusal of the tax inspector to issue a certificate allowing it to receive payments without deduction of tax was a breach of Article 1 of the First Protocol. It was held that an interference with property, even for the securing of the payment of taxes, had to strike a proper balance between the general interest and the protection of fundamental rights. On the facts the

interference was not arbitrary or disproportionate and there was no discrimination between the sub-contractor and those of its competitors in a similar position.

- In *R (Williamson) v Secretary of State for Education and Employment* [2003] 1 All ER 385 the appellants were teachers and parents who wished corporal punishment to be administered to their children because, they contended, it was based on Christian principles. They sought a declaration that the abolition of corporal punishment in all schools was a breach of their rights under Articles 8, 9 and 10 and under Article 2 of the First Protocol. The Court of Appeal held that although a complete ban on corporal punishment would interfere with Convention rights there was no interference when the ban was confined to schools because the punishment could be performed by the teachers themselves. The imposition of corporal punishment was not 'expressive content' under Article 10 and Article 8 had no application.

- In *R (Ullah) v Special Adjudicator* [2002] EWCA Civ 1856 the Court of Appeal held that a decision to remove an asylum seeker to a country that did not respect his rights under Article 9 would not be unlawful where the nature of the interference with the right to practise religion that was anticipated fell short of ill-treatment within the terms of Article 3. When considering a decision to deport, the court was not required to recognise any article of the Convention other than Article 3.

- In *R (Beeson) v Secretary of State for Health* [2002] EWCA Civ 1812 the claimant complained that the decision-making procedure of a local authority under the National Assistance Act 1948, where the decision was made by one independent member and two councillors, was not 'independent'. The Court of Appeal, reversing the decision at first instance (see Supplement, para 11.68) held that viewed as a whole, and taking into account the availability of judicial review, the procedure satisfied the requirements of Article 6.

- In *R (D) v Secretary of State for the Home Department* [2002] EWHC Admin 1805 the claimant was a discretionary life prisoner who had been made the subject of a restriction direction under the Mental Health Act 1983. The Mental Health Review Tribunal could not direct a patient's discharge but could notify the Secretary of State that a patient was entitled to be discharged, though the claimant had no statutory right to have his case referred to the Parole Board. It was held that Article 5(4) required the claimant to have access to a court which had power to direct his release. As a result, a declaration of incompatibility was made.

- In *Waite v United Kingdom* (Judgment of 10 December 2002) the applicant complained that the procedure by which the Parole Board had revoked his licence was unfair because he had not been given an oral hearing. The Court held that where characteristics relating to the applicant's personality and level of dangerousness were in issue Article 5(4) required an oral hearing. Since the applicant had no enforceable right to compensation there was also a breach of Article 5(5).

- In *Re Deep Vein Thrombosis and Air Travel Group Litigation* [2002] EWHC 2825 QB it was held that the Warsaw Convention (which limits personal injury claims by air passengers) was a substantive and not a procedural limitation and, as a result, Article 6 of the Convention was not engaged. Article 8 did not require the state to provide a civil remedy.
- In *Obasa v United Kingdom* (Judgment of 16 January 2003) the United Kingdom was found to be in breach of the 'reasonable time' requirement of Article 6(1) in relation to Employment Tribunals which, including appeals, took over seven years.
- In *R v H* [2003] UKHL 1 the House of Lords considered the question whether the procedure for deciding if a defendant was fit to stand trial under section 4 of the Criminal Procedure (Insanity) Act 1964 was incompatible with Article 6. It was held that the purpose and function of the procedure under the 1964 Act was not to decide whether the accused person had committed a criminal offence and Article 6(2) and (3) had no application.
- In *Holder v Law Society*, *The Times*, 29 January 2003, the Court of Appeal allowed the Law Society's appeal against the judge's refusal to strike the action out (see Supplement, para 18.101A). The Court of Appeal held that, although the intervention of the Law Society in the claimant's legal practice involved an interference with his rights under Article 1 of the First Protocol, it was justified in the public interest. The statutory scheme under the Solicitors Act 1974 complied with the Convention.
- In *Van de Ven v Netherlands* (Judgment of 4 February 2003) it was held that the regime under which the applicant was held in a high-security prison, including routine weekly strip searches with other strict security measures, amounted to a breach of Article 3.
- In *Jones v University of Warwick*, *The Times*, 7 February 2003, the Court of Appeal considered an application to exclude evidence obtained by trespassing in the claimant's house and infringing her privacy contrary to Article 8. It was held that a breach of Article 8 did not require the exclusion of evidence. As the conduct of the defendants was not so outrageous that the defence should be struck out, the case should be heard and the evidence placed before the trial judge.
- In *Peck v United Kingdom* (Judgment of 28 January 2003) the Court held that the disclosure by a local authority of CCTV footage taken in a public place of the applicant's attempted suicide was a breach of Article 8 (see Supplement, para 12.164). Although the applicant was in the street he was not there for the purposes of participating in a public event and there were no relevant or sufficient reasons to justify the disclosure of the footage. Judicial review did not provide the applicant with an effective remedy. As a result, there were breaches of Articles 8 and 13 and the applicant was awarded just satisfaction of €11,800 in respect of non-pecuniary loss.

- In *Mudie v Kent Magistrates' Court* (4 February 2003) the Court of Appeal held that condemnation proceedings under the Customs and Excise Management Act 1979 were not 'criminal proceedings' and no penalty was imposed. As a result, the appellants were not entitled to legal aid in these proceedings.
- In *Clark v Kelly, The Times*, 12 February 2003, the Privy Council held that Article 6 required that any advice given by a clerk to the justices in private on matters of law, practice or procedure should be regarded as provisional until the substance of the advice had been repeated in open court and the parties had been given the opportunity to comment on it.
- In *R (KB) v Mental Health Review Tribunal* [2003] EWHC Admin 193 Stanley Burnton J considered the circumstances in which damages should be awarded by the English courts for breaches of Article 5. The cases concerned breaches resulting from delays in hearing applications by the Mental Health Review Tribunal. He held that the English courts should award damages to compensate for injury but an award was not obligatory in every case of breach. Exemplary damages could not be awarded nor could damages for loss of a chance of a favourable tribunal decision. Damages were not to be calculated on an arithmetic rate per day. In some cases the judge held that a finding of a breach of Article 5(4) amounted to sufficient just satisfaction and in other cases sums in the range of £750 to £4,000 were awarded.
- In *Cream Holdings Ltd v Banerjee* [2003] EWCA Civ 103 the Court of Appeal considered the effect of the provisions of section 12(3) of the Act that relief affecting the exercise of the right of freedom of expression should not be granted unless the court is satisfied that the application 'is likely to establish that publication should not be allowed' (see Supplement, para 15.243). The Court held that the test under section 12(3) was not on the 'balance of probabilities' but whether a real prospect of success had been convincingly established.
- In *Matthews v Ministry of Defence* [2003] UKHL 4 the House of Lords held that the issue of a certificate under section 10 of the Crown Proceedings Act 1947 which had the effect of barring the claimant's claim against the Crown formed part of the substantive law. As a result, there was no infringement of Article 6 and the claimant's appeal was dismissed. (For the decision of the Court of Appeal, see Supplement, para 11.303.)
- In *Runa Begum v Tower Hamlets LBC* [2003] UKHL 5 the House of Lords held that the requirements of Article 6 were satisfied if the appellate court had full jurisdiction over an administrative decision but this did not necessarily mean jurisdiction to re-examine the merits of the case. The test as to whether it was necessary to have an independent fact-finder was whether, consistently with the rule of law and constitutional propriety, the relevant decision-making powers could be entrusted to administrators. If so, it did not matter that they needed to make findings of fact. The appeal was, therefore, dismissed. (For the Court of Appeal decision, see Supplement, para 11.304A.)

TABLES OF CASES

A. Alphabetical – All Cases

B. Chronological and Numerical

1. European Commission of Human Rights

2. European Court of Human Rights

3. European Court of Justice and Court of First Instance

TABLES OF LEGISLATION AND TREATIES

A. UK Statutes

B. UK Statutory Instruments

C. National Legislation from Other Jurisdictions

1

THE CONSTITUTIONAL PROTECTION OF HUMAN RIGHTS

C. The Status of Rights in English Law at Common Law

(1) Introduction

1.20 For a fuller discussion of the status of rights in English law, see A W B Simpson, *Human Rights and the End of Empire: Britain and the Genesis of the European Convention* (Oxford University Press, 2001), 14–41.

(3) Fundamental rights and statutory construction

1.25 See also D Dyzenhaus, M Hunt and M Taggart, 'The Principle of Legality in Administrative Law: Institutionalisation as Constitutionalisation' (2001) 1 OUCLJ 1.

In *R v Worcester County Council, ex p SW* [2000] 3 FCR 174, para 18, Newman J held that the principle of legality was a principle of construction which had an exact parallel in the presumption of constitutionality which applied in the interpretation of provisions passed by a parliament subject to the terms of a written constitution (see *A-G (Gambia) v Jobe* [1984] AC 689). See also *R (Morgan Grenfell) v Special Commissioners of Income Tax* [2002] 2 WLR 1299 where the House of Lords held that legal professional privilege was a fundamental human right and could only be overridden by express words or by necessary implication.

(4) Civil rights and administrative law decisions

1.31   See also *R (Daly) v Secretary of State for the Home Department* [2001] 2 AC 532.

(5) 'Common law' rights

1.33   n128: See, generally, C Forsyth (ed), *Judicial Review and the Constitution* (Hart Publishing, 2000) which contains a number of the important essays mentioned in the Main Work which consider the extent to which *ultra vires* is the central justification for judicial review.

1.34   For a discussion of Sir John Laws' views, see J A G Griffith, 'The Brave New World of Sir John Laws' (2000) 63 MLR 159; see also J A G Griffith, 'The Common Law and the Political Constitution' (2001) 117 LQR 42 (discussing Sir Stephen Sedley's views), and S Sedley, 'The Common Law and the Political Constitution: A Reply' (2001) 117 LQR 68. In his dissenting judgment in *R (International Transport Roth) v Secretary of State for the Home Department* [2002] 3 WLR 344 Laws LJ expressed the view (at para 71) that, in its present state of evolution, the British system may be said to stand at an intermediate stage between parliamentary and constitutional supremacy. Parliament remains the sovereign legislature— there is no superior text to which it must defer (leaving aside the refinements flowing from membership of the European Union) and there is no statute which by law it cannot make. But, at the same time, the common law has come to recognise and endorse the notion of constitutional, or fundamental, rights. These are broadly the rights given expression in the Convention for the Protection of Human Rights and Fundamental Freedoms, but their recognition in the common law is autonomous. In his lecture, 'The Human Rights Act Two Years On: Analysis', delivered on 1 November 2002, Lord Irvine commented on this analysis as follows:

> It may be that Sir John's description of 'an intermediate stage' is a prediction that we are only half-way on a constitutional journey and that, in the fullness of time, we will leave Parliamentary supremacy behind altogether. If so, I do not join in that prediction. The present arrangements were crafted as a settlement. They do not call for, or imply, further legislation, and I do not predict any. They represent our reconciliation of effective rights protection with Parliamentary sovereignty.

n152: See, generally, T R S Allan, *Constitutional Justice* (Oxford University Press, **1.37** 2001).

In *R (Daly) v Secretary of State for the Home Department* [2001] 2 AC 548, 549, **1.38** paras 30–1, Lord Cooke said:

> . . . it is of great importance, in my opinion, that the common law by itself is being recognised as a sufficient source of the fundamental right to confidential communication with a legal adviser for the purpose of obtaining legal advice. Thus the decision may prove to be in point in common law jurisdictions not affected by the Convention. Rights similar to those in the Convention are of course to be found in constitutional documents and other formal affirmations of rights elsewhere. The truth is, I think, that some rights are inherent and fundamental to democratic civilised society. Conventions, constitutions, bills of rights and the like respond by recognising rather than creating them.
>
> To essay any list of these fundamental, perhaps ultimately universal, rights is far beyond anything required for the purpose of deciding the present case. It is enough to take the three identified by Lord Bingham: in his words, access to a court; access to legal advice; and the right to communicate confidentially with a legal adviser under the seal of legal professional privilege. As he says authoritatively from the woolsack, such rights may be curtailed only by clear and express words, and then only to the extent reasonably necessary to meet the ends which justify the curtailment. The point that I am emphasising is that the common law goes so deep.

D. The Bill of Rights Debate

(1) The campaign for a Bill of Rights

For the full history of British involvement in the drafting of the Convention, see **1.41** A W B Simpson, *Human Rights and the End of Empire: Britain and the Genesis of the European Convention* (Oxford University Press, 2001), chs 11–15.

n171: See E Wicks, 'The United Kingdom Government's Perception of the ECHR at the Time of Entry' [2000] PL 438.

E. Parliamentary Sovereignty and the Entrenchment of a Bill of Rights

(3) Methods of entrenchment

n293: See also J Fudge, 'The Canadian Charter of Rights: Recognition, **1.79** Redistribution and the Imperialism of the Courts', in T Campbell, K Ewing and A Tomkins (eds), *Sceptical Essays in Human Rights* (Oxford University Press, 2001).

1.80   n299: See A Butler, 'Judicial Review, Human Rights and Democracy', in G Hushcroft and Paul Rishsworth (eds), *Litigating Rights* (Hart Publishing, 2002); J Allan, 'The Effect of a Statutory Bill of Rights where Parliament is Sovereign: The Lesson from New Zealand', in T Campbell, K Ewing and A Tomkins (eds), *Sceptical Essays in Human Rights* (Oxford University Press, 2001).

F. The Nature of Rights Protection Under the Human Rights Act

(2) The constitutional protection of human rights

1.89   In *Thoburn v Sunderland City Council* [2002] 3 WLR 247 Laws LJ (at para 62) defined a constitutional statute as one which: (a) conditions the legal relationship between citizen and state in some general, overarching manner; or (b) enlarges or diminishes the scope of what we would now regard as fundamental constitutional rights.

1.90   The Human Rights Act has been described by Lord Bingham as 'an important constitutional instrument' (*Brown v Stott* [2001] 2 WLR 817, 835). In the same case Lord Steyn described the Convention as 'our Bill of Rights' (at 839). Similarly, in *R v Offen* [2001] 1 WLR 253, 275, Lord Woolf CJ stressed that it is important to recognise that the 1998 Act is a constitutional instrument introducing Convention rights into domestic law. In *McCartan Turkington Breen v Times Newspapers* [2001] 2 AC 277, 297, Lord Steyn said that the Act was a constitutional measure designed to buttress freedom of expression. It fulfils the function of a Bill of Rights in our legal system; there is general agreement that it is a constitutional measure.

See, generally, J Jowett, 'Beyond the Rule of Law: Towards Constitutional Judicial Review' [2000] PL 671; G Huscroft, 'Rights, Bills of Rights and the Role of Courts and Legislatures', in G Huscroft and P Rishworth (eds), *Litigating Rights* (Hart Publishing, 2002).

1.91   See also Lord Steyn's lecture, 'Democracy through Law' [2002] EHRLR 723.

2

THE IMPACT OF UNINCORPORATED HUMAN RIGHTS TREATIES

B. The Convention and Changes to Domestic Law

n22: The derogation has since been withdrawn; see Supplement, para 6.93.   **2.08**

C. The Impact of the Convention in the English Courts

(1) Introduction

See also D Dyzenhaus, M Hunt and M Taggart, 'The Principle of Legality in   **2.10**
Administrative Law: Institutionalisation as Constitutionalisation' (2001) 1
OUCLJ 1 and K Knop, 'Here and There: International Law in Domestic Courts'
(2000) 32 NYU Journal of International Law and Politics 501.

n32b: See also *Lewis v A-G of Jamaica* [2000] 3 WLR 1785 discussed at Supplement, paras 2.15 and 2.34A.

(2) The Convention as an aid to construing statutes

2.15 However, in *Matadeen v Pointu* [1999] AC 98, 114G–H, the Privy Council when considering the effect of the International Covenant on Civil and Political Rights in the domestic law of Mauritius said that it is 'a well-recognised canon of construction that domestic legislation, including the Constitution, should if possible be construed so as to conform to such international instruments'.

In *Lewis v A-G of Jamaica* [2000] 3 WLR 1785, 1805C, the Privy Council, referring to the American Convention on Human Rights, said that 'it is now well established that domestic legislation should as far as possible be interpreted so as to conform to the state's obligation under such a treaty'.

These *dicta* appear to be a radical departure from the orthodox view that treaty obligations are only taken into account where a statute is ambiguous; see Main Work, paras 2.13–2.15. The issue is not expressly addressed in the judgments and it is to be noted that none of the authorities referred to in the Main Work were discussed by the Privy Council. However, the Court of Appeal in *R v Lyons and Others* [2002] HRLR 18, para 52, reaffirmed the principle that human rights obligations under international law 'will be overridden by a clear contrary directive in a statute' and, making express reference to *Lewis*, remarked that that principle was not contradicted by 'any of the divergent views expressed by members of the Privy Council in recent years'.

(6) The Convention and Community law

2.26 **n90:** See also Article 6(2) (formerly Article F(2)) of the Treaty on European Union which is referred to in the Main Work, para 1.28.

2.29 Rather than seeking accession to the Convention (which would have required amendments to both the Convention and the EU Treaty), the institutions of the EU have made a declaration known as the 'EU Charter of Fundamental Rights' (which was signed on 7 December 2000 at the start of the EU summit in Nice). The fifth paragraph of the Preamble states that the Charter purports to 'reaffirm' rights derived, *inter alia*, from the Convention. Article 51(1) provides that:

> The provisions of this Charter are addressed to the institutions and bodies of the Union with due regard for the principle of subsidiarity and to the Member States only when they are implementing Union law. They shall therefore respect the rights, observe the principles and promote the application thereof in accordance with their respective powers.

The Charter is to be found in the Appendix to this Supplement.

The Charter provides that insofar as it contains rights which correspond to rights guaranteed by the Convention, 'the meaning and scope of those rights shall be the same as those laid down by the said Convention' (Article 52(3)). Although the provisions of the Charter are not formally binding, they have been referred to and relied upon in proceedings before the European Court of Justice and the Court of First Instance (see paras 27 and 28 of the Opinion of Advocate-General Tizzano in *BECTU v Secretary of State for Trade and Industry*, C-173/99, 8 February 2001; paras 125–7 of the Opinion of Advocate-General Mischo in *Booker Aquaculture Ltd v Hydro Seafood*, C-20/00, 20 September 2001; *max.mobil Telekommunikation Service GmbH v Commission*, T-54/99, 30 January 2002; para 39 of the Opinion of Advocate-General Jacobs in *Union de Pequenos Agricultores v Council*, C-50/00 P, 21 March 2002; and para 124 of the Opinion of Advocate-General Jacobs in *Ministre de l'économie, des finances et de l'industrie v GEMO SA*, C-126/01, 30 April 2002).

Reference to the Charter has also been made in the English Administrative Court, although not as 'a source of law in the strict sense'; see *R (Robertson) v City of Wakefield Metropolitan Council* [2002] QB 1052.

For a general discussion of the Charter, see K Feus (ed), *The EU Charter of Fundamental Rights: Text and Commentaries* (Federal Trust, 2000); T Eicke, 'The European Charter of Fundamental Rights: Unique Opportunity or Unwelcome Distraction' [2000] EHRLR 280; T Kyriakou, 'The Impact of the EU Charter of Fundamental Rights on the EU System of Protection of Rights: Much Ado About Nothing?' [2001] 5 Web JCLI; I Rogers, 'From the Human Rights Act to the Charter: Not Another Human Rights Instrument to Consider?' [2002] EHRLR 343; and E Wicks, 'Declaratory of Existing Rights: The UK's Role in Drafting a European Bill of Rights, Mark II' [2001] PL 527.

(7) The Convention and administrative discretion

In *Lewis v A-G of Jamaica* [2000] 3 WLR 1785 the applicants complained that the way in which the prerogative of mercy had been exercised was unfair. The Privy Council (at 1806G) held that: **2.32**

> In considering what natural justice requires, it is relevant to have regard to international human rights norms set out in treaties to which the state is a party whether or not those are independently enforceable in domestic law.

The Privy Council went on to say that, when a state had acceded to international human rights treaties with the right of individual petition, the protection of law entitled the petitioner to complete the procedure and have the reports by international human rights organisations considered when the prerogative of mercy was being exercised. This approach is difficult to reconcile with the views expressed in *R v Secretary of the State for the Home Department, ex p Brind* [1991] AC 696 where the House of Lords rejected the argument that an administrative discretion must be exercised in accordance with the European Convention on Human Rights. The *Brind* case was not expressly discussed in *Lewis* although it was cited in argument.

2.40   n138: *R v DPP, ex p Kebilene* is now reported at [2000] 2 AC 326.

n139: The remarks of Lord Bingham CJ are now reported at [2000] 2 AC 326, 339.

D. The Impact of Other Human Rights Treaties

(2) The Universal Declaration of Human Rights

2.42   For the full history of the drafting of the Universal Declaration, see A W B Simpson, *Human Rights and the End of Empire: Britain and the Genesis of the European Convention* (Oxford University Press, 2001), chs 7–9, a work which was cited by Lord Bingham giving the principal speech of the Privy Council in *Procurator Fiscal v Watson and Another; HM Advocate v JK* 2002 SLT 229.

nn147–9: See also *Reyes v The Queen* [2002] 2 WLR 1034.

(3) The International Covenant on Civil and Political Rights

2.44   For a full discussion of the Covenant, see S Joseph, J Schultz and M Castan, *The International Covenant on Civil and Political Rights: Cases, Materials and Commentary* (Oxford University Press, 2001).

n161: See also *R (Farrakhan) v Secretary of State for the Home Department* [2002] 3 WLR 481.

2.45   In *R (Mullen) v Secretary of State for the Home Department* [2002] 1 WLR 1857 the Administrative Court held that a 'miscarriage of justice' under section 133 meant a wrongful conviction of an innocent accused, so that compensation was only payable to those ultimately proved innocent. See also *R (Christofides) v Secretary of State for the Home Department* [2002] 1 WLR 2769 in which it was held that there was no entitlement to compensation where a conviction for one offence had been substituted for another.

(4) The United Nations Convention on the Rights of the Child

2.50A   The Child Convention has been held by United Kingdom courts to inform the interpretation and application of the European Convention in cases concerning children. In *Procurator Fiscal v Watson and Another; HM Advocate v JK* 2002 SLT 229 the Privy Council held that the requirement in Article 6 of the Convention that the trial of a criminal charge be held within a reasonable time must, when dealing with children, be read in the light of the Child Convention and the United Nations Standard Minimum Rules for the Administration of Juvenile Justice ('the Beijing Rules'). In *R (SR) v Nottingham Magistrates' Court* [2001] EWHC Admin 802 the Administrative Court took a variety of provisions of the Child Convention into account when considering the application of Articles 8 and 14 of the Convention to a 16-year-old accused.

(7) Treaties dealing with social and economic rights

n234: See, generally, K Ewing, 'Social Rights and Human Rights: Britain and the Social Charter: The Conservative Legacy' [2000] EHRLR 91.   **2.57**

For a general discussion, see M Craven, 'The Justiciability of Economic, Social   **2.58** and Cultural Rights' and N Blake, 'Citing International Instruments in Cases Concerning Economic, Social and Cultural Rights', in Burchill, Harris and Owers (eds), *Economic, Social and Cultural Rights: Their Implementation in United Kingdom Law* (University of Nottingham Human Rights Law Centre, 1999).

The ILO has now adopted 183 Conventions and 191 Recommendations. The   **2.60** United Kingdom has now ratified 85 Conventions.

(8) European materials other than the Convention

There is a large volume of other European human rights materials produced by   **2.60A** the Council of Europe, the parent body of the European Court of Human Rights. In particular, the Assembly of the Council passes resolutions and makes recommendations on the full range of human rights issues. Recommendations are considered by the Committee of Ministers which also makes recommendations to the Contracting States. In recent years these have covered matters such as 'The right of rejected asylum seekers to an effective remedy in the context of Article 3 of the European Convention on Human Rights' (Recommendation No R (98)13) and 'On Measures concerning media coverage of election campaigns' (Recommendation No R (99)15). Recommendations on conscientious objection, along with a number of other international materials, were considered in passing by the Court of Appeal in *Sepet v Secretary of State for the Home Department* [2001] EWCA Civ 681, paras 35ff. In *A v B plc* [2002] 3 WLR 542, para 11(xii), the Court of Appeal referred to the general guidance to be found in Council of Europe Resolution 1165 of 1998 ('The Right to Privacy').

Article 1 of the European Convention on Social and Medical Assistance 1953 (ETS No 14) provides that nationals of the Contracting Parties:

who are lawfully present in any part of its territory to which this Convention applies and who are without sufficient resources shall be entitled equally with its own nationals and on the same conditions to social and medical assistance . . . provided by the legislation in force from to time to time in that part of its territory.

This Convention was considered in *Kaya v London Borough of Haringey* [2002] HRLR 1 in which it was held that the applicant, an asylum seeker granted temporary admission under the Immigration Act 1971, was not 'lawfully present' in the United Kingdom. He could not, therefore, take advantage of the Convention.

E. The Limits of Applicability of Unincorporated Treaties

2.68 See, generally, D O'Brien and V Carter, 'Constitutional Rights, Legitimate Expectations and the Death Penalty' [2000] PL 573.

3

THE HUMAN RIGHTS ACT:
INTERPRETATION AND SYNOPSIS

B. The Construction of Constitutional Instruments

(1) Introduction

n23: See N Roberts, 'The Law Lords and Human Rights: The Experience of the   **3.07**
Privy Council in Interpreting Bills of Rights' [2000] EHRLR 147.

(2) General principles

(b) The 'generous approach'

In *Reyes v The Queen* [2002] AC 235, para 26, Lord Bingham gave important   **3.14**
guidance on the proper approach to constitutional interpretation:

11

when . . . an enacted law is said to be incompatible with a right protected by a Constitution, the court's duty remains one of interpretation . . . Decided cases around the world have given valuable guidance on the proper approach of the courts to the task of constitutional interpretation: see, among many other cases, *Weems v United States* (1910) 217 US 349, 373, *Trop v Dulles* (1958) 356 US 86, 100–101, *Minister of Home Affairs v Fisher* [1980] AC 319, 328, *Union of Campement Site Owners and Lessees v Government of Mauritius* [1984] MR 100, 107, *Attorney General of The Gambia v Momodou Jobe* [1984] AC 689, 700–701, *R v Big M Drug Mart Ltd* [1985] 1 SCR 295, 331, *S v Zuma* 1995 (2) SA 642, *S v Makwanyane* 1995 (3) SA 391 and *Matadeen v Pointu* [1999] 1 AC 98, 108. It is unnecessary to cite these authorities at length because the principles are clear. As in the case of any other instrument, the court must begin its task of constitutional interpretation by carefully considering the language used in the Constitution. But it does not treat the language of the Constitution as if it were found in a will or a deed or a charterparty. A generous and purposive interpretation is to be given to constitutional provisions protecting human rights. The court has no licence to read its own predilections and moral values into the Constitution, but it is required to consider the substance of the fundamental right at issue and ensure contemporary protection of that right in the light of evolving standards of decency that mark the progress of a maturing society: see *Trop v Dulles* 356 US 86, 101. In carrying out its task of constitutional interpretation the court is not concerned to evaluate and give effect to public opinion, for reasons given by Chaskalson P in *S v Makwanyane* 1995 (3) SA 391, 431, para 88:

> Public opinion may have some relevance to the inquiry, but, in itself, it is no substitute for the duty vested in the courts to interpret the Constitution and to uphold its provisions without fear or favour. If public opinion were to be decisive, there would be no need for constitutional adjudication. The protection of rights could then be left to Parliament, which has a mandate from the public, and is answerable to the public for the way its mandate is exercised, but this would be a return to parliamentary sovereignty, and a retreat from the new legal order established by the 1993 Constitution. By the same token the issue of the constitutionality of capital punishment cannot be referred to a referendum, in which a majority view would prevail over the wishes of any minority. The very reason for establishing the new legal order, and for vesting the power of judicial review of all legislation in the courts, was to protect the rights of minorities and others who cannot protect their rights adequately through the democratic process. Those who are entitled to claim this protection include the social outcasts and marginalised people of our society.

n37a: The remarks of Lord Hope in *R v DPP, ex p Kebilene* are now reported at [2000] AC 326 at 381.

(e) Comparing the approaches

3.23A In *R v Hughes* [2002] 2 AC 259, para 35, the Privy Council applied the principle that in constitutional instruments exceptions to rights that individuals might otherwise have (like all other constitutional derogations) should be given a strict and narrow (rather than a broad) construction.

(3) The effect of prior law and practice

In *Gairy v A-G of Granada* [2002] 1 AC 167 the Privy Council held that historic **3.24** common law doctrines which restricted the liability of the Crown or its amenability to suit could not stand in the way of effective protection of fundamental human rights which had been guaranteed under the constitution.

In *Pinder v The Queen* [2002] 3 WLR 1443 the Privy Council took the view that **3.26** although flogging was inhuman and degrading treatment, it nevertheless remained constitutional under the transitional provisions of the constitution of the Bahamas. However, in a strong dissenting judgment Lord Nicholls and Hope expressed the view (at para 60) that never was there a more telling instance of the 'austerity of tabulated legalism' (see *Minister of Home Affairs v Fisher* [1980] AC 319, 328) than in *Pinder* itself where the constitutionality of inhuman punishment was said to depend, at least in part, on the inference to be drawn from the niceties of an argument based on redundancy of language. They went to say that this approach, if adopted, would tragically impoverish the spirit of the Constitution of the Bahamas.

(5) Interpretation of rights instruments in other common law jurisdictions

(a) Canada

In *Montreal v Quebec* (2000) 8 BHRC 478 the Supreme Court considered the **3.30** principles of interpretation to be applied to the Charter, stressing the inadequacy of a grammatical analysis and the importance of contextual interpretation.

C. The Provisions of the Human Rights Act

(2) The Human Rights Act before commencement

n102: *R v DPP, ex p Kebilene* is now reported at [2000] 2 AC 326. **3.37**

However, in *R v Lambert* [2001] 3 WLR 206 the House of Lords held that the Act **3.39** did not apply retrospectively to a summing up made before the Act came into force. See also *R v Kansal (No 2)* [2001] 3 WLR 1562 and *R v Lyons* [2002] 3 WLR 1562. These cases are discussed further at Supplement, para 3.75A.

nn105, 106a, 106c: See Supplement, para 3.37, n102, above.

(5) Section 2: Taking account of Convention jurisprudence

(b) The construction of section 2

In relation to the different weight to attach to the various types of decisions iden- **3.47A** tified in section 2(1), see *R v Secretary of State for Work and Pensions, ex p Carson*

[2002] 3 All ER 994 in which it was held by Stanley Burnton J that decisions of the European Commission on Human Rights 'are not of the same level as those of the court. Where, however, there is a clear and constant line of decisions of the Commission that are not inconsistent with those of the court, good reason is required if this court is to decline to follow them' (para 38).

3.50   In *R (Alconbury Developments Ltd) v Environment Secretary* [2001] 2 WLR 1389, 1399, para 26, Lord Slynn said that 'In the absence of some special circumstances it seems to me that the court should follow any clear and constant jurisprudence of the European Court of Human Rights.'

Some indication of the type of 'special circumstances' which might find favour with the courts was given by Lord Hoffmann in the same case when he said (at para 76):

> The House is not bound by the decisions of the European court and, if I thought that . . . they compelled a conclusion fundamentally at odds with the distribution of powers under the British constitution, I would have considerable doubt as to whether they should be followed.

In *Aston Cantlow Parochial Church Council v Wallbank* [2002] Ch 51, para 44, the Court of Appeal said that:

> Our task is not to cast around in the European Human Rights Reports like black-letter lawyers seeking clues. In the light of s 2(1) of the Human Rights Act 1998 it is to draw out the broad principles which animate the Convention.

In *Brown v Stott* [2001] 2 WLR 817, 855, Lord Hope expressed caution about the use of Canadian authorities and emphasised the need to take account of the statutory framework when doing so.

In *R (Anderson) v Secretary of State for the Home Department* [2002] 2 WLR 1143 the claimants challenged the controversial role of the Home Secretary in fixing a tariff for mandatory life prisoners where the executive is effectively exercising a judicial sentencing function. The difficulty they faced when arguing the case before the Court of Appeal was an earlier unsatisfactory decision of the European Court of Human Rights in *Wynne v United Kingdom* (1994) 19 EHRR 333. Although the Court of Appeal took the view that the claimant's arguments were correct and that *Wynne* was wrongly decided, it nevertheless decided to follow the case, primarily on the ground of judicial comity; see Simon Brown LJ at paras 65, 66 and Buxton LJ at paras 89–93.

By the time that *Anderson* came to be argued before the House of Lords at [2002] 3 WLR 1800, the Grand Chamber of the Court of Human Rights had reversed the *Wynne* decision in *Stafford v United Kingdom* (2002) 35 EHRR 32. Lord Bingham (at para 18) stated that while the duty under section 2(1)(a) is to take into account any judgment of the European Court, whose judgments are not strictly binding, the House of Lords would not without good reason depart from the principles laid down in a carefully considered judgment of the court sitting as a Grand Chamber (see *R (Alconbury Developments Ltd) v Secretary of State for the Environment, Transport and the Regions* [2001] 2 WLR 1389, 1399, para 26).

In contrast, in *R (Amin) v Secretary of State for the Home Department* [2002] 3 WLR 505, para 62, the Court of Appeal stressed that it was not bound to apply Strasbourg case law, particularly in relation to an adjectival provision which was not expressly set out in the Convention (the duty to investigate under Article 2). Laws LJ in *Runa Begum v Tower Hamlets LBC* [2002] 1 WLR 2491, para 17, also emphasised that the terms of section 2 were designed to encourage the development of domestic principles.

In *R v Botmeh* [2001] 1 WLR 531 the Court of Appeal accepted that, pursuant to section 2 of the Human Rights Act, it would rarely be appropriate for the English courts to adopt a standard of protection which is lower than that set in the Strasbourg case law (para 16).

For a case in which an English court declined to follow certain aspects of a European Court decision, see *R v Spear* [2002] 3 WLR 437 in which the House of Lords considered *Morris v United Kingdom* (2002) 34 EHRR 1253 in relation to the compatibility of courts-martial procedures with Article 6. As a result of the decision in *Spear*, it is now the practice of the European Court of Human Rights to adjourn its hearing pending the outcome of any relevant domestic proceedings in the English courts.

n358c: *R v DPP, ex p Kebilene* is now reported at [2000] 2 AC 326.

(c) Proving a relevant Convention decision   **3.51**

The rules for citation of authority are *different* from the draft rules which appear in Appendix C of Main Work, Vol 2. The Practice Direction, *Miscellaneous Provisions Relating to Hearings*, which supplements CPR, Part 39, reproduced in the Appendix to this Supplement, states that:

• The authority cited should be an authoritative and complete report.
• The party must give to the court and any other party a list of the authorities he intends to cite and copies of the reports not less than three days before the hearing. (Section 2(1) of the Human Rights Act 1998 requires the court to take account of the authorities listed here.)
• Copies of the complete original text issued by the European Court and Commission either paper-based or from the Court's database of judgments (HUDOC) may be used.

(8) Section 10: Remedial action

3.56 The Mental Health Act (Remedial) Order 2001, SI 2001/3712, which came into force on 26 November 2001, amends sections 72(1) and 73(1) by moving the word 'not' in each provision. The effect is that the wording now requires the Mental Health Review Tribunal to satisfy itself of the existence of criteria justifying detention, rather than to presume their existence at the outset. See, further, Supplement, para 10.182.

(10) Sections 14 to 17: Derogations and reservations

3.63 The Human Rights Act (Amendment) Order 2001, SI 2001/1216, which came into force on 1 April 2001, amended the Human Rights Act 1998 to reflect the withdrawal by the UK Government of the derogation from Article 5(3) of the Convention on Human Rights which was originally preserved by section 14(1)(a) of, and set out in Part I of Schedule 3 to, the 1998 Act. The withdrawal of the derogation was effective from 26 February 2001 and followed the implementation of Schedule 8 to the Terrorism Act 2000.

However, in November 2001 an Order was made pursuant to section 14 of the Human Rights Act to derogate from Article 5(1) of the Convention in relation to detention under the Anti-Terrorism, Crime and Security Act 2001 on the basis that there was a terrorist threat to the United Kingdom following the attacks in the United States of 11 September 2001 (see the Human Rights Act 1998 (Designated Derogation) Order 2001, SI 2001/3644). The Human Rights Act 1998 was amended by the Human Rights Act 1998 (Amendment No 2) Order 2001, SI 2001/4032, to insert the derogation.

It was held by the Special Immigration Appeals Commission in *A and Others v Secretary of State for the Home Department* [2002] HRLR 45 that this derogation was not itself unlawful but that that the provision of the Anti-Terrorism Act operated in a manner which was discriminatory in breach of Article 14 and in relation to which there had been no derogation. However, the Court of Appeal (*The Times*, 29 October 2002) decided that the power to detain foreign nationals only on the ground that they posed a risk to national security did not breach Article 14.

For a discussion of the derogation and, in particular, of the adequacy of parliamentary scrutiny, see 'Opinion 1/2002 of the Commissioner for Human Rights Mr Alvaro Gil-Robles on Certain Aspects of the United Kingdom 2001 Derogation from Article 5 para 1 of the European Convention on Human Rights' Comm DH (2002) 7.

(11) Sections 20 to 22: Supplemental matters

3.75 The remarks of Lord Hobhouse in *R v DPP, ex p Kebilene* are now reported at [2000] AC 326 at 398.

The text of the Main Work has been superseded by the decision of the House of **3.75A**
Lords in *R v Lambert* [2001] 3 WLR 206. In that case the House of Lords adopted
the reasoning of the Court of Appeal in *Wilson v First County Trust (No 2)* [2001]
3 WLR 42 and held that the Human Rights Act did not apply retrospectively to
the summing up of a trial heard before the Act came into force. Lord Slynn (at para
6) observed that the Act did not come into force until the day appointed by the
Secretary of State and since there was a presumption against retrospectivity in legislation, it is not to be assumed *a priori* that Convention rights, however com-
mendable, are to be enforced in national courts in respect of past events. Section
6 of the Act did not deal specifically with acts which took place before October
2000 whereas section 22(4) did so. Section 7(6) of the Act distinguishes between
a public authority and 'an appeal against the decision of a court' whereas section
22(4) extends the application of section 7(1)(b) *only* when proceedings are
brought by a public authority.

The House of Lords therefore declined to apply the *dictum* of Lord Steyn in *R v
DPP, ex p Kebilene* [2000] 2 AC 326 at 368, which is set out at Main Work, para
3.75A, and decided that section 22(4) does not apply to an appeal in relation to
court decisions taken prior to October 2000. However, Lord Hope (at paras
104–7) distinguished a breach of Convention rights by the act of a court (such as
summing up in a criminal trial) from an alleged breach of Convention rights by a
prosecuting authority; in relation to a breach by the prosecuting authority, retrospective reliance on Convention rights under section 7(1)(b) is permitted by section 22(4) at each stage of an appeal (including an appeal to the House of Lords).

The decision in *R v Lambert* was considered by the House of Lords in *R v Kansal
(No 2)* [2001] 3 WLR 1562. In that case the majority took the view that *Lambert*
had not been correctly decided on the question of the retrospective effect of the
Human Rights Act (see Lord Lloyd at para 17, Lord Steyn at para 26 and Lord
Hope at para 72.) Nevertheless, a differently constituted majority determined
(with only Lord Hope dissenting) that there was no compelling reason to depart
from the decision of the majority in *Lambert*. The House of Lords does not appear
to have considered criminal cases in which it departed from its own decisions (see,
for example, *R v Shivpuri* [1987] AC 1, 23A–C). It should also be borne in mind
that the effect of the decision in *Lambert* is that criminal convictions arrived at in
breach of the United Kingdom's international obligations before October 2000
cannot be reconsidered by the criminal courts. The conclusion is a surprising and
unsatisfactory one.

In *R v Lyons* [2002] 3 WLR 1562 the House of Lords rejected the argument that
convictions which the Court of Human Rights had decided were unfair as being
in breach of Article 6 were unsafe under section 2 of the Criminal Appeals Act
1995. The statutory procedure could not be overridden by giving direct effect to
the Convention as an international convention.

D. The Weaknesses of the Human Rights Act

(1) Introduction

3.76 See, generally, T Campbell, K Ewing and A Tomkins (eds), *Sceptical Essays on Human Rights* (Oxford University Press, 2001).

(2) The limitations of the European Convention model

3.79 In *The Struggle for Civil Liberties* (Oxford University Press, 2001), ch 1, Ewing and Gearty develop their criticisms of human rights instruments by distinguishing between human rights which protect the autonomy of the individual (such as the right to private life or freedom of conscience) and civil liberties which facilitate participation in the community (such as freedom of expression). They argue that the tendency to conflate civil liberties with human rights is deeply and profoundly mistaken; and that the main purpose of civil liberties is to develop an active political culture: it is about freedom *to* rather than freedom *from*.

3.80 n235: See G Van Bueren, 'Including the Excluded: The Case for an Economic, Social and Cultural Rights Act' [2002] PL 456.

n240: See R Bellamy, 'Constitutive Citizenship versus Constitutional Rights: Republican Reflections on the EU Charter and the Human Rights Act', in T Campbell, K Ewing and A Tomkins (eds), *Sceptical Essays on Human Rights* (Oxford University Press, 2001).

n246: See *Government of South Africa v Grootboom* (2000) 11 BCLR 1169.

n247: See *Ministry of Health v Treatment Action Campaign*, 5 July 2002; and see I Hare, '*Ministry of Health v Treatment Action Campaign*: The South African Aids Pandemic and the Constitutional Right to Health Care' [2002] EHRLR 624.

(3) The limitations of the Human Rights Act

3.81 See, generally, R Clayton, 'Does the Human Rights Act Guarantee Effective Remedies?', in J Jowell and J Cooper (eds), *Delivering Rights: How the Human Rights Act is Working and for Whom* (Hart Publishing, 2003).

3.88 For a discussion of the impact of the Parliamentary Committee on Human Rights and of Parliamentary scrutiny generally, see D Feldman, 'Parliamentary Scrutiny of Legislation and Human Rights' [2002] PL 323 and A Lester, 'Parliamentary Scrutiny under the Human Rights Act 1998' [2002] EHRLR 432.

n282: See S Beckett and I Clyde, 'A Human Rights Commission for the United Kingdom: The Australian Experience' [2000] EHRLR 131.

4

THE HUMAN RIGHTS ACT AND STATUTE LAW

B. The Rule of Construction

(1) Introduction: the scope of section 3(1)

In *R v Lambert* [2001] 3 WLR 206, 242, para 110, Lord Hope accepted that the **4.04** interpretative obligation in section 3(1) applied to the provisions of the Human Rights Act 1998 in exactly the same way as it applies to any other statute.

(5) The rule of construction in New Zealand

n66: See A Butler, 'Interface between the Human Rights Act 1998 and other **4.23** Enactments: Pointers from New Zealand' [2000] EHRLR 249.

In *R v Poumako* [2000] 2 NZLR 695 the New Zealand Court of Appeal applied a **4.26A** narrow interpretation of the retrospective effect of criminal legislation in order to interpret it in line with section 6 of the Bill of Rights Act despite the fact that this interpretation was not what was intended when the retrospective legislation was enacted (see, generally, A Butler, 'Declaration of Incompatibility or Interpretation Consistent with Human Rights in New Zealand' [2001] PL 28). In *R v Pora* (2000) 6 HRNZ 129 the Court of Appeal again took a restrictive approach to the retrospective effect of criminal legislation; the broad interpretation taken by the minority is difficult to justify. See, further, A Butler, 'Implied Repeal, Parliamentary Sovereignty and Human Rights in New Zealand' [2001] PL 586.

It is strongly arguable that the New Zealand courts cannot provide an effective remedy for human rights violations since section 4 of the New Zealand Bill of Rights Act preserves parliamentary sovereignty where legislation is inconsistent with the Bill of Rights Act; see A Butler, 'Judicial Review, Human Rights and Democracy', in G Huscroft and P Rishworth (eds), *Litigating Rights: Perspectives from Domestic and International Law* (Hart Publishing, 2002).

(6) The effect and the limits of the 'rule of construction'

4.27   n79a: Generally on section 3(1), see H Fenwick, 'The Interpretative Obligation under Section 3 of the Human Rights Act 1998' [2001] SL Rev 8; R Clayton, 'The Limits of What is Possible: Statutory Construction under the Human Rights Act [2002] EHRLR 559; D Rose and C Weir, 'Interpretation and Incompatibility: Striking the Balance under the Human Rights Act', in J Cooper and J Jowell, *Delivering Rights? How the Human Rights Act is Working and For Whom* (Hart Publishing, 2003). On the relationship between Parliament and the judiciary, including the limits, if any, of the interpretative powers of the courts under section 3(1), see T Campbell, 'Incorporation Through Interpretation', in T Campbell, K Ewing and A Tomkins (eds), *Sceptical Essays on Human Rights* (Oxford University Press, 2001); A Young, 'Judicial Sovereignty and the Human Rights Act 1998' (2002) 61 CLJ 53; C Gearty, 'Reconciling Parliamentary Democracy and Human Rights' (2002) 118 LQR 248; and D Vick, 'Deontological *Dicta*' [2002] MLR 279.

4.28   There has been considerable uncertainty about whether section 3(1) applies to all cases coming before the courts after 2 October 2000 irrespective of when the activities which formed the subject matter of the those cases took place. In *Pye (Oxford) v Graham* [2002] Ch 804 Mummery LJ at 821, para 43, and Keane LJ at para 48, expressed the view *obiter* that section 3 had retrospective effect, but when the case came to be argued before the House of Lords at [2002] 3 WLR 221 it was conceded that section 3 was not retrospective. However, in *Wilson v First National Trust (No 2)* [2002] QB 74 the Court of Appeal distinguished between:

- a claimant alleging under section 7(1) of the Human Rights Act that a public authority has acted incompatibly with Convention rights under section 6(1) where a retrospective claim is defeated by section 22(4) of the Act (for a further discussion of that provision, see Supplement, para 3.75A); and

- the duty of the court under section 6(1) when making a declaration of incompatibility to examine the facts as they are at the time of making the order.

The approach taken in *Wilson (No 2)* was applied by the Court of Appeal in *Pearce v Governing Body of Mayfield School* [2001] ICR 198 where it provided some support for the view that the Sex Discrimination Act 1975, read subject to section 3 of the Human Rights Act, prohibited discrimination against homosexuals; see, further, Supplement, para 17.148. However, the Court of Appeal refused to allow the appeal because the acts of discrimination took place before 2 October 2000.

The nature of the interpretative obligation under section 3 was extensively analysed by Lord Steyn in *R v A (No 2)* [2002] 1 AC 45, 67, 68, paras 44, 45. Lord Steyn stressed that it will sometimes be necessary under section 3 to adopt an interpretation which is linguistically strained, not only by reading down the express language of the statute but by the implication of provisions. A declaration of incompatibility was a measure of last resort. It must be avoided unless it is plainly impossible to do so; if a *clear* limitation on Convention rights is stated *in terms*, such an impossibility will arise (see *R v Home Secretary, ex p Simms* [2000] 2 AC 115, 132 *per* Lord Hoffmann).

By contrast, Lord Hope in *R v A (No 2)* [2002] 1 AC 45, 87, para 108, took a more cautious approach:

> The rule of construction which section 3 lays down is quite unlike any previous rule of statutory interpretation. There is no need to identify an ambiguity or absurdity. Compatibility with Convention rights is the sole guiding principle. That is the paramount object which the rule seeks to achieve. But the rule is only a rule of interpretation. It does not entitle the judges to act as legislators. As Lord Woolf CJ said in *Poplar Housing Association v Donoghue* [2001] QB 48 section 3 does not entitle the court to legislate; its task is still one of interpretation. The compatibility is to be achieved only so far as this is possible. Plainly this will not be possible if the legislation contains provisions which expressly contradict the meaning which the enactment would have to be given to make it compatible. It seems to me that the same result must follow if they do so by necessary implication, as this too is a means of identifying the plain intention of Parliament.

No general principles can be extracted from the judgments of Lords Slynn, Clyde and Hutton. Nevertheless, the House of Lords went on to decide that section 41(3)(c) of the Youth Justice and Criminal Evidence Act 1999 was subject to the implied provision that evidence and questioning required to ensure a fair trial under Article 6 should not be treated as inadmissible.

For a discussion of *R v A*, see J Spencer, 'Rape Shields and the Right to a Fair Trial' (2001) 60 CLJ 452; and P Mirfield, 'Human Wrongs?' (2002) 118 LQR 20.

In *R v Lambert* [2001] 3 WLR 206, 233, 235, Lord Hope again stressed the need to employ section 3 in a way which respected the will of the legislature and preserved the integrity of statute law. He made a number of general observations about the use of section 3 (at paras 79–81):

- resort to it would not be possible where the legislation contains provisions which expressly contradict the meaning which the enactment would have to be given to make it compatible;
- great care had to be given to identifying the word or phrase which, in its ordinary meaning, would be incompatible and how it is to be construed to make it compatible;
- the ways in which the court could carry out its task included: stating the effect of the provision without altering the ordinary meaning, expressing the words in different language or reading words into the provision (which had to be carefully distinguished from amendment).

Lord Hope also discussed (at para 81) the techniques to be used when construing legislation in accordance with section 3. He noted the three approaches set out in Main Work, para 4.28:

- a strained or non-literal construction may be adopted;
- words may be 'read in' by way of addition to those used by the legislator;
- words may be 'read down' to give them a narrower construction than their ordinary meaning would bear.

He then suggested a number of possible techniques that may be used by the courts:

- it may be enough to say what the effect of the provision is without altering the ordinary meaning of the words used (see *Brown v Stott* (2000) JR 328, 355B–C *per* Lord Justice General);
- words used will be required to be expressed in different language in order to explain how they are to be read in a way that is compatible: the exercise is one of translation into compatible language from language which is incompatible (see, for example, *Vasquez v The Queen* [1994] 1 WLR 1304);
- it may be necessary to read words in to explain the meaning that must be given if it is to be compatible (see, for example, *R v A (No 2)* [2001] 2 WLR 1546).

In *R v Lambert* the House of Lords applied section 3 to construe the words 'if he proves' in section 28(3) of the Misuse of Drugs Act 1971 to mean 'if he gives sufficient evidence' (and the words 'to prove' as 'to give sufficient evidence'). Statutory language which, in its natural and ordinary meaning, placed a legal burden on the defendant was, therefore, construed as placing only an evidential burden.

In *Poplar Housing and Regeneration Community Association Ltd v Donoghue* [2002] QB 48, 72, 73, para 75, Lord Woolf CJ also set out some general principles concerning the application of section 3:

- unless the legislation would otherwise be in breach of the Convention, section 3 can be ignored so that the court should always first ascertain whether, absent section 3, there would be any breach of Convention rights;
- if the court has to rely on section 3, it should limit the extent of the modified meaning to that which it is necessary to achieve compatibility;
- section 3 does not entitle the court to *legislate*; its task is still one of interpretation, but interpretation in accordance with section 3;
- the views of the parties and of the Crown as to whether a 'constructive' interpretation should be adopted cannot modify the task of the court; if section 3 applies, the court is required to adopt the section 3 interpretation;
- where, despite the strong language of section 3, it is not possible to achieve a result which is compatible with Convention rights, the court is not *required* to grant a declaration and presumably in exercising its discretion to grant a declaration, the court will be influenced by the usual considerations which apply to the grant of declarations.

In *Re S (Care Order: Implementation of Care Plan)* [2002] 2 AC 291 the House of Lords once more considered the limits of the interpretative provision contained in section 3(1) and effectively adopted the approach of Lord Hope in *R v A (No 2)* and *R v Lambert*. Lord Nicholls held that, while section 3(1) is a 'powerful tool', its reach is not unlimited. Lord Nicholls stressed that section 3 is concerned with *interpretation* not legislation and that the courts should be mindful of its outer limit and the aim of the Human Rights Act of preserving Parliamentary sovereignty. It was for Parliament to enact and amend statutes, not the courts. In identifying the outer limits of section 3 Lord Nicholls held that 'a meaning which departs substantially from a fundamental feature of an Act of Parliament is likely to have crossed the boundary between interpretation and amendment. This is especially so where the departure has important practical repercussions which the court is not equipped to evaluate' (para 40). Lord Nicholls also added the following general observation:

> [w]hen a court, called upon to construe legislation, ascribes a meaning and effect to the legislation pursuant to its obligation under s 3, it is important the court should identify clearly the particular statutory provision or provisions whose interpretation leads to that result. Apart from all else, this should assist in ensuring the court does not inadvertently stray outside its interpretation jurisdiction (para 41).

In the case itself, the House of Lords held that the Court of Appeal had overstepped the appropriate limits of section 3(1) and had effectively *legislated* in relation to the Children Act 1989.

A slightly different issue arose in *Adan v Newham LBC* [2002] 1 WLR 2120 in relation to homelessness appeals to the county court. The Court of Appeal had to consider whether the jurisdiction of the county court (which exercised powers akin to judicial review) was sufficient to cure a breach of Article 6 where the primary facts were disputed. Although Hale LJ construed the statutory provision as being compatible with Article 6, that construction was rejected by Brooke LJ and David Steel J as being constitutionally improper: the provision showed that Parliament had decided that local authorities, not the courts, should be the final arbiter of the facts. However, this reasoning is open to question. *Adan* was not a case where a section 3 interpretation was contradicted by necessary implication. A *constitutional* objection to interpreting legislation in a manner compliant with the Convention cannot be derived from the Human Rights Act itself.

It appears from the cases that the following principles should be applied where a court is asked to construe legislation in accordance with section 3:

- It is necessary to identify with precision the particular statutory provision which is said to contravene Convention rights; see *R v A (No 2)* [2001] 2 WLR 1546 *per* Lord Hope at 1582, 1583, para 110, and again in *R v Lambert* [2001] 3 WLR 206, para 80. See also *Re S (Care Order: Implementation of Care Plan)* [2002] 2 AC 291 *per* Lord Nicholls at 313, 314, para 41.
- The court should next ascertain whether, absent section 3, there is any breach of Convention rights; see *Poplar Housing Association v Donoghue* [2001] QB 48, para 75; *R v A (No 2) per* Lord Hope, para 58.
- When the court comes to apply section 3, the touchstone is compatibility with Convention rights.
- However, the principal focus is to identify *possible* meanings to be given to the legislation in question.
- The court can interpret legislation under section 3 by 'reading in' Convention rights (by *implying* words in a statute).
- It is *not* possible under section 3 to interpret legislation compatibly if the construction conflicts with its express words.
- It is also *not* possible under section 3 to interpret legislation compatibly if it conflicts with a statute by *necessary* implication.

In *R v Offen* [2001] 1 WLR 253 the Court of Appeal interpreted section 2 of the Crime (Sentences) Act 1997 (the power to impose an automatic life sentence following a conviction for a second serious offence) in accordance with section 3 of the Human Rights Act and adopted a broad interpretation of the phrase 'exceptional circumstances' by reading in Articles 3 and 5. The case is discussed further at Supplement, para 11.347.

The Court of Appeal in *Cachia v Faluyi* [2002] 1 WLR 1966 read down the word 'action' in section 2(3) of the Fatal Accidents Act 1976 as meaning 'served process' in order to permit dependent children bringing proceedings based on a second writ issued within the limitation period where the first writ had been issued but not served.

In *O'Hagan v Rea* (2001) SLT (Sh Ct) 30, when considering section 35 of the Education (Scotland) Act 1980, the Sheriff's Court applied section 3 to the interpretation of the words 'reasonable excuse' in relation to a parent who was charged with a criminal offence because of his child's truancy. It was held that the narrow interpretation of this term established by the authorities was incompatible with Article 6(2) but that section 3 could be used to give the section a 'wide meaning' to render it compatible.

The decision in *Brown v Procurator Fiscal* was overruled by the Privy Council in *Stott v Brown* [2001] 2 WLR 817 which decided there was no breach of Article 6. For a fuller discussion, see Supplement, para 11.346.

In *Hooper v Secretary of State for Work and Pensions* [2002] UKHRR 785 Moses J noted the far-reaching interpretative power conferred by section 3(1) as analysed in *R v Lambert* and *R v A (No 2)*. He held, however, that there was a significant distinction between cases concerning the requirements of a fair criminal trial, such as *R v A (No 2)* and *R v Lambert*, where the courts might be regarded as authoritative experts, and cases concerning social and economic policy in respect of which they are not. *Hooper* itself, dealing with different benefits available to widows and widowers, was held to fall within the latter category. It was held that as such cases require the decision-maker to be in a position to foresee the *effects* of the adaptation of legislation, it was a matter for Parliament and not the courts. Moses J thus declined to interpret the legislation in question compatibly and instead made a declaration of incompatibility.

In *Goode v Martin* [2002] 1 WLR 1828 CPR 17.4 was interpreted under section 3 to allow the claimant to amend her pleadings after the expiry of the limitation period where the amendment consisted of a response to the defendant's version of events.

In *R (RA) v Secretary of State for the Home Department* [2002] EWHC Admin 1618 it was held that section 41(3) of the Mental Health Act 1983 could be read so as to render it compatible with Article 5.

4.28A n82a: The remarks of Lord Bingham CJ in *R v DPP, ex p Kebilene* are now reported at [2000] 2 AC 326, 344; the remarks of Laws LJ are now reported at ibid, 356.

(8) The doctrine of *Pepper v Hart*

4.37 In *R v Environment Secretary, ex p Spath Holme* [2001] 2 AC 349, 391, Lord Bingham stressed the need for compliance with all three conditions laid down by Lord Browne-Wilkinson in *Pepper v Hart*. He went on to say (at 393) that where the issue turned on the scope of a statutory power (as opposed to the meaning of a statutory expression) it was most unlikely that statements by the responsible minister would be of assistance:

No doubt the minister would seek to give helpful answers. But it is most unlikely that he would seek to define the legal effect of the draftsman's language, or to predict all the circumstances in which the power might be used, or to bind any successor administration.

See also *R (Westminster City Council) v National Asylum Support Service* [2002] 1 WLR 2956, para 22.

Lord Steyn has argued that *Hansard* may be relevant as an aid to the interpretation of section 3 of the Human Rights Act *against* the executive; see J Steyn, '*Pepper v Hart*: A Re-examination' (2001) 21 OJLS 59.

C. Statements of Compatibility

4.42 In *R v A (No 2)* [2002] 1 AC 45, 75, para 69, Lord Hope expressed the view that statements of compatibility are no more than expressions of opinion by the minister; they are not binding on the court, nor do they have any persuasive authority.

D. Declarations of Incompatibility

(2) The power to make a declaration of incompatibility

4.46 n126: See Thomas and Kellar, 'Joining the Crown in Civil Proceedings under the Human Rights Act 1998' (2001) JR 135.

In relation to subordinate legislation, see, generally, R Allen and P Sales, 'Joint Note for the Court of Appeal in *R v Lord Chancellor, ex p Lightfoot*' [2000] PL 361; and D Squires, 'Challenging Subordinate Legislation under the Human Rights Act' [2000] EHRLR 116.

It has been suggested *obiter* in several cases that the procedure for making a declaration of incompatibility cannot extend to breaches of *positive* rights. In *Re S (Care Order: Implementation of Care Plan)* [2002] 2 AC 291, 322, para 82, Lord Nicholls considered a potential breach of the right of access to the court under Article 6 in relation to the Children Act where, for example, a child was unable to bring proceedings because there was no parent or guardian willing and able to question the local authority's care decision. He pointed out (at 322, paras 85, 86):

> The Convention violation now under consideration consists of a failure to provide access to a court as guaranteed by article 6(1). The absence of such provision means that English law may be incompatible with article 6(1). The United Kingdom may be in breach of its treaty obligations regarding this article. But the absence of such provision from a particular statute does not, in itself, mean that

the statute is incompatible with article 6(1). Rather, this signifies at most the existence of a lacuna in the statute . . . This is the position so far as the failure to comply with article 6(1) lies in the absence of effective machinery for protecting the civil rights of young children who have no parent or guardian able and willing to act for them. In such cases there is a statutory lacuna, not a statutory incompatibility.

In *R (J) v Enfield LBC* [2002] 2 FLR 1 Elias J also took the view, *obiter*, that the procedure for making a declaration of incompatibility could not be invoked where there was a breach of a positive right. In that case the claimant proved that the failure of a local authority to accommodate herself and her child breached Article 8. The family was subject to immigration control and the local authority had no power to provide accommodation. Elias J concluded that it would be inappropriate to grant a declaration because it was a *body* of legislation taken together which was incompatible with Article 8; and he also rejected the argument that the court ought to identify the particular statutory provision which is most closely linked to the Convention right infringed so that the fast-track procedure could be utilised.

By contrast, in *R (Rose) v Secretary of State for Health* [2002] UKHRR 785 Scott Baker J considered whether a declaration of incompatibility could be made in relation to a statutory *scheme* which failed to protect Convention rights or whether only individual offending provisions of primary legislation could be declared incompatible. He left the matter open, concluding that a final decision would be premature given the case before him.

The difficulty about applying the procedure for making a declaration of incompatibility to primary legislation arises because of the definition of 'primary legislation' in section 4. Primary legislation, as defined by section 4(1) and (2), is framed on the basis that a *particular* provision of primary legislation is incompatible with Convention rights, unlike the position with secondary legislation defined under section 4(3), (4). Nevertheless, there are counter-arguments indicating that the procedure for making a declaration of incompatibility can cover breaches of positive rights. Section 4(2) should be read and given effect under section 3 so far as it is possible to make it compatible with Convention rights. Furthermore, the Human Rights Act should be interpreted in a broad and generous way to give effect to fundamental rights; see Main Work, para 3.14A.

In *Wilson v First County Trust* [2001] QB 407 the question of making a declaration of incompatibility was adjourned for a further hearing (*Wilson v First County (No 2)* [2002] QB 74) where the Court of Appeal decided to grant a declaration because: **4.47**

• it was necessary to make a declaration to give effect to the order stating that section 127(3) of the Consumer Credit Act 1974 was incompatible with Article 6 and Article 1 of the First Protocol; and

- a declaration would serve the legislative purpose under the Human Rights Act by providing a basis for the government making a remedial order.

A declaration of incompatibility was made in *R (H) v Mental Health Review Tribunal* [2002] QB 1 where it was held that that sections 72 and 73 of the Mental Health Act 1983 were incompatible with Article 5(1) and (4). Subsequently, the Secretary of State made the Mental Health Act 1983 (Remedial) Order 2001, SI 2001/3712, on 18 November 2001.

In *R (International Transport Roth) v Secretary of State for the Home Department* [2002] 3 WLR 344 the Court of Appeal held that the statutory scheme which penalised carriers of illegal immigrants into the UK under the Immigration and Asylum Act 1999 breached Article 6 and made a declaration of incompatibility.

In *Hooper v Secretary of State for Work and Pensions* [2002] UKHRR 785 Moses J decided that sections 36 to 38 of the Social Security Contributions and Benefits Act 1992 were discriminatory against widowers and therefore incompatible with Article 14, read together with Article 1 of the First Protocol, and granted a declaration. He again made a declaration in *Wilkinson v Inland Revenue Commissioners* (2002) STC 347, holding that section 262 of the Income and Corporations Taxes Act 1988 discriminated against widowers.

However, the declaration of incompatibility in *R v Secretary of State for the Environment, ex p Alconbury* (made by the Divisional Court at [2001] JPL 291) that the planning system breached Article 6 was reversed by the House of Lords at [2001] 3 WLR 1389. Similarly, the decision of Keith J in *Matthews v Ministry of Defence, The Times*, 30 January 2002, that the bar on taking proceedings against the Crown under section 10 of the Crown Proceedings Act 1947 breached the right of access to the court under Article 6 was reversed by the Court of Appeal at [2002] 3 All ER 513.

In relation to Orders in Council being defined as primary legislation under section 21, see, generally, P Billings and B Pontin, 'Prerogative Powers and the Human Rights Act: Elevating the Status of Orders in Council' [2001] PL 21.

4.50 In *RSPCA v Attorney-General* [2001] 3 All ER 530, para 37, Lightman J expressed the view that the RSPCA rules may constitute subordinate legislation under section 21(1) of the Human Rights Act because they are an 'instrument made under primary legislation'.

4.52 The views expressed in the Main Work that the court must satisfy itself that *primary* legislation prevents the removal of the incompatibility were accepted by Richards J; see *R (Bono) v Harlow District Council* [2002] 1 WLR 2475.

(3) Jurisdiction to make declarations of incompatibility

In *Poplar Housing and Regeneration Community Association Ltd v Donoghue* [2002] **4.53**
QB 48, paras 9, 10 and 28, the Court of Appeal took the view that, when a county
court was dealing with a matter which might result in a declaration of incompatibility being sought on appeal there could be substantial advantages in giving a decision summarily.

It was held in *R v Secretary of State for the Home Department, ex p Kurdistan Worker's Party and Others* [2002] EWHC Admin 644 that the fact that a tribunal, in that case the Proscribed Organisations Appeal Commission, does not have power to make a declaration of incompatibility does not generally render proceedings before it inappropriate or render an application for judicial review appropriate. The appropriate course is still generally to pursue the proceedings before the inferior tribunal and then on appeal to the High Court or Court of Appeal and apply for a declaration, rather than to apply for judicial review directly.

n137: *R v DPP, ex p Kebilene* is now reported at [2000] 2 AC 326.

In *Whittaker v P & D Watson* [2002] ICR 1244 the EAT considered an appeal **4.54**
from an employment tribunal which had stayed a claim under the Disability
Discrimination Act 1995. The tribunal had concluded that it did not have jurisdiction to deal with the claim and that section 7 of the 1995 Act, which excluded
small businesses from liability under the Act, was incompatible with the Human
Rights Act. The EAT, dismissing the applicant's appeal, held that neither it nor the
employment tribunal had the jurisdiction to decide whether legislation was incompatible with Convention rights. The applicant was, however, given permission to appeal to the Court of Appeal, which does have the required jurisdiction.
It was suggested that parties seeking a declaration of incompatibility should have
their cases determined on paper by the President of the EAT who, where appropriate, could adjourn or dismiss the appeal, giving permission to appeal to the
Court of Appeal to determine the issue of compatibility.

For an example of a remedial order, see the the Mental Health Act 1983 **4.59**
(Remedial) Order 2001, SI 2001/3712, made on 18 November 2001 by the
Secretary of State for Health. It followed the declaration of incompatibility made
by the Court of Appeal in *R (H) v London North and East Region Mental Health
Review Tribunal* [2001] 3 WLR 512 in relation to the burden of proof for discharge from detention in hospital pursuant to the Mental Health Act 1983.

It was held in *Thoburn v Sunderland City Council* [2002] 3 WLR 247 that section **4.60**
10(2) and 10(3) apply to future legislation as well as to legislation already passed.

5

HUMAN RIGHTS AND PUBLIC AUTHORITIES

B. The Definition of Public Authorities Under the Act

(2) Types of public authorities

The distinction between standard public authorities, functional public authori- **5.08**
ties and courts and tribunals drawn in the Main Work was adopted and approved

by Lord Woolf CJ in *Poplar Housing and Regeneration Community Association Ltd v Donoghue* [2002] QB 48, 68, para 63.

C. Functional Public Authorities

(1) The definition of functional authorities

5.27 The definition of who should be a public authority and what is a public function for the purposes of section 6 should be given a generous interpretation; see *Poplar Housing and Regeneration Community Association Ltd v Donoghue* [2002] QB 48, 67, para 58 (*per* Lord Woolf CJ). However, the fact that a body performed an activity which otherwise a public body would be under a duty to perform did not mean that such performance was necessarily a public function. The defendant had been granted a tenancy of a property by the London borough of Tower Hamlets pending a decision as to whether she was intentionally homeless. The property had subsequently been transferred to the claimant housing association. Following a determination by the council that the claimant was intentionally homeless, the association issued a summons for possession under section 21(4) of the Housing Act 1996. The defendant alleged that this amounted to a breach of Article 8. The court held that in all the circumstances of this 'borderline' case (para 66) the housing association was so closely assimilated with the council that it was performing public and not private functions. The council had created the association to take a transfer of local authority housing stock, five of its board members were also members of the council, and the association was subject to the guidance of the council as to the manner in which it acted towards the defendant. The court also had regard to the fact that the transfer of the property from the council to the association had taken place during the currency of the defendant's tenancy, and 'it was intended that she would be treated no better and no worse off than if she remained a tenant of [the council].' The association therefore 'stood in relation to her in very much the position previously occupied by [the council]' (para 65).

In *R (Heather) v Leonard Cheshire Foundation* [2002] 2 All ER 936 the Court of Appeal considered whether the defendant care provider constituted a 'public authority' under section 6. Pursuant to a power under the National Assistance Act 1948, a local authority engaged the defendant to provide residential accommodation to the claimants to meet its statutory obligation. The claimants argued that the defendant's decision to close the home was contrary to Article 8. Lord Woolf CJ held that 'on the approach adopted in *Donoghue*' the defendant was not performing a public function. The local authority was contracting out to a voluntary service provider which had no statutory powers of its own and, with the exception of the source of funding, there was no material distinction between the nature of the services provided by the defendant to residents funded by a local authority and those provided to residents funded privately. The defendant was not 'standing in the shoes of the local authorities' (para 35). The court in *Heather* observed that the result of its ruling was that the defendant was not subject to challenge under the Human Rights Act 1998, even though the local authority would have been if it had been responsible for making the same decision. The claimants' submission that this circumstance militated in favour of a finding that the function was public was, however, dismissed as circular, the court choosing to emphasise, as it had done in *Donoghue* (at para 60), the continuing obligation of the local authority to the individual(s) concerned under the Convention in respect of that function, regardless of the delegation of its performance.

The approach taken by the Court of Appeal in *Poplar Housing* and *Leonard Cheshire* is not compelling. It is difficult to reconcile with the expansive views of Lord Irvine in moving the Bill who said 'We have also decided that we should apply the Bill to a wide rather than a narrow range of public authorities so as to provide as much protection as possible to those who claim their rights have been infringed' and those of Jack Straw MP; see, further, Main Work, para 5.03. (These statements are themselves admissible on the *Pepper v Hart* principles; see Main Work para 4.35 ff.) It is also strongly arguable that a broad and generous interpretation of the meaning of 'public authorities' would extend its scope to private bodies which provide 'contracted out' services and would operate in the public interest.

The managers of a private psychiatric hospital which was registered both as a mental nursing home under the Registered Homes Act 1984, and to receive patients liable to be detained under the Mental Health Act 1983, were held to be a public authority in *R (A) v Partnerships in Care Ltd* [2002] 1 WLR 2610. The claimant challenged the decision by the managers to cease the treatment of personality disorders in one of its wards. In support of that ruling, Keith J remarked that under the 1983 and 1984 Acts, the managers were a body 'upon whom important statutory functions are devolved' (para 17), and that, by virtue of regulations made under the 1984 Act, 'the statutory duty . . . to provide adequate professional staff and adequate treatment facilities was cast *directly* on the hospital' (para 24). It was also a matter of public interest for patients detained under the 1983 Act to receive the care and treatment that they needed to satisfy the criteria for rehabilitation.

See, generally, D Oliver, 'The Frontiers of the State: Public Authorities and Public Functions under the Human Rights Act' [2001] PL 476; C McDougall, ' "The Alchemist's Search for the Philosopher's Stone": Public Authorities and the Human Rights Act One Year On' [2002] JR 23; M Carss-Fisk, 'Public Authorities: The Developing Definition' [2002] EHRLR 319; K Marcus, 'What is Public Power? The Court's Approach to the Public Authority Definition under the Human Rights Act', in J Cooper and J Jowell (eds), *Delivering Rights? How the Human Rights Act is Working and for Whom* (Hart Publishing, 2003).

n112c: *R v Servite Homes, ex p Goldsmith* is now reported at [2001] LGR 55.

n112e: *R v Mutham House School, ex p R* is now reported at [2000] LGR 255.

(2) The exclusion of private acts of functional public authorities

5.29 Conversely, a private hospital making decisions about whether facilities can and should be provided, and adequate staff made available, to treat NHS patients was held to be performing acts of a public nature; see *R (A) v Partnerships in Care Ltd* [2002] 1 WLR 2610. See, further, Supplement, para 5.27.

5.34 Several of the suggestions in this paragraph are supported by the reasoning of Keith J in *R (A) v Partnerships in Care Ltd* [2002] 1 WLR 2610; see, further, Supplement, para 5.27. The function of the managers of a private hospital in deciding whether facilities could and should be provided, and adequate staff made available, to enable relevant treatment to take place was described as 'the subject of specific statutory underpinning directed at the hospital'. Keith J also drew an analogy between the role of the hospital and that of a private company selected to run a prison, holding that, as with a private prison, the nature of the hospital's function was 'a matter of public concern and interest'.

(4) Religious bodies

5.36 A parochial church council was found to be a public authority in *Aston Cantlow Parochial Church Council v Wallbank* [2002] Ch 51, 62, para 35, where the Court of Appeal (Sir Andrew Morritt V-C) said:

> It is an authority in the sense that it possesses powers which private individuals do not possess to determine how others should act. Thus, in particular, its notice to repair has statutory force. It is public in the sense that it is created and empowered by law; that it forms part of the church by law established; and that its functions include the enforcement through the courts of a common law liability to maintain its chancels resting upon persons who need not be members of the church. If this were to be incorrect, the PCC would nevertheless, and for the same reasons, be a legal person certain of whose functions, chancel repairs among them, are functions of a public nature.

See, further, D Oliver, 'Chancel Repairs and the Human Rights Act' [2001] PL 651.

D. The Human Rights Act and the Courts

(2) Courts and tribunals

5.43 In *Austin Hall Building v Buckland Securities* [2001] BLR 272, H H J Bowsher QC held that an adjudicator in a building dispute exercising functions pursuant to the Housing Grants Construction and Regeneration Act 1996 was not a 'court or tribunal' for the purpose of section 6 of the Human Rights Act because 'proceedings before an adjudicator are not legal proceedings' falling within section 21 of the Human Rights Act (para 40). The judge dealt with the definition of 'legal proceedings' as follows (para 35):

> Legal proceedings result in a judgment or order that in itself can be enforced. If the decision at the end of legal proceedings is that money should be paid, a judgment is drawn up that can be put in the hand of the Sheriff or Bailiff and enforced. That is not the case with an adjudicator. The language of the 1996 Act throughout is that the adjudicator makes a decision. He does not make a judgment. Nor does he make an 'award' as an arbitrator does though he can order that his decision be complied with. Proceedings before an arbitrator are closer to court proceedings because an award of an arbitrator can in some circumstances be registered and enforced without a judgment of the court. But the decision of an adjudicator, like the decision of a certifier, is not enforceable of itself. Those decisions, like the decisions of a certifier, can be relied on as the basis for an application to the court for judgment, but they are not in themselves enforceable.

The Court of Appeal in *R v Mushtaq* [2002] EWCA Crim expressed the view that a jury in a criminal trial is not a separate public authority; the court acting collectively bears the shared responsibility for ensuring a fair trial.

(5) Indirect horizontal application of human rights

(d) Germany

5.73 n269: See also R Brinktrine, 'The Horizontal Effect of Human Rights in German Constitutional Law: The British Debate on Horizontality and the Possible Role Model of the German Doctrine of "*mittelbare Dritwirkung der Grundrechte*" ' [2001] EHRLR 421; and R English, 'Protection of Privacy and Freedom of Speech in Germany', in M Colvin (ed), *Developing Key Privacy Rights* (Hart Publishing, 2002).

(6) The court as a public authority under the Human Rights Act

(b) Views concerning the effect of section 6(3)

5.79 The effect of section 6(3) continues to be the subject of considerable debate: see, for example, A Lester and D Pannick, 'The Impact of the Human Rights Act on Private Law: The Knight's Move' 116 LQR 380; J Beatson and S Grosz, 'Horizontality: A Footnote' 116 LQR 385; N Bamforth, 'The True "Horizontal Effect" of the Human Rights Act 1998' 117 LQR 34; D Oliver, 'The Human Rights Act and the Public Law/Private Law Divide' [2000] EHRLR 343; T Raphael, 'The Problem of the Horizontal Effect' [2000] EHRLR 393; T De La Mare and K Gallifant, 'The Horizontal Effect of the Human Rights Act 1988' [2001] JR 29; M Hunt, 'The "Horizontal Effect" of the Human Rights Act:

Moving Beyond the Public–Private Distinction', in J Jowell and J Cooper (eds), *Understanding Human Rights Principles* (Hart Publishing, 2001); I Hare, 'Vertically Challenged: Private Parties, Privacy and the Human Rights Act' [2001] EHRLR 526; and A Young, 'Remedial and Substantive Horizontality: The Common Law and *Douglas v Hello!*' [2002] PL 221.

(c) Analysis of the effect of section 6(3)

5.81 **Procedural horizontality.** A striking example of a tribunal failing to regulate its own procedures to act in conformity with the Convention is provided by *R (A) v Lord Saville (No 2)* [2002] 1 WLR 1249. The Court of Appeal held that the Bloody Sunday Inquiry tribunal had breached the rights of soldier–witnesses under Article 2 of the Convention by requiring them to give evidence in Londonderry.

5.83 **Remedial horizontality.** Section 12 of the Human Rights Act requires the court to satisfy itself of certain specified matters if it is considering whether to grant 'any relief which, if granted, may affect the exercise of the Convention right to freedom of expression'. In *A v B plc* [2002] 3 WLR 542 the Court of Appeal was required to consider the balance between the Article 8 rights of the claimant, a professional footballer, and the defendant newspaper's Article 10 rights when deciding the defendant's appeal against an interim injunction to prevent publication of stories addressing the claimant's extramarital affairs. In the course of allowing the appeal, the Court laid down detailed guidelines for the exercise of judicial discretion in the light of the provisions both of section 12 of the Human Rights Act, and of Articles 8 and 10 of the Convention.

5.84 **Direct statutory horizontality.** The principle of direct statutory horizontality has been applied, for example, in *Wilson v First County Trust* [2001] QB 407 and *Wilson v First County Trust (No 2)* [2001] 3 WLR 42 where the Court of Appeal decided that the bar against enforcing a credit agreement breached the right of access to the court under Article 6 and the right to enjoy property under Article 1 of the First Protocol.

5.85 In the Main Work it is suggested that section 6(1) of the Human Rights Act requires a court to undertake the act of statutory construction in accordance with section 3 of the Act. Lord Hope expresses the same view in *R v Lambert* [2001] 3 WLR 206, para 114, which is discussed further at Supplement, para 5.114.

5.88 **The development of the common law.** In *Douglas v Hello! Ltd* [2001] 2 WLR 992, 1015–17, paras 83–91, Brooke LJ stated that horizontality arose because of positive duties imposed by Convention rights as a result of Article 1 of the Convention; the extent to which positive duties are based on Article 1 of the Convention is, however, open to question (see, generally, Main Work, paras 6.97–6.100). Sedley LJ said (at 1027, para 133) that section 12(4) of the Act:

... puts beyond question the direct applicability of at least one article of the Convention as between one private party to litigation and another—in the jargon, its horizontal effect. Whether this is an illustration of the intended mechanism of the entire Act, or whether it is a special case (and if so, why), need not detain us here.

Keene LJ said at 1035–6, para 166, that:

> Since the coming into force of the Human Rights Act 1998, the courts as a public authority cannot act in a way which is incompatible with a Convention right: section 6(1). That arguably includes their activity in interpreting and developing the common law, even where no public authority is a party to the litigation. Whether this extends to creating a new cause of action between private persons and bodies is more controversial, since to do so would appear to circumvent the restrictions on proceedings contained in section 7(1) of the Act and on remedies in section 8(1).

In *Loutchansky v Times Newspapers Ltd* [2002] QB 321 the Court of Appeal scrutinised the 'multiple publication rule' in the common law of defamation in order to establish whether it was in conflict with Article 10 of the Convention. It was held that this rule was compatible with Convention rights.

New causes of action in private law.   In *Venables v News Group Newspapers*   **5.98** [2001] Fam 430 Dame Butler-Sloss P held that, although the Convention does not give rise in private law proceedings to free-standing causes of action based on Convention rights, the court was obliged in such cases to act compatibly with Convention rights in adjudicating on common law causes of action.

There has been some debate about whether the courts would feel obliged to recognise a new tort of breach of privacy following the coming into force of the Human Rights Act (see Main Work, para 12.165ff). The recent case law reveals three distinct views about the availability and desirability of a new tort of invasion of privacy:

- That there is no common law tort of invasion of privacy and the courts are prevented by binding Court of Appeal authority from developing one (*Wainwright v Home Office* [2002] 3 WLR 405).
- That there is no tort and no need to develop one because in 'the great majority of situations, if not all situations, where the protection of privacy is justified . . . an action for breach of confidence now will . . . provide the necessary protection' (*A v B plc* [2002] 3 WLR 542).
- That a new tort is required and is now available, or is developing, in part at least as a result of the impetus provided by the Human Rights Act 1998 (*Douglas v Hello!* [2001] QB 967; *H (A Healthcare Worker) v Associated Newspapers Limited* [2002] EWCA Civ 195, para 40).

The outcome of the debate between these different views remains unclear; see, generally, H Tomlinson (ed), *Privacy and the Media* (Matrix, 2002), ch 1.

E. The Acts of a Public Authority

(1) The 'act' of a public authority

5.100 In *R v Lambert* [2001] 3 WLR 206, 243, para 114, Lord Hope said that the word 'act' should be given a broad and purposive meaning and includes the manner of the decision-taking exercise and the process of the reasoning leading up to it.

(3) The exclusion of liability for acts required by primary or delegated legislation

5.105A n379a: *R v DPP, ex p Kebilene* is now reported at [2000] 2 AC 326.

5.105B Section 6(2)(b) applies where a public authority is acting to give effect to, or enforce, a statutory provision which cannot be read or given effect to in a way which is compatible with Convention rights. The scope of section 6(2)(b) has been considered in several cases. In *R v Kansal (No 2)* [2002] AC 69, 113–14, para 88, Lord Hope rejected the argument that it was open to a prosecutor to exercise his discretion authorising the use of evidence from compulsory questioning by choosing *not* to adduce the evidence. Similarly, in *R (Alconbury) v Secretary of State for the Environment* [2001] JPL 291 the Divisional Court decided it was not legitimate to read down a legislative discretion so as to *extinguish* it. By contrast, in *R (Friends Provident) v Secretary of State for the Environment* [2001] 1 WLR 1450, paras 98 and 100, Forbes J *obiter* accepted the submission that the Secretary of State's discretion to call in a planning inquiry to ensure compliance with Article 6 only arose in some cases, where, for example, there were significant issues of fact to be decided. Thus, not *every* refusal to call in a planning application was necessarily incompatible with Article 6; and section 6(2)(b) did not apply. These authorities were extensively analysed by Moses J in *R (Wilkinson) v IRC* [2002] STC 347 where it was argued that section 6(2)(b) arose because primary legislation could be read or given effect in a way which was compatible with Convention rights: a discretionary provision to grant widow's bereavement allowance to a widower could be read down so that it *only* authorised the exercise of the power in a way which was compatible with Convention rights. However, Moses J held that compatibility could not be achieved by removing the power altogether and treating the provision conferring a power to give equal treatment to widowers as if it was a duty to treat them equally.

The decision in *Brown v Procurator Fiscal* was overruled by the Privy Council in *Brown v Stott* [2001] 2 WLR 817 which decided there was no breach of Article 6. For a fuller discussion, see Supplement, para 11.346.

5.106 The impact of the Act on delegated legislation is examined by R Allen and P Sales, 'Joint Note for the Court of Appeal in *R v Lord Chancellor, ex p Lightfoot*' [2000]

PL 361 in which it was accepted by the Crown that where enabling legislation does not compel subordinate legislation which is incompatible with Convention rights, officials acting under the subordinate legislation would be bound by section 6(1) to give effect to Convention rights.

The views expressed in the Main Work that a public authority can only escape liability under section 6(2)(b) if the *enabling* legislation deprived it of any discretion to act was accepted by Richards J in *R (Bono) v Harlow DC* [2002] 1 WLR 2475, paras 33–4. **5.107**

(6) The impact on the common law and the rules of precedence

In *R v Lambert* [2001] 3 WLR 206, 243, para 114, Lord Hope said that the word 'act' should be given a broad and purposive meaning. Section 6(1) of the Act states that a public authority must not act incompatibly with a Convention right and requires that a court carries out the 'act' of statutory construction otherwise than in accordance with section 3(1) of the Human Rights Act. A decision based on the application of a statute and the development of the common law is also an act by the court and is subject to the prohibition in section 6(1). Section 6(1) also affects matters of substance so that it will be unlawful within the meaning of section 6(1) for a court (including an appeal court) to determine a criminal charge on an interpretation of a statute which ignores section 3(1) or on a proposition of law which is incompatible with a Convention right. **5.114**

In *Aston Cantlow Parochial Church Council v Wallbank* [2002] Ch 51 the Court of Appeal held that the common law liability to carry out repairs to the chancel of a parish church was incompatible with Article 1 of the First Protocol and Article 14.

(7) Are there non-justiciable acts under the Human Rights Act?

See P Billings and B Pontin, 'Prerogative Powers and the Human Rights Act: Elevating the Status of Orders in Council' [2001] PL 21. **5.118**

In *R (Marchiori) v Environment Agency* [2002] EWCA Civ 3 the Court of Appeal confirmed that questions of the merits and demerits of government defence policy were non-justiciable. However, Laws LJ, giving the leading judgment, made the following *obiter* remarks (at paras 40 and 41): **5.119A**

> a statute might itself require the courts to review high policy decisions (or decisions involving judgment of deeply controversial social questions) upon which traditionally they would advisedly have had no voice. That I think was the position in *Operation Dismantle*. In this jurisdiction such a state of affairs may most obviously arise in the execution of the judges' duty under the Human Rights Act 1998.

F. Acts Which are 'Incompatible' with Convention Rights

(1) The meaning of 'incompatible'

5.121A n435e: The remarks of Lord Bingham CJ in *R v DPP, ex p Kebilene* are now reported at [2000] 2 AC 326, 344; the remarks of Laws LJ are now reported at ibid, 356.

n435f: The remarks of Lord Hope are now reported at [2000] 2 AC 326, 386, 388.

G. 'Judicial Deference' and the Human Rights Act

(3) The views of a public authority

5.132 n471: *R v Broadcasting Standards Commission, ex p BBC* is now reported at [2000] 3 WLR 1327.

5.133 n474a: The remarks of Lord Hope in *R v DPP, ex p Kebilene* are now reported at [2000] 2 AC 366, 381.

(4) 'Judicial deference under the Act': conclusion

5.134 In a number of cases it has been emphasised that deference should be accorded to the decisions of the legislature where the context justifies it (see, for example, *Brown v Stott* [2001] 2 WLR 817, 834–5 (Lord Bingham); 842–3 (Lord Steyn)). Similarly, in *R v Lambert* [2001] 2 WLR 211, 219, Lord Woolf CJ observed that:

> . . . the legislation is passed by a democratically elected Parliament and therefore the courts under the Convention are entitled to and should, as a matter of constitutional principle, pay a degree of deference to the view of Parliament as to what is in the interest of the public generally when upholding the rights of the individual under the Convention.

In *Poplar Housing and Regeneration Community Association Ltd v Donoghue* [2002] QB 48, para 69, Lord Woolf CJ expressed comparable views concerning whether the ability of a housing association to obtain possession on mandatory grounds under the Housing Act 1988 in relation to premises let as an assured shorthold tenancy was a disproportionate interference with Article 8:

> There is certainly room for conflicting views. . . . However, in considering whether Poplar can rely on Article 8(2), the Court has to pay considerable attention to the fact that Parliament intended when enacting section 21(4) of the 1988 Act to give preference to the needs of those dependent on social housing as a whole over those in the position of the defendant. The economic and other implications of any policy in this area are extremely complex and far-reaching. This is an area where, in our judgments, the courts must treat the decisions of Parliament as to what is the public interest with particular deference.

In his dissenting judgment in *International Transport Roth GmbH v Secretary of State for the Home Department* [2002] 3 WLR 344, paras 81–7, Laws LJ formulated some general principles to be applied when judges ascertain the degree of deference to be paid to the democratic powers of government:

- greater deference should be paid to an Act of Parliament than the decision of the executive or a subordinate measure; see Lord Woolf CJ in *R v Lambert* [2001] 2 WLR 211, para 16; and *Poplar Housing and Regeneration Community Association v Donoghue* [2002] QB 48, para 69;
- there is more scope for deference where the Convention itself requires a balance to be struck and much less so where rights are expressed in unqualified terms; see *R v DPP, ex p Kebilene* [2002] 2 AC 326, para 80 *per* Lord Hope;
- greater deference will be due where the subject matter is peculiarly within the constitutional responsibility of democratic government—such as the defence of the realm (see eg *Chandler v DPP* [1964] AC 763, 790, 798 *per* Lord Reid and Viscount Radcliffe and *Marchiori v Environmental Agency* [2002] EWCA Civ 3, paras 31–8, discussed at Supplement, para 119A) or immigration control—and less when it lies within the constitutional responsibility of the court (such as the field of criminal justice); and
- greater deference is due where the subject matter lies more readily within the actual or potential expertise of the democratic powers (such as governmental decisions in the area of macro-economic policy; see *R v Secretary of State for the Environment, ex p Nottinghamshire CC* [1986] AC 240; *R v Secretary of State for the Environment, ex p Hammersmith and Fulham LBC* [1991] 1 AC 521).

Thus, in *R (Hirst) v Secretary of State for the Home Department* [2002] 1 WLR 2929, a case concerning whether a prisoner's Article 10 rights had been breached by a policy requiring all conversations with the press to be recorded for vetting purposes, Elias J stated that the courts will take a much more deferential approach to the application of the proportionality principle where the deprivation of the right formed part of the prisoner's punishment, 'particularly where it reflects the democratic will' (para 39). See also *R (Pearson) v Secretary of State for the Home Department* [2001] HRLR 31, paras 20–3.

The Court of Appeal in *R (Mahmood) v Secretary of State for the Home Department* [2001] 1 WLR 840 and *R (Isiko) v Secretary of State for the Home Department* [2001] HRLR 295 took a highly deferential approach towards the proportionality principle. However, in *R v A (No 2)* [2001] 2 WLR 1546 and *R (Daly) v Secretary of State for the Home Department* [2001] 2 WLR 1622 the House of Lords applied a stricter test whilst emphasising that its application would be affected by the context. However, in *R (Samaroo) v Home Secretary* [2001] UKHRR 1150 the Court of Appeal again took a deferential approach towards the proportionality principle when applying *Daly*. *Samaroo* was cited with approval and applied by the Court of Appeal in *R (Ponting) v Governor of HM Prison Whitemoor* [2002] EWCA Civ 224.

In *R (Prolife Alliance) v BBC* [2002] 2 All ER 756 the Court of Appeal considered the margin of discretion to be granted to the BBC when reviewing its decision to refuse permission to the Prolife Alliance to air their party election broadcast in the lead-up to the 2001 general election. The Court (at para 37, *per* Laws LJ) shed some light upon the relationship between factual context and the extent of deference to be granted to a public authority:

> Where the context is broadcast entertainment, I would accept without cavil that in the event of a legal challenge to a prohibition the courts should pay a very high degree of respect to the broadcasters' judgment, given the background of the [Broadcasting Act] 1990, [Broadcasting Act] 1996, the BBC Agreement, the codes of guidance and the BSC adjudications. Where the context is day-to-day news reporting the broadcasters' margin of discretion may be somewhat more constrained but will remain very considerable. But the *milieu* with which we are concerned with in this case, the cockpit of a general election, is inside the veins and arteries of the democratic process. The broadcasters' views are entitled to be respected, but their force and weight are modest at best.

In *R (Farrakhan) v Secretary of State for the Home Department* [2002] 3 WLR 481 the Court of Appeal, without citing *Samaroo*, relied principally upon its conclusion that a 'particularly wide margin of discretion' should be accorded to the Secretary of State when upholding his decision to refuse the claimant, the spiritual leader of the Nation of Islam, entry to the UK.

These cases are discussed more fully at Supplement, para 6.81A, and see, generally, P Craig 'The Courts, the Human Rights Act and Judicial Review' [2001] 117 LQR 589. See also J Jowell, 'Due Deference under the Human Rights Act', in J Cooper and J Jowell (eds), *Delivering Rights? How the Human Rights Act is Working and for Whom* (Hart Publishing, 2003), who argues that the deference that the courts should give to the bodies they are reviewing rests not on their superior *constitutional* competence but on the relative *institutional* competence of the courts and other bodies to decide the matter, in the context of the particular right under review.

6

GENERAL PRINCIPLES UNDER THE CONVENTION

B. The Interpretation of the Convention

(2) Construing the Convention

(a) Construing the Convention as a treaty

6.17 **Special meaning.**   The concept of autonomous meaning as a rule for interpreting international treaties was extensively discussed by the House of Lords in *R v Secretary of State for the Home Department, ex p Adan* [2001] 2 WLR 143 (in the context of analysing the Geneva Convention and Protocol relating to the Status of Refugees (1951) (Cmd 9171) and (1967) (Cmnd 3906)).

(c) The Convention as a 'living instrument'

6.24 In *Stafford v UK* (2002) 35 EHRR 22 the Court reconsidered its analysis of the mandatory life sentence for murder in *Wynne v UK* (1994) 19 EHRR 333 'in the light of present day conditions'. The Court held that 'the finding in *Wynne* that the mandatory life sentence constituted punishment for life can no longer be regarded as reflecting the real position in the domestic criminal justice system of the mandatory life prisoner'. Accordingly, the UK government was in breach of Article 5(4) in failing to provide for review by a court of the lawfulness of the claimant's detention following expiry of the tariff element of the sentence. Similarly, in *Goodwin v United Kingdom* (2002) 35 EHRR 18 the Court re-examined the lack of legal recognition given to a post-operative transsexual against current scientific and social conditions and concluded that Article 8 had been breached, differing from the views taken by the Court in *Cossey v United Kingdom* (1980) 13 EHRR 622; *Rees v United Kingdom* (1986) 9 EHRR 56; and *Sheffield and Horsham v United Kingdom* (1990) 13 EHRR 163.

6.26 See also *Jokela v Finland* (Judgment of 21 May 2002) in which the Court held that the right to peaceful enjoyment of possessions contained in Article 1 of Protocol 1 included 'the expectation of a reasonable consistency between interrelated albeit separate decisions concerning the same property'. See, further, Supplement, para 6.30.

6.27 The cautious approach of the Court towards the implication of Convention rights was evident in its refusal to imply a right to die by assisted suicide into Article 2 in *Pretty v UK* (2002) 12 BHRC 149.

(d) The principle of effectiveness

6.30 In *Jokela v Finland* (Judgment of 21 May 2002) the Court relied upon the principle of effectiveness to hold that the right to peaceful enjoyment of possessions in Article 1 of Protocol 1 included 'the expectation of a reasonable consistency between interrelated albeit separate decisions concerning the same property' where its value had been assessed at very different levels for expropriation and inheritance tax purposes.

C. The Doctrine of 'Margin of Appreciation'

(3) Margin of appreciation and the Human Rights Act

The views expressed in the Main Work concerning the role of the 'margin of appreciation' in a general sense under the Human Rights Act were adopted and approved by Lord Hutton in *R v Lambert* [2001] 3 WLR 206, 272, para 195. **6.37**

See also *Brown v Stott* [2001] 2 WLR 817, 835 in which Lord Bingham said that while a national court does not accord the margin of appreciation recognised by the Court of Human Rights as a supra-national court, it will give weight to the decisions of a representative legislature and a democratic government within the margin of discretion accorded to those bodies. **6.38**

D. The Doctrine of Proportionality

(2) Proportionality under the Convention

(b) The principle of proportionality

In the important case of *Hatton and Others v United Kingdom* (2002) 34 EHRR 1 the Court stated (at para 97) that: **6.47**

> It considers that States are required to minimise, as far as possible, the interference with . . . rights by seeking to achieve their aims in the least onerous way as regards human rights.

The Court found (at para 106) that the steps taken by the government to improve the noise climate from night flights at Heathrow airport were not *necessary* in the absence of any serious attempt to evaluate the extent or impact of the interference with the applicants' sleep patterns and the absence of any prior specific and complete study with the aim of finding the least onerous solution as regards human rights.

(3) Proportionality in English administrative law

In *R (Alconbury Developments Ltd) v Environmental Secretary* [2001] 2 WLR 1389, 1407, para 53, Lord Slynn remarked that the time had come to recognise proportionality as part of administrative law. Lord Slynn's suggestion was followed by the Court of Appeal in *R (Tucker) v Secretary of State for Social Security* [2001] EWCA Civ 1646. **6.54**

See, generally, M Elliott, 'The HRA 1998 and Standard of Substantive Review' [2002] JR 97; M Fordham, 'Common Law Proportionality' [2002] JR 110; and R Clayton, 'Proportionality and the HRA 1998: Implications for Substantive Review' [2002] JR 124.

(4) Proportionality in European Community Law

(b) The necessity test

6.60   In *Gough v Chief Constable of Derbyshire* [2002] QB 459, paras 72–80, Laws LJ carried out a detailed analysis of the proportionality principle. He emphasised that a court is making a secondary judgment and it must respect the margin of discretion of the original decision-maker; that it is not legitimate for a decision-maker to override a Community right except on substantial and objective grounds of the public interest; and that the decision-maker must choose a means which constitutes the least interference consistent with its public policy aim.

(8) Proportionality under the Human Rights Act

(b) The proportionality principle

6.81A   In *R (Mahmood) v Secretary of State for the Home Department* [2001] 1 WLR 840 and *R (Isiko) v Secretary of State for the Home Department* [2001] HRLR 295 the Court of Appeal treated proportionality as equivalent to *Wednesbury* unreasonableness; it decided that the proper test was to ask whether the public authority's view of the proportionality of an interference with a Convention right was within the range of responses open to a reasonable decision-maker. However, in *R v A (No 2)* [2001] 2 WLR 1546 and *R v Secretary of State for the Home Department, ex p Daly* [2001] 2 AC 532 the House of Lords held that proportionality required the court to examine:

- whether the legislative objective is sufficiently important to justify limiting the fundamental right;
- whether the measures designed to meet the legislative objective are rationally connected to it; and
- whether the means used to impair the freedom are no more than is necessary to accomplish that objective.

In a concurring judgment in *Daly* (at 546–8) Lord Steyn drew the following distinctions between proportionality and the principle of *Wednesbury* unreasonableness. First, the doctrine of proportionality may require the reviewing court to assess the balance which the decision-maker has struck, not merely whether it is within the range of rational or reasonable decisions. Secondly, the proportionality test may go further than the traditional grounds of review inasmuch as it may require attention to be directed to the relative weight accorded to interests and considerations.

Thirdly, even the heightened scrutiny test developed in *R v Ministry of Defence, ex p Smith* [1996] QB 517 is not necessarily appropriate to the protection of human rights (see *Smith and Grady v United Kingdom* (1999) 29 EHRR 493 and Main Work, para 21.178). However, Lord Steyn went on to emphasise that proportionality does not mean a shift to merits review, and that the intensity of review will depend on the subject matter in hand, even in cases involving Convention rights.

In the important case of *R (Samaroo) v Home Secretary* [2001] UKHRR 1150 the Court of Appeal examined the ramifications of the *Daly* principles when assessing whether a decision to deport the claimant was a proportionate interference with the right of respect for family life. Dyson LJ took the view that what proportionality requires in any particular case will usually have to be considered in two stages:

- can the objective of the measure be achieved by means which are less interfering with an individual's rights? and
- does the measure have an excessive or disproportionate effect on the interest of the affected individual?

Dyson LJ then stated that, when addressing this second issue, the task for the decision-maker is to strike a fair balance between the legitimate aim in question and the individual's Convention rights; and the function of the court is to decide whether this fair balance has been struck, recognising and allowing that the decision-maker has a discretionary area of judgment. The particular factors the court will consider when deciding whether to defer to the decision-maker's judgment will include:

- the nature of the right, that is, is it an unqualified or a qualified right;
- the extent to which the issue requires consideration of social, economic and political factors;
- the extent to which the court has a special expertise, for example, in criminal matters;
- where the rights have a high degree of constitutional protection such as freedom of expression and access to the courts.

Dyson LJ went on to hold that the court should give the Secretary of State a significant margin of discretion in assessing the proportionality of his decision to deport the claimant: the right to family life was not absolute or one which required high constitutional protection; the court did not have the expertise to judge how effective a deterrent is a policy of deporting foreign nationals convicted of serious drug offences once they had served their sentence; and the Court of Human Rights had on many occasions upheld deportations made against drug trafficking offences, even when they involved the most serious interferences with Article 8 rights. He concluded that it is not incumbent on the Secretary of State to *prove* that the withholding of a deportation order would seriously undermine his policy of deterring crime and disorder. Proof is not required. The justification must be 'convincingly established' and the court should consider the matter in a realistic manner, always keeping in mind that the decision-maker is entitled to a significant margin of discretion. The Secretary of State must show he has struck a fair balance; and the court will interfere if the weight accorded by the decision-maker to particular factors is unfair and unreasonable.

It is submitted that the *Samaroo* decision is unsatisfactory in a number of respects. First, Dyson LJ does not elaborate on his reasons for holding that the legitimate aim of deterring crime and disorder cannot be achieved by an alternative means which interferes less with Convention rights; or explain the justification for moving straight to the second stage of considering whether the interference with the claimant's right to family life was proportionate or excessive. In *R (Hirst) v Secretary of State for the Home Department* [2002] 1 WLR 2929, paras 33–6, Elias J expressed the view that there is no room for a court to consider the principle that a right should be minimally impaired where the executive decides to remove it as a deliberate and considered response (such as denying the right to freedom of expression to a prisoner or deciding that deportation is the only appropriate response for a conviction for serious drug offences). However, this analysis is open to question. The fact that the executive has concluded that denying the essence of a right is appropriate is the *very* circumstance in which it may be appropriate for a court to consider whether there is a *less* drastic means of accomplishing the objective in question. Furthermore, this approach is difficult to reconcile with the approach taken by the House of Lords in *R v Shayler* [2002] 2 WLR 754 (which is discussed further below).

Secondly, the benevolent approach taken by Dyson LJ in *Samaroo* to proportionality contrasts strongly with the close factual analysis adopted by the Canadian courts when considering the proportionality of interferences with rights and freedoms under the Canadian Charter of Rights: see, for example, *RJR McDonald v Canada (A-G)* [1995] 3 SCR 199 and *Thomson Newspapers v Canada* [1998] 1 SCR 877, and see also Main Work, para 6.66.

However, in *R (Ponting) v Governor of HM Prison Whitemoor and Another* [2002] EWCA Civ 224 the Court of Appeal applied Dyson LJ's approach in *Samaroo* when considering whether various provisions of the governor's 'compact' on computer use with the (unsuccessful) claimant–prisoner breached his rights under Articles 6 and 8.

The approach to proportionality advocated in *Daly* was further considered by the House of Lords in the important case of *R v Shayler* [2002] 2 WLR 754 in the course of determining whether sections 1 and 4 of the Official Secrets Act 1989 were incompatible with Article 10. It was argued that the possibility of a judicial review of a decision to refuse authorisation to disclose relevant information did not provide effective protection of the claimant's Article 10 rights. Lord Bingham, quoting from *Daly* at length, emphasised that, when reviewing an alleged violation of a Convention right, 'the court will now conduct a much more rigorous and intrusive review than was once thought to be permissible' (para 33). Lord Hope cited with approval the three-stage approach approved in *Daly*, stating at para 61:

> As these propositions indicate, it is not enough to assert that the decision taken was a reasonable one. A close and penetrating examination of the factual justification for the restriction is needed if the fundamental rights enshrined in the Convention are to remain practical and effective for everyone else who wishes to exercise them.

Lord Hope proceeded to set out (at para 79) the questions a court should ask itself when reviewing a refusal to authorise disclosure of relevant information:

> (1) What, with respect to that information, was the justification for interference with the Convention right? (2) If the justification was that this was in the interests of national security, was there a pressing social need for that information not to be disclosed? And (3) if there was such a need, was the interference with the Convention right which was involved in withholding authorisation for the disclosure of that information no more than was necessary?

The Court of Appeal adopted such a rigorous approach in *R (Prolife Alliance) v BBC* [2002] 2 All ER 756 when reviewing a decision by the BBC to refuse permission to the Prolife Alliance to air a party election broadcast which showed images of abortion operations. Laws LJ, giving the leading judgment of the Court, scrutinised and rejected the factual justifications put forward for the decision, remarking (at para 43) that:

> there is nothing gratuitous sensational or untrue in the appellant's intended [party election broadcast]. It is certainly graphic and, as I have said, disturbing. But if we are to take political free speech seriously, those characteristics cannot begin to justify the censorship that was done in this case.

The approach in this case can, however, be contrasted with that taken in *R (Farrakhan) v Secretary of State for the Home Department* [2002] 3 WLR 481 where the Court of Appeal acknowledged *Daly* to be the 'best source of guidance in judicial review cases where human rights are in play' (para 65). The Court did not, however, embark upon a close factual analysis of the proportionality of the Secretary of State's decision to refuse the claimant, the spiritual leader of the Nation of Islam, entry into the UK, which decision was challenged on grounds that it violated Article 10. The Court chose instead to uphold the decision by according a 'particularly wide margin of discretion' to the Secretary of State (para 71). In its anxiety to avoid 'substituting its own decision for that of the decision maker' the Court failed to make any assessment of its own as to whether the Secretary of State's justification for the decision was 'convincingly established', even on the basis adopted in *Samaroo* (to which no reference was made). It is submitted that the degree of deference shown by the Court was such that, in practice, the intensity of review was no greater than would have resulted from applying the *Wednesbury* test, an outcome which is inconsistent with *Daly*, *Samaroo* and *Shayler* (the last of which was also not referred to by the Court).

In many cases the court will have to consider cases where public authorities are plainly on their face acting disproportionately. For example, in *R (Daly) v Secretary of State for the Home Department* [2001] 2 AC 532 where a policy that required prisoners always to absent themselves when legally privileged material is being searched was held to be disproportionate; and *A v Secretary of State for the Home Department* [2002] HRLR 45 where the Special Immigration Appeals Commission decided that the power to detain foreign nationals only on national security grounds was discriminatory and breached Article 14 because it was disproportionate.

The proportionality issue which arose in *Gough v Chief Constable of Derbyshire* [2002] 3 WLR 289 was rather different. In that case, however, it was unclear whether the public authority would necessarily be acting disproportionately if it followed the statutory scheme. Lord Phillipps MR (at paras 84–6) said:

> In our judgment these statutory provisions, if given their natural meaning, are capable of being applied in a manner which is harsh and disproportionate. If a low standard of proof is applied at the first stage, there is a danger of individuals being made subject to banning orders on evidence which is too slender to justify the restrictions on their freedom which these entail. The requirement to demonstrate 'special circumstances' could also lead the FBOA, or the magistrates' court on appeal, to refuse to grant permission to leave the country for a purpose which, while innocuous, would not naturally be said to constitute 'special circumstances'.
>
> However, the question is not whether the statutory provisions are capable of being interpreted in a manner which has disproportionate effect. The question is whether they are capable of being interpreted in a manner that is proportionate. Those who have to apply them are under a duty to give them an interpretation which is compatible with the requirements of European Community law and of the Human Rights Convention if this can be achieved.
>
> We have concluded that the scheme itself, if properly operated, will satisfy the requirements of proportionality.

Thus, a public authority is obliged to interpret provisions which might potentially be disproportionate in a way compatible with the Convention. It is probably immaterial whether this obligation arises because the public authority is duty bound to interpret legislation compatibly under section 3 or duty bound to apply it compatibly under section 6.

In *London Regional Transport v Mayor of London* [2003] EMLR 4, paras 56–7, Sedley LJ described the role of the proportionality principle in the following terms when considering the test for striking the balance between recognising the legitimacy of ordering disclosure of confidential information if it served the public interest in the free flow of information and ideas:

> Is it to be in Coke's phrase (4 Inst 41) the golden and straight metwand of the law or the uncertain and crooked cord of discretion? The contribution which Article 10 and the jurisprudence of the European Court of Human Rights can make towards an answer is, in my view, real.
>
> It lies in the methodical concept of proportionality. Proportionality is not a word found in the text of the Convention: it is the tool—the metwand—which the Court has adopted (from 19th-century German jurisprudence) for deciding a variety of Convention issues including, for the purposes of the qualifications to Articles 8 to 11, what is and is not necessary in a democratic society. It replaces an elastic concept with which political scientists are more at home than lawyers with a structured inquiry. Does the measure meet a recognised and pressing social need? Does it negate the primary right or restrict it more than necessary? Are the reasons given for it logical?

See, generally, M Fordham and T de la Mare, 'Identifying the Principles of Proportionality', in J Jowell and J Cooper (eds), *Understanding Human Rights Principles* (Hart Publishing, 2001); P Craig, 'The Courts, the Human Rights Act and Judicial Review' [2001] 117 LQR 589; R Clayton, 'Regaining a Sense of Proportion: The Human Rights Act and the Proportionality Principle' [2001] EHRLR 504; N Blake, 'Importing Proportionality: Clarification or Confusion' [2002] EHRLR 19; and I Leigh, 'Taking Human Rights Proportionately: Judicial Review, the Human Rights Act and Strasbourg' [2002] PL 265.

E. The Nature of Convention Rights

(2) Derogations from Convention rights

The Human Rights Act (Amendment) Order 2001, SI 2001/1216, which came into force on 1 April 2001, amended the Human Rights Act 1998 to reflect the withdrawal by the UK Government of the derogation from Article 5(3) of the Convention which was originally preserved by section 14(1)(a) of, and set out in Part I of Schedule 3 to, the 1998 Act. The withdrawal of the derogation was effective from 26 February 2001 and followed the implementation of Schedule 8 to the Terrorism Act 2000. **6.93**

By the Human Rights Act 1998 (Amendment No 2) Order 2001, SI 2001/4032, which came into force on 20 December 2001, Part I of the Human Rights Act 1998 was amended to contain a new derogation from Article 5. The derogation is made in respect of the extended powers of arrest and detention of suspected terrorists, pending deportation, accorded by the Anti-terrorism, Crime and Security Act 2001, which was passed in the wake of the terrorist attack on New York on 11 September 2001. The derogation is expressed to be from Article

5(1)(f), as interpreted by the Court in *Chahal v United Kingdom* (1996) 23 EHRR 413. The Court held in *Chahal* that detention which is on its face lawful under Article 5(1)(f), because it is done with a view to deportation or extradition, will cease to be permissible if deportation proceedings are not prosecuted with due diligence. Section 23 of the 2001 Act permits detention of a suspected international terrorist under the Immigration Act 1971 even where his removal or departure from the United Kingdom is prevented 'whether temporarily or indefinitely by a point of law which wholly or partly relates to an international agreement, or a practical consideration'.

The legality of the derogation is open to some doubt, as there is apparently no evidence of a specific threat to the United Kingdom. In October 2001, the Home Secretary himself informed the House of Commons that 'there is no immediate intelligence pointing to a specific threat to the United Kingdom' (HC Deb, col 925, 15 October 2001). See, further, Tomkins, 'Legislating against Terror: The Anti-Terrorism, Crime and Security Act 2001' [2002] PL 205; and Wadham, 'The Anti-Terrorism, Crime and Security Act 2001' Arch News 2002, 1, 5.

In *A and Others v Secretary of State for the Home Department* [2002] HRLR 45 the Special Immigration Appeals Commission decided that there was a public emergency threatening the life of the United Kingdom which justified derogating from the Convention under Article 15 of the Convention, but went on to hold that the power to detain foreign nationals only on national security grounds was discriminatory and breached Article 14. This decision was reversed by the Court of Appeal at [2002] UKHRR 1141.

(5) Positive obligations imposed by Convention rights

6.99 It has been suggested that there are five main positive duties under the Convention:

- a duty to place a legal framework which provides effective protection for Convention rights;
- a duty to prevent breaches of Convention rights;
- a duty to provide information and advice relevant to a breach of Convention rights;
- a duty to respond to breaches of Convention rights; and
- a duty to provide resources to individuals to prevent breaches of their Convention rights.

See, further, K Starmer, 'Positive Obligations under the Convention', in J Jowell and J Cooper (eds), *Understanding Human Rights Principles* (Hart Publishing, 2001).

6.100 In *Hatton and Others v United Kingdom* (2002) 34 EHRR 1 the Court, referring to *Powell & Rayner v United Kingdom* (1990) 12 EHRR 355, stated (at para 96) that 'whatever analytical approach is adopted—the positive duty or an interference—the applicable principles regarding justification under Article 8(2) are broadly similar.'

The nature of positive obligations was considered by the House of Lords in *R (Pretty)* **6.100A**
v DPP [2002] 1 AC 800. The question of whether a positive obligation exists depends on striking a fair balance between the general interests of the community and interests of the individual; see *Pretty, per* Lord Bingham at 1608, 1609, para 15; *per* Lord Hope at 1636, para 92. Striking a fair balance depends on whether the obligation in question is proportionate, and Lord Hope stated (at paras 92–7) that a public authority will show that it has acted proportionately if it proves:

- that the objective which is sought to be achieved is sufficiently important to justify limiting the fundamental right;
- that the means chosen to meet the objective are rational, fair and not arbitrary; and
- that the means used to impair the right are no more than is necessary to accomplish that objective and are as minimal as reasonably possible.

(6) The burden of proof

The courts have, however, placed upon public authorities the burden of establish- **6.102**
ing justification for interference with Convention rights. See, for example, *Kelly v BBC* [2001] Fam 59, 68, 69 *per* Munby J; *R (Samaroo) v Home Secretary* (2001) UKHRR 1150, para 29 *per* Dyson LJ (approving the judgment of Thomas J); and *R (KB and Others) v Mental Health Review Tribunal and Another* [2002] EWHC Admin 639, para 47 *per* Stanley Burnton J.

F. General Restrictions and Limitations on Convention Rights

(2) Restrictions on the political activities of aliens

In *R (Farrakhan) v Secretary of State for the Home Department* [2002] 3 WLR 481 **6.110**
the Court of Appeal described Article 16 as 'something of an anachronism half a century after the agreement of the Convention' (para 70), and held that it did not have direct impact upon the question of the compatibility with Article 10 of the Secretary of State's decision to refuse the claimant entry into the United Kingdom.

(5) Implied restrictions on Convention rights: the 'inherent limitations' doctrine

In *Re A (Children) (Conjoined Twins: Surgical Separation)* [2001] 2 WLR 480 **6.121**
the Court of Appeal rejected the argument that Article 2 contained an implied

limitation that the right could be violated if it was in conflict with another person's Article 2 right. Brooke LJ noted (at 571G) that the doctrine of inherent limitation appeared to be in its infancy as a matter of Convention law and said:

> I would be reluctant to hold, unless and until compelled to do so, that a right as fundamental as the right identified in article 2 can be subject to an implied limitation which destroys its value.

G. Interference with Qualified Rights

(2) 'Prescribed by law'

(a) Introduction

6.127 n492a: The principles which apply to statutory bodies do not affect the Crown which (like a private individual) is free to do whatever it chooses unless this is expressly prohibited; see, for example, *R v Secretary of State for Health ex p C* (2000) 1 FLR 627.

(b) The Convention approach

6.134 **Foreseeability.** For the meaning of 'prescribed by law', see also *Vgt Verein gegen Tierfabriken v Switzerland* (2001) 10 BHRC 473, paras 55–8, where the Court held that a commercial which contained only pictorial information of pigs in their natural surroundings and then in cramped pens could be prohibited from being broadcast for being 'political advertising'; the Court held that the interference was prescribed by law and had been formulated with sufficient precision as 'political' because the commercial reflected controversial opinions. However, in *NF v Italy* (Judgment of 2 August 2001) the Court decided that it was not foreseeable for a judge to be disciplined for his membership of the Freemasons under a directive which prohibited him from undermining the judiciary.

6.135 *Hashman and Harrup v United Kingdom* is now reported at (2000) 30 EHRR 241.

(3) 'Prescribed by law' under the Human Rights Act

6.143A In *B v Chief Constable of Avon and Somerset* [2001] 1 WLR 340 the Divisional Court decided that a sex offender order which prohibited the applicant from contacting, communicating, associating or befriending a person under 16 was sufficiently precise to be 'prescribed by law'. In *R (Rath) v Advertising Standards Authority* [2001] HRLR 436 the Authority's Code of Practice was held to be 'prescribed by law' because it had the underpinning of subordinate legislation and was readily accessible.

In *R v Perrin* [2002] EWCA Crim 747 the Court of Appeal held that the offence of publishing an obscene article under section 2(1) of the Obscene Publications

Act 1959 was 'prescribed by law' and rejected the argument that the definition of obscenity in section 1(1) of the Act was too imprecise to satisfy the requirement of foreseeability.

In *R v Shayler* [2002] 2 WLR 754 Lord Hope described (at para 56) the proper approach to ascertain whether a measure is 'prescribed by law' in the following terms:

> The principle of legality requires the court to address itself to three distinct questions. The first is whether there is a legal basis in domestic law for the restriction. The second is whether the law or rule in question is sufficiently accessible to the individual who is affected by the restriction, and sufficiently precise to enable him to understand its scope and foresee the consequences of his actions so that he can regulate his conduct without breaking the law. The third is whether, assuming that these two requirements are satisfied, it is nevertheless open to the criticism on the Convention ground that it was applied in a way that is arbitrary because, for example, it has been resorted to in bad faith or in a way that is not proportionate. I derive these principles, which have been mentioned many times in subsequent cases, from *The Sunday Times v United Kingdom* (1979–1980) 2 EHRR 245, para 49 and also from *Winterwerp v The Netherlands* (1979) 2 EHRR 387, 402–403, para 39 and *Engel v The Netherlands (No 1)* (1976) 1 EHRR 647, 669, paras 58–59 which were concerned with the principle of legality in the context of article 5(1): see also *A v The Scottish Ministers* 2001 SLT 1331, 1336L–1337B (PC).

For a recent discussion of the principle of legal certainty and the requirement of accessibility, see *Shum Kwok Sher v HKSAR* [2002] HKCFA 17, paras 60–5, *per* Sir Anthony Mason NPJ. See, generally, H Mountfield, 'The Concept of Lawful Interference with Fundamental Rights', in J Jowell and J Cooper (eds), *Understanding Human Rights Principles* (Hart Publishing, 2001).

(5) 'Necessary in a democratic society'

The House of Lords approved and applied the Court's 'three-fold test' in *R v*   **6.147**
Shayler [2002] 2 WLR 754, paras 23, 57, 58, 97.

When a public authority seeks to justify an interference it must properly establish the grounds. As Munby J said in *Kelly v BBC* [2001] Fam 59, 70:

> . . . if those who seek to bring themselves within paragraph 2 of article 10 are to establish 'convincingly' that they are—and that is what they have to establish—they cannot do so by mere assertion, however eminent the person making the assertion, nor by simply inviting the court to make assumptions; what is required . . . is proper evidence.

In *R (Samaroo) v Home Secretary* [2001] UKHRR 1150 Dyson LJ stressed that the court must consider this question in a realistic manner, always keeping in mind that the decision-maker has a significant margin of discretion. The case is discussed further at Supplement, para 6.81A.

H. 'Waiver' of Convention Rights

(4) Waiver under the Human Rights Act

6.162   The failure of defendants to challenge the impartiality and independence of temporary sheriffs during the course of their criminal trials in Scotland prior to the decision in *Starrs v Procurator Fiscal* [2000] HRLR 191 was held not to be a waiver of rights in *Millar v Procurator Fiscal* [2001] UKPC 4. Lord Bingham expressed the view (at para 31) that, in the context of an entitlement to a fair hearing before an independent and impartial tribunal, waiver amounted to a voluntary, informed and unequivocal election by a party not to claim the right or raise an objection. He also formulated (at paras 33–8) some general propositions in relation to proving waiver of a right:

- If a criminal defendant or his agent wishes to take a point on the qualification of the trial court, it should be taken timeously as a plea in bar of trial. If such a point is not taken, the omission to do so shall be taken to show an intention to abandon or waive the point *unless* the circumstances show that it was not intended to abandon or waive it or that the omission resulted from ignorance or misapprehension which provided a reasonable explanation of the failure to take it.
- If knowledge of some material matter is absent, even an express intention to waive a right may readily be recognised as insufficient to constitute a binding abandonment of the right.
- Ignorance of the law cannot be sufficient to found a plea of waiver.
- The more obvious it is that a point is available to be taken, the more readily it may be inferred that that the failure to take it represented a deliberate intention not to take it.

Lord Bingham held (at para 38) that agents could only be taken to have waived the rights of their clients if they made a voluntary, informed and unequivocal election; and that there was no evidence to show they appreciated, or must be taken to have appreciated, the eventual outcome of *Starrs* or a decision to similar effect.

In *R v Hayward* [2001] 3 WLR 125, 135, para 22, Sir Christopher Rose V-P stated that a criminal defendant has the right to be present at trial and to be legally represented but went on to say (at para 18):

> Those rights can be waived, separately or together, wholly or in part, by the defendant himself. They may be wholly waived if, knowing, or having the means of knowledge as to, when and where his trial is to take place, he deliberately and voluntarily absents himself and/or withdraws instructions from those representing him.

The Court of Appeal's finding of waiver was not challenged on appeal to the House of Lords (*sub nom R v Jones* [2002] 2 WLR 524). That finding was, however, treated with some caution by their Lordships on the facts, particularly by Lords Hoffmann and Rodger, as there had been no evidence that the appellants had known what the consequences of absconding would be.

In *Doncaster BC v Hancock, Independent*, 9 April 2001, it was held that an applicant who had not asked for a public hearing of a detailed assessment before a costs judge had impliedly waived his right to a public hearing. In *Austin Hall Building v Buckland Securities* [2001] BLR 272 H H J Bowsher QC held that the claimant had waived his right to a public hearing before an adjudicator in a building dispute exercising functions pursuant to the Housing Grants Construction and Regeneration Act 1996.

See, generally, G Morris, 'Fundamental Rights: Exclusion by Agreement' (2001) 30 ILJ 49.

7

THE RIGHT TO LIFE AND THE
ABOLITION OF THE DEATH PENALTY

B. The Right in English Law

(2) The obligation to protect life

(b) The protection of life and the unborn child

For a comprehensive discussion of the law relating to abortion and miscarriage, **7.09**
see *Smeaton v Secretary of State for Health* [2002] EWHC Admin 610 (Munby J).

C. The Law Under the European Convention

(1) The scope of the right

Article 2 will only be engaged in cases of non-fatal physical ill-treatment in excep- **7.34**
tional circumstances (*Ilhan v Turkey* (2002) 34 EHRR 36). But see *Makratzis v
Greece* (Decision of 18 October 2001) in which an Article 2 complaint based on a
non-fatal shooting was held to be admissible.

n94: See also *McShane v United Kingdom* (2002) 35 EHRR 23, para 93: 'The text of Article 2, read as a whole, demonstrates that it covers not only intentional killings but also situations where it is permitted to "use force" which may result, as an unintended outcome, in the deprivation of life.'

The meaning of Article 2 was extensively analysed by the Court of Appeal in *Re A (Children) (Conjoined Twins: Surgical Separation)* [2001] 2 WLR 480 which is discussed further at Supplement, para 7.54.

7.34A The right to life is so fundamental in all human rights instruments that the German courts were entitled to interpret criminal legislation to make former East German government officials responsible for the intentional killing of people who had died whilst trying to escape from the country (*Streletz and Others v Germany* (2001) 33 EHRR 751). A state policy which flagrantly infringed Article 2 could not be covered by Article 7.

(2) The obligation to protect life

(a) Introduction

7.35 See also *Keenan v United Kingdom* (2001) 10 BHRC 319, para 88.

(b) Positive duty to protect life

7.37 The duty to take positive measures to protect life arises in particular when the state has been warned of the risk but fails to avert it (*Akkoc v Turkey* (2002) 34 EHRR 51). In *Mastromatteo v Italy* (Decision of 14 September 2000) the applicant complained that her son had been killed in the course of a bank robbery by gang members who were on prison leave. The complaint was held to be admissible. The limits of the positive duty are illustrated by the case of *Ivison v United Kingdom* (Decision of 16 April 2002) in which a complaint was considered in relation to a girl, working as a prostitute, who was murdered. The case was found to be inadmissible. The fact that the girl's mother had informed the authorities of her concern for her daughter's welfare if she continued to consort with two particular individuals was not held to be sufficient to show the existence of a specific risk of danger to her life in respect of which the authorities could be held responsible for failing to take preventative measures. The Court also did not consider that the scope of Article 2 could be extended to place a general obligation on the authorities to protect persons from falling under harmful influences of a criminal or immoral nature.

7.38 There should be an effective investigation when individuals have been killed as a result of the use of force. The essential purpose of such investigation is to secure the effective implementation of domestic laws which protect the right to life (*Jordan v United Kingdom* (2001) 11 BHRC 1, para 105). For such an investigation to be effective a number of requirements must be fulfilled (paras 106–9):

- the persons responsible for the investigation must be independent of those implicated in the events—this must be 'practical independence';
- the investigation must be effective in the sense that it is capable of leading to a determination as to whether or not the force was justified and to the identification and punishment of those responsible;
- a requirement of promptness and reasonable expedition is implicit in this context;
- there must a sufficient element of public scrutiny of the investigation and, in particular, the next of kin of the victim must be involved to the extent necessary to safeguard their legitimate interests.

The inquest procedures in Northern Ireland did not comply with these requirements for a number of reasons including a lack of independence of the police officers investigating the incident from those implicated in it, a lack of public scrutiny and transmission of information to the victim's family, the absence of legal aid for the inquest, and non-disclosure of the witness statements.

In *Edwards v United Kingdom* (2002) 12 BHRC 190 the Court considered a complaint of a violation of Article 2 after a prisoner, C, whose parents were the applicants, was killed by a fellow inmate. The killing was found to be a breach of the positive obligation to protect an individual whose life was at risk from the criminal acts of another. The Court noted that those in custody were in a particularly vulnerable position and found that in the instant case the placing of a dangerously unstable prisoner in a cell with C breached his Article 2 rights. There was also found to be a breach of the procedural obligation to investigate pursuant to Article 2. The inquiry which had been conducted was unable to compel the attendance of witnesses. It was also held in private, preventing the applicants attending or asking questions.

In *McShane v United Kingdom* (2002) 35 EHRR 23 a complaint was made by the wife of a man killed during the policing of riots in Northern Ireland. The UK government submitted that as the death was the result of an accident, Article 2 was not engaged. The Court rejected this argument, holding that as the death was the result of a use of force by the state it was covered by Article 2, notwithstanding that it may have been unintentional. The Court also found that the investigation conducted had been inadequate: the investigators lacked independence, there was an inability to compel crucial witnesses to attend the inquest, a failure to allow a verdict that could play a role in securing a criminal prosecution, the non-disclosure of various documents, and delay. The Court also held that the availability of civil proceedings did not discharge the state's obligation as such proceedings are not undertaken at the initiative of the state and do not involve the identification and punishment of alleged perpetrators.

In *Calvelli v Italy* (Judgment of 17 January 2002) the Court considered a complaint by the parents of a child who they alleged had died as a result of medical negligence. The parents claimed that there had been an insufficient investigation to satisfy Article 2. The Court held that Article 2 was engaged in the context of allegations of a death in hospital and that proper investigatory procedures had to be put in place. The parents had civil proceedings available to them, which they chose to settle. Had they been successful in such civil proceedings, disciplinary action against the doctors could have followed. Under these circumstances the Court found that the Article 2 requirement was satisfied. On Article 2 and medical negligence, see also the admissibility decisions in *Powell v UK* (Decision of 4 May 2000) and *Eriksson v Italy* (Decision of 26 October 1999).

7.41   In *Keenan v United Kingdom* (2001) 10 BHRC 319, para 89, the Court said that:

> the scope of the positive obligation must be interpreted in a way which does not impose an impossible or disproportionate burden on the authorities. Not every claimed risk to life therefore can entail for the authorities a Convention requirement to take operational measures to prevent that risk from materialising. For a positive obligation to arise, it must be established that the authorities knew or ought to have known at the time of the existence of a real and immediate risk to the life of an identified individual from the criminal acts of a third party.

As a result, it held that there was no breach of the positive obligation in failing to take steps to prevent the suicide of a mentally ill prisoner.

In *Sieminska v Poland* (Decision of 29 March 2001) the Court accepted that the positive obligations of the state

> include a requirement for hospitals to have regulations for the protection of their patients' lives and also the obligation for establishing the cause of a death which occurs in hospital and any liability on the part of the medical practitioners concerned.

In *Nitecki v Poland* (Decision of 21 March 2002) it was accepted that where an individual was denied health care, in circumstances in which the state undertakes to make its provision available to the general population, there could be a breach of Article 2. On the facts of the case itself, however, there was held to be no breach and it was declared inadmissible. See also *Calvelli v Italy* (Judgment of 17 January 2002), discussed at Supplement, para 7.38, on state obligations in relation to medical negligence.

7.43   In *Pretty v United Kingdom* (2002) 12 BHRC 149 the Court held (as the House of Lords had done in *R (Pretty) v DPP* [2002] 1 AC 800) that Article 2 did not confer a 'right to die'. The UK was not in breach of the Convention in making the assistance of suicide illegal.

(e) Deaths in custody

7.44   If the state is unable to provide an explanation for the death of a person who is taken into custody in good health then there may be two separate violations of Article 2: in respect of the death and in respect of a failure to carry out an investigation (see

Velikova v Bulgaria, Judgment of 18 May 2000; *Tanli v Turkey*, Judgment of 10 April 2001; *Salman v Turkey* (2002) 34 EHRR 17). A similar result was reached when an individual 'disappeared' while in state custody (*Cicek v Turkey*, Judgment of 27 February 2001; *Akdeniz v Turkey*, Judgment of 31 May 2001). In *Anguelova v Bulgaria* (Judgment of 13 June 2002) a breach of Article 2 was found when the deceased had died four hours after arriving at a police station. The Court found that there had been a failure to provide timely medical care and failure to conduct an effective investigation.

However, there was no breach of the positive duty to protect life where a prisoner who had not given any indication of suicidal tendencies, committed suicide in police custody despite regular inspections of his cell (*Tanribilir v Turkey*, Judgment of 16 November 2000). The Court held that, in such a case, an applicant must show that the authorities had failed to take reasonable steps to prevent the suicide in circumstances where they knew or ought to have known that there was a clear and immediate risk to life. See also *Aronica v Germany* (Decision of 18 April 2002) in which the claim of a breach of Article 2 by a suicidal prisoner was held to be inadmissible on the facts, and *Edwards v United Kingdom* (2002) 12 BHRC 190 in which a breach was found after a prisoner was killed after mistakenly being placed in the same cell as another who was dangerous and unstable.

(3) Exceptions to the right to life

(c) 'No more than absolutely necessary'

The *McCann* case was distinguished in *Brady v United Kingdom* (Decision of 3 April 2001). The applicant's son had been shot during a police operation to prevent what was believed to be an armed robbery after he had made what had been interpreted as a threatening movement. The officer honestly believed it was necessary to shoot the deceased to protect himself. As a result, the use of lethal force could be regarded as 'absolutely necessary' within the meaning of Article 2(2)(a). **7.52**

In *Gül v Turkey* (2002) 34 EHRR 28, it was held that the firing of about 50 shots at the door of the deceased's flat by members of the security forces during a search operation went beyond what was 'absolutely necessary' and constituted a breach of Article 2. **7.53**

D. The Impact of the Human Rights Act

(1) Introduction

In relation to the separation of conjoined twins, Article 2(1) confirms rather than alters the existing law (*Re A (Children) (Conjoined Twins: Surgical Separation)* **7.54**

63

[2001] 2 WLR 480). In that case the Court of Appeal suggested that the word 'intentionally' in Article 2 should be given an autonomous meaning and should, therefore, apply only where the purpose of the prohibited action is to cause death. However, it rejected the argument that Article 2 was subject to an implied limitation to the effect that the right could be violated if it conflicted with another person's Article 2 rights (at 571, *per* Brooke LJ). For a critical discussion of this case, see J Black-Branch, 'Being Over Nothingness: The Right to Life under the Human Rights Act' (2001) 26 EL Rev Human Rights Survey, HR/22.

(2) UK cases

7.55 The United Kingdom has been found to be in breach of Article 2 on eight occasions (*McShane v United Kingdom* (2002) 35 EHRR 23; *Edwards v United Kingdom* (2002) 12 BHRC 190; *Jordan v United Kingdom* (2001) 11 BHRC 1; *McKerr v United Kingdom* (2002) 34 EHRR 553; *Shanaghan v United Kingdom* (Judgment of 4 May 2002); *Kelly v United Kingdom* (Judgment of 4 May 2002); *Keenan v United Kingdom* (2001) 10 BHRC 319; and *McCann v United Kingdom* (1995) 21 EHRR 97).

7.58 See also *Brady v United Kingdom* (Decision of 3 April 2001), discussed at Supplement, para 7.52.

7.60 See also *Jordan v United Kingdom* (2001) 11 BHRC 1, discussed at Supplement, para 7.38; *Keenan v United Kingdom* (2001) 10 BHRC 319, discussed at Supplement, para 7.41; *McShane v United Kingdom* (2002) 35 EHRR 23, discussed at Supplement, para 7.38; and *Edwards v United Kingdom* (2002) 12 BHRC 190, discussed at Supplement, para 7.38.

(3) General impact issues

(a) Introduction

7.61A In *R (Amin) v Secretary of State for the Home Department* [2002] 3 WLR 505 the Court of Appeal considered the investigatory obligation pursuant to Article 2. It examined two cases dealing with the state's investigative obligations following death in custody. In one case, the prisoner had committed suicide in prison, in the other he was murdered by his cellmate. It was conceded by the Secretary of State, and the concession was accepted as correct by the Court, that Article 2 was triggered by death as a result of state negligence as well as death through the state's use of force. The Court also held that the kind of investigation which satisfies the Article 2 requirement will not be fixed and uniform, but will depend on the nature of the allegation made against the state—with investigation of an allegation of deliberate killing requiring a higher level of scrutiny than an allegation of death through negligence. In relation to *Amin* (murder of prisoner by a fellow prisoner) the Court held that the investigation, taken as a whole, had satisfied the Article 2 requirements. In relation to *Middleton* (suicide) the Court held that in cases in which Article 2 applied, an inquest jury was entitled to return what would, in effect, be a rider identifying the nature of the neglect that they have found.

The approach taken by the Court of Appeal in relation to the procedural obligation to investigate under Article 2 is open to question. The four specific procedural obligations identified by the Court of Human Rights in *Jordan v United Kingdom* (2001) 11 BHRC 1 (see Supplement, para 7.38) have been consistently followed in a number of Strasbourg cases (see the cases also decided on 4 May 2001: *Kelly v United Kingdom*, paras 95–8; *Shanaghan v United Kingdom*, paras 89–92; *McKerr v United Kingdom*, paras 112–15; *Edwards v United Kingdom* (2002) 12 BHRC 190, paras 70–4; *McShane v United Kingdom* (2002) 35 EHRR 23, paras 94–8) and appear to be fundamental elements of that procedural obligation. Secondly, there is a danger of formulating the obligation at such a high level of generality that it becomes devoid of specific content.

It has been suggested that English self-defence law is incompatible with Article 2   **7.61B** because it allows an honest but unreasonable mistake to ground an acquittal on the basis of self-defence whereas, under Article 2, the mistaken belief must be based on good reasons; see F Leverick, 'Is English Self-defence Law Incompatible with Article 2 of the ECHR?' [2002] Crim LR 347.

(b) Health care

It has been held that where the continuance of medical care of a patient in a per-   **7.64** manent vegetative state would not be in his best interests, there was no breach of Article 2 if that care was withdrawn (*NHS Trust A v M* [2001] 2 WLR 942). A patient may, provided he has mental capacity, refuse treatment even if this places his life at risk. This will not lead to a breach of Article 2; see *B v An NHS Hospital Trust* [2002] EWHC Fam 429.

(4) Specific areas of impact

(a) Immigration

In *R v Secretary of State for the Home Department, ex p Njai*, 1 December 2000   **7.68** (Rafferty J) it was held that the removal of the applicant from the United Kingdom to Gambia, where he would be unable to obtain treatment for his schizophrenia, constituted a breach of Article 2.

(aa) Media law

In *Venables v News Group Newspapers* [2001] Fam 430 the court took Article 2   **7.69A** into account when deciding whether to grant an injunction to restrain publication of information relating to two convicted murderers. It was held that the risk to their lives from the criminal acts of third parties was such that an injunction should be granted against the whole world. The court was obliged to grant the injunction because it knew of the existence of a real and immediate risk to the lives of the claimants (at 1066–167, paras 83–6).

(ab) Mental health law

7.69B   The Court of Session has held that Article 2 will generate a duty to consider the protection of the life of members of the public when a determination is made as to whether to release a mentally disordered patient (*Anderson v Scottish Ministers* (2000) 8 BHRC 590).

In *R (T) v Mental Health Tribunal* [2002] EWHC Admin 247 the risk to T of being attacked by a patient being considered for discharge was insufficient to engage Article 2. It has been held that there was no breach of Article 2 when a mental patient who suffered from Hepatitis C was not allowed condoms (*R (H) v Ashworth Health Authority* [2001] EWHC Admin 872).

(b) Planning and environment

7.70   It has been held that it would be an unwarranted extension of Article 2 to hold that it imposes a duty on a highway authority to treat roads in order to prevent the natural formation of ice as a result of climatic conditions (*Sandhar v Department of Environment*, 21 March 2001, QBD).

(c) Police law

7.72   It was held in *R v Director of Public Prosecutions, ex p Manning* [2001] QB 330 that given the importance of Article 2(1) there had to be compelling grounds for not giving reasons as to why a prosecution was not going to follow a death in custody.

In *Orange v Chief Constable of West Yorkshire* [2002] QB 347 the Court of Appeal held that the decision in *Keenan v United Kingdom* (2001) 10 BHRC 319, discussed further at Supplement, para 7.41, did not extend the scope of the duty of care owed by the police at common law to a person in custody. This decision appears to be consistent with the approach of the Court of Human Rights in *Tanribilir v Turkey* (Judgment of 16 November 2000); see, further, Supplement, para 7.44.

It was held in *Chief Constable of the Greater Manchester Police v McNally* [2002] 2 Cr App Rev 37 that when considering whether to disclose information relating to a police informer in civil proceedings the court should consider the informer's right to life pursuant to Article 2. The risk to the informer should be considered along with the fair trial rights of the parties to the civil proceedings and other factors. In *R (Green) v Police Complaints Authority* [2002] UKHRR 293 the Court of Appeal held that an individual complainant has no right to participate in an investigation by the Police Complaints Authority, notwithstanding that the complaint raised a duty pursuant to Article 2 to investigate an allegation that a police officer had tried to kill the complainant. It was held that the Article 2 duty was satisfied by the provision of a thorough and independent investigation, the ability of the complainant to contribute evidence and his being kept informed of the progress of the investigation. He had no right to have disclosed to him witness statements gathered in the course of the investigation until, at least, its conclusion.

(d) Prison law

The case of *R v Director of Public Prosecutions, ex p Manning* [2001] QB 330 concerned the death of a prison inmate following the forcible search of his person for drugs. Lord Bingham said (at para 33):

7.72A

> . . . the right to life is the most fundamental of all human rights. It is put at the forefront of the Convention. The power to derogate from it is very limited. The death of a person in the custody of the state must always arouse concern, as recognised by section 8(1)(c), (3)(b) and (6) of the Coroners' Act 1988, and if the death resulted from violence inflicted by agents of the state that concern must be profound.

In that case an inquest was held to constitute a sufficient inquiry into the death of the prisoner. However, in *R (Wright) v Secretary of State for the Home Department* [2002] HRLR 1 it was held that the inquest had been insufficient. Jackson J derived a number of propositions from the authorities:

1. Articles 2 and 3 enshrine fundamental human rights. When it is arguable that there has been a breach of either article, the state has an obligation to procure an effective official investigation.
2. The obligation to procure an effective official investigation arises by necessary implication in Articles 2 and 3. Such investigation is required, in order to maximise future compliance with those articles.
3. There is no universal set of rules for the form which an effective official investigation must take. The form which the investigation takes will depend on the facts of the case and the procedures available in the particular state.
4. Where the victim has died and it is arguable that there has been a breach of Article 2, the investigation should have the general features identified by the court in *Jordan v United Kingdom* at paragraphs 106 to 109.
5. The holding of an inquest may or may not satisfy the implied obligation to investigate arising under Article 2. This depends upon the facts of the case and the course of events at the inquest.

In the circumstances of the case, the inquest did not constitute an effective official investigation. As a result, Jackson J made a mandatory order for an independent official inquiry into the death of the prisoner.

This case can be contrasted with *R (Amin) v Secretary of State for the Home Department* [2002] 3 WLR 505, discussed at Supplement, para 7.61A, in which the Court of Appeal held that the requirements of Article 2 had been met in a case in which the Prison Service had accepted fault and expressly invited the family to become involved in an inquiry. It was said the 'investigative obligation' was a flexible one and that publicity and family participation were not discrete compulsory requirements to be fulfilled in every case. As a result, insofar as proposition 4 from *Wright* suggested a 'universal formula' for all investigations it was incorrect. For a discussion of *Amin*, see Supplement, para 7.61A.

7.72B In *R (Bloggs) v Secretary of State for the Home Department* [2002] EWHC Admin 1921 it was held that the decision of the Home Secretary to move a prisoner from a protected witness unit ('PWU') to a mainstream prison was not in breach of his Article 2 rights. Although the claimant had been placed at greater risk by this move that risk was not unreasonable. A different conclusion was reached in *R (F) v Chief Constable of Norfolk Police* [2002] EWHC Admin 1738 in which the claimant complained that he had not been placed in a PWU. It was held that, although in order for there to be a positive obligation to protect a person from harm by third parties it had to be shown that there was a real and immediate risk to the claimant's life, it did not have to be shown that the danger was going to occur in the near future. Where a prisoner had previously been admitted to a PWU it was incumbent on the Prison Service to satisfy itself that the risk was no longer such as to require readmission. As a proper risk assessment had not been carried out the decision was quashed.

(e) Euthanasia

The House of Lords held in *R (Pretty) v DPP* [2002] 1 AC 800 that Article 2 did not confer a 'right to die'. The European Court of Human Rights reached a similar conclusion (*Pretty v United Kingdom* (2002) 12 BHRC 149). A patient may, however, provided they have mental capacity, refuse treatment even if this places their life at risk; see *B v An NHS Hospital Trust* [2002] EWHC Fam 429.

(f) Other

7.72C It was held by the Court of Appeal in *R (A) v Lord Saville of Newdigate* [2002] 1 WLR 1249 that in deciding whether witnesses to the Bloody Sunday Inquiry should be permitted to give their evidence away from Londonderry the threshold of a 'real and immediate' threat to life to engage Article 2 was set too high. It sufficed that the witnesses had good cause to fear for their lives. This should then be balanced against the adverse consequences of the inquiry being required to move venue.

Appendix 3: Human Rights Cases in Other Jurisdictions

(2) Human Rights Committee

For a discussion of Article 6 of the ICCPR, see S Joseph, J Schultz and M Castan, **7.91**
*The International Covenant on Civil and Political Rights: Cases, Materials and
Commentary* (Oxford University Press, 2001), ch 8.

(3) India

The right to a healthy environment and to sustainable development are implicit   **7.94**
in the right to life. The right to access to drinking water is fundamental to life
and, as a result, there is a duty on the state under Article 21 to provide clean
drinking water to its citizens. Where an industrial concern sought to establish a
factory within 10km of two reservoirs, the precautionary principle applied so
that it was required to establish that there would be no danger of pollution
(*Andhra Pradesh Pollution Control Board v Nayudu (No 2)* [2002] 3 LRC 275,
Supreme Court).

(7) South Africa

In *Carmichele v Ministry of Safety and Security* 2001 (10) BCLR 995 the   **7.105A**
Constitutional Court held that if the police and prosecutors had an immunity
against claims in negligence arising out of a failure to prevent the commission of
life-threatening crimes it would be inconsistent with the Constitution and its values, including the right to life. See also Supplement, para 11.510A.

In *Govender v Minister of Safety and Security* (2001) (11) BCLR 1197 the Supreme
Court of Appeal held that a statutory provision permitting the use of reasonable
force in apprehending a fleeing suspect did not authorise a police officer to use
lethal force. Olivier JA said (at para 21) that

> in giving effect to [the statutory provision permitting force], and in applying the
> constitutional standard of reasonableness the existing (and narrow) test of propor-
> tionality between the seriousness of the relevant offence and the force used should
> be expanded to include a consideration of proportionality between the nature and
> degree of the force used and the threat posed by the fugitive to the safety and secu-
> rity of the police officers, other individuals and society as a whole. In so doing, full
> weight should be given to the fact that the fugitive is obviously young, or unarmed,
> or of slight build, *etc*, and where applicable, he could have been brought to justice
> in some other way. In licensing only such force, necessary to overcome resistance
> or prevent flight, as is 'reasonable', [the statutory provision] implies that in certain
> circumstances the use of force necessary for the objects stated will nevertheless be
> unreasonable. It is the requirement of reasonableness that now requires interpreta-
> tion in the light of constitutional values. Conduct unreasonable in the light of the
> Constitution can never be 'reasonably necessary'.

That statutory provision was analysed in detail by the Constitutional Court in *S v Walters* (2002) (7) BCLR 663. A subsection which permitted deadly force in arrests for trivial offences such as shoplifting, or for serious but non-violent offences such as fraud, was struck down in its entirety.

8

RIGHT NOT TO BE SUBJECT TO TORTURE OR INHUMAN OR DEGRADING TREATMENT

C. The Law Under the European Convention

(1) Introduction

For a general discussion of Article 3, see *Pretty v United Kingdom* (2002) 12 **8.14** BHRC 149, paras 50–4.

n36: The principle that Article 3 enshrines one of the fundamental values of a democratic society was recently emphasised in *Labita v Italy* (Judgment of 6 April 2000).

In *Labita v Italy* (Judgment of 6 April 2000) the Court held, adopting a standard **8.15** of proof of 'beyond reasonable doubt', that where a prisoner had alleged degrading treatment in prison involving physical and mental ill-treatment, a failure to provide any medical evidence or evidence of a complaint at a reasonably appropriate time or in appropriate circumstances meant that the applicant had failed to produce sufficient evidence of a breach of Article 3. See also *Berlinski v Poland* (Judgment of 20 June 2002).

n39: See also *Akkoc v Turkey* (2002) 34 EHRR 51.

(2) State liability

8.19 In *Indelicato v Italy* (Judgment of 18 October 2001) although allegations of ill-treatment in custody failed to establish 'degrading treatment' under Article 3, the shortcomings of the subsequent investigations into those allegations did constitute a breach of the applicant's Article 3 rights.

8.20 The positive obligation of the state under Article 3 does not extend to an obligation to sanction the taking of the life of a person who is suffering (*Pretty v United Kingdom* (2002) 12 BHRC 149). Article 3 does not require a state party to provide a civil remedy to a victim of torture allegedly carried out in a country not party to the Convention (*Al-Adsani v United Kingdom* (2002) 12 BHRC 89, para 40).

(3) Torture

8.23 In *Akkoc v Turkey* (2002) 34 EHRR 51 blindfolding and stripping the prisoner, forcing her to walk naked between wardens, the use of electric shocks, hot and cold water treatments, and threats of ill-treatment to the prisoner's children, were found to amount to torture.

In *Peers v Greece* (2001) 10 BHRC 364 it was held that poor prison conditions, lack of privacy and basic hygiene did not amount to torture but was degrading treatment (see also Supplement, para 8.45A).

In *Denizci v Cyprus* (Judgment of 23 May 2001) ill-treatment and beating of detainees which had not been shown to have been carried out for the purposes of extracting confessions was held to be inhuman treatment but not torture (para 386) (see also *Egmez v Cyprus* (2002) 34 EHRR 29.

(4) Degrading and inhuman treatment and punishment

(a) Inhuman treatment

8.28 n82: See also *Dulaş v Turkey* (Judgment of 30 January 2001) (destruction of 70-year-old's home and possessions in front of her eyes held to be inhuman treatment); *Bilgin v Turkey* (2002) 35 EHRR 39; and *DG v Ireland* (2002) 35 EHRR 33 (detention of a minor in a penal institution because no therapeutic unit available and handcuffing held not to be in breach of Article 3).

In *Cyprus v Turkey* (2001) 11 BHRC 45 Greeks living in the Karpas area of Northern Cyprus were compelled to live in a situation of isolation and were controlled and restricted in their movements. The Court held that there was

> an inescapable conclusion that the interferences at issue were directed at the Karpas Greek-Cypriot community for the very reason that they belonged to this class of persons. The treatment to which they were subjected during the period under consideration can only be explained in terms of the features which distinguish them from the Turkish-Cypriot population, namely their ethnic origin, race and religion. . . . the situation in which the Karpas Greek-Cypriots live and are compelled to live: isolated, restricted in their movements, controlled and with no prospect of renewing or developing their community. The conditions under which that population is condemned to live are debasing and violate the very notion of respect for the human dignity of its members (para 309).

The Court accepted that a complaint of discriminatory treatment gave rise to a separate issue under Article 3 (relying on *Abdulaziz, Cabales and Balkandali v United Kingdom* (1985) 7 EHRR 471). It went on to hold that the treatment of the Karpas Greek-Cypriots attained a level of severity which amounted to degrading treatment.

The detention of a minor not charged with any offence in a penal institution could, of itself, constitute 'inhuman and degrading treatment'; see *Aerts v Belgium* (1998) 5 BHRC 382, paras 64–6.

In *Z v United Kingdom* (2001) 10 BHRC 384 abused children whose claim for negligence against a local authority was struck out (*X (Minors) v Bedfordshire County Council* [1995] 2 AC 633 (see, further, Main Work, para 11.44)) brought claims in Strasbourg alleging, amongst other things, a breach of Article 3. It was said that the United Kingdom had failed to ensure their safety at the hands of their parents. The children had first been referred to social services in 1987 because of concerns about their treatment but were not placed into emergency care until 1992. There was no dispute before the Court that the abuse suffered reached the necessary threshold to amount to inhuman and degrading treatment. The Court found that the system had failed the children and accordingly there had been a breach of Article 3. The Court made pecuniary awards of between £4,000 and £100,000, with £32,000 to each for non-pecuniary damage, and £39,000 for costs and expenses. **8.28A**

In *Cyprus v Turkey* (2001) 11 BHRC 45 the Court considered a large number of complaints arising out of the Turkish military intervention. An Article 3 complaint was made by relatives of missing Greek Cypriots in relation to the failure by the Turkish authorities to investigate the circumstances of their disappearance. The Court held that 'the silence of the authorities of the respondent State in the face of the real concerns of the relatives of the missing persons attains a level of severity which can only be categorised as inhuman treatment within the meaning of Article 3' (para 157).

In *Rehbock v Slovenia* (Judgment of 28 November 2000) the applicant had been arrested for suspected drug smuggling. He was unarmed and did not offer violence. He was arrested by six men with shotguns and pistols who dragged him onto the bonnet of a car, cuffed his hands behind his back and hit him with cudgels and fists. He suffered a double fracture of the jaw and facial contusions. The force used was excessive and unjustified and caused serious suffering which amounted to inhuman treatment. A doctor had been summoned after he had asked for one and, although painkilling medication was not provided on several occasions when requested, this mistreatment did not constitute a breach of Article 3.

In *JM v United Kingdom* (Judgment of 28 September 2000) the applicant was a rape victim who complained that the rapist, who had chosen to defend himself, cross-examined the applicant for six days, having been granted access to medical details and personal information about her. A friendly settlement was reached on the basis of an *ex gratia* payment.

(b) Inhuman punishment

8.31 Mandatory life sentences have been held not to constitute a breach of Article 3. See Supplement, para 8.71.

(5) Individuals in detention

(c) Conditions of detention

8.45A In *Dougoz v Greece* (2001) 10 BHRC 306 the applicant complained of being confined in an overcrowded and dirty cell with insufficient sanitary and sleeping facilities, scarce hot water, no fresh air or natural daylight and no exercise yard. It was held that this amounted to degrading treatment contrary to Article 3.

In *Peers v Greece* (2001) 10 BHRC 364 the Court noted that the prison conditions the applicant complained of, which included an inability to use a toilet in private, days of little or no light or ventilation, failure to supply soap and toilet paper 'diminished the applicant's human dignity and arose in him feelings of anguish and inferiority capable of humiliating and debasing him and possibly breaking his physical or moral resistance' (para 75).

The failure on the part of the authorities to take steps to improve conditions denoted a 'lack of respect for the applicant which amounted to degrading treatment under Article 3'. The Court emphasised that the fact that the conditions were not aimed at degrading the prisoner was only one factor to take into account and the absence of such purpose could not conclusively rule out a finding of violation (para 74).

In *Price v United Kingdom* (2002) 34 EHRR 1285 the claimant, a four-limb-deficient thalidomide victim with numerous health problems, was committed for contempt of court in civil proceedings. She was kept in conditions in which she was dangerously cold, risked developing pressure sores and was unable to go to the toilet or keep clean without the greatest difficulty. It was held that this constituted degrading treatment contrary to Article 3.

Detention in the open for a period of a week, with significant privations and some beatings was a breach of Article 3 (*Akdeniz v Turkey*, Judgment of 31 May 2000, para 98). In *Kalashnikov v Russia* (Judgment of 15 July 2002) the Court found that conditions of infestation, poor ventilation, a lack of privacy in communal toilet arrangements, acute overcrowding and generally crammed and insanitary conditions—combined with the length of detention—amounted to 'degrading treatment' and a breach of Article 3.

However, ill treatment must attain a minimum level of severity and must go beyond the inevitable element of suffering and humiliation connected with legitimate punishment so that there was no breach of Article 3 when a prisoner who, although confined in a small dormitory, had freedom of movement during the day and, despite inadequate sanitary facilities, was able to keep himself clean (*Valašinas v Lithuania* (2002) 12 BHRC 266). In *Bollan v United Kingdom* (Decision of 4 May 2000) a prisoner had committed suicide after being told that she would be kept in her cell until she calmed down. There was no reason to suspect that she would commit suicide and the confinement in her own cell could not be considered as amounting to ill-treatment.

(d) Medical treatment of detainees

In *Keenan v United Kingdom* (2001) 10 BHRC 319 the Court considered the treatment of a potential suicide in an English jail. The applicant was the mother of a prisoner who had committed suicide. She alleged breaches of Articles 2 and 3 in the Prison Service's failure to prevent her son's suicide after his conviction for assault. He died by self-asphyxia during the course of his detention. He had been medically monitored by the prison doctor and the Court found that the prison authorities did all that could reasonably be expected of them once he had started to display signs of suicidal tendencies—they had placed him in hospital care and watched over him. At the time of his death there had been no diagnosis of schizophrenia. As such there had been no violation of Article 2. However, the Court found that the inmate had been subjected to inhuman and degrading treatment, in breach of Article 3. It commented that a lack of proper medical treatment could amount to treatment contrary to Article 3. In assessing whether the treatment had not reached the appropriate standard consideration should be given to the vulnerability of those suffering from mental illness and the difficulty this caused them in terms of complaining about that treatment. The Court found that there was a lack of medical notes about the monitoring of the deceased and that the psychiatrist had seen him on 29 April but not again before his suicide on 15 May. The

8.50A

prison doctor (not qualified in psychiatry) had reverted to an earlier course of medication without reference to a specialist which had resulted in an assault on prison officers by the deceased and a consequential increase in his sentence. The Court regarded this increase as inappropriate given his state of mind and how close he was to his release date. Overall, they found that the treatment of the deceased was not compatible with the standard expected in order to avoid a violation of Article 3. The Court ordered the UK to pay £10,000 general damages and £21,000 costs and expenses.

This case can be contrasted with *Kudla v Poland* (2001) 10 BHRC 269 in which the applicant who was held on remand for three years suffered from chronic depression and had twice attempted suicide in prison. He was detained on remand for a period of four months despite a psychiatric opinion that this could jeopardise his life because of the likelihood of a further suicide attempt. The Court held that the applicant was not subjected to ill-treatment which attained the minimum level of severity to come within the scope of Article 3.

(6) Extradition and deportation

8.58 Deporting an Iranian woman back to her home country where she would face stoning to death or flogging due to unsubstantiated allegations of adultery against her would breach her Article 3 rights (*Jabari v Turkey* (2000) 9 BHRC 1). Furthermore, the 'automatic and mechanical application' of a five-day time limit for asylum applications was 'at variance with the protection of the fundamental value embodied in Article 3' (para 40).

The Court went on to hold that, because of the importance of Article 3, the notion of an effective remedy under Article 13 requires an independent and rigorous scrutiny of a claim that substantial grounds exist for fearing a real risk of treatment contrary to Article 3 (para 50).

In *Hilal v United Kingdom* (2001) 33 EHRR 31 it was held that the deportation of the applicant to Tanzania would breach Article 3 as he would face a serious risk of being subjected there to torture or inhuman and degrading treatment. The applicant had been mistreated in Zanzibar and the Government argued that he would be secure in mainland Tanzania. The Court rejected this argument holding that the 'internal flight' did not offer a reliable guarantee against the risk of ill-treatment.

In contrast, in *Bensaid v United Kingdom* (2001) 33 EHRR 205 the Court held that the return of a schizophrenic applicant to Algeria where he would have difficulties in obtaining medication did not constitute a breach of Article 3. The risk that the applicant would suffer a deterioration in his condition on return to Algeria was to a large extent speculative.

(7) European Committee for Prevention of Torture

The United Kingdom is party to the European Convention for the Prevention of **8.58A**
Torture and Inhuman Treatment or Punishment (see Main Work, para 2.54).
The Committee for the Prevention of Torture and Inhuman or Degrading
Treatment or Punishment ('CPT') was set up under the Torture Convention. It
has published a document containing the substantive sections of its various general reports entitled *The CPT Standards* (Council of Europe, 2002) (available on
the Council of Europe website at www.cpt.coe.int/en/docsstandards.htm). This
deals with standards under eight headings: police custody; imprisonment; training of law enforcement personnel; health care services in prisons; foreign nationals detained under aliens legislation; involuntary placement in psychiatric
establishments; juveniles deprived of their liberty; and women deprived of their
liberty.

The CPT visited the United Kingdom in February 2001 and produced a report
dated 18 April 2002 (CPT/Inf (2002) 6) which made a number of recommendations and requests for information. In February 2002 the CPT visited the persons
detained under the provisions of the Anti-Terrorism, Crime and Security Act
2001 (see, further, Supplement, para 10.51).

See, generally, J Murdoch, 'The European Convention for the Prevention of
Torture and Inhuman or Degrading Treatment or Punishment: Activities in
2001' (2002) 27 EL Rev Human Rights Survey, HR/47.

D. The Impact of the Human Rights Act

(1) Introduction

The United Kingdom was also found to be in breach of Article 3 in *Price v United* **8.59**
Kingdom (2002) 34 EHRR 1285, discussed at Supplement, para 8.45A; *Hilal v
United Kingdom* (2001) 33 EHRR 31, discussed at Supplement, para 8.58; in
Keenan v United Kingdom (2001) 10 BHRC 319, discussed at Supplement, para
8.50A; and in *Z v United Kingdom* (2001) 10 BHRC 384, discussed at
Supplement, para 8.28A.

(2) United Kingdom cases in Strasbourg

(b) Deportation and extradition

A violation was found in *Hilal v United Kingdom* (2001) 33 EHRR 31 (see **8.62**
Supplement, para 8.58). In contrast, there was no breach in the case of *Bensaid v
United Kingdom* (2001) 33 EHRR 205 (see Supplement, para 8.58).

(d) Conditions of detention

8.68   The Court found the United Kingdom to be in breach of Article 3 as a result of a failure to provide proper medical attention for a suicidal prisoner (*Keenan v United Kingdom* (2001) 10 BHRC 319; see, further, Supplement, para 8.50A). A breach was found in *Price v United Kingdom* (2001) 34 EHRR 1285 in relation to the detention of a severely disabled person in police custody (see, further, Supplement, para 8.45A).

(e) Other cases

8.68A   A violation of Article 3 was found when a local authority failed to take proper steps to protect abused children; see *Z v United Kingdom* (2001) 10 BHRC 384, discussed further at Supplement, para 8.28A. The eviction of a person from temporary hotel accommodation by a local authority was not of sufficient severity to engage Article 3 (*O'Rourke v United Kingdom,* Decision of 26 June 2001).

(3) Impact of the Human Rights Act

(a) General

8.69   In *Husain v Asylum Support Adjudicator* [2001] EWHC Admin 852 Stanley Burnton J considered (at para 53) that the question as to whether the withdrawal of all support and benefits from a destitute asylum seeker because of his misconduct was contrary to his Article 3 rights was a difficult one, but did not decide the point. In *Reynolds v Secretary of State for Work and Pensions* [2002] EWHC Admin 426, para 42, Wilson J treated those remarks as supporting the contention that such treatment did potentially breach Article 3, but held that the low level of payments in the case before him, £41.35 per week, 'wholly fails' to reach the necessary 'depth' of ill-treatment.

(b) Criminal law

8.71   In *R v Offen* [2001] 1 WLR 253 the Court of Appeal interpreted the power (formerly under section 2 of the Criminal (Sentences) Act 1997 and now under section 109 of the Powers of Criminal Courts (Sentencing) Act 2000) to impose an automatic life sentence following a conviction for a second serious offence in accordance with section 3 of the Human Rights Act and adopted a broad interpretation of the phrase 'exceptional circumstances'. Such an approach did not contravene the prohibition on inhuman and degrading treatment.

In *R (Lichniak) v Secretary of State for Home Department* [2002] 3 WLR 1834 the House of Lords rejected the argument that mandatory life sentences constituted a breach of Article 3. Lord Bingham took the view (at para 16) that the complaints were not of sufficient gravity to engage Article 3. In *R v Drew* [2002] 2 Cr App

R(S) 45 the Court of Appeal confirmed that the imposition of an automatic sentence of life imprisonment under section 109 of the Powers of Criminal Courts (Sentencing) Act 2000 was not incompatible with Article 3. The Court of Appeal held that this must apply in circumstances where the offender, although suffering from a mental illness sufficient for a hospital order to have been made under the Mental Health Act 1983 had not the terms of section 109 prevented it, was shown at trial to have formed the necessary *mens rea* for the offence. It should be noted that on 10 July 2002 the Appeal Committee of the House of Lords granted provisional permission to appeal this decision.

In *R v H (Assault of a Child: Reasonable Chastisement)* [2002] 1 Cr App R 59 the Court of Appeal considered the question of the extent to which the defence of 'reasonable chastisement' must be modified in the light of the decision of the Court of Human Rights in *A v United Kingdom* (1998) 27 EHRR 611. It was held that, in accordance with the Article 3 case law, the judge should direct the jury that, when they are considering the reasonableness or otherwise of chastisement they must consider the nature and context of the defendant's behaviour, its duration, its physical and mental consequences in relation to the child, the age and personal characteristics of the child and the reasons given by the defendant for administering punishment. Such a direction was a proper incremental development of the common law and did not give rise to a breach of Article 7 of the Convention.

In *R v Weir* [2001] 1 WLR 421 the House of Lords considered Article 3 in relation to the position of the victims of crime. The DPP had lodged an appeal against the quashing of a murder conviction one day late. It was argued that the House of Lords should exercise its discretion to allow the appeal in any event, having consideration for the interests of victims and potential victims, and possible ill-treatment or torture of them. This argument was dismissed by the House of Lords which pointed out that the Convention was conceived to protect private citizens against the abuse of power by state and public authorities rather than to strengthen the rights of prosecutors against private citizens.

In *R (Pretty) v Director of Public Prosecutions* [2001] 1 AC 800 the House of Lords **8.71A** held that the refusal of the Director to give an undertaking that he would not consent to the prosecution of the applicant's husband for assisting her suicide did not constitute a breach of any positive obligation of the state under Article 3. The positive obligations of the state under Article 3 were not absolute and the United Kingdom was not obliged to ensure that a competent terminally ill person who was unable to take her own life was entitled to assistance without the person giving the assistance risking prosecution.

(ba) Health care

8.71B   The withdrawal of medical treatment from patients in a permanent vegetative state is not degrading and inhuman treatment. Article 3 requires the victim to be aware of the inhuman or degrading treatment which he or she is experiencing or at least to be in a state of physical or mental suffering (*NHS Trust A v M* [2001] 2 WLR 942, 956, para 49).

(bb) Media law

8.71C   The right to be free from degrading and inhuman treatment is a fundamental one which the Court will take into account when making orders which restrict publication of information. Thus, in *Venables v News Group Newspapers* [2001] Fam 430 the fact that there was a serious risk to the rights of the claimants under Article 3 (and Article 2) was a decisive factor in support of the grant of an injunction.

(c) Immigration

8.73   The Court of Appeal has held that even where a Mental Health Review Tribunal had decided it was appropriate for an asylum seeker to continue his detention under the Mental Health Act 1983, it would not be a breach of Article 3 to deport him back to Malta where the level of care might be lower (*X v Secretary of State for the Home Department* [2001] 1 WLR 740).

In contrast, where an applicant originally from Gambia was suffering from schizophrenia and there was 'credible medical evidence' that the lack of medical facilities there would reduce his life expectancy, it was held that there was a breach of Articles 2 and 3 where deportation would result in a significant risk of suicide (*R v Chief Immigration Officer, ex p Njai*, 1 December 2000 (Rafferty J)). In *Dhima v Immigration Appeal Tribunal* [2002] EWHC Admin 80, para 25, there was no duty on the Contracting State to 'near guarantee' the deportee's safety, but the sufficiency of the protection provided by the destination state was to be considered when a complaint was made under Article 3. Relying on the decision of the House of Lords in *Horvath v Secretary of State for the Home Department* [2001] AC 489 Auld J held (at paras 29–37) that there was a 'broad symmetry' in the application to both human rights and refugee cases of this 'sufficiency of protection' test, as derived from *HLR v France* (1997) 26 EHRR 29. In *Secretary of State for the Home Department v Kacaj* [2002] EWCA Civ 314 a case was remitted back to the Immigration Appeal Tribunal because there was a legitimate ground for doubt as to whether that test had properly been applied.

(d) Mental health law

8.77   In *R (Wilkinson) v Broadmoor Special Hospital Authority* [2002] 1 WLR 419 the Court of Appeal held that in a case where allegations were made concerning breaches of human rights, including Article 3, in relation to compulsory medical treatment under sections 57 and 58 of the Mental Health Act 1983, the right approach on an application for judicial review was for the court to reach its own view as to whether or not the treatment ought to be given. The issue was whether the defendant could show 'medical necessity' sufficient to justify what would otherwise be a breach of Article 3. Accordingly, the Court of Appeal gave directions for medical witnesses to be cross-examined.

In *S v Airedale National Health Service Trust* [2002] EWHC Admin 1780 Stanley Burnton J did not need to consider the application of the evidential test suggested in *Wilkinson* but was of the view (at para 79) that although the use of seclusion in mental hospitals was capable of amounting to a breach of Article 3 (and Article 8), it did not achieve the necessary level of 'minimum severity' on the facts of the case before him. A similar decision as to the lack of 'minimum severity' in a seclusion case was reached by Sullivan J in *R (Munjaz) (No 2) v Ashworth Hospital Authority* [2002] EWHC Admin 1521. Applications for permission to appeal have been lodged in both *Munjaz* and *S*.

(f) Prison law

In *R v Governor of HMP Frankland, ex p Russell* [2000] HRLR 512 Lightman J decided that there was nothing degrading or objectionable about requiring prisoners to wear uniform. However, he took the view that punishing prisoners for refusing to wear uniforms by providing one meal a day served in a cell constituted inhuman and degrading treatment in breach of Article 3.

8.80

In *Russell v Home Office*, 2 March 2001, Crane J held that there is little, if any, difference between the approach of the Court of Human Rights and the approach of an English court in cases where injury has resulted to a person in custody. If a man enters custody uninjured and is later found while in custody to have injuries for which no plausible explanation is provided by those responsible for his custody, the court in appropriate circumstances would be likely to draw the inference that his custodians must have caused those injuries. The judge held that assaults on recaptured prisoners amounted, in that case, to degrading treatment or punishment.

In *R (Wright) v Secretary of State for the Home Department* [2002] HRLR 1 Jackson J held that a failure to provide prompt medical attention to a prisoner in a cell is a breach of Article 3 and, as a result, the prison authorities are under an obligation to carry out an independent and open inquiry (see, further, Supplement, para 7.72A).

In *Napier v The Scottish Ministers* [2002] UKHRR 308 an interim injunction was granted ordering the transfer of a prisoner from Barlinnie Prison to a prison which complied with Article 3. The prisoner complained that the cell was grossly inadequate in living space, lighting and ventilation, that the sanitary arrangements involved 'slopping out', that the extent to which he was confined in his cell was excessive and that the periods of exercise and recreation outside the cell were inadequate.

See also *Price v United Kingdom* (2002) 34 EHRR 1285, discussed at Supplement, para 8.45A.

Appendix 1: The Canadian Charter of Rights

(3) 'Cruel and unusual'

(c) *Grossly disproportionate*

8.91 **Mandatory minimum sentences.** n251: The Supreme Court upheld the minimum mandatory sentences in *R v Morrissey* [2001] 3 LRC 336 and *R v Latimer* [2001] 3 LRC 593 (father who killed severely disabled 12-year-old daughter convicted of second-degree murder, and convicted for ten years).

8.92A In *R v Wust* [2000] SCC 18 the Supreme Court held that minimum mandatory sentences must be interpreted in a manner consistent with the full context of the sentencing scheme, including statutory remission. Thus, the appellant in that case was entitled to have taken into account time served in custody before sentence.

(d) *Other circumstances*

8.98A Extradition from Canada to a country in which the death penalty might be imposed does not violate the guarantee against cruel and unusual punishment (*Kindler v Canada* [1993] 4 LRC 85). However, the values underlying section 12 form part of the balancing exercise when the court is considering whether extradition would violate the principles of fundamental justice under section 7. Fundamental justice required that, in every case, the Canadian authorities were bound to ask for and obtain an assurance that the death penalty would not be imposed as a condition of extradition (*Minister of Justice v Burns* (2001) 11 BHRC 314). The deportation of a refugee to face a substantial risk of torture would generally violate section 7 of the Charter (*Suresh v Canada (Minister for Citizenship and Immigration)* [2002] SCC 1). For an example of a case where the risk of torture was not made out, see *Ahani v Canada (Minister of Citizenship and Immigration)* [2002] SCC 2.

Appendix 3: Human Rights Cases in Other Jurisdictions

(1A) Human Rights Committee

Article 7 of the International Covenant on Civil and Political Rights provides that   **8.106A**

> No one shall be subjected to torture or cruel, inhuman or degrading treatment or punishment. In particular, no one shall be subjected without his consent to medical or scientific experimentation.

Article 10 provides that persons in detention shall be treated with humanity and dignity. These provisions are supplemented by the United Nations Convention against Torture and Other Cruel, Inhuman or Degrading Treatment or Punishment 1984. In General Comment 20 the Human Rights Committee stated that, under paragraph 2 of Article 7,

> It is the duty of the State party to afford everyone protection through legislation and other measures as may be necessary against the acts prohibited by article 7 whether inflicted by people in their official capacity, outside their official capacity or in a private capacity.

For a discussion of Articles 7 and 10 of the ICCPR, see S Joseph, J Schultz and M Castan, *The International Covenant on Civil and Political Rights: Cases, Materials and Commentary* (Oxford University Press, 2001), ch 9.

(5) Belize

In *Reyes v Queen* [2002] 2 WLR 1034 the Privy Council considered section 102   **8.111** of the Criminal Code, which required a mandatory sentence of death to be passed on the defendant on conviction of murder by shooting. After a full consideration of the authorities from a number of jurisdictions it was held that, by precluding any judicial consideration of the humanity of condemning the defendant to death, this provision subjected him to inhuman or degrading punishment. This defect could not be remedied by the subsequent opportunity to seek mercy from the executive. This decision was applied in the St Lucia case of *R v Hughes* [2002] 2 WLR 1058 and in the St Christopher and Nevis case of *Fox v The Queen* [2002] 2 WLR 1077 which were heard immediately afterwards.

(6A) Hong Kong

The mandatory life sentence for murder does not constitute 'degrading and inhu-   **8.112A** man punishment'; see *Lau Cheong v HKSAR* [2002] HKCFA 18.

(9A) Fiji

The decision in *Taito Rarasea v State* (2002) 3 CHRLD 126 (High Court) con-   **8.115B** cerned the reduction of a prisoner's food rations for two weeks, as punishment for the fact that the prisoner had escaped lawful custody. The court declared that such a reduction in rations was degrading and inhuman treatment or punishment, relying in part on Article 11(1) of the International Covenant on Economic, Social and Cultural Rights, which recognised everyone's right to adequate food. It was held that any treatment or punishment that impinges upon the inherent dignity of the individual will constitute cruel, inhuman and degrading treatment.

(10A) Malaysia

8.116A In *Abdul Ghani Haroon v Ketua Polis Negara* (2002) 3 CHRLD 124 the High Court held that the deliberate and unreasonable denial of access to a person in detention to family members was cruel, inhuman and oppressive to both the detainees and their families.

(11) Namibia

8.119 It is unlawful to place prisoners in chains, even after they have attempted to escape (*Namunjepo v Commanding Officer* [2000] 3 LRC 360, Namibian Supreme Court).

(12A) Seychelles

8.121A Article 16 of the Constitution of the Seychelles provides that 'Every person has a right to be treated with dignity worthy of a human being and not be subjected to torture, cruel, inhuman or degrading treatment or punishment.'

In *Charles v A-G* [2001] 2 LRC 169 the petitioner claimed that during detention in an army camp he had been subjected to assaults and torture by soldiers. He provided photographs showing injuries to his wrists and neck. In the absence of corroborative medical evidence there was no *prima facie* case of torture.

(12B) St Lucia

8.121B In *Harding v Superintendent of Prisons* (2002) 3 CHRLD 128 it was held that the shackling of a prisoner for 24 hours a day was a form of torture. It was also held that confining the claimant to a solitary cell for an extended period without access to exercise or sunlight constituted unreasonable punishment and was inhumane and repugnant to the values and attitudes of a civilised society.

(15) South Africa

8.124 In *S v Dodo* 2001 (5) BCLR 423 (CC) the Constitutional Court considered a statutory provision which provided for mandatory life imprisonment unless the court was satisfied that there were 'substantial and compelling circumstances' justifying the imposition of a lesser sentence. Ackermann J reviewed the mandatory minimum sentencing provisions in a number of jurisdictions and concluded that the legislature and the executive have a legitimate interest, role and duty in relation to sentencing. He held that the punishment which was 'cruel, inhuman or degrading' involved some degree of impairment of human dignity. This right would only be violated if the sentence legislated was grossly disproportionate to the sentence merited. The challenged legislation did not require such a sentence and was not, therefore, unconstitutional.

In *Mahomed v President of Republic of South Africa* (2001) 11 BHRC 314 the **8.124A** Constitutional Court held that the deportation or extradition of a person to the United States where he faced the death penalty would infringe his constitutional right not to be subjected to cruel, inhuman or degrading punishment.

The imposition of indeterminate sentences on habitual criminals was declared to be unconstitutional in *S v Niemand* (2001) (11) BCLR 1181. The Constitutional Court adopted a remedy of 'reading in', so that a maximum limit was imposed. However, the Supreme Court of Appeal upheld indeterminate sentences for dangerous criminals in *Bull v The State* (2000) 6 BCLR 551.

See also *Govender v Minister of Safety and Security* (2001) (11) BCLR 1197 (use of force in apprehending a fleeing suspect), discussed at Supplement, para 7.105A.

(18A) Uganda

An exclusion order which banned a person convicted of witchcraft from his vil- **8.131A** lage, thereby depriving him of shelter, the means of subsistence and other necessities of life, as well as access to his family, was dehumanising and degrading; see *A-G v Abuki* [2000] 1 LRC 63.

9

FREEDOM FROM SLAVERY, SERVITUDE AND FORCED LABOUR

We are not aware of any developments having occurred that materially alter the law and practice as set out in Chapter 9 of the Main Work.

10

THE RIGHT TO LIBERTY

B. The Rights in English Law

(5) Powers of arrest and detention

(c) Arrest

Arrest with warrant.   In *Henderson v Chief Constable of Cleveland* [2001] 1 WLR 1103 the Court of Appeal held that where an arrest is carried out in the execution of a default warrant, the failure to take the person arrested immediately before a court (should a court be sitting) was not unlawful and did not render his continuing detention on the arrest warrant unlawful.   **10.31**

Arrest without warrant.   Where an arrest is based on an entry on the police national computer, the test of reasonableness should be applied to the officer making the arrest, not the officer who put the information in the computer (see *Hough v Chief Constable of Staffordshire, The Times*, 14 February 2001).   **10.33**

10.38   The Prevention of Terrorism (Temporary Provisions) Act 1989 was repealed by the Terrorism Act 2000, subject to section 2(2) of, and Schedule 1 to, that Act, which preserved in force various provisions of the 1989 Act, including those discussed in the Main Work, para 10.38, until 20 July 2001. The 2000 Act reforms and extends previous counter-terrorist legislation, and puts many of its provisions, unchanged, on a permanent basis. Under section 41 of the 2000 Act, which came into force on 19 February 2001, a constable has power to arrest without a warrant 'a person whom he reasonably suspects to be a terrorist'. 'Terrorist' is defined in section 40(1) of the Act as including a person who is or has been concerned in the commission, preparation or instigation of acts of terrorism. The application of the arrest power is not restricted geographically. 'Terrorism' is defined to include actions which are unconnected with the United Kingdom, its government, its people or their property (section 1(4)).

See, generally, C Chatterjee, 'The Terrorism Act 2000: An Analysis' (2002) 39 Amicus Curiae 19; JJ Rowe, 'The Terrorism Act 2000' [2001] Crim LR 527.

(e) Detention of suspected terrorists

10.49   The Prevention of Terrorism (Temporary Provisions) Act 1989 was repealed by the Terrorism Act 2000, although the provisions discussed in the Main Work at paras 10.49 and 10.50 remained in force until 20 July 2001 (see Supplement, para 10.38). The legislative provisions dealing with the detention of suspected terrorists are now contained in the Terrorism Act 2000, and came into force on 19 February 2001. A person arrested under section 41 of the 2000 Act (see Supplement, para 10.38) can be detained for up to 48 hours (section 41(3)). This period can be extended for further periods, not exceeding seven days, by a designated district judge on the application of a police officer of at least the rank of superintendent (Schedule 8, paras 29 and 36). There are special provisions for the review of detention by a 'review officer' (Schedule 8, Part II).

10.50   When a person arrives in or is seeking to enter or leave Great Britain or Northern Ireland, he may be examined by an examining officer for the purpose of determining whether he appears to be a person concerned in the commission, preparation or instigation of acts of terrorism (section 53(1), Schedule 7, para 2). A person who is to be examined may be detained on the authority of an examining officer. Such detention may not last longer than nine hours from the time when the examination begins (Schedule 7, para 6(4)).

(f) Other powers of detention

10.51   Under section 23 of the Anti-Terrorism, Crime and Security Act 2001, a 'suspected international terrorist' who is detained under the Immigration Act 1971, pending examination and pending a decision to give or refuse leave to enter, may be detained:

despite the fact that his removal or departure from the United Kingdom is prevented (whether temporarily or indefinitely) by—
(a) a point of law which wholly or partly relates to an international agreement, or
(b) a practical consideration

A 'suspected international terrorist' for the purposes of the 2001 Act is a person who
has been certified by the Secretary of State on the basis that he reasonably believes
that that person's presence in the United Kingdom is a risk to national security and
reasonably suspects that the person is or has been concerned in the commission,
preparation or instigation of acts of terrorism, is a member of or belongs to an international terrorist group, or has links with an international terrorist group (section
21(1), (2)). An 'international terrorist group' is a group which is subject to the control or influence of persons outside the United Kingdom, and which the Secretary
of State suspects is concerned in the commission, preparation or instigation of acts
of international terrorism (section 21(3)). Section 23 of the 2001 Act has been the
subject of a formal derogation from Article 5 by the United Kingdom (see
Supplement, para 6.93). See, generally, A Tomkins, 'Legislating against Terror: The
Anti-Terrorism, Crime and Security Act 2001' [2002] PL 205; J Wadham, 'The
Anti-Terrorism, Crime and Security Act 2001' (2002) Archbold News 1, 5.

These provisions were considered by the Court of Appeal in *A and Others v
Secretary of State for Home Affairs* [2002] HRLR 45 on an appeal from a decision
of the Special Immigration Appeals Tribunal on an appeal against a decision by
the Home Secretary to issue certificates in respect of 11 persons. The Court rejected the argument that there was no 'public emergency threatening the life of the
United Kingdom' that justified derogation from the Convention. A belief that the
risk of a terrorist attack in the United Kingdom was greater than in other states
that were also signatories to the Convention was reasonable given the material
available. The Court of Appeal allowed the Secretary of State's appeal against the
tribunal's decision that the measures were discriminatory in effect (see also the
discussion at Supplement, paras 6.93 and 17.164).

(6) Deprivation of liberty by court order

(b) Detention pending trial

n178: See now the Law Commission report, *Bail and the Human Rights Act 1998* **10.57**
(Law Com No 269).

In *R v Leeds Crown Court, ex p Wardle* [2001] 2 WLR 865 the House of Lords held **10.60**
that when a new charge has been laid in the magistrates' court on the last day of
the custody time limit of the original charge, the true question was whether the
new charge had been brought solely for the purpose of avoiding the custody time
limit and the prosecutor must demonstrate that the new charge was necessary. In

R (Eliot) v Reading Crown Court [2002] 1 Cr App R 32 it was held that 'Bail Act considerations' (ie, considerations whether or not to grant bail in the first place) could not properly be taken into account as a factor capable of giving rise to good and sufficient cause for extending custody time limits.

(d) Imprisonment and other orders on conviction

10.68 **n233:** A 'discretionary lifer' is, however, only entitled to the reports available to a Category Review Team in exceptional cases; see *Williams v Secretary of State for the Home Department, The Times,* 1 May 2002.

10.69 In *Stafford v United Kingdom* (2002) 35 EHRR 22 the Court rejected the analysis of discretionary and mandatory life sentences which it had made in *Wynne v United Kingdom* (1994) 19 EHRR 333. See, further, Supplement, para 10.167.

(e) Detention of mental patients

10.71 **Powers of detention.** When a Mental Health Review Tribunal had ordered the discharge of a patient, it was unlawful to readmit the patient to hospital under sections 2 or 3 of the Mental Health Act 1983 even though the relevant professionals had not satisfied themselves that, where it was practicable for them to do so, there had been a relevant change of circumstances; see *R v East London and the City Mental Health NHS Trust, ex p von Brandenburg* [2001] 3 WLR 588.

(7) Compensation for unlawful detention

10.78 In *North Kent Magistrates v Reid,* 4 April 2001 (Park J), a claim for false imprisonment against a magistrates' court was struck out on the basis that there was no prospect of showing that the magistrates had acted in bad faith.

n282: *R v Secretary of State for the Home Department, ex p Chahal (No 2)* is now reported at [2000] HRLR 261.

C. The Law Under the European Convention

(2) The substance of the guarantees

10.89 **n316a:** *Riera Blume v Spain* is now reported at (2000) 30 EHRR 632.

(3) Permissible deprivation of liberty

(c) Substantive law of detention

10.93 The detention of an individual awaiting expulsion who posed no danger to the public and who was not at risk of absconding was in breach of Article 5(1) (*Dougoz v Greece* (2002) 34 EHRR 61).

In *Conka v Belgium* (2002) 34 EHRR 54 the Court emphasised the need to protect the individual from arbitrariness and held that a conscious decision to deprive overstayers of their liberty by misleading them about the true reasons for attending a police station was not compatible with Article 5.

Article 5(1)(a): Detention after conviction.   By contrast, in *Stafford v United*   **10.96**
Kingdom (2002) 35 EHRR 32 the Secretary of State sought to justify the continued detention of a prisoner under a mandatory life sentence based upon the risk of further, non-violent, offending. The Court found there to be an insufficient causal connection between that risk and the original sentence for murder in 1967. The applicant's release on licence had been allowed by the Secretary of State in 1979, following which the applicant had been imprisoned again for a fraud offence. The Court noted that the applicant had served the sentence found to be appropriate by the trial court for the fraud offence, and that there was 'no power under domestic law to impose indefinite detention on him to prevent future non-violent offending' (para 82).

Article 5(1)(d): Detention of minors.   See also *DG v Ireland* (2002) 35 EHRR   **10.112**
33 in which the Court held that the applicant minor's detention in a penal institution for periods totalling approximately seven weeks did not amount to an interim custody measure preliminary to a regime of supervised education where it had been ordered on two occasions in the absence of any specific proposal for secure and supervised education, and on the third occasion on the basis of 'a proposal for temporary accommodation which, in any event, turned out to be neither secure nor appropriate' (para 84).

A complaint that the detention of a minor suffering from an untreatable psycho-   **10.113**
pathic disorder was a breach of Article 5(1)(d) was held inadmissible in *Koniarska v United Kingdom* (Decision of 12 October 2000).

Article 5(1)(e): Detention of persons in special circumstances.   The term 'al-   **10.114A**
coholics' was considered by the Court in *Witold Litwa v Poland* (2001) 33 EHRR 1267. The Court held that 'alcoholics' included 'persons who are not medically diagnosed as "alcoholics", but whose conduct and behaviour under the influence of alcohol pose a threat to public order or themselves' (para 61). In that case, the detention of the applicant for six hours in a 'sobering-up centre' after he was assessed to be 'moderately intoxicated' was held to constitute a breach of his Article 5 rights.

For detention to be lawful under Article 5(1)(e) it is necessary that less severe mea-   **10.120**
sures have been considered and found to provide insufficient safeguards (*Varbanov v Bulgaria*, Judgment of 5 October 2000).

(4) The rights of a person arrested or detained

(b) Information as to reasons for arrest (Article 5(2))

10.127   While Article 5(2) requires the imparting of information 'promptly' it does not require that it be done 'immediately' (*HB v Switzerland*, Judgment of 5 April 2001).

(c) Rights of those on remand

10.133   **Scope of the rights.**   Article 5(3) does not include a right to be brought repeatedly before a judge; see *Grauzinis v Lithuania* (2002) 35 EHRR 144.

n467: See also *Kudla v Poland* (2001) 10 BHRC 259 and *Ilowiecki v Poland* (Judgment of 4 October 2001).

10.134   **Right to be brought promptly before a judge.**   A 'judicial officer' for the purpose of Article 5(3) is required to be an individual who is independent of the parties and of the executive (*HB v Switzerland*, Judgment of 5 April 2001). Article 5(3) is not complied with when national law merely gives the applicant the possibility of lodging an application challenging the lawfulness of his detention; see *Sabeur Ben Ali v Malta* (2002) 34 EHRR 693.

10.136   Only in exceptional circumstances will the holding of an individual for over four days without release or appearance before a judicial authority be acceptable for the purposes of Article 5(3) (*Tas v Turkey* (2001) 33 EHRR 15).

n477: The Court also works to a rule of thumb that ordinarily the period of detention before a person is brought before a judge should not be longer than four days; see, for example, *Tas v Turkey* (2001) 33 EHRR 15.

10.143   **The right to a trial within a reasonable time.**   In *Jablonski v Poland* (Judgment of 21 December 2000) it was emphasised that, when deciding whether a person should be released or detained, the judicial authorities must consider alternative methods of ensuring his appearance at trial. This obligation does not give a court a choice between either bringing the accused to trial within a reasonable time or granting him provisional release, even subject to guarantees. Until conviction the accused is presumed innocent and the purpose of Article 5(3) essentially is to require his provisional release once continued detention ceases to be reasonable. The Court went on to find that the failure to consider alternative preventative measures (such as bail or police supervision) breached Article 5(3).

10.144   Detention in custody for five years and 11 months was a breach of Article 5(3) despite the fact that the case was a complex one; see *Erdem v Germany* (2002) 35 EHRR 383 and *Jecius v Lithuania* (2002) 35 EHRR 400.

(d) Right to contest the lawfulness of detention (Article 5(4))

Introduction. It was held in *Douiyeb v Netherlands* (2000) 30 EHRR 790 that the mere fact that there has been no violation under Article 5(1) of the Convention does not mean that there is no violation under Article 5(4). **10.145**

Procedural requirement. In *DN v Switzerland* (2002) 63 BMLR 221 Article 5(4) was breached by a failure to provide an independent and impartial tribunal. A complaint was made by a patient seeking release from a psychiatric hospital that a psychiatric expert sitting as a member of the tribunal considering his release had also been the only person to subject him to a psychiatric examination. In the case of a person whose detention falls within the ambit of Article 5(1)(c), a hearing is required; see *Trzaska v Poland* (Judgment of 11 July 2000); *Grauzinis v Lithuania* (2002) 35 EHRR 144, para 31; *Wloch v Poland* (2002) 34 EHRR 229; and *Cesky v Czech Republic* (2001) 33 EHRR 181. **10.152**

Article 5(4) does not guarantee a right to appeal against decisions ordering or extending detention, but where domestic law provides for a system of appeal the appellate body must also comply with Article 5(4); see *Grauzinis v Lithuania* (2002) 35 EHRR 144. **10.153**

The failure to give the accused the material from the file of a criminal investigation relevant to the lawfulness of detention has been found to breach Article 5(4) in a number of cases. In *Alva v Germany* (Judgment of 13 February 2001), the Court acknowledged that the need for criminal investigations to be conducted efficiently might imply the need for secrecy in order to prevent tampering with evidence and undermining the course of justice. However, that legitimate aim cannot be pursued at the expense of substantial restrictions on the rights of the defence. Information essential for determining the lawfulness of the detention should therefore be made available in an appropriate manner to a suspect's lawyer. See also *Lietzow v Germany* (Judgment of 13 February 2001) and *Schöps v Germany* (Judgment of 13 February 2001). **10.154**

n553: See also *Lanz v Austria* (Judgment of 31 January 2002) and *Migon v Poland* (Judgment of 25 June 2002).

Speedy determination. Although the clock normally starts to run from the institution of Article 5(4) proceedings, the Court stated in *Igdeli v Turkey* (Judgment of 10 June 2002) that 'where a person has to wait for a period to challenge the lawfulness of his custody, there may be a breach of Article 5(4)' (para 34). The Court accordingly concluded that a seven-day detention with no opportunity for challenge breached not only Article 5(3) but also Article 5(4). It is difficult to reconcile this ruling with a natural reading of Article 5(4). In relation to the meaning of the word 'speedily' in Article 5(4) the Court has held that a 10-day period, following the request for the release of information, for the prosecution to **10.155**

file its observations, followed by a further 10 days before the court reached its decision was excessive and in breach of the Convention (*GB v Switzerland* (2002) 34 EHRR 265); and see also *MB v Switzerland* (Judgment of 30 November 2000). In *Szeloch v Poland* (Judgment of 22 February 2001), detention for a period of four years and three months in relation to suspicion for manslaughter and sex abuse against children was held to breach Article 5(4) as a failure to display 'special diligence' in the conduct of proceedings.

10.157 A delay of 24 days between a request for release on trial and the release itself for a detainee in a psychiatric institution was held to be in violation of Article 5(4) in *LR v France* (Judgment of 27 June 2002). A gap of two years between considerations of whether to release a prisoner serving a discretionary life sentence, who had completed rehabilitatory work required of him, was found to be too long by the Court and in breach of Article 5(4) (*Oldham v United Kingdom* (2001) 31 EHRR 813).

In proceedings concerning a review of psychiatric detention, the complexity of the medical issues is a factor which may be taken into account when assessing compliance with Article 5(4) (see *Musial v Poland* (2000) 31 EHRR 29, para 47; see also *Vodenicarov v Slovakia*, Judgment of 21 December 2000).

D. The Impact of the Human Rights Act

(2) UK cases

(a) Introduction

10.161 The United Kingdom has now been found to be in breach of Article 5 on 16 occasions.

n604: See also *V and T v United Kingdom* (1999) 30 EHRR 121 (sentences at Her Majesty's Pleasure breach Article 5(4)); *Oldham v United Kingdom* (2001) 31 EHRR 813 (two-year delay between Parole Board reviews of the sentence of a discretionary lifer was in breach of Article 5(4)); *O'Hara v United Kingdom* (2002) 34 EHRR 32 (detention for six days and 13 hours without charge breached Article 5(3)); *Hirst v United Kingdom, The Times,* 3 August 2001 (delays between Parole Board reviews of detention of discretionary lifer were in breach of Article 5(4)); *Stafford v United Kingdom* (2002) 35 EHRR 32 (detention of applicant and absence of review of detention after expiry of tariff period of mandatory life sentence breached Article 5(1) and (4) respectively). *Caballero v United Kingdom* is now reported at (2000) 30 EHRR 643. *Curley v United Kingdom* is now reported at (2000) 31 EHRR 401. See also *SBC v United Kingdom* (2002) 34 EHRR 619 which followed *Caballero* in deciding that the refusal of bail under section 25 of the Criminal Justice and Public Order Act 1994 breached Article 5(3) and (5).

(b) *Terrorism cases*

n610: The Human Rights Act (Amendment) Order 2001, SI 2001/1216, which came into force on 1 April 2001, amended the Human Rights Act 1998 to reflect the withdrawal by the UK Government of the derogation from Article 5(3) of the Convention which was originally preserved by section 14(1)(a) of, and set out in Part I of Schedule 3 to, the 1998 Act. The withdrawal of the derogation was effective from 26 February 2001 and followed the implementation of Schedule 8 to the Terrorism Act 2000. The UK has since derogated from Article 5(1)(f); see Supplement, para 6.93.

10.163

(d) *Life prisoners*

In *Stafford v United Kingdom* (2002) 35 EHRR 32 the Court reassessed the application of the Convention to the mandatory life sentence for murder in the United Kingdom. The Court rejected the distinction drawn in *Wynne* between mandatory and discretionary life sentences, holding that 'the finding in *Wynne* that the mandatory life sentence constituted punishment for life can no longer be regarded as reflecting the real position in the domestic criminal justice system of the mandatory life prisoner' (para 79). The Court went on to hold that Article 5(4) required the lifer's continued detention beyond the tariff period set by the Secretary of State to be reviewed 'by a body with power to release or with a procedure containing the necessary safeguards including, for example, the possibility of an oral hearing' (para 89). As to the Secretary of State's discretion to fix further periods of imprisonment, the Court stated as follows (at para 80):

10.167

> Once the punishment element of the sentence (as reflected in the tariff) has been satisfied, the grounds for the continued detention, as in discretionary life and juvenile murderer cases, must be considerations of risk and dangerousness. Reference has been made by Secretaries of State to a third element—public acceptability of release—yet this has never in fact been relied upon. As Lord Justice Simon Brown forcefully commented in the case of *Anderson and Taylor* ([2002] 2 WLR 1143), it is not apparent how public confidence in the system of criminal justice could legitimately require the continued incarceration of a prisoner who had served the term required for punishment for the offence and was no longer a risk to the public.

n622a: *Curley v United Kingdom* is now reported at (2000) 31 EHRR 401; see also *V and T v United Kingdom* (1999) 30 EHRR 121 where the Court held that sentences at Her Majesty's Pleasure breach Article 5(4).

10.168

(e) *Other applications*

The refusal to review a prisoner's detention within two years breached Article 5(4); see *Oldham v United Kingdom* (2001) 31 EHRR 813. A challenge to section

10.169

25 has been held admissible as potentially breaching Article 5(3) and (5); see *SBC v United Kingdom* (Decision of 5 September 2000).

10.170A   n629a: *Caballero v United Kingdom* is now reported at (2000) 30 EHRR 643.

(3) The impact on remedies for wrongful detention

(b) *Compensation for wrongful detention*

10.175A   Damages for judicial acts are discussed in detail in the Law Commission report, *Damages under the Human Rights Act 1998* (Law Com No 266), Appendix A.

(4) Specific areas of impact

(a) *Criminal law*

10.177   In *R v Leeds Crown Court, ex p Wardle* [2001] 2 WLR 865 the House of Lords held that a new custody time limit commencing, for the purposes of regulation 4 of the Prosecution of Offences (Custody Time Limits) Regulations 1987, following substitution in the magistrates' court of a charge of manslaughter in place of a charge of murder, did not breach Article 5.

n643: See the Law Commission report, *Bail and the Human Rights Act 1998* (Law Com 269), discussed at Supplement, para 10.178.

n647a: *Caballero v United Kingdom* is now reported at (2000) 30 EHRR 643.

n648: See the views expressed in the Law Commission report, *Bail and the Human Rights Act 1998* (Law Com 269), discussed at Supplement, para 10.178.

10.178   In circumstances in which the prosecution were acting with due diligence and expedition to obtain evidence it has been held that the extension of custody time limits do not breach Article 5; see *Wildman v DPP*, *The Times*, 8 February 2001.

In general, the domestic procedure for bail has been found to be compatible with the Convention. In *R (DPP) v Havering Magistrates' Court* [2001] 1 WLR 805 it was held that there was no breach of Article 5 provided that a justice evaluated material before him in the context of the consequences to the defendant and, in particular, took account of the fact that where hearsay evidence was relied on, it had not been subject to cross-examination. It was further held that a defendant should be given a fair opportunity to comment on the material upon which the proceedings were based, that the justice was not limited to considering only evidence that was admissible in the strict sense, and that the facts upon which his decision was based did not need to be proved to the criminal standard of proof.

The Law Commission has now published its report, *Bail and the Human Rights Act 1998* (Law Com 269), which considers the impact of the Act in detail. The

Commission has produced *Suggested Guidance for Bail Decision-Takers*; see Part XIII of the report. The Law Commission's examination of Convention case law led it to conclude (para 2.37):

- That continuing detention can only be justified in the following circumstances where the detention is necessary in pursuit of one of five legitimate purposes where the accused would: (1) refuse to attend trial; (2) interfere with evidence or witnesses or otherwise obstruct the course of justice; (3) commit an offence while on bail; (4) be at risk against which he would be inadequately protected; and (5) where a disturbance to public order would result (para 2.29).
- A legitimate purpose only exists where there is a real risk that the feared event will occur if the defendant is released on bail.
- Detention will only be necessary if that risk could not be adequately addressed, to the point where detention would no longer be necessary, by the imposition of appropriate bail conditions.
- The court refusing bail should give reasons for finding that detention is necessary. Those reasons should be closely related to the individual circumstances pertaining to the defendant and be capable of supporting the court's conclusions.

As a result the Law Commission reached the following conclusions about bail:

- Pre-trial detention for the purpose of preventing a defendant from committing an offence while on bail can be compatible with Article 5(1)(c) and (3) provided that it is a necessary and proportionate response to a real risk that, if released, the defendant would commit an offence on bail. Previous convictions and other circumstances may be relevant, but the decision-maker must consider whether it may properly be inferred from them that there is a real risk that the defendant will commit the offence (para 3.11).
- The power to refuse bail under paragraph 2A of Part 1 of Schedule 1 to the Bail Act (that is, if the offence is indictable or triable either way and the defendant appears to be on bail in criminal proceedings) can only be applied in a Convention-compliant manner if the court relies on another ground of detention. The Commission took the view that a court should not refuse bail solely on the ground that paragraph 2A applied and recommended its amendment (paras 4.10–4.12).
- Refusal of bail for a defendant's own protection (whether from harm from others or self-harm) can be compatible with the Convention where detention is necessary to address a real risk that, if granted bail, the defendant would suffer harm by others or self-harm against which the detention could provide protection; and there are exceptional circumstances in the nature of the alleged offence and/or the conditions or context in which it is alleged to have been committed (para 5.10).

- In the absence of authority, the Commission saw no reason why a court decision to order detention because of self-harm could not be compatible with Article 5 even where the circumstances giving rise to the risk are unconnected with the alleged offence, provided the court is satisfied that there is a real risk of self-harm, and that a proper medical examination will take place rapidly so that the court may then consider exercising its powers of detention under the Mental Health Act 1983 (para 5.11).
- Refusal of bail because of a lack of information under paragraph 5 of Part 1 of Schedule 1 to the Bail Act can be compatible with Article 5 provided that detention is for a short period, which is no longer than necessary to enable the required information to be obtained; and the lack of information is not due to a failure of the prosecution, the police, the court or another state body to act with 'special diligence'. Where these tests are met, the requirements for lawful detention prescribed above will not apply. After that short period of time, a lack of information that is not due to a failure of a state body to act with 'special diligence' may be taken into account as a factor militating in favour of detention, in support of the existence of another Convention-compliant ground for detention (paras 6.13–6.16).
- Section 7(5) of, and paragraphs 5 and 6 of Part 1 of Schedule 1 to, the Bail Act can be interpreted compatibly with Article 5. The court should not refuse to grant bail simply because the defendant has been arrested under section 7 of the Act. The provisions should be applied so that bail is only refused where it is necessary for a purpose defined under Article 5, and the circumstances leading to a defendant being arrested under section 7 may properly be taken into account as a possible reason for deciding that detention is necessary for that purpose (para 7.33). The repeal of paragraph 6, and the amendment of paragraph 5, of Part 1 of Schedule 1, was recommended (para 7.35).
- The power to grant bail in only exceptional circumstances under section 25 of the Criminal Justice and Public Order Act 1994 should be construed as meaning that where the defendant would not, if released on bail, pose a real risk of committing a serious offence, this constitutes an 'exceptional circumstance' so that bail may be granted. There may be other 'exceptional circumstances' which permit bail to be granted and that even if an 'exceptional circumstance' exists, bail may be withheld on a Convention-compatible ground (paras 8.46–8.48).
- A court should not detain a person where there is another way to achieve that aim which will interfere with the defendant's liberty to a lesser extent. Thus, a defendant must be released, if need be subject to conditions, unless that would create a risk of a kind which can, in principle, justify pre-trial detention and that risk cannot, by imposing suitable bail conditions, be averted or reduced to a level at which it would not justify detention (para 9A.25).
- When deciding to impose conditional bail, a court should, to comply with Article 5, only impose a condition for a purpose that Article 5 recognises as

justifying detention; a bail condition should only be imposed where, if the defendant were to break that condition (or be reasonably thought to do so), it may be necessary to arrest the defendant in order to pursue the purpose for which the condition was imposed; and decision-makers should state reasons for imposing bail conditions and specify the purpose for which any conditions are imposed (para 9B.36).

- Although Article 5(4) is unlikely to be infringed simply because the defendant was not present, provided he is represented, a court should not hear a bail application where his presence is essential to fair proceedings (para 11.14);
- Although it is not necessary to hear sworn evidence in most cases, the court should consider whether fairness requires calling evidence on oath to decide the application (para 11.27).
- The duty of disclosure will be complied with by applying *Wildman v DPP, The Times*, 8 February 2001 and paragraph 34 of the Attorney-General's guidance on *Disclosure of Information in Criminal Proceedings* (November 2000) (para 11.34).
- Reconsideration of bail should take place at least every 28 days to comply with Article 5(4) (para 12.9).
- The court should be willing, at regular intervals of 28 days, to consider arguments that in a particular case the passage of time amounts to a change of circumstances so as to require a fully argued bail application (para 12.23).

n648a: See the views expressed in the Law Commission report, *Bail and the Human Rights Act 1998* (Law Com 269), paras 4.10–4.12, discussed at Supplement, para 10.178.

n648b: See the views expressed in the Law Commission report, *Bail and the Human Rights Act 1998* (Law Com 269), para 7.33, discussed at Supplement, para 10.178.

n651: See the views expressed in the Law Commission report, *Bail and the Human Rights Act 1998* (Law Com 269), para 9B.36, discussed at Supplement, para 10.178.

n651a: See the views expressed in the Law Commission report, *Bail and the Human Rights Act 1998* (Law Com 269), para 3.11, discussed at Supplement, para 10.178.

n651b: See the views expressed in the Law Commission report, *Bail and the Human Rights Act 1998* (Law Com 269), para 3.11, discussed at Supplement, para 10.178.

n652: See the views expressed in the Law Commission report, *Bail and the Human Rights Act 1998* (Law Com 269), para 5.10, discussed at Supplement, para 10.178.

10.178A   The Court of Appeal in *R v Grant* [2002] QB 1030 decided that the detention of a person charged with murder who had been found to have done the act charged but was under a disability and was unfit to be tried was not 'arbitrary' for the purposes of Article 5(1)(e). The right to make an immediate application to a Mental Health Review Tribunal and the other protections operating following admission to hospital ensured compliance with Article 5(4). However, it expressed the view *obiter* at paras 53, 54 that it was questionable whether the procedures under section 4 give proper effect to the second of the conditions laid down for detention under Article 5(1)(e); see Main Work, para 10.117. They do not specifically address whether it can be reliably shown that the person suffers from a mental disorder sufficiently serious to warrant detention. The procedures under the Criminal Procedure (Insanity) Act 1964 are not directed specifically to that question. It therefore may be possible for a person to be found unfit to be tried without his suffering from a mental disorder sufficiently serious to warrant detention.

The House of Lords in *R (Lichniak) v Secretary of State for the Home Department* [2002] 3 WLR 1834 decided that mandatory life sentences were not so arbitrary as to breach Article 5. The House of Lords examined the legitimacy of the aim of the detention and its proportionality and concluded that there was no breach of Article 5.

(b)   Immigration

10.179   In *R (Saadi) v Secretary of State for the Home Department* [2002] 1 WLR 3131 the House of Lords confirmed the decision of the Court of Appeal that the detention of asylum seekers who were not likely to abscond could be justified under Article 5(1)(f), overturning a controversial ruling to the contrary by Collins J at first instance. The claimants were Kurdish asylum seekers who alleged that their detention in a 'reception centre' was not justified under Article 5(1)(f) because it was not 'to prevent their effecting an unauthorised entry into the country', neither were they 'people against whom action was being taken with a view to deportation or extradition'. The House of Lords took the view that the Government could detain asylum seekers without breaching Article 5 until their application was authorised. Until that time their entry was unauthorised. Furthermore, it was not necessary to show that the applicant was evading immigration control. Accordingly, even though a person who does not seek to deceive an immigration officer, or to pass out of the area of immigration control without presenting himself to an immigration officer, does not constitute an illegal entrant (*R v Naillie* [1993] AC 674; he may nonetheless be detained under Article 5(1)(f) pending the determination of his application. See, further, C de Than, 'Detention of Asylum Seekers Does Not Violate Article 5' (2002) 66(2) J Crim L 140.

By the Human Rights Act 1998 (Amendment No 2) Order 2001, SI 2001/4032, which came into force on 20 December 2001, the United Kingdom derogated from its obligation under Article 5(1)(f), as interpreted by the court in *Chahal v*

United Kingdom (1996) 23 EHRR 413, to prosecute deportation proceedings with due diligence. The derogation applies in respect of the continued detention of suspected international terrorists under the Immigration Act 1971, which is permitted under section 23 of the Anti-terrorism, Crime and Security Act 2001, even where their removal or departure from the United Kingdom is prevented 'whether temporarily or indefinitely by a point of law which wholly or partly relates to an international agreement, or a practical consideration'. In *A and Others v Secretary of State for the Home Department* [2002] UKHRR 1141 the Court of Appeal held that the derogation was lawful; see Supplement, para 3.63.

(d) Mental health law

In *R (H) v Secretary of State for the Home Department* [2002] QB 1 the Court of Appeal declared that sections 72(1) and 73(1) of the Mental Health Act 1983 were incompatible with Article 5(1) and (4) of the Convention in that, for the Mental Health Review Tribunal to be obliged to order a patient's discharge, the burden is placed upon the patient to prove that the criteria justifying his detention in hospital for treatment no longer exist; and that Article 5(1) and (4), by contrast, require the tribunal to be positively satisfied that all the criteria justifying the patient's detention in hospital for treatment continue to exist before refusing a patient's discharge. By the Mental Health Act (Remedial) Order 2001, SI 2001/3712, which came into force on 26 November 2001, sections 72(1) and 73(1) were amended simply by moving the word 'not' in each provision. The effect is that the wording now requires the tribunal to satisfy itself of the existence of criteria justifying detention, rather than to presume their existence at the outset. **10.182**

It was held by the Court of Session in *Anderson v Scottish Ministers* [2002] UKHRR 1 that it was not incompatible with Article 5 to detain a mental patient on the basis of public protection, even if that individual could not be treated, and that the Mental Health (Public Safety and Appeals) Scotland Act 1999 was compatible with the Convention. **10.185**

In *S v Airedale NHS Trust*, *The Times*, 5 September 2002, Scott Baker J took the view that the unnecessary seclusion of a mental patient did not *per se* give rise to a breach of Article 5 or the tort of false imprisonment since seclusion affected the terms of a patient's detention but did not amount to detention as such.

It has been held that the Mental Health Review Tribunal exhibits sufficient attributes of a court to satisfy the requirements of Article 5(4) and that there is no incompatibility as between the Mental Health Act 1983 and Article 5(1) in relation to compulsory admission to hospital (*R v East London and the City Mental Health NHS Trust, ex p von Brandenburg* [2001] 3 WLR 588). **10.187**

In *R v Mental Health Review Tribunal London South and South West Region, ex p C* [2002] 1 WLR 176 the Court of Appeal held that the tribunal's practice of listing cases for eight weeks from the date of the application was a breach of Article 5(4). A period of eight weeks was an administrative convenience rather than a necessity. Although there was nothing wrong with a maximum of eight weeks, the listing procedures must be tailored to the exigencies of individual cases. A fixed period of eight weeks had led to some applications not leading to as speedy a decision as was required by Article 5(4). In *R (KB) v Mental Health Tribunal* [2002] EWHC Admin 639 the claimants, patients detained under the Mental Health Act 1983, complained that long delays (27 weeks in one case) between their applications for review of their detention and the review hearings were in breach of Article 5(4). The delays resulted from repeated adjournments of the hearings. Stanley Burnton J held that the correct approach in such cases was as follows (para 46):

> [F]irst, to consider whether the delays in question are, on the face of it, inconsistent with the requirement of a speedy hearing. If they are, the onus is on the State to excuse the delay. It may do so by establishing, for example, that the delay has been caused by a sudden and unpredictable increase in the workload of the tribunal, and that it has taken effective and sufficient measures to remedy the problem. But if the State fails to satisfy that onus, the claimant will have established a breach of his right under Article 5.4.

An increase that had been obvious for some time required the state to take adequate measures to assure compliance with Article 5(4) if it was not to be in breach. Stanley Burnton J went on to consider the workload of the Mental Health Review Tribunals, the evidence available to the state relating to delays, the shortage of medical members and tribunal staff, the common practice of cancelling or adjourning hearings to accommodate urgent cases, and the adequacy of IT provision. The judge concluded that the Secretary of State could not have been taken by surprise by the delays and, as a result, the basic responsibility for the delays experienced by patients was that of central government in failing to provide adequate resources.

In *R (B) v Mental Health Review Tribunal* [2002] EWHC Admin 1553 it was held that delays of over eight months in hearing a case were a breach of Article 5(4).

In *R (A) v Secretary of State for the Home Department, The Times*, 5 September 2002, Crane J held that it was possible to read section 41(3)(c)(i) of the Mental Health Act 1983 compatibly with Article 5. The Secretary of State was under a duty to respond with reasonable promptness to a recommendation from the Mental Health Review Tribunal. The tribunal had recommended the patient be conditionally discharged but deferred directing that discharge until appropriate accommodation became available. A requirement on the Secretary of State to consent to the patient's leave of absence under section 17 of the Act might cause some delay. However, it did not follow that such a delay would be unreasonable. Nevertheless, any delay following a justifiable delay which occurred afterwards was unlawful.

Where a health authority, despite the exercise of all reasonable endeavours, is un- **10.188** able to procure for a patient the level of care in the community which the tribunal considered to be a pre-requisite for discharge from hospital, it does not breach Article 5 if detention of the patient continues (*R v Camden and Islington Health Authority, ex p K* [2001] 3 WLR 553). In *R (H) v Secretary of State for the Home Department*, *The Times*, 24 May 2002, the Court of Appeal departed from the decision of the House of Lords in *Secretary of State v Home Department (Oxford Regional Mental Health Review Tribunal)* [1988] AC 120. The Court ruled that that case was potentially in conflict with Article 5(4) as its effect was to prevent a tribunal revisiting its decision to defer conditional discharge even where it proved impossible to make the necessary arrangements for the patient to comply with the proposed conditions. The Court accordingly held that the original tribunal decision should be treated as provisional, and 'the tribunal should monitor progress towards implementing it to ensure that the patient was not left in limbo for an unreasonable length of time'. See also *R (C) v Secretary of State for the Home Department* [2002] 3 WLR 967.

A Mental Health Review Tribunal is the body which discharges the United Kingdom's obligations under Article 5(4) in relation to mental patients. In the absence of material circumstances of which the tribunal is not aware when it orders discharge, it is not open to the professionals, at any rate until and unless the tribunal's decision has been quashed by a court, to re-section a patient (see *R (Ashworth Hospital Authority) v Mental Health Review Tribunal* [2002] EWCA Civ 923).

(e) Police law

Breach of the peace.   n720a: *Hashman and Harrup v United Kingdom* is now re- **10.197** ported at (2000) 30 EHRR 241.

Terrorism cases.   The derogation referred to in the Main Work is no longer in **10.200** place (see Supplement, para 6.93).

(f) Prison law

It was held by the Court of Appeal in *Banks v Secretary of State for the Home* **10.201** *Department* [2002] EWHC Admin 381 that Articles 5 and 6 do not apply to the discretionary recall of a prisoner released on licence from a determinative sentence. Article 5(4) had been satisfied by the original trial process and any appeal. See also *R (West) v Parole Board* [2002] EWHC Admin 769.

The deprivation of the liberty of a prisoner which forms part of his sentence is justified under Article 5(1)(a). As a result, the imposition of additional days of imprisonment on a prisoner for disciplinary reasons (*R (Greenfield) v Secretary of State for the Home Department* [2001] 1 WLR 1731 (Div Ct)) and a change of his security categorisation (*R v Secretary of State for the Home Department, ex p Sunder* [2001] EWHC Admin 252) did not breach Article 5. This decision is difficult to reconcile with the views expressed in *Ezeh and Connor v United Kingdom* (2002) 35 EHRR 691 which held that the imposition of additional days of imprisonment was in substance a fresh deprivation of liberty even though it was referable to the original sentence.

In *R (Giles) v Parole Board and Another* [2002] 3 All ER 1123 1 (allowing an appeal against the decision of Elias J at [2002] 1 WLR 654) it was held that Article 5(4) did not apply to the element of a determinate sentence which depended on personal characteristics of the defendant under section 2(2)(b) of the Criminal Justice Act 1991 (now section 80(2)(b) of the Powers of Criminal Courts (Sentencing) Act 2000 (protection of the public)). The decision to impose the longer term was plainly a judicial decision which was subject to appeal so that the supervision required by Article 5(4) was incorporated into the decision.

The House of Lords in *R (Lichniak) v Secretary of State for the Home Department* [2002] 3 WLR 1834 decided that mandatory life sentences were not so arbitrary as to breach Article 5. The House of Lords examined the legitimacy of the aim of the detention and its proportionality and concluded that there was no breach of Article 5.

10.203   In *R (Noorkoiv) v Secretary of State for the Home Department* [2002] 1 WLR 3284 it was held that the system for listing hearings before a discretionary lifer panel within three months of the tariff date breached Article 5(4). The Court of Appeal observed that much shorter periods than three months had been condemned by the Strasbourg court, and held that references to the Parole Board should be made before the end of the tariff period so that if the board wished to direct release it could do so either on the expiry of the tariff period, or as soon as practical thereafter. The Secretary of State and the Parole Board could not excuse delays that would otherwise be in breach of Article 5(4) simply by pointing to a lack of resources provided by other arms of government.

The Court of Appeal held in *R v HMP Life Panel, ex p MacNeil* [2001] EWCA Civ 448 that a review after two years of a mandatory life prisoner recalled from release on licence after a violent incident did not breach Article 5(4); the unreasonableness of any delay depends upon the particular circumstances of every case.

10.204   In *R v Offen* [2001] 1 WLR 253 the Court of Appeal held that the imposition of mandatory sentences under section 2 of the Crime (Sentences) Act 1997 (now section 109 of the Powers of Criminal Courts (Sentencing) Act 2000) is not in breach of Article 5 provided that the 'exceptional circumstances' test for not imposing the sentence is read so as to include any person who does not provide a significant risk to the public.

(g) Other applications

In *Re K (A Child) (Secure Accommodation Order: Right to Liberty)* [2001] 2 WLR **10.204A**
1141 the Court of Appeal held that while a secure accommodation order
amounted to a deprivation of liberty it was not incompatible with Article 5 since
Article 5(1)(d) rendered permissible the detention of a child 'by lawful order for
the purpose of educational supervision'. Educational supervision was to be interpreted widely so as to encompass many aspects of the exercise by a local authority
of parental rights over a child.

Appendix 1: The Canadian Charter of Rights

(2) Liberty and Security

(b) 'Liberty'

In *Blencoe v British Columbia Human Rights Commission* [2000] 2 SCR 307 the **10.209**
majority of the Supreme Court said that section 7 of the Charter must be interpreted broadly and that the liberty interest is not restricted to mere freedom from
physical restraint and includes the right to make fundamental personal choices,
free from state interference. As a result, it has been held that the issuing of a deportation order engages section 7 (*Romans v The Minister of Citizenship and
Immigration* [2001] FCT 466). However, driving a vehicle on the highway is not
an interest protected by section 7 (*Buhlers v British Columbia (Superintendent of
Motor Vehicles)* (1999) 132 CCC (3d) 478, BCCA).

Nor is there any infringement of Charter rights when school authorities search **10.210**
students, where the authorities have reasonable grounds for believing that a school
rule had been violated, provided that the search is reasonable (*R v M* [2000] 2
LRC 580). Attendance at the office of the school's Vice-Principal was not detention for Charter purposes, therefore the students did not have rights to counsel.

(3) Protection from arbitrary detention or imprisonment

The refusal to grant day parole to a prisoner did not amount to an arbitrary de- **10.220**
tention. Conditional release was an enhancement, not a deprivation of liberty
(*Bonamy v Canada (National Parole Board)* [2001] CRDJ 340).

Appendix 2: The New Zealand Bill of Rights Act

(2) Liberty of the person

The New Zealand Court of Appeal held in *Bennett v Superintendent of Rimutaka* **10.240A**
Prison [2002] 1 NZLR 616 that solitary confinement of prisoners, or classification

of maximum security, was not a new detention for the purposes of section 23(1) of the New Zealand Bill of Rights. Nor were *habeas corpus* remedies available to such prisoners. The prisoners in that case had argued that *habeas corpus* should be available, because other means of challenging the legality of their treatment, such as judicial review, were inadequate. Judicial review, it was argued, was inadequate because remedies were discretionary, and the burden of proof was placed on the detainee. In contrast, *habeas corpus* as a writ of right was given priority by court staff and judicial officers because of its significance. The court rejected those arguments, holding that unlawful treatment while an inmate is detained did not render the detention unlawful. The remedy was the cessation of the unlawful element, not the cessation of the detention. Further, in truly urgent cases, applications for interim relief could be heard as speedily as *habeas corpus*.

See also *McVeagh v Attorney General* [2002] 2 LRC 35 (there was no breach of the ICCPR provisions requiring an effective remedy for breach of rights when *habeas corpus* provisions were unavailable to a detainee in a mental health hospital; the availability of an action for false imprisonment was sufficient).

(3) Rights of a person arrested

10.242 The right to consult a lawyer continues throughout the detention process, as does the obligation on police officers to facilitate enforcement of that right (*Rae v Police* [2000] 3 NZLR 452, NZ CA).

10.244 The principles governing bail were discussed in *B v Police* [2000] 1 NZLR 31.

Appendix 3: Human Rights Cases in Other Jurisdictions

(1A) Botswana

10.245A Section 3 of the Constitution provides for a fundamental right to liberty and section 5 provides that no person shall be deprived of his personal liberty save as authorised by law in specified circumstances. These include '(c) in execution of the order of a court to secure the fulfilment of any obligation imposed on him by law'.

In *Noor v Botswana Co-operative Bank* [2001] 3 LRC 472 it was held that civil imprisonment for debt was within the terms of this provision because the relevant domestic legislation did not allow imprisonment where the debtor could not pay for genuine lack of means (*Coetzee v Government of South Africa* [1994] 4 LRC 220 and *Ciulla v Italy* (1989) 13 EHRR 346 distinguished).

(2) Hong Kong

A mandatory sentence of life imprisonment for murder did not amount to arbitrary detention contrary to Article 5 of the Hong Kong Bill of Rights (*HKSAR v Pun Ganga Chandra* (2001–2) HKC 192).

10.247

(4A) Inter-American Commission on Human Rights

The case of *Coard v United States* [2001] 9 BHRC 150 concerned claims by Grenadians who had been detained during the US military intervention in 1983. It was argued that the United States had violated a number of articles of the American Declaration of Rights and Duties of Man 1948 including Articles I (right to life, liberty and personal security), XVII (right to recognition of civil rights) and XXV (right to protection from arbitrary arrest). The Commission accepted that the internment of civilians for security reasons could be permissible (by reference to Article 78 of Geneva Convention IV). However, the petitioners were not afforded access to a review of the legality of their detention with the least possible delay and, as a result, the Commission found a deprivation of rights under Articles I, XVII and XXV.

10.251A

(8) Sri Lanka

In *Weerawansa v A-G* [2001] 1 LRC 407 the Supreme Court held that there had been breaches of Article 13(1) and (2) because there were no proper grounds for suspicion and the petitioner had not been brought before a magistrate. It was held to be essential that a suspect be brought into the presence of a judge and have the opportunity to communicate with him.

10.261

11

FAIR TRIAL RIGHTS

B. The Rights in English Law

(2) Right of access to the courts

(a) Introduction

See, generally, A Le Sueur, 'Access to Justice Rights in the United Kingdom' [2000] EHRLR 457 and D Squires, 'Access to a Court after *Witham*, *Lightfoot* and *Saleem*' [2001] JR 38.   **11.15**

It has been held that there is a fundamental right of access to tribunals (see *R v Home Secretary, ex p Saleem* [2001] 1 WLR 443). As Hale LJ said (at 458A):   **11.18A**

> In this day and age a right of access to a tribunal or other adjudication mechanism established by the state is just as important and fundamental as a right of access to the ordinary courts.

(d) Immunities

11.44A **Negligence immunity.** It remains unclear whether the shift of emphasis in negligence cases will now be reversed in the light of *Z v United Kingdom* (2001) 10 BHRC 384 in which the Court of Human Rights refused to follow *Osman* (see Supplement, para 11.162). One consequence of *Osman* is that the English courts are now careful to avoid discussions of 'immunity' in the negligence context and have emphasised that 'policy' questions are part of the assessment; see *Kane v New Forest District Council* [2001] 3 All ER 914 and *K v Secretary of State for the Home Department* [2002] EWCA Civ 893. See also C Newdick, 'Damages for Public Authority Negligence: Public Interests and the Human Rights Act' [2002] Tort LR 127.

11.45 For a case in which the 'assumption of responsibility' test was applied, see *Cowan v Chief Constable of Avon and Somerset* [2002] HLR 44 (no assumption of responsibility to tenant who was unlawfully evicted by landlord when police had been called to deal with breach of peace); and see also *Brooks v Commissioner of Police for the Metropolis* [2002] EWCA Civ 407.

(3) Fair trial rights in general

(b) Independent and impartial tribunal

11.63 **Independence.** The Report of the Review of Tribunals (*Tribunals for Users: One System, One Service*, March 2001) has recommended that, in order to ensure the independence of statutory tribunals they should be organised into a coherent system to sit alongside the ordinary courts, with administrative support provided by the Lord Chancellor's Department. It also recommended that appointments to tribunals should be made by the Lord Chancellor using the same system as for judicial appointments (see, generally, Chapter 2, 'A More Independent System').

11.65A In *R (Bewry) v Norwich City Council* [2002] HRLR 21 Moses J held that there is a common law right to a hearing before a tribunal which is independent and impartial. The common law provided no less protection for the applicant's rights than Article 6. Given that the members of a housing benefit review board were city councillors, and it was the city council that was resisting that claimant's claim for housing benefit, the board lacked the appearance of independence and impartiality. It could not be said that the members of the board were independent when deciding issues of fact. As a result, in spite of what the judge described as 'the clarity and care demonstrated by the decision', the decision of the board was quashed. Some doubt has been cast on this decision in the light of the approach of the Court of Appeal to Article 6 in *Runa Begum v Tower Hamlets* [2002] 1 WLR 2491; see, generally, Supplement, para 11.303.

Impartiality. For a critique of the 'automatic disqualification' principle see A   **11.67**
Olowofoyeku, 'The *Nemo Judex* Rule: The Case Against Automatic
Disqualification' [2000] Public Law 456; and see *Ebner v Official Trustee in
Bankruptcy* [2001] 2 LRC 369, HC Aust, discussed at Supplement, para 11.464.

In *Re Medicaments (No 2)* [2001] 1 WLR 700 the Court of Appeal held that   **11.68**
Convention jurisprudence required a modest adjustment of the test for bias in *R
v Gough*. The court must first ascertain all the circumstances which had a bearing
on the suggestion that the judge was biased. It must then ask whether those circumstances would lead a fair-minded and informed observer to conclude that
there was a real possibility, or a real danger, the two being the same, that the tribunal was biased. This adjustment was approved by the House of Lords in *Magill
v Porter* [2002] 2 WLR 37, with the deletion of the reference to a 'real danger'.
Further, it noted that from the standpoint of the fair-minded and informed observer:

- protestations of lack of bias are unlikely to be helpful; and
- whilst the complainer's fears are clearly relevant at the initial stage when the
  court has to decide whether the complaint is one that should be investigated,
  they lose their importance once the stage is reached of looking at the matter objectively. At that stage what is decisive is whether any fears expressed by the
  complainer are objectively justified. See also *Taylor v Lawrence* [2002] 3 WLR
  640.

In *R (Hussain) v Asylum Support Adjudicator* [2001] EWHC Admin 852 Stanley
Burnton J considered the issue of what information is to be ascribed to the fair-
minded and informed observer. He found it difficult to reconcile the test formulated by the Court of Appeal in *R v Spear* [2001] 2 WLR 1692 that takes account
of *all* the relevant facts (including, presumably, those that are not available to the
public) with the requirement of an appearance of independence. He preferred and
applied the test formulated by Lindsay J in *Scanfuture UK Ltd v Secretary of State
for Trade and Industry* [2001] IRLR 416 which ascribed to the observer only such
information as could be acquired by a persistent, even dogged, member of the
public. The 'fair-minded and informed observer' is a not a lawyer but is informed
about the practice of the courts; see *Sengupta v Holmes* [2002] EWCA Civ 1104,
but cf *Daktaras v Lithuania* (2002) 34 EHRR 1466.

A number of unsuccessful challenges to the independence and impartiality of decision-makers have been made:

- The chief constable of a police force was not disqualified from hearing a disciplinary case against a police officer although that officer had brought proceedings against the force (*R (Bennion) v Chief Constable of Merseyside* [2001] IRLR
  442).

- An appeal panel dealing with school exclusions, partly set up by the education authority and which took action based on guidance from the Secretary of State was 'independent and impartial'; see *R (S) v Brent London Borough Council* [2002] EWCA Civ 693.
- A Professional Conduct Committee of the General Medical Council constituted to consider a charge that the applicant had lied to an earlier hearing before a differently constituted committee; see *R (Nicolaides) v General Medical Council* (2001) Lloyd's Med Rep 525 (Sir Richard Tucker).
- The trial of an offence by court-martial was not in itself incompatible with the right of an accused under Article 6(1) of the Convention to a fair hearing by an independent and impartial tribunal. The safeguards designed to ensure the independence and impartiality of the members of courts-martial, including the oath taken by them and their obligation to observe the directions of the judge advocate, were adequate (*R v Spear* [2002] 3 WLR 437; see also *R v Skuse* [2002] EWCA Crim 991).
- Lay members of employment tribunals (*Scanfuture UK Ltd v Secretary of State for Trade and Industry* [2001] IRLR 416) and lay members of VAT and duties tribunals (*Ali and Begum v The Commissioners of Customs and Excise*, 30 May 2002, VAT and Duties Tribunal, Stephen Oliver QC).
- The role of the judge advocate at a naval court-martial who, unlike his army and air force counterparts, is not appointed from the ranks of civilian barristers in private practice but is a barrister serving in the Navy, did not breach the requirement of an 'independent and impartial' tribunal (*R v Skuse* [2002] EWCA Crim 991).
- A judge who was an acquaintance of the chief constable (a witness for the prosecution) was not required to withdraw from the proceedings. The Court of Appeal said that the fair-minded and informed observer would be conscious that the relationship was a formal one and, more importantly, that the credibility of the chief constable was not in issue (*R v Mason and Others* [2002] EWCA Crim 385).
- Asylum support adjudicators, although appointed by the Home Office, in practice enjoyed considerable security of tenure (appointment could only be terminated by the Home Secretary on limited specified grounds with the consent of the Lord Chancellor) and therefore satisfied the requirement of independence under Article 6. In any event, it was held that any lack of independence was cured by the availability of judicial review since the issue before the adjudicator was likely to be whether the Secretary of State had reasonable grounds to come to his decision rather than a dispute as to primary facts (*R (Hussain) v Asylum Support Adjudicator* [2001] EWHC 852).
- Where the representative of one of the parties to a tribunal application had previously sat with members of the tribunal hearing the case (see *Skelton v Christian Salvesen* [2002] All ER(D) 137 (July), EAT). In that case Lord

Johnston said that a distinction must be drawn between professional and social acquaintances; with the former, there is no presumption of bias and, in any event, public policy prevented the argument succeeding because otherwise lay members of tribunals would never be able to appear in cases, whether as a representative or to give evidence. Similarly, in *Lawal v Northern Spirit* [2002] ICR 1507 the Court of Appeal held that a lay member of the Employment Appeal Tribunal was not biased merely because he had previously sat as a lay member with counsel for one of the parties who sat as a part-time chairman of the Employment Appeal Tribunal.

- The fact that a judge had used the services of the claimant's solicitors during the trial to amend a will already held by them would not be regarded by a fair-minded and informed observer as raising a possibility of bias (*Taylor v Lawrence* [2002] 3 WLR 640). If a fair-minded and informed person might regard the judge as biased, or if the position was borderline, the judge should make full disclosure.
- The fact that a judge had refused permission to appeal on paper did not mean that there was a real possibility of bias if he sits on the substantive hearing (*Sengupta v Holmes* [2002] EWCA Civ 1104).

However, challenges based on lack of independence and impartiality have been successful in several cases:

- The Crown Court Rules which set out the constitution of the Crown Court when hearing an appeal against a decision of licensing magistrates were held to be unlawful because in practice the appeal panel would include two magistrates belonging to the same licensing committee as the magistrates who made the decision appealed against. Such a panel lacked the objective appearance of independence and impartiality; see *R (Chief Constable of Lancashire and Gosling) v Preston Crown Court* [2002] 1 WLR 1332.
- A Housing Benefit Review Board which included councillors as members was held not to be 'independent' (*R (Bewry) v Norwich City Council* [2002] HRLR 21 and *R (Bono) v Harlow District Council* [2002] 1 WLR 2475). The position has now been solved by the introduction of a new system of appeal to an independent tribunal.
- The decision-making procedure of a local authority under the National Assistance Act 1948 where the decision was made by one independent member and two councillors was not 'independent' (*R (Beeson) v Dorset County Council* [2002] HRLR 369).

(c) Fair hearing

Prior notice of the case. An alleged contemnor has a common law right to adequate written notice of what is being alleged against him (*Newman v Modern Bookbinders* [2000] 2 All ER 814. See also *Commissioners for Customs and Excise v Togher* [2001] EWCA Civ 474).

11.72

11.73 **Adequate time to prepare.**   The requirement of a fair and public hearing did not extend to necessitating the presence of a litigant in person at a directions hearing and a refusal to adjourn such a hearing due to his ill health was not a breach of Article 6 (*Toofanny v Parkside Health NHS Trust,* 5 June 2001, EAT).

11.75 **A hearing.**   The right to an oral hearing is usually associated with, and flows from, a right to a public hearing. However, in *R v Special Commissioner, ex p Morgan Grenfell* [2002] 2 WLR 255, para 50, CA, it was said that where the Inland Revenue applies to the Special Commissioner pursuant to section 20 of the Taxes Management Act 1970 for consent to issue a notice for the production of documents subject to legal professional privilege, Article 6 does not require the Commissioner to afford the intended recipient an oral hearing. The possibility of an oral hearing was excluded by the nature of the process in question (para 50). The point was not pursued on the appeal to the House of Lords at [2002] 2 WLR 1299; see Supplement, para 12.173.

11.76 **Legal representation.**   A litigant in person should be allowed to have the assistance of a *McKenzie* friend unless the judge is satisfied that fairness and the interests of justice do not require him to have that assistance (*R v Bow County Court, ex p Pelling* [1999] 1 WLR 1807). See also H Grant, 'Commissions of Inquiry: Is there a Right to be Legally Represented?' [2001] PL 377.

11.76A **Calling and cross-examination of witnesses.**   In *FSA v Rourke* [2002] CP Rep 14 Neuberger J stated that the right to cross-examine witnesses could not be an absolute right in civil proceedings, otherwise any summary procedure would be 'doomed'.

(d) Public hearing

11.80 The principle of open justice has to be balanced against considerations of national security, the right to life and the right to protection against torture and/or inhuman or degrading treatment when considering whether proceedings for breach of confidence against a former soldier in Northern Ireland should be held in open court; see *Secretary of State for Defence v Times Newspapers Ltd,* 28 March 2001 (Blofeld J).

In *R (Amvac Chemical UK Ltd) v The Secretary of State for the Environment, Food and Rural Affairs and Others* [2001] EWHC Admin 1011 Crane J stated that Article 6 provides a slightly stricter test than CPR 39.2. However, he held on the facts that no sufficient grounds for a hearing in private had been made out, applying either the CPR test or the Article 6 test. He noted that a public hearing would not defeat the object of the hearing, no confidential information of significance had been identified and there was no special reason to fear than any reporting of the case would be unbalanced.

(e) Hearing within a reasonable time

See also *Re Blackspur Group* [2001] 1 BCLC 653, discussed at Supplement, para **11.86**
11.333, and see also *Davies v United Kingdom* (2002) 35 EHRR 720, discussed at
Supplement, para 11.219.

(f) Reasoned judgment

A judicial decision which affects the substantive rights of the parties should be rea- **11.89**
soned. Although the judge is not obliged to deal with every argument he should
identify the issues the resolution of which were vital to his conclusion and the
manner in which they were resolved should be explained. Article 6(1) requires
that the reason for an award of costs should be apparent either from reasons or by
inference from the circumstances in which it is made (*English v Emery Reimbold &
Strick* [2002] 1 WLR 2409). In order to comply with Article 6, an applicant seeking permission to appeal from an arbitration award on a point of law under section 69 of the Arbitration Act 1996 should, at the very least, be told which of the
threshold tests he had failed (*North Range Shipping v Seatrans Shipping* [2002] 1
WLR 2397). See also Supplement, para 11.313.

A disciplinary body has no general duty to give reasons for its decisions on matters
of fact where the essential issue is one of credibility or the reliability of evidence
(*Gupta v General Medical Council* [2002] 1 WLR 1691).

(4) Fair trial rights in criminal cases

(f) The presumption of innocence

For a discussion of the recent cases on 'reverse onus' provisions and Article 6, see **11.119**
Supplement, para 11.347.

(h) Other rights in relation to the trial

In *R v Hayward* [2001] 3 WLR 125 the Court of Appeal stated that a defendant **11.126**
had a general right to attend and be represented in criminal proceedings. Those
rights could be waived wholly or in part. Only in rare and exceptional cases could
the discretion to proceed in the absence of the defendant or his lawyers be exercised, particularly if the defendant was unrepresented. In the exercise of that discretion the judge had to consider fairness to both defence and prosecution and all
the relevant circumstances. The judge had to ensure, where the discretion to proceed was exercised, that the trial remained fair, exposing the weaknesses in the
prosecution case and warning the jury not to draw any adverse inference from the
absence of the defendant. The House of Lords upheld the decision of the Court of
Appeal. However, unlike the Court of Appeal, it held that 'the seriousness of the
offence' was not a matter relevant to the exercise of that discretion. Whether the
offence charged is serious or relatively minor, the judge's overriding concern

should be to ensure that the trial, if conducted in the absence of the defendant, will be as fair as circumstances permit and lead to a just outcome (*R v Jones* [2002] 2 All ER 113). See, generally, P W Ferguson, 'Trial in Absence and Waiver of Human Rights' [2002] Crim LR 554. However, where a defendant had plainly not voluntarily absented himself from the trial the threshold of prejudice and unfairness was a comparatively low one. The fact that the defendant is a juvenile is an important factor in considering whether a trial *in absentia* is unfair; see *R (On the Application of R) v Thames Youth Court* [2002] EWHC Admin 1670.

(i) Exclusion of illegally obtained evidence

11.131   The House of Lords in *Attorney-General's Reference (No 3 of 1999)* [2001] 2 WLR 56 pointed out that, apart from express statutory provisions, nowhere in the Commonwealth, or indeed in Convention law, is there any general principle that unlawfully obtained evidence is not admissible.

For a general discussion of the principles relating to the exclusion of illegally obtained evidence, see *R v Shaheed* [2002] 2 NZLR 377. The majority of the New Zealand Court of Appeal concluded that, in place of the *prima facie* exclusion rule, admissibility should be determined by conducting a balancing exercise in which, as a starting point, appropriate and significant weight is given to the breach of a right guaranteed by the Bill of Rights Act; see, generally, Supplement, para 21.130.

11.132   In *R v P* [2001] 2 All ER 58 the House of Lords held that the criteria for determining fairness under Article 6 were the same criteria that would be applied when considering an application for exclusion of evidence under section 78 of the Police and Criminal Evidence Act 1984 (see also *R v Bailey* [2001] EWCA Crim 733). A defendant was not entitled to have unlawfully obtained evidence excluded simply because it had been so obtained. His entitlement was to an opportunity to challenge the use and admission of the evidence and a judicial assessment of the effect of its admission on the fairness of the trial.

In *R v Looseley* [2001] 1 WLR 2060 the House of Lords held that in relation to the exercise of the judicial discretion conferred by section 78 of the Police and Criminal Evidence Act 1984 and the exercise of the power to stay proceedings as an abuse of process of the court, the principles of English law which have developed are in conformity with Article 6; see also Supplement, para 11.353.

There is no policy of English law excluding telephone intercepts independent of the Interception of Communications Act 1985 and such evidence lawfully obtained abroad can be admitted (*R v P* [2001] 2 All ER 58 and *R v Wright* [2001] EWCA Crim 1394). The admission into evidence of conversations between suspected offenders who were covertly recorded whilst they were under arrest and detained in police cells was held by the Court of Appeal in *R v Mason and Others*

[2002] EWCA Crim 385 not to constitute a breach of Article 6. The rights to remain silent and not to incriminate oneself were not contravened if a person chose to volunteer information about offences which he has committed. The Court said that the police did no more than arrange a situation which was likely to result in the suspected offenders volunteering confessions. They were not tricked into saying what they did even though they were placed in a position where they were likely to do so.

In *Attorney-General's Reference (No 3 of 1999)* [2001] 2 WLR 56 Lord Hutton said **11.134** that in exercising the discretion under section 78 the interests of the victim and the public must be considered as well as the interests of the defendant.

(5) Retrospective criminal laws

In *R v Offen* [2001] 1 WLR 253 it was held that the provisions of section 2(2) of **11.149A** the Crime (Life Sentences) Act 1997 (now section 109 of the Powers of the Criminal Courts (Sentencing) Act 2000) providing for automatic second life sentences in the case of convictions for a second 'serious offence' were not contrary to Article 7. The sentence was being imposed for the second offence, not the first.

C. The Law Under the European Convention

(2) Proceedings covered by Article 6

(a) Introduction

The Court in *Beer v Austria* (Judgment of 6 February 2001) held that Article 6(1) **11.157** was applicable to costs proceedings, provided that the legal costs which form the subject matter of the proceedings were incurred during the resolution of a dispute which involved the determination of civil rights and obligations. See also *Ziegler v Switzerland* (Judgment of 21 February 2002).

Article 6 applies to 'interim proceedings' which have the effect of partially determining the rights of the parties by 'causing irreversible prejudice' to a party's interests (see *Markass v Cyprus* [2002] EHRLR 387). In *Markass* the Court applied Article 6 to an application to set aside an *ex parte* injunction but the point was not specifically discussed in the final judgment (2 July 2002) which simply proceeded on the basis that Article 6 was applicable.

Stage at which Article 6 applies. In *Brennan v United Kingdom* (2002) 34 **11.158** EHRR 18 the Court said that Article 6, especially Article 6(3)(c), may be relevant before a case is sent for trial if and insofar as the fairness of the trial is likely to be seriously prejudiced by an initial failure to comply with its provisions. See, further, Supplement, para 11.245. In *Weixelbraun v Austria* (Judgment of 20

December 2001) the Court held that Article 6(2) applied to compensation proceedings following a final acquittal. This case is discussed further at Supplement, para 11.237A.

(b) Civil rights and obligations

11.160 **Introduction.** In *GJ v Luxembourg* [2000] BPIR 1021 the applicant was held to be entitled to bring a complaint under Article 6(1) concerning the liquidation of the limited liability company in which he held 90 per cent of the shares. The complaint was in relation to the activities of the liquidators, consequently it was impossible for the company, as a legal personality, to bring the complaint.

11.162 **Disputes.** In *Z v United Kingdom* (2001) 10 BHRC 384 the Court held that the government's submission that there was no arguable civil right for the purposes of Article 6 once the House of Lords had ruled that no duty of care arose was of relevance to any claims which were lodged or pursued subsequently by other plaintiffs. The House of Lords' decision did not remove, retrospectively, the arguability of the applicants' claims.

11.163 **The nature of 'civil rights and obligations'.** The concept of 'civil rights and obligations' was analysed by the House of Lords in *R (Alconbury Developments Ltd) v Secretary of State for the Environment, Transport and the Regions* [2001] 2 WLR 1389. Lord Hoffmann pointed out that, although the original intention appears to have been to limit it to 'private law rights' the Convention case law, beginning with *Ringeisen v Austria (No 1)* (1971) 1 EHRR 455, had clearly extended it to administrative decisions (paras 77–81). This was, however, subject to the 'substantial modification of the full judicial model' (para 84): in the case of administrative decisions Article 6 would be complied with if the decision was subject to subsequent control by a judicial body that has full jurisdiction. This approach was supported by the Court of Human Rights when the issue went to Strasbourg (*Holding & Barnes plc v United Kingdom*, Decision of 12 March 2002). It was held that the availability of judicial review was enough to ensure compliance with Article 6 and, as a result, the application was manifestly ill-founded.

The right to enjoy a good reputation and the right to have the justification of attacks upon such reputation determined by a court are civil rights under Article 6(1) (*Werner v Poland*, Judgment of 15 November 2001).

11.169 In *Göç v Turkey* (Judgment of 11 July 2002) the Grand Chamber held that the applicant's dispute with the Treasury over the level of compensation to which he was entitled under the statutory compensation scheme for unlawful detention concerned a dispute involving a civil right within the meaning of Article 6(1).

11.172 **Cases outside Article 6.** In *Pellegrin v France* (2001) 31 EHRR 651 a Grand Chamber stated that in determining the applicability of Article 6 to public servants it should adopt a functional criterion based on the nature of the employee's duties and responsibilities. The Court has to ascertain

> whether the applicant's post entails—in the light of the nature of the duties and responsibilities appertaining to it—direct or indirect participation in the exercise of the powers conferred by public law and duties designed to safeguard the general interests of the state or of other public authorities (para 66).

The Court said that the police and armed forces were obvious examples of employment which fell outside the scope of Article 6. See, also, *Fogarty v United Kingdom* (2002) 34 EHRR 302.

This means that Article 6 has no application to disputes concerning:

* the dismissal of an employee of the Ministry of Co-operation and Development who was posted abroad, undertaking public finance work (*Pellegrin v France* (2001) 31 EHRR 651);
* the pay and conditions of judges (*Kajanen and Tuomaala v Finland*, Judgment of 19 October 2000; *Conti v Italy*, Judgment of 11 April 2001; *Pitkevich v Russia*, Judgment of 8 February 2001);
* military pensions (*R v Belgium*, Judgment of 27 February 2001) or military discipline (*Duman v Turkey*, Judgment of 5 December 2000);
* the employment of a local authority director of personnel (*ET v Finland*, Judgment of 7 September 2000);
* the employment of a lecturer employed by the Polish National Fire Service (*Kepka v Poland*, Judgment of 11 July 2000).

However, in *Frydlender v France* (2001) 31 EHRR 52 the Court held that a dispute concerning the employment of an employee in the French economic development office did involve a 'civil right'. Similarly, claims by a civil servant in the administrative courts for judicial review of decisions to refuse him extended sick leave, to suspend payment of salary and to put him on notice to return to work were within Article 6 because they related to 'purely economic rights' (*Benkessiouer v France* (2001) 33 EHRR 1317). These cases were discussed by the Court of Appeal in *Matthews v Ministry of Defence* [2002] 1 WLR 2621 in which it was concluded that the effect of *Pellegrin* was confined to disputes about conditions of employment.

n685: In *Ferrazzini v Italy* (2002) 34 EHRR 1068 a Grand Chamber considered whether, in the light of changed attitudes as to the legal protection that falls to be accorded to individuals in their relations with the state, Article 6(1) should not be extended to cover disputes as to the lawfulness of the decisions of the tax authorities. The Court, by a majority (11–6), refused to take this step, holding that tax disputes fell outside the scope of civil rights and obligations despite their pecuniary aspects (paras 29–30). However, the dissenting judges pointed out that although the original intention was to exclude disputes between individuals and governments from Article 6, its scope had gradually been extended to cover a wide range of such disputes. After a full analysis of the scope of Article 6(1), they concluded that tax matters should now fall within its scope.

However, it should be noted that in *Ali and Begum v The Commissioners for Customs and Excise* (30 May 2002) Stephen Oliver QC held that the *Ferrazzini* decision was not applicable in the United Kingdom, at least insofar as rights and obligations relating to VAT are concerned. He preferred the reasoning of the minority for four reasons (para 25). First, there is no place in the laws of the United Kingdom for a 'public law' relationship, distinct from civil rights and obligations, between taxpayer and the tax authorities. Second, in the United Kingdom, tax does not belong to the 'hard core of public authority prerogative' but was imposed by Parliament. Thirdly, the tax relationship frequently gives rise to a civil right and claim against the state, for example, tax recovery rights. Fourth, *Ferrazzini* was concerned with direct taxes, in contrast VAT was a product of the EU and the rights and obligations between a taxable person and the state which arose from the application of a VAT code were new and were not within the contemplation of the framers of the Convention.

11.173   The setting up or adjustment of financial support for housing associations involves the public authority prerogatives of the state which cannot be regarded as directly affecting civil rights and obligations (*Woonbron Volkhuisvestingsgroep v Netherlands* (2002) 35 EHRR CD 161).

n689: In *Maaouia v France* (2000) 9 BHRC 205 the Court stated that decisions regarding the entry, stay and deportation of aliens do not concern the determination of an applicant's civil rights or obligations or of a criminal charge against him, within the meaning of Article 6(1). The fact that the decision incidentally has major repercussions on an applicant's private and family life or on his prospects of employment cannot suffice to bring those proceedings within the scope of civil rights protected by Article 6.

11.176   **n711:** The case of *Lauko v Slovakia* is now reported at (2001) 33 EHRR 994; and see also *Kadubec v Slovakia* (2001) 33 EHRR 1016.

(c) Criminal charges

11.179   Prison disciplinary hearings before the prison governor are criminal in nature (see *Ezeh and Connors v United Kingdom* (2002) 35 EHRR 691). The Court found that the nature of the charges against the applicants (threats of violence and assault), together with the nature of and severity of the potential and actual penalties (awards of seven and 40 additional days' imprisonment), were such as to lead to the conclusion that both were subject to criminal charges within the meaning of Article 6(1). The governor's refusal of the applicants' request to be legally represented at their hearings was, therefore, a breach of their rights under Article 6(3)(c).

The nature of a 'charge'.   In *Quinn v Ireland* (Judgment of 21 December 2000) **11.180** the Court held that whilst the applicant had not been formally charged under domestic law when he was questioned about his movements under section 52 of the Offences Against State Act, he was at that point 'substantially affected', since failure to answer the questions could lead to a penalty of six months' imprisonment, and therefore 'charged' for the purposes of Article 6(1) with the offences to which the questions related, even though no criminal proceedings as regards those offences were pursued against him.

(3) Article 6(1) guarantees

(b) Right of access to the courts

General.   In *Palumbo v Italy* (Judgment of 30 November 2000) the Court stated **11.185** that the 'right to a court' guaranteed by Article 6 also protects the implementation of final, binding judicial decisions. Accordingly, it said the execution of a judicial decision should not be prevented, invalidated or unduly delayed. In *Vasilopoulou v Greece* (Judgment of 21 March 2002) the Court found a violation of Article 6(1) where the state authorities refused to pay damages awarded against it in civil proceedings.

Effectiveness.   In *X v United Kingdom* (1984) 6 EHRR 136 the Commission **11.189** summarised the '*Airey*' principle in this way:

> Only in exceptional circumstances, namely where the withholding of legal aid would make the assertion of a civil claim practically impossible, or where it would lead to an obvious unfairness of the proceedings, can such a right be invoked by virtue of Article 6(1) of the Convention.

See also the discussion of this case in *R v Legal Services Commission, ex p Jarrett* [2001] EWHC Admin 989 which is considered further at Supplement, para 11.306.

In *P and Others v United Kingdom* (2002) 12 BHRC 615 the Court held that the principles of effective access to court and fairness required that the applicants received the assistance of a lawyer in care proceedings of 'exceptional complexity' extending over 20 days in which the documentation was voluminous and which required a review of highly complex expert evidence relating to the applicants' fitness to parent their daughter.

In *Burdov v Russia* (Judgment of 7 May 2002) the European Court of Human Rights held that it was not open to a state authority to cite lack of funds as an excuse for not honouring a judgment debt. While a delay in the execution of a judgment may be justified in particular circumstances, the delay must not be such as to impair the essence of 'the right to a court' protected under Article 6(1). That right would be rendered illusory if a Contracting State's domestic legal system allowed a final, binding judicial decision to remain inoperative to the detriment of one party thus precluding the applicant from benefiting from the success of the litigation.

In *McVicar v United Kingdom* (2002) 35 EHRR 22 the Court considered a complaint that the unavailability of legal aid in defamation proceedings was a violation of the right to effective access to a court under Article 6(1). The Court held that the question whether or not Article 6(1) required legal representation to an individual litigant depended on the specific circumstances of the case and, in particular, whether the individual would be able to present his case properly and satisfactorily without the assistance of a lawyer. The applicant was the defendant and, as a result, the issue was not one of access but one of fairness, although the test was the same. The applicant was a well-educated and experienced journalist who had the assistance of an experienced defamation lawyer until the outset of the trial. In the circumstances, the applicant was not denied a fair trial by reason of his ineligibility for legal aid.

11.191 **Restrictions on access.**   In *Clunis v United Kingdom* (Decision of 11 September 2001) the Court said that the striking-out procedures under the CPR did not of themselves offend the principle of access to a court. In such a procedure, the claimant is generally able to submit to the court the arguments supporting his claims on the law and the court will rule on those issues at the end of an adversarial procedure.

The refusal of an appeal court to hear an appeal because the appellant had failed to deposit a sum of money was a disproportionate hindrance to the right of access to a court. The applicant should have received legal aid and an exemption from the deposit requirement but did not do so because of judicial negligence (*García Manibardo v Spain* (2002) 34 EHRR 196).

When a criminal court ordered the confiscation of the property of a person who was not the defendant and who was not informed of the hearing there was a breach of the Article 6(1) right of access to court (*Baumann v France* (2002) 34 EHRR 1041).

11.192 In *Kreuz v Poland* (2001) 11 BHRC 456 it was held that the requirement that a party to civil proceedings pay a court fee of six to seven per cent of the value of the claim was a disproportionate restriction on his right of access to court.

11.192A In *Escalano v Spain* (Judgment of 25 January 2000) the Court held that the particularly strict interpretation of a procedural rule (in relation to limitation) deprived the applicants of the right of access to the court to have their claims for compensation examined.

In *Devlin v UK* (2002) 34 EHRR 1029 the Court held that the issue by the **11.193** Secretary of State of a section 42 certificate certifying that the refusal to employ D had been on the grounds of national security, which had the effect of barring the Employment Tribunal's jurisdiction, constituted a disproportionate restriction on the applicant's right of access to the court. See also *Devenney v United Kingdom* (2002) 35 EHRR 643.

The operation of the doctrine of state immunity does not qualify a substantive **11.194** right under domestic law but operates as a procedural bar on the national court's power to determine the right (see *Al-Adsani v United Kingdom* (2002) 12 BHRC 89; *Fogarty v United Kingdom* (2002) 34 EHRR 302; and *McElhinney v Ireland* (2002) 12 BHRC 114). The Convention had to be interpreted in harmony with the rules of international law relating to the grant of state immunity. As a result, claims against the United Kingdom failed by majorities of sixteen-to-one in three Grand Chamber cases:

- In *Al-Adsani* a claim in the English courts against Kuwait in respect of allegations of torture in Kuwait.
- In *McElhinney* a claim in the Irish courts against the United Kingdom government in respect of the actions of a soldier at a border checkpoint.
- In *Fogarty*, a claim for sex discrimination by an employee of the US embassy in London against the US government.

In *Z v United Kingdom* (2001) 10 BHRC 384 the Court reviewed its reasoning in **11.195** *Osman v United Kingdom* (1999) 29 EHRR 245, in the light of Lord Browne-Wilkinson's speech in *Barrett*, and found that the ruling of the House of Lords that there was no duty of care did not disclose the operation of an immunity. The Court concluded that the inability of the applicants to sue the local authority flowed, not from an immunity, but from the applicable principles governing the substantive right of action in domestic law. Consequently, there was no restriction on access to a court of the kind contemplated in *Ashingdane v United Kingdom* (1985) 7 EHRR 528. Once the House of Lords had ruled on the arguable legal issues that brought into play the applicability of Article 6(1) of the Convention, the applicants could no longer claim any entitlement under Article 6(1) to obtain any hearing concerning the facts. Such a hearing would have served no purpose, unless a duty of care in negligence had been held to exist in their case. The Court said it was not for them to find that this should have been the outcome of the striking out proceedings since this would effectively involve substituting their own views as to the proper interpretation and content of domestic law. The Court went on to say that, irrespective of the position in domestic law, it was not persuaded that the decision disclosed an immunity in fact or practical effect due to its allegedly sweeping or blanket nature. The decision concerned only one aspect of the exercise of local authorities' powers and duties and could not be regarded as an arbitrary removal of the courts' jurisdiction to determine a whole range of civil claims. However, the Court found that there was a violation of the applicants' right to an effective remedy under Article 13, since the applicants did not have available to them an appropriate means of obtaining a determination of their allegations that the local authority failed to protect them from inhuman and degrading treatment and the possibility of obtaining an enforceable award of compensation for the damage suffered thereby. For a study of the Court's Article 6 jurisprudence and a critique of the *Osman* decision, see C Gearty, 'Unravelling *Osman*' (2001) 64 MLR 159.

In *Reid v United Kingdom* (Decision of 21 June 2001) the Court considered a complaint that the 'immunity' of the Crown Prosecution Service from actions in negligence (see *Elguzouli-Daf v Commissioner of Police* [1995] QB 335 and Main Work, para 11.43) was a breach of the right of access to a court under Article 6. The Court rejected the argument based on *Osman* and concluded that 'the inability of the applicant to sue the CPS flowed not from an immunity but from the applicable principles governing the substantive right of action in domestic law'. As a result, it was held that the application was 'manifestly ill-founded'.

It is submitted that there are powerful arguments in favour of the approach taken in *Osman*. In an opinion dissenting on this issue Judges Rozakis and Palm suggested that it was important to distinguish between an absence of access to the court and the circumstances justifying a proportionate denial of it. They found it difficult to accept that

> the creation of new case-law barring the examination of the case on its merits was proportionate to the need for adequate protection of individuals (and society generally) against negligence by public authorities.

They drew attention to the fact that, in *Osman*, the Court was mainly concerned with the fact that the applicants in a very serious case of possible substantive human rights violations did not have the opportunity to air their grievances before a court and suggested that the two cases were indistinguishable. This point is not met by the majority's suggestion that *Osman* should have been decided in the applicant's favour under Article 13 because the remedy provided by the English law was being restricted by what is, in substance and effect, an 'immunity' for state officials.

It is noteworthy that, in the case of *Carmichele v Ministry of Safety and Security* 2001 (10) BCLR 995 (CC) the South African Constitutional Court held that if the police and prosecutors had an immunity against claims in negligence arising out of a failure to prevent the commission of life-threatening crimes then this would be inconsistent with the Constitution and its values. It is submitted that the 'public policy' barriers to negligence actions against public bodies are similarly inconsistent with Article 6 and that in cases in which it is alleged that negligence has led to serious interference with a person's Convention rights, liability should not be subject to 'blanket' exclusions.

Access following administrative decisions. In *Kingsley v United Kingdom*   **11.197**
(2002) 35 EHRR 177 the Grand Chamber stated that where a complaint is made
of a lack of impartiality on the part of the decision-making body, the concept of
'full jurisdiction' requires that the reviewing court not only considers the complaint but has the ability to quash the impugned decision and the power either to
make the decision itself or to remit the case for a fresh decision by an impartial
body. The case is discussed further at Supplement, para 11.199.

In *Chapman v United Kingdom* [2001] 10 BHRC 48 the Court found that the   **11.198**
scope of review of the High Court which was available to the applicant after a public procedure before a planning inspector was sufficient to comply with the requirement of access to an independent tribunal under Article 6(1). It enabled a
decision to be challenged on the basis that it was perverse, irrational, had no basis
on the evidence or had been made with reference to irrelevant factors, which provided an adequate judicial control of the administrative decisions in issue.

In *Kingsley v United Kingdom* (2002) 35 EHRR 177, also discussed at Supplement,   **11.199**
para 11.197, the applicant claimed that the Gaming Board's panel that determined
he was not a 'fit and proper person' to hold the Board's certificate of approval was
not impartial. On review, Jowitt J and the Court of Appeal stated that even if satisfied that the Panel's decision lacked impartiality, they could not quash the decision
and remit the case for a new decision because, under the doctrine of 'necessity', the
decision would have to stand as it had to be made by the Gaming Board and could
not be delegated to an independent tribunal. The Court held that in such circumstances, the reviewing court did not have 'full jurisdiction' within the meaning of
the case law of Article 6 when it reviewed the Panel's decision. For a discussion of
this case, see I Leigh, 'Bias, Necessity and the Convention' [2002] PL 407.

In *De Ponte Nascimento v United Kingdom* (Decision of 31 January 2002) the
Court said that the requirements of the consolidated Court of Appeal (Civil
Division) Practice Direction, as it applied in the applicant's case, that he would be
granted leave for a second tier appeal only if it had a realistic prospect of success
and raised a point of principle or disclosed some other reason why it should be
heard, were reasonable and proportionate measures taken in pursuit of the fair
and efficient administration of justice. The Court noted that Article 6(1) does not
guarantee a particular outcome in any case or that the 'right result' will be reached.

In *Eliazer v The Netherlands* (Judgment of 16 October 2001) the Court held that
the domestic law of the Netherlands which precluded any appeal to the Supreme
Court against judgments pronounced following proceedings which had been
conducted in the defendant's absence did not violate Article 6(1). The state's interest in ensuring that as many cases as possible were tried in the presence of the
accused before allowing access to the Supreme Court outweighed the accused's
concern to avoid the risk of being arrested by attending his trial.

In *Hoffman v Germany* [2002] 1 FLR 119 the Court held that the fact that a father was unable to appeal further because of the exclusion of a second appeal in child access proceedings where the child was born out of wedlock amounted to a denial of access to a court. See also *Sommerfeld v Germany* (Judgment of 11 October 2001).

(c) Right to a fair hearing

11.206 **Right to be present at an adversarial oral hearing.** In *Göç v Turkey* (2002) 35 EHRR 134 the Court stated that the applicant's right to adversarial proceedings means, in principle, the opportunity to have knowledge of, and comment on, all evidence adduced or observations filed, even by an independent member of the national legal service, such as the Principal Public Prosecutor in that case, with a view to influencing the court's decision on his appeal. This decision was upheld by the Grand Chamber (Judgment of 11 July 2002) which also said that the applicant should have been afforded an oral hearing in his claim for compensation resulting from his unlawful detention. Whilst the fact and length of the detention, as well as his financial and social status could be established without the need to hear the applicant, the essentially personal nature of his experience which was also relevant to the determination of the appropriate level of compensation required that he be heard.

11.209 **Right to equality of arms.** A breach of the principle of equality of arms was found in *Beer v Austria* (Judgment of 6 February 2001) where the applicant was not notified of an appeal against a costs order which had been filed. The Court stated that even if in appeal proceedings on a costs order the possibility to present legal and factual arguments may be limited, it is for the parties to say whether or not a document calls for their comment.

In *Fischer v Austria* (17 January 2002) the Court found a violation of the principle of equality of arms where the Supreme Court dismissed the applicant's appeal, after obtaining the comments of the Procurator General without informing him of the submissions or giving him an opportunity to respond to them. It rejected the government's submission that the comments did not affect the decision. The principle of equality of arms does not depend on quantifiable unfairness flowing from a procedural inequality. It is a matter for the defence to assess whether a submission deserves a reaction. See also *Lanz v Austria* (Judgment of 31 January 2002).

The Court also found a breach where the applicant was not given the opportunity to comment on the observations of his opponent in costs proceedings (*Zeigler v Switzerland*, Judgment of 21 February 2002). Whether the observations had any effect on the appeal court's judgment was of little consequence. There was a breach of the principle of equality of arms where the appeal court heard the appeal in the applicant's absence, despite his request for an adjournment (supported by medical certificate) and considered new evidence which because of his absence he could not comment on (*Komanicky v Slovakia*, Judgment of 4 June 2002).

In *PG and JH v UK* (Judgment of 25 September 2001) the Court said that the entitlement to disclosure of relevant evidence under Article 6(1) is not an absolute right. However, as a general principle, only such measures restricting this right which are strictly necessary are permissible under Article 6(1).

In *Smokovitis v Greece* (Judgment of 11 April 2002) the Court stated that while in principle the legislature is not precluded in civil matters from adopting new retrospective provisions to regulate rights arising under existing laws, the principle of the rule of law and the notion of fair trial enshrined in Article 6 preclude any interference by the legislature—other than on compelling grounds of the general interest—with the administration of justice designed to influence the judicial determination of a dispute. Thus Greece was held to have infringed the applicant's rights under Article 6(1) by intervening in a manner (passing legislation extinguishing pending salary claims against public bodies) which was decisive to ensure that the outcome of proceedings to which it was a party was favourable to it. See also *Vasilopoulou v Greece* (Judgment of 21 March 2002).

In *Kutic v Croatia* (Judgment of 1 March 2002) the Court found a violation where the government passed legislation staying all claims for damages resulting from terrorist acts pending the enactment of new legislation. The Court acknowledged that a situation might arise where a significant number of legal suits claiming large sums of money are lodged against a state which may call for some regulation. However, more than six years had passed and no legislation had been enacted. In the circumstances, even allowing for the margin of appreciation to which the state was entitled, the applicant had been deprived of his right to a court.

Freedom from self-incrimination.   In *IJL v United Kingdom* (2001) 33 EHRR **11.211** 225 it was held that the use of statements in criminal proceedings which defendants were compelled to give to inspectors appointed by the Department of Trade and Industry breached the right against self-incrimination.

In *JB v Switzerland* (Judgment of 3 May 2001), the Court found a breach of the freedom from self-incrimination when the applicant had been compelled to provide documents concerning his income after tax evasion proceedings had been commenced. The proceedings were criminal in nature (*AP, MP and TP v Switzerland* (1997) 26 EHRR 541) and any additional untaxed income disclosed by the compelled documents could have constituted tax evasion. The Court emphasised that its decision did not concern the question as to whether the state could oblige a taxpayer to give information for the sole purpose of securing a correct tax assessment (para 63). See, further, Supplement, para 11.236.

In *PG and JH v UK* (Judgment of 25 September 2001) the Court held that the use of voice samples, obtained in breach of Article 8, which did not include any incriminating statements, may be regarded as akin to blood, hair or other physical or objective specimens used in forensic analysis and to which the privilege against self-incrimination does not apply.

11.212 A failure by the trial judge when summing up to give due weight to the applicant's reliance on legal advice to explain his refusal to answer police questions was a breach of Article 6(1) (*Beckles v United Kingdom, The Times*, 15 October 2002). No separate protection against self-incrimination exists in civil cases under Article 6(1), the matter falling to be considered under the general aspect of fairness (*Vernon v United Kingdom* (2000) 29 EHRR CD 264).

11.213 **The right to legal assistance.** In *McVicar v United Kingdom* (2002) 35 EHRR 22 the Court held that the applicant was not prevented from presenting his defence effectively to the High Court, nor was he denied a fair hearing, by reason of the unavailability of legal aid in defamation proceedings. The Court said that the case was not sufficiently complex to require a person in the applicant's position to have legal assistance under Article 6(1).

11.214 **Right to fair presentation of evidence.** In *CG v United Kingdom* (2002) 34 EHRR 789 the Court agreed with the English Court of Appeal that the judicial interventions of the trial judge, although excessive and undesirable, did not render the trial proceeding as a whole unfair. The applicant's counsel was never prevented from continuing with the line of defence that he was attempting to develop. In addition the Court attached importance to the fact that the applicant's counsel was able to address the jury in a final speech which lasted for 45 minutes and that the substance of the applicant's defence was reiterated in the trial judge's summing up.

11.218 **Right to a reasoned judgment.** In *Mousaka v Golden Seagull Maritime Inc* [2001] 1 WLR 395 David Steel J summarised the Strasbourg jurisprudence in relation to the giving of reasons as follows:

- Article 6 obliges the court to give reasons. The extent of this duty varies according to the nature of the decision and the circumstances of the case.
- Full reasons should be given for a decision on the merits, although even then it is not necessary to provide a detailed answer to every argument.
- Although Article 6 applies to the appeal process, it does not guarantee a right of appeal: nonetheless any limitation on the right of appeal must be imposed pursuant to a legitimate aim, proportionately applied.
- If a right of appeal is rejected, the applicant must be made aware of the grounds on which the decision was reached: in many cases this may take the form of an endorsement of the lower court's decision.

• Where there are legitimate restraints on a right of appeal, such as the need for it to be a matter of general importance, it is sufficient for the court to refer to these limitations.

In *Hirvisaari v Finland* (Judgment of 27 September 2001) the Statutory Pension Board dismissed the applicant's appeal against the decision to reduce his full disability pension on the basis that whilst his health was deteriorating, the applicant was still partly capable of work. The Court held that this reasoning was inadequate since the reference to his deteriorating health in a decision confirming his right only to a reduced pension must have left the applicant with a certain sense of confusion. This confusion was not clarified by the appeal court which dismissed the applicant's appeal, endorsing the reasoning of the Board.

(d) A hearing within a reasonable time

A delay of two years between the applicant's original sentence and the subsequent sentence, following an Attorney-General's reference, was held to amount to a breach of the reasonable time requirement under Article 6(1) (*Howarth v United Kingdom* (2001) 31 EHRR 37.

11.219

There was no violation of the reasonable time requirement in a complex case, arising out of the Guinness takeover, where the proceedings lasted about four-and-a-half years in total, including appeals (*IJL v United Kingdom* (2001) 33 EHRR 225).

In *Futterer v Croatia* (Judgment of 20 December 2001) the Court said that when assessing the reasonableness of the length of time in question, in addition to the complexity of the case and the conduct of the parties, the court should also consider the importance of what is at stake for the applicant in the litigation. In *Mikulic v Croatia* (2002) 11 BHRC 689 the Court held that the applicant's right to have her paternity established or refuted and thus to have her uncertainty as to the identity of her natural father eliminated required the national authorities to act with particular diligence in ensuring the progress of the proceedings in view of what was at stake for the applicant. The Court found a breach notwithstanding the delay attributable to the defendant who had repeatedly ignored appointments for DNA tests and failed to attend court hearings.

In *Kreps v Poland* (Judgment of 26 July 2001) the European Court said that where persons were kept in detention during proceedings, the authorities were under a duty to exercise specific diligence, and whether that duty had been complied with was, it said, a relevant factor in assessing the reasonableness of the length of proceedings. In *Davies v United Kingdom* (2002) 35 EHRR 720 the Court said that given that the applicant was a company director and that disqualification proceedings would have had a considerable impact on his reputation and on his ability to practise his profession 'special diligence' was called for in bringing the proceedings to an end expeditiously.

In *Alithia v Cyprus* (Judgment of 11 July 2002) the Court said that expeditious proceedings were necessary in order to prevent the applicants, a newspaper and its editor in chief, from remaining in a protracted state of uncertainty in a libel case which could have a prejudicial effect on the reputation, credibility and circulation of the newspaper.

In *Góç v Poland* (Judgment of 16 April 2002) the Court said that the applicant's advanced age was a relevant consideration in assessing whether the authorities had determined his application to have works carried out to the gas supply in his apartment within a reasonable time.

Criminal proceedings brought against a doctor lasting over six years was held not to be unreasonable in view of the complexity of the case; see *Calvelli v Italy* (Judgment of 7 January 2002).

11.221   In civil cases violations on the grounds of delay have included the following:

- a delay of nine years and eight months in employment proceedings (including a wait of six years for a decision of the Conseil d'État) (*Frydlender v France* (2001) 31 EHRR 52);
- land consolidation proceedings of more than 22 years, despite the inherent complexity of such proceedings and the fact that the applicant himself contributed to a certain extent to their length (*Walder v Austria*, Judgment of 30 January 2001); and see also *Van Vlimmeren v Netherlands* [2001] RVR 34 (violation where land consolidation proceedings had not concluded after seven years));
- a period of two years to hear an appeal against an interim order issued on an *ex parte* basis (*Markass Car Hire Ltd v Cyprus*, Judgment of 2 July 2002);
- a delay of ten years and 11 months in disciplinary proceedings (*Luksch v Austria*, Judgment of 13 December 2001);
- a period of eight years and three months in maintenance proceedings. The Court noted the particular importance of the claim to the applicant and that the appellate court twice had to refer the case back to the first instance court on account of procedural defects (*Gollner v Austria*, Judgment of 17 January 2002);
- a period of ten years for proceedings before the civil courts and the German Constitutional Court (*Klein v Germany* (2002) 34 EHRR 16).

In a criminal cases violations have included the following:

- a period of 11 years between the commencement of preliminary investigations and judgment in 'white-collar crime proceedings' of 'exceptional complexity involving very complex facts and a large number of suspects' (*Rosslhuber v Austria*, Judgment of 28 November 2000);
- a period of four years for proceedings for abuse of power and misconduct in public office which were of a 'certain complexity' (*Di Donato v Italy*, Judgment of 26 April 2001);

- a period of five years in a case of theft and fraud (*Giannangeli v Italy*, Judgment of 5 July 2001);
- a period of eight years between arrest and judgment in tax evasion and smuggling proceedings which were both legally and factually complex (*Schweighofer v Austria*, Judgment of 9 October 2001);
- shareholder liability proceedings lasting ten years and ten months, including six-and-a-half years before the regional court (*Schreder v Austria*, Judgment of 13 December 2001);
- a period of four years and ten months in criminal proceedings where the conviction had been appealed three times and remitted back to the district court twice (*Maurer v Austria*, Judgment of 17 January 2002);
- a period of four years in relation to criminal proceedings which were reopened after conviction, time running from the date of reopening (*Loffler v Austria* (2002) 34 EHRR 49).

(e) *Independent and impartial tribunal established by law*

Impartial. The mere fact that a judge had also made pre-trial decisions in a case **11.228** could not be taken as in itself justifying fears as to his impartiality (*Pullicino v Malta* [2001] EHRLR 95). Furthermore, the fact that a judge was a member of the Freemasons would not, of itself, raise doubts about his impartiality in a case where a witness or party was also a Freemason (*Salaman v United Kingdom* [2001] EHRLR 85).

There have been findings of violations of Article 6(1) due to a failure to meet the objective test of impartiality in a number of recent cases:

- In *Wettstein v Switzerland* (Judgment of 21 December 2000) it was held that an applicant who was involved in two proceedings against different local authorities that overlapped in time and in which the part-time judge in one acted for the opposing party in the other could have legitimate concerns that the judge would not approach his case with the requisite impartiality.
- In *Werner v Poland* (Judgment of 15 November 2002) the Court held that there were objective reasons for the applicant to believe that the court making the decision to dismiss him from his post as judicial liquidator lacked impartiality where one of its members had made the recommendation for his removal which led to the court hearing the case.
- In *Morris v United Kingdom* (2002) 34 EHRR 1253 the Court held that the court-martial system established by the Armed Forces Act 1996 did not provide the appellant with an independent and impartial tribunal. It said that the safeguards established by the new system were insufficient to exclude the risk of outside pressure being brought to bear on the two relatively junior serving officers who sat on the applicant's court-martial. In particular, it noted that those officers had no legal training and remained subject to army discipline and reports. There

was also no statutory or other bar to their being made subject to external army influence when sitting on the case. Further, the automatic review of conviction and sentence by a non-judicial 'reviewing authority' undermined the status of the court-martial as a 'tribunal'. The Court said that these two fundamental flaws were not cured by the applicant's subsequent appeal to the Court-Martial Appeal Court, since that appeal did not involve any rehearing of the applicant's case, but simply determined that leave to appeal should be refused. See, further, Supplement, para 11.296.

- In *Tierce v San Marino* (2002) 34 EHRR 672 there was a lack of impartiality when the same judge conducted both the judicial investigation and the trial at first instance.

- In *Daktaras v Lithuania* (2002) 34 EHRR 1466 there was a violation when a *cassation* petition to the Supreme Court was lodged by the president of the criminal division of that court because he was, in effect, taking up the prosecution case. Furthermore, although the president did not sit as a member of the court which determined the *cassation* petition, he chose the judge *rapporteur* and the members of the court (cf the decision of the Court of Appeal in *Sengupta v Holmes* [2002] EWCA Civ 1104). See, further, Supplement, para 11.68.

n972: *Castillo Algar v Spain* is now reported at (2000) 30 EHRR 827.

(f) Right to a public hearing and the public pronouncement of judgment

11.230   **Public hearing.**   In *Riepan v Austria* (Judgment of 14 November 2000) the Court stated that a trial will only comply with the requirement of publicity if the public is able to obtain information about its date and place and if this place is easily accessible to the public. The Court observed that the holding of a trial outside a regular court room, in particular in a place like a prison to which the general public in principle has no access, presents a serious obstacle to its public character. In such a case, the state is under an obligation to take compensatory measures in order to ensure that the public and the media are duly informed about the place of the hearing and are granted effective access. In *Riepan* the Court stated that the lack of a public hearing before a trial court could only be remedied by a complete rehearing before the appeal court. This provision was breached in *Guisset v France* (2002) 34 EHRR 47 when disciplinary proceedings against a former ambassador accused of budget irregularities were held in private.

11.231   In *Riepan v Austria* (Judgment of 14 November 2000) the Court said that cases in which security concerns justify excluding the public from a trial are rare. Such concerns were a common feature of many criminal proceedings.

11.232   In *B v United Kingdom* (2002) 34 EHRR 529 the Court rejected the submission that the presumption in favour of a private hearing in cases under the Children

Act was inconsistent with Article 6. It stated that it was essential in such cases that the parents and other witnesses should feel able to express themselves candidly on highly personal issues without fear of public curiosity or comment. It also noted that the courts have a discretion to hold proceedings under the Children Act in public if merited by the special features of the case.

Public pronouncement of judgment.   In *B v United Kingdom* (2002) 34 EHRR   **11.234**
529 (discussed also at Supplement, para 11.232) the Court said that there was no right under Article 6 to the public pronouncement of judgments in residence applications under the Children Act. The Court said that a literal interpretation of the terms of Article 6(1) concerning the pronouncement of judgments would not only be unnecessary for the purposes of public scrutiny but would invalidate the purpose of holding the hearing in private and thus ultimately might even frustrate the primary aim of Article 6(1), to secure a fair hearing.

(4) Minimum standards of fairness in criminal proceedings

(b) Presumption of innocence

In *Heaney and McGuiness v Ireland* (2001) 33 EHRR 12 the Court held that the   **11.236**
threat and imposition of a criminal sanction (a single prison sentence) on the applicants because they failed to supply information (account for their movements at a particular time) to the authorities investigating the alleged commission of criminal offences by them destroyed the very essence of their privilege against self-incrimination and their right to remain silent, which could not be justified by security and public order concerns. See also *Quinn v Ireland* (Judgment of 21 December 2000).

A fresh examination of the question of guilt in compensation proceedings follow-   **11.237A**
ing a final acquittal constitutes a breach of Article 6(2) (*Sekanina v Austria* (1994) 17 EHRR 221). The Court also found a breach in *Weixelbraun v Austria* (Judgment of 20 December 2001) where the applicant's claim for compensation, following his acquittal, was dismissed because the suspicion that he was guilty had not been entirely dissipated, ie he had not proved his innocence. The Court held that the applicant could rely on Article 6(2) when challenging the decision in compensation proceedings irrespective of the fact that the contested decision had been given after his acquittal had become final. The decision on the right to compensation could be regarded as a consequence and, to some extent, the concomitant of the decision on criminal responsibility of the accused.

In *Pham Hoang v France* (1992) 16 EHRR 53, paras 35–6, the Court held that the   **11.238**
effect of various presumptions of the Customs Code was not to breach the Article 6(2) rights of a person accused of drug smuggling. The presumption of responsibility was rebuttable.

In *Phillips v United Kingdom* (2001) 11 BHRC 280 the Court rejected a complaint that the presumptions made in an inquiry into the means of a convicted drug trafficker during confiscation proceedings under the Drug Trafficking Act 1994 were a breach of Article 6(2). The Court held that, although Article 6(2) applied to the whole of criminal proceedings, the right to be presumed innocent only applied to the particular offence 'charged' and that

> Once an accused has properly been proved guilty of that offence, Article 6(2) can have no application in relation to allegations made about the accused's character and conduct as part of the sentencing process unless the accusations are of such a nature and degree as to amount to the bringing of a new 'charge' (para 35).

The Court also held that Article 6(2) was not applicable to confiscation proceedings. It went on to hold that Article 6(1) was applicable and the right to be presumed innocent formed part of the general notion of a fair hearing but was not absolute (para 40). On the facts, it was held that the operation of the presumptions in relation to the applicant was confined within reasonable limits. For a critical discussion of this decision, see A Ashworth, 'Burdens of Proof and Confiscation Orders' [2001] 7 Arch News 5.

A refusal to pay statutory compensation to an acquitted person on the basis that the suspicion against him had not been dispelled violated the presumption of innocence in Article 6(2) (*Lamanna v Austria*, Judgment of 10 July 2001; see also *Sekanina v Austria* (1994) 17 EHRR 221 and *Oppegard v Norway* (2000) 29 EHRR CD 223). However, in a case where admissions had been made in the course of a criminal investigation which was discontinued this was sufficient to rebut the presumption of innocence and justified the refusal of compensation (*Annemersbedrijf Gebroedes van Leeuwen BV v Netherlands* (2000) 29 EHRR CD 96).

A requirement that a defendant provides an explanation for his conduct when the prosecution had not been able to establish a convincing *prima facie* case shifted the burden of proof and was a breach of Article 6(2) (*Telfner v Austria* (2002) 34 EHRR 207).

11.240 The presumption of innocence may be infringed not only by a judge or court but also by other public authorities including prosecutors. This is particularly so when the prosecutor performs quasi-judicial functions; see *Daktaras v Lithuania* (2002) 34 EHRR 1466 (no violation on the facts).

In *Butkevicius v Lithuania* (Judgment of 26 March 2002) the Court held that public statements made by public officials following the applicant's arrest amounted to declarations of his guilt which served to encourage the public to believe him guilty and prejudged the assessment of the facts by the competent judicial authority contrary to Article 6(2).

(c) Information as to the accusation (Article 6(3)(a))

11.241

The Court in *T v Austria* (Judgment of 14 November 2000) held that the applicant's rights under Article 6(3)(a) and (b) were violated by the imposition of a fine for abuse of process, in circumstances where he had not been informed of the Court's suspicion that he had made false or incomplete statements in his legal aid request. In *Mattoccia v Italy* [2001] EHRLR 89 the Court found a breach of Article 6(3)(a) in a case where the applicant had been accused of committing a sexual offence 'in Rome in November 1985'. Although the prosecution became aware of more precise dates and the place of the alleged offence they did not convey the details to the applicant. The adequacy of the information had to be assessed in the light of Article 6(3)(b). In all the circumstances, the applicant had not had proper notice of the charge.

In *Sipavicius v Lithuania* (Judgment of 21 February 2002) the Court found a breach of Article 6(3)(c) where the court at first instance had when giving judgment reclassified the offence with which the applicant was charged and convicted him without giving him sufficient time to prepare his defence. However, the Court held the breach was cured by the appellate process since the applicant had the opportunity to advance before the Court of Appeal and the Supreme Court his defence in respect of the reformulated charge.

(d) Adequate time and facilities to prepare a defence (Article 6(3)(b))

11.243

In *Zoon v The Netherlands* (Judgment of 7 December 2000) the Court found that the applicant's defence rights were not unduly affected by the absence of a complete judgment or by the absence of a detailed enumeration of the items of evidence relied on to ground his conviction, in circumstances where the applicant and his counsel would have been able to make an informed assessment of the possible outcome of any appeal in light of the judgment in abridged form and of the evidence contained in the case file.

(e) Defence in person or through legal assistance (Article 6(3)(c))

11.245

In *Brennan v United Kingdom* (2002) 34 EHRR 507 the Court said that although Article 6 will normally require that the accused be allowed to benefit from the assistance of a lawyer at the initial stages of police interrogation, this right is not explicitly set out in the Convention and may be subject to restriction for good cause. The Court said that whilst the recordings of interviews and attendance of a lawyer provide a safeguard against police misconduct, they are not an indispensable precondition of fairness under Article 6(1). It held that the adversarial procedure conducted before the trial court was capable of bringing to light any oppressive conduct by the police. The question in each case is whether the restriction, in the light of the entirety of the proceedings, has deprived the accused of a fair hearing. On the facts, the Court found that the presence of the police officer within hearing distance during the applicant's first consultation with his solicitor infringed his right to an effective exercise of his defence rights under Article 6(3) read in conjunction with Article 6(1). See also *Berlinski v Poland* (Judgment of 20 June 2002).

Surveillance by an investigating judge of an accused's contacts with his lawyer was said to be a serious interference with an accused's right to a fair trial which required 'very weighty reasons' to justify such conduct. The risk of collusion (interference with witnesses and evidence) had been raised to justify the applicant's detention on remand, but that risk could not, without more, justify the surveillance of the applicant's contact with his lawyer (*Lanz v Austria*, Judgment of 31 January 2002). Sufficient reasons were given in *Kempers v Austria* (Judgment of 27 February 1997) where the applicant was suspected of being the member of a gang and utmost confidentiality was necessary in order to catch the other members.

In *RD v Poland* (Judgment of 18 December 2001) the Court found a violation of Article 6(3)(c) where the Court of Appeal communicated its refusal of free legal assistance to the accused eight working days before the expiry of the time limit for the submission of his appeal. The shortness of time left to the applicant for appointing a lawyer of his choice and for preparing for the appeal did not give him a realistic opportunity of having his case brought to and defended in the court in a 'concrete and effective way'.

See also *Ezeh and Connors v United Kingdom* (2002) 35 EHRR 691, discussed at Supplement, para 11.179, where the Court found the prison governor's refusal of the applicants' request to be legally represented at their hearings to have breached their rights under Article 6(3)(c).

(f) Examination of witnesses (Article 6(3)(d))

11.252 In *Birutis v Lithuania* (Judgment of 28 March 2002) the Court said that whilst the use of statements made by anonymous witnesses to found a conviction is not in all circumstances incompatible with Article 6(3)(d), the Convention effectively prohibits a conviction based solely on anonymous evidence. On the facts the Court found the domestic court's failure to question anonymous witnesses and scrutinise the manner and circumstances in which the statements were obtained infringed Article 6(3)(d).

In *SN v Sweden* (Judgment of 2 July 2002) the Court said, having regard to the special features of criminal proceedings concerning sexual offences, Article 6(3)(d) cannot be interpreted as requiring in all cases that questions be put directly by the accused or his representative, through cross-examination or other means. On the facts, the Court noted that the videotape of the police interview with the alleged victim was shown during the trial and appeal hearings, and in the circumstances it held that these measures were sufficient to have enabled the accused to challenge the victim's statements and his credibility in the course of the criminal proceedings.

In *Kok v Netherlands* (Decision of 4 July 2000) the Court said that, when assessing whether the procedures followed in the questioning of an anonymous witness had been sufficient to counterbalance the difficulty caused to the defence, due weight had to be given to the extent to which the anonymous testimony had been decisive in convicting the applicant.

In *PS v Germany* (Judgment of 20 December 2001) the Court found a violation of Article 6(3) where the applicant's conviction for sexual abuse of a child was based solely or to a decisive extent on depositions made by a person whom the applicant had had no opportunity to examine, either during the investigation or at trial.

In *Visser v Netherlands* (Judgment of 14 February 2002) the Court found a breach of Article 6(3)(d) where the appellate court failed to carry out an examination into the seriousness and well-foundedness of the reasons for preserving the anonymity of the witness when it decided to use the witness statement made before the investigating judge in evidence against the applicant. The Court could not be satisfied that the interest of the witness in remaining anonymous could justify limiting the rights of the defence to the extent that they were limited.

(g) Assistance of an interpreter (Article 6(3)(e))

There was a breach of Article 6(3)(e), taken together with Article 6(1), when no interpreter was available during the sentencing process, even though the applicant's counsel had agreed to proceed without an interpreter being present (*Cuscani v United Kingdom* (2003) 36 EHRR 2). **11.255**

(5) The provisions of Article 7

(a) Introduction

In *Streletz, Kessler and Krenz v Germany* (2001) 33 EHRR 751 the Court considered applications by former leaders of East Germany (the GDR) who had been prosecuted for the deaths of people who had attempted to cross the border from East to West before 1989. The Court held, at para 87, that **11.258**

> a State practice such as the GDR's border-policing policy, which flagrantly infringes human rights and above all the right to life, the supreme value in the international hierarchy of human rights, cannot be covered by the protection of Article 7(1) of the Convention. That practice . . . cannot be described as 'law' within the meaning of Article 7.

The applicants, who had created a practice which flagrantly disregarded the principles of legality in the GDR, could not invoke the protection of Article 7.

(c) Interpretation of criminal law

11.260 The Court has stressed the inevitable element of judicial interpretation of the criminal law; see *Streletz, Kessler and Krenz v Germany* (2001) 33 EHRR 751, para 82.

D. The Impact of the Human Rights Act

(2) United Kingdom cases

(a) Introduction

11.269 The Court has now found the United Kingdom in breach of Article 6 on 36 occasions.

> **n1137:** See also: *Moore v United Kingdom* (2000) 29 EHRR 728; *Kingsley v United Kingdom* (2002) 35 EHRR 177; *IJL v United Kingdom* (2001) 33 EHRR 225; *Howarth v United Kingdom* (2001) 31 EHRR 37; *Mills v United Kingdom* (Judgment of 5 June 2001); *Atlan v United Kingdom* (2002) 34 EHRR 833; *Brennan v United Kingdom* (2002) 34 EHRR 507; *Devlin v United Kingdom* (2002) 34 EHRR 1029; *Morris v United Kingdom* (2002) 34 EHRR 1253; *Devenney v United Kingdom* (2002) 35 EHRR 643; *Ezeh and Connors v United Kingdom* (2002) 35 EHRR 691; *Davies v United Kingdom* (2002) 35 EHRR 720; *P and Others v United Kingdom* (2002) 12 BHRC 615; *Cuscani v United Kingdom* (2003) 36 EHRR 2; *Beckles v United Kingdom, The Times*, 15 October 2002; *Somjee v United Kingdom* (Judgment of 15 October 2002); and *Foley v United Kingdom* (Judgment of 22 October 2002).

> *Magee v United Kingdom* is now reported at (2000) 8 BHRC 646; *Averill v United Kingdom* is now reported at (2000) 8 BHRC 430.

(b) Access to the courts

11.274 A breach of Article 6 was found where the administrative decision was not reviewable in a court which could quash the decision and make a fresh decision or remit the case to a fresh decision-maker (*Kingsley v United Kingdom* (2002) 35 EHRR 177, discussed further at Supplement, paras 11.197 and 11.199).

11.276 The Court has not followed its approach in *Osman*; see *Z v United Kingdom* (2001) 10 BHRC 384, discussed at Supplement, para 11.195.

(d) The conduct of criminal proceedings

11.288 The use of compelled statements in subsequent criminal proceedings was found to be a breach in *IJL v United Kingdom* (2001) 33 EHRR 225, discussed at Supplement, para 11.211.

11.292 For a recent case on prosecution disclosure, see *Atlan v United Kingdom* (2002) 34 EHRR 833, discussed at Supplement, para 11.341.

The confiscation procedure under the Drug Trafficking Act 1994 does not breach **11.295** Article 6(1) or (2) (*Phillips v United Kingdom* (2001) 11 BHRC 280, discussed further at Supplement, para 11.238).

The Armed Forces Act 1996 abolished the position of the convening officer and **11.296** split the functions previously performed by the convening officer between three bodies: the higher authority, the prosecuting authority and the court administration officer. The latter was independent of both the higher authority and the prosecuting authority and selected the court-martial's members for each particular case. The new system has been considered by both the House of Lords and the Strasbourg court. In *Morris v United Kingdom* (2002) 34 EHRR 1253, discussed at Supplement, para 11.228, the Court rejected criticism of the role of the Permanent President but held that the roles of the junior officers (sitting on the court-martial) and that of the reviewing authority did not satisfy the requirement of independence and impartiality. The position was reviewed by the House of Lords in *R v Spear* [2002] 3 WLR 437 which held that there were sufficient safeguards to guarantee the independence and impartiality of the court-martial system, and it noted that the European Court in *Morris* had not been provided with all of the information relating to these safeguards. In *R v Skuse* [2002] EWCA Crim 991 the Court of Appeal rejected the argument that the naval judge-advocate, a serving officer, was not 'independent and impartial'. A fair-minded and informed observer, possessed of the facts would conclude that there were sufficient guarantees to exclude any real possibility of a danger of bias.

A breach of the 'reasonable time requirement' under Article 6(1) was found in **11.297A** *Howarth v United Kingdom* (2001) 31 EHRR 37; see, further, Supplement, para 11.219.

(3) General impact issues

(a) Introduction

In *Magill v Porter* [2002] 2 WLR 37 Lord Hope, with whose speech the rest of **11.303** their Lordships agreed, stated that the Article 6(1) rights to a fair trial, to a public hearing and to a hearing within a reasonable time are separate and distinct rights. Thus, he said a complaint that one of these rights has been breached cannot be answered by showing that the others were not.

In *Brown v Stott* [2001] 2 WLR 817, 836B–C, Lord Bingham said, in relation to express and implied rights contained in Article 6(2) and (3):

> . . . while the overall fairness of a criminal trial cannot be compromised, the constituent rights comprised, whether expressed or implicitly, within article 6 are not themselves absolute. Limited qualification of these rights is acceptable if reasonably directed by national authorities towards a clear and proper public objective and if representing no greater qualification than the situation calls for.

In *R v A (No 2)* [2002] 1 AC 45 Lord Steyn said:

> It is well established that the guarantee of a fair trial under Article 6 is absolute: a
> conviction obtained in breach of it cannot stand . . . The only balancing permitted
> is in respect of what the concept of a fair trial entails: here account may be taken of
> the familiar triangulation of interests of the accused, the victim and society.

In *R v Skuse* [2002] EWCA Crim 991 the Court-Martial Court of Appeal reviewed the recent authorities dealing with the appropriate remedy for a breach of
Article 6(1) and stated that the position was not clear. It expressed the tentative
view that had it found a breach of the independence requirement it would not
have been bound to hold the conviction unsafe. However, in *R v Spear* [2002] 3
WLR 437 the House of Lords held that where a breach of the requirement of independence and impartiality was found a conviction should be quashed. This is
consistent with the views expressed by the Privy Council in *Millar v Dickson*
[2002] 1 WLR 1615 and *Mills v HM Advocate* [2002] 3 WLR 1597. The area
where there is uncertainty as to the appropriate remedy for a breach of Article 6(1)
concerns a breach of the reasonable time requirement (discussed at Supplement,
para 11.344).

In *Re S (Children: Care Order: Implementation of Care Plan)* [2002] 2 AC 291 Lord
Nicholls said that, by virtue of the Human Rights Act 1998, Article 8 rights are
now part of the civil rights of parents and children for the purposes of Article 6(1).
This is because under section 6 of the Act, it is unlawful for a public authority to
act inconsistently with Article 8. The same reasoning would apply to all of the
other Convention rights incorporated by the Human Rights Act. Lord Nicholls
also noted that Article 6(1) does not itself guarantee any particular content for
civil rights and obligations in the substantive law of Contracting States. Similarly
in *Fogarty v UK* (2002) 34 EHRR 302 the Strasbourg court said that Article 6(1)
cannot by way of interpretation create a substantive civil right which has no legal
basis in the domestic law.

In *Matthews v Ministry of Defence* [2002] 1 WLR 2621 the Court of Appeal said
that the judge was right to restrict the effect of the decision in *Pellegrin* (see
Supplement, para 11.172) to employment disputes. The *Pellegrin* criteria were not,
it said, intended to exclude claims in tort from the application of Article 6. The
Court of Appeal went on to dismiss a claim that section 10 of the Crown
Proceedings Act 1947 infringed Article 6 insofar as it precluded a serviceman from
bringing a claim in tort against the Ministry of Defence. The Court said that
Article 6(1) cannot be engaged by a provision of the substantive law of a state which
provides that certain groups will be under no civil liability in circumstances where
others would be under such liability. Any other conclusion it said would be to hold
that the Convention is capable of rendering unlawful substantive laws of a state on
the ground that they are discriminatory, notwithstanding no fundamental right

under the Convention is in play. Consequently, it held that since section 10 of the Crown Proceedings Act 1947 was a substantive provision, its effect was that the serviceman had no effective cause of action in negligence. As a result, the serviceman had no civil right which engaged the provision of Article 6(1).

In *R (Hussain) v Asylum Support Adjudicator* [2001] EWHC Admin 852 Stanley Burnton J said:

> Article 6 does not apply to the exercise by public authorities of their discretion, as distinguished from their compliance with their obligations owed to citizens. Obligations give rise to rights; discretionary payments and discretionary support do not. A line has to be drawn between those decisions which, in a democratic society, must be given to an independent and impartial tribunal and those which need not. Article 6 draws this line by restricting the requirement to the determination of criminal charges and civil rights and obligations. A right by definition is something to which the citizen is entitled, to which he has an enforceable claim. A discretionary benefit, one a government may give or refuse as it wishes, cannot be the subject of a right.

It was held that a destitute asylum seeker who is receiving support under Part VI of the Immigration and Asylum Act 1999 has a civil right, within the meaning of Article 6, to the continuation of support subject to regulation 20 of the Asylum Support Regulations 2000, SI 2000/704. This reasoning was approved by the Court of Appeal in *Runa Begum v Tower Hamlets London Borough Council* [2002] 1 WLR 2491. The Court noted that the regime established by Part VII of the Housing Act was not confined to the conferment of discretions upon the local authority which in administering the scheme had to resolve a series of matters which sat at different points on a spectrum between what is wholly objective and what is wholly subjective. In such circumstances he said there was no 'brightline rule' as to when Article 6 applied but he concluded that the subject matter of the scheme, dealing with the urgent provision of living accommodation for persons who will often be gravely disadvantaged (or the refusal to provide it), so touches their well-being that the homeless person's civil rights and obligations are engaged by a determination under the scheme. In this regard he said it is not a necessary incident of a 'civil right' attracting the protections of Article 6(1) that the law allows its owner to maintain an action for damages to make the right good (ie it may be wider than the common law concept of cause of action).

In *R (Beeson) v Dorset County Council* [2002] HRLR 369 Richards J held that the issue under regulation 25 of the National Assistance (Assessment of Resources) Regulations 1992, SI 1992/2977, as to whether the applicant was entitled to have the value of his house left out of account in the assessment of his liability to pay for accommodation which the authority was under a statutory duty to provide was an issue involving his civil rights and obligations within the meaning of Article 6(1). This decision was upheld by the Court of Appeal at [2002] EWCA Civ 448 on the basis that the local authority was concerned with the question as to what premises the claimant would occupy as his home and upon what terms.

A decision to exclude a child from a secondary school or deny admission is not a determination of civil rights under Article 6 (*R (B) v Head Teacher and Governing Body of Alperton Community School* [2001] ELR 359).

11.304A The House of Lords in *Magill v Porter* [2002] 2 WLR 37 recognised that there was some force in the criticism that, where accusations of wilful misconduct are involved, the auditor is required to act under the Local Government and Finance Act 1982 not only as an investigator but also as a prosecutor and as judge. However, it held that this problem was solved by the right of appeal from the auditor's decision to the Divisional Court which not only had power to quash the decision, but also had power to rehear the case, and to take a fresh decision itself in the exercise of the powers given to the auditor. Further, their Lordships stated that any errors of law made by the Divisional Court did not lead inevitably to that court's decision being set aside, such errors could be corrected on appeal.

In *R (Alconbury Developments Ltd) v Secretary of State for the Environment, Transport and the Regions* [2001] 2 WLR 1389 the House of Lords, in allowing an appeal from the decision of the Divisional Court, held that where the courts have jurisdiction to conduct a judicial review of the lawfulness and fairness of a decision, a Government minister can be both a policy- and a decision-maker without there being a violation Article 6(1). As Lord Slynn said (at para 49):

> the question . . . is whether there is a sufficient judicial control to ensure a determination by an independent and impartial tribunal subsequently. [The Court of Human Right's] judgments . . . do not require that this should constitute a rehearing on an application by an appeal on the merits . . . What is required on the part of the [Court] is that there should be a sufficient review of the legality of the decisions and of the procedures followed.

However, the position may be different where the decision-maker makes findings of primary fact and is not independent from the parties. Unfortunately, the case law in this area has been inconsistent and it is difficult to distil clear principles.

• There have been a number of planning cases where the absence of a public fact-finding inquiry has not resulted in a breach of Article 6; see *Vetterlein v Hampshire County Council* [2002] JPL 289; *R (Malster) v Ipswich Borough Council* [2002] PLCR 14; and *Friends Provident v Secretary of State for Transport* [2002] 1 WLR 1450. However, in *R (Kathro) v Rhonda Cybnon Taff CBC* [2002] Env LR 15 Richards J stated *obiter* that the absence of any public inquiry in the decision-making process of a local planning authority meant there was a real possibility that, in certain circumstances, a decision of an authority which was not itself an independent tribunal would not be subject to sufficient judicial control to satisfy Article 6. See also Supplement, para 11.381A.

- In *R (Bewry) v Norwich City Council* [2002] HRLR 21 Moses J took the view that the Administrative Court 'cannot cure the often imperceptible effects of the influence of the connection between the fact-finding body and a party to the dispute since it has no jurisdiction to reach its own conclusion on the primary facts; still less any power to weigh the evidence' (para 64). See also *R (Bono) v Harlow DC* [2002] 1 WLR 2475.

- In *Ali and Begum v The Commissioners of Customs and Excise* (30 May 2002) Stephen Oliver QC held that Article 6 required the VAT Tribunal to construe paragraph 4(2) of Schedule 11 to the Value Added Tax Act 1994 in a manner that enabled it to substitute its findings of primary fact where the evidence demands it when reviewing the reasonableness of a Commissioner's decision to require security. See also *Dannatt v Customs and Excise Commissioners* (30 May 2002).

- In *R (Brogan) v Metropolitan Police* [2002] EWHC 2127 Davis J held that where the police refused to grant a special exemption to the claimant's licensee of a public house, the police were not making a primary finding of fact and judicial review provided a sufficient review process to comply with Article 6.

The Court of Appeal in *Adan v London Borough of Newham* [2002] 1 WLR 2120 held, *obiter*, that the county court did not have 'full jurisdiction' on an appeal pursuant to section 204 of the Housing Act 1996, which gives a dissatisfied homeless applicant a right to appeal 'on any point of law' arising from the decision of the local authority reviewing officer, so that there would be an Article 6 irregularity in the procedure taken as a whole. However, in *Runa Begum v Tower Hamlets London Borough Council* [2002] 1 WLR 2491 the Court of Appeal, considering the same provisions of the Housing Act 1996, disagreed with the reasoning of all the members of the Court in *Adan*. Laws LJ, with whom Lord Woolf CJ and Dyson LJ agreed, said that in determining whether the review court possessed 'full jurisdiction' it was necessary to examine the statutory scheme as a whole, including the extent to which the first instance process might be relied on to produce fair and reasonable decisions. He said:

> Where the scheme's subject matter generally or systematically involves the resolution of primary fact, the court will incline to look for procedures akin to our conventional mechanisms for finding facts: rights of cross-examination, access to documents, a strictly independent decision-maker. To the extent that procedures of that kind are not given by the first instance process, the court will look to see how far they are given by the appeal or review; and the judicial review jurisdiction (or its equivalent in the shape of a statutory appeal on law) may not suffice. Where however the subject-matter of the scheme generally or systematically involves the weighing of policy issues and regard being had to the interests of others who are not before the decision-maker, then for the purposes of Article 6 the court will incline to be satisfied with a form of inquisition at first instance in which the decision-maker is more of an expert than a judge (I use the terms loosely), and the second instance appeal is in the nature of judicial review.

He observed that schemes which involve findings of fact are likely directly to engage civil rights, whereas schemes where judgment, discretion and issues of policy predominate are more likely to be ones in which decisions under it 'determine or affect' civil rights. Applying this approach to the Housing Act regime, Laws LJ said that the scheme, judged as a whole, lay towards the end of the spectrum where judgment and discretion, rather than fact-finding, played the predominant role. Furthermore, he took the view that the judge had ample power to decide whether the review officer's decision was one which was properly available to her on the evidence which she had. Because the first instance process did not of itself fulfil Article 6, Laws LJ indicated that the judge was perfectly entitled, within the jurisdiction given by section 204, to subject the earlier decision to a close and rigorous analysis. Consequently, he held that section 204 in its context conferred 'full jurisdiction' on the judge and that therefore the scheme complied with Article 6(1).

This conclusion was reached, despite Laws LJ's acceptance that Mrs Begum's case involved 'sharp issues of fact' which fell for determination. However, he said that the compliance of the statutory scheme could not vary from case to case, according to the degree of factual dispute arising, because of the principle of legal certainty. However, it is open to question whether this approach is consistent with the Strasbourg jurisprudence which states that in assessing compliance with Article 6 it is necessary to have regard to the 'subject matter of the decision appealed against' (eg *Bryan v UK* (1995) 21 EHRR 342) or with the comments of Lord Nicholls in *Re S (Children: Care Order: Implementation of Care Plan)* [2002] AC 291, discussed at Supplement, para 11.365. It is submitted that the critical issue of whether judicial review is sufficient to comply with Article 6 must depend upon whether the dispute of primary fact arises in relation to an individual's rights or interests or whether it raises an issue which depends on evaluating the public interest; see, generally, Schiemann and M Andenas (eds), *Policy Making and Decision Taking: Human Rights and English Public Law after Alconbury* (British Institute of Comparative Law, 2003).

Nevertheless, the *Runa Begum* case was followed and applied by the Court of Appeal in *R (Adlard and Others) v Secretary of State for the Environment, Transport and Regions* [2002] 1 WLR 2515. In that case it was held that the rights of objectors under Article 6 are not violated if a local planning authority refuses to accord them a public hearing, or indeed any form of oral hearing. The combination of the authority's initial decision-making process and judicial review by the High Court is sufficient to ensure compliance with Article 6.

It appears that, as a result of the Court of Appeal decisions in *Runa Begum* and *Adlard*, even when the decision of an administrative body which is not independent is 'fact sensitive', the availability of judicial review will ensure that the whole process complies with Article 6.

(b) Access to the courts and immunities

'Access to court' points have been argued on a number of occasions since 2 **11.306**
October 2000. The arguments have been unsuccessful in the following areas:

- *Sovereign immunity*: A state is not precluded from granting immunity to a foreign state in accordance with its international obligations. Article 6 forbids a Contracting State from denying individuals the benefits of its powers of adjudication; it does not extend the scope of those powers (*Holland v Lampen-Wolfe* [2000] 1 WLR 1573).
- *Exclusive jurisdiction clauses*: In *OT Africa v Fayad Hijazy* [2001] 1 Lloyd's 76 Aikens J stated that Article 6 does not give a litigant an unfettered choice of the tribunal in which to pursue or defend his civil rights.
- *Vexatious litigants*: The Court of Appeal in *Ebert v Official Receiver* [2001] EWCA Civ 340 stated that the general principles relating to the grant or refusal of leave to appeal to vexatious litigants under section 42 of the Supreme Court Act 1981 complied with the requirements of Article 6. In *A-G v Wheen* [2001] IRLR 91 it was held that an order under section 33 of the Employment Tribunals Act 1996 preventing the institution of proceedings without permission did not breach Article 6.
- *Time limits*: In *J & PM Dockeray (A Firm) v Secretary of State for the Environment, Food and Rural Affairs* [2002] EWHC Admin 420 Collins J held that the rigid application of the 14-day time limit for appeal against the valuation of livestock under the Foot and Mouth Disease (Ascertainment of Value) (No 4) Order 2001, SI 2001/1242, was a legitimate and proportionate interference with the right of access to the appeal process and did not breach Article 6.
- *Rules relating to service*: In *Anderton v Clwyd County Council* [2002] EWCA 933 the Court of Appeal rejected the argument that by refusing to admit uncontroverted evidence of the fact that the defendant received the claim form before the end of the period for service and before a 'deemed day' of service, which occurred after the end of the period, the claimant asserting a civil right is precluded from access to the court. The Court of Appeal said that any interference with the right of access was not a consequence of a system of disproportionately strict rules but a result of the claimant waiting until the end of a generous period allowed for issuing and serving the claim form and then serving the document without regard to the rules as to when service will be deemed to be effected.

However, 'access to court' arguments have found favour in other areas:

- *Security for costs*: In *Nasser v United Bank of Kuwait* [2001] EWCA Civ 556 the Court of Appeal held that the rules for the provision of security for costs on an appeal were within Article 6. The issue in each case was whether security was objectively justified having regard to the circumstances and the potential burden on the party providing the security. The grant of permission to appeal denoted at least a 'real prospect' of the case succeeding. In such circumstances an appellant's ease of access to appellate justice was to be given greater priority in accordance with the aim of the CPR generally and Article 6 (see also *McAteer v Lismore (No 2)* [2000] NI 477).

- *Legal aid*: The Directions and Guidance under the Access to Justice Act 1999 are wrong to the extent that they fail to indicate that there was a discretion to grant legal aid in cases in which the withholding of legal aid would make the assertion of a civil claim practically impossible or would lead to an obvious unfairness in the proceedings (*R v Legal Services Commission, ex p Jarrett* [2002] ACD 160). In *R (Alliss) v Legal Services Commission* [2002] EWHC Admin 2079 Jackson J held that Article 6 was breached by withdrawing a legal aid certificate where there was an imminent trial involving complex issues of fact and law and no material change of circumstances.

- *Construction of statutes and rules of court limiting access to the courts*: In *Cachia v Faluyi* [2001] 1 WLR 1966 the Court of Appeal held that a provision of the Fatal Accidents Act 1976 barring a second action 'in respect of the same subject matter of complaints' had to be construed, in the light of Article 6, as not applying where the first writ had been issued but not served. Brooke LJ commented (at para 21) that the case was

  > a very good example of the way in which the enactment of the Human Rights Act now enables English judges to do justice in a way which was not previously open to us.

  In *Goode v Martin* [2002] 1 WLR 1828 the Court of Appeal said it was necessary to interpret CPR 17.4(2) so as to permit the court to allow a claimant to amend her statement of claim after the expiry of the limitation period where the amendment consisted of a response to the defendant's version of events. The Court held that a narrower interpretation would impose an impediment on the claimant's access to the court that would have to be justified.

11.307 The position in relation to 'negligence immunity' is now unclear as a result of the decision of the Court of Human Rights in *Z v United Kingdom* (2001) 10 BHRC 384, discussed at Supplement, para 11.195, which refused to follow *Osman* and accepted the government's submission that the 'just and reasonable requirement' was not an immunity but was an essential element of the tort. It is submitted that this decision fails to recognise the practical effect of the requirement in relation to claims against public authorities where claims which would otherwise succeed are refused on 'policy' grounds. Under the influence of *Osman* the courts have been more careful in assessing the 'just and reasonable requirement' in every case, rather than relying on a 'blanket' approach (see, for example, *Barrett v Enfield* [2001] 2 AC 550) but it is not clear whether this trend is continuing; see, generally, A

Lidbetter and J George, 'Negligent Public Authorities and Convention Rights: The Legacy of *Osman*' [2001] ERLR 599.

(c) Independence and impartiality

Independence.   In *International Transport Roth GmbH v Home Secretary* [2002]   **11.309**
3 WLR 344 a majority of the Court of Appeal held that the fixed-penalty regime imposed by the Immigration and Asylum Act 1999 offends the carrier's right to have his penalty determined by an independent tribunal. The scheme, it said, makes the Secretary of State judge in his own cause.

The Court of Session in *R v United Kingdom Central Council for Nursing, Midwifery & Health Visiting, ex p Tehrani* [2001] IRLR 208 held that it was not necessary that the respondent's professional conduct committee should itself meet all the requirements of an independent and impartial tribunal, given that an automatic right of appeal to the Court of Session lay from any order striking the name of one of its members from the register.

In *Millar v Dickson* [2002] 1 WLR 1615 the Privy Council held that the failure to   **11.310**
raise the point taken in *Starrs v Ruxton* was not an implicit waiver of the right to trial by an independent and impartial tribunal. (On waiver under the Human Rights Act, see, further, Supplement, para 6.162.)

In *R v Spear* [2001] 2 WLR 1692 it was held that a part-time judge advocate's lack   **11.311A**
of security of tenure did not undermine his impartiality or independence. Such appointments were made and terminated by the Judge Advocate-General who was wholly independent of the executive.

The Court of Appeal in *R v Acton Youth Court* [2001] 1 WLR 1828 said that district judges and justices should not normally disqualify themselves from hearing a trial merely because they had ruled in favour of the prosecution's *ex parte* application for non-disclosure on the ground that it attracted public interest immunity.

In *Clark v Kelly* [2000] SLT 1038 the applicant sought to challenge the independent and impartiality of district (magistrates') courts on the ground that the clerk was a member of the tribunal and was not independent. This argument was rejected on the ground that the clerk's role was confined to that of legal adviser and providing justices with necessary information. See also *Mont v United Kingdom* [2002] EHRLR 270 (complaint that the role of the justices' clerk was in breach of Article 6 held inadmissible); *R (Hussain) v Asylum Support Adjudicator* [2001] EWHC 852, discussed at Supplement, para 11.68; and *Morris v UK* (2002) 34 EHRR 1253, discussed at Supplement, para 11.228.

Impartiality.   In *Re Medicaments (No 2)* [2001] 1 WLR 700 (approved by the   **11.312**
House of Lords in *Magill v Porter* [2002] 2 WLR 37) the Court of Appeal held

that Convention jurisprudence required a modest adjustment of the test for bias in *R v Gough*. See, further, Supplement, para 11.68.

In the Scots case of *Stott v Minogue* [2001] SLT (Sh Ct) 25 the Sheriff's Court held that Article 6 did not entitle an accused to request a positive declaration by a judge that he was not connected to the Freemasons. Taken together, the judicial oath and the ethical duty of judges to disclose a conflict provided sufficient proof of impartiality to satisfy Article 6. See also *Salaman v United Kingdom* [2001] EHRLR 85, also noted at Supplement, para 11.228.

(d) Impact on civil proceedings

11.313   The right to a fair and reasonable opportunity to put one's case does not mean that a litigant is entitled to an unlimited and uncontrolled chance to address the court (*Attorney-General v Covey*, *The Times*, 2 March 2001). Where permission to appeal from a decision of a lower court is refused a litigant is entitled under Article 6 to a reasoned decision for the refusal (*Hyams v Plender (Practice Note)* [2001] 1 WLR 32).

In *English v Emery Reimbold & Strick* [2002] 1 WLR 2409 the Court of Appeal said that Article 6(1) will be violated if a judgment leaves it unclear whether the court in question has addressed a contention advanced by a party that is fundamental to the resolution of the litigation. The reasons must be sufficient to demonstrate that the essential issues raised have been addressed by the court and how those issues have been resolved. However, it said there will be some circumstances in which the reason for the decision will be implicit from the decision itself. In such circumstances Article 6 will not be infringed if the reason for the decision is not expressly spelt out by the judicial tribunal. The Court of Appeal in *English* said that decisions on liability for costs given without reasons will only comply with Article 6 if the reason for the decision in respect of costs is clearly implicit from the circumstances in which the award is made.

The Court of Appeal in *North Range Shipping Limited v Seatrans Shipping Corporation* [2002] 1 WLR 2397 held that Commercial Court judges should give brief reasons on a refusal of leave to appeal to the High Court from the decision of arbitrators under section 69 of the Arbitration Act 1996. An unsuccessful applicant should be told which of the threshold tests under section 69(3) for leave he has failed and where the challenge is on the basis that the arbitrators' decision is obviously wrong, Article 6 may, in addition, require further brief reasons.

In *Woodhouse v Consignia* [2002] 1 WLR 2558 the Court of Appeal said that when deciding whether it is just to remove a stay imposed on an action by the operation of CPR PD 52, para 19, judges must remember that if a stay remains in place, they are depriving the claimant of access to the court. They should not, therefore, latch on to one or two considerations (such as the length of any delay) to the exclusion of all others. They must carry out the necessary balancing exercise methodically and explain how they reached their ultimate decision. The Court said that provided judges make their decisions within the framework provided by CPR 3.9 and 1.1, they are unlikely to fall foul of Article 6(1) in this regard.

In *Hart v Relentless Records* [2002] EWHC Ch 1984 Jacob J took the view that a judge's meeting with counsel in the judge's corridor to urge settlement and express a view on the strength of the claimant's case was not evidence of bias but represented active case management. Informal meetings of this kind were not within the scope of Article 6. **11.315**

The decision of a Special Commissioner to consent to the issue of a notice, under section 20 of the Taxes Management Act 1970, for the production of legally privileged material is not a decision that determines the intended recipient's civil rights (*R v Special Commissioner, ex p Morgan Grenfell* [2000] 1 All ER 535, Ch D). The possibility of an oral hearing is excluded by the very nature of the process in question (*R v Special Commissioner, ex p Morgan Grenfell* [2001] STC 497, CA (the applicant successfully appealed to the House of Lords at [2002] 2 WLR 1299 but not on these issues which were not argued on the appeal)). **11.317**

It has been held that the procedure under the Debtors Act 1869 which can lead to imprisonment for failure to comply with orders to pay money is to be treated as 'criminal proceedings'. The 'judgment summons' procedure in use in the Family Division was not compatible with Article 6 (*Mubarak v Mubarak* [2001] 1 FLR 698). A new procedure for such applications has now been laid down (see *Practice Direction (Committal Applications)* [2001] 2 All ER 704). **11.318A**

The Scottish courts have rejected the argument that the unpredictability of jury damages awards means that trial with a jury must be unfair; see *McLeod v British Railways Board* [2001] SLT 238 (a personal injury case).

In *Stevens Associates v The Aviary Estate, The Times*, 2 February 2001, Pumfrey J held that Article 6 of the Convention did not entitle a person to litigate the same issue more than once. Once an action had been struck out, it was entirely proper for a court to regulate its procedure in such a way as to prevent the same issues being revisited without the costs of the earlier action having been paid.

In *Rowland v Bock* [2002] EWHC 692 Newman J held that the master, in refusing to allow one of the parties to give his evidence by videolink, in circumstances where he could not return to the United Kingdom to attend the hearing without the risk of arrest, had failed to pay sufficient regard to Article 6 and the need to see that the parties were on an equal footing.

In *Maronier v Larmer* [2002] EWCA Civ 774 the Court of Appeal said that English courts should apply a strong presumption that the procedures of other signatories of the Convention were compliant with Article 6. However, where a judgment emanates from a country which does not apply the Convention the court must check that the guarantees in Article 6 have been complied with before recognising the judgment (*Pellegrini v Italy* (2002) 35 EHRR 44).

(e) Impact on judicial review proceedings

11.320 **Judicial review procedure.**   In *R (Burkett) v London Borough of Hammersmith and Fulham* [2002] 1 WLR 1593 Lords Steyn and Hope expressed some doubt as to whether the provision in CPR 54.5(1) that the claim form in an application for judicial review must be filed 'promptly' is sufficiently certain to comply with the right to a fair hearing within a reasonable time in Article 6(1). Lord Hope said that the principle of legality required that any law or rule which restricts Convention rights must be formulated with sufficient clarity to enable the citizen to foresee the consequences which a given action may entail and so regulate his conduct accordingly.

11.324 **Review of decisions determining Article 6 rights.**   In *R (Alconbury Developments Ltd) v Secretary of State for the Environment, Transport and the Regions* [2001] 2 WLR 1389, para 169, Lord Clyde said:

> The suggestion was advanced that, if the respondents were correct in their contention that the present proceedings are in breach of article 6(1), the scope of judicial review might somehow be enlarged so as to provide a complete remedy. . . . I consider that it might well be difficult to achieve a sufficient enlargement to meet the stated purpose without jeopardising the constitutional balance between the role of the courts and the role of the executive.

See also Lord Nolan at para 62 and the different approaches of the majority and minority of the Court of Appeal in *Adan v London Borough of Newham* [2002] 1 WLR 2120, discussed at Supplement, para 11.304A.

(4) Specific areas of impact

(a) Commercial law

11.327 **Introduction.**   Article 6 does not apply to proceedings before an adjudicator appointed under the Housing Grants, Construction and Regeneration Act 1996 since such proceedings do not result in a final determination (*Elanay Contracts v The Vestry* [2001] Build LR 33) or because an adjudicator is not a 'public authority' (*Austin Hall Building v Buckland Securities* [2001] Build LR 372, H H J Bowsher QC).

The Court of Appeal in *Wilson v First County Trust (No 2)* [2001] 3 WLR 42 declared that section 127(3) of the Consumer Credit Act 1974 was incompatible with the Human Rights Act. The Court held that the absolute bar to enforcement in the case of a credit agreement which does not contain the prescribed terms is a disproportionate restriction on the right of the lender, which exists in all other cases, to have the enforceability of his loan determined by the court.

See also *North Range Shipping Limited v Seatrans Shipping Corporation* [2002] 1 WLR 2397, discussed at Supplement, para 11.218.

n1345: The Financial Services and Markets Act received Royal Assent in 2000 (not, as stated in the Main Work, 1999).

The Court of Appeal in *Berry Trade Limited v Moussavi and Others* [2002] 1 WLR 1910 held that the judge had erred in failing to adjourn a committal application in insolvency proceedings on the ground that the appellant had refused to accept an offer of funding from the applicant seeking committal. The appellant had a right to make an application for legal aid to fund legal representation in the committal proceedings and was waiting for the Legal Services Commission to consider his application. To refuse the request for an adjournment in those circumstances was contrary to Article 6.

Regulatory proceedings involving 'criminal charges'. In *R (Fleurose) v*   **11.331**
Securities and Futures Authority Ltd [2002] IRLR 297 the Court of Appeal held that disciplinary proceedings instituted by the SFA against the appellant, a registered trader, for improper trading in financial markets, the maximum penalty for which was an unlimited fine, did not involve the determination of a criminal offence or charge. The Court placed reliance on its judgment in *Han & Yau v Commissioners of Customs and Excise* [2001] 1 WLR 2253 where it stated that

> where the offence is limited to a restricted group, as is generally the case in relation to disciplinary offences, the Court is unlikely to classify a charge under the applicable disciplinary or regulatory code as criminal, at least unless it involves or may lead to loss of liberty.

n1365: In *Re Blackspur Group* [2001] 1 BCLC 653 the fact that proceedings   **11.333**
under section 6 of the Company Directors Disqualification Act 1986 had been on foot for over eight years was held not to be contrary to Article 6. Four years of that time were accounted for by criminal proceedings and a very large proportion of the time that had elapsed since was due to the various interlocutory activities of the defendant, which the court said were not engaged in so as to obtain, but rather to avoid, a hearing within a reasonable time, or at all. See also *Secretary of State for Trade and Industry v Staton* [2001] CP Rep 1. However, in *Davies v United Kingdom* (2002) 35 EHRR 720 the Court of Human Rights held that the civil rights and obligations of one of the Blackspur directors, who although not a defendant in the criminal proceedings had had his disqualification proceedings stayed until after the conclusion of the criminal trial, were not determined within a reasonable time. The *Davies* decision is discussed at Supplement, para 11.220.

11.334　**Regulatory proceedings involving 'civil rights and obligations'.**　Where the livelihood and professional reputation of a person are at stake and in the absence of overriding public interest considerations it is a violation of Article 6 for a disciplinary hearing to continue when the person is too ill to put her own case (*Brabazon-Drenning v United Kingdom Central Council for Nursing, Midwifery and Health Visiting* [2001] HRLR 6). Since the Human Rights Act 1998 came into force, any tendency to read down rights of appeal in disciplinary cases is to be resisted (*Ghosh v General Medical Council* [2001] 1 WLR 1915, PC) and for the purposes of Article 6 the Privy Council has full jurisdiction (see also *Preiss v General Dental Council* [2001] 1 WLR 1926, PC). In the case of proceedings before the General Medical Council time begins to run for Article 6 purposes when the medical practitioner is notified that the matter has been referred to the Preliminary Proceedings Committee (*General Medical Council v Pembrey* [2002] EWHC Admin 1602).

In *R (Nicolaides) v General Medical Council* (2001) Lloyd's Med Rep 525 Sir Richard Tucker held that Article 6 was not engaged in relation to professional conduct proceedings where the outcome was a reprimand as there was no determination of the civil right to practise. He held that the question as to whether Article 6 was engaged depended on the actual outcome of the case, not on what the outcome might have been (para 31). It is submitted that this conclusion is incorrect: if a person's right to practise is, potentially, at risk then Article 6 should be applicable.

In *Ali and Begum v The Commissioners of Customs and Excise* (30 May 2002) Stephen Oliver QC held, notwithstanding the decision of the European Court in *Ferrazzini v Italy*, that the obligations imposed by the tax and the default surcharge assessments, the penalty notices and the notices of requirement to provide security under the Value Added Tax Act 1994, are civil obligations under Article 6(1); see Supplement, para 11.172.

(b) Criminal law

11.338　**Introduction.**　In *Hinds v Attorney-General of Barbados* [2002] 2 WLR 470, para 18, the Privy Council noted that whilst the right to a fair trial under Article 6 is absolute, this does not mean that every legal error, every irregularity, every deviation from good practice and every departure from procedural propriety in the course of a trial must deprive a defendant of a fair hearing. In this regard, questions of degree are relevant, as are the facts of a particular case and the circumstances of a particular defendant.

In *R v Weir* [2001] 1 WLR 421 the House of Lords rejected the DPP's argument that to deny him an extension of time in which to seek leave to appeal from the Court of Appeal was to deny him effective access to a court, and deny him an opportunity which would have been open to a defendant. The civil rights of the DPP were not in issue and he was not charged with a criminal offence.

It is of vital importance that criminal proceedings are seen to be fair. The Administrative Court quashed a conviction where an unrepresented disabled defendant had been kept waiting all day before the hearing began and had not had the opportunity to make closing submissions (*R (King) v Isleworth Crown Court* [2001] ACD 51).

The Lord Chief Justice has issued a Practice Direction to justices' clerks to ensure that trials in the magistrates' courts are fair (*Practice Direction (Justices: Clerk to Court)* [2000] 1 WLR 1886). This provides, *inter alia*, that in order to ensure a fair trial, any advice other than that given in open court was provisional until submissions from the parties had been heard.

In *R v Kirk, The Times*, 26 June 2002, the Court of Appeal held that the fact that a man aged over 23 had no defence under section 6(3) of the Sexual Offences Act 1956 for an offence of unlawful intercourse with a girl under 16 contrary to section 6(1) of the Act, did not make the defence discriminatory, disproportionate or incompatible with Articles 6 or 14 of the European Convention on Human Rights.

Definition of 'criminal charge'. In *International Transport Roth GmbH v* **11.339**
Secretary of State for the Home Department [2002] 3 WLR 344 the Court of Appeal held that there was essentially a single question: 'what is the essential character of the scheme?' (see Simon Brown LJ at para 34, Laws LJ at para 94 and Jonathan Parker LJ at para 160). Simon Brown LJ said that the classification of proceedings between criminal and civil is secondary to the more directly relevant question of just what protections are required in the particular case to achieve a fair trial. Since the various procedural safeguards provided by Article 6 are not ultimately dependent upon such a classification, he questioned whether the classification exercise should be attempted at all. However, Laws LJ disagreed stating that the issue whether the proceedings were to be regarded as effectively imposing criminal liability, and so exacting criminal sanctions, was critical to determining whether or not the Article 6 guarantees were satisfied. Simon Brown and Jonathan Parker LJJ both laid particular stress on the fixed penalty nature of the scheme they were examining. Jonathan Parker LJ took the view that, because the penalty was fixed where liability has been determined, no account can be taken of the facts of particular cases, or of the circumstances of a particular defendant. Nor is there scope for mitigation. He said it was not possible to remedy this unfairness by using section 3 of the Human Rights Act to substitute a maximum penalty for a fixed penalty, thereby allowing a proper degree of flexibility to the sentencer, as that would be too radical an alteration to the scheme to be regarded as interpretation. Simon Brown LJ also emphasised that the unfairness of the provision of a fixed

penalty for a strict liability offence which he said could not stand unless it can be adjudged proportionate in all cases having regard to the culpability involved. Laws LJ, dissenting, said that the real case being made was that in the name of the rule of law Article 6 effectively forbids a legislative scheme so unfair, or draconian, as the fixed penalty regime. He said it was difficult to find authority to the effect that the substance of 'civil rights and obligations' within Article 6 is subject to qualifications in the name of fairness.

The courts have considered the question as to whether particular proceedings give rise to 'criminal charges' in a number of cases. The following have been held not to constitute criminal charges under Article 6:

- An allegation of breach of bail conditions under section 7(5) of the Bail Act 1976 (*R (DPP) v Havering Magistrates' Court* [2001] 1 WLR 805).
- An application for a sex offender order under section 2 of the Crime and Disorder Act 1998 (*B v Chief Constable of Avon and Somerset Constabulary* [2001] 1 WLR 340).
- An application for an anti-social behaviour order under section 1 of the Act (*R (McCann) v Crown Court at Manchester* [2001] 1 WLR 358) (because such orders are not about crime and punishment but were aimed at the protection of an identified section of the community, and therefore were not criminal proceedings).
- Proceedings for the condemnation of goods forfeited by Customs and Excise (*Goldsmith v Commissioners of Customs and Excise, The Times*, 12 June 2001). It was said that none of the usual consequences of a criminal conviction followed from condemnation and forfeiture proceedings. There was no conviction or finding of guilt. The person concerned was not subject to any other penalty, apart from the consequences of the forfeiture and the loss of the goods.
- Prison disciplinary proceedings conducted by the prison governor. In *R (Al-Hassan) v Secretary of State for the Home Department* [2002] 1 WLR 545 the Court of Appeal held that the imposition by a prison governor of 21 days' additional imprisonment was close to the borderline but within the margin of discretion to be extended to the prison authorities. However, the position has been significantly altered by the Court's decision in *Ezeh and Connors v United Kingdom* (2001) 35 EHRR 691; see Supplement, para 11.384.
- The power to impose an unlimited fine for improper trading in financial markets (*R (Fleurose) v Securities and Futures Authority Ltd* [2002] IRLR 297).
- The recategorisation of a prisoner by the review committee which took into account matters constituting a criminal offence (*R (Sunder) v Secretary of State for the Home Department* [2001] EWHC Admin 252).
- Default surcharge penalties, misdeclaration penalties and late registration penalties imposed under the Value Added Tax Act 1994 (*Ali and Begum v The Commissioners of Customs and Excise*, 30 May 2002).

- A decision by the Commissioners to demand a restoration fee for the return of a seized vehicle to a third party (*Dannatt v Customs and Excise Commissioners*, 30 May 2002).
- Proceedings under sections 4 and 4A of the Criminal Procedure (Insanity) Act 1964. In any event the Court of Appeal said they did not infringe Article 6. The 1964 Act, as amended by the Criminal Procedure (Insanity and Unfairness to Plead) Act 1991, to protect accused persons with a disability fairly balanced the public interest in ascertaining whether the alleged acts had been committed and in identifying and treating those who had committed the acts and their interests (*R v M and Others* [2001] EWCA 202).
- Measures of the kind provided for by section 20 of the Local Government Finance Act 1982 (surcharge of loss incurred or deficiency caused by wilful misconduct on the part of members or senior officers of local authorities), which apply to persons having a special status or responsibility and are compensatory and regulatory rather than penal in character, lie outside the criminal sphere for the purposes of Article 6 (*Magill v Porter* [2002] 2 WLR 37).
- An anti-social behaviour order is neither a conviction or a condemnation that a person is guilty of an offence and is not a criminal charge; *R (McCann) v Manchester Crown Court* [2002] 3 WLR 1313. The House of Lords went on to hold that insofar as an anti-behaviour order was a civil right within the scope of Article 6(1), the use of hearsay evidence was not unfair and a breach of Article 6.
- The decision of the Parole Board whether to recall a prisoner released on licence (*R (West) v Parole Board, The Times*, 21 November 2002, CA).

In *Gough v Chief Constable of Derbyshire* [2002] 3 WLR 389 it was held that a football banning order is not a 'penalty' for the purposes of Article 7. The Court of Appeal upheld the Divisional Court's finding that proceedings for the imposition of international banning orders under the Football (Spectators) Act 1989, as amended by the Football (Disorder) Act 2000, were civil not criminal in character. However, the Court said that while the orders were made in civil proceedings they impose serious restraints on freedoms that the citizen normally enjoys. Thus, while technically the civil standard of proof applies, that standard should reflect the consequences that will follow if the case for the banning order is made out. This should lead the magistrates to apply an exacting standard of proof that will, in practice, be hard to distinguish from the criminal standard.

The following have been held to be 'criminal charges' for the purposes of Article 6:

- A determination by tax commissioners to penalise a defaulting taxpayer (*King v Walden (Inspector of Taxes)* [2001] STC 822). The amount of the fine was potentially very substantial and designed to punish defaulting taxpayers.

- The imposition of a civil evasion penalty in respect of VAT or excise duty (*Han & Yau v Customs & Excise Commissioners* [2001] EWCA Civ 1048; see also the decision of the Court of Human Rights in *Georgiou (t/a Marios Chippery) v United Kingdom* [2001] STC 80 and P Baker, 'Taxation and the ECHR' [2000] BTR 211).

- Contempt of court proceedings for breaches of injunctions of the civil courts (*Mubarak v Mubarak* [2001] 1 FLR 698, also discussed at Supplement, para 11.318A). It should be noted, however, that this does not make such proceedings 'criminal' for the purposes of the double jeopardy rule (*DPP v Tweddell* [2001] EWHC Admin 188, approved in *London Borough of Barnet v Hurst* [2002] EWCA Civ 1009).

- The penalty regime imposed by the Immigration and the Asylum Act 1999 on those responsible for clandestine entrants to the United Kingdom (*International Transport Roth GmbH v The Secretary of State for the Home Department* [2002] 3 WLR 344).

- The House of Lords held in *R (Anderson) v Secretary of State for the Home Department* [2002] 3 WLR 1800 that the decision of the Home Secretary to fix the tariff for mandatory life prisoners was within the scope of Article 6.

In *Re M (A Child) Secure Accommodation Order* [2001] FCR 692 the Court of Appeal held that, although proceedings for a secure accommodation order were not criminal proceedings within the meaning of Article 6, a child facing such an application was to be given the minimum rights to a fair trial set out in Article 6(3).

11.341 **Disclosure and public interest immunity.** In *Atlan v United Kingdom* (2002) 34 EHRR 833 it was held that the disclosure of undisclosed material *ex parte* to the Court of Appeal was not sufficient to remedy the unfairness of the applicant's trial (applying *Rowe and Davis v United Kingdom*, discussed at Main Work, para 11.292).

In *R v Dervish* [2001] EWCA Crim 2789 the Court of Appeal held that the public interest in protecting the identity of an informant had to be balanced against the right of the defendant to a fair trial. If there is material which might assist the defence in any way in the conduct of its defence, then the necessity for the defendant to have a fair trial outweighs the other interests in the case and the prosecution must either produce the undisclosed material or discontinue the prosecution.

In *R v Brushett* (2001) Crim LR 471 the Court of Appeal summarised the applicable principles relating to the disclosure of material by the prosecution as follows:

- It is a fundamental aspect of the right to a fair trial that criminal proceedings should be adversarial and that there should be equality of arms between prosecution and defence;

- The right to an adversarial trial means that both prosecution and defence should be given the opportunity to have knowledge of, and comment on, the evidence of the other party;
- Article 6(1) and the English law require that the prosecution should disclose to the defence all material evidence in their possession for or against the accused;
- The entitlement to disclosure is not an absolute right;
- Only such measures restricting the right of the defence which are strictly necessary are permissible under Article 6(1);
- Any difficulties caused to the defence by the limitation of its rights must be sufficiently counterbalanced by the procedures followed by the judicial authorities; and
- Decision-making procedure must, so far as is possible, provide adversarial proceedings and equality of arms and incorporate adequate safeguards for the defence.

n1413: *Jasper v United Kingdom* is now reported at (2000) 30 EHRR 441.   **11.342**

Equality of arms.   In *Wildman v DPP*, *The Times*, 8 February 2001, the   **11.342A**
Divisional Court held that the defendant's right to equality of arms was not breached by the prosecution's failure to disclose the whole of the evidence in its possession to the defence before: (a) an application for bail; or (b) arguments relating to custody time limits.

The Court of Appeal in *R v Smith (Joe)* [2001] 1 WLR 1031 held that it was permissible for a judge when determining the question of whether or not an officer had reasonable grounds to suspect a defendant of involvement in an offence to take into account evidential matters put before the judge by the prosecution in an *ex parte* hearing but not disclosed to the defence where there is no other evidence in the case at the time of the ruling. This did not offend against the principle of equality of arms in Article 6.

In *R v C* [2001] EWCA Crim 1529 it was held that a failure by the prosecution to disclose statements made by the complainant in unrelated proceedings which could have damaged her credibility was not a breach of the principle of equality of arms and did not prevent the defendant from having a fair trial.

In *R (Ramda) v Secretary of State for the Home Department* [2002] EWHC 1278 the Divisional Court quashed the decision of the Home Secretary to extradite the applicant in circumstances where he had relied on materials of which the applicant had no knowledge.

Hearing within a reasonable time.   In *Magill v Porter* [2002] 2 WLR 37 the   **11.344**
House of Lords held that the right in Article 6(1) to a determination within a reasonable time is an independent right which is not to be seen as part of the overriding right to a fair trial, nor does it require the person concerned to show that he

has been prejudiced by the delay. Lord Hope, with whom the rest of their Lordships agreed, stated that Article 6(1) creates a number of rights which, although closely related, can and should be considered separately. Thus, he said it is no answer to a complaint that one of the rights was breached that the others were not. The only question, he concluded, was whether, having regard to all the circumstances of the case, the time taken to determine the person's rights and obligations was unreasonable. In *Dyer v Watson* [2002] 3 WLR 1488 the Privy Council stated that 'the threshold of proving a breach of the reasonable time requirement is a high one, not easily crossed' (para 52). Lord Bingham outlined the approach in any case where a breach is alleged. The first step is to consider the period of time which has elapsed. It is only if that period is one which, on its face and without more, gives grounds for real concern is it necessary for the court to enquire any further. If that high threshold is passed, first, the court must look into the detailed facts and circumstances of the particular case, and, second, the state must explain and justify any lapse of time which appears to be excessive. However, Lord Bingham noted that there is no obligation on the state to show that it has acted 'with all due diligence and expedition', but a marked lack of expedition, if unjustified, will point towards a breach of the reasonable time requirement. Similarly, Lord Rodger said that the 'test is whether the proceedings have been, or can be, completed within a reasonable time, not whether they could or should have been completed sooner'.

The Privy Council in *Darmalingum v The State* [2000] 1 WLR 2303 held that the right to a 'fair hearing within a reasonable time by an independent and impartial tribunal' contains three separate guarantees. Thus the Board said that it is no answer to a complaint that there was a breach of a disposal within a reasonable time that the defendant was convicted after a fair hearing by a proper court. The Board stated that even where the defendant's guilt was 'manifest' that factor could not justify or excuse a breach of the guarantee of a disposal within a reasonable time. However, in *Flowers v The Queen* [2000] 1 WLR 2396 the Privy Council stated that the right to a fair trial within a reasonable time is not a separate guarantee but, rather, that the three elements form part of one embracing form of protection afforded to the individual, which itself must be balanced against the public interest in the attainment of justice. Consequently, in deciding whether the defendant's conviction should be quashed because of a lengthy period of delay the Board held that it was entitled to take into account the consideration that the defendant was 'clearly guilty of a very serious crime'. The Privy Council considered these conflicting decisions in *Mills v HM Advocate* [2002] 3 WLR 1597. It held that the right to a fair trial within a reasonable time was a separate guarantee and concluded that the proposition in *Flowers* that the choice of remedy should be influenced by balancing the interests of the defendant against the public interest was incorrect. On the other hand, it said that the proposition in *Darmalingum* that the normal remedy is to quash the conviction goes too far. Rather, it is simply one of a variety of possible remedies, the choice between which must depend on the circumstances of each case (see also *Dyer v Watson* [2002] 3 WLR 1488, para 121). It noted that different considerations apply in a case of pre-trial delay to the case of delay between the date of conviction and an appeal. In this regard it said that there was no precedent for the setting aside of a conviction which has been upheld on appeal as a sound conviction on the ground that there was an unreasonable delay between the date of conviction and the hearing of the appeal. On the facts it held that a reduction of the appellant's sentence by nine months in order to compensate him for the effects of the delay between his conviction and the hearing of his appeal was an appropriate and sufficient remedy. The issue of the appropriate remedy for a breach of the reasonable time requirement in respect of pre-trial/conviction delay did not arise in *Mills* and, although discussed, was not decided by the Privy Council in *Dyer v Watson* [2002] 3 WLR 1488.

In *R v HM Advocate* 2002 SLT 834 the High Court of Justiciary, Appeal Court, held that pre-trial delay which breached the reasonable time requirement did not automatically require discontinuance of the trial. Discontinuance was not the only available remedy, the entire criminal process could still comply with the Convention.

In *Attorney-General's Reference (No 2 of 2001)* [2001] 1 WLR 1869 the Court of Appeal stated that the relevant time for determining whether a charge was brought within a reasonable time would, ordinarily, commence when the defendant was charged or served with a summons. However, there would be situations where a broader approach would be necessary to give effect to Article 6(1). There could be a period prior to being formally charged where the accused has been substantially affected by the actions of the state so as to be in substance in no different position from a man who had been charged (see, for example, *Deweer v Belgium* (1980) 2 EHRR 439). The Court of Appeal held that, in general, proceedings could not be stayed on the ground that there had been a breach of the reasonable time requirement in Article 6(1) unless the accused could demonstrate prejudice arising from the delay.

The High Court of Justiciary in *Mitchell v HM Advocate* [2001] SCCR 110 held that a delay of nearly two years in the bringing of a prosecution for social security fraud did not violate Article 6; the trial occurred within a reasonable time. This case did not merit a high prioritisation in the prosecutor's list. There was no failure or unreasonableness in the prosecution's handling of the matter. See also *HM Advocate v McGlinchey* [2000] SLT 995; *Smith v HM Advocate* (2000) SCCR 926; and *HM Advocate v Workman* (2000) JC 383.

In *Magill* the House of Lords held that a period of eight years and five months from the commencement of the auditor's investigation to the decision of the

Divisional Court in the appeal from the auditor's decision did not breach the reasonable time requirement. Particular significance was placed on the fact that it had not been suggested that the auditor had caused the delay at any stage by inactivity and the need for a thorough investigation given the importance of the investigation to all parties, including those who were at risk of being surcharged, and its obvious political sensitivity.

In *Valentine v HM Advocate* [2002] JC 58 the High Court of Justiciary held that a delay of 23 months between the commencement of the investigation and trial did not breach the defendant's right to a fair trial within a reasonable period of time.

In *Attorney-General's Reference (No 2 of 2001)* [2001] 1 WLR 1869 the Court of Appeal stated that ordinarily the commencement of proceedings to determine whether a charge was brought within a reasonable time was either when a defendant was summoned or charged. However, there would be situations where a broader approach would be necessary to give effect to Article 6(1). There could be a period prior to being formally charged where the accused has been substantially affected by the actions of the state so as to be in substance in no different position from a man who had been charged (see, for example, *Deweer v Belgium* (1980) 2 EHRR 439). The Court of Appeal held that, in general, proceedings could not be stayed on the ground that there had been a breach of the reasonable time requirement in Article 6(1) unless the accused could demonstrate prejudice arising from the delay. The relevant time would, ordinarily, commence when the defendant was charged or served with a summons. However, in some cases a broader approach had to be taken.

11.344A **Pre-trial publicity.** In *Montgomery v HM Advocate* [2001] 2 WLR 779 the Privy Council stated that in determining the effect of pre-trial publicity under Article 6 the only issue to be addressed was the right of the defendant to a fair trial; no assessment of the weight to be given to the public interest came into the exercise. It said that the decisive question was whether the doubts raised about the impartiality of the tribunal were objectively justified, and was not confined to the residual effect of the pre-trial publicity on the minds of each juror since account had to be taken of the role which the trial judge would play to ensure that the defendants would receive a fair trial. In most cases the likely effect of any warnings or directions given to the jury would be the critical issue.

11.346 **Right to silence and self-incrimination.** The Privy Council upheld the appeal of the Procurator Fiscal in *Brown v Stott* [2001] 2 WLR 817. It decided that the right not to incriminate oneself is not an absolute right and that section 172(2)(a) did not represent a disproportionate legislative response to the problem of maintaining road safety. Emphasis was placed on the fact that section 172(2)(a) provides for the putting of a single question, the answer to which cannot of itself incriminate the suspect, since it is not without more an offence to drive a car. It was noted that the section does not sanction prolonged questioning about the facts alleged to give rise to criminal offences (as was the case in *Saunders v United Kingdom* (1996) 23 EHRR 313) and the penalty for declining to answer under the section is moderate and non-custodial. Finally, if there was any evidence of improper coercion or oppression such as might give rise to unreliable admissions the trial judge would have ample power to exclude evidence of the admission.

For a discussion of *Brown v Stott*, see R Pillay, 'Self-incrimination and Article 6: The Decision of the Privy Council in *Procurator Fiscal v Brown*' [2001] EHRLR 78.

In *DPP v Wilson, The Times*, 21 March 2001, the Court of Appeal held that, following *Brown*, there was no ground under Article 6 for excluding a response to a section 172(2)(b) notice which requires a person to identify the driver at the time of the alleged offence.

It has been suggested that the reasoning in *Brown v Stott* and *DPP v Wilson* is inconsistent with the decision of the Court of Human Rights in *Heaney and McGuinness v Ireland* (2001) 33 EHRR 12 decided two weeks after *Brown* but before *Wilson* (see A Ashworth, 'The Self-Incrimination Saga' [2001] 5 Arch News 5). In *Heaney and McGuinness* it was held that the threat of a prison sentence for failing to provide potentially incriminating information destroyed the 'very essence' of the privilege against self-incrimination and as a result was a breach of Article 6. This point was not considered in *Brown* or *Wilson*. It is arguable that, whereas an adverse inference drawn from a failure to provide information may be permissible, the imposition of a penalty will normally destroy the 'very essence' of the privilege (see, generally, A Jennings, 'Self-Incrimination and the Right to Silence', in Starmer, Strange and Whittaker (eds), *Criminal Justice, Police Powers and Human Rights* (Blackstone, 2001), 215).

In *R v Everson* [2001] EWCA Crim 896 the Court of Appeal decided that the defendant's right of silence was not breached where the judge directed the jury not to convict on silence alone but did not expressly tell the jury not to convict mainly on the basis of the defendant's failure to speak at interview. It observed, however, that the JSB specimen direction should be revised to include that requirement; see also *R v F (Mark Frank)* [2001] 1 Cr App R 17.

In *Attorney-General's Reference (No 7 of 2000)* [2001] 2 Cr App R 286 the Court of Appeal held that the use by the Crown, in criminal proceedings against a bankrupt for an offence under the Insolvency Act 1986, of documents which were delivered to the Official Receiver under compulsion but which did not contain statements made by the bankrupt under compulsion, did not violate the bankrupt's right to a fair trial.

The Court of Appeal in *R v Kearns* [2002] 1 WLR 2815 carried out an extensive survey of the recent Strasbourg and domestic jurisprudence on the scope of the right to silence and the right not to incriminate oneself and concluded that there was an important distinction between the compulsory production of documents or other material which had an existence independent of the will of the suspect or accused person and statements that he has had to make under compulsion. In the former case there is no infringement of the right to silence and the right not to incriminate oneself; see *Attorney-General's Reference (No 7 of 2000)* [2002] 2 Cr App R 286. In the latter kind of situation there could be an infringement depending on the circumstances. A law will not be likely to infringe the right to silence or not to incriminate oneself if it demands the production of information for an administrative purpose or in the course of an extrajudicial enquiry. However if the information so produced is or could be used in subsequent judicial proceedings, whether criminal or civil, then the use of the information in such proceedings could breach those rights and so make the trial unfair. Whether that is the case would depend on all the circumstances of the case, but in particular

- whether the information demanded is factual or an admission of guilt; and
- whether the demand for the information and its subsequent use in proceedings is proportionate to the particular social or economic problem that the relevant law is intended to address.

The Court of Appeal held that section 354(3)(a) of the Insolvency Act 1986, which makes it an offence if a bankrupt fails to account for a loss once he has been requested to do so by the Official Receiver, did not breach the right to remain silent or not to incriminate oneself because: (a) the demand was made in the course of an extrajudicial procedure not in order to provide evidence to enable another charge to be proved; (b) the information obtained could not be used in subsequent criminal proceedings against the bankrupt; (c) even if section 354(3)(a) did infringe the right to silence and/or the right not to incriminate oneself, this limited restriction was justified as it was intended to deal with the social and economic problem of bankrupts. The Court said that there was an obvious need for a statutory regime that imposes a duty on a bankrupt to co-operate in providing full and accurate information to the person charged with administering the bankrupt's estate. Equally clearly, that duty should be backed up by appropriate statutory sanctions to ensure that the duty is carried out properly. Section 354(3)(a) was a proportionate legislative response to the problem of administering and investigating bankrupt estates. See also *Beckles v United Kingdom*, *The Times*, 15 October 2002).

In *R v Allen* [2001] 4 All ER 768 the House of Lords held that a request for information under section 20(1) of the Taxes Management Act 1970 could not constitute a violation of the right against self-incrimination.

For a general discussion of these issues, see A Jennings, A Ashworth and B Emmerson, 'Silence and Safety: The Impact of Human Rights Law' [2000] Crim LR 879.

Presumption of innocence. In *Parker v DPP* [2001] RTR 16 the Divisional   **11.347**
Court held that the irrebuttable presumption, under section 15 of the Road
Traffic Act 1988, that the quantity of alcohol at the time of driving was no less
than that in the sample taken at the police station, did not infringe the presumption of innocence under Article 6(2).

In *R v Williams (Gary Ian)*, *The Times*, 30 March 2001, the Court of Appeal said
that an insignificant omission of an element of the offence from the judge's direction to the jury did not amount to a breach of Articles 6(1) or (2) of the
Convention. A legal misdirection or non-direction was not significant unless it
was possible that the jury would have acquitted but for the error of law.

In *R v Lambert* [2001] 2 WLR 211, 220, para 19, the Court of Appeal held that
the requirement under section 2 of the Homicide Act 1957 on the defendant to
prove, on the balance of probabilities, that he is suffering from diminished responsibility did not contravene Article 6. However, the decision of the Court of
Appeal that the presumptions in sections 5(4) and 28 of the Misuse of Drugs Act
1971 placing a legal burden on the accused were compatible with Article 6(2) was
reversed by the House of Lords at [2001] 3 WLR 206. It was pointed out that the
imposition of a legal burden meant that the accused must be convicted even if he
persuaded the jury that it was as likely to be true as not that he did not know that
packages in his possession contained drugs. As a result, the transfer of the legal
burden of proof did not satisfy the principle of proportionality. However, the
House of Lords applied section 3 of the Human Rights Act to interpret sections
5(4) and 28 as placing only an evidential burden on the accused; see, further,
Supplement, para 4.28.

The Divisional Court in *L v DPP* [2002] 3 WLR 863 held that the imposition of
a legal burden on the defendant under section 139 of the Criminal Justice Act
1988 to prove on the balance of probabilities that he had good reason for carrying
a knife in a public place was consistent with Article 6(2) in view of the strong public interest in bladed articles not being carried in public without good reason. The
court noted that, in contrast to sections 28(2) and (3) of the Misuse of Drugs Act
1971, under section 139 the prosecution had to prove that the defendant *knowingly* had the offending article in his possession.

The Court of Appeal in *R v Carass* [2002] 1 WLR 1714 held that in relation to the
offence under section 206(1) of the Insolvency Act 1986 of concealing property
or debts in anticipation of the winding up of a company, the burden under section
206(4) on the defendant 'to prove' that he had no intent to defraud should, pursuant to section 3(1) of the Human Rights Act, be read as 'adduce sufficient evidence', there being no justification for the imposition of a persuasive burden in
relation to this important element of the offence. In *R v Daniel* [2002] EWCA
Crim 959 the Court of Appeal considered itself bound by the decision in *Carass*

to hold that section 352 of the Insolvency Act 1986 which provides that a person is not guilty of an offence under section 354 (concealment by a bankrupt of a debt due to him) if he proves that he had no intent to defraud or conceal the state of his affairs, imposed an evidential burden of proof on the defendant. However, the Court of Appeal said that but for *Carass* it could not have construed section 352 as imposing only an evidential burden. Auld LJ, giving the judgment of the Court, said that the words 'if he proves' must, as a matter of plain English, mean more than the evidential raising of an issue for the prosecution to refute beyond reasonable doubt. He cautioned against the courts striving for compatibility by so changing the meaning of those words as to give them a sense that they could not, in the sense intended by section 3(1), possibly bear.

The Court of Appeal in *Gough v Chief Constable of Derbyshire* [2002] 3 WLR 389 held that it was permissible under Article 6 to require a person subject to an international banning order to demonstrate that foreign travel during the period of a prescribed match was not for the purpose of attending the match. The object of the foreign travel is likely to be within the exclusive knowledge of the would-be traveller, and proof of the object should not involve untoward difficulty.

In *International Transport Roth GmbH v Home Secretary* [2002] 3 WLR 344 a majority of the Court of Appeal held that the burden imposed on carriers to show that they did not know, and had no reasonable grounds of suspecting, that an illegal entrant was concealed in their vehicle was not a disproportionate interference with the carrier's rights under Article 6(2).

In *Sliney v Havering LBC* [2002] EWCA Crim 2558 the Court of Appeal decided that the legal burden placed on the defendant under section 92(5) of the Trade Marks Act 1994 was necessary, just and proportionate.

11.350 **Legal advice.** In *R (M and La Rose) v Commissioner of Police* [2001] EWHC Admin 553 (permission to appeal refused at [2001] EWCA Civ 1825) it was held that the provision of a cell (rather than an interview room) was only a 'theoretical or illusory' breach of Article 6(3)(b) of the Convention. Similar reasoning was applied when the only telephone available to the applicant to call his solicitor was on the desk of the custody sergeant, who remained present throughout the call. In the circumstances, there was no violation of the confidentiality of solicitor–client communications and the applicant had not been denied adequate facilities for the preparation of his defence.

The Court of Appeal in *R v Thakrar* [2001] EWCA Crim 1096 held that the mere fact that the appellant's solicitors had fallen below the level of reasonably competent solicitors in the way in which they had prepared for the trial did not itself mean that the appellant's conviction was unsafe. On the facts the appellant had not been prejudiced by the way his defence was advanced at trial, and he had not been deprived of a fair trial.

In *McLean v Procurator Fiscal* [2001] 1 WLR 2425 the defendants complained that they had been deprived of effective legal assistance in criminal proceedings by the fixed payment system under Scottish criminal legal aid. The Privy Council held that, in the absence of proof that the fixed fee system had given rise to actual or inevitable prejudice at trial, there was no breach of Article 6.

In *R v Oates* [2002] 1 WLR 2833 the Court of Appeal held that Article 6(3)(c) did not require that the appellant be granted legal aid to renew orally her application for leave to appeal against her murder conviction where there were no exceptional circumstances.

In *R (Van Hoogstraten) v Governor of Belmarsh Prison, The Times*, 5 November 2002, the refusal of the governor to allow a prison visit from an Italian advocate instructed by the claimant as his legal adviser breached Article 6(3).

Conduct of trial.   The House of Lords decided in *R v A* [2000] 1 WLR 789   **11.352** that, as a general rule, the effect of the admission or exclusion of evidence on the fairness of a trial was to be judged after its completion in the context of the proceedings as a whole. However, it was undesirable that a vulnerable witness (such as the complainant in a rape trial) should be exposed to the risk of having to give evidence again if the first trial was found to be unfair; and Lord Hope also expressed the view that any question of incompatibility with Article 6 was an issue of general public importance likely to affect the other trials and that it was in the interests of all parties that the issue be determined in advance of the trial.

In *R v A (No 2)* [2001] 2 WLR 1546 the House of Lords held that the test of admissibility of evidence of previous sexual relations between an accused and a complainant under section 41(3)(c) of the Youth Justice and Criminal Evidence Act 1999 was whether the evidence (and questioning in relation to it) was so relevant to the issue of consent that to exclude it would endanger the fairness of the trial under Article 6 of the Convention. If that test was satisfied, the evidence should not be excluded.

The House of Lords in *R (McCann) v Manchester Crown Court* [2002] 3 WLR 1313 held that Article 6(1) does not require the automatic exclusion of hearsay evidence consisting of statements from individuals who could not—or would not, because they were too frightened—be identified on the basis that anti-social behavior orders affected civil rights.

The Court of Appeal in *R v Loveridge, The Times*, 3 May 2001, held that the admission of evidence, in that case video recordings, that had been obtained in breach of Article 8 was only relevant to the safety of a conviction if it had interfered with the right of the defendant to a fair hearing.

In *HM Advocate v Smith (Peter Thomson)* [2000] SCR 910 the High Court of Justiciary held that, although the anonymity of witnesses would not of itself be incompatible with a fair trial, police officers as anonymous witnesses should only be used in exceptional circumstances. Anonymity of police officers could be justified where it was strictly necessary to ensure operational effectiveness and where defence rights were respected. On the facts, an application for police officers to give evidence anonymously was allowed.

In *R v Porter* [2001] EWCA Crim 2699 the Court of Appeal stated that judges would do well to reflect before incautiously refusing applications for adjournments so that expert evidence can be made available to the defence. The Court said that the interests of defendants and the need for vigilance in complying with Article 6 call for careful analysis of the implications before a ruling is given.

11.353   *Agents provocateurs.*   In *R v Shannon* [2001] 1 WLR 51 the Court of Appeal rejected the argument that trials involving incitement or instigation by an *agent provocateur* were by definition unfair under Article 6. This approach was approved by the House of Lords in *R v Looseley* [2001] 1 WLR 2060 in which it was made clear that the English law of entrapment had not been modified by the right to a fair trial under Article 6. Although entrapment was not a defence, a prosecution founded on entrapment was an abuse of the court's process. When deciding whether conduct amounts to 'state-created crime' the question was whether, in all the circumstances, the conduct of the police was so seriously improper as to bring the administration of justice into disrepute. The House of Lords did not accept that the *Teixeira de Castro* case (see Main Work, para 11.216) stated any general principle that there was a breach of Article 6 whenever police officers gave a person an opportunity to break the law and he took advantage of that opportunity in circumstances in which it appeared that he would have behaved in the same way had someone else given him the opportunity. If a person freely takes advantage of an opportunity to break the law given to him by a police officer, the police officer is not to be regarded as being guilty of 'entrapment'.

11.354   **Interpreters.**   In *R (Bozkurt) v Thames Magistrates' Court* [2002] RTR 15 the Divisional Court said that it was undesirable for the same interpreter to translate during the drink-drive procedure at a police station and then to translate for the same defendant when interviewed by the court duty solicitor, without the defendant's consent. In those circumstances the interpreter was a potential prosecution witness who might be called to give evidence that the proper procedures has occurred at the station. However, the court held that the defendant was fully protected from any prejudice or unfairness by the interpreter's duty of confidentiality in respect of what had occurred at the interview and by the judge's ability to exclude unfair evidence at the trial.

The giving of reasons.   In *R (Jermyn) v Wirral Magistrates' Court* [2001] Cr App   **11.354A**
R(S) 485 the Administrative Court held that the general rule, that magistrates
were not under a duty to give reasons for their decision to commit a defendant to
the Crown Court for sentence, withstood Article 6(1) or (3)(b) of the European
Convention of Human Rights because any person committed for sentence still
had the opportunity in the Crown Court to make full representation as to the appropriate punishment.

Sentencing.   In *HM Advocate v McIntosh* [2001] 3 WLR 107 the Privy Council   **11.355**
held that a person against whom a confiscation order was sought under section
3(2) of the Proceeds of Crime (Scotland) Act 1995 was not 'charged' or 'accused
of' any 'criminal offence' and therefore Article 6(2) had no application to the
prosecutor's application for a confiscation order.

The Privy Council in *McIntosh* expressly disagreed with the conclusion of the
Court of Appeal in *R v Benjafield* [2001] 3 WLR 75 that Article 6(2) was a specific
example of the more general obligations in Article 6(1) and therefore the confiscation procedure had to be considered on the assumption that it was subject to the
requirements of both Article 6(1) and (2). The approach of the Court of Appeal
in *Benjafield* would, however, appear to be consistent with that adopted by the
Court of Human Rights in *Zoon v Netherlands* (Judgment of 7 December 2000)
where the Court stated that

> As the requirements of 6(3) are to be seen as particular aspects of the right to a fair
> trial guaranteed by Article 6(1), the Court will examine the applicant's complaints
> under 6(1) and 3(b) taken together.

See also *Quinn v Ireland* (Judgment of 21 December 2000).

The Privy Council stated that since Article 6(1) does not cease to apply on conviction, but continues during the imposition of sentence and any appeal, the defendant in any application for a confiscation order, following his conviction for a
drug trafficking offence, would be entitled to all the protection afforded to him by
Article 6(1). That in itself, would ensure that any reverse onus provision was fairly
applied in the given case.

See also *Phillips v United Kingdom* (2001) 11 BHRC 280, discussed further at
Supplement, para 11.238.

The House of Lords in *R v Benjafield; R v Rezvi* [2002] 2 WLR 235 held, following
Phillips v UK and *McIntosh v Lord Advocate*, that confiscation proceedings under
section 77AA of the Criminal Justice 1988 Act and section 4(3) of the Drug
Trafficking Act 1994 are part of the sentencing process following a conviction and
does not involve a fresh criminal charge. Consequently, Article 6(2) is not engaged,
although the accused remains entitled to the protection afforded by Article 6(1).
In that regard their Lordships stated that the burden imposed on the defendant to

establish the innocent source of his assets under the confiscatory procedures devised by Parliament are a fair and proportionate response to the need to protect the public interest. Critical to this conclusion, it said, was that under both Acts, the judge must be astute to avoid injustice. If there is or might be a serious or real risk of injustice, he must not make a confiscation order.

In *R (Anderson) v Secretary of State for the Home Department* [2002] 3 WLR 1800 the House of Lords held that the setting of the tariff in the case of a mandatory life prisoner was a sentencing exercise and therefore should be subject to the constraints of Article 6 following the decision of the European Court in *Stafford v United Kingdom* (2002) 35 EHRR 32. The House of Lords went on to grant a declaration of incompatibility.

In *R (West) v Parole Board, The Times*, 21 November 2002, the Court of Appeal held that the decision of the Parole Board to recall a prisoner released on licence was not a criminal charge within the scope of Article 6(1).

11.356 **Appeals.** In *R (Shields) v Crown Court at Liverpool* [2001] UKHRR 610 it was held that the fact that decisions made in the course of a criminal trial were not susceptible to judicial review was not a breach of Article 6. The defendant had a right of appeal at the conclusion of the trial and, if the trial was unfair, the conviction would be quashed. See also *R (Regentford) v Canterbury Crown Court* [2001] HRLR 18.

11.357 *R v Davis and Rowe* is now reported at [2001] 1 Cr App R 8. In *R v Williams (Gary Ian), The Times*, 30 March 2001, it was held that a breach of Article 6(2) did not render a conviction automatically unsafe and the court was entitled to inquire whether the result would have been different if the jury had been properly directed.

For a general discussion of the change in the 'safety test' on appeals, see A Jennings, A Ashworth and B Emmerson, 'Silence and Safety: The Impact of Human Rights Law' [2000] Crim LR 879.

Whilst the right to a fair trial guaranteed by Article 6 is an absolute right, the subsidiary rights comprised within that article are not absolute. Consequently, it is always necessary to consider all the facts and the whole history of the proceedings in a particular case to judge whether a defendant's right to a fair trial has been infringed or not (*R v Forbes* [2001] 2 WLR 1, HL). If on such consideration it is concluded that a defendant's right to a fair trial has been infringed, a conviction will be held to be unsafe within the meaning of section 2 of the Criminal Appeal Act 1968. See also *R v Togher, The Times*, 21 November 2000.

In *R v Lambert* [2001] 3 WLR 206 the majority of the House of Lords held that an alleged breach of Convention rights by the trial court could not be relied upon as a ground of appeal in respect of a conviction which took place before the Act came into force. The Convention could only be relied on if the alleged breach was by the prosecuting authority. See, generally, Supplement, para 3.75A. This decision was followed, with some reluctance, by a majority of the House of Lords in *R v Kansal (No 2)* [2001] 3 WLR 1562; see further Supplement, para 3.75A. Furthermore, in *R v Lyons* [2002] UKHL 44 the House of Lords decided that the convictions of the defendants were not unsafe under section 2 of the Criminal Appeal Act 1968 even though the European Court held in *Saunders v United Kingdom* (1996) 23 EHRR 313 and *IJL v United Kingdom* (2000) 33 EHRR 11 that the admission of evidence breached Article 6.

In *R v Craven* [2001] 2 Cr App R 12 the prosecution's failure to disclose fingerprint evidence rendered the trial unfair. However, this was cured on appeal as the Court of Appeal was able to look at and consider all the evidence including evidence which was unavailable at trial.

(c) Education

In *R v Richmond LBC, ex p JC* [2001] ELR 21, CA, it was held that the right to express a preference as to the school that a child should attend belonged to the child's parents. However, it said that the right could not properly be described as a 'civil right' for the purposes of Article 6.   **11.358**

In *R v Hertfordshire County Council, ex p A* [2001] ELR 239 Maurice Kay J held that a school governors' disciplinary panel was entitled to use one of the local authority's in-house solicitors as a legal adviser during the hearing. Article 6 was not violated because the panel had not been overly influenced by the legal adviser so that it could no longer be regarded as independent and impartial.

In *R (B) v Head Teacher and Governing Body of Alperton Community School* [2001] ELR 359 Newman J decided that Article 6 did not apply to exclusion proceedings by the Independent Appeal Panel because they were disciplinary and did not involve the determination of a criminal charge.

In *R (S) v Brent London Borough Council* [2001] EWHC Admin 384 Scott Baker J held that a local authority's involvement in the setting up of an independent appeal panel that heard cases involving the exclusion of pupils from school and received guidance on exclusion and reinstatement from the Secretary of State for Education did not breach the common law duty to ensure independence and impartiality. The Court of Appeal at [2002] EWCA Civ 693 agreed and noted that there may in any event be difficulties in the light of the present Strasbourg jurisprudence in holding that a school exclusion appeal panel is a body which determines a pupil's civil rights, whether as to education or to a reputation (*S v Brent London Borough Council* [2002] EWCA Civ 693).

In *R v Secretary of State for Education and Employment, ex p B, The Times*, 8 June 2001, Newman J held that Article 6 did not apply to exclusion proceedings by the Independent Appeal Panel because they were disciplinary and did not involve the determination of a criminal charge.

(d) Employment, discrimination and disciplinary bodies

11.361   The Employment Appeal Tribunal in *Scanfuture UK Ltd v Secretary of State for Trade and Industry* [2001] IRLR 416 held that new procedures for appointing lay members of employment tribunals, for a renewable period of three years, which included an element of open competition, and a different system of removal which included judicial involvement, meant that those tribunals were now compliant with Article 6.

In *Robinson v The Home Office*, 3 May 2002, the Employment Appeal Tribunal held that the applicant was deprived of a fair trial when her application for an adjournment was refused and her claim on the merits dismissed in her absence notwithstanding the fact she had submitted a medical certificate indicating she was medically unfit to attend the hearing.

In *Lawal v Northern Spirit* [2002] ICR 1507 the Employment Appeal Tribunal held that a lay member of it was not biased merely because he had previously sat as a lay member with one of the parties' counsel who sat as its part-time chairman. See also *Skelton v Christian Salvesen* [2002] All ER(D) 137, EAT, also discussed at Supplement, para 11.68.

In *Melbourne v Ministry of Defence*, 14 January 2002, the Employment Appeal Tribunal held that in view of *Pellegrin v France* it was legitimate to exclude members of the armed services from access to an employment tribunal to complain of unfair dismissal.

A two-year delay in commencing disciplinary proceedings against a general practitioner (from the date of notification of the complaint) was held not to be a breach of the reasonable time requirement (*Haikel v General Medical Council* [2002] Lloyd's Med Rep 415). The Privy Council said that only in exceptional circumstances would a stay be granted in such proceedings on the grounds of delay, in view of the important countervailing public interest that allegations and serious misconduct should be heard and determined rather than stayed.

In *Madan v The General Medical Council* [2001] Lloyd's Rep Med 539 the Administrative Court held that Article 6 was engaged by a hearing before the Interim Orders Committee of the General Medical Council to determine whether a doctor charged with misconduct should be suspended or made subject to any other interim order pending determination of the charge. The court held that Article 6 required the committee to weigh the interests of the doctor against the need for public protection and to consider whether a suspension order was proportionate to the risk identified. The Privy Council in *Chaudhury v GMC* [2002] UKPC 41 agreed that the Interim Orders Committee was a tribunal which determined a civil right of the doctor, namely his right to practise medicine. However it reserved its position on whether the Committee in coming to its decision whether to suspend registration had to comply with the Convention doctrine of proportionality. In this regard, Lord Hutton said that in relation to determinations by a committee of the Council there is little or no difference between the requirement of the common law that the committee must act in a way which is fair and reasonable and the Convention doctrine of proportionality.

(e) Family law

In *Re M (A Child) (Secure Accommodation Order)* [2001] FCR 692 the Court of Appeal stated that the minimum rights described in Article 6 should be afforded as a matter of procedural fairness to a child facing an application for a secure accommodation order. However, it said the procedural fairness must be measured against the realities of the case. In *Re S (A Child) (Adoption Proceedings: Joinder of Father)* [2001] 1 FLR 302 it was held that a failure to join a child's father as a respondent to adoption proceedings would arguably infringe his right to a fair trial under Article 6. See also *Re S* (2001) 1 FLR 302 and *Re H (A Child) (Adoption: Disclosure)* [2001] 1 FLR 646 which are discussed further at Supplement, para 13.156; and *B v United Kingdom* (2002) 34 EHRR 529, discussed at Supplement, paras 11.232 and 11.234.

11.364

The Court of Appeal in *Re D (A Child)* [2002] EWCA Civ 448 said that Article 6 reinforced section 1(2) of the Children Act 1989 by giving an entitlement to a fair hearing within a reasonable time. It noted that Strasbourg jurisprudence made it clear, in relation to children, that time must not be allowed to go by that would itself be determinative of the case.

In *Re S (Children: Care Order: Implementation of Care Plan)* [2002] 2 AC 291 Lord Nicholls identified two circumstances concerning childcare decisions made by a local authority pursuant to its powers under the Children Act 1989 in which the right of access to a court under Article 6 is capable of being infringed:

- the absence of effective machinery for protecting the civil rights of young children who have no parent or guardian able and willing to become involved in questioning a care decision made by a local authority. Such children, in practice, have no way of initiating judicial review proceedings to challenge the decision; and
- the inability of parents and children alike to challenge in court (by way of appeal) care decisions, however fundamental, made by a local authority while a care order is in force.

Lord Nicholls said it was doubtful whether judicial review will always meet the standard of judicial control required by Article 6(1) even if the review is conducted with the heightened scrutiny discussed in *R (Daly) v Secretary of State for the Home Department* [2001] 2 AC 532. He noted, however, that the level of judicial control required by Article 6(1) will depend upon the extent to which the particular decision affects those private law rights of the parent and children which they have retained after the child has been taken into care.

The right to a fair trial is not confined to the 'purely judicial' part of the proceedings and, if a jointly instructed expert's report was likely to influence the court's assessment of fact, there might be a breach of Article 6 if a litigant was denied the opportunity to examine and comment on documents considered by the expert and to cross-examine witnesses interviewed by the expert; see *Re C (Care Proceedings: Disclosure of Local Authority's Decision-Making Process)* [2002] 2 FCR 673 (Munby J).

11.366 In *Clibbery v Allan* [2002] 2 WLR 1511 the Court of Appeal held that a rule prohibiting the disclosure of family proceedings relating to property and finance in chambers would inappropriately interfere with rights under Article 6 (and Article 10). An injunction restraining the respondent from publicising such proceedings was discharged; see also Supplement, paras 15.245 and 15.274. Butler-Sloss P emphasised that 'long established principles of open justice . . . are entirely consistent with the Convention and which our exceptions do not . . . breach' (para 81).

In *R (S) v Plymouth City Council* [2002] 1 WLR 2583 the Court of Appeal noted the importance of a mother's right of access to legal advice to enable her to decide whether or not to exercise a right (to apply for the discharge of guardianship of her mentally handicapped son) which is likely to lead to legal proceedings against her (an application to displace her as the nearest relative) if she does so. In the absence of a clear and proper public objective against disclosure, the Court said that proper access to legal advice required that she should have access to the confidential information which would be relevant to the court's decision. On the facts the Court of Appeal held that the mother's right to respect for her family life coupled with her right to a fair trial constituted legitimate aims of interference with the son's right to respect for his private life.

11.366A It has been held that the 'judgment summons' procedure in use in the Family Division was not compatible with Article 6 (*Mubarak v Mubarak* [2001] 1 FLR 698) and as a result *Practice Direction (Committal Applications)* [2001] 2 All ER 704 has been given. This makes clear (at para 2) that

> In any family proceedings . . . in which a committal order may be made, including proceedings for the enforcement of an existing order by way of judgment summons or other process, full effect will be given to the Human Rights Act 1998 and to the

rights afforded under that Act. In particular, [Article 6 of the Convention] . . . is fully applicable to such proceedings.

(f) Health care

In *R (Wilkinson) v The Responsible Medical Officer, Broadmoor Hospital* [2002] 1 **11.367** WLR 419 the Court of Appeal held that the Administrative Court hearing a challenge brought by a detained mental-health patient against a decision for compulsory treatment should conduct a merits review on the evidence in order to comply with the requirements of Article 6.

In *R (Wooder) v Feggetter* [2002] 3 WLR 591 the Court of Appeal held that where a mental patient was to be given medical treatment against his consent, the doctor whose second opinion was required under section 58 of the Mental Health Act 1983 had to give written reasons for granting the necessary certificate.

(g) Housing

In *R (McLellan) v Bracknell Forest District Council* [2002] 2 WLR 1448 the Court **11.368** of Appeal held that Chapter 1 of Part V of the Housing Act 1996, which provided for introductory tenancies in the public housing sector, was compatible with Article 6, since the High Court was a court which had full jurisdiction in respect of the right of appeal from the review decision of the local housing authority. There was no question of making or applying policy, the reviewing officer simply determined whether the reasons for seeking possession were good.

In *St Brice v Southwark LBC* [2001] 1 WLR 1537 the Court of Appeal rejected the argument that issuing a warrant of possession without notice to the tenant was a breach of Article 6. The tenant's right to possession had been previously determined against him when a suspended possession order was made and the issue of the warrant was simply a step authorised to be taken to enforce the earlier order.

In *R (Cumpsty) v Rent Service* [2002] EWHC Admin 2526 Pitchford J decided that the scheme governing the determination of local reference rent provides a tenant with a fair and public hearing before an independent and impartial tribunal subject to the local authority and rent officer providing sufficient reasons.

Housing benefit review boards have been replaced by independent appeal tri- **11.369** bunals under Schedule 7 to the Child Support, Pensions and Social Security Act 2000 with effect from 2 July 2001. The view expressed in the Main Work that housing benefit review boards do not comply with the Article 6 obligation to ensure an independent and impartial tribunal was confirmed by the decision of Moses J in *R (Bewry) v Norwich City Council* [2002] HRLR 21 in which it was also held that the boards were not 'independent and impartial' at common law (see Supplement, para 11.65A).

(ha) Immigration and asylum

11.376A   In *R (Ramda) v The Secretary of State for the Home Department* [2002] EWHC
1278 the Divisional Court rejected the argument that the applicant could rely on
recourse to the European Court of Human Rights to correct any failure on the
part of the country seeking his extradition to accord him a fair trial. The
Divisional Court said the sole question in such cases was whether the approach
taken by the requesting state's courts to, in this case, the receipt of confession evidence, will itself be such as to create a real risk of a fundamentally unfair trial.

(hb) Local government law

11.371   **Licensing.**   In *R (Brogan) v Metropolitan Police* [2002] EWHC 2127 Davis J
held that where the police refused to grant a special exemption to the claimant's licensee of a public house, there was from an objective point of view no independent and impartial tribunal. However, the police were not making a primary
finding of fact and judicial review provided a sufficient review process to comply
with Article 6.

(i) Planning and environmental law

11.377   **Introduction.**   See *Chapman v United Kingdom* (2001) 10 BHRC 48, discussed
at Supplement, para 11.198.

11.380   **Plan-making powers.**   The processes by which the Secretary of State for the
Environment makes decisions under the Town and Country Planning Act 1990
and orders under the Transport and Works Act 1992, the Highways Act 1980 and
the Acquisition of Land Act 1981 were held to be compatible with Article 6 by the
House of Lords in *R (Alconbury Developments Ltd) v Secretary of State for the
Environment, Transport and the Regions* [2001] 2 WLR 1389. Their Lordships said
that planning matters are essentially matters of policy and expediency and not of
law. Consequently, whilst the Secretary of State is not impartial in the manner required by Article 6 because in each case his policy is in issue, their Lordships held
that the High Court's power to review the lawfulness and fairness of the decision
was sufficient to remedy the position.

In *Friends Provident Life Office v Secretary of State for the Environment, Transport
and the Regions* [2002] 1 WLR 1450 Forbes J said that there was no reason in principle why Article 6 should not extend to the administrative decision-making
process relating to a third party's objections to a planning application, provided it
directly affected his civil rights. He held that the planning authority's procedures,
when taken with the High Court's power of review, constituted a composite
process which met the requirements of Article 6. Similarly, in *R (Adlard and
Others) v Secretary of State for Environment, Transport and Regions* [2002] 1 WLR
2515 the Court of Appeal held that the rights of objectors under Article 6 are not

violated if a local planning authority refuses to accord them a public hearing, or indeed any form of oral hearing. The combination of the authority's initial decision-making process and judicial review by the High Court is sufficient to ensure compliance with Article 6. See also *R (Aggregate Industries UK Ltd) v English Nature* [2002] EWHC 908 and see, generally, J Findlay and S Bird, '*Alconbury* a Year On: Article 6 Challenges Face Stiff Uphill Struggle after Court of Appeal *Begum* and *Adlard* Adopts a Schematic Approach' [2002] JPL 1045; and T Corner and P Brown, 'Applying *Alconbury*: Article 6, Third Parties and Development Plans' [2002] JPL 661.

In *Bovis Homes Ltd v New Forest District Council* [2002] EWHC Admin 483 Ouseley J held that although the planning authority's adoption of a local plan affected a developer's rights to use and develop property, it did not give rise to a determination of them. Accordingly Article 6 was not engaged by that decision.

A delay of three years and six months in determining an application for planning permission was held to breach the applicant's right to have its civil rights determined within a reasonable time (*UK Coal Mining Ltd v Secretary of State for Local Government, Transport and the Regions* [2001] EWHC 912).

In *R (Ward) v Monmouthshire County Council* [2002] EWCA Civ 1915 the Court of Appeal held that the service of a notice of entry under section 64 of the Land Drainage Act 1991 and the availability of judicial review without more satisfied the landlord's rights under Article 6.

Land development. When a local authority determines its own planning application, its decision might not be subject to sufficient control by the court if there are disputed issues of fact (*R (Kathro) v Rhondda Cynon Taff County Borough Council* [2002] Env LR 15). In relation to fact-finding the differences between a planning authority and the Secretary of State were potentially important since there is no equivalent of the planning inspector in the local planning authority's decision-making process. Contrast *R (Vetterlien) v Hampshire County Council* [2001] EWHC Admin 560 where Sullivan J held that the procedure adopted by a local authority when granting planning permission to construct an energy recovery unit and waste transfer station, together with judicial review, were sufficient to meet the requirements of Article 6. **11.381A**

(k) Prison law

In *R (Daly) v Secretary of State for Home Department* [2001] 2 AC 532 the House of Lords held that there was no justification for routinely excluding all prisoners whilst their privileged correspondence was searched. **11.384**

The House of Lords in *R (Anderson) v Secretary of State for the Home Department* [2002] 3 WLR 1800 held that the setting of the tariff in the case of a mandatory life prisoner was a sentencing exercise and therefore should be subject to the constraints of Article 6 following the decision of the European Court in *Stafford v United Kingdom* (2002) 35 EHRR 32. The House of Lords went on to grant a declaration of incompatibility.

In *R (Al-Hassan) v Secretary of State for the Home Department* [2002] 1 WLR 545 the Court of Appeal held that prison disciplinary proceedings conducted by the prison governor were not criminal proceedings under Article 6 but took the view that the imposition by a prison governor of 21 days of additional imprisonment was close to the borderline but within the margin of discretion to be extended to the prison authorities. However, in *Ezeh and Connor v United Kingdom* (2002) 35 EHRR 691 a period of seven days was found to be a criminal charge (see Supplement, para 11.179). As a result the Government enacted the Prison (Amendment) Rules 2002, SI 2002/2116, which require a governor who is considering imposing a disciplinary penalty of additional days to refer the charge to an adjudicator.

Newman J in *Al-Hasan* said at first instance ([2001] HRLR 706) that the prisoners would have had no greater right to legal representation under Article 6(3) than they had under the common law, as stated in *R v Secretary of State for the Home Department, ex p Tarrant* [1985] 1 QB 251. This decision cannot be reconciled with *Ezeh and Connors v United Kingdom* (2002) 35 EHRR 691 which held that the refusal of the governor to allow prisoners legal representation at the disciplinary hearing breached Article 6(3)(c).

The Court of Appeal held in *R (West) v Parole Board, The Times*, 21 November 2002, that a decision of the Parole Board to recall a prisoner released on licence was not a criminal charge under Article 6(1).

In *R (Ponting) v Governor of HM Prison Whitemoor* [2001] EWHC Admin 241 Newman J accepted that it was possible that, according to the nature of a disability, a prisoner's case preparation could be seriously and substantially damaged by restricted access to computer facilities. However, the Court of Appeal at [2002] EWCA Civ 224 held that the conditions in the compact regulating the prisoner's use of the computer did not breach his right of access to the court.

Appendix 1: The Canadian Charter of Rights

(2) The scope of the rights

(a) Fundamental justice

11.391 It is a principle of fundamental justice that only voluntary conduct should attract the penalty and stigma of criminal liability. A limitation on the defence of duress to a person who commits an offence 'under compulsion of threats of immediate death or bodily harm from a person who is present when the offence is committed' offended section 7 of the Charter (*R v Ruzic* [2001] 3 LRC 703). An extradition hearing and the exercise of the discretion to surrender a fugitive had to comply with the principles of fundamental justice (*USA v Cobb* [2001] SCC 19). The failure of the Justice Minister to request an assurance that the death penalty would not be imposed before an extradition was a breach of the accused's right to fundamental justice (*USA v Burns* [2001] SCCDJ 50).

The common law rule of 'jury secrecy' did not infringe a defendant's rights to fundamental justice under section 7 (*R v Pan* [2001] SCC 42). Section 7 does not give a person charged with sex offences against children a right to challenge jurors for cause on the ground of partiality (*R v Find* [2001] SCC 32).

(3) Criminal trial guarantees

(b) Section 11(b): trial within a reasonable time

The right to a trial within a reasonable time includes the right to be sentenced within a reasonable time (*R v MacDougall* [2000] 1 LRC 390). **11.397**

The decision in *R v MacDougall* [2000] 1 LRC 390 concerned delay in sentencing caused by the judge's illness. The court held that two competing interests had to balanced, namely the need to proceed with utmost care and caution when considering the removal of a judge seised with a case, in order to protect judicial independence and fairness to the accused, and the need to protect the rights of the accused. **11.399**

(d) Section 11(d): presumption of innocence

In *Little Sisters Book and Art Emporium v Canada (Minister of Justice)* [2001] 2 LRC 436 the Supreme Court struck down a reverse onus clause, whereby an importer of allegedly obscene materials was required to disprove obscenity. **11.405**

n1633a: See also *R v Stone* [1992] 2 SCR 290 (defence of automatism).

(e) Section 11(d): fair and public hearing

In *R v Mills* [1999] 2 SCR 638 the Supreme Court upheld legislation which limited the production of records in sexual offence proceedings. Under that legislation, the accused was required to establish that the records were likely to be relevant at trial, or to the competence of a witness testifying, and that disclosure was in the interests of justice. Further, judicial inspection of the documents was required to determine where and to what extent the documents should be produced. In *R v McClure* [2001] SCC 14 the court rejected an attempt by the defendant in a sexual abuse case to obtain the litigation files of a complainant against **11.406** him who had also instituted civil litigation. The court noted that solicitor–client privilege was a principle of fundamental importance to the administration of justice as a whole. Despite its importance, however, the privilege was not absolute and, in limited circumstances, could yield to allow an accused to make a full answer and defence. The appropriate test for determining whether to set aside solicitor–client privilege was the 'innocence-at-stake test', which was a stringent test. The privilege should be infringed only where core issues going to the guilt of the accused were involved and there was a genuine risk of a wrongful conviction.

The guidelines in *Seaboyer* were subsequently codified by sections 76.1 and 276.2 of the Criminal Code. In *R v Darrach* [2001] 1 LRC 536 the defendant contended that section 276, which excluded evidence, violated his right to make full answer and defence under section 7 of the Charter and his right to presumption of innocence. The Supreme Court held that the provisions were not unconstitutional but enhanced the fairness of the hearing by excluding misleading evidence. The principles of fundamental justice enshrined in the Charter protected the complainant's rights as well as those of the accused.

A confidentiality order should only be made when: (a) such an order is necessary in order to prevent a serious risk to the proper administration of justice because reasonably alternative measures will not prevent the risk; and (b) the salutary effects of the publication ban outweigh the deleterious effects on the rights and interests of the parties and the public, including the effects on the right to free expression, the right of the accused to a fair and public trial, and the efficacy of the administration of justice; see *Sierra Club of Canada v Canada (Minister of Finance)* [2002] SCC 41.

(f) Section 11(d): Independent and impartial tribunal

11.409A   A challenge to the independence of the Liquor Control and Licensing Branch was rejected by the Supreme Court in *Ocean Port Hotel Ltd v British Columbia (General Manager, Liquor Control and Licensing Branch)* [2001] SCC 52. The court noted that administrative bodies were to be treated differently to superior courts, and that, absent constitutional constraints, the degree of independence of a particular decision-maker was to be determined by its enabling statute. Superior courts, by virtue of their role as courts of inherent jurisdiction, were constitutionally required to possess objective guarantees of both individual and institutional independence. The same constitutional imperative applied to the provincial courts. Administrative tribunals, by contrast, lacked this constitutional distinction from the executive. They were created precisely for the purpose of implementing government policy, which could require them to make quasi-judicial decisions. Given their primary policy-making function, however, it was properly the role and responsibility of Parliament and the legislatures to determine the composition and structure required by a tribunal to discharge the responsibilities bestowed upon it. While tribunals may sometimes attract Charter requirements of independence, as a general rule they did not attract those requirements.

Legislation which affected the tenure and financial security of judges was successfully challenged in *Mackin v New Brunswick* [2002] SCC 13. The Supreme Court stated that financial security required that judges' salaries be provided for by law and that neither the executive nor the legislative branch of government should arbitrarily encroach on that right in a manner which affected the independence of the courts. Any measure taken by a government that affected any aspect of the remuneration conditions of judges would automatically trigger the application of the principles relating to the institutional dimension of financial security. In particular, governments had a constitutional duty to use an independent, effective and objective body for recommendations on salary reductions, increases or freezes for judges. See also *R v Find* [2001] SCC 32 (juror challenges in child sexual abuse case dismissed) and *Re Therrien* [2001] SCC 35 (procedures for removing a judge upheld).

(4) Freedom from self-incrimination

In *R v Liew* [1999] 3 SCR 227, on the other hand, an inculpatory conversation to an undercover police officer was held to be admissible. The Supreme Court noted that although the officer was undercover, the exchange did not amount to an interrogation and the police officer did not prompt, coax or cajole the defendant's statements, nor was the defendant vulnerable to the officer as there was no relationship of trust between them.   **11.419**

Appendix 2: The New Zealand Bill of Rights Act

(1) Introduction

In *Drew v A-G* [2000] 3 NZLR 750 the High Court held that there was no right to legal representation in prison disciplinary proceedings that led to seven days' loss of remission, as such proceedings were not criminal proceedings. Alternatively, even if such proceedings were criminal proceedings, denial of legal representation at such proceedings was justifiable in a free and democratic society.   **11.422**

(2) The guarantees

(b) Fairness: sections 24 and 25

Section 25(a): fair and public hearing before an independent and impartial court.   It should be noted that a Minister's certificate that material is subject   **11.437**

to public interest immunity is not conclusive (*Choudry v A-G* [2000] 2 LRC 427).

n1751: See also *R v Poumako* [2000] 2 NZLR 695 (concerning retroactive penalties).

In *R v Griffin* [2002] 1 LRC 503 the Court of Appeal set aside a conviction and ordered a new trial because the defendant's psychologist had been unable to examine the complainant's mental state. The defendant had been charged with having unlawful intercourse with a severely subnormal woman. One of the essential elements of the offence was that the complainant was severely mentally subnormal to the extent that she was incapable of living an independent life or of guarding herself against serious exploitation or common physical dangers. The prosecution adduced medical evidence as to the complainant's mental status, but the defendant's expert had not been allowed to interview her or carry out tests on the grounds that her family had not consented, and it would therefore infringe her right under section 10 of the Bill of Rights not to be subject to 'medical or scientific experimentation' without consent. The court noted that the complainant's mental state was an essential ingredient of the offence, and the central issue at trial. Further, the complainant's subnormality was more finely balanced in this case than in others, and capable of *bona fide* argument.

A regulation prohibiting legal representation at prison disciplinary proceedings before a Visiting Justice was struck down by the Court of Appeal in *Drew v Attorney General* [2001] NZCA 207 (12 July 2001). In reaching its conclusion, the court relied on the facts that:

- the decision-makers hold judicial office and exercise judicial power;
- they follow a procedure which is essentially that of a court;
- they may have to resolve difficult issues of fact and law;
- the prisoners may not be able—if unrepresented—to address effectively those issues, to the disadvantage both of themselves and the decision-maker; and
- the penalties may be substantial and in the regular criminal justice system they would call for legal representation.

11.451   **Sub-section 25(g): benefit of a lesser penalty.**   In *R v Teina Pora* (2001) 6 HRNZ 129 the Court of Appeal ruled that where a statute clearly intended to impose a retroactive penalty, courts would give effect to it. In that case it was held that a later statute imposing a minimum period of parole ineligibility in the case of certain types of murder did not override a general statutory provision against retroactive penalties which reflected New Zealand's commitment to Article 15(1) of the International Covenant on Civil and Political Rights.

Appendix 3: Human Rights Cases in Other Jurisdictions

(1) Introduction

11.462 n1779: In *Dickerson v US* (2000) 8 BHRC 407 the Supreme Court upheld *Miranda* as announcing a constitutional rule which could not be superseded legislatively.

(1A) Human Rights Committee

11.462B Article 14 of the International Covenant on Civil and Political Rights (see Main Work, Vol 2, 146–7) provides for rights of fair trial in similar terms to Article 6 and the Seventh Protocol, Articles 2, 3 and 4 of the Convention. Article 15 of the Covenant is in similar terms to Article 7 of the Convention. For a discussion of Articles 14 and 15 of the Covenant, see S Joseph, J Schultz and M Castan, *The International Covenant on Civil and Political Rights: Cases, Materials and Commentary* (Oxford University Press, 2001), ch 14, 'Right to a Fair Trial: Article 14', and ch 15, 'Prohibition of Retroactive Criminal Laws: Article 15'.

(2) Australia

11.463 In *Brownlee v Queen* [2001] HCA 36 the High Court held that the Constitutional right to jury trial did not include trial according to the ancient common law rules which required the jury to be discharged if one member became incapable of continuing to act, and did not permit the jury to separate after retirement.

11.464 In *Ebner v Official Trustee in Bankruptcy* [2001] 2 LRC 369 the High Court held that the principle of trial by an independent and impartial tribunal was fundamental to the Australian judicial system. There was no separate and free-standing rule of automatic disqualification where the judge had a pecuniary interest and no requirement of law that a judge had to disclose an interest in, or association to, a case. However, the *Dietrich* principle does not require legal representation on a review of a deportation decision (*Van Cuong Ngyuen v Minister for Immigration and Multicultural Affairs* [2000] FCA 1265).

11.466A The right to silence is protected by section 20(2) of the Evidence Act 1995 ('any direction concerning the failure of an accused to give evidence should not suggest that the accused was, or believed himself to be, guilty of the offence'). The case of *Azzopardi v R* [2001] 4 LRC 385 concerned a direction by a trial judge in a murder case whereby the jury was invited to conclude from the defendant's failure to testify that any doubt about the prosecution's case could be discounted more easily and that its evidence could more readily be accepted as true. The High Court allowed the defendant's appeal and ordered a retrial, holding that section 20 prohibited any prejudicial comment on the defendant's failure to give evidence.

(2A) Barbados

11.466B   In *Hinds v Attorney-General of Barbados* [2002] 2 WLR 470 the Privy Council considered section 18(12) of the Constitution of Barbados which provides that the constitutional right of a person charged to defend himself in person or by a legal representative shall be construed as entitling a person to legal representation at public expense. It was held that, although not every criminal defendant of insufficient means was entitled to legal aid, his right to a fair hearing guaranteed by section 18(1) was not qualified. Although many cases might fairly be heard without the defendant being represented, the more serious the charge, the more complex the case and the greater the potential penalty the more likely that legal representation of the defendant, if he so desired, would be necessary for the hearing to be fair.

(3A) Botswana

11.467A   The decision of the Botswana Court of Appeal in *Makuto v State* [2000] 5 LRC 183 involved differential sentences for rapists who were HIV-positive. The standard sentence for rape was 10 years, whereas the sentence for rapists who tested positive for HIV prior to sentencing, but had been unaware of that status at the time of the offence, was 15 years. The court struck down the differential sentencing, because it could not be shown that the defendants had been HIV-positive at the time of the attack. On the other hand, the court upheld the sentence of 20 years for rapists who had been aware of their HIV status at the time of the offence.

(4) Hong Kong

(b) Scope of the rights

11.470A   In *Tse Wai Chun Paul v Solicitors Disciplinary Tribunal* [2001] HKCFI 854 the High Court rejected an argument that the Solicitors Disciplinary Tribunal was required to hold its hearings in public. The fact that the applicant could appeal to the Court of Appeal from the tribunal, or seek judicial review of the tribunal's decision, meant that the procedures considered as a whole complied with the fair trial provisions of the Bill of Rights. In reaching its decision, the High Court relied on the decision of the House of Lords in *R v Alconbury Developments v Secretary of State for the Environment, Transport and Regions* [2001] 2 WLR 1389.

(c) The presumption of innocence

11.471   The presumption of innocence does not prevent the 'derivative use' of compulsorily obtained self-incriminating materials (*HKSAR v Lee Ming Tee* [2001] HKCFA 18).

(d) The right to legal assistance

A court's unfettered discretion to order an unsuccessful defendant in criminal tri-   **11.474**
als to pay prosecution costs is not contrary to the Hong Kong Bill of Rights (*Au Chi Wai v HKSAR* [2000] 2 HKLRD 278).

There is a residual discretion to exclude a voluntary confession obtained by undercover police officers if its use at the trial would be unfair to the accused
(*Secretary of Justice v Lam Tat Ming* (2000–2) HKC 693, Ct of Final Appeal).

(f) Other rights

The common law offence of misconduct in a public office is sufficiently certain to   **11.475A**
be constitutional in accordance with the Bill of Rights Ordinance (*Shum Kwok Sher v HKSAR* [2002] HKCFA 17).

(6) Ireland

An applicant who sought to keep his name secret in legal proceedings was unsuc-   **11.483A**
cessful in *Re Ansbacher (Cayman) Ltd* [2002] IEHC 27. The court held that the
right to a public trial outweighed in that case the rights to privacy or confidentiality.

(7) Jamaica

The right to be tried within a reasonable time is not an absolute right. It had to be   **11.484**
balanced against the public interest in the attainment of justice and, as a result, the
court is entitled to take into account the fact that a serious offence had taken place.
The court had to take into account the length of the delay, the reason for the delay,
the defendant's assertion of his right and the prejudice to the defendant (*Flowers v R* [2000] 1 WLR 2396, PC).

(7A) Lesotho

A statutory provision which provided that in certain courts no party could be   **11.487A**
legally represented was inconsistent with the constitutional right to a fair trial.
Although there was no implied constitutional right to representation in all civil
proceedings, there was an implied right when the requirements of a fair trial made
it appropriate (*Attorney-General of Lesotho v Mopa* (2002 (6) BCLR 645, CA)).

(8) Mauritius

In *Darmalingum v The State* [2000] 1 WLR 2303 the applicant had been arrested   **11.488**
in 1985, tried in 1993 and had his appeal determined in July 1998. The Privy
Council held that these delays were infringements of the applicant's right to a fair
trial within a reasonable time under section 10(1) of the Constitution. It said that

the only disposal which would properly vindicate the constitutional rights of the defendant was the quashing of the conviction.

(9A) Nigeria

11.491A Where it is sought to terminate an employee's employment because that employee has allegedly committed theft, and the employee denies such theft, the issue of whether theft has been committed must be determined by a court exercising criminal jurisdiction: *Geidem v NEPA* [2001] 2 NWLR 45 (Nigeria Court of Appeal).

(12) South Africa

(b) The presumption of innocence

11.501 In *State v Manamela* [2000] 5 LRC 65 the Constitutional Court declared unconstitutional a reverse onus clause imposed on recipients of stolen goods, whereby the onus was on the recipients to show that they had reasonable grounds for believing that the person from whom they received the goods was authorised to deal with those goods. The court adopted a remedy of 'reading in'. In *Singo v S* 2002 (8) BCLR 793 the Constitutional Court considered the validity of summary proceedings whereby an accused person who failed to appear in court at the time and on the date fixed by a warning so to appear was guilty of an offence, unless the accused then satisfied the court that the failure was not due to his or her fault. In a unanimous decision written by Ngcobo J, the Court found a breach of the presumption of innocence, which was not justifiable under the general limitations clause. The right to silence was also breached, but the Court found that breach to be justifiable.

(d) Access to the court

11.505 A statutory provision which required written notice to be served within 90 days of the commission of a wrong alleged against a local authority was a material limitation on an individual's constitutional right of access to the court which could not be justified. The active protection of the right of prospective litigants to approach a court for adjudication of their claims outweighed the governmental interests concerned (*Moise v Transitional Local Council of Greater Germiston* (2001) 11 BHRC 474; and see also *Potgieter v Lid Van Die Uitvoerende Raad: Gesondheid, Provinsiale Regering Gauteng* 2001 (11) BCLR 1175). However, a provision which required taxpayers to pay VAT assessed by the commissioners before the determination of disputes (the 'pay now, argue later' provision) insofar as it was a limitation on the right of access to the court was justifiable (*Metcash v Commissioner for the South African Revenue Service* (2001) 11 BHRC 497).

11.505A In *Van der Walt v Metcash Trading Limited* 2002 (5) BCLR 454 the Supreme Court of Appeal had treated two applications for leave to appeal differently on two successive days, even though the applications were based on substantially identical facts. A majority of the Constitutional Court held that this differential treatment did not breach any constitutional right of the applicants, including the rights of access to court and equality. Justice Goldstone, in a judgment with which the majority of the court concurred, held that while it was unfortunate that contrary orders should be issued in substantially identical cases, there was nothing to suggest that either of the orders were arbitrary. The panels were required to exercise a discretion in determining the prospects of success on appeal. In exercising such a discretion, reasonable minds may well differ. That did not make either order incorrect.

Legislation which permitted customs authorities to seize and sell goods in the possession of customs debtors, even when those goods belonged to third parties, was declared an unlawful deprivation of property, contrary to section 25 of the Constitution, in *First National Bank of SA Limited v Commissioner for the South African Revenue Services* 2002 (7) BCLR 702. The Court also added that such legislation might be contrary to the right of access to courts, because the authorities could seize and sell goods without having to invoke court processes beforehand.

Rate collection procedures were upheld in *De Beer NO v North Central Local Council* 2001 (11) BCLR 1109 (court order was required before property could be sold; judicial control rendered procedures fair).

(c) Other issues

In *S v Mamabolo* (2001 5 BCLR 449) the Constitutional Court held that the sum-   **11.510A**
mary contempt procedure used in relation to 'scandalising the court' was an unjustifiable infringement of constitutionally protected rights to a fair trial under section 35(3). In *Carmichele v Ministry of Safety and Security* 2001 (10) BCLR 995 (CC) the Constitutional Court held that for police and prosecutors to have an immunity against claims in negligence arising out of a failure to prevent the commission of life-threatening crimes would be inconsistent with the Constitution and its values.

In *Van Rooyen v S and Others* 2002 (8) BCLR 810 the Constitutional Court dealt   **11.510B**
with the institutional independence and constitutional legitimacy of South Africa's magistracy. Most of the challenged statutory provisions concerning the magistracy were upheld, but some provisions dealing with the assignment of certain powers to magistrates and their removal from office were found to be unconstitutional. Chief Justice Chaskalson, writing for a unanimous Court, considered that the core of judicial independence was the complete freedom of individual judicial officers to hear and decide the cases that come before them, with no outside interference or attempt to interfere with the way in which judicial officers conduct their cases and make their decisions. The required safeguards should include security of tenure and a basic degree of financial security.

A statute permitting hearsay evidence to be admitted in criminal trials, in certain circumstances including where it was necessary in the interests of justice, was held to be constitutional in *Ndhlovu v State* (Supreme Court of Appeal, 31 May 2002).

In *Singo v State* (2002) 12 BHRC 702 it was held that a statute which provided that a person who culpably failed to comply with a warning to appear in court and where the burden was on the accused to prove that it was not his fault was unconstitutional. Having regard to the importance of the right to be presumed innocent and the fact that the state could achieve its objective by less intrusive means, the imposition of the legal burden on the accused could not be justified.

(13A) Tanzania

11.512A In *Ndyanabo v Attorney-General* [2002] 3 LRC 541 the Court of Appeal declared that a provision of the Elections Act which required the deposit of security for costs before an election petition could be lodged was unconstitutional. The statutory provision effectively denied access to justice to indigent petitioners.

(14) Trinidad and Tobago

11.513 In *Ferguson v A-G of Trinidad and Tobago* [2001] 3 LRC 631 the Privy Council said that the guarantees of due process, protection of the law and a fair hearing under sections 4 and 5 of the Constitution were of generous width and capable of applying to the treatment of an accused at a preliminary inquiry.

(c) Other fair trial rights

11.517A In *Boodram v State of Trinidad and Tobago* [2002] Cr App R 103 the Privy Council said that where it had been demonstrated that counsel's incompetence or failure to perform his duties were of a fundamental nature, an appellate court should proceed with great care before concluding that even if the incompetence or failures had not occurred the jury's verdict would inevitably have been the same.

(15) Zimbabwe

(c) Presumption of innocence

11.521 In *State v Shikunga* [2000] 1 SA 616 the Zimbabwe Supreme Court, applying the decision of the South African Constitutional Court in *S v Zuma* 1995 (4) BCLR 401 (see Main Work, para 11.497), declared that a statutory provision imposing the burden on the accused to disprove the voluntariness of a confession was contrary to the presumption of innocence.

Summary proceedings for contempt in which the accused was required to show cause why an order should not be made merely shifted the burden of adducing evidence, as opposed to the burden of persuasion, to the accused (*Re Chinamasa* (2001) 9 BHRC 519).

(d) Other cases

In *Re Chinamasa* (2001) 9 BHRC 519 the Supreme Court held that the High **11.525** Court was an 'independent and impartial tribunal' for the purposes of determining an allegation of 'scandalising the court'. However, a person charged with such contempt was entitled to the same protections under section 18 as a person charged with an ordinary criminal offence. The accused was entitled to be acquitted if there was a reasonable doubt as to his guilt.

In *Movement for Democratic Change v Chinamasa* [2001] 3 LRC 673 the Supreme Court emphasised that the right of full and unimpeded access to courts is of cardinal importance for the adjudication of justiciable disputes.

12

THE RIGHT TO RESPECT FOR PRIVACY AND THE HOME

B. The Rights in English Law

(1) Introduction

In *Douglas v Hello! Ltd* [2001] QB 967, para 110, Sedley LJ expressed the view **12.06** that the point has been reached where it can be said with confidence that the law recognises and will appropriately protect personal privacy. However, there has been some debate about whether the courts would recognise a new tort of breach of privacy following the coming into force of the Human Rights Act (see Main Work, paras 12.165ff). The recent case law reveals three distinct views about the availability and desirability of a new tort of invasion of privacy:

- That there is no common law tort of invasion of privacy and the courts are prevented by binding Court of Appeal authority from developing one (*Wainwright v Home Office* [2002] 3 WLR 405).
- That there is no tort of invasion of privacy and no need to develop one because in 'the great majority of situations, if not all situations, where the protection of

privacy is justified . . . an action for breach of confidence now will . . . provide the necessary protection' (*A v B plc* [2002] 3 WLR 542).

- That a new tort is required and is now available, or is at least developing, in part as a result of the impetus provided by the Human Rights Act 1998 (*Douglas v Hello!* [2001] QB 967; *H (A Healthcare Worker) v Associated Newspapers Limited* [2002] EWCA Civ 195, para 40). In *Campbell v MGN* [2003] 2 WLR 80 although the claimant chose not to pursue a claim for damages for infringement of privacy the Court of Appeal said that the unjustifiable publication of information relating to an aspect of an individual's private life which he does not choose to make public 'would better be described as breach of privacy rather than breach of confidence' (para 70).

The outcome of the debate between these different views remains unclear. See, generally, H Tomlinson (ed), *Privacy and the Media* (Matrix, 2002), ch 1, and M Tugendhat and I Christie (eds), *The Law of Privacy and the Media* (Oxford University Press, 2002).

In New Zealand a tort of breach of privacy has now been formulated; see *P v D* [2000] 2 NZLR 591 and *L v G* [2002] DC Reg 234, discussed at Supplement, para 12.244, and see, generally, R Tobin, 'Privacy and Freedom of Expression in New Zealand', in M Colvin (ed), *Developing Key Privacy Rights* (Hart Publishing, 2002).

n30: See the decision of the Court in *Khan v United Kingdom* (2000) 8 BHRC 310.

(2) Intrusion into the home: entry, search and seizure

(b) Interference with land and goods

12.14 In *Costello v Chief Constable of Derbyshire* [2001] 1 WLR 1437 the Court of Appeal held that a person's right of possession to goods was entitled to equal legal protection regardless of whether possession was obtained unlawfully by theft or by some other unlawful means.

(e) Powers of search and seizure of goods

12.21 The powers of entry, search and seizure following arrest conferred by sections 18 and 19 of the Police and Criminal Evidence Act 1984 are confined to domestic offences and there is no statutory power to search the premises of a person arrested under a provisional warrant issued under the Extradition Act 1989. There is, however, a common law power of search and seizure in such cases which had not been revoked by the 1984 Act. The exercise of the power was in accordance with the common law, and was for the legitimate aim of preventing crime and, subject to the safeguard that its use was dependent on the issue of an arrest warrant, so as to make it proportionate to that aim, it did not infringe Article 8 (*R v Commissioner of Police for the Metropolis, ex p Rottman* [2002] 2 WLR 1315, HL); see Supplement, para 12.177.

(3) The misuse of personal information

(a) Introduction

The protection of rights to personal information may also be enforced by public bodies on behalf of individuals in its care. In *Broadmoor Special Hospital Authority v Robinson* [2000] QB 775 the Court of Appeal held that a public body which was exercising a statutory responsibility in the public interest could, in the absence of any statutory implication to the contrary, apply to the court for an injunction to prevent interference with its public responsibilities. The court therefore had jurisdiction to grant an injunction which enabled a special hospital to perform its statutory duties to treat patients, maintain security and to provide a therapeutic environment by restraining an activity outside the hospital provided the activity had a sufficiently significant impact on hospital security or its treatment of a patient. However, the hospital could not bring proceedings to protect other patients' rights to privacy or confidence or prevent distress to the victim's family unless these complaints interfered with the performance of its duties. As a result in *Ashworth Security Hospital v MGN* [2001] 1 WLR 515 the Court of Appeal held that it had jurisdiction to order disclosure of the identity of the individual who provided medical information from the hospital medical database about the murderer, Ian Brady, on the principle established by *Norwich Pharmacal v Customs & Excise* [1974] AC 133. The decision of the Court of Appeal was upheld by the House of Lords (*Ashworth Hospital Authority v MGN* [2002] 1 WLR 2033) on the basis that while the exercise of the jurisdiction to require a third party who was involved in wrongdoing, here a journalist, to identify the wrongdoer was subject to Article 10, in the exceptional circumstances of the case itself the order to disclose was justifiable, in part because of the importance attached to confidentiality of such medical records pursuant to Article 8. The question of whether the order was compatible with Article 10 is discussed at Supplement, paras 15.76 and 15.78.

12.26

(b) Breach of confidence

'Circumstances of confidence'. In *A v B plc* [2002] 3 WLR 542 it was said that:

12.32

> A duty of confidence will arise whenever the party subject to the duty is in a situation where he either knows or ought to know that the other person can reasonably expect his privacy to be protected.

This is what Sedley LJ described in *Douglas v Hello!* [2001] QB 967, para 126, as 'an artificial relationship of confidentiality between intruder and victim'. Such a 'duty of confidence' is indistinguishable from a tortious duty not to intrude into privacy. See also *Campbell v MGN* [2003] 2 WLR 80, paras 69–70.

12.33 **Misuse of the information.**   In *Douglas v Hello! Ltd* [2001] QB 967 the claim was based on an exclusive agreement made between Michael Douglas and Catherine Zeta-Jones with a magazine to publish photographs of their wedding which was breached when another magazine decided to publish them. An injunction was granted for breach of confidence in *Venables v News Group Newspapers* [2001] Fam 340 to protect the life and well-being of the two youths who had murdered the infant, James Bulger. The two cases are discussed further at Supplement, para 12.202.

(c) Disclosure of information by public bodies

12.38 The checks provided by a consultancy service which advised local authorities and voluntary organisations on the suitability of those they proposed to employ in childcare posts were found not to be unlawful in *R v Secretary of State for Health, ex p C* [2000] HRLR 400 and *R v Worcester County Council, ex p SW* [2000] HRLR 702. In *R v C & D, ex p A* [2001] 1 WLR 461 Turner J held that the duty to act fairly was not engaged when information concerning allegations of sex abuse against an individual who had applied to be a school teacher was passed from one police authority to another (declining to follow *R v Local Police Authority in the Midlands, ex p L M* [2000] 1 FLR 612). He took the view that the local educational authority had a pressing need to receive the information and that the decision to pass the information to it was neither illegal nor irrational.

n174: *R v Local Police Authority in the Midlands, ex p LM* is now reported at [2000] 1 FLR 612

(d) Confidential files

12.44 In *Baker v Secretary of State for the Home Department* [2001] UKHRR 1275 the Information Tribunal held that the Home Secretary did not have reasonable grounds for issuing a certificate giving the Security Service blanket exemption from revealing in response to a request under section 7(1)(a) of the Data Protection Act 1998 whether it was holding or processing personal data about an individual. The exemption was wider than was necessary to protect national security and as a result failed the 'proportionality test'.

n201: In *Campbell v MGN Ltd* [2003] 2 WLR 80 the Court of Appeal held that section 32 provided a general exemption to the media, both before and after publication. Morland J's decision at first instance at [2002] EMLR 617 that the media was only protected prior to publication had been the source of considerable concern and the confirmation that the exemption is a general one is a welcome one for the media.

The Data Protection Commissioner has been renamed the Information **12.45** Commissioner; see paragraph 1 of Schedule 2 to the Freedom of Information Act 2000.

(e) Access to personal information

The Freedom of Information Act 2000 has now been enacted. However, only a **12.46** few provisions are now in force: see section 87 of the Act and the Freedom of Information Act 2000 (Commencement No 1) Order 2001, SI 2001/1637. Section 1 creates two rights against public authorities where an individual requests information: a right to be informed in writing whether the public authority holds information of the description specified in the request, and a right to have the information confirmed to him. However, section 2 and Part II of the Act contain exemptions which limit these duties. Public authorities are defined in sections 2–6 of, and Schedule 1 to, the Act. At present neither the right under section 1 nor the enforcement procedure under Part IV are in force.

n214: The Access to Personal Files (Social Services) Regulations 1989, SI 1989/206, as amended by SI 1991/1587, have now lapsed. An application for personal information should be made under the Data Protection Act 1998.

n215: The Access to Personal Files (Housing) Regulations 1989, SI 1989/503, have now lapsed. An application for personal information should be made under section 7 of the Data Protection Act 1998.

(4) Photography, surveillance and telephone tapping

(b) Photography

The publication of a covertly taken photograph of a model leaving a meeting of **12.53** Narcotics Anonymous was not a breach of confidence although the Court of Appeal gave strong hints that the position might have been different if the claim had been for invasion of privacy (*Campbell v MGN* [2003] 2 WLR 80, paras 29–34, 54). In *Theakston v MGN* [2002] EMLR 398 an injunction was granted to restrain the publication of photographs of the claimant taken in a brothel. The judge refused to restrain publication of the story of what had taken place; see, further, Supplement, para 12.202.

(c) Surveillance

The authorisation procedure under section 93 of the Police Act 1997 has been **12.60** amended by section 75 of the Regulation of Investigatory Powers Act 2000. The Regulation of Investigatory Powers Act regulates for the first time directed surveillance, intrusive surveillance and use of covert intelligence sources (as defined in section 26). The authorisation procedure for such surveillance is contained in Part II of the Act.

12.61   The Regulation of Investigatory Powers Act 2000 now regulates directed surveillance, intrusive surveillance and use of covert intelligence sources (as defined in section 26).

12.62   The Regulation of Investigatory Powers Act 2000 is now in force. A complaint about the conduct of intelligence services or in relation to surveillance and covert human intelligence sources under Part II of the Act must be made to the Tribunal under section 65 of the Act. Section 65(2)(a) states that the Tribunal is the only appropriate tribunal for the purposes of section 7(1)(a) of the Human Rights Act. Section 17 provides that, subject to section 18, no evidence shall be adduced, question asked, assertion or disclosure made or other thing done in, for the purposes of or in connection with any legal proceedings which in any manner:

- discloses the contents of an intercepted communication (from which its origin in anything falling within section 17(2) may be inferred); or
- tends to suggest that anything that has occurred (or may have occurred or will be going to occur) which falls within the scope of section 17(2).

(d) Intercepting letters and telephone tapping

12.66   The Interception of Communications Act 1985 has been repealed and replaced by the Regulation of Investigatory Powers Act 2000. The power of the Secretary of State to grant a warrant is now contained in section 5 of that Act.

12.68   Under section 1 of the Regulation of Investigatory Powers Act 2000 it is an offence, without lawful authority, to intercept any communication in the course of its transmission by a public post office or by a public or private telecommunications system. A communication can be lawfully intercepted without a warrant in the limited circumstances defined by sections 3 or 4 and under the rather broader conditions under the Telecommunications (Lawful Business Practice) (Interception of Communications) Regulations 2000, SI 2000/2699 (which, for example, may entitle interception to establish the existence of facts to detect unauthorised use of the telecommunications system).

12.69   Section 9(1) of the Interception of Communications Act 1985 has been repealed and replaced by section 17 of the Regulation of Investigatory Powers Act 2000. Section 17 provides that, subject to section 18, no evidence shall be adduced, question asked, assertion or disclosure made or other thing done in, for the purposes of or in connection with any legal proceedings which in any manner:

- discloses the contents of an intercepted communication (from which its origin in anything falling within section 17(2) may be inferred); or
- tends to suggest that anything that has occurred (or may have occurred or will be going to occur) which falls within the scope of section 17(2).

A complaint in relation to an intercepted communication or in relation to the acquisition and disclosure of communications data under Part I of Chapter II of the Act must be made to the Tribunal under section 65 of the Act. Section 65(2)(a) states that the Tribunal is the only appropriate tribunal for the purposes of section 7(1)(a) of the Human Rights Act. The Tribunal will exercise its jurisdiction under section 67 in accordance with the procedure defined by section 68.

Section 7(8) of the Interception of Communications Act 1985 has been repealed **12.70** and replaced by section 67(8) of the Regulation of Investigatory Powers Act 2000 which states that, except to such extent as the Secretary of State may by order otherwise provide, determinations, awards, orders and other decisions of the Tribunal (including decisions as to whether they have jurisdiction) shall not be subject to appeal or liable to be questioned in any court.

The Regulation of Investigatory Powers Act 2000 is now in force. The effect of the **12.70A** Act is considered at Supplement, paras 12.60–12.62, 12.66 and 12.68–12.70.

(5) Privacy and the media

(a) Introduction
For a general discussion of privacy and media regulation, see H Tomlinson (ed), **12.71** *Privacy and the Media: The Developing Law* (Matrix, 2002), ch 6.

(b) Press regulation
The Code of Practice was further amended and the latest version is dated 1 **12.72** December 1999.

In *R (Ford) v Press Complaints Commission* [2002] EMLR 95 an application for **12.74** permission for a judicial review of the PCC's dismissal of a privacy complaint failed. The judge accepted that it was arguable that the PCC was a public authority but took the view that there was no arguable case as, despite the provisions of the Human Rights Act, the courts should continue to defer to the decisions of regulators. The decision is a doubtful one as the judge failed to take into account the positive obligations of the courts to protect Article 8 rights. The PCC's specialist knowledge is of limited relevance to the consideration of an issue such as invasion of privacy. It is submitted that the point was clearly arguable and that permission should have been given.

(c) Regulation of broadcasting
n303: *R v Broadcasting Standards Commission, ex p BBC* is now reported at **12.76** [2001] QB 885.

The Government has proposed a radical reform of the system for regulation of the **12.77A** electronic media; see *A New Future for Communications* (12 December 2000, Cm

5010). It is proposed that a single regulator, OFCOM, will take responsibility for all regulatory functions. The paving Act, the Office of Communications Act 2002, is already in force and the Government has now published a draft Communications Bill which contains a new formulation of the regulator's duties in relation to privacy; see Supplement, para 15.92.

C. The Law Under the European Convention

(1) The scope of the right

(a) Introduction

12.83 **n315:** *R v Broadcasting Standards Commission, ex p BBC* is now reported at [2001] QB 885 and was applied in *R v Loveridge* [2001] 2 Cr App R 591.

(b) Private life

12.84 **Introduction.** The Court has taken an expansive view of the scope of 'private life' on several occasions. In *Amann v Switzerland* (2000) 30 EHRR 843, para 65, the Court reiterated that the scope of 'private life' was broad enough to include professional and business activities (this case is discussed further at Supplement, paras 12.105 and 12.128). A similar approach was taken in *Rotaru v Romania* (2000) 8 BHRC 449 which is discussed at Supplement, para 12.90. Compare the *dicta* of Newman J in *R v Worcester County Council, ex p SW* [2000] HRLR 702, 717–19 which are discussed at Supplement, para 12.148.

In *Pretty v United Kingdom* (2002) 12 BHRC 149, para 61, the Court said:

> the concept of 'private life' is a broad term not susceptible to exhaustive definition. It covers the physical and psychological integrity of a person *(X. and Y. v. the Netherlands* (1985) 8 EHRR 235 para 22). It can sometimes embrace aspects of an individual's physical and social identity *(Mikulic v. Croatia,* judgment of 7 February 2002, para 53). Elements such as, for example, gender identification, name and sexual orientation and sexual life fall within the personal sphere protected by Article 8 (see e.g. *B. v. France* (1992) 16 EHRR 1 para 63; *Burghartz v. Switzerland* (1994) 18 EHRR 101 para 24; *Dudgeon v. the United Kingdom* (1981) 4 EHRRR 149 para 41, and *Laskey, Jaggard and Brown v. the United Kingdom* (1997) 24 EHRR 39 para 36). Article 8 also protects a right to personal development, and the right to establish and develop relationships with other human beings and the outside world (see, for example, *Burghartz v. Switzerland,* Commission's report, op. cit., para 47; *Friedl v. Austria,* (1994) 21 EHRR 83 Commission's report, para 45). Though no previous case has established as such any right to self-determination as being contained in Article 8 of the Convention, the Court considers that the notion of personal autonomy is an important principle underlying the interpretation of its guarantees.

The Court went on to hold that the notion of personal autonomy contained in Article 8(1) included the right to conduct one's life in a manner of one's own choosing. Pursuit of activities that were physically or morally harmful fell within the ambit of Article 8(1) and limitation of the pursuit required justification. The Court therefore held that the legal prohibition which prevented Mrs Pretty from exercising her choice to avoid an undignified and distressing death from an assisted suicide breached Article 8(1) but found that the interference was justified under Article 8(2). The Court therefore declined to follow the House of Lords in *R (Pretty) v DPP* [2002] 1 AC 800 which had held that Article 8 was directed at the protection of personal automony while an individual was alive but did not confer the right to decide how or when to die.

In *PG and JH v United Kingdom* (Judgment of 25 September 2001), para 56, the Court also stressed that private life is a broad term not suspectible to exhaustive definition. The Court then observed (paras 57–8):

> There are a number of elements relevant to a consideration of whether a person's private life is concerned in measures effected outside a person's home or private premises. Since there are occasions when people knowingly or intentionally involve themselves in activities which are or may be recorded or reported in a public manner, a person's reasonable expectations as to privacy may be a significant, though not necessarily conclusive factor. A person who walks down the street will, inevitably, be visible to any member of the public who is also present. Monitoring by technological means of the same public scene (e.g. a security guard viewing through close circuit television) is of a similar character. Private life considerations may arise however once any systematic or permanent record comes into existence of such material from the public domain. It is for this reason that files gathered by security services on a particular individual fall within the scope of Article 8 even where the information has not been gathered by any intrusive or covert method (see *Rotaru v. Romania* (2000) 8 BHRC 449 at paras 43–44). The Court has referred in this context to the Council of Europe's Convention of 28 January 1981 for the protection of individuals with regard to automatic processing of personal data, which came into force on 1 October 1985, whose purpose is 'to secure in the territory of each Party for every individual . . . respect for his rights and fundamental freedoms, and in particular his right to privacy, with regard to the automatic processing of personal data relating to him' (Article 1), such data being defined as 'any information relating to an identified or identifiable individual' (Article 2) (see *Amman v. Switzerland* 5, ECHR 2000–2, §§ 65–67, where the storing of information about the applicant on a card in a file was found to be an interference with private life, even though it contained no sensitive information and had probably never been consulted).
>
> In the case of photographs, the Commission previously had regard, for the purpose of delimiting the scope of protection afforded by Article 8 against arbitrary interference by public authorities, to whether the taking of the photographs amounted to an intrusion into the individual's privacy, whether the photographs related to private matters or public incidents and whether the material obtained was envisaged for a limited use or was likely to be made available to the general public (see *Friedl v. Austria*, (1994) 21 EHRR 83 paras 49–52). Where photographs were taken of an applicant at a public demonstration in a public place and retained by the police in a file, the Commission found no interference with private life, giving weight to the fact that the photograph was taken and retained as a record of the demonstration and no

action had been taken to identify the persons photographed on that occasion by means of data processing (see *Friedl v. Austria* above paras 51–52).

The Court therefore concluded that the recording of voices when a criminal defendant is being charged and when in his police cell interfered with his right to respect for private life.

12.86   **Physical and moral integrity.**   It was held in *DG v Ireland* (2002) 35 EHRR 33 that 'private life', for the purpose of Article 8, includes the moral and physical integrity of a prisoner deprived of his or her liberty, and that there may be circumstances in which Article 8 could be regarded as affording protection in respect of conditions of detention even if they do not attain the level of severity required for a breach of Article 3. However, it was held that normal restrictions and limitations consequent on prison life and discipline during lawful detention are not matters which would constitute a violation of Article 8. In the case itself it was held that the conditions complained of did not breach Article 8. In *Nowicka v Poland* (Decision of 16 October 2001) a claim that there had been a breach of Article 8 in relation to conditions of detention and a psychiatric examination in custody was held to be admissible. See also *Pretty v United Kingdom* (2002) 12 BRHC 149, discussed at Supplement, para 12.84.

12.87   **Personal identity.**   A refusal to allow an individual to adopt a child does not interfere with his right to develop personality pursuant to Article 8 (*Frette v France*, Judgment of 26 February 2002).

n331: It was held in *Mikulic v Croatia* [2002] 1 FCR 720 that paternity proceedings which lasted some five years breached a child's Article 8 rights as the prolonged uncertainty as to her identity failed to respect her private life.

In *Roche v United Kingdom* (Decision of 23 May 2002) a failure to provide the applicant with documents about tests conducted into the effects of chemical weapons, in which he had participated some years earlier, was admissible under Article 8.

12.90   **Personal information.**   In *Rotaru v Romania* (2000) 8 BHRC 449, para 43, the Court said that public information could fall within the scope of private life where it is systematically collected and stored in files held by the authorities. It was said to be 'all the truer' where such information concerned a person's distant past.

In *Roche v United Kingdom* (Decision of 23 May 2002) a failure to provide the applicant with documents about tests conducted into the effects of chemical weapons, in which he had participated some years earlier, was admissible under Article 8.

12.92   **Personal sexuality.**   In *ADT v United Kingdom* (2000) 9 BHRC 112 it was held that the criminalisation of homosexual acts in private where more than two people were present was an interference with 'private life'. The Court rejected the

Government's argument that because a number of individuals were present and the activities were videotaped the activities were not 'private'.

In *GL and AV v Austria* and *SL v Austria* (Decisions of 22 November 2001) claims that the existence of a higher age of consent for male homosexual relations than was enforced for lesbian or heterosexual relations was in breach of Articles 8 and 14 were held to be admissible. The claims in *GL and AV* were brought by adults prosecuted for having sexual relations with underage boys while the claim in *SL* was brought by an underage boy wishing legally to engage in homosexual relations.

In *Brown v United Kingdom* (Decision of 4 June 2002) the applicant complained about his discharge from the armed forces, on the basis that he was homosexual, and the prior investigation into his sexuality. The United Kingdom accepted that the applicant's discharge was a breach of Article 8. In relation to the investigation the Court noted that the applicant had been asked about his sexuality and that his answers were recorded and circulated to certain officers. It found the complaint that this constituted a breach of Article 8 to be admissible.

n350: *Lustig-Prean v United Kingdom* is now reported at (1999) 29 EHRR 449.

n351: *Smith v United Kingdom* is now reported at (1999) 29 EHRR 493.

The Court returned to the question of the position of transsexuals in *Goodwin v* **12.93** *United Kingdom* (2002) 35 EHRR 447. The Grand Chamber held, this time, that the failure legally to recognise a gender reassignment was a breach of Article 8. The failure to recognise the new gender identity interfered with Article 8(1) and there were insufficient factors of public interest to justify it after re-examining the lack of legal recognition given to a post-operative transsexual against current scientific and social conditions. The Grand Chamber therefore differed from the views taken by the Court in *Cossey v United Kingdom* (1980) 13 EHRR 622; *Rees v United Kingdom* (1986) 9 EHRR 56; and *Sheffield and Horsham v United Kingdom* (1990) 13 EHRR 163.

In *Van Kuck v Germany* (Decision of 18 October 2001) the Court considered a claim by a transsexual that her rights under Article 8 had been breached after a German court refused to allow her to claim a reimbursement for her sex change from a health insurance company. The basis of the alleged breach of Article 8 was that the German court had made assumptions about the applicant's personality and sexual identity based upon misconstrued facts and thus failed to respect her private life. The claim was found to be admissible.

(c) 'Home'

Where an individual had not lived in a place as a 'home' for more than ten years **12.97** prior to the alleged interference they could not claim a breach of Article 8 (see *Iordanou v Turkey*, Decision of 25 June 2002).

12.99 In *Hatton v United Kingdom* (2002) 34 EHRR 1 the Court again considered a claim that Article 8 was breached in relation to noise at Heathrow Airport. This time, the Court held that there was a breach of the applicants' Article 8 rights as not enough was being done to reduce noise levels. It held that despite the margin of appreciation left to the state, it considered that there had been a failure to strike a fair balance between the United Kingdom's economic well-being and the applicants' effective enjoyment of their right to respect for their homes and their private and family lives. The matter is due to be reconsidered by a Grand Chamber shortly. For a discussion of *Hatton*, see G Jones and J Pike, 'Proportionality and Planning: A Difficult and Nice Point' [2002] JPL 908 and see, generally, M McMereux, 'Deriving Environmental Rights from the European Convention on Human Rights and Fundamental Freedoms, (2001) 21 OJLS 521.

(d) 'Correspondence'

12.102 **Interference with postal correspondence.** It was held in *Faulkner v United Kingdom* (2002) 35 EHRR 686 that a failure to send a letter from a prisoner to the Scottish Minister of State constituted an interference with his Article 8 rights which was not justified under the circumstances. See also *Puzinas v Lithuania* (Judgment of 14 March 2002) in which it was held that opening and censoring a prisoner's correspondence with his wife and an international institution was not justified and breached Article 8.

In *AB v Netherlands* (Judgment of 29 January 2002) a prisoner complained that his letters to the European Commission on Human Rights had been opened, that he was not permitted to correspond with his representative, a former inmate, and that he was only permitted to send a total of two to three letters per week from the prison. The Court held that no justification had been presented for interfering with communication with the Commission, and found a breach of Article 8. The Court also held that a blanket prohibition on correspondence with former prisoners could not be justified. However, the Court declined to find a breach of Article 8 in relation to the limit on the number of letters a prisoner could write a week. It was noted that the limitation did not prevent the prisoner maintaining contact with those outside prison and, bearing in mind that the state paid for the writing materials and postage, some limit on the number of letters that could be sent was permissible.

12.103 In *Messina v Italy* (Judgment 28 September 2000) the Court found that the interferences with correspondence and family visits which had been placed on a prisoner charged and convicted of Mafia-style activities were proportionate. In *Rehbock v Slovenia* (Judgment of 28 November 2000), the Court held that the monitoring of the applicant's correspondence during his detention on remand in Slovenia constituted an unjustified interference with his right of correspondence.

Searches and seizures. In *Buck v Germany* (Decision of 7 May 2002) the **12.104** Court considered a complaint relating to the search of the applicant's business and the seizure of documents. The search and seizure had been part of an investigation to determine whether the applicant's son had been driving a van which it was alleged had been speeding. The applicant complained that, given the relatively trivial nature of the offence and the damage to his business and reputation from the seizure of the documents, the action of the state had been disproportionate and in breach of Article 8. The claim was found to be admissible.

Telephone tapping. In order to establish a breach of Article 8 in relation to **12.105** telephone tapping, the applicant must provide sufficient *prima facie* evidence that such tapping has occurred; see *Lesnik v Slovakia* (Decision 8 January 2002). In *Amann v Switzerland* (2000) 30 EHRR 843 the Court held that the interception and recording of the applicant's telephone conversation by the Public Prosecutor's Office interfered with his right to private life and correspondence under Article 8. The consequent creation and storage of an index card in the name of the defendant were also both held to interfere with his right to private life. However, in *PG and JH v United Kingdom* (Judgment of 25 September 2001) the Court held that telephone metering (ie obtaining information concerning the numbers called on a telephone) was an interference with Article 8 which was in accordance with the law and proportionate. In *Greuter v Netherlands* (Decision of 19 March 2002) a telephone tap of the partner of a suspect in a criminal investigation was found to be justified for the purpose of Article 8.

In *MM v Netherlands* (Decision of 21 May 2002) the Court considered a case in which a telephone conversation was recorded by the alleged victim of a crime. It was argued on behalf of the Netherlands that as the recording was the result of actions by a private party, Article 8 was not engaged. The recording was made, however, on the advice of the police who had provided and installed the recording equipment. Under these circumstances the Court held that the complaint of a breach of Article 8, on the basis that the recording had not followed the correct procedures, was admissible.

(e) 'Respect'

Positive action to prevent interference by a private individual. In *A v United* **12.114** *Kingdom* (Decision of 5 March 2002) the Court considered a complaint that there had been a failure to respect the applicant's private life in circumstances in which she was prevented, by Parliamentary privilege, from bringing proceedings in relations to disparaging comments made against her by a Member of Parliament, in Parliament, which she claimed were untrue. The complaint was found to be admissible.

(2) Justification under Article 8(2)

(c) 'In accordance with the law'

12.128 In *Amann v Switzerland* (2000) 30 EHRR 843 the Court held that Swiss law did not set out with sufficient clarity the scope and conditions of the exercise of the discretionary power of the Public Prosecutor's Office to intercept telephone calls and to create and store records regarding persons who had been monitored (see also *Rotaru v Romania* (2000) 8 BHRC 449).

(d) 'Necessary in a democratic society' for a legitimate aim

12.141 **For the prevention of disorder or crime.**   The tapping of a telephone can be necessary for the prevention of crime, and lawful, even if the telephone is that of the partner of a suspect rather than the suspect himself (*Greuter v Netherlands*, Decision of 19 March 2002, claim held inadmissible).

12.142 n521: *Foxley v United Kingdom* is now reported at (2000) 8 BHRC 571.

12.144 **For the protection of health or morals.**   In five cases, *Chapman v United Kingdom, Coster v United Kingdom, Beard v United Kingdom, Lee v United Kingdom* and *Smith v United Kingdom* (2001) 33 EHRR 18 the Court decided that the occupation of caravans by gypsies was an integral part of their ethnic identity and that enforcement proceedings for breach of planning permission and the planning decisions themselves interfered with their right to private and family life. However, the Court found that the interferences were pursued for the legitimate aim of protecting the rights of others through preserving the environment. It considered that domestic authorities had a wide margin of appreciation concerning the planning considerations attaching to a particular site (see *Buckley v United Kingdom* (1996) 23 EHRR 101). The planning inspectors had identified strong environmental factors relating to the applicants' use of land which outweighed their individual interest. The Court also noted that gypsies were at liberty to camp on any caravan site with planning permission. Although there were insufficient sites which gypsies found acceptable and affordable and on which they could lawfully place their caravans, the Court was not persuaded that there were no alternatives available to the applicants. It did not accept that, because statistically, the number of gypsies were greater than the number of places available in authorised gypsy sites, a decision not to allow the applicants to install their caravans constituted a breach of Article 8. Nor could Article 8 be interpreted to impose on the United Kingdom an obligation to make available to the gypsy community an adequate number of suitably equipped sites. Article 8 did not give a right to be provided with a home.

In *Pretty v United Kingdom* (2002) 12 BHRC 149 it was held that a ban on assisting suicide, although an interference for the purpose of Article 8(1), was justified as it protected the life and health of others, in particular of those who might not be able to make informed decisions about ending their life.

For the protection of the rights and freedoms of others.   In the context of the   **12.146** publication of a photograph of a politician presented in a disparaging manner, the Court held that while such publication might interfere with the right to private life, a state was entitled not to prevent it on the basis that such freedom of expression was required to protect Article 10 rights, which are of particular significance in the context of political campaigning (*Schussel v Austria*, Decision of 21 February 2002).

D. The Impact of the Human Rights Act

(1) Introduction

In *R v Worcester County Council, ex p SW* [2000] HRLR 702, 717–19, discussed   **12.148** at Supplement, para 12.38, Newman J dealt with the scope of Article 8 although the case was argued before the Human Rights Act came into effect. He stated that:

- The notion of 'private life' is broad enough to include, to a certain degree, activities which can be seen to be an aspect of the development of an individual's personality, for example, in establishing relationships, even though the activities have occurred in a business or professional context.
- The effect, where appropriate, of including activities occurring in a business or professional context within Article 8 is limited and selective.
- It recognises the conduct as being within private life. It does not extend it to an individual's business or professional life.
- Activities occurring within an individual's business or professional life will be encompassed within Article 8 where the dividing line between them is not clearly distinguishable, for example, where it can be seen that it has occurred in a place where access to the public is excluded and some domestic authority has been exercised.

He went on to hold that material gathered by an employer about the suitability of the applicant as a teacher is material recording the public performance of the teacher and involves no element of private life. However, the reasoning of Newman J is difficult to reconcile with the approach taken by the Court in *Lustig-Prean v United Kingdom* (1999) 29 EHRR 449 and *Smith and Grady v United Kingdom* (1999) 29 EHRR 493 and in subsequent cases.

The Court of Human Rights continues to take an expansive view of the scope of Article 8; see Supplement, para 12.84. In particular, the Court in *Pretty v United*

Kingdom (2002) 12 BHRC 149 held that the legal restriction which prevented Mrs Pretty from avoiding, by an assisted suicide, an undignified and distressing death breached Article 8(1). The Court did not follow the approach of the House of Lords in *R (Pretty) v DPP* [2002] 1 AC 800 which had held that Article 8 was directed at the protection of personal automony while an individual was alive but did not confer the right to decide how or when to die.

(2) United Kingdom cases

(a) Introduction

12.152 The United Kingdom has been found to have violated the right to respect for private life, home and correspondence on 28 occasions to date.

> **n548:** The violations since 1 September 2000 were in the following cases: *Armstrong v United Kingdom* (Judgment of 16 July 2002); *Goodwin v United Kingdom* (2002) 35 EHRR 447; *I v United Kingdom* (Judgment of 11 July 2002); *Faulkner v United Kingdom* (2002) 35 EHRR 686; *Hatton v United Kingdom* (2002) 34 EHRR 1; *PG and JH v United Kingdom* (Judgment of 25 September 2001); *MG v United Kingdom* (Judgment of 24 September 2002); *Taylor-Sabori v United Kingdom* (Judgment of 22 October 2002); *Beck, Copp and Bazeley v United Kingdom* (Judgment of 22 October 2002); *Perkins and R v United Kingdom* (Judgment of 22 October 2002; and *Allan v United Kingdom, The Times,* 12 November 2002.
>
> *Lustig-Prean v United Kingdom* is now reported at (1999) 29 EHRR 449 and *Smith and Grady v United Kingdom* is now reported at (1999) 29 EHRR 493. *Khan v United Kingdom* is now reported at (2000) 8 BHRC 310. *Foxley v United Kingdom* is now reported at (2000) 8 BHRC 571. *ADT v United Kingdom* is now reported at (2000) 9 BHRC 112.

(c) Telephone tapping and surveillance

12.154 See also *Armstrong v United Kingdom* (Judgment of 16 July 2002).

(d) Privacy and sexual relationships

12.159 On 8 January 2001, the Sexual Offences (Amendment) Act 2000 came into force reducing the age of consent for homosexual acts between consenting males to 16. As a result and at the request of both parties, the application in *Sutherland v United Kingdom, The Times,* 13 April 2001, was struck out on 27 March 2001.

(e) Other applications

12.164 **Personal privacy.** In *Peck v United Kingdom* (Decision of 15 May 2001) a complaint concerning a local authority's release to the press of CCTV footage of the claimant's attempted suicide was held to be admissible (for the English case, see Main Work, para 12.201).

(3) General impact issues

(a) *Privacy and the common law*

See, generally, Supplement, para 12.06. See also: R Singh and J Strachan, 'The **12.165** Right to Privacy in English Law' [2002] EHRLR 129; M Colvin (ed), *Developing Key Privacy Rights* (Hart Publishing, 2002); H Tomlinson (ed), *Privacy and the Media: The Developing Law* (Matrix, 2002); and M Tugendhat and I Christie (eds), *The Law of Privacy and the Media* (Oxford University Press, 2002).

In *Wainwright v The Home Office* [2002] 3 WLR 405 the Court of Appeal held **12.167** that there was no right to privacy at common law. The current debate on this issue is discussed at Supplement, para 12.06.

n599: *R v Broadcasting Standards Commission, ex p BBC* is now reported at [2001] QB 885. See also *R v Loveridge* [2001] 2 Cr App R 29.

(b) *The impact on civil procedure*

In *St Merryn Meat v Hawkins* [2001] CP Rep 116 (Mr Vos QC) it was held that **12.171** the obtaining of evidence by telephone taps on home telephones was a breach of the defendant's Article 8 rights even though it had not been undertaken by a public authority. This had not been disclosed to the court and, as a result, search and freezing orders made without notice were discharged.

On the balancing of competing interests of privacy and good reputation of two **12.172** private parties and freedom of expression of the press in relation to a decision on the revelation of medical documents in libel proceedings, see *Chase v News Group Newspapers* [2002] EWHC 1101, QB. The case is discussed at Supplement, para 15.31, in relation to Article 10.

It was held by the House of Lords in *R v Special Commissioner of Income Tax, ex p* **12.173** *Morgan Grenfell* [2002] 2 WLR 1299 that legal professional privilege was a fundamental human right recognised by the common law and that the courts would construe general words in a statute as overriding such fundamental human rights only if expressly stated by a statute or required by necessary implication. Section 20(1) of the Taxes Management Act 1970 contained no express reference to legal professional privilege, and there was no necessary implication that legal professional privilege needed to be excluded by it. It would have been irrational for Parliament to have preserved legal professional privilege for documents in the hands of the lawyer, but not for documents, which could be copies or originals of the same documents, in the hands of the taxpayer.

The Court of Appeal decided in *South Coast Shipping v Havant BC* [2002] 3 All ER 779 that CPR PD 47, para 40.14, on disclosure of documents in relation to disputes as to costs, was compatible with Article 8.

n611: The House of Lords in *R (Daly) v Secretary of State for the Home Department* [2001] 2 AC 532 overruled the Court of Appeal decision in *R v Home Secretary, ex p Simms* [1999] QB 349 by holding that the policy permitting prison officers to examine a prisoner's legally privileged material in his absence was unlawful.

(c) The right of access to personal information

12.174 In *R (Addinell) v Sheffield City Council* [2000] ACD 331 Sullivan J took the view that it was an unwarranted extension of the principle established by *Gaskin v United Kingdom* (1989) 12 EHRR 36 for a parent to obtain access to the social services files of his son who had died in council care.

In *R (Gunn-Russo) v Nugent Care Society* [2002] 1 FLR 1 Scott Baker J held that the disclosure of adoption records by a voluntary adoption agency required a balancing exercise to be conducted between disclosure and confidentiality. The case is discussed further at Supplement, para 13.156.

Article 8 is engaged in circumstances in which a child born through artificial insemination wishes to discover the identity of his biological parents; see *R (Rose) v Secretary of State for Health* [2002] EWHC Admin 1593 (Scott Baker J).

The commercial use of the electoral register breached the Article 8 rights of an individual who wished to be on the register but not to have his details used in such a way; see *R (Robertston) v City of Wakefield Metropolitan Council* [2002] 2 WLR 889.

In *Baker v Secretary of State for the Home Department* [2001] UKHRR 1275 it was held to be disproportionate under Article 8 for the Security Service to refuse to deny or confirm on a blanket basis that it held personal data in response to a request for access under section 7 of the Data Protection Act 1998.

(4) Specific areas of impact

(a) Commercial law

12.176 **n622:** *R v Broadcasting Standards Commission, ex p BBC* is now reported at [2001] QB 885.

(b) Criminal law

12.177 In *R v Commissioner of Police for the Metropolis, ex p Rottman* [2002] 2 WLR 1315 the House of Lords held that a police officer who had arrested a person in or on his premises pursuant to a warrant of arrest issued under section 8 of the Extradition Act 1989 had power to search those premises for, and to seize, any goods or documents which he reasonably believed to be material evidence in relation to an extradition crime in respect of which a warrant was issued. Such a search and seizure was not in breach of Article 8, notwithstanding that it is governed by the common law rather than the Police and Criminal Evidence Act 1984.

In *R (Marper) v Chief Constable of South Yorkshire* [2002] 1 WLR 3223 it was held that section 64 of the Police and Criminal Evidence Act 1984, which allows the police to maintain on file DNA and fingerprint samples of individuals, even if those individuals have not been convicted of any crime, is not incompatible with Article 8. It was held that even if the right to privacy was infringed, that infringement was justified for the purposes of Article 8(2).

In *R v Pearce* [2001] 1 WLR 1553 the Court of Appeal decided that the fact that the cohabitee and child of the defendant to a murder charge were compellable witnesses did not breach his Article 8 rights.

It was held by the House of Lords in *R (Pretty) v DPP* [2002] 1 AC 800 that the fact that assisting suicide was a criminal offence did not breach the Article 8 rights of an individual to choose their own personal identity. The House of Lords questioned whether Article 8 was engaged at all, but in any event found any interference to be justifiable and proportionate. The somewhat different approach of the Court of Human Rights is discussed at Supplement, para 12.84.

Where a Rastafarian claimed that he used cannabis on religious grounds, Article 8 did not require a stay of proceedings, nor were questions of proportionality and necessity questions for the jury (*R v Taylor* [2002] 1 Cr App R 519). For a case which raised a similar issue in South Africa, see Supplement, para 14.127.

The courts have continued to deal with the admissibility of evidence obtained in **12.178** breach of Article 8 as an issue of fairness under section 78 of the Police and Criminal Evidence Act. The suggestion made in the Main Work that a stricter test should be applied because the Human Rights Act creates constitutional rights has therefore not been adopted. In two cases the House of Lords rejected the defendant's attempt to overturn his conviction on the grounds that it was based upon evidence obtained in breach of Article 8. In *Attorney-General's Reference (No 3 of 1999)* [2001] 2 WLR 56 a DNA sample taken from the defendant on his arrest for an offence for which he had been acquitted was, contrary to section 64(3B)(b) of the Police and Criminal Evidence Act 1984, used in the investigation of a subsequent offence. The House of Lords held that the admission of a second DNA sample which had been taken during that investigation did not give rise to an unlawful interference with the defendant's rights under Article 8. In *R v P* [2001] 2 WLR 463 the House of Lords decided that recordings of telephone conversations between a national of another country and the appellants which had been lawfully intercepted in that country by its prosecuting authorities were admissible in evidence at the appellants' trial in England. Similarly, the Court of Appeal in *R v Bailey* [2001] EWCA Crim 733 took the view that tape recordings made by the police in breach of various statutory requirements might nevertheless be admissible under section 78. In *R v Loveridge* [2002] Cr App R 591 the Court of Appeal ruled that convictions were safe even though the police had unlawfully videotaped the defendant and adduced evidence from a facial-mapping expert to compare the video with a CCTV video taken of a robbery.

In *R v McLeod* [2002] EWCA Crim 989 the Court of Appeal held that notwithstanding that the use of a covert listening device to record a conversation was probably in breach of Article 8, the evidence gathered from the recording should not be held to be inadmissible pursuant to section 78 of the Police and Criminal Evidence Act 1984.

On the disclosure of personal information of parties in sex assault trials, see J Temkin, 'Digging the Dirt: Disclosure of Records in Sexual Assault Cases' (2002) 61 CLJ 126.

12.180 It was held in *R (Craven) v Secretary of State for the Home Department* [2001] EWHC Admin 850 that the release of a life prisoner on licence on condition that he did not go to a certain area, to prevent accidental contact with the family of the victim, was not in breach of his rights under Article 8.

n627a: *Khan v United Kingdom* is now reported at (2000) 8 BHRC 310.

(d) Employment and discrimination

12.187 **Collection and use of personal data on employees.** See Newman J in *R v Worcester County Council, ex p SW* [2000] HRLR 702, 716–20, regarding the potential application of Article 8 to the Department of Health's Consultancy Service Index (an advisory service open to various public and private bodies which provides information on the suitability of potential childcare employees). The case is discussed further at Supplement, para 12.148. In *De Keyser v Wilson* [2000] IRLR 234 the EAT held that references to the applicant's personal life in a letter of instruction sent to a medical expert in an unfair dismissal case did not breach Article 8.

The Information Commissioner has issued a draft *Employment Practices Code* which deals with the use of personal data in employer/employee relationships. This takes a very restrictive view as to the extent to which monitoring and surveillance can be conducted in the workplace. The draft code suggests that, in order to comply with the DPA, employers must:

- Assess the impact of the monitoring on the privacy, autonomy and other legitimate rights of staff and should not introduce monitoring in which any adverse impact is out of proportion to the benefits.
- If comparable benefits can reasonably be achieved by another method with less adverse impact, adopt that method.

- Target any monitoring on those areas where it is actually necessary and proportionate to achieving the business purpose. (The draft code says that monitoring of all staff will not be justified if the purpose of the monitoring is to address a risk that is posed only by a few.)
- Not use personal information collected through monitoring for purposes other than those for which the monitoring was introduced and staff were told about unless the information is such that no reasonable employer could ignore it, ie it reveals criminal activity or gross misconduct.
- Remember that information collected through monitoring can be misleading, misinterpreted or even deliberately falsified as well as being inaccurate because of equipment malfunction. If the information is to be used in a way that might have an adverse impact on employees, they should be presented with the information and given an opportunity to challenge or explain it before it is used.

Sexual orientation discrimination.   The Court of Appeal's decision in *Pearce v Governing Body of Mayfield School* [2002] ICR 188 provides some support for the view that the Sex Discrimination Act 1975, read subject to section 3 of the Human Rights Act so as to make it compatible with Articles 8 and 14, extends to sexual orientation discrimination. The case is discussed further at Supplement, para 17.148.   **12.188**

See, generally, R Wintemute, 'Lesbian and Gay Inequality 2000: The Potential Impact of the Human Rights Act 1998 and the Need for an Equality Act 2002' [2000] EHRLR 603.

(f) Health care

In *A Health Authority v X* [2001] UKHRR 1213 Munby J decided that Article 8 required a health authority to show a compelling public interest when seeking disclosure of confidential patient records disclosed in care proceedings for the purpose of investigating allegations that doctors had breached their terms of service. He took the view that GP records could be disclosed in compliance with Article 8 only if: they were *bona fide* and reasonably required for the proper exercise of their regulatory functions; there was a compelling public interest in their disclosure which satisfied the criteria of necessity and proportionality; and there were efficient and adequate safeguards against abuse. The Court of Appeal at [2002] 2 All ER 780 held that Munby J had correctly balanced the public interest in effective disciplinary procedures against the confidentiality of the documents and had correctly used his power to attach conditions to the disclosure.   **12.192A**

(g) Housing law

In *Poplar Housing and Regeneration Community Association Ltd v Donoghue* [2002] QB 48 the Court of Appeal held that a registered social landlord was a functional public authority. It stated (at para 59) that the fact that a body performed an activity which otherwise a public body would be under a duty to perform did not mean   **12.193** that such performance was necessarily a public function. However, it held that in all the circumstances of the case the housing association was so closely assimilated with the council that it was performing public and not private functions.

Premises can be a 'home' notwithstanding that the claimant has no legal or equitable interest in it (*London Borough of Harrow v Qazi* [2002] UKHRR 316). The courts have rejected a number of arguments, based on Article 8, to the effect that there is a right to a home:

- Article 8 does not provide any remedy solely because an individual is homeless; see *R (Morris) v London Borough of Newham* (2002) 27 EG 143. Article 8 does not confer a right to be provided with a home nor to succeed to a tenancy.
- Article 8, read in conjunction with Article 14, cannot be used to interpret the Housing Act 1985 so as to permit a claimant outside the class of relatives so entitled under the 1985 Act to succeed to the tenancy of a dead relative (*Michalak v Wandsworth London Borough Council* [2002] 4 All ER 1136).
- Given the competing claims to the resources of a local authority, Article 8 cannot be used to interpret section 17 of the Children Act 1989 so as to *require* a local authority to provide a home for a mother and her children (*R (W) v Lambeth London Borough Council* [2002] 2 All ER 901).

The introductory tenancy scheme, contained in the Housing Act 1996, which enables local authorities operating the scheme to terminate tenancies in the first 12 months by issuing the appropriate notice, was compatible with Article 8 (*R (McLellan) v Bracknell Forest Borough Council, ex p McLellan* [2002] 2 WLR 144, CA).

On the relation between the transfer of property following divorce pursuant to the Matrimonial Causes Act 1973, and the confiscation of a home pursuant to the Drug Trafficking Act 1994, in the light of rights under Article 8, see *HM Customs and Excise v MCA* [2002] EWCA Civ 1039.

See, generally, I Loveland, 'When is a House not a Home under Article 8 ECHR' [2002] PL 221; and I Loveland, 'Rethinking the Rule in *Hammersmith v Monk* from a Human Rights Perspective' [2002] EHRLR 327.

n682: *R v Servite Homes, ex p Goldsmith* is now reported at [2001] LGR 55.

12.195 In *Marcic v Thames Water Utilities Ltd* [2001] 3 All ER 698 H H J Havery QC decided that the failure of the defendant to carry out works to bring to an end repeated flooding on the claimant's home was a breach of Article 8 which it failed to justify. A subsequent application for a reconsideration of the judgment was refused (see *Marcic v Thames Water Utilities (No 2)* [2001] 2 WLR 1000). The decision was upheld by the Court of Appeal at [2002] 2 WLR 932. The Court also held that the flooding was a nuisance as well as a breach of Article 8.

In *Lee v Leeds City Council* [2002] 1 WLR 1488 the Court of Appeal accepted there may be cases in which property let by a local authority was in such poor condition that a failure to repair breached Article 8. However, the Court went on to hold that, on the facts, the condition did not reach such a level. Furthermore, the condition was not such as to require other legislation to be interpreted, in the light of Article 8, to alter the duty of a local authority landlord to undertake repairs.

In *McKenna v British Aluminium, The Times*, 25 April 2002 Neuberger J held that claims made by children, who had no proprietary rights in their home, in relation to factory emissions and noise pollution could arguably be made under Article 8 even though they could not be maintained in nuisance or on strict liability based on *Rylands v Fletcher*.

In *Castle Vale Housing Action Trust v Gallagher* (2001) 33 HLR 72 the Court of **12.196** Appeal doubted whether Article 8 made any difference to the way the court approached the question of the reasonableness of making a possession order in respect of residential property occupied under a secured tenancy. However, Article 8 did reinforce the importance of only making an order depriving someone of his home in circumstances where a clear case was made out. In *Lambeth LBC v Howard* (2001) 33 HLR 58 the Court of Appeal said that a possession order for modest rent arrears is unlikely to be disproportionate and the issue will depend on striking a fair balance between the rights of the individual and the interests of the community. In *Sheffield City Council v Hopkins* [2002] HLR 12 the Court of Appeal stated that when exercising its discretion under section 85 of the Housing Act to suspend the execution of a warrant, the discretion should be used to further the policy of Part IV of the Act reinforced by Article 8 which was only to evict after a serious breach of the tenancy agreement where it was reasonable to do so and where the tenant had been proved to breach any condition of suspension. The Court of Appeal decided in *St Brice v Southwark LBC* [2002] 1 WLR 1537 that once a county court had made a possession order against a council tenant, his right under Article 8 had been complied with; a local authority did not therefore breach Article 8 by evicting him without notice by a warrant of possession obtained under the possession order.

Where a housing association sought a mandatory order for possession under section 21 of the Housing Act 1988, the Court of Appeal decided that the statutory provision was necessary in a democratic society under Article 8(2); see *Poplar Housing and Regeneration Community Association Ltd v Donoghue* [2002] QB 48. The limited role of the court under section 21(4) was a legislative policy decision and was a policy area where the decisions of Parliament as to the public interest should be treated with particular deference.

In *Somerset County Council v Isaacs* [2002] EWHC Admin 1014 it was argued that the express statutory exclusion (the Caravan Sites Act 1968 and the Mobile

Homes Act 1983) of gypsies provided with accommodation on local authority land from the security of tenure enjoyed by the occupiers of caravans on privately owned land breached Article 8. It was argued that this exclusion prevented the court from investigating the justification, or lack of it, of an eviction. It was held, however, that as an alleged infringement of Article 8 could be raised before the county court or the Administrative Court on judicial review, the lack of security of tenure would not itself result in any infringement of Article 8 rights. In any event, the court held, there was sufficient evidence that the denial of security of tenure was proportionate and in the pursuit of a legitimate aim.

In *Sheffield City Council v Smart* [2002] HLR 34 the Court of Appeal considered two cases of individuals who had become unintentionally homeless and were then provided with a non-secure tenancy pursuant to the Housing Act 1996 by local authorities. In both cases the authorities subsequently served notices to quit. The Court of Appeal held that in the possession proceedings which followed the county court was entitled to assume, unless something exceptional had occurred after the notice to quit was served, that the Housing Act itself struck the correct balance of interests pursuant to Article 8(2) and the court need not review the matter *ab initio.*

(h) Immigration law

12.198 The application of Article 8 in relation to immigration cases has been considered by the Court of Appeal in *R (Mahmood) v Home Secretary* [2001] 1 WLR 840 and *R (Isiko) v Secretary of State for the Home Department* [2001] HRLR 295. However, these cases must be treated with considerable caution because the approach they take towards the proportionality principle has been superseded by the stricter test applied by the House of Lords in *R v A (No 2)* [2002] 1 AC 45 and *R (Daly) v Secretary of State for the Home Department* [2001] 2 AC 532. In relation to alleged breaches of Article 8 in the country to which an immigrant would be returned, see *R (M, A, Z) v Immigration Appeal Tribunal* [2002] EWCA Civ 952, CA.

(i) Local government law

12.199 An obligation under Article 8 may arise when a health authority seeks to move residents of a mental health institution against their will; see *R v Brent, Kensington, Chelsea and Westminster Mental Health NHS Trust, ex p C* [2002] EWHC Admin 1262. In the case itself it was held that no breach of Article 8 had occurred.

On local authority liability in relation to homelessness and Article 8, see *R (Morris) v London Borough of Newham* [2002] EWHC Admin 1262.

In *R (J & P) v West Sussex County Council* [2002] EWHC Admin 1143 it was held that a decision by a local authority to reveal that an individual had been convicted of sexually abusing children to the daughter of the individual's partner engaged Article 8 but was justified for the purposes of Article 8(2).

In *R (J) v Enfield LBC* [2002] FLR 1 Elias J held that a local authority has a discretionary power to grant financial assistance for the acquisition of accommodation pursuant to the Local Government Act 2000. This power becomes a *duty* in circumstances in which Article 8 breaches are at issue.

(j) Media law

As suggested in the Main Work, the Human Rights Act 1998 has had a considerable impact on media law in relation to 'privacy' issues. There have been several important cases since the Human Rights Act came into force: **12.202**

- In *Douglas v Hello! Ltd* [2001] QB 967 the Court of Appeal set aside an interlocutory injunction restraining *Hello!* magazine from publishing pictures of the Douglas–Zeta-Jones wedding, the exclusive rights to which had been sold to *OK!* magazine.
- In *Mills v Mirror Group Newspapers* [2001] EMLR 957 an injunction restraining the publication of the claimant's home address was refused in the absence of evidence of apprehended harm.
- In *Venables v News Group Newspapers* [2001] Fam 340 the applicants (notoriously convicted of murdering the infant, James Bulger) were granted injunctions against the whole world to prevent the publication of information which might lead to their identification.
- In *Theakston v MGN Ltd* [2002] EMLR 398 Ouseley J refused an injunction to restrain the publication of a story concerning the activities of a television presenter in a brothel, but granted an injunction to restrain the publication of photographs.
- In *A v B plc* [2002] 3 WLR 542 the Court of Appeal discharged an injunction to restrain publication of a story about the sexual activities of a premier league footballer. The Court took into account the fact that the relationship had been a transient one, that the other parties to the relationship wished to disclose it and the fact that the claimant was a well-known premiership footballer who was a club captain.
- In *Campbell v Mirror Group Newspapers* [2003] 2 WLR 80 the claimant complained about the publication of photographs and a story about drug treatment. The claimant was a well-known model who had falsely denied that she took drugs. It was accepted that, given the public interest in knowing that the claimant's denials of drug addiction were false, the newspaper was entitled to publish the story. The Court of Appeal held that publication of the fact that the claimant was attending meetings of Narcotics Anonymous was not a breach of confidence. In the context this information was not of 'sufficient significance to shock the conscience and justify the intervention of the court' (para 56).

Furthermore, if publication of confidential information is justifiable in the public interest, the journalist must be given reasonable latitude as to the manner in which the information is conveyed to the public (para 64).

In every case where privacy rights are relied on, media defendants respond by relying on the right to freedom of expression. In considering a conflict between these two rights the result of section 12(4) of the Human Rights Act 1998 is that the court must have particular regard to any relevant privacy codes (see *Douglas v Hello! Ltd* [2001] QB 967; *A v B plc* [2002] 3 WLR 542, para 11(iv)). In *A v B plc* the Court of Appeal emphasised the need for all interferences with freedom of expression, particularly freedom of the press, to be justified. Although the Court quoted, with apparent approval, a Council of Europe resolution which said that the rights to privacy and freedom of expression are not 'in any hierarchical order, since they are of equal value' (para 11(xii)), its decision has been generally understood as treating freedom of expression as having priority over the right to privacy. However, in *Campbell v MGN* [2003] 2 WLR 80, the Court of Appeal emphasised that the fact that the Court in *A v B plc* had commended the Council of Europe guidance on striking a balance (para 40). The principles to be applied in cases in which expression and privacy are in conflict await definitive exposition by the courts.

On privacy and freedom of expression in relation to private parties, such as the media, see A Young, 'Remedial and Substantive Horizontality: The Common Law and *Douglas v Hello! Ltd*' [2002] PL 232 and I Hare, 'Verticality Challenged: Private Parties, Privacy and the Human Rights Act' [2001] EHRLR 526. Generally, on the law relating to privacy and freedom of expression, see R Singh and J Strachan, 'The Right to Privacy in English Law' (2002) EHRLR 129; M Colvin (ed), *Developing Key Privacy Rights* (Hart Publishing, 2002); H Tomlinson (ed), *Privacy and the Media: The Developing Law* (Matrix, 2002); and M Tugendhat and I Christie (eds), *The Law of Privacy and the Media* (Oxford University Press, 2002).

On the requirement of a journalist to reveal a source in the context of the leaking of confidential medical information, see the decision of the House of Lords in *Ashworth Hospital Authority v MGN* [2002] 1 WLR 2033, discussed at Supplement, para 15.76.

(k) Mental health law

12.203   In relation to the obligation pursuant to Article 8 which arises when a health authority seeks to move residents of a mental health institution against their will, see *R (C) v Brent, Kensington, Chelsea and Westminster Mental Health NHS Trust* [2002] EWHC Admin 181. In the case itself it was held that no breach of Article 8 had occurred.

It was held in *R (E) v Ashworth Hospital Authority* [2002] AC 149 that restrictions on a male patient of a mental institution dressing as a woman were not in breach of Article 8. There was no breach of Article 8 when a mental patient who suffered from Hepatitis C was not permitted to be provided with condoms in a secure hospital (*R (H) v Ashworth Health Authority* [2001] EWHC Admin 872).

(l) Planning and environmental law

Introduction.　n719: *R v Leicestershire County Council, ex p Blackfordby and Boothorpe Action Group* is now reported at [2001] Env LR 35.　　**12.207**

It was held in *Clark v Secretary of State for Environment, Transport and the Regions* [2002] EWCA Civ 819 that a refusal of planning permission to safeguard the Green Belt complied with Article 8.

Enforcement powers.　In *Porter v South Bucks DC* [2002] 1 WLR 1359 the　**12.208** Court of Appeal held that the decision as to whether to grant an injunction to restrict an actual or apprehended breach of planning control should be exercised in a manner which is compliant with the Article 8 rights of those affected. The judge must balance the impact of the injunction, if infringing upon Article 8(1) rights, against any justification pursuant to Article 8(2) in a manner which is structured and articulated. See G Jones and J Pike, 'Proportionality and Planning: A Difficult and Nice Point' [2002] JPL 908.

In *R (Ward) v London Borough of Hillingdon* [2001] LGR 457 Stanley Burnton J applied the decision of the European Court of Human Rights in *Chapman v United Kingdom, The Times*, 30 January 2001 (discussed at Supplement, para 12.146), and decided that the decision to evict gypsies from a caravan site was proportionate under Article 8(2).

n723: The Court rejected the applications in *Chapman v United Kingdom, Coster v United Kingdom, Beard v United Kingdom, Lee v United Kingdom and Smith v United Kingdom* (2001) 10 BHRC 48 which are discussed at Supplement, para 12.146. The UK compromised *Varey v United Kingdom*.

Statutory nuisance.　In *Marcic v Thames Water Utilities* [2002] 2 WLR 932 the　**12.209** Court of Appeal held that a failure by the public authority to prevent flooding of the claimant's home was both a statutory nuisance and a breach of the authority's positive obligations under Article 8.

(m) Police law

Introduction.　It was held in *R (Fuller) v Chief Constable of Dorset Police* [2002]　**12.210** 3 All ER 57 that the power of the police, pursuant to sections 61 and 62 of the Public Order Act 1994, to direct trespassers living on land to move, was not incompatible with Article 8.

12.211 **The Interception of Communications Act.** The Interception of Communications Act 1985 has been repealed and replaced by the Regulation of Investigatory Powers Act 2000 which is discussed further at Supplement, paras 12.60–12.62, 12.66 and 12.68–12.70.

12.214 **Regulation of other forms of surveillance.** The Regulation of Investigatory Powers Act 2000 is now in force and regulates directed surveillance, intrusive surveillance and use of covert intelligence sources (as defined in section 26). The authorisation procedure for such surveillance is contained in Part II of the Act. The procedure for making a complaint under the Act is discussed further at Supplement, para 12.62.

12.215 The Regulation of Investigatory Powers Act 2000 is now in force and regulates directed and intrusive surveillance. The procedure for making a complaint and the jurisdiction of the Tribunal are discussed at Supplement, para 12.69.

12.216 **Search warrants.** For a search found to be incompatible with Article 8, see *R (Paul Da Costa & Co) v Thames Magistrates' Court* [2002] Crim LR 504.

In *R (Pamplin) v Law Society* [2001] EWHC Admin 300 Newman J held that the disclosure by the police to the Law Society of the prosecution file relating to the applicant was not a breach of his Article 8 rights. The mere fact that the information was confidential did not engage Article 8 because the file centred on the applicant's public life as a provider of legal services.

12.218A **Other areas of police activity.** In *R (Marper) v Chief Constable of South Yorkshire* [2002] 1 WLR 3223 the Court of Appeal decided that the retention of fingerprints and DNA samples after a suspect was cleared of an offence interfered with Article 8(1). The interference was not substantial but real and the justification was proportionate. It was also argued that the retention of the samples was discriminatory and breached Article 14. See, further, Supplement, para 17.166.

(n) Prison law

12.219 In *N v Governor of HM Dartmoor Prison*, *The Times*, 19 March 2001, Turner J held that disclosure by a prison governor to a local authority and the probation service of a spent sex offence committed by the claimant against a child was justified under Article 8(2) because such disclosure was necessary in order to protect children. In *R (N) v Ashworth Special Educational Authority*, *The Times*, 26 June 2001, the random monitoring of telephone calls by patients in a high security hospital was an interference with the right to privacy which went no further than was necessary to achieve a legitimate aim.

In *R (Ponting) v Governor of HMP Whitemoor* [2002] EWCA Civ 2224 it was held that a prisoner, given access to a computer but subject to various conditions relating to its use, did not have his Article 8 rights breached because of the conditions.

(o) Sex offender orders

In *B v Chief Constable of Avon and Somerset* [2001] 1 WLR 340 Lord Bingham CJ **12.219A**
decided that sex offender orders were not incompatible with Article 8 since they
were authorised by section 2 of the Crime and Disorder Act 1998, had the legitimate object of preventing crime and protecting the public and extended no more
than was strictly necessary to serve their intended purpose. In *Jones v Greater
Manchester Police Authority* [2001] EWHC Admin 189 the appellant, a 63-year-
old man with 30 convictions relating to sexual offences against young males in
England and abroad, asked the court to set aside a sex offender order made against
him pursuant to section 2 of the Crime and Disorder Act 1998. The order prohibited the appellant for the remainder of his life from entering any public park,
children's playground or public swimming bath and from being in the company
of any person under the age of 18 years. It also prevented him from leaving the
country without first notifying the police and obtaining the permission of the
court. The appeal was made on the grounds that, *inter alia*, the order gave rise to
a disproportionate interference with the appellant's right to a private life pursuant
to Article 8. Dismissing the appeal, Latham LJ acknowledged that the purpose of
the order was to protect the public from serious harm and held that the interference with Article 8 rights was justified in the light of the appellant's age and long
history of offences. In addition, although the order had been made for life, it was
open to the appellant to apply subsequently to vary the order.

(p) Tax law

In *R v Commissioners of Inland Revenue, ex p Banque Internationale à Luxembourg* **12.219B**
[2000] STC 708 the bank sought to quash statutory notices served by the
Commissioners requiring it to produce documents relating to various large-scale
corporate tax avoidance schemes (which were being financed by the bank).
Lightman J held that insofar as the notices interfered with rights protected by
Article 8(1), there was sufficient justification for the purpose of Article 8(2) because
the notices were necessary in a democratic society for protecting the taxation system and, in particular, were necessary to enable the Commissioners to take appropriate remedial action in relation to sophisticated corporate tax avoidance schemes.

(q) Social security law

It was held in *R (Reynolds) v Secretary of State for Work and Pensions* [2002] EWHC **12.219C**
Admin 426 that the broadly worded principles articulated in Article 8 are not suitable for a challenge as to the level of a social security payment. It was held that, in
any event, had there been an interference with the right to private and family life
it would, on the facts, have been justified.

In *R (Plumb) v Secretary of State for Social Security* [2002] EWHC Admin 1125 it
was held that Article 8 could be engaged in circumstances in which a *deduction* was

made from social security which it was alleged infringed upon family life. A distinction was drawn between such a case and one in which a claimant sought to use Article 8 to found a positive claim for a benefit to which he or she was not yet entitled. The case itself involved a deduction from the claimant's jobseeker's allowance to pay for child support. It was found, however, that the deduction did not infringe Article 8 rights and that in any event it was justified for the purpose of Article 8(2).

Appendix 1: The Canadian Charter of Rights

(1) Introduction

12.220 See, generally, M Russell, 'The Impact of the Charter on Privacy and Freedom of Expression in Canada', in M Colvin (ed), *Developing Key Privacy Rights* (Hart Publishing, 2002).

(4) Section 8 analysis: a two-step process

(b) *'Reasonable expectation of privacy'*

12.237 **The existence of a 'search' or 'seizure'.**   Citizens have a reasonable expectation of privacy with respect to bodily integrity. In the absence of statutory authority, police could take blood and hair samples from suspects only with the informed consent of those suspects (*R v Arp* [2000] 2 LRC 119). The persons consenting had to be aware of their rights, and the consequences of consent. In *Arp*, consent to samples being taken for the purposes of one murder investigation was held to cover the use of those samples for a subsequent murder investigation. The mere fact that police recover lost or stolen property is insufficient to support an inference that the owner voluntarily relinquished his expectation of privacy in the item; see *R v Law* 2002 SCC 10 (before a stolen safe was returned to its owner, a police officer unconnected with the theft investigation, but who suspected the owner of violating tax laws, photocopied some financial documents found in the safe. The Supreme Court held that there had been a violation of the right to privacy).

There was no breach of section 8 when a customs declaration was disclosed to unemployment authorities which showed that the appellant had been on holiday outside Canada while receiving unemployment benefits (*Smith v Canada* [2001] SCC 88).

12.243 **The reasonableness of the search or seizure.**   A forced bedpan vigil by customs officers of a detainee suspected to have ingested pellets of drugs was held to amount to a reasonable search in *R v Monney* [1999] 6 BHRC 336. A strip search (and intimate search) of an arrested suspect, on the other hand, was declared unreasonable in *Golden v R* (2002) 12 BHRC 295. The majority of the court stated that the fact that the police had reasonable and probable grounds to carry out an arrest did not confer on them the automatic authority to carry out a strip search, even where the strip search met the definition of being 'incident to lawful arrest'. In addition to reasonable and probable grounds justifying the arrest, the police must establish reasonable and probable grounds justifying the strip search.

Appendix 2: The New Zealand Bill of Rights Act

(1) Introduction

In *P v D* [2000] 2 NZLR 591 a journalist informed a public figure that he was **12.244** preparing a newspaper article concerning his treatment at a psychiatric hospital and an injunction was sought to prevent publication. Although the claim for breach of confidence failed, Nicholson J held the tort of breach of privacy was established by public disclosure of private facts which are highly offensive and objectionable to a person of reasonable sensibilities subject to the nature and extent of legitimate interest in the public disclosure of the information. Such factors had to be balanced against the right to freedom of expression under section 14 of the New Zealand Bill of Rights Act. In *L v G* [2002] DCR 234 it was held that the publication of sexually explicit photographs of the claimant was an invasion of her privacy, despite the fact that she could not be identified. Damages of NZ$2,500 were awarded for invasion of privacy.

See, generally, R Tobin, 'Privacy and Freedom of Expression in New Zealand', in M Colvin (ed), *Developing Key Privacy Rights* (Hart Publishing, 2002).

(2) The interpretation of section 21

In *R v Holford* [2001] 1 NZLR 385 the court admitted evidence which had been **12.252** illegally obtained by private investigators who were trespassers as its admission did not result in unfairness.

In *R v Kappely* [2001] 1 NZLR 7 the Court of Appeal reiterated that, when con- **12.253** sidering the reasonableness of a search under a warrant, neither validity nor legality were the sole determinant. The search in that case was unreasonable under section 21 and the evidence inadmissible because:

- the warrant was not validly issued (because there was no adequate evidential basis);
- the warrant was not validly executed as it did not authorise the search of the particular premises; and
- it would have been practical for the officers to observe the premises while a new warrant was obtained which correctly identified the address.

See also *R v Thompson* [2001] 1 NZLR 129.

(3) Electronic surveillance

(b) Participant recording

12.257   See also *R v Smith* [2000] 3 NZLR 456, NZ CA, in which the evidence of an informer, fitted with a video camera, was held admissible against a suspected drugs trafficker.

Appendix 3: Human Rights Cases in Other Jurisdictions

(1) Introduction

12.258   In *Re C* (2001) 10 BHRC 131 the German Constitutional Court held that the publication of three photographs of Princess Caroline of Monaco with her children taken in publicly accessible places was a breach of her privacy rights. It was said that the decisive criterion for differentiating between the private and the public sphere was whether the individual was in a situation where he reasonably believed that he could not be observed by the public.

See, generally, R English, 'Protection of Privacy and Freedom of Speech in Germany', in M Colvin (ed), *Developing Key Privacy Rights* (Hart Publishing, 2002).

12.259   n852: See also *Stenberg v Carhart* (2000) 120 Sup Ct 2597.

12.259A   In *Kyllo v United States* (11 June 2001) the Supreme Court held that the Fourth Amendment was violated when the Government used, without warrant, a thermal imaging device to explore details of a private home. The use of this device was a 'warrantless search'.

(1A) Australia

12.259B   In *Lenah Game Meats v Australian Broadcasting Corporation* [2001] HCA 63 the claimant sought an injunction to restrain the broadcast of video film which had been obtained by trespassers in a meat processing plant. The High Court refused to grant an injunction. The majority held that the claimant had no cause of action. The judges who considered whether there was a developing tort of invasion of privacy in Australian law held that, even if there was, it would not avail a corporation.

See D Lindsay, 'Freedom of Expression, Privacy and the Media in Australia', in M Colvin (ed), *Developing Key Privacy Rights* (Hart Publishing, 2002).

(4) Ireland

12.265   An applicant in legal proceedings who sought to keep secret his name in those proceedings was unsuccessful in *Re Ansbacher (Cayman) Ltd* [2002] IEHC 27. The court held that the right to a public trial outweighed in that case the rights to privacy or confidentiality.

(4A) Malta

In *Ellul v Advocate General* (2002) 3 CHRLD 335 the Malta Constitutional Court held that identity documents of a transsexual other than the birth certificate should be amended. The court accepted that there was a breach of Article 8 of the European Convention on Human Rights, and that any documents issued by the state or any state authority identifying the applicant, with the exception of birth certificates, such as identity cards and passports should indicate the applicant's new gender. Birth certificates, however, were intended to record a historic fact and the state was right to keep their contents as objective and determinate as possible. Although the birth certificate should not be changed, a document should be attached to it stating that all of the applicant's other documents have been modified to reflect her new sex and name.

12.265A

(5) South Africa

In *Investigation Directorate v Hyundai Motor Distributors* (2000) (10) BCLR 1079 the Constitutional Court held that statutory powers of search and seizure in support of preparatory investigations were not in breach of the privacy rights in section 14 of the Constitution. The Court construed the relevant provisions as providing that a warrant could only be obtained if there was reasonable suspicion that an offence had been committed. It was held that the right to privacy was potentially applicable to a corporation. The guarantee became more intense as it moved towards the intimate personal sphere of the life of human beings and less intense as it moved away from that core. A search and seizure by competition authorities was held to have breached constitutional privacy rights in *Pretoria Portland v Competition Commission* (31 May 2002). The Supreme Court of Appeal found that the appellants had been hampered in their efforts to have the search warrant set aside. The court also relied on the impropriety of the invitation to television companies surreptitiously to enter the premises.

12.267

13

THE RIGHT TO MARRY AND TO FAMILY LIFE

B. The Rights in English Law

(2) Marriage and divorce

(a) Introduction

In *Bellinger v Bellinger* [2002] 2 WLR 411 the Court of Appeal confirmed that a 'marriage' between a man and a woman who was born a man is not a valid marriage. See also *W v W (Physical Inter-sex)* [2001] 2 WLR 674. **13.05**

See, generally, S Leech and R Young, 'Marriage, Divorce and Ancillary Relief under the Human Rights Act 1998: An Introduction' [2001] EHRLR 300.

(c) The right to divorce

On 16 January 2001 the Lord Chancellor's Department announced that it was proposed that Part II of the Family Law Act 1996 would be repealed. As a result, the provisions, described at Main Work, para 13.10, will not be introduced. **13.10**

(3) Rights of children

(c) Parental responsibility orders

13.21 The appropriate procedure for a child conceived by *in vitro* fertilisation was considered in *Re D (A Child: Parental Responsibility: IVF Baby)* [2001] 1 FLR 972.

(e) Public law children proceedings

13.30 **Introduction.** In *R (W) v Lambeth LBC* [2002] 2 All ER 901 the Court of Appeal decided that a local authority had a power (but not a duty) to provide housing to a family who were intentionally homeless, declining to follow *R (A) v Lambeth LBC* [2001] EWCA Civ 1624.

(4) Family rights in other areas

(a) Medically assisted reproduction and surrogacy arrangements

13.50 In *Centre for Reproductive Medicine v Mrs U* (2002) 1 FLR 927 the Court of Appeal decided that a widow was unable to use her deceased husband's sperm where he had withdrawn his consent for its use and storage after his death and that decision was not invalid.

(d) 'Family' and statutory rights

13.69 In *Mendoza v Ghaidan* [2002] 4 All ER 1162 the Court of Appeal decided that the survivor of a same-sex couple who could succeed to a statutory tenancy could qualify as a spouse under the Rent Act. The Court of Appeal relied on Article 14 of the Convention; and declined to follow *Fitzpatrick v Sterling Housing Association* [2001] AC 27.

C. The Law Under the European Convention

(2) The right to marry and form a family

(a) The scope of the right

13.76 In *R (Pretty) v DPP* [2002] 1 AC 800, para 6, Lord Bingham expressed the view that, contrary to the view expressed in the Main Work, he would infer that Article 12 conferred a right not to marry.

13.79 A claim that the length of divorce proceedings had effectively prevented the applicant from remarrying, in breach of Article 12, was held to be inadmissible as the applicant had not established that she actually wanted to remarry and was prevented from doing so (*Truszkowska v Poland*, Decision of 11 December 2001).

(c) The position of transsexuals

The Court of Human Rights returned to the question of transsexual marriages in **13.86**
Goodwin v United Kingdom and *I v United Kingdom* (2002) 35 EHRR 447. It
held, this time, recognising the major social shifts in relation to marriage, that preventing a transsexual marrying as their post-operative gender was a breach of
Article 12.

(e) The right to found a family

n369: In *Frette v France* (Judgment of 26 February 2002) it was held that Article **13.88**
8 did not confer a right to adopt. The Court did however consider that a refusal of
an adoption due to the applicant's homosexuality could be an infringement of
Article 8 read in conjunction with Article 14, though on the facts of the case it was
found that any discriminatory effect was justified.

(3) The meaning of family life under Article 8

A child's right to know its paternity may come within the ambit of 'private life' so, **13.101**
for example, a failure to establish paternity leading to a prolonged uncertainty as
to identity constituted a breach of Article 8 (*Mikulic v Croatia* [2002] 1 FCR
720).

It has been held that where a relationship between a father and child does amount
to 'family life', there was a breach of Article 8 read in conjunction with Article 14
when the father was treated less favourably because he was not married to the
mother of the child in relation to contact; see *Sahin v Germany; Sommerfeld v
Germany and Hoffman v Germany* [2002] 1 FLR 119 and see, further,
Supplement, para 17.122.

In *Haas v Netherlands* (Decision of 18 June 2002) the Court considered a complaint by the applicant who claimed to be the illegitimate child of P. On P's,
death his estate had passed to his nephew under the rules of intestacy. P had not
recognised the applicant as his son during his life, they had never lived together
and no paternity test had been conducted. Nevertheless P did *treat* the applicant
as his child in various ways. The Court found the claim for a breach of Article 8,
on the basis of interference with 'family life', to be admissible. The complaint was
also found admissible as a breach of Article 14 read in conjunction with Article
8.

Where the applicant's children were adults and no longer dependent, a court was
unwilling to find that his deportation interfered with his 'family life' (*Mir v
Switzerland*, Decision of 26 March 2002 (application inadmissible)).

On Article 8 and paternity tests, see *Mikulic v Croatia* [2002] 1 FCR 720 and see, **13.103**
further, Supplement, para 12.87.

(e) The extended family

13.110 In *GHB v United Kingdom* [2000] EHRLR 545 it was accepted that family life in Article 8 was broad enough to encompass ties between grandparents and grandchildren. However, a lesser degree of scrutiny was required to restrictions on grandparents' access to their grandchildren.

(5) The right of respect for family life

(b) The obligations imposed on the state to respect family life

13.115 In *Chapman v United Kingdom* (2001) 10 BHRC 48 the Court decided that the occupation of caravans by gypsies was an integral part of their ethnic identity and that enforcement proceedings for breach of planning permission and the planning decisions themselves interfered with their right of respect for private and family life. For a discussion of these cases, see Supplement, para 12.146.

13.117 For the right to respect for family life when children are removed into public care, see *K and T v Finland* [2000] EHRLR 536 and *L v Finland* [2000] EHRLR 541 which are discussed further at Supplement, para 13.131A.

13.118 In *Glaser v United Kingdom* [2000] 3 FCR 193 the applicant complained that Article 8 had been breached by the mother's persistent non-compliance with contact orders, ultimately moving from England to Scotland. The Court decided that there was no absolute obligation to ensure contact with non-custodial parents after a divorce. The crucial question was whether the authorities had taken all necessary steps to facilitate contact within the special circumstances of the case. The difficulties of enforcement resulted from the unilateral acts of the mother in relocating out of the jurisdiction with the children. There was therefore no violation of Article 6 or Article 8. See also *K and T v Finland* [2000] EHRLR 536 which is discussed further at Supplement, para 13.131A.

n468: Cf *Petersen v Germany* (Decision of 6 December 2001) in which a change to a child's surname, objected to by the father, did not interfere with the father's Article 8(1) rights on the basis that in this case the surname did not constitute an outer sign of the bond between the applicant and his son. The applicant was also not permitted to bring a claim, in relation to the change of surname, on behalf of his son as he was found to lack standing.

(c) Respect for family life in care cases

13.119 A failure to involve parents sufficiently in the process leading to a child being taken into care can constitute an interference for the purpose of Article 8 (*P, C and S v United Kingdom* (2002) 35 EHRR 1075). And see, generally, *Venema v The Netherlands* (Judgment of 17 December 2002).

It was held in *Sahin v Germany* [2002] 1 FLR 119 that a failure directly to ask a child whether she wished to have contact with her father, in the course of a contact dispute, breached the father's right fully to participate in the process and thus violated his Article 8 rights. Similarly in *Sommerfeld v Germany* [2002] 1 FLR 119 it was held that a failure by the court to obtain expert psychological evidence to evaluate a child's apparently fixed desire not to have contact with her father was a breach of his Article 8 rights.

It was held in *Buchberger v Austria* (Judgment of 20 December 2001) that a mother had been insufficiently involved in the decision-making process leading to her children being taken into care in breach of Article 8. The decision regarding the children had been taken in proceedings in which fresh evidence was presented to the court which the mother was not informed about and to which she was given no chance to respond.

(d) Respect for family life in immigration cases

See *Al-Nashif v Bulgaria* (Judgment of 20 June 2001) on the procedural requirements for a deportation interfering with family life. **13.121**

In *Mensah v Netherlands* (Decision of 9 October 2001) the Court found inadmissible a claim that a refusal to grant residence permits to two sons was a breach of Article 8. It was reiterated that Article 8 does not invariably require residency to be granted to facilitate unification of a family and on the facts the Court found that no breach of Article 8 had occurred. See also *Adnane v Netherlands* (Decision of 6 November 2001) and *Kaya v Netherlands* (Decision of 6 November 2001) in which similar claims were held to be inadmissible. **13.124**

(e) Respect for family life in prisoner cases

In *Messina v Italy* (Judgment of 28 September 2000) the Court found that restrictions on family visits to a prisoner who had been charged and convicted for Mafia-type activities were proportionate interferences with his right of respect for family life. **13.126**

In *Ploski v Poland* (Decision of 4 December 2001) a claim was made that a refusal to allow a prisoner to attend the funerals of his parents was a breach of Article 8. The claim was found to be admissible.

In *Kleuver v Norway* (Decision of 30 April 2002) the Court considered the case of an imprisoned mother separated from her baby. The Court declined to determine whether, as a general rule, states are required to provide facilities in which female prisoners and their babies can be kept together. The Court noted that the applicant knew she was pregnant when embarking upon the criminal activity for which she was later imprisoned. It also noted that the applicant had been placed in a high-security unit due to the nature of her crime, a drugs offence, and the fact she had attempted escape. It noted further that the period of separation complained of was only three months. Under these circumstances the Court found that the complaint of a breach of Article 8 was inadmissible. It also found inadmissible the complaint that various other features of the applicant's incarceration, such as the use of handcuffs and body searches, were a violation of Article 8.

(6) Justification for interference with family life

(a) Introduction

13.128 A decision denying a father access to his son on the basis that contact would be harmful to the son was not justified in the absence of psychological evidence which had not been obtained (*Elsholz v Germany* [2000] 2 FLR 486). The case has re-emphasised that the ending of contact between parent and child is only justified in exceptional circumstances (*Scozzari v Italy* [2000] 2 FLR 771). The refusal to extend a father's resident permit so that he could have trial visits with his child pre-judged the court's decision on access and Article 8 was breached by his subsequent deportation where there was no immediate need for his removal and which prevented him from forming a meaningful relationship with his child (*Ciliz v Netherlands*, Judgment of 13 July 2000).

In *Meads v United Kingdom* (Decision of 9 October 2001) a claim that an eviction was in breach of Article 8 was held to be inadmissible. It found that there was a legitimate interest in protecting the rights of banks providing mortgages and the eviction itself was not disproportionate.

(b) The public care cases

13.129 Article 8 requires that all relevant evidence be disclosed promptly. In this case a failure in relation to a transcript and interview with a child was held to be in breach of the Convention. The applicant was deprived of an adequate involvement in the decision-making process concerning the care of her daughter (*TP and KM v United Kingdom* [2000] 2 LGLR 181, para 83).

In relation to a failure to involve parents sufficiently in the process leading to a child being taken into care, see *P, C and S v United Kingdom* (2002) 35 EHRR 1075 and *Buchberger v Austria* (Judgment of 20 December 2002). In *P, C and S v United Kingdom* the Court held that extraordinary and compelling reasons are required to justify taking a newborn child directly into care. Such reasons were not established in the case itself and a breach of Article 8 was found. The Court also found that a breach of Article 8 had occurred on the basis that the parents had not been sufficiently involved in the care proceedings.

The various procedural steps necessary to respect family life when action is taken to protect a child in an emergency were extensively reviewed in *Venema v The Netherlands* (Judgment of 17 December 2002).

A claim that the removal of a child from the family home for three months was a **13.130**
breach of Article 8 in circumstances in which the local authority perceived a real
risk of sexual abuse was held to be inadmissible (*MB and GB v United Kingdom*,
Decision of 23 October 2001).

In *K and T v Finland* [2001] 2 FLR 707 the Court accepted that, when making **13.131A**
emergency care orders, it may not be possible because of the urgency of the situation to involve those who have custody of the child in the decision-making
process. However, taking a newborn child into public care at the moment of its
birth is an extremely harsh measure and calls for extraordinarily compelling reasons. The Court also emphasised that the guiding principle under Article 8 is that
a care order is a temporary measure to be discontinued as soon as circumstances
permit and that any measures implementing temporary care should be consistent
with the ultimate aim of reuniting the natural parents and the child. The minimum to be expected is that the authorities examine the situation from time to
time to see whether there has been any improvement in the family situation. The
possibilities of reunification will be progressively diminished and eventually destroyed if the biological parents and children are not allowed to meet each other at
all, or only rarely, so that no natural bonding occurs. In contrast, in *L v Finland*
[2000] 2 FLR 118 it was found that the care order was justified and proportionate. The decision-making process leading to the children being taken into care had
involved the applicant parents to a degree sufficient to provide them with the requisite protection of their interests. The mother and father had separated before the
requests for revocation of the care orders were made and, in the circumstances, the
national authorities could consider the maintenance of the orders to be in the best
interests of the children.

(c) The deportation of non-national family members

In *El Boujaidi v France* (2000) 30 EHRR 223 the Court ruled that a family ac- **13.132**
quired in France by the applicant *after* an exclusion order was made was not relevant to a consideration of Article 8.

In order for a deportation, which interferes with family life, to be justified it must
be 'prescribed by law'. Even where national security is at stake, measures interfering with family life have to be subject to some form of adversarial proceedings before an independent body competent to review the reasons for the decision and
the relevant evidence. Where there was no evidence of an independent inquiry
having been conducted and no reasons had been given to the applicants, or their
lawyer, to justify the decision to deport, the interference was not justified and was
in breach of Article 8 (*Al-Nashif v Bulgaria*, Judgment of 20 June 2002).

In *Boujlifa v France* (2000) 30 EHRR 419 the Court held that there was no breach **13.134**
of Article 8 where the applicant, who had been in France from the age of five, was

deported after committing a crime. The Court took account of the seriousness of the crime, the fact that he did not have a wife and children in France and that he 'did not show any desire to acquire French nationality at the time he was entitled to do so' (para 44) and held that deportation was lawful even though the applicant's whole family lived in France and that he had not been to Morocco, his place of birth, since he was five years of age.

In *Boultif v Switzerland* (2001) 33 EHRR 50 the Court set out some general principles to be applied where the main obstacle to expelling the applicant was the difficulty for spouses to stay together and, in particular, for a spouse and/or the children to live in the other's country of origin. In assessing whether expulsion is necessary and proportionate, the Court will consider:

- the nature and seriousness of the offence committed by the applicant;
- the length of the applicant's stay in the country from which he is going to be expelled;
- the time elapsed since the offence was committed as well as the applicant's conduct in that period;
- the nationalities of the various individuals concerned;
- the applicant's family situation such as the length of the marriage;
- other factors expressing the effectiveness of the couple's family life;
- whether the spouse knew about the offence at the time he or she entered into a family relationship;
- whether there are children of the marriage; and
- the seriousness of the difficulties which the spouse is likely to encounter in the country of origin (although the mere fact that a person might face certain difficulties in accompanying her or his spouse cannot in itself exclude an expulsion).

In *Jakupovic v Austria* (Decision of 15 November 2001) a claim was made that a residence prohibition following the commission of a crime was a disproportionate interference with family life was found to be admissible.

D. The Impact of the Human Rights Act

(1) Introduction

13.135A In *R v Secretary of State for Health, ex p L* [2001] 1 FLR 406 Scott Baker J held that none of the Convention cases show that the relationship between an uncle or an aunt with a nephew or a niece *necessarily* amounts to 'family life' within the meaning of Article 8. 'Family life' is an elastic concept that depends very much on the facts of the individual case. However, the onus of establishing family in each case is on the claimant. The case is discussed further at Supplement, para 13.178. See also *GHB v United Kingdom* [2000] EHRLR 545 which is discussed at Supplement, para 13.110.

(2) United Kingdom cases

(a) Introduction

The United Kingdom was found to be in breach of the right to respect for family life in *TP and KM v United Kingdom* [2000] 2 LGLR 181.   **13.136**

It was held in *R v Governor of Wakefield Prison, ex p Banks* [2002] 1 FCR 445 that the relationship between a nephew and his uncle, who had been in prison since before the nephew was born, did not constitute 'family life' for the purposes of Article 8. Thus, a restriction on visits by the nephew did not breach the Convention.

(4) Specific areas of impact

(a) Criminal law

In *R v Gwent Magistrates, ex p Stokes* [2001] EWHC Admin 569 it was held that a   **13.147A**
committal order for 12 days for non-payment of fines and compensation orders in relation to a single mother with four children was a disproportionate interference with the right to respect for family life.

(c) Family law

On a court order of confidentiality in a matrimonial case not involving children   **13.150**
and the requirement to balance Articles 8 and 10 in determining whether to make the order, see *Clibbery v Allan* [2002] 1 All ER 865, discussed at Supplement, para 15.274.

In *Re S (Children: Care Order: Implementation of Care Plan)* [2002] 2 AC 291 the   **13.151**
House of Lords heard an appeal from the Court of Appeal's far-reaching judgment in *Re W and B (Children)* [2001] 2 FLR 582 and considerably lessened its scope as far as the Human Rights Act is concerned. The House of Lords accepted that in both the making of care orders, under the Children Act 1989, and the discharging of local authorities' obligations to children in its care, Article 8 rights can be breached. Taking children into care generally interferes with the Article 8 rights of both parents and children and will need to be justified pursuant to Article 8(2). It is also possible that a care order could be initially justified, but then cease to be so as events unfold, leading to a breach of Article 8. This did not however detract from the 'cardinal principle' (*per* Lord Nicholls at 204) of the Children Act that the court is not empowered under the Act to interfere with the way in which a local authority discharges its obligations once it has parental responsibility for a child in care. The fact that the Children Act does not itself contain mechanisms

for the ongoing monitoring of a local authority's discharge of its obligation to children in care, did not render it incompatible with Article 8. If Article 8 violations occurred, proceedings could be brought directly under the Human Rights Act. The case is discussed further at Supplement, para 13.154A.

The involvement of parents in care proceedings will generally be necessary to comply with Article 8. In *Re C (Care Proceedings: Disclosure of Local Authority's Decision-Making Process)* [2002] 2 FCR 673 the court found that while there were substantial shortcomings in the mother's involvement at particular junctures of the care proceedings, when the process was considered overall, there was no breach of Article 8.

13.152   Where an application is made for a care order, the Court of Appeal stressed in *In re O (Supervision Order)* [2001] 1 FLR 923 that the issue must be considered under Article 8 so that any intervention between children and parents is proportionate to the legitimate aim in question.

13.154   In *Payne v Payne* [2001] 1 WLR 1826 the Court of Appeal decided that where an application was made under section 13(1)(b) of the Children Act 1989 to allow a child to be removed from the country, the established principles should be applied and were unaffected by Article 8.

13.154A   In *Re S and W (Children)* [2002] 2 All ER 192 the House of Lords considered the interpretation of the Children Act 1989 by the Court of Appeal in *Re W and B (Children)* [2001] EWCA Civ 757. The Court of Appeal had held that in order to read the Children Act compatibly with the Convention, parts of care plans should be 'starred' such that if the local authority failed to discharge the most important elements of its obligations to the child the matter could be returned to the court. The Court of Appeal also held that trial judges could use powers to make interim care orders in order to supervise the local authority's treatment of children in its care. The House of Lords held that these innovations went beyond the powers of the court to read legislation compatibly pursuant to section 3 of the Human Rights Act (see Supplement, para 4.28). While it urged Parliament to consider the manner in which local authorities are monitored in the discharge of their obligations to children in care, the House of Lords held that interpreting the Children Act so as to require court supervision of local authorities through starred care plans was an impermissible *legislative* innovation from the court. The House of Lords also held that interim care orders were to be used only to safeguard the welfare of children until such time as the court was ready to make a final order and not to facilitate ongoing supervision by the courts.

13.154B   Where a local authority is investigating child protection under section 47 of the Children Act, it had a wide margin of appreciation under Article 8 (*R (S) v Swindon Borough Council* [2001] EWHC Admin 334).

Private law cases. In *Re H (Children) (Contact Order) (No 2)* [2002] 1 FLR 22   **13.155**
Wall J said that the proper application of the checklist in section 1(3) of the
Children Act was equivalent to the balancing exercise required in the application
of Article 8 and was a useful cross-check to ensure that a proposed order was in ac-
cordance with the law, necessary for the protection of the rights and freedoms of
others and proportionate. See, generally, S Leech and R Young, 'Marriage,
Divorce and Ancillary Relief under the Human Rights Act 1998: An
Introduction' [2001] EHRLR 300.

Adoption. In *Re H (A Child) (Adoption: Disclosure)* [2002] 1 FLR 646 it held   **13.156**
that where an unmarried mother and father had a sufficient relationship to constitute a *de facto* family, the placement of a child for adoption without informing
the father that proceedings were taking place constituted a breach of Article 8. In
B (A Child) (Adoption Order) [2001] 2 FLR 89 the Court of Appeal said that making an adoption order in favour of foster parents where the father maintained a
close relationship with his son was a disproportionate interference with the father's Article 8 rights.

A judge has an unfettered discretion to join any person in adoption proceedings
and was entitled to join a natural father even where there is no marriage and no
parental responsibility to avoid a complaint about breaching Articles 6 and 8 (*Re
S* [2001] 1 FLR 302). In *Re H (A Child) (Adoption: Disclosure)* [2001] 1 FLR 646
Dame Elizabeth Butler-Sloss P held that notice should ordinarily be given to the
natural father; if there were close ties, Articles 6 and 8 might be relevant.
Similarly, in *R (A Child) (Adoption Proceedings: Joinder of Father)* [2001] FLR
302 the Court of Appeal held that it was appropriate to join the father in the proceedings since to do otherwise might breach Articles 6 and 8; the father had
strong views about the adoption and any future challenge might be disastrous for
the child's stability.

Article 8 does not positively require that a child's relatives are informed or consulted before making an adoption order and Holman J decided on the facts in *Z
County v R* [2001] 1 FLR 365 that he should preserve the confidentiality of the
mother who had concealed her pregnancy from her family. The Court of Appeal
expressed the view in *B v RP* [2001] 1 FLR 589 that an adoption order was undoubtedly an interference with the right of respect for family life and such an intervention is only necessary if there is a pressing social need and the action was
proportionate to that need.

In *R (Gunn-Russo) v Nugent Care Society* (2001) 1 FLR 1 Scott Baker J said that
the disclosure of adoption records by a voluntary adoption agency required a balancing exercise to be conducted between disclosure and confidentiality. The
Secretary of State had no power to compel the agency to disclose the records nor a
duty to make available an appeal procedure if the agency decided not to disclose.

He went on to hold that domestic law in this area was compatible with Article 8. On the facts of the case the adoption agency had failed to give proper consideration to the specific circumstances of the case on a document-by-document basis and Scott Baker J quashed its decision.

In *Re X (Children) (Adoption: Confidentiality)* [2002] 2 FLR 476 the Court of Appeal held than an order maintaining the anonymity of prospective parents during adoption proceedings was not in breach of Article 8.

A local authority which adopted a policy which financially discriminated against foster carers who were related to the children they fostered was found to be unlawful in *R (R) v Manchester City Council* [2002] 1 FLR 433 on public law grounds. It was also held to breach Articles 8 and 14 by failing to be necessary and proportionate.

It was held by the House of Lords in *Re B (A Child) (Sole Adoption by Unmarried Father)* [2002] 1 WLR 258 that section 15 of the Adoption Act 1976 which sets out the circumstances in which *one* parent can adopt a child, allows the correct balance to be struck for the purposes of Article 8 and need not be read down.

13.160A **Unmarried fathers.** In *R (Denson) v Child Support Agency* [2002] 1 FLR 938 it was argued that a liability order sought by the Child Support Agency in relation to the claimant's arrears was in breach of his Article 8 rights. The claim was rejected on the basis that the order did not infringe the right to private or family life and in any event was proportionate and in pursuit of a legitimate aim.

(d) Housing

13.161 On the relationship between the transfer of property following divorce, pursuant to the Matrimonial Causes Act 1973 and the confiscation of a home pursuant to the Drug Trafficking Act 1994, in the light of rights under Article 8, see *HM Customs and Excise v A* [2002] 3 FCR 481, CA.

13.162 In *Poplar Housing and Regeneration Community Association Ltd v Donoghue* [2002] QB 48 the Court of Appeal rejected the claim that the ability of a housing association to obtain possession on mandatory grounds under the Housing Act 1988 in relation to premises let as an assured shorthold tenancy was a disproportionate interference with Article 8.

In *Ekinci v London Borough of Hackney* [2002] HLR 2 the Court of Appeal held that there was no breach of Article 8 where Parliament had enacted a scheme of priorities for homeless people to be determined by local authorities whose resources were inevitably limited. In assessing priorities Parliament was entitled to take into account considerations such as vulnerability, which may or may not have an impact on family life.

In *Sheffield City Council v Hopkins* [2002] HLR 12 the Court of Appeal stated that **13.163**
when exercising its discretion under section 85 of the Housing Act to suspend the
execution of a warrant, the discretion should be used to further the policy of Part
IV of the Act, reinforced by Article 8, which was only to evict after a serious breach
of the tenancy agreement where it was reasonable to do so and where the tenant
had been proved to breach any condition of suspension. In *St Brice v Southwark
LBC* [2002] 1 WLR 1537 the Court of Appeal decided that once a county court
had made a possession order against a council tenant, his Article 8 rights had been
complied with; a local authority therefore did not infringe those rights by evicting
him without notice by a warrant of possession obtained under the possession
order.

(da) Education

In *CB v Merton London Borough Council* [2002] ELR 441 Sullivan J held that a de- **13.163A**
cision of the Special Educational Needs Tribunal to specify a certain residential
school in a child's statement of special education needs did not constitute an interference with the parent's right of respect for family life.

(db) Housing

The Court of Appeal held in *Michalak v Wandsworth London Borough Council* **13.163B**
[2002] 4 All ER 1136 that the list of family members who were entitled to succeed
to a secure tenancy under section 113 of the Housing Act 1985 is exhaustive. The
exclusion of more distant relatives was not incompatible with Articles 8 or 14.
However, in *Mendoza v Ghaidan* [2002] 4 All ER 1162 the Court of Appeal decided that a same-sex cohabitee was entitled to succeed to a Rent Act tenancy by
relying on Article 14.

(e) Immigration

A considerable number of Article 8 challenges have been made to decisions in im- **13.164**
migration and asylum cases, particularly in deportation cases.

A breach of Article 8 was found in *B v Secretary of State for the Home Department*
[2000] 2 CMLR 1086, a case heard prior to the Human Rights Act coming into
force. The Court of Appeal held that it was disproportionate under Article 8 to deport a man despite his conviction for child sex abuse as he had been in this country since 1962.

Most challenges to deportation orders based on Article 8 have been unsuccessful:

- A decision to deport was unsuccessfully challenged under Article 8 in *R v
  Secretary of State for the Home Department, ex p Hakansoy* [2001] Imm AR 16.
- In *R v Secretary of State for the Home Department, ex p Seri* [2001] Imm AR 169
  Dyson J held that a decision to refuse to grant exceptional leave to remain in the
  United Kingdom was justified under Article 8(2).

- It was held by the Court of Appeal in *R (Mahmood) v Secretary of State for the Home Department* [2001] 1 WLR 840 and *R (Isiko) v Secretary of State for the Home Department* [2001] HRLR 295 that, provided the Secretary of State had taken into account all the relevant facts, it was not necessarily a breach of Article 8 to deport an illegal immigrant even if that meant interfering with his family life. In *Isiko* the Court of Appeal found that the policy contained in DP3/96 in relation to removing an individual who marries after the commencement of enforcement proceedings was lawful. These two decisions must be treated with caution because the House of Lords has subsequently adopted a much stricter test of proportionality in *R (Daly) v Secretary of State for the Home Department* [2001] 2 WLR 1622. This proportionality issue is discussed further at Supplement, para 6.81A.
- In *R (Samaroo) v Home Secretary* (2001) UKHRR 1150 the Court of Appeal approached the question of whether deportation was a proportionate interference with the right of respect for family life by examining whether the Home Secretary had struck a fair balance between the claimant's right and the prevention of crime and disorder bearing in mind that he had a discretionary area of judgment. It was not necessary for the Home Secretary to show that the risk of crime and disorder outweighed the violation of the Convention right; instead he had to justify a derogation from a Convention right and the justification had to be convincingly established. The view taken by Dyson LJ as to the proportionality principle is discussed further at Supplement, para 6.81A.
- In *Nwokoye v Secretary of State for the Home Department* [2002] SLT 128 the Scottish Court of Session decided that a deportation order did not breach Article 8 even though its effect was to bring a father's contact with his child to an end.

The other Article 8 complaints have covered a variety of fields. In *R (McCollum) v Secretary of State for the Home Department* [2001] ACD 58 Turner J rejected the argument that a decision to refuse entry to a long-standing homosexual partner on the basis that he was not entitled to be treated as a member of the family was a breach of Article 8. In *R (Akhbari) v Secretary of State for the Home Department* [2001] EWHC Admin 407 Harrison J decided that where a child's asylum application was inextricably linked to that of her parents and they were subject to a removal order, the Secretary of State was justified in taking the view that the family unit should be maintained and there was no breach of Article 8. In *R (Montana) v Secretary of State for the Home Department* [2001] 1 WLR 552 the Court of Appeal stated that the withholding of citizenship did not necessarily constitute interference with, or failure to respect, family life. Although different citizenships within the family unit could result in practical difficulties, this did not necessarily preclude contact or the development of family ties. In *R (Harris) v Secretary of State for the Home Department* [2001] EWHC Admin 225 the applicant was refused leave to re-enter after visiting his terminally ill father on the ground that he had committed a large number of offences. Collins J held, *inter alia*, that the decision to refuse him leave to re-enter could not be justified under Article 8(2).

In *R (M, A, Z) v Immigration Appeal Tribunal* [2002] Imm AR 560 it was argued that the treatment a deported individual would receive in the country to which they were to be sent would breach Article 8. It was held that only flagrant breaches of Article 8 in the foreign country might prevent a deportation being lawful and, contrary to the claimant's submissions, that even in such circumstances the court should consider whether the deportation was nonetheless justified pursuant to Article 8(2).

On the jurisdiction to consider Article 8 at different stages of immigration law proceedings, see *R (Nyakonya) v Immigration Appeal Tribunal* [2002] EWHC Admin 1544.

In *Carpenter v Secretary of State for the Home Department* [2002] 2 CMLR 64 it was argued before the European Court of Justice that a decision to deport the wife of an English national contravened article 49 of the EC Treaty (formerly article 59) and Council Directive EEC 73/148 on the basis that the deportation would render it considerably harder for the husband to move freely within the Community to offer services. When the husband travelled in the Community as part of his work, his wife stayed at home to look after his children from a previous marriage. The court held that since the directive did not govern the right of residence of members of the family of a provider of services, it needed to consider whether such a right might be inferred from the principles or other rules of Community law. It held that the Community legislature had recognised the importance of ensuring the protection of the family life of nationals in order to eliminate obstacles to the exercise of the fundamental freedoms guaranteed by the EC Treaty. It found that the decision to deport constituted an unjustified interference with Article 8 of the Convention which was among the rights which, pursuant to the court's settled case law, restated by the Preamble to the Single European Act and by article 6(2) of the EU Treaty, were protected in Community law.

In *R (Drita) v Secretary of State for the Home Department*, *The Times*, 11 November 2002, Lightman J decided that a decision to accommodate the claimant in a hostel free of charge did not breach Article 8 and even if it amounted to an interference, the interference was proportionate.

(f) Local government law

Access to information. See now also *MG v United Kingdom* (Judgment of 24 September 2002).   **13.170**

Community care. It was held in *Ali v Birmingham City Council* [2002] HLR 51 that it was not in breach of Article 8 for a local authority to offer accommodation   **13.171**

to children only, and not to their mothers, or as an alternative to offer the cost of passage back to the Netherlands, the claimants' home country.

(g) Prison law

13.178   In *R v Secretary of State for the Home Department, ex p Mellor* [2002] QB 13 the Court of Appeal decided that a prisoner had no right under Articles 8 or 12 to be allowed to give a sample of semen to be used artificially to inseminate his wife. In *R v Secretary of State for Health, ex p L* [2001] 1 FLR 406 it was held that it was not irrational, nor a breach of Article 8, to have a policy restricting child visits to patients at high-security hospitals.

In *R (P, Q and QB) v Secretary of State for the Home Department* [2001] 1 WLR 2002 the Court of Appeal examined the blanket prison policy of removing a child from his or her mother at 18 months. It said that the following principles would be derived from the Strasbourg cases in relation to prisoners and the right to respect for family life:

- the right was not one which a prisoner necessarily lost by reason of his detention;
- in considering whether the state's reasons for interfering with that right were relevant and sufficient, the court must be entitled to take account of the reasonable requirements of prison organisation and security and the desirability of maintaining a uniform regime in prison which avoided any appearance of arbitrariness or discrimination;
- whatever the justification for a prison rule, Convention law required the court to consider the application of that rule to an individual case to decide whether a particular interference was proportionate; and
- the more serious the intervention, the more compelling the justification must be.

The Court of Appeal went on to decide that the aim of the policy was to promote the welfare of the child and held that the court could intervene in an exceptional case if the effect of the policy could not fulfil its objectives in relation to a particular child because its impact was catastrophic.

The view was expressed in *R (Banks) v Governor of Wakefield Prison* [2002] 1 FCR 445 that a restriction on visits by children to prisoners who were deemed to pose a risk to children was justifiable for the purpose of Article 8. On the facts of the case it was found that the relationship between the prisoner and his nephew, the child in question, did not in any event constitute 'family life' for the purpose of Article 8. See, further, Supplement, para 13.136.

In *R (Craven) v Secretary of State for the Home Department* [2001] EWHC Admin 813 Stanley Burnton J held that the imposition of an exclusion zone on a convicted murderer to minimise the risk of accidental contact between him and his victim's family could be necessary in a democratic society.

(h) Social security law

On claims that the level of social security, or deductions from it, interfere with private and family life, see *R (Reynolds) v Secretary of State for Work and Pensions* [2002] EWHC Admin 426 and *R (Plumb) v Secretary of Social Security* [2002] EWHC Admin 1125.

13.178A

Appendix 1: The Canadian Charter of Rights

(2) The Charter rights of children

In *KLW v Winnipeg Child and Family Services* (2000) 9 BHRC 370 the Supreme Court considered the compatibility of child protection legislation with the Charter. A statutory provision which allowed for the warrantless apprehension of children in non-emergency situations did not violate the principles of fundamental justice provided that it was construed to provide for a minimum threshold of a 'risk of serious harm' and a prompt post-apprehension hearing.

13.180

(5) Duties of care in tort

In *Dobson (Litigation Guardian of) v Dobson* [1999] 2 SCR 753 the Supreme Court decided that a pregnant woman did not owe a duty of care in tort to her unborn child. The court noted that the actions of a pregnant woman, including driving, were inextricably linked to her familial role, her working life, and her rights of privacy, bodily integrity and autonomous decision-making. Moreover, the judicial recognition of this cause of action would involve severe psychological consequences for the relationship between mother and child, as well as the family unit as a whole. The imposition of tort liability in this context would have profound effects upon every pregnant woman and upon Canadian society in general. Such after-the-fact judicial scrutiny of the subtle and complicated factors affecting a woman's pregnancy could make life for women who are pregnant or who are merely contemplating pregnancy intolerable. The best course, therefore, was to allow the duty of a mother to her foetus to remain a moral obligation which, for the vast majority of women, was already freely recognized and respected without compulsion by law.

13.185A

Appendix 3: Human Rights Cases in Other Jurisdictions

(1A) Hong Kong

Article 23(1) of the Hong Kong Bill of Rights Ordinance provides that

13.188A

> The family is the natural and fundamental group unit of society and is entitled to be protected by society and the State.

This is, however, subject to a reservation in relation to immigration legislation. As a result, orders for the removal of a family member who was not a permanent resident do not involve an interference with the fundamental right to family life (*Chan To Foon v Director of Immigration* [2001] 320 HKCU 1).

(2) Ireland

13.189 In *North Western Health Board v W (H)* [2001] IESC 70 the Irish Supreme Court refused to intervene when the parents of a baby withheld their consent to a particular test being carried out on the infant. The test was a standard one, and its purpose was to establish whether their child had certain biochemical or metabolic disorders which could be extremely serious but were also treatable if identified at an early stage. A majority of the court held that the circumstances did not oust the natural authority of the family, especially as the legislature had not chosen to make the test mandatory.

(2A) Namibia

13.196A The Supreme Court of Namibia held in *Chairperson of the Immigration Selection Board v Frank* (2001) 3 CHRLD 179 that article 10 (anti-discrimination) of the constitution did not prohibit discrimination on the ground of sexual orientation. The court relied on the absence in article 10 of any express reference to sexual orientation, unlike the comparable provision in the South African constitution. The court also ruled that article 14 (protection of the family) did not apply to a homosexual relationship. Again, the court relied on the absence of any express reference to homosexual relationships in that article, and the lack of specific protection for homosexuals in the relevant provisions of the African Charter and the ICCPR.

(3) South Africa

13.197 A ban on the adoption of children by non-South Africans was declared unconstitutional in *Minister for Welfare and Population Development v Fitzpatrick* [2001] 1 LRC 292 because it was contrary to section 28(2) of the Constitution, which provides that the child's best interests are of paramount importance in every matter concerning the child.

13.198 In *Dawood v Minister of Home Affairs* 2000 (8) BCLR 887 the Constitutional Court held that, although there is no express constitutional provision protecting the right to family life or the right of cohabitation, legislation interfering with the marriage relationship would clearly infringe the right to dignity. In *Makinana v Minister of Home Affairs* 2001 (6) BCLR 581 it was held that statutory provisions which required foreign spouses of South African residents to obtain work permits was unconstitutional as contravening the right to dignity.

Certain immigration provisions were declared unconstitutional in *Booysen v Minister of Home Affairs* [2002] 2 LRC 232 as being contrary to the right to dignity, because they failed to give proper recognition to the importance of family life, particularly the reciprocal rights and duties of the spouses to cohabitation and to financial support. Those provisions concerned the obligation of foreign spouses, married to South Africans or permanent residents, when seeking to work in South Africa to apply for a work permit while outside the country and then not to enter the country until the work permit had been issued; and the requirement that work permits would only be issued to such spouses if they did not pursue an occupation for which a sufficient number of persons were available in South Africa.

14

FREEDOM OF THOUGHT, CONSCIENCE AND RELIGION

B. The Rights in English Law

(3) Religious worship and education in schools

It was held in *Williamson v Secretary of State for Education* [2002] 1 FLR 493 that **14.13A** it was not possible to describe the support for the imposition of corporal punishment in schools as a manifestation of belief within Article 9. See also Supplement, paras 15.267 and 19.87.

(7) Religious freedom in other areas

In *R (Pretty) v DPP* [2002] AC 800 the House of Lords rejected the argument that **14.35A** Article 9 entitled an individual to be assisted to commit suicide as a manifestation of her beliefs. It was held that Article 9 does not entitle an individual to *practise* whichever beliefs they hold. This analysis was accepted by the Court of Human Rights in *Pretty v United Kingdom* (2002) 12 BHRC 149.

14.35B   In *R v Taylor* [2002] 1 Cr App R 37 the Court of Appeal held that the prosecution of a member of the Rastafarian religion for the possession of cannabis was not a violation of Article 9, notwithstanding that it was claimed that the cannabis was used for the purpose of worship. It was held that Article 9 was not violated where legislation of general application happened to prohibit conduct encouraged or required by a religious belief.

C. The Law Under the European Convention

(1) The scope of the right

(b) 'Thought, conscience and religion'

14.40   On the definition of religion and belief under Article 9 see, generally, C Evans, *Freedom of Religion Under the European Convention on Human Rights* (Oxford University Press, 2001), ch 4.

(c) 'Manifestation'

14.44   Rites and acts of worship include having animals killed by ritual slaughter, though not necessarily the right to take part in the slaughter (*Jewish Liturgical Association Ch'are Shalom ve Tsedek v France* (2000) 9 BHRC 27). It was made clear in *Metropolitan Church of Bessarabia v Moldova* (2002) 35 EHRR 13 that religious beliefs are often manifested in communities. Interpreting Article 9 in the light of Article 11, the Court held that Article 9 included the right to organise such religious communities. The Court also reiterated the principle that a church or ecclesiastical body can bring a claim on behalf of its adherents.

See, generally, C Evans, *Freedom of Religion Under the European Convention on Human Rights* (Oxford University Press, 2001), ch 6.

14.46   The activities of an applicant, a member of the Algerian Islamic Salvation Front, in broadcasting messages in favour of this organisation did not constitute an expression of religious belief within the meaning of Article 9. As a result, the threatened confiscation of the applicant's telephones did not infringe his freedom of religion (*Zaoui v Switzerland*, Decision of 18 January 2001).

14.47   It appears that the result of *Arrowsmith* is that the manifestation of belief will only be protected if the religion or belief *requires* a particular form of manifestation (see C Evans, *Freedom of Religion Under the European Convention on Human Rights* (Oxford University Press, 2001), 115–17). It will not be sufficient to show that the behaviour is merely permitted or encouraged by the religion (see, for example, *Khan v United Kingdom* (1986) 48 DR 253).

In *Pretty v United Kingdom* (2002) 12 BHRC 149 the Court noted, in relation to a 'belief' that individuals should be permitted to assist suicide, that not all opinions or convictions constitute beliefs in the sense protected by Article 9(1), particularly where the alleged belief is not manifested through worship, teaching, practice or observance as described in the second sentence of the first paragraph. The Court further noted that the term 'practice' as employed in Article 9(1) does not cover every act which is motivated or influenced by a religion or belief.

In *Pichon and Sajous v France* (Decision of 2 October 2001) the Court considered a complaint by pharmacists who had been convicted for refusing to distribute contraceptive pills. The applicants claimed that, as the refusal had been a manifestation of their religious beliefs, the conviction was in breach of Article 9. The case was held to be inadmissible as pharmacists, in their professional/public capacity, were not entitled to impose on others their religious convictions in this manner.

(2) The nature of the protection

(a) Negative protection

It seems that the right to religious practice and observance protected by Article 9 is **14.49** not violated if such practice is rendered more difficult, but not impossible, by the actions of the state (*Jewish Liturgical Association Ch'are Shalom ve Tsedek v France* (2000) 9 BHRC 27). A refusal to recognise a church constituted an interference with Article 9(1) in circumstances in which only recognised religions could be practised in the country (*Metropolitan Church of Bessarabia and Others v Moldova* (2002) 35 EHRR 13). It was no answer for the state to assert that in its view the same religious beliefs could be manifested within a different organisation or church.

n182a: *Thlimmenos v Greece* is now reported at (2000) 9 BHRC 12. **14.51A**

(b) Positive protection

See also *Dubowska v Poland* (Decision of 18 April 1997) (complaint of a failure to **14.52** bring criminal charges for publicly insulting religious feelings inadmissible).

See, generally, C Evans, *Freedom of Religion Under the European Convention on Human Rights* (Oxford University Press, 2001), 69–72. In the *Metropolitan Church of Bessarabia and Others v Moldova* (2002) 35 EHRR 13 it was held that a failure to protect the assets of a religious organisation, through a refusal to register it, could be a breach of Article 9.

(3) Justifiable limitations

(a) Absolute right to believe

For a discussion of the doctrine of the *'forum internum'*, see C Evans, *Freedom of* **14.54** *Religion Under the European Convention on Human Rights* (Oxford University Press, 2001), 72–9.

n192: In *Bozhilov v Bulgaria* (Decision of 22 November 2001) a complaint that there was a breach of Article 9 following a failure to select an individual for an appointment to an inter-governmental organisation because of his political views was held inadmissible.

14.55 For a discussion of the position of the state church under Article 9, see C Evans, *Freedom of Religion Under the European Convention on Human Rights* (Oxford University Press, 2001), 80–7.

(b) Restrictions upon manifestation of belief

14.56 Interference with the selection of a religious leader, which was arbitrary and based on a seemingly unfettered discretion, was found to be in breach of Article 9 (*Hasan and Chaush v Bulgaria* (2002) 34 EHRR 55). However, the right to practise religion free from state interference, as recognised in *Hasan and Chaush*, does not give a right to be officially recognised as the sole organisation representing a religious community to the exclusion of others (*The Supreme Holy Council of the Muslim Community v Bulgaria*, Decision of 13 December 2001).

14.58 **n204:** *Buscarini v San Marino* is now reported at (2000) 30 EHRR 208.

14.59 In *Dahlab v Switzerland* (Decision of 15 February 2001) the applicant, a Muslim teacher, complained that a prohibition on her wearing a headscarf at work was a breach of her Article 9 rights. The complaint was held inadmissible on the basis that the ban on the applicant's wearing a headscarf while teaching had not been imposed because she was a woman but had pursued the legitimate aim of ensuring the neutrality of state primary education.

(c) Conscientious objection

14.62 In *Stefanov v Bulgaria* (Judgment of 3 May 2001) the applicant was a Jehovah's witness who complained about being convicted for refusing to serve in the army. A friendly settlement was agreed. The Bulgarian government agreed to obtain an amnesty for all those convicted of such offences. On conscientious objection, see Gilbert, 'The Slow Development of the Right to Conscientious Objection to Military Service Under the European Convention on Human Rights' (2001) 5 EHRLR 554.

D. The Impact of the Human Rights Act

(2) United Kingdom cases

(a) Introduction

14.68 **n227:** *Buscarini v San Marino* is now reported at (2000) 30 EHRR 208.

(3) General impact

The Consistory Courts of the Dioceses of the Church of England (constituted **14.76A** under the Ecclesiastical Jurisdiction Measure 1963) are courts within the meaning of section 6 of the Human Rights Act (see Supplement, para 5.42). In *Re Durrington Cemetery* [2000] 3 WLR 1322 the Chichester Consistory Court took Article 9 into account when granting a faculty permitting the remains of a practising Jew who had been buried in consecrated ground to be exhumed for reinterment in a Jewish cemetery. The Chancellor said that 'this court would be seriously at risk of acting unlawfully under the Human Rights Act 1998 were it to deny the freedom of the orthodox Jewish relatives of the late Mr Saunders to manifest their religion in practice and observance by securing the reinterment of his cremated remains in a Jewish cemetery'.

In *Re Crawley Green Road Cemetery, Luton* [2001] HRLR 431 a widow who was a humanist wished to remove her husband's ashes from consecrated ground where they had been buried. Neither she nor her husband had realised that the cemetery was consecrated ground. The Consistory Court of St Albans held that it would be acting incompatibly with her rights under Article 9 if it were to deny her the right to remove the ashes.

Under section 13 of the Charities Act 1993 the court has jurisdiction to make a **14.76B** scheme dividing the assets of a charity for the furtherance of the objects of the charity. It has been held that the balancing nature of the jurisdiction is consistent with Article 9(2) which recognised that the freedom of any group to manifest its religion is limited by the need to protect the similar rights of other groups (*Varsani v Jesani*, 31 July 2001 (Patten J)).

(4) Specific areas of impact

(b) Education

However, in *Dahlab v Switzerland* (Decision of 15 February 2001) the Court of **14.78** Human Rights held that a complaint by a Muslim teacher against a prohibition on wearing a headscarf at work was inadmissible.

The prohibition of corporal punishment in schools by section 548 of the **14.79** Education Act 1996 was not a breach of the Article 9 rights of parents because, although such punishment was in accordance with the parents' faith, it did not embody or define their Christian beliefs (*Williamson v Secretary of State for Education* [2002] 1 FLR 493).

(c) Employment and discrimination

n269a: *Thlimmenos v Greece* is now reported at (2000) 9 BHRC 12. **14.81**

(h) Immigration law

14.86A   In *R v Special Adjudicator, ex p Ullah* [2002] EWHC Admin 1584 Harrison J considered a refusal to grant asylum in circumstances in which it was claimed that if the applicant was returned to Pakistan, he would not be free to practise his religion. It was held that in order for such a decision to be a breach of the Convention the denial of Article 9 rights in the country to which the individual would return had to be 'flagrant', which was not found on the facts of the instant case. Harrison J also held that a breach of Article 9 in the context of immigration could be justified by the need for immigration controls.

Appendix 1: The Canadian Charter of Rights

(1) Scope of the right

14.90   The naming of swearing on the Bible as one of the options for attesting to the truth of testimony in court does not violate freedom of religion as there was no coerced conformity to religious doctrine. The defendant was free to affirm. In any event, the legislation impaired the Charter right to freedom of religion as little as was reasonably possible (*R v Anderson* [2001] CRDJ 315 (Man Prov Court)).

(2) Justifiable limitations

(b) Sunday closing

14.93   See also *R v Hy & Zel's Supermarket Drug Store* (2000) 48 WCB (2d) 154 (Ontario Superior Court).

(c) Religious education

14.98A   In *BC College of Teachers v Trinity Western University* (2001) 10 BHRC 425 the British Columbia College of Teachers ('BCCT') had refused to approve a teacher application programme by a university associated with the Evangelical Free Church of Canada on the ground that the university discriminated against homosexuals. The Supreme Court (L'Hereux-Dube J dissenting) held that the decision was unlawful. The BCCT had failed to take into account the impact of its decision on the freedom of religion of the members of the university. The case is discussed further at Supplement, para 17.183.

(d) Other issues

14.102A   Although Canadian prisons provided religious diets to inmates they refused to provide vegetarian diets. In *Maurice v A-G of Canada* (2002) ACWS (3d) 472 the Federal Court held that there was an entitlement for a vegetarian diet, based on freedom of conscience.

Appendix 3: Human Rights Cases in Other Jurisdictions

(1) Introduction

In *Watchtower Bible and Tract Society v Village of Stratton* (17 June 2002) the **14.108**
Supreme Court held that an ordinance which prevented canvassers from going on
to private property to promote any 'cause' without first obtaining a permit from
the Mayor's office was a violation of the First Amendment. It was pointed out that,
for over 50 years, the Supreme Court had invalidated restrictions on door-to-door
canvassing by Jehovah's Witnesses. In *Levitan v Ashcroft* (8 March 2002, DC Cir)
the court held that a religious practice did not need to be mandated by a prisoner's
religion in order to qualify for protection under the First Amendment. The practice involved in that case was the drinking of wine during communion.

(3A) Cayman Islands

In *Grant (Guardian ad litem of Shemiah Grant) v The Principal, John A Cumber* **14.112A**
Primary School (2001) 3 CHRLD 138 the Court of Appeal held that
Rastafarianism qualified as a religion and that the wearing of dreadlocks were an
essential part of the observance of the religion. As a result, the court quashed a de-
cision to expel a Rastafarian from school for offending the dress code as being
Wednesbury unreasonable.

(4) Human Rights Committee

In *Ross v Canada* (2001) 10 BHRC 219 it was held that the transferring of a **14.113**
teacher who published books and pamphlets containing controversial religious
opinions to non-teaching duties was a justifiable limitation on the manifestation
of his beliefs. For a full discussion of Article 18 of the ICCPR, see S Joseph, J
Schultz and M Castan, *The International Covenant on Civil and Political Rights:
Cases, Materials and Commentary* (Oxford University Press, 2001), ch 17.

(5) India

An excessively noisy religious service which disturbed the peace of the others **14.116**
could not be justified as being consistent with the enjoyment of rights by others as
no religion prescribes that prayers must be performed through amplifiers or by
beating drums (*Church of God (Full Gospel) in India v KKR Majestic Colony Welfare
Association* (2000) 3 CHRLD 237).

(8) South Africa

The right to freedom of religion has internal limits and does not, therefore, con- **14.126**
fer unfettered freedom to choose a grave site or to take a grave site without the

consent of the owner of the land; see *Nkosi v Bhrmann* 2002 (6) BCLR 574 (SCA).

14.127 In *Prince v President of Cape Law Society* (2002) 12 BHRC 1 the Constitutional Court, by a majority of five to four, dismissed the appeal from the decision of the Supreme Court of Appeal and refused to declare that provisions of section 4(b) of the Drugs Act and section 22A(10) of the Medicines Act were invalid to the extent that they do not allow for an exemption for the religious use, possession and transportation of cannabis by *bona fide* Rastafari. There were important dissenting judgments by Ngcobo and Sachs JJ.

14.127A In *Christian Education v Minister of Education* (2000) 9 BHRC 53 the Constitutional Court rejected a claim that a blanket prohibition on corporal punishment was interference with the constitutional right of freedom of religion. The appellant was a voluntary association representing Christian schools who claimed that corporal punishment was a vital aspect of Christian religion. It was held that the restriction served the interest of protecting pupils from degradation and indignity.

15

FREEDOM OF EXPRESSION

A. The Nature of the Right

In *McCartan Turkington Breen v Times Newspapers* [2001] 2 AC 277, 297, Lord **15.01**
Steyn described freedom of expression as 'the primary right in a democracy' saying that 'without it an effective rule of law is not possible'.

n1: See, generally, J Beatson (ed), *Freedom of Expression and Freedom of Information: Essays in Honour of Sir David Williams* (Oxford University Press, 2000).

B. The Right in English Law

(1) Introduction

In *McCartan Turkington Breen v Times Newspapers* [2001] 2 AC 277, 297, Lord **15.06**
Steyn said that even before the coming into operation of the Human Rights Act

1998 the principle of freedom of expression attained the status of a constitutional right with attendant high normative force. It has recently been described as 'a fundamental right which has been recognised at common law for very many years' (*R v Shayler* [2002] 2 WLR 754, para 21).

15.12A   The Human Rights Act 1998 reinforces and gives greater weight to the protection of freedom of expression which was already established by case law (see *Venables v News Group* [2001] Fam 430, para 36). The Act is a 'constitutional' measure which buttresses freedom of expression so that any curtailment of it must be convincingly established by a compelling countervailing consideration, and the means employed must be proportionate to the end sought to be achieved (*McCartan Turkington Breen v Times Newspapers* [2001] 2 AC 277).

(2) Prior restraint

(c) Breach of confidence and other claims

15.18   The position has now been changed by section 12(3) of the Human Rights Act which provides that an interim injunction which might affect the exercise of the right to freedom of expression should not be granted unless the applicant is 'likely to establish that publication should not be allowed'. This is a higher test than that in *American Cynamid*. It has been said that the difference between 'likely' and 'real prospect of success' is small (see *A v B plc* [2002] 3 WLR 542, para 11(iii); *Imutran Ltd v Uncaged Campaigns Ltd* [2001] EMLR 563; and see also Supplement, para 15.243). It is submitted that in a case where Article 10 is engaged, an interim injunction should not be granted unless the claimant shows that it is more probable than not that an injunction will be granted at trial (see *Theakston v MGN Ltd* [2002] EMLR 398, para 45).

15.21A   The principles to be applied when considering whether or not to grant an injunction restraining the publication of confidential information were considered in the case of *London Regional Transport v The Mayor of London*, 31 July 2001 where Sullivan J applied the 'conscience test' (derived from *R v Department of Health, ex p Source Informatics Ltd* [2000] 1 All ER 786, 796): would (or should) the confidant's conscience be troubled by disclosure of the confidence? In the Court of Appeal at [2003] EMLR 4, para 55, Sedley LJ stressed the importance of the Article 10 right to receive and impart information:

> Whether or not undertakings of confidentiality have been signed, both domestic law and Art 10(2) would recognise the propriety of suppressing wanton or self-interested disclosure of confidential information; but both correspondingly recognise the legitimacy of disclosure, undertakings notwithstanding, if the public interest in the free flow of information and ideas will be served by it.

He went on to suggest that the 'proportionality principle' (see Main Work, paras 6.72ff and Supplement, para 6.81A) furnishes a 'more certain guide' to whether or not disclosure should be made than does the 'conscience test' (para 58). In other words, in cases involving public authorities, disclosure should only be restricted if:

- it meets a recognised and pressing social need;
- it does not negate or restrict the right to freedom of expression more than is necessary; and
- the reasons given for it are logical.

(This summary of the proportionality test derives from para 57 of the judgment.)

The approach applies whether the court is considering an express confidentiality undertaking or an implied obligation. In *A v B plc* [2002] 3 WLR 542 the Court of Appeal gave 'Guidelines' to assist judges in determining applications for interim injunctions in breach of confidence cases. The Court of Appeal made it clear that, regardless of the quality of the material which it is intended to publish, *prima facie* the court should not interfere with its publication. However, the 'Guidelines' are expressed in general terms and provide no specific guidance for judges or litigants. The Court said that what is required is not 'a technical approach to the law but a balancing of the facts'. This means that, in practice, it is difficult to predict whether a particular breach will be restrained. In *The Jockey Club v Buffham* [2002] 2 WLR 178 Gray J refused an injunction on the grounds of public interest, holding that on the facts the public interest in freedom of access to information outweighed the right of confidence.

When a newspaper had given undertakings not to publish confidential material **15.21B** derived from a former member of the security services, it was entitled to a variation excluding information in the public domain. It was not necessary for it to obtain clearance from the Attorney-General before publishing (*Attorney-General v Times Newspapers* [2001] 1 WLR 885). When an injunction is granted to restrain the publication of allegedly confidential material pending trial a third party who, with knowledge of the order, publishes the information commits a contempt of court because the purpose of making the order was intentionally frustrated (see *Attorney-General v Times Newspapers* [1992] 1 AC 191). However, the court could not render it a criminal offence for a newspaper to fail to obtain clearance from the Attorney-General before publishing material to which there could manifestly not be the slightest ground of objection. The contrary conclusion would be a breach of Article 10 (see *Attorney-General v Punch Ltd* [2001] 2 WLR 1713, para 108).

(3) Protection of reputation: defamation

(d) *Defences to an action for defamation*

Justification.   It has been held that the requirement that the defendant bears the **15.31** burden of proving the truth of the sting of the libel (rather than justifying some lesser allegation) is consistent with Article 10:

> To require a defendant . . . to be able to justify not a diminished version of a damaging assault on a claimant's reputation but the essence or substance or sting of that assault is not in our judgment a disproportionate invasion of the right of free expression. It meets the legitimate purpose, recognised by Article 10(2), of protecting people from the publication of damaging and unjustified falsehoods (*Berezovsky v Forbes* [2001] EMLR 1030, para 12).

The Court of Appeal rejected the argument that the decision in *Bergens Tidende v Norway* (2001) 31 EHRR 16 had altered the course of Convention jurisprudence on this subject. This is consistent with the approach of the Court of Human Rights in *McVicar v United Kingdom* (2002) 35 EHRR 566. In *Chase v News Group Newspapers* [2002] EWCA Civ 1772 the Court of Appeal considered the argument that the principles relating to justifying an allegation of 'reasonable grounds for suspicion' were incompatible with Article 10. It held that the requirements that the defence should focus upon some conduct of the individual claimant that in itself gave rise to suspicion, and that post-publication material could not be relied on, were justified restrictions on freedom of expression. Furthermore, it was held that the 'repetition' rule, in the context of a plea of justification, was not contrary to Article 10 but that appropriate use could be made of hearsay evidence under the Civil Evidence Act 1995.

15.32 **Fair comment.**   It appears that in order to rebut the defence of fair comment a claimant must show that the defendant did not have a genuine belief in what is said. In contrast to the position in relation to qualified privilege, it is not sufficient to show that the defendant was actuated by spite, animosity, intent to cause injury or other ulterior motive. This was the view of Lord Nicholls in the Hong Kong case of *Cheng Albert v Tse Wai Chun Paul* (2001) 10 BHRC 525 (Hong Kong Court of Final Appeal), and it has been held that this approach should be adopted by the English courts; see *Sugar v Associated Newspapers*, 6 February 2001 (Eady J) and *Branson v Bower (No 2)* [2001] EMLR 809 (Eady J), para 11.

15.34 **Qualified privilege.**   A press conference is a public meeting within the meaning of section 7 of, and paragraph 9 of the Schedule to, the Defamation Act 1952. The reference in the statute to 'public meeting' had to be interpreted in a manner which gave effect to the intention of the legislature in the social and other conditions which obtain today. The construction of the statute, which was 'always speaking', had to be considered in the light of the basic principles of the legal system as it has evolved, which included the law of freedom of expression (*McCartan Turkington Breen v Times Newspapers* [2001] 2 AC 277; for a discussion of this case, see I Loveland, 'Freedom of Political Expression: Who Needs the Human Rights Act?' [2001] PL 233).

n113: In relation to the modern law of qualified privilege, see, generally, *Loutchansky v Times Newspapers* [2002] QB 321, paras 9–27, and *Loutchansky v Times Newspapers (Nos 2–5)* [2002] 2 WLR 640.

In *McCartan Turkington Breen v Times Newspapers* [2001] 2 AC 277, 300 Lord **15.36** Cooke said that the opinions in *Reynolds* were intended to ensure that the common law of England harmonised with human rights jurisprudence in general and the European Convention on Human Rights in particular. It was accepted by the Court of Appeal in *Loutchansky v Times Newspapers* [2002] QB 321, para 45, that the common law principles of qualified privilege as developed in *Reynolds* were compatible with Article 10. However, *Reynolds* continues to attract criticism. In *Lange v Atkinson* [2000] 3 NZLR 385, 399, the New Zealand Court of Appeal expressed the view that *Reynolds* 'appears to alter the structure of the law of qualified privilege in a way which adds to the uncertainty and chilling effect almost inevitably present in this area of the law' (see, further, Supplement, para 15.333, and see the discussion of this point at Main Work, para 15.249). For discussions of *Reynolds*, see I Loveland, '*Reynolds v Times Newspapers* in the House of Lords' [2001] PL 351 and 'A New Legal Landscape: Libel Law and Freedom of Political Expression in the United Kingdom' [2000] EHRLR 476; K Williams, 'Defaming Politicians: The Not So Common Law' (2000) 63 MLR 748; F Trindade, 'Defamatory Statements and Political Discussion' (2000) 116 LQR 185; R Milne, 'Press Freedom and Qualified Privilege' (2000) 5 Comms L 124; K Rimmel, 'A New Public Interest Defence For the Media' (2000) 11 Ent LR 36; K Schilling, 'The Americanisation of English Libel Laws' (2000) 11 Ent LR 48.

It has been said that when a libel is published abroad and republished in England the appropriate standards of 'responsible journalism' will be those of the original place of publication rather than English standards (see *Lukowiak v Unidad Editorial SA* [2001] EMLR 1043).

n121a: The *GKR* case at first instance is now reported as *GKR Karate v Yorkshire Post (No 2)* [2000] EMLR 410.

The defence of '*Reynolds* qualified privilege' has been considered in several recent cases. In *Loutchansky v Times Newspapers (Nos 2–5)* [2002] 2 WLR 640 the Court of Appeal identified a number of considerations which 'are likely to figure prominently in the court's thinking' in deciding in a given case whether the standard of responsible journalism has been satisfied' (para 41):

- the fact that, if a publication is privileged it will, to all intents and purposes, provide the publishers with a complete defence;
- setting standards of journalistic responsibility too low would inevitably encourage too great a readiness to publish defamatory matter: journalists should be rigorous, not lax, in their approach; but
- setting the standard too high would be damaging to society because it would deter newspapers from discharging their proper function of keeping the public informed.

In *Bonnick v Morris* [2002] 3 WLR 820 the Privy Council made it clear that the purpose of *Reynolds* privilege is to provide proper protection for responsible journalism when reporting matters of public concern. The standard had to be applied in a practical and flexible manner. Lord Nicholls said that it would introduce unnecessary and undesirable legalism and rigidity if the objective standard of responsible journalist had to be applied in all cases by reference to the 'single meaning' of the words.

The defence failed in the following cases: *Gilbert v MGN* [2000] EMLR 680; *Grobbelaar v News Group* [2001] EWCA Civ 33; *Baldwin v Rusbridger* [2001] EMLR 1062 (Eady J); *English v Hastie*, 21 January 2002 (Gray J); *Field v Local Sunday Newspapers* [2002] EWHC 336. However, the defence has been successful in several cases: *Lukowiak v Unidad Editorial SA* [2001] EMLR 1043 (Eady J); *Al Fagih v HH Saudi Research & Marketing* [2002] EMLR 215 and *Bonnick v Morris* [2002] 3 WLR 820.

15.37   In *Lillie & Reed v Newcastle City Council* [2002] EWHC 1600 Eady J held that the authors of a report alleging serious child abuse by the claimants were 'malicious', despite the fact that they honestly believed in the truth of the charges which were made, because they were not acting in good faith:

> They abused the occasion for which they had striven so hard to ensure that blanket protection. Its four members consciously, after a detailed consideration of the material assembled before them, set out to misrepresent the state of the evidence available to support their joint belief that [the claimants] . . . were child abusers (and indeed abusers on a massive scale) and to give readers the impression that statements by parents and/or children had been corroborated by police inquiries (para 1370).

This arguably involves a substantial extension of the traditional concept of malice as 'knowing or reckless falsity' and its limits remain to be worked out.

(e) Remedies

15.39   It has been recognised that exorbitant awards of damages have a 'chilling effect' on the exercise of the right of freedom of expression (*Skrine v Euromoney* [2001] EMLR 434, 443, para 36 (Morland J)).

(4) Comment on court proceedings: contempt of court

(d) Breach of undertakings or orders that restrict court reporting

15.62   **Orders for postponement of trial reporting.**   n202: See also *R v Sherwood, ex p Telegraph Group* [2001] EWCA Crim 1075.

15.67   **Orders to prevent publication of the names of parties.**   n222a: *R v Secretary of State, ex p Wagstaff and Associated Newspapers* is now reported at [2001] 1 WLR 292.

15.69   **Restriction of publication of information concerning children.**   The power to dispense with anonymity has to be exercised with great caution; see, generally,

McKerry v Teesdale and Wear Valley Justices [2001] EMLR 127. An 'anonymity' order under section 39 of the Children and Young Persons Act 1933 will only be justified if Article 10 is met—the restriction must fulfil the tests in Article 10(2). However, if the order is properly made then its enforcement will not violate Article 10 (see *Briffet v DPP* [2002] EMLR 203). When considering whether to make such an order in proceedings for an anti-social behaviour order each case must be considered on its merits, but evidence as to the effects on members of the offender's family is not, *prima facie*, relevant (*R (T) v Crown Court at St Albans* [2002] EWHC Admin 1129).

(e) *Protection of journalistic sources*

Although section 10 refers only to 'the source of information contained in a pub-   **15.74** lication' it appears that the protection only extends to 'confidential journalistic sources'; see, for example, the discussion in *Goodwin v United Kingdom* (1996) 22 EHRR 123 considered at Main Work, para 15.77.

n256: See also *Ashworth Hospital Authority v MGN* [2001] 1 WLR 515 (interests   **15.76** of justice did not cover just narrow purposes of administration of justice but all interests which were justiciable). The decision of the Court of Appeal was upheld by the House of Lords at [2002] 1 WLR 2033 on the basis that while the exercise of the jurisdiction to require a third party who was involved in wrongdoing, in this case a journalist, to identify the wrongdoer was subject to Article 10, in the exceptional circumstances of the case itself the order to disclose was justifiable. See also *Interbrew SA v Financial Times* [2002] 1 Lloyd's Rep 542 in which exceptional circumstances existed so as to require a journalist to identify a source (upheld by the Court of Appeal at [2002] EWCA Civ 274, but see the comments of Lord Woolf on this decision in *Ashworth Hospital Authority v MGN* [2001] 1 WLR 515, paras 50–8).

See also *Ashworth Hospital Authority v MGN* [2001] 1 WLR 515 (disclosure order   **15.78** to protect the confidentiality of medical records, discussed further at Supplement, para 15.76), upheld by the House of Lords at [2002] 1 WLR 2033.

(5) Obscenity and indecency

(a) *Introduction*

It was held by the Court of Appeal in *R v Perrin* [2002] EWCA Crim 747 that   **15.80** there had been no violation of Article 10 after a defendant was convicted of publishing an obscene article contrary to the Obscene Publications Act 1959. The Court held that because Parliament was 'entitled to conclude' that restrictions on the publication of obscene material was necessary in a democratic society, the restriction was justified under Article 10(2). It is submitted that this is not the correct test and that the Court should have considered whether the interference was, in fact, justified on the evidence.

(c) Other obscenity and indecency offences

15.90 In *R v Smethurst* [2002] 1 Cr App Rep 6 it was held that the offence of making indecent photographs of children contrary to section 1(1)(a) of the Protection of Children Act 1978 did not contravene Article 10. The offence was 'there for the prevention of crime, for the protection of morals and, in particular for the protection of children from being exploited' which, the court said 'is undoubtedly a matter which is necessary in a democratic society'. The court did not go on to analyse the proportionality of the sanctions. The same area was the subject of a careful and detailed analysis by the Supreme Court of Canada in *R v Sharpe* [2001] 2 LRC 665, discussed at Supplement, para 15.307A.

(6) Media regulation and censorship

(a) Introduction

15.92 The Government has proposed a radical reform of the system for regulation of the electronic media; see *A New Future for Communications* (12 December 2000, Cm 5010). It is proposed that a singular regulator, OFCOM, will take responsibility for all regulatory functions. The paving Act, the Office of Communications Act 2002, is already in force and the Government has now published a draft Communications Bill. The key changes which are proposed include:

- the transfer of functions from the five existing regulators (ITC, BSC, Radio Authority, Radio Communications Agency and OFTEL) to OFCOM, the new regulator for the industry; and
- the removal of the requirement for the licensing of telecommunications systems and the introduction of a new regulatory regime for electronic communications networks, electronic communications services and associated facilities.

Clause 3(1)(g) of the Bill provides that OFCOM's duties shall include:

> to secure, so far as practicable and in the manner that best takes account of the need to guarantee an appropriate level of freedom of expression, that all persons are provided with adequate protection from—
> (i) unfair treatment in programmes included in television and radio services; and
> (ii) unwarranted infringements of privacy . . .

This is a curious provision which appears to provide a broadcaster who infringes privacy with at least three separate and cumulative arguments, namely, that it was not 'practicable' to avoid the infringement, that prevention of such an infringement would not take account of freedom of expression and that the infringement was 'warranted'. It is doubtful whether such a 'hedged' right to privacy strikes a proper balance between Articles 8 and 10.

(7) Freedom of expression and the criminal law

(a) Introduction

Criminal conduct designed to express political views, such as cutting the wire at a nuclear weapons establishment, may be protected by Article 10 of the Convention (*Hutchinson v Newbury Magistrates*, 9 October 2000, DC). See also *Percy v DPP* [2002] Crim LR 835, discussed at Supplement, para 15.121

15.111

(b) Blasphemous libel

The Irish Supreme Court held that it was difficult to reconcile the view that blasphemy could be carried out without any intent with the freedom of expression, and the freedom of religion, and declined to follow *Whitehouse v Gay News* [1979] AC 617 (see *Corway v Independent Newspapers* [2000] 1 ILRM 426, discussed at Supplement, para 5.369A).

15.113

(e) Other criminal offences

Racial hatred.   In *Percy v DPP* [2002] Crim LR 835 the appellant was a protester against US military policy who had defaced the American flag. She was convicted of using threatening, abusive and insulting words or behaviour likely to cause distress contrary to section 5 of the Public Order Act 1986. The Administrative Court overturned the conviction, holding that it was incompatible with Article 10 of the Convention. The behaviour had been insulting but there had been no risk of disorder and a high threshold had to be overcome before interference with an individual's Article 10 rights was permitted. The restriction was not 'strictly necessary'.

15.121

(9) Freedom of information

Article 10 does not mean that there is a general right to receive information in the absence of willingness to impart the information (*R v Bow County Court, ex p Pelling* [2001] 1 UKHRLR 165, para 36). It was held in *R v Secretary of State, ex p Wagstaff and Associated Newspapers* [2001] 1 WLR 292, in relation to the inquiry into the murders carried out by Dr Shipman, that given the right to receive information provided by Article 10, it was irrational to hold that inquiry in private without sufficient justification. In *Wagstaff* the court was of the view that there is a presumption in favour of a public inquiry. However, this view was rejected in *Persey v Secretary of State for Environment, Food and Rural Affairs* [2002] 3 WLR 704. In *Persey* the claimants sought an order that the Government carry out a public inquiry into the handling of the foot and mouth outbreak. The Administrative Court held that the decision to hold the inquiry in private was not irrational and that Article 10 of the Convention was not engaged by such a decision. Article 10 prohibited interference with freedom of expression but imposed no positive

15.136A

obligation on the Government to provide an open forum to achieve the wider dissemination of information. The claimants did not have any right under Article 10 to require a public authority to gather information which they would have an interest in receiving, still less to require the public authority to gather that information in any particular form or manner, ie by public rather than private inquiry. Furthermore, even if the decision constituted a restriction on the claimants' or media's right to freedom of expression it was capable of being justified under Article 10(2). The Government's decision was one which was open to it to take and it could not be impugned as irrational or otherwise unlawful. (See also *R (Howard) v Secretary of State for Health* [2002] 3 WLR 738.)

(10) Community law

15.136B   Freedom of expression as embodied in Article 10 is among the general principles of law the observance of which is ensured by the Court of Justice (see, for example, *Ter Voort* [1992] ECR I-5485, Judgment, para 35; *Commission v Netherlands* [1991] ECR I-4069, Judgment, para 30). This includes commercial expression (*R v Secretary of State for Health, ex p Imperial Tobacco Ltd* [2000] All ER (EC) 769, Opinion of Advocate General, paras 153–4). However, restrictions on the freedom of expression on the ground of protection of health are permitted in the Community legal order. Thus restrictions on the advertising of alcoholic beverages to consumers under Swedish law were justified on this ground (*Konsumentombudsmannen (KO) v Gourmet International Products AB* [2001] All ER (EC) 308).

C. The Law Under the European Convention

(2) Scope of the right

(a) Introduction

15.140   n448: See also *Nicol and Selvanayagam v United Kingdom* (Decision of 11 January 2001).

15.141   nn452, 455 and 457: *Lehideux v France* is now reported at (2000) 30 EHRR 665.

15.144   n463: Cf *Volkmer v Germany* (Decision of 22 November 2001) which held that the dismissal of a teacher for political activity in the former East Germany which was an abuse of authority was not a breach of Article 10 and *Petersen v Germany* (Decision of 22 November 2001) in which it was held that the dismissal of a professor of modern history from East Germany for lack of professional qualifications was also not in breach of Article 10.

n464: *Rekvenyi v Hungary* is now reported at (2000) 30 EHRR 519. *Wille v Liechtenstein* is now reported at (2000) 30 EHRR 558.

(b) The relationship with Article 10 and other Convention rights

nn477a and 481a–c: *Wille v Liechtenstein* is now reported at (2000) 30 EHRR 558.   **15.148**

(c) The right to hold opinions and to impart information

In *Roche v United Kingdom* (Decision of 23 May 2002) a claim that the failure to   **15.149**
provide information on medical tests done on the applicant some years previously
was a violation of Articles 8 and 10 was declared admissible.

(d) Freedom of the press and mass media

nn498 and 502a: *Bergens Tidende v Norway* is now reported at (2001) 31 EHRR   **15.154**
16.

The Court has found violations of Article 10 in a number of recent cases involv-   **15.156**
ing the media:

- In *News Verlag GmbH v Austria* (2000) 31 EHRR 246 it was held that an injunction prohibiting the publication of a photograph of a criminal suspect was a
  breach of Article 10. The absolute prohibition on the use of the photograph went
  further than was necessary to protect the suspect from defamation or against violation of the presumption of innocence. It was important to bear in mind that
  Article 10 protects the form in which ideas and information are conveyed. The
  Court emphasised the essential functions of the press in imparting information
  (see also the admissibility decisions in *Krones Verlag GmbH v Austria*, Judgment
  of 15 May 2001, and *Unabhängige Initiative Informationsvielfat v Austria*,
  Judgment of 26 February 2002).
- In *Da Silva v Portugal* (2002) 34 EHRR 56 the applicant was the manager of a
  daily newspaper which had published an article attacking a candidate in a local
  election in strong terms. He was found guilty of criminal libel and fined. The
  Court found a violation of Article 10. It pointed out that journalists could resort to a degree of exaggeration or even provocation. The applicant had reproduced extracts of articles by the candidate and had, therefore, acted in
  accordance with the rules of the journalistic profession.
- In *Du Roy and Malaurie v France* (Judgment of 3 October 2000) the applicants
  had been fined for publishing information in relation to the joinder of civil parties in criminal proceedings. The ban on such publication was absolute and was
  said to be necessary in the interests of the proper administration of justice. The
  Court pointed out that the case concerned political figures and there were other
  ways of protecting the rights of the accused. The conviction of the journalists
  was not a reasonably proportionate way of pursuing the legitimate aim of protecting the interests of justice.

- In *Thoma v Luxembourg* (Judgment of 29 March 2001) it was held, after one journalist quoted a defamatory remark made by another, that it was a disproportionate interference with his Article 10 rights to require him formally to distance himself from the quoted remark. See, further, Supplement, para 15.252.

The decision in *Bergens Tidende* can be contrasted with that in *Verdens Gang and Aase v Norway* (Decision of 16 October 2001) in which allegations of professional misconduct made against a doctor had also resulted in a successful claim for damages by the doctor against the newspaper. In that case the complaint was held to be inadmissible because the article was factually incorrect and biased and the applicant newspaper and journalist had not taken sufficient steps to fulfil their obligations to verify the complaints which had been made by the patients. The newspaper had not waited for the doctor to be released from his obligation of professional confidence before publishing. In the circumstances, the interest of the doctor in protecting his professional reputation was not counterbalanced by an important public interest in the freedom of the press to impart information of legitimate public concern.

n506a: *Bergens Tidende v Norway* is now reported at (2001) 31 EHRR 16.

(e) The licensing power

15.159   The state has a relatively wide margin of appreciation in relation to licensing decisions; see *Skyradio AG and Others v Switzerland* (Decision of 27 September 2001) (Article 10 claim inadmissible).

15.160   The refusal to grant a licence to operate a television transmitter was an interference with the right to freedom of expression. However, this interference was justified insofar as the Convention permits states to regulate broadcasting by means of a licensing system. The necessity for the interference was not established until the applicant was provided with a viable alternative to terrestrial television in the form of cable television (*Tele 1 Privatfernsehgesellschaft mbH v Austria* [2001] EHRLR 223).

15.161   In *United Christian Broadcasting v United Kingdom* (Decision of 7 November 2000) a complaint that a statutory provision (paragraph 2(7) of Part 11 of Schedule 2 to the Broadcasting Act 1990) prohibited religious or political bodies from holding national radio licences was held to be inadmissible. The purpose of the restriction was to avoid discrimination between religions and could not be said to be arbitrary. The Court also took into account the fact that religious groups were not restricted from applying for licences for local radio broadcasting. In *Brook v United Kingdom* [2001] EHRLR 106 the applicant complained that the Foreign Office's failure to grant him a short-wave radio licence was an unjustified interference with his Article 10 right to impart information. The Court held that the requirements of Article 10(2) were satisfied. The proportionality test was met because the applicant had the alternative of applying for an AM or FM licence.

(3) Types of expression

(b) Political expression

On the importance of free expression in the context of politics, see also *Jerusalem v Austria* (Judgment of 27 February 2001). In relation to political expression it has been held that it is important to distinguish between advocating violence and legitimate discussion of potentially inflammatory topics. In *Sener v Turkey* (Judgment of 18 July 2000) the Court held that a discussion of the problems between Kurds and Turks fell on the latter side of the line and that the state had given insufficient weight to the public's right to information in breach of Article 10 (see also *Erdogdu v Turkey* (2002) 34 EHRR 1143 and *Özgur Gündem v Turkey* (2001) 31 EHRR 1082). In *Unabhängige Initiative Informationsvielfalt v Austria* (Judgment of 26 February 2002) the Court held that in the context of political discussion even comments of a polemic nature were protected by Article 10.

15.164

In *Vgt Verein gegen Tierfabriken v Switzerland* (2001) 10 BHRC 473 the Court considered the effect of a prohibition on political advertising on the applicant association which sought to promote the protection of animals. The Court held that the domestic authorities had failed to demonstrate in a relevant and sufficient manner why the grounds generally advanced in support of the prohibition on political advertising also served to justify the ban on the applicant's proposed television commercials. This is an important decision which may lead to a relaxation of the rules governing political advertising in the United Kingdom.

15.165

A publisher can be required to prove that there is a sufficient factual basis for a value judgement but this is not a high hurdle. Thus in *Dichand v Austria* (Judgment of 26 February 2002) the fact that the applicants published harsh criticism of a politician in strong and polemical language on a slim factual basis did not mean that they lost the protection of Article 10 which protects information or ideas which offend, shock or disturb.

15.166

An individual may be a public figure, even if his appearance is not known to the public. Thus it was held that the publication of a photograph of a politician accused of impropriety was protected by Article 10 even if his appearance was not widely known (*Krone Verlag Gmbh & Co Kg v Austria*, Judgment of 26 February 2002). While criticism of civil servants could in certain circumstances receive greater protection than criticism of private individuals, it generally received lesser protection than criticism of politicians (*Nikula v Finland* (2002) 12 BHRC 519).

15.167

(d) Commercial expression

In *Stambuk v Germany* (Decision of 22 October 2000) a doctor complained that he was disciplined in breach of Article 10 for co-operating with a newspaper article which appeared to advertise his practice. He claimed that such a prohibition

15.175

was not 'necessary', insofar as its aims were the prevention of competition among doctors rather than the protection of health, and was disproportionate insofar as it covered co-operation with the press as well as direct advertising. The complaint was held to be admissible.

(4) Justifying limits on expression

(b) Interferences

15.182 An order that there be a right of reply is an interference under Article 10 (see *Ediciones Tiempo SA v Spain* (1989) 62 DR 247).

(d) 'Prescribed by law'

15.188 n596: The rules relating to the registration of the titles of periodicals in Poland were not formulated with sufficient precision to enable the applicant to regulate his conduct; see *Gaweda v Poland* (2002) 12 BHRC 486.

15.189 n604: *Hashman and Harrup v United Kingdom* is now reported at (2000) 30 EHRR 241.

(e) 'Necessary in a democratic society'

15.191 The question of whether an interference is 'necessary in a democratic society' is considered on a 'case by case' basis. In a number of cases, the Court has found that the particular sanction imposed was disproportionate to the legitimate aim:

- *Bobo v Spain* (2001) 31 EHRR 50 concerned an employee of state television in Spain who had been dismissed for making critical and abusive remarks about the management of the television station. The Court held that there was no reasonable relationship of proportionality between the sanction imposed and the legitimate aim pursued. Although discipline would have been justified, dismissal was too severe a sanction.
- In *Maronek v Slovakia* (2001) 10 BHRC 558 the Court held that a judgment for defamation in respect of a letter which was made public, and which contained allegations of dishonesty, was a disproportionate interference with the Article 10 rights of the writer who had acted in good faith, raised matters of public interest and most of whose allegations had been published earlier in a newspaper. One of the bases for the decision was the fact that the applicant had been required to pay damages and costs of 25 times the average monthly salary, which in English terms would be roughly £40,000. Insofar as the majority decision is more widely based it was subject to powerful criticism in the Concurring Opinion in which three of the seven judges joined.

By contrast, where the interference is of a less serious nature, a breach of Article 10 is less likely. Thus a complaint about an injunction which required the applicant to refer to 'current differences of opinion' when discussing scientifically proven results concerning the safety of microwave ovens was held to be inadmissible, in part, because of the minor nature of the interference with freedom of expression (*Hertel v Switzerland*, Decision of 17 January 2001).

An important consideration in relation to proportionality is whether the statements being made are statements of fact or value judgments. Because the truth of the latter is not susceptible to proof restrictions are much harder to justify. This point has been considered in several recent cases:

- In *Feldek v Slovakia* (Judgment of 12 July 2001) the applicant had been sued for libel by a government minister who he had accused of having a fascist past. The Court found that the statement was a value judgment, the truth of which was not susceptible of proof. It rejected the argument that a value judgement could only be considered as such if it was accompanied by the facts on which the judgment was based (para 86). As a result it was held (at para 87) that the Slovak court did not convincingly establish any pressing social need for putting the protection of the personal rights of a public figure above the applicant's right to freedom of expression and the general interest of promoting this freedom when issues of public interest are concerned.
- In *Perna v Italy* (Judgment of 25 July 2001) the applicant journalist had suggested that a judge who was a member of the Communist Party had sworn a judicial oath to God, the law and Communist Party headquarters. This was a critical opinion couched in provocative language but with a factual basis, namely the judge's political militancy. A finding of aggravated defamation was a breach of Article 10. However, there was no violation in relation to allegations concerning the complainant's participation in a plan to gain control of public prosecutors' offices.
- In *Dichand v Austria* (Judgment of 26 February 2002) the fact that the applicants published harsh criticism of a politician in strong and polemical language on a slim factual basis did not mean that they lost the protection of Article 10 which protects information or ideas which offend, shock or disturb.

These cases can be contrasted with *Tammer v Estonia* (2001) 10 BHRC 543. The applicant was a journalist who had made insulting remarks about the wife of a former prime minister of Estonia who had held public positions. The applicant was convicted of the criminal offence of 'insult' and fined. The Court accepted that the words used were value judgments but said that they could have been formulated without resort to insulting expressions. It was held that, taking into account the margin of appreciation, domestic authorities were entitled to interfere with the exercise of the applicant's rights. The reasoning in the *Tammer* case is difficult to follow and it is suggested that it is not of general application.

(f) Objective of the interference

15.198   **National Security, territorial integrity or public safety.**   See also *Erdogdu v Turkey* (2002) 34 EHRR 1143.

n646:   *Incal v Turkey* is now reported at (2000) 29 EHRR 449.

n647:   See also *Ibrahim Aksoy v Turkey* (Judgment of 10 October 2000). *Ceylan v Turkey* is now reported at (2000) 30 EHRR 73; *Surek v Turkey* is reported at (1999) 7 BHRC 339; *Arslan v Turkey* is reported at (2001) 31 EHRR 264; *Baskaya and Okçuoglu v Turkey* is reported at (2001) 31 EHRR 10.

15.201   **Prevention of disorder or crime.**   In *Marlow v United Kingdom* (Decision of 5 December 2000) the Court concluded that the prosecution of the writer of a book which incited others to grow cannabis pursued the legitimate aim of the prevention of crime. In *Ekin v France* (Judgment of 17 July 2001) it was held that a ban on the publication and sale of a book about the Basque conflict on the grounds of a potential danger to public order was disproportionate to the legitimate aim. In *Nicol and Selvanayagam v United Kingdom* (Decision of 11 January 2001) it was accepted that the arrest, detention and subsequent imprisonment of protestors who were seeking to disrupt an angling competition was a serious interference with the right of freedom of expression but, in the circumstances, it was not disproportionate. There was a real risk of disorder if similar protests took place and the imprisonment for 21 days was a result of the failure to agree to a bind over which was designed to avoid a 'real risk' of further protest.

n653:   *Incal v Turkey* is now reported at (2000) 29 EHRR 449; *Janowski v Poland* is now reported at (2000) 29 EHRR 705. Cf *Osmani and Others v Former Yugoslav Republic of Macedonia* (Decision of 11 October 2001) in which an interference with freedom of expression in the context of incitement to political violence was found to be proportionate and the complaint was therefore inadmissible.

15.204   **Protection of the reputation or the rights of others.**   **n663:** *Nilsen and Johnsen v Norway* is now reported at (2000) 30 EHRR 878.

n664a: *Bergens Tidende v Norway* is now reported at (2001) 31 EHRR 16.

15.206   **n669:**   *Rekvenyi v Hungary* is now reported at (2000) 30 EHRR 519.

15.208   The conviction of defence counsel for 'negligent defamation' following criticism of the public prosecutor in court was a breach of Article 10 (*Nikula v Finland* (2002) 12 BHRC 519). It should be for defence counsel, subject to supervision of the court, to assess the relevance and usefulness of a defence argument without being influenced by the potential 'chilling effect' of even a relatively light criminal sanction or an obligation to pay damages or costs. In *Lesnik v Slovakia* (Decision of 8 January 2002) a complaint that a conviction for criticism of a public prosecutor was in breach of Article 10 was found to be admissible. However, a fine imposed on a lawyer for the making of defamatory remarks about a magistrate during his own disciplinary process was found not to be in breach of Article 10 and his complaint held inadmissible (*Kubli v Switzerland*, Decision of 21 February 2002).

n672: *Lehideux v France* is now reported at (2000) 30 EHRR 665.

n674: *Janowski v Poland* is now reported at (2000) 29 EHRR 705.

A complaint that a criminal investigation aimed at obtaining disclosure of a jour-   **15.211**
nalist's sources was in breach of Article 10 was declared admissible in *Roemen and Schmidt v Luxembourg* (Decision of 12 March 2002).

Maintaining the authority and impartiality of the judiciary.   See also *Perna v*   **15.214**
Italy (Judgment of 25 July 2001), para 15.191, discussed at Supplement, para 15.191.

In *Nikula v Finland* (2002) 12 BHRC 519 the Court held that while counsel's freedom of expression in court was not unlimited it could only be lawfully re-stricted in exceptional circumstances. In the case itself a lawyer had been con-victed of defamation following criticism in court of the prosecutor in a case in which both were involved. This was found to be a breach of Article 10.

See also *Hurter v Switzerland* (Decision of 21 February 2002) in which the disci-plinary punishment of a lawyer for making serious allegations against the Court of Appeal in documents lodged in court on his client's behalf was held to be pro-portionate and his claim for breach of Article 10 inadmissible. In part the fact that the appellant was a lawyer rendered interference more likely to be proportionate as lawyers have obligations to maintain public confidence in the judiciary. See also *Wingerter v Germany* (Decision of 21 March 2002).

D. The Impact of the Human Rights Act

(2) United Kingdom cases

(a) Introduction

The United Kingdom has not been found to be in breach of Article 10 in the pe-   **15.218**
riod 1 June 2000 to 1 December 2002.

(e) Defamation

In *McVicar v United Kingdom* (2002) 35 EHRR 22 the Court held that the denial   **15.229**
of legal aid to defend defamation proceedings was not a violation of Article 6(1) and that such ineligibility was not a violation of Article 10. It also held that the burden of proof on a defendant in defamation proceedings constituted a justified restriction on freedom expression under Article 10(2).

(g) Other applications

15.236 n753: *Hashman and Harrup v United Kingdom* is now reported at (2000) 30 EHRR 241.

A complaint under Article 10 was held inadmissible in *United Christian Broadcasting v United Kingdom* (Decision of 7 November 2000) on the basis that the restriction was not disproportionate as religious groups could apply for local licences and that it was necessary to ensure that there was no discrimination in the allocation of the very limited national radio spectrum. In *Marlow v United Kingdom* (Decision of 5 December 2000) the conviction of a writer of a book which incited others to grow cannabis was held to be justified on the ground that the prosecution pursued the legitimate aim of the prevention of crime and was a proportionate response to a 'pressing social need'.

(3) General impact issues

Introduction

15.237 The general impact of Article 10 has been considered in a number of recent cases. The importance of the right to freedom of expression has been acknowledged in many cases (for example, *McCartan Turkington Breen v Times Newspapers* [2001] 2 AC 277). The extent to which Article 10 requires specific 'justification' of an interference on the facts of each case remains controversial. In *Ashdown v Telegraph Group* [2002] QB 546, paras 15–18, Morritt V-C rejected the argument that where Article 10 was engaged the facts of each case have to be considered to determine whether a restriction goes further than is necessary in a democratic society. In contrast, in *Loutchansky v Times Newspapers* [2002] QB 321, para 46, after considering *Sunday Times v United Kingdom* (1979) 2 EHRR 245, para 65, the Court of Appeal held that it was necessary to consider the application of general principles to the facts of each case in order to determine whether a particular interference with freedom of expression was justified under Article 10(2).

Restrictions on freedom of expression in the public interest must be 'strictly proved' (*R v Secretary of Health, ex p Wagstaff* [2001] 1 WLR 292). As Munby J said in *Kelly v BBC* [2001] Fam 59, 67:

> . . . if those who seek to bring themselves within paragraph 2 of article 10 are to establish 'convincingly' that they are—and that is what they have to establish—they cannot do so by mere assertion, however eminent the person making the assertion, nor by simply inviting the court to make assumptions; what is required . . . is proper evidence . . .

(See also *Venables v News Group* [2001] Fam 430 and *Re X (A Child)* [2001] 1 FCR 541. Contrast the views expressed by Dyson LJ in *R (Samaroo) v Home Secretary* [2001] UKHRR 1150, discussed at Supplement, para 6.81A.)

However, this approach has not always been followed in practice. Despite the high constitutional importance of the right to freedom of expression, the courts have continued to accord a substantial margin of discretion to the executive in freedom of expression cases and have not rigorously imposed the requirement of 'convincing evidence'. Thus, in the surprising case of *R (Farrakhan) v Secretary of State for the Home Department* [2002] 3 WLR 481 the Court of Appeal accepted that one reason for the decision of the Home Secretary to exclude the claimant from the United Kingdom was to prevent him from exercising his right to freedom of expression and that, as a result, the restriction had to be justified under Article 10(2). The matter could also have been approached on the basis of an interference with the right of the claimant's United Kingdom followers to 'receive information' (see, for example, *Benjamin v Minister of Information and Broadcasting* [2001] 1 WLR 1040, Supplement, para 15.347A). The Court of Appeal then held that the exclusion on the ground that the claimant's visit 'might provide a catalyst for disorder' was a proportionate restriction of freedom of expression despite the absence of any 'convincing evidence' of a significant risk of disorder. The decision was, effectively, upheld on the traditional *Wednesbury* basis that it was within the Home Secretary's 'margin of discretion'. Although the House of Lords refused permission to appeal, it is submitted that the Court of Appeal's judgment does not embody the correct approach to the review of decisions which interfere with the right to freedom of expression.

(a) Section 12 of the Human Rights Act

15.243   Section 12(3) requires the court to look at the merits of the case and not merely to apply the *American Cyanamid* test (*Douglas v Hello! Ltd* [2001] QB 967, para 150; see also *Imutran Ltd v Uncaged Campaigns Ltd* [2001] EMLR 563; *Theakston v MGN* [2002] EMLR 398; and *A v B plc* [2002] 3 WLR 542). The section does not require the court to give priority to Article 10 rights over all others, it simply directs the court to look at the merits of the case on an interim application (*Douglas*, at 1031–3, paras 149–53, *per* Keene LJ).

15.244   Where the balance between privacy and freedom of expression does not clearly point in one direction, interim relief should generally be refused (*A v B plc* [2002] 3 WLR 542, para 12). It has been suggested that, because the Convention right to freedom of expression is qualified in favour of the reputation and rights of others (which includes the right to respect for private life under Article 8), when considering an injunction against the media, 'privacy' and 'reputation' rights are as relevant as freedom of expression (*Douglas v Hello! Ltd* [2001] QB 967, para 133). As section 12(4) directs attention to 'any relevant privacy code', it is likely that any newspaper which breached paragraph 3 of the Press Complaints Commission's Code of Practice would have its claim to freedom of expression 'trumped' by privacy considerations (*Douglas v Hello! Ltd* [2001] QB 967, para 94, *per* Brooke LJ).

15.245 When considering a conflict between freedom of expression and privacy the court must take relevant privacy codes into account under section 12(4) (see *Douglas v Hello! Ltd* [2001] QB 967; and see also *Mills v Mirror Group Newspapers* [2001] EMLR 957 (Lawrence Collins J)). In *Mills* an injunction restraining the publication of the claimant's home address was refused in the absence of evidence of apprehended harm. The judge also took into account the fact that the newspaper indicated that it had no intention of publishing and that it would abide by the Press Complaints Commission's Code of Practice. However, in *A v B plc* [2002] 3 WLR 542 the Court of Appeal emphasised that the privacy codes were only one factor and discouraged reliance on individual decisions of the PCC (para 11(xiv) and (xv)). See, generally, H Tomlinson (ed), *Privacy and the Media: The Developing Law* (Matrix, 2002), ch 4. The Court of Appeal went on to say that the fact that under section 12(4) the court was required to have particular regard to whether it would be in the public interest for material to be published did not mean that the court was justified in interfering with freedom of the press because there was no identifiable special public interest in any particular material being published. Regardless of the quality of the material published the court should, *prima facie*, not interfere with its publication.

In *Clibbery v Allan* [2002] 2 WLR 1511 it was held that the principle of open justice applied to family courts and the exclusion of the public had to be objectively justified. Cases involving children and ancillary relief were automatically protected from publication but there was no prohibition on publication of other family proceedings save in cases in which the parties were under a compulsion to disclose documents.

On the balancing exercise between privacy and expression in cases of alleged breach of confidence, see *A v B plc* [2002] 3 WLR 542 in which the Court of Appeal held that what was required, generally, was a weighing of all the material facts rather than a technical legal approach; and see also *Campbell v MGN Ltd* [2003] 2 WLR 80; and *The Jockey Club v Buffham* [2002] 2 WLR 178.

On the law relating to privacy and freedom of expression, see, generally, R Singh and J Strachan, 'The Right to Privacy in English Law' (2002) 2 EHRLR 129; M Colvin (ed), *Developing Key Privacy Rights* (Hart Publishing, 2002); H Tomlinson (ed), *Privacy and the Media: The Developing Law* (Matrix, 2002); and M Tugendhat and I Christie (eds), *The Law of Privacy and the Media* (Oxford University Press, 2002).

n776: *Nilsen and Johnsen v Norway* is now reported at (2000) 30 EHRR 878.

The effect of section 12(4) is that Article 10 is 'horizontally' applicable as between parties to private litigation (*Douglas v Hello! Ltd* [2001] QB 967, para 133; see also *McCartan Turkington Breen v Times Newspapers* [2001] 2 AC 277; *Venables v News*

Group Newspapers [2001] Fam 430; and *Mills v Mirror Group Newspapers* [2001] EMLR 957).

It was held in *Imutran Ltd v Uncaged Campaigns Ltd* [2001] EMLR 563 that section 12(4) does not require the courts to place greater weight on freedom of expression than they already do but that it does require the courts to give it specific and separate consideration. In *Ashdown v Telegraph Group* [2002] Ch 149, para 27, the Court of Appeal said that

> section 12 does no more than underline the need to have regard to contexts in which [Strasbourg jurisprudence] has given particular weight to freedom of expression while at the same time drawing attention to considerations which may nonetheless justify restricting that right.

This approach appears to give Article 10 too little weight and, it is submitted, that the effect of section 12(4) is that the court should not grant relief which impedes the right to freedom of expression unless there are cogent grounds for doing so, supported by evidence.

15.246 In relation to the significance of the status of the individual claiming privacy rights, it was held in *A v B plc* [2002] 3 WLR 542 that while a public figure (in this case a footballer) was entitled to privacy in certain circumstances, it should also be recognised that he had to expect and accept that his actions would be more closely scrutinised than a member of the general public. The injunction was discharged. In *Theakston v MGN Ltd* [2002] EMLR 398 Ouseley J considered the significance of the fact that the claimant asserting a right to privacy was a television presenter of programmes for younger viewers. This, taken with the fact that privacy was being claimed in relation to acts taking place in a brothel, which could not be considered a private place, led to the refusal of the injunction to restrain the publication of the article. However, the court did grant an injunction to restrain the publication of photographs that had been taken without his consent. For a discussion of these decisions, see H Tomlinson (ed), *Privacy and the Media: The Developing Law* (Matrix, 2002), paras 2.17–2.19.

(b) Defamation

15.247 The judges have been generally cautious in applying Convention principles to the law of libel. In *Branson v Bower*, 21 November 2000, Eady J dealt with the general impact of the Human Rights Act 1998 on the law of defamation in the following terms:

> It is important, however, to recognise that the European Convention has not been directly incorporated into English law. The courts must take these matters into account when applying domestic law but they should not be regarded as bypassing our long-established principles. We should use European jurisprudence to assist us in testing, from time to time, whether our own laws are consistent with the rights guaranteed under the Convention. European decisions, however, are often difficult

to apply by analogy because they are tied to their own facts . . . In this jurisdiction it happens that we have a civil law of defamation that is sophisticated and highly developed and includes a range of defences for the media.

However, in *Berezovsky v Forbes (No 2)* [2001] EMLR 45, para 11, the Court of Appeal refused to 'rest on the laurels of earlier judicial statements . . . that the English common law already conforms with Article 10'. See also *Branson v Bower* [2001] EMLR 800, para 6.

15.252 The impact of Article 10 on a number of aspects of the law of defamation has been considered in the case law since 2 October 2000:

- **Publication:** The rule that each separate communication of defamatory words gives rise to a separate cause of action has been held to be consistent with Article 10, even when it is applied to publication on the Internet (*Loutchansky v Times Newspapers (Nos 2–5)* [2002] 2 WLR 640).

- **Justification:** The requirement that the defendant prove the truth of a defamatory allegation has been held to be compatible with Article 10(2), meeting 'the legitimate purpose, recognised by Article 10(2) of protecting people from the publication of damaging and unjustified falsehoods' (*Berezovsky v Forbes (No 2)* [2001] EMLR 45, para 12). This conclusion was confirmed by the decision of the Court of Human Rights in *McVicar v United Kingdom* (2002) 35 EHRR 22 in which it was held that the requirement to prove that the allegations made in the article were substantially true on the balance of probabilities constituted a justified restriction on freedom of expression under Article 10(2) in the interests of the protection of reputation. (See also *Khumalo v Holomisa* (2002) 12 BHRC 538, discussed further at Supplement, para 15.373, in which the South African Constitutional Court reached a similar conclusion.) Furthermore, in *Chase v News Group Newspapers* [2002] EWHC 1101 it was held that the principle that it was impermissible to rely on hearsay for the purpose of a plea in justification was within the state's margin of appreciation for the purposes of Article 10(2). Eady J also declined to depart from the rules that a defence of justification must focus upon some conduct of the individual claimant and that it cannot involve matters postdating publication.

- **Repetition Rule:** In *Mark v Associated Newspapers* [2002] EMLR 38 the Court of Appeal rejected the argument that the repetition rule was incompatible with the decision of the Court of Human Rights in *Thoma v Luxembourg* (Judgment of 29 March 2001) that journalists cannot be 'systematically and formally' required to 'distance themselves from the content of a defamatory quotation'. Simon Brown LJ held that any supposed tension had been resolved by the decision in *Al Fagih v HH Saudi Research and Marketing* [2002] EMLR 215 which made it clear that the 'repetition rule' does not limit the scope of qualified privilege at common law.

- **Reference:** The test as to whether the words complained of in fact refer to the claimant is objective and, at common law, the liability for 'unintentional defamation' is strict (*Hulton v Jones* [1910] AC 20). However, the application of this principle to 'lookalike' photographs is incompatible with Article 10 and, as a result, the strict liability rule is not applicable to 'lookalikes' (*O'Shea v MGN* [2001] EMLR 943 (Morland J)). This is one of the rare cases in which the common law has been changed to take account of Convention rights.

- **Fair comment:** The common law of fair comment appears to be consistent with Article 10 (see *Branson v Bower* [2001] EMLR 800). Where a defendant makes 'comments', the defence is made out if he can show (1) that he expressed the opinions honestly; and (2) that he did so upon facts accurately stated. It has been said that this is consistent with the Convention jurisprudence (*Branson v Bower (No 2)* [2001] EMLR 809 (Eady J)).

- **Qualified privilege:** It has been said that the principles of qualified privilege in English law are compatible with Article 10 (*Loutchansky v Times Newspapers* [2002] QB 321; and see also *Loutchansky v Times Newspapers (Nos 2–5)* [2002] QB 783 (the House of Lords refused permission to appeal in both cases)). In *Al Fagih v HH Saudi Research and Marketing* [2002] EMLR 215 the Court of Appeal reiterated that the English law relating to qualified privilege, as set out in *Reynolds*, was compatible with Article 10. This includes its application in the context of political speech. In the context of *Reynolds* qualified privilege the 'single meaning' rule does not apply—in each case the question is 'was the article a piece of responsible journalism?'. (See also *Bonnick v Morris* [2002] 3 WLR 820, discussed at Supplement, para 15.370A.)

- **Remedies:** It has been held that the combination of Articles 6 and 10 does not give a claimant a right to seek a 'declaration of falsity' (*Loutchansky v Times Newspapers (No 6)* [2002] EMLR 44). Gray J rejected the argument that there was a right of access to the court to determine the 'reputation' in cases where the defendant had a 'privilege' defence.

A number of areas remain to be considered including the common law rule that a defendant cannot, in mitigation of damage, lead evidence of specific acts of misconduct (the rule in *Scott v Sampson* (1882) 8 QBD 491) or of other defamatory publications to the same effect (*Associated Newspapers v Dingle* [1964] AC 371). The result of this rule is that a defendant cannot, in practice, lead evidence as to the claimant's actual reputation or the reputation he deserves. It is arguable that this rule (which has been mitigated, in part, by the decision in *Burstein v Times Newspapers* [2001] 1 WLR 579) is incompatible with Article 10.

(c) Freedom of information

It has been held, in relation to the BBC's attempt to gain access to encrypted images from the Lockerbie trial, that the right to receive and impart information **15.253** does not extend to receiving television signals which those broadcasting them did not wish to be received (*BBC Petitioners (No 2)* [2000] SLT 860). See also *Roche v United Kingdom* (Decision of 23 May 2002), discussed at Supplement, para 15.149. There is no general right to receive information under Article 10 (*R v Bow County Court, ex p Pelling* [2001] 1 UKHRLR 165, para 36) and the Government is not under a positive obligation to hold inquires in public (*Persey v Secretary of State for Environment, Food and Rural Affairs* [2002] 3 WLR 704 and *Howard v Secretary of State for Health* [2002] 3 WLR 738), but see *R (Wagstaff and Others) v Secretary of State for Health* [2001] 1 WLR 292 and see, generally, Supplement, para 15.136A.

(4) The impact

(a) Commercial law

15.254 It has been held that the Advertising Standards Authority code is sufficient for the requirements that interference be 'prescribed by law' and that in the instant case the interference with Article 10 rights was justified (*R v Advertising Standards Authority Ltd, ex p Matthias Rath BV* [2001] EMLR 582).

In general, the provisions of the Copyright Act 1988 strike a proper balance between the right to free expression and the needs of a democratic society, which included the recognition and protection of private property (*Ashdown v Telegraph Group* [2002] QB 546). However, two types of case in which freedom of expression might lead to a modification of the present approach have been identified:

- information of public interest relating to an event in the past (where the 'fair dealing rule' cannot apply). In such a situation freedom of expression could be accommodated by refusing to grant an injunction (para 46); and
- in cases where there is the clearest public interest in giving effect to the right of freedom of expression a 'public interest defence' should be available (para 58, disapproving the approach of Aldous LJ in *Hyde Park Residence v Yelland* [2001] Ch 143).

It was held in *Psychology Press v Flanagan and Another* [2002] EWHC 1205 that a refusal to allow an author under contract with the claimant to publish a competitor book, while an interference with the right to freedom of expression, was justified as upholding the 'sanctity of contract' (para 41).

(b) Criminal law

15.259 **Obscenity and indecency.** It was held by the Court of Appeal in *R v Perrin* [2002] EWCA Crim 747 that the offence of publishing an obscene article contrary to the Obscene Publications Act 1959 was compatible with Article 10 as such an offence had a legitimate purpose, was prescribed by law and 'Parliament was entitled to conclude that the prescription was necessary in a democratic society' (para 52). The Court did not consider whether this conclusion was correct but found that it was within the 'discretionary area of judgment'.

Official secrets.   It would be a breach of Article 10 for the court to find that there   **15.260**
has been a criminal offence where a newspaper failed to obtain clearance from the Attorney-General before publishing material which might not raise the slightest ground for objection (*Attorney-General v Punch Ltd* [2001] 2 WLR 1713, 1742, para 108).

It has also been held by the Court of Appeal that a newspaper cannot be required to seek confirmation from the Attorney-General that facts which it intends to publish are in the public domain (*Attorney-General v Times Newspapers* [2001] 1 WLR 885).

The suggestion in this paragraph of the Main Work that the Official Secrets Act   **15.261**
1989 was difficult to reconcile with Article 10 was rejected by the House of Lords in *R v Shayler* [2002] 2 WLR 754, *per* Lord Hope at para 42. It was held that sections 1(1) and 4(1), (3) of the 1989 Act were compatible with Article 10 and declined to read a 'public interest' defence into them. Although the prosecution of a former member of the security services for unlawfully disclosing documents was an interference with his right to freedom of expression, the House of Lords found that it was necessary in the pursuit of legitimate ends. The court noted that the ban on disclosure was not absolute and disclosure could be made to particular individuals or, following official authorisation, to the general public. If such authorisation was declined, the decision could be judicially reviewed and would itself have to be compatible with Article 10.

Public order.   In *Percy v DPP* [2002] Crim LR 835 it was held that a conviction   **15.263**
pursuant to section 5 of the Public Order Act 1986 for burning an American flag at an American airbase was contrary to Article 10 (see also Supplement, para 15.121).

n836: *Hashman and Harrup v United Kingdom* is now reported at (2000) 30 EHRR 241.

When a newspaper published racist criticism of a person which would, foresee-   **15.266A**
ably, be likely to stimulate a racist reaction by readers, its potential exposure to a claim under the Protection from Harassment Act 1997 was not a breach of Article 10 (*Thomas v News Group Newspapers* [2002] EMLR 4). See J Coad, 'Harassment by the Media' [2002] Ent LR 18.

(c) Education law

The abolition of corporal punishment in school was held not to infringe the par-   **15.267**
ent's right to freedom of expression, notwithstanding that it was asserted that the

imposition of corporal punishment was a part of the parent's beliefs (*Williamson v Secretary of State for Education* [2002] 1 FLR 493). See, further, Supplement, para 19.87.

(d) Employment and discrimination

15.268   For the relationship between Article 10 and employment law, see, generally, L Vickers, *Freedom of Speech and Employment* (Oxford University Press, 2002).

(e) Family law

15.274   In *Clibbery v Alan* [2001] 2 FCR 577, Mumby J held that when proceedings relating to money or property (as opposed to children) are heard in chambers in the Family Division it is not unlawful or a contempt of court for one of the parties to make public disclosure of what has gone on in chambers. This decision was upheld by the Court of Appeal on the facts at [2002] 2 WLR 1511. However it was said that, although Munby J had taken the correct approach in rejecting the blanket imposition of confidentiality in a case not involving children and instead balancing Article 8 and Article 10 interests, he had expressed his general propositions too widely.

(g) Media law

15.277   **Introduction.**   On the relationship between privacy under Article 8 and free expression as it pertains to the media, see *Douglas v Hello! Ltd* [2001] QB 967; *A v B plc* [2002] 3 WLR 542; and *Campbell v MGN Ltd* [2003] 2 WLR 80. See, further, H Tomlinson (ed), *Privacy and the Media* (Matrix, 2002), ch 1, and M Tugendhat and I Christie (eds), *The Law of Privacy and the Media* (Oxford University Press, 2002); and see also Supplement, paras 12.33 and 12.202).

15.280   In *Ashworth Hospital Authority v MGN* [2002] 1 WLR 2033 the House of Lords emphasised that section 10 of the Contempt of Court Act 1981 and Article 10 of the Convention had a common purpose in seeking to enhance the freedom of the press by protecting journalistic sources and that the approach was the same under both. An order for disclosure must be proportionate and necessary. On the facts, however, it was held that, in relation to the disclosure of confidential medical records about a patient, the public interest was sufficiently strong to justify disclosure of the journalist's source.

15.282   **Reporting restrictions.**   It was held in *Venables and Another v News Group Newspapers Ltd* [2001] Fam 430 that an injunction against the whole world to prevent the identities and future whereabouts of the killers of James Bulger being disclosed was not a breach of Article 10.

15.285A   **Regulation of broadcasting.**   In *R (Prolife Alliance) v BBC* [2002] 3 WLR 1080 the Court of Appeal considered a decision by the BBC not to transmit a party broadcast by a registered political party opposed to abortion on the basis that its graphic content offended taste and decency. The Court of Appeal held that the decision was unlawful as it failed to take into account the fundamental importance of political debate, especially in the context of elections. It held that it would be very rare that freedom of expression in elections could be lawfully interfered with on the grounds of taste and decency alone.

(h) Prison law

A policy which denied a prisoner the right to contact the media by telephone whenever his purpose was to comment on matters of legitimate public interest was a breach of Article 10; see *R (Hirst) v Secretary of State for the Home Department* [2002] 1 WLR 2929. The fact that the prisoner was able to use other means of communication, such as the post, did not prevent the breach. There was found to be no breach of Article 10 when the prison authorities insisted on being allowed to read a draft autobiography of a prisoner intended for publication when the draft was sent to and from prison (*R (Nilsen) v HM Prison Whitemoor* [2002] EWHC Admin 668).

15.286

(i) Immigration law

The Court of Appeal held that where the Home Secretary exercises his power pursuant to the Immigration Act 1971 to refuse entry to, or expel, an alien *solely* to prevent the alien expressing his opinions within the United Kingdom, the power must be exercised compatibly with Article 10 (*R (Farrakhan) v Secretary of State for the Home Department* [2002] 3 WLR 481). In the case itself, it was held that the refusal of entry was lawful as it complied with Article 10(2), being proportionate and in pursuit of a legitimate aim. See also Supplement, para 15.237.

15.287A

Appendix 1: The Canadian Charter of Rights

(1) Introduction

See, generally, M Russell, 'The Impact of the Charter on Privacy and Freedom of Expression in Canada', in M Colvin (ed), *Developing Key Privacy Rights* (Hart Publishing, 2002).

15.290

(2) Justifiable limitations

(c) Types of restrictions on expression

Reporting restrictions. A publication ban should only be ordered when: (a) such an order is necessary in order to prevent a serious risk to the administration of justice, because reasonable alternative measures will not prevent the risks; and

15.301

(b) the salutary effects of the ban outweigh the deleterious effects on the rights and interests of the parties and the public. The burden of displacing the presumption of openness rests on the party seeking the ban. Applying these tests, the Supreme Court overturned a ban on the publication of information about undercover police operations in a specific case but upheld a ban on information tending to identify particular officers involved in the administration for a period of one year. As a matter of general practice, the identity of police officers should not be shrouded in secrecy forever; see *The Vancouver Sun v R* [2001] SCC 77.

15.305A Reporting restrictions were further considered in *R v ONE* [2001] SCC 77 and *R v Mentuck* [2002] 1 LRC 413. In those cases, reporting restrictions had been made concerning: (1) the police *modus operandi*; and (2) the names of particular undercover police officers. The court stated that the test to be applied in deciding whether an order banning publication should be made was as follows:

- such an order is necessary in order to prevent a serious risk to the proper administration of justice, because reasonable alternative measures will not prevent the risk; and
- the salutary effects of the publication ban outweigh the deleterious effects on the rights and interests of the parties and the public, including the effects on the right to free expression, the right of the accused to a fair and public trial, and the efficacy of the administration of justice.

Applying that test, the court held that the one-year reporting restrictions on the names of the undercover officers were justified, but that the restrictions on the *modus operandi* of the police were not justified.

15.307A *R v Sharpe* [2001] 2 LRC 665 concerned a challenge to the criminalisation of 'child pornography'. This was defined to include visual representations that show a person who is, or is depicted as being, under the age of 18 years and is engaged in, or is depicted as being engaged in, explicit sexual activity and visual representations the dominant characteristic of which is the depiction, for a sexual purpose, of a sexual organ or the anal region of a person under the age of 18 years. 'Child pornography' also included visual representations and written material that advocated sexual activity with a person under the age of 18 years that would be an offence under the Code. The Supreme Court upheld that legislation, except for two instances that raised little or no risk of harm to children, namely: (1) written materials or visual representations created and held by the accused alone, exclusively for personal use; and (2) visual recordings created by or depicting the accused that do not depict unlawful sexual activity and are held by the accused exclusively for private use.

15.307B In *Little Sisters Book and Art Emporium v Canada (Minister of Justice)* [2001] 2 LRC 436 the Supreme Court considered a challenge based on freedom of expression brought by gay rights groups following Customs seizures of pornographic materials. The freedom of expression argument was unsuccessful. The court held that the 'national community standard of tolerance test', for determining whether materials were obscene, did not discriminate against the gay and lesbian community. A concern for minority expression was one of the principal factors which had led to the adoption of the national community test in the first place. The Canadian community specifically recognised in the Charter that equality (and with it, the protection of sexual minorities) is one of the fundamental values of Canadian society. The standard of tolerance of this same Canadian community for obscenity could not be reasonably interpreted as seeking to suppress sexual expression in the homosexual community in a discriminatory way. However, the challenge was successful on the basis that the placing of the burden of proof on the defendant to disprove obscenity did not constitute a reasonable limit on the appellant's freedom of expression.

Racial hatred.   'Wilful blindness' meets the strict *mens rea* requirement for the offence of wilfully promoting racial hatred (see *R v Harding* (2001) 49 WCB (2d) 68 (Ont Superior Ct of Justice)).   **15.308**

Commercial expression.   A city by-law which capped the number of new outdoor billboard signs was an interference with freedom of expression but was justifiable under section 1 as its objectives were pressing and substantial (*Urban Outdoor Trans Ad v Scarborough (City)* [2001] CRDJ 322 (Ont CA)). A city bylaw which prohibited advertising signs outside industrial zones was, on the other hand, struck down in *R v Guignard* [2002] SCC 14. The appellant had erected a sign on one of his buildings, expressing his dissatisfaction with the services of an insurance company; the court held that consumers have the freedom to criticise products or services, which may take the form of 'counter-advertising'. In *Vann Niagra v Oakville (Town)* [2002] CRD Lexis 162 (Ont CA) a blanket provision on billboard signs was struck down under section 2.   **15.311**

Picketing.   Secondary picketing is generally lawful unless it involves tortious or criminal conduct (*RWDSU, Local 558 v Pepsi-Cola Canada Beverages (West) Ltd* [2002] SCC 8).   **15.318A**

Other restrictions on expression.   The power to deport for membership of a terrorist organisation did not breach the right to free speech (*Suresh v Canada (Minister for Citizenship and Immigration)* [2002] SCC 1).   **15.321A**

Appendix 2: The New Zealand Bill of Rights Act

(1) Introduction

See, generally, R Tobin, 'Privacy and Freedom of Expression in New Zealand', in M Colvin (ed), *Developing Key Privacy Rights* (Hart Publishing, 2002).   **15.323**

(2) **Justifiable limitations**

(a) *Introduction*

15.328 **n999a:** *Moonen v Film and Literature Board of Review* is now reported at [2000] 2 NZLR 9. Following the decision of the Court of Appeal in *Moonen* the Film and Literature Board of Review reconsidered the classification in the light of the judgments and again held that the material was objectionable. Mr Moonen's appeal against that decision was dismissed by the High Court and the Court of Appeal on the basis that there was no error of law (*Moonen v Film and Literature Board of Review (No 2)* [2002] NZAR 358 and [2002] 2 NZLR 754).

(b) *Restrictions on expression*

15.329 **Prior restraint.** In *Beadle v Allen* [2000] NZFLR 639 a restraining order was made under the Harassment Act in relation to a former patient who sent large numbers of faxes to her former doctor and others containing allegations of improper treatment and sex abuse. It was held that this order was a justifiable limitation on the appellant's freedom of expression.

In *A-G for England and Wales v R* [2002] 2 NZLR 91 the Court of Appeal declined to grant the British Government an injunction prohibiting publication of a book by an SAS soldier but held that there was no defence to a claim for an account of profits. In refusing an injunction, the court relied in part on the soldier's right to freedom of expression.

Where a person was awaiting trial for murder he had standing to apply for an injunction restraining the publication of an article which might prejudice a fair trial. The rights to freedom of expression and fair trial had to be balanced but when an article strongly suggested that the same person had committed both the murder with which the claimant was charged and another murder there was a real and substantial risk it would prejudice the claimant's trial (*Burns v Howling at the Moon Magazines* [2002] 1 NZLR 381). See also Supplement, para 15.338.

n999b: See also *Beckett & Ors v TV3 Network Services* [2000] NZAR 399.

15.333 **Defamation.** The New Zealand Court of Appeal has now reheard *Lange v Atkinson* [2000] 3 NZLR 385. The court maintained the position in its earlier judgment for the following reasons (at 339, paras 38 and 40):

> First, the *Reynolds* decision appears to alter the structure of the law of qualified privilege in a way which adds to the uncertainty and chilling effect almost inevitably present in this area of law. We are not persuaded that in the New Zealand situation matters such as the steps taken to verify the information, the seeking of comment from the person defamed, and the status or source of the information, should fall within the ambit of the enquiry into whether the occasion is privileged. Traditionally such matters are not of concern to that question in the kind of setting

presently under discussion. In particular, source and status may be relevant, but only in the area of reports of meetings and suchlike. For the reasons expressed in our earlier judgment, we do not consider it necessary, nor would it be in accord with principle, to import into this enquiry, for the limited purposes of the specific subject matter now under discussion but not otherwise, a specific requirement of reasonableness . . .

Secondly, there are significant differences between the constitutional and political context in New Zealand and in the United Kingdom in which this body of law operates. They reflect societal differences. Thirdly, the position of the press in the two countries does appear to be significantly distinct. And, fourthly, this is an area of law in which Parliament has essentially left it to the courts to develop the governing principles and apply them to the evolving political social and economic conditions.

Contempt. A decision to prohibit the publication of the name of a prominent businessman and philanthropist found in possession of substantial quantities of cannabis was quashed in *Lewis v Wilson & Horton Ltd* [2001] 2 LRC 205. There was no basis upon which it could be concluded that the risk of damage to the appellant outweighed the interests of freedom of expression.   **15.335**

In *Television New Zealand v R* (2000) 6 HRNZ 192 the Court of Appeal considered an application by TVNZ for access to a videotaped interview of a convicted murderer which it proposed to use in the course of a documentary on child abuse. The court considered that the principle of open justice and freedom of expression had to be balanced against the legitimate privacy interests of the accused. The court refused to interfere with the judge's refusal to grant the application.   **15.338**

In *R v Burns (Travis)* [2002] 1 NZLR 387 the Court of Appeal granted an order suppressing publication of the appellant's name and other details pending the hearing of his appeal against his conviction for murder because of prejudice to a possible retrial. The order had initially been made because the appellant had been a witness in an earlier murder trial. However, the Court of Appeal refused to continue the order after the appeal had been dismissed (*R v Burns (Travis) (No 2)* [2002] 1 NZLR 410). See also Supplement, para 15.329.

Obscenity and pornography. In *Living Word Distributors v Human Rights Action Group* [2001] 2 LRC 233 the Court of Appeal considered an application by a human rights organisation which objected to the importation of religious videos which stigmatised homosexuals. The Court of Appeal quashed the decision of the Film and Literature Board of Review banning the videos. In exercising their censorship role the Board had to take into account the right freely to impart and receive information under section 14.   **15.340**

Police powers. In *Stemson v Police* [2002] NZAR 278 it was held that loud complaints in a benefits offices did not constitute disorderly conduct. Although the appellant's conduct was troubling to the complainant and to members of the public it   **15.342**

was no more than a vehement exercise of his right to freedom of expression under section 14. As a result, the appeal against conviction for disorderly conduct was allowed.

For a discussion of expression and assembly, see R Hart, 'The Mobs Are Out: The Right to Protest on Public Roads' (2001) 9 University of Auckland Law Review 311.

15.342A **Expression and privacy.**   In *P v D* [2001] 2 NZLR 591 the High Court considered that the public disclosure of private facts which were highly offensive and objectionable to a reasonable person was a breach of privacy. These factors balanced the right to freedom of expression in section 14. There was minimal legitimate public interest in disclosure of the fact that a public figure had been treated in a psychiatric hospital and a permanent injunction was granted. In *L v G* [2002] DCR 234 it was held that the publication of sexually explicit photographs of the claimant was an invasion of her privacy, despite the fact that she could not be identified. Damages of NZ$2,500 were awarded for invasion of privacy. See, generally, R Tobin, 'Privacy and Freedom of Expression in New Zealand', in M Colvin (ed), *Developing Key Privacy Rights* (Hart Publishing, 2002).

In *R v Mahanga* [2001] 1 NZLR 641 the Court of Appeal upheld the trial judge's decision to refuse the media access to a videotaped interview which had been played during the course of a trial. The privacy rights of the convicted person outweighed the interests in open justice and freedom of speech. These interests had been fulfilled during the course of the trial by the opportunity to see the interview being played in court.

Appendix 3: Human Rights Cases from Other Jurisdictions

(1) Introduction

15.347 In *City of Erie v Pap's AM tdba 'Kandyland'* (2000) 529 US 49 the Supreme Court held that, although nude dancing attracted First Amendment protection, it could be prohibited on the basis of its undesirable 'secondary effects' (see P Rumney, '*City of Erie at al v Pap's AM tdba "Kandyland"*': Low-Value Speech and the First Amendment' [2001] Public Law 158).

In *Hill v Colorado*, 29 June 2000, the Supreme Court upheld a statute which made it unlawful 'knowingly to approach' a person within 100 feet of a health care facility to pass a 'leaflet or handbill to, display a sign to, or engage in oral protest, education or counselling'. This restriction was 'content neutral' because it regulated the places where speech may occur not speech itself and made no reference to the content of the demonstrator's speech. The restriction was 'narrowly tailored' to the state's interest and left open ample alternative communication channels (applying *Ward v Rock against Racism* (1989) 491 US 781).

In *United States v Playboy*, 22 May 2000, the Supreme Court struck down a statute requiring cable operators primarily dedicated to sexually oriented programming to block transmission or to limit it to hours when children were unlikely to be viewing. It was held that this violated the First Amendment because it did not employ the least restrictive means for dealing with the problem.

In *Bartnicki v Vopper*, 21 May 2001, the Supreme Court considered a publication of illegally recorded telephone conversations. It held that the criminalisation of the publication of illegally obtained information of public concern was contrary to the First Amendment (applying the 'Pentagon Papers' case, *New York Times v United States* (1971) 403 US 713).

The relationship between the 'free speech clause' and the 'establishment clause' was considered in *Good News Club v Milford Central School*, 11 June 2001. The respondent school had denied the petitioners use of its building for religious meetings for children. The Supreme Court held that the club's free speech rights had been violated and there was no realistic danger that the community would think that the school was endorsing religion. The school made its limited public forum available to other organisations.

In *Detroit Free Press v Ashcroft* (3 April 2002) a district court in Michigan granted newspapers a preliminary injunction preventing the disclosure of post-11 September proceedings for the removal of non-US citizens (mainly Muslim men), and requiring the production of transcripts of previous closed proceedings.

See also *Boy Scouts of America v Dale* (2000) 8 BHRC 535, discussed at Supplement, para 16.147.

(1A) Anguilla

Article 11 of the Constitution of Anguilla contains a qualified right of freedom of expression which includes the freedom to receive and impart ideas and information. In *Benjamin v Minister of Information and Broadcasting* [2001] UKPC 8 the Privy Council held that a government decision to suspend a radio programme which had criticised a decision to establish a national lottery was a breach of this provision. Although there is no absolute and generalised right to speak, the suspension of a regular radio programme to stop discussion of a controversial issue was a breach of Article 11. The rights of both the broadcaster and the participatory listeners were infringed (reliance was place on *Fernando v Sri Lanka Broadcasting Corporation* (1996) 1 BHRC 104, as to which, see Supplement, para 15.380). **15.347A**

(2) Antigua and Barbuda

In *Observer Publications v Matthew* [2001] UKPC 11 the appellant's application for a telecommunications licence had not been determined five years after it was **15.350** made. The Privy Council held that there was a plain breach of the appellant's right to freedom of expression and ordered that a radio broadcasting licence be issued. However, a system of business licences which covered those in professional practice did not interfere with rights of freedom of expression (*A-G v Goodwin* [2001] 2 LRC 1, 14 (the licensing system was struck down on other grounds)).

(3A) Dominica

15.355A In *Cable & Wireless (Dominica) v Marpin Telecoms* (2000) 9 BHRC 486 the Privy Council accepted that a telecommunications monopoly could potentially be an unjustifiable breach of freedom of expression. The question for local courts to consider was whether the licence granting a monopoly made provision for protecting the rights and freedoms of others.

(3B) Grenada

15.355B Section 10 of the Constitution protects freedom of expression. In *Commissioner of Police v Worme*, 9 November 2000 (Alleyne J), the High Court declared that the section of the Criminal Code creating the offence of intentional libel was null and void because it could not be justified under section 10. The purported offence created was committed if the matter complained of imputed any kind of misconduct in public office and the Crown were unable to justify an offence of such breadth.

(4) Hong Kong

(a) Introduction

15.358 The decision of the Court of Appeal in *HKSAR v Ng Kung Siu* holding that a law prohibiting flag desecration was contrary to Article 19 was overturned by the Court of Final Appeal at (2000) 8 BHRC 244. It was held that in Hong Kong's new constitutional order there were legitimate societal interests in protecting the national and regional flags which fell within the concept of 'public order'. The prohibition of flag desecration was not a wide restriction on freedom of expression and was a justifiable and constitutional restriction. In *HKSAR v Tsui Ping Wing* (2000–3) HKC 247 it was held that the although the use of abusive language was protected under Article 19, it attracted the lowest degree of protection. A restriction on the use of abusive language by taxi drivers was necessary for the respect of the rights of others, for the protection of public order and for the protection of public morals.

(b) Defamation

15.359 The Court of Final Appeal has rejected the argument that a court ordering a defendant to apologise in a discrimination case would *necessarily* breach the defendant's freedom of expression. Instead, the circumstances of each individual case would need to be considered; see *Ma Bik Yung v Ko Chuen*, [2001] HKCFA 46.

In *Cheng Albert v Tse Wai Chun Paul* (2001) 10 BHRC 525 the Court of Final Appeal held that, in order to rebut the defence of 'fair comment' in defamation proceedings, a claimant had to prove that the defendant did not, in fact, hold the opinion which was expressed. Lord Nicholls NPJ said (at 533D) that

> The purpose for which the defence of fair comment exists is to facilitate freedom of expression by commenting on matters of public interest. This accords with the constitutional guarantee of freedom of expression. And it is in the public interest that everyone should be free to express his own, honestly held, views on such matters . . .

This analysis has been adopted in first instance cases in England (see Supplement, para 15.32).

(6) India

In *Narmada Bachao Andolan v Union of India* (1999) 8 SCC 308 the Supreme Court held that the offence of scandalising the court was compatible with Article 19. It was said that   **15.365**

> Courts are not unduly sensitive to fair comment or even outspoken comments being made regarding their judgments and orders made objectively, fairly and without any malice, but no one can be permitted to distort orders of the court and deliberately give a slant to its proceedings, which have the tendency to scandalise the court or bring it to ridicule, in the large interest of protecting the administration of justice (at 313).

Article 105(2) of the Indian Constitution contains a separate provision guaranteeing freedom of speech and voting in Parliament. In *Rao v State* [1999] 3 LRC 297 the Supreme Court held that this freedom was independent of Article 19, and unrestricted by the exceptions contained therein. The court held that Members of Parliament alleged to have taken bribes in order to vote in a particular manner were immune from prosecution.   **15.365A**

(7) Ireland

A priest failed in his attempt to prosecute for blasphemous libel, following the publication of a newspaper cartoon (*Corway v Independent Newspapers* [2000] 1 ILRM 426, Irish Supreme Court). The court stated that it was difficult to see how the common law crime of blasphemy, which related to established religion, could exist in the current constitutional framework. The court declined to follow *Whitehouse v Lemon* [1979] AC 617 and noted that it was difficult to reconcile the view that blasphemy could be carried out without any intent with the freedom of expression and the freedom of religion. It was the role of the legislature to define   **15.369A** the crime of blasphemy. In the absence of such legislation, and the present uncertain state of the law, the court would not authorise institution of a criminal prosecution for blasphemy. In any event, the court was of the view that in the instant case, no insult to the blessed sacrament was intended, and no jury could reasonably conclude such insult existed, or was intended to exist.

(7A) Jamaica

15.370A Section 22 of the constitution of Jamaica provides that

> (1) Except with his own consent, no person shall be hindered in the enjoyment of his freedom of expression, and for the purposes of this section the said freedom includes the freedom to hold opinions and to receive and impart ideas and information without interference, and freedom from interference with his correspondence and other means of communication.
> (2) Nothing contained in or done under the authority of any law shall be held to be inconsistent with or in contravention of this section to the extent that the law in question makes provision—
>> (a) which is reasonably required—
>>> (i) in the interests of defence, public safety, public order, public morality or public health; or
>>> (ii) for the purpose of protecting the reputations, rights and freedoms of other persons, or the private lives of persons concerned in legal proceedings, preventing the disclosure of information received in confidence, maintaining the authority and independence of the courts, or regulating telephony, telegraphy, posts, wireless broadcasting, television or other means of communication, public exhibitions or public entertainments; or
>> (b) which imposes restrictions upon public officers, police officers or upon members of a defence force.

This provision was considered by the Privy Council in *Bonnick v Morris* [2002] 3 WLR 820 where it was held that the law relating to qualified privilege as declared in *Reynolds v Times Newspapers* [2001] 2 AC 127 was consistent with it. As a result, a journalist who published a false defamatory imputation but who was acting reasonably had a complete defence.

(9) South Africa

(b) Defamation

15.373 In *Khumalo v Holomisa* (2002) 12 BHRC 538 the Constitutional Court considered whether the constitution required a development in the common law of defamation. The court held that despite the fundamental importance of freedom of expression to a democratic society it was not a paramount value and had to be construed in the context of other constitutional values, in particular, human dignity, freedom and equality. The law of defamation sought to strike a balance between the value of human dignity and the protection of freedom of expression. The difficulty of proving the truth of defamatory statements and leaving the proof of falsity to the defendant does cause a 'chilling effect' on the publication of information. However, this chilling effect is reduced considerably by the defence of 'reasonable publication' (established in *National Media Ltd v Bogoshi* [1999] 3 LRC 617). The court concluded:

> to hold . . . that the plaintiffs may never succeed unless they can establish that a defamatory statement was false would clearly put plaintiffs at risk. It would desta-bilise the careful balance struck between plaintiff's and defendant's interests achieved by the . . . defence of reasonable publication (para 44).

As a result, the applicants had not demonstrated that the common law was incon-sistent with the provisions of the constitution.

(f) Contempt of court

In *State v Mamabolo* (2001) 10 BHRC 493 the Constitutional Court held that the form of contempt known as 'scandalising the court' was compatible with the con-stitutional guarantee of freedom of expression although the scope for a conviction was very narrow indeed. It must be shown that the offending conduct, viewed contextually, really was likely to damage the administration of justice. It was, how-ever, held that the summary procedure for dealing with allegations of scandalising the court was in breach of the constitutional right to a fair trial.   **15.376A**

(g) Censorship of hate speech

The decision of the Constitutional Court in *Islamic Unity Convention v Independent Broadcasting Authority* 2002 (5) BCLR 433 (CC) concerned a com-plaint by the South African Jewish Board of Deputies that a radio interview broad-cast by the Islamic Unity Convention was likely to breach a provision in the Code of Conduct of the Independent Broadcasting Authority. That provision prohibited broadcasting likely to prejudice relations between sections of the population. The court held that the code's provision was too intrusive and made serious inroads into the right of freedom of expression, and declared the provision unconstitutional and invalid. The declaration of invalidity was made subject to the proviso that no pro-tection is given to the broadcasting of material that amounts to propaganda for war, the incitement of imminent violence or the advocacy of hatred that is based on race, ethnicity, gender or religion, and that constitutes incitement to cause harm.   **15.376B**

(10) Sri Lanka

(d) Media regulation

In *Fernando v Sri Lanka Broadcasting Corporation* (1996) 1 BHRC 104 the pe-titioner claimed that the bringing to an end of a series of educational radio   **15.380** programmes allowing listener participation and dealing with current affairs, human rights and ethnic issues, was an infringement of his right to expression under Article 14(1)(a) of the constitution. The right to freedom of expression included the right to obtain and record information necessary for the purposes of expression although, in the absence of express constitutional provision, it did not include the right to information *simpliciter*. However, the freedom of expression of the petitioner, as participatory listener, had been infringed because the stoppage of the programmes prevented further participation by him.

(e) Other cases

15.381 In *Jayantha Adikari Egodawele v Commissioner of Elections* [2002] 3 LRC 1 the Supreme Court held that the right to take part in public affairs and to vote at elections guaranteed by section 25 of the International Covenant on Civil and Political Rights 1966 were an essential part of the freedom of expression recognised by Article 14 of the constitution. See also *Karunatilleke v Dissanayake* [1999] 1 Sri LR 157.

(11) Zimbabwe

(e) Other cases

15.386 In *Chavundka v Minister of Home Affairs* (2000) 8 BHRC 390 the Supreme Court declared unconstitutional the offence of publishing a false statement likely to cause fear, alarm or despondency among the public, or a section of the public. The court noted that there should be particular vigilance about vagueness when freedom of expression was in issue. The offence in this case contained no requirement that the public be harmed, the offence was speculative and overbroad. However, in *Re Chinamasa* (2000) 9 BHRC 519 the court upheld the charge and procedure of contempt committed by scandalising the court. Given that the aim of the contempt proceedings were to protect the administration of justice, the court ruled that the proceedings were a justifiable interference with freedom of expression.

16

FREEDOM OF ASSEMBLY AND ASSOCIATION

B. The Rights in English Law

(2) Restrictions on assembly

(c) Criminal offences

n54: The threat of violence under section 3 of the Public Order Act 1986 (affray) **16.16**
has to be towards a person or persons present at the scene. This means that the possession of petrol bombs for later use was insufficient (*I v DPP* [2001] 2 WLR 765).

(d) Regulatory powers

Protection from harassment. In *Silverton and Others v Gravett and Others*, 19 **16.35**
October 2001 (H H J Bentley QC) it was held that the prohibitions on harassment imposed by the Protection from Harassment Act 1997 did not breach the
rights of freedom of association under Article 11.

(4) Trade unions and the right to strike

(a) Introduction

16.41 **n156:** See now *Wilson v United Kingdom* (2002) 35 EHRR 523.

(b) The 'right to strike'

16.43 A dispute over the proposed privatisation of a local authority housing and advice service is a 'trade dispute' within the meaning of sections 219 and 244 of the Trade Union and Labour Relations (Consolidation) Act 1992 (*Unison v Westminster City Council* [2001] ICR 1046). However, a dispute over the terms on which an employer proposed to transfer its business to an unidentified third party was not (*University College London Hospitals NHS Trust v Unison* [1999] ICR 204). As a result, an injunction was granted to prevent strike action. The trade union subsequently made an unsuccessful application to the Court of Human Rights; see Supplement, para 16.80.

(c) The regulation of trade unions

16.46 In *Midland Mainline Ltd v National Union of Rail, Maritime & Transport Workers* [2001] IRLR 813 the Court of Appeal gave guidance on the construction of a trade union's obligations in relation to pre-strike ballots under the Trade Union and Labour Relations (Consolidation) Act 1992.

(d) The rights to recognition and consultation

16.49 **n182:** See *GMB v Man Truck & Bus UK Ltd* [2000] IRLR 636 (EAT) in which it was held that sections 188 and 195 of the 1992 Act should be interpreted so as to impose a duty of consultation even where the employer dismisses only in order to impose new terms and conditions and offers immediate re-engagement on those new terms.

(5) Other restrictions on freedom of association

(b) National security

16.52 The Prevention of Terrorism (Temporary Provisions) Act 1989 and the Northern Ireland (Emergency Provisions) Act 1996 have ceased to have effect by virtue of section 2 of the Terrorism Act 2000. The Terrorism Act 2000 lists proscribed organisations at Schedule 2. These provisions came into force on 19 February 2001 by virtue of the Terrorism Act 2000 (Commencement No 3) Order 2001, SI 2001/421. The list of proscribed organisations in Schedule 2 to the Terrorism Act contains 14 organisations and another 21 organisations were added to it by the Terrorism Act (Proscribed Organisations) (Amendment) Order 2001, SI 2001/1261.

Sections 4 to 6 of the Terrorism Act 2000 set out the statutory appeal which is available to an organisation included in Schedule 2. These provisions were considered in *R (Kurdistan Workers Party and Others) v Secretary of State for the Home Department* [2002] EWHC Admin 644 in which Richards J refused the claimants permission to bring judicial review proceedings against the Secretary of State to challenge the lawfulness of the claimants' proscription under Schedule 2 to the 2000 Act. It was held that the claimants should avail themselves of the statutory appeal scheme before bringing judicial review proceedings. The claimants' statutory appeals are due to be heard shortly.

C. The Law Under the European Convention

(2) Assembly

(b) Limitations on assembly

In *Stankov v Bulgaria* (Judgment of 2 October 2001) a number of meetings of an or- **16.62**
ganisation which aimed to unite Macdeonians on a regional and cultural basis had been prohibited on the grounds of an alleged threat to public order and because the association imperilled Bulgaria's territorial integrity. The Court held that the probability that separatist declarations would be made at the meetings could not justify a ban on them. It stressed the fact that freedom of assembly and the right to express one's views through it are among the paramount values in a democratic society:

> Sweeping measures of a preventive nature to suppress freedom of assembly and expression other than in cases of incitement to violence or rejection of democratic principles—however shocking and unacceptable certain views and words used may appear to the authorities, and however illegitimate the demands made may be—do a disservice to democracy and often even endanger it (para 97).

On the evidence there was no indication that the association's meetings were likely to become a platform for the propagation of violence and, as a result, it was held that authorities overstepped their margin of appreciation and that measures banning meetings were not necessary in a democratic society.

Steps taken by the police to evacuate a church occupied by 200 illegal immigrants did not constitute a violation of the right to freedom of assembly (*Cisse v France*, Judgment of 9 April 2002). Although the parish priest had not asked the police to intervene and the means deployed in their intervention had been abrupt and indiscriminate, the fear of the authorities that the situation might deteriorate rapidly and could not continue much longer was not unreasonable. In any event, the immigrants' presence with its symbolic and testimonial value had been tolerated sufficiently long for the interference not to appear unreasonable in the instant case after such a lengthy period.

(3) Association

(b) The meaning of 'association'

16.67 **n244:** See also *OVR v Russia* (Decision of 3 April 2000) in which it was held that a notary association was not an association within the meaning of Article 11 and *Koll v Austria* (Decision of 4 July 2002) in which it was held that a tourism federation was an institution of public law and so could not be considered an association within the meaning of Article 11.

(e) Right to form and join trade unions

16.76 In *Schettini v Italy* (Decision of 9 November 2000) the Court emphasised that

> if members of a trade union have a right, in order to protect their interests, that the trade union should be heard, Article 11 leaves each State a free choice of the means to be used towards this end. While the concluding of collective agreements is one of these means, there are others. What the Convention requires is that under national law trade unions should be enabled, in conditions not at variance with Article 11, to strive for the protection of their members' interests.

A difference in treatment between different unions can be justified by the legitimate aim of securing the viability and effectiveness of the bargaining and a difference based on the degree of representation is 'reasonable and objective'.

In *Sanchez Navajas v Spain* (Decision of 21 June 2001) the applicant was a trade union official who had been refused a credit of 15 hours for the study of new legislation on union elections. The Court held that a requirement that workers' representatives should, in principle, be entitled to appropriate facilities in order to enable them to carry out their trade union functions quickly and effectively could be derived from Article 11, read in the light of Article 28 of the European Social Charter (see Main Work, Vol 2, p 117). However, on the facts the applicant had not demonstrated that the study of the new legislation was strictly necessary for the exercise of his trade union functions and, as a result, there was no interference with his Article 11 rights.

(f) Interference with freedom of association

16.78 A prohibition of a strike is a restriction on a union's power to protect the occupational interests of its members and is, therefore, an interference with Article 11 rights (*Unison v United Kingdom* [2002] IRLR 497). The interference was, however, justified and the Court ruled the complaint inadmissible; see Supplement, para 16.80.

(g) Restrictions on freedom of association

16.80 In *Refah Partisi v Turkey* (2002) 35 EHRR 56 the Court held (by a majority of four to three) that a ban on the Refah Partisi (the 'Welfare Party') in Turkey was not a breach of Article 11. The Turkish Constitutional Court had made an order dissolving the party on the ground that it had become 'a centre of activities against the principle of secularism'. The Court held that when campaigning for changes in legislation or to the legal or constitutional structures of the state, political parties continued to enjoy the protection of Article 11 provided they complied with two conditions:

- the means used to those ends had to be lawful and democratic; and
- the proposed changes had to be compatible with fundamental democratic principles.

It was held that the sanctions imposed on the applicants could reasonably be considered to meet a pressing social need for the protection of democratic society, since, on the pretext of giving a different meaning to the principle of secularism, the leaders of the Refah Partisi had declared their intention to institute Islamic law (the *Sharia*), a system of law that was in marked contrast to the values embodied in the Convention. They had also left no doubt about their position regarding recourse to force in order to come to power and, more particularly, to retain power.

The dissenting minority (Judges Fuhrmann, Loucaides and Bratza) pointed out that the Refah Partisi was the fifteenth political party dissolved by the Constitutional Court and the fourth case to come before the Court of Human Rights. They suggested four principles could be derived from the case law:

1. That although Article 11 has an autonomous role it must also be considered in the light of Article 10: the protection of opinions and the freedom to express them was one of the objectives of the freedom of association. Freedom of expression protected opinions which were offensive, shocking or disturbing.
2. The state has an obligation to organise free elections by secret ballot at reasonable intervals under Article 3 of the First Protocol in order to ensure the free expression of the opinion of the people on the choice of the legislature. This requires the free competition of a plurality of political parties representing all shades of opinion.
3. In relation to political parties, the exceptions to Article 11 had to be construed strictly, and only convincing and compelling reasons could justify restrictions on their freedom of association.
4. One of the characteristic principles of democracy is the possibility which it offers to resolve a country's problems by dialogue and without recourse to violence. The fact that a political programme was incompatible with the present principles and structures of the state does not mean that it is contrary to the democratic rules.

Applying these principles, the minority took the view that the dissolution of the Refah Partisi was disproportionate to the legitimate aim pursued. There was no convincing evidence that it was intending to put into effect a political programme which was incompatible with Convention norms or which would destroy secular society. The reasoning of the minority is convincing.

The case can be contrasted with the more recent decision of the Court in *Yazar and Others v Turkey* (36 EHRR 6 2002) which concerned the decision of the Turkish Constitutional Court to ban the People's Labour Party ('the HEP'). The Court held that, since the HEP had not advocated any policy which could have undermined the country's democratic regime and had not urged or sought to justify recourse to force, its dissolution could not be considered to reflect a pressing social need.

16.81   The applicant in *Grande Oriente d'Italia de Palazzo Giustiniani v Italy* (2002) 34 EHRR 629 was an Italian association grouping several Masonic lodges which has been in existence since 1805 and is affiliated to the Universal Freemasons. It complained that a law which obliged candidates for public office to declare that they are not members of the Freemasons was a violation of Article 11. The Court held that this measure was not 'necessary in a democratic society': the search for a fair balance must not lead to a position in which individuals were discouraged from exercising their right of association for fear of prejudicing their applications for public office.

In *NF v Italy* (2002) 35 EHRR 106 the applicant was an Italian magistrate who had been disciplined for his Masonic links. The Court found that the law under which he had been disciplined was not sufficiently clear to allow even a person as well informed of the law as the applicant to realise that a magistrate joining an official Masonic lodge could face disciplinary action. As a result, the interference was not 'prescribed by law' under Article 11(2). See also *Maestri v Italy* (Decision of 4 July 2002).

The prohibition of a strike designed to persuade an employer to impose conditions on the transferee of its business pursued the legitimate aim of protecting the rights of the employer (although the employer was an NHS Trust and was, therefore, a public authority). In all the circumstances, the prohibition on the ability to strike was a proportionate measure which was 'necessary in a democratic society' to protect the rights of the NHS Trust and the complaint was held to be inadmissible (*Unison v United Kingdom* [2002] IRLR 497).

In *Gorzelik v Poland* (Judgment 20 December 2001) it was held that a refusal to register an association claiming to represent a national minority was necessary and proportionate. The Court took into account the fact that the applicant could have obtained registration by slightly changing the name of their association and by amending a single provision of the memorandum of association. The Court pointed out that pluralism and democracy are, by the nature of things, based on a compromise that requires various concessions by individuals and groups of individuals. The latter must sometimes be prepared to limit some of their freedoms so as to ensure the greater stability of the country as a whole (para 66).

(i) Positive protection of freedom of association

In *Wilson v United Kingdom* (2002) 35 EHRR 523 the applicants complained **16.83** about the 'de-recognition' of unions for collective bargaining purposes and the offers of more favourable conditions of employment to employees agreeing not to be represented by unions. The Court rejected the argument that Article 11 entailed compulsory collective bargaining—the freedom of a union to make its voice heard did not extend to the imposition on an employer of an obligation to recognise a trade union (para 44). However, United Kingdom law permitted employers to offer inducements to employees who relinquished the right to union representation. As a result, it was possible for an employer to undermine or frustrate a union's ability to strive for the protection of the interests of its members. The United Kingdom had, therefore, failed in its positive obligation to secure enjoyment of Article 11 rights. The Court has, in general, taken a cautious approach towards the 'trade union' provisions of Article 11 and *Wilson* is one of the very few Article 11 cases where a complaint by a trade union has succeeded.

D. The Impact of the Human Rights Act

(2) United Kingdom cases

(b) Assembly

In *Gypsy Council v United Kingdom* (Decision of 14 May 2002) it was held that the **16.88** prohibition of the Horsmonden Horse Fair was necessary in a democratic society. Where large gatherings are concerned the impact on the community as a whole could legitimately be taken into consideration. The fair had been growing in size through the years and in 2000 the police had identified concerns about the disruption to the local community caused by the 'sheer volume' of visitors, indiscriminate parking, littering, a background level of increased crime and road closures. The authorities made available a site some 20 miles from Horsmonden where large numbers of persons could assemble without causing disruption and the police permitted a limited procession to take place in Horsmonden.

(c) Association

The United Kingdom was found to be in breach of Article 11 in *Wilson v United* **16.89** *Kingdom* (2002) 35 EHRR 523.

(3) Impact of Article 11 on the law relating to assembly

(a) Introduction

16.93   See, generally, H Fenwick and G Phillipson, 'Public Protest, the Human Rights Act and Judicial Responses to Political Expression' [2000] PL 627.

n319: See also *Director of Public Prosecutions v Jones* [2002] EWHC Admin 110 in which the court held that even where the conditions imposed on a public assembly were *ultra vires* the police powers under section 14 of the Public Order Act 1986, this did not make the notice invalid. The unlawful conditions could simply be severed from the notice.

n332: See also *McBride v UK* (Decision of 5 July 2001) which followed and approved the reasoning in *Steel*.

(4) Impact of Article 11 on the law relating to association

(b) Trade unions

16.109   In *National Union of Rail, Maritime and Transport Workers v London Underground Ltd* [2001] IRLR 228 the Court of Appeal pointed out that Article 11 still leaves each state with the freedom to determine the means by which members' interests are protected but that these may be subject to regulation at national level. Robert Walker LJ refused to accept that notice requirements under the Trade Union and Labour Relations (Consolidation) Act 1992 (as amended) breached Article 11 as they could not be said to be oppressive or disproportionate.

(c) Other forms of association

16.110   In *R (L) v Governors of J School* [2001] ELR 411 it was held that the exclusion of a pupil from school was not a violation of his rights of association under Article 11 which did not include a right merely to share the company of others. In any event, any infringement was proportionate and necessary to safeguard the rights of the other pupils.

Appendix 1:   The Canadian Charter of Rights

(3) Association

(a) Definition and scope

16.126A   The exclusion of agricultural workers from statutory trade union and collective bargaining rights was declared unconstitutional in *Dunmore v Ontario (Attorney General)* 2001 SCC 94.

(b) Negative freedom

Legislation which required construction workers to be members of certain unions   **16.131A**
was upheld in *R v Advance Cutting & Coring Ltd* 2001 SCC 70.

Appendix 3: Human Rights Cases from Other Jurisdictions

(1) Introduction

In *Boy Scouts of America v Dale* (2000) 8 BHRC 535 the Supreme Court held that   **16.147**
requiring the Boy Scouts to accept a gay rights activist as an adult member violated
their First Amendment rights of expressive association. If an association engaged
in expressive activity, the First Amendment was implicated, and forced inclusion
of an unwanted person in the group infringed its freedom of expressive association.

The Supreme Court also struck down an interference with freedom of association
in *California Democratic Party v Jones*, 26 June 2000. California had imposed a
'blanket primary' system, allowing all voters to choose among all candidates in
primaries. It was held that this violated the political party's rights to free association. There were no compelling state interests justifying the intrusion.

(6A) Solomon Islands

In *Folotalu v Attorney-General* [2002] 3 LRC 699 the High Court held that the re-   **16.158A**
quirement of the payment of a deposit of SB$5,000 for candidates at parliamen-
tary elections was inconsistent with the constitutional right of freedom of
association.

(11) Zimbabwe

The forced attendance of farmers and farm workers at local ZANU (PF) branch   **16.165**
meetings was a breach of their rights of freedom of association guaranteed by section 21 of the Constitution (*Commercial Farmers Union v Minister of Lands,
Agriculture and Resettlement* [2001] 2 LRC 521, 533).

17

FREEDOM FROM DISCRIMINATION IN RELATION TO CONVENTION RIGHTS

B. The Right in English Law

(2) Sex discrimination

(a) The meaning of discrimination

Direct discrimination. In *Khan v Chief Constable of Yorkshire* [2001] ICR 1065   **17.13**
the House of Lords overturned the decision of the Court of Appeal. Where victimisation is concerned, the question is: was the treatment afforded to the victim 'by reason that' the complaint had been brought? The reason for not providing a reference was the legal advice given which said that it would not be appropriate where the Chief Constable was in litigation with the complainant. The House of Lords accepted that where the reason for the refusal was the need on the part of the Chief Constable to preserve his position pending the outcome of the litigation,

his refusal to provide the claimant with a reference did not amount to victimisation under the Race Relations Act.

The words 'treats or would treat' in the discrimination legislation mean that an applicant can succeed where he or she can only point to a hypothetical comparator. This is a matter of law rather than discretion on the part of the tribunal (see *Chief Constable of West Yorkshire Police v Vento* [2002] IRLR 177 (EAT), approved by the Court of Appeal in *Balamoody v UK Central Council for Nursing, Midwifery and Health Visiting* [2002] IRLR 288).

17.14 **n48:** For further discussion of the appropriate comparator in the light of *MacDonald v Ministry of Defence* [2001] IRLR 431 and *Pearce v Governing Body of Mayfield School* [2001] ICR 198, see Supplement, para 17.148.

17.17A **Burden of proof.** The Sex Discrimination (Indirect Discrimination and Burden of Proof) Regulations 2001, SI 2001/2660, implemented the Burden of Proof Directive (97/80/EC) by inserting section 63A into the Sex Discrimination Act 1975 which provides that, where a complainant proves facts from which an employment tribunal could conclude, in the absence of an adequate explanation from the respondent, that an act of unlawful discrimination has been committed, the tribunal must uphold the complaint unless the respondent proves it did not or should not be treated as having committed that act. Section 66A of the Sex Discrimination Act, as amended, makes similar provision for county court cases, but only in relation to employment-related discrimination (broadly defined). These provisions, which came into effect on 12 October 2001, are regarded by some as a reversal of the burden of proof. Given, however, that an inference of discrimination could previously be drawn where a claimant established less favourable treatment and a difference of sex, in the absence of an explanation from the employer (*King v Great Britain China Centre* [1992] ICR 516), the only real difference the provision has made in practice is that tribunals may be a little more ready to draw such an inference.

17.18 **Indirect discrimination.** The definition of indirect discrimination in the Sex Discrimination Act 1975 was amended by the Sex Discrimination (Indirect Discrimination and Burden of Proof) Regulations 2001, SI 2001/2660, insofar as it applies to the employment context (broadly defined). Section 1(2) of the Act now provides that indirect discrimination will be taken to occur where an employer applies to a woman a 'provision, criterion or practice' which he or she applies or would apply equally to a man but which: (a) is such that it would be to the detriment of a considerably larger proportion of women than of men; (b) which he or she cannot show to be justifiable irrespective of the sex of the person to whom it is applied; and (c) which is to her detriment.

In *Harvest Town Circle Ltd v Rutherford* [2001] IRLR 599 the EAT accepted that section 109 of the Employment Rights Act 1996 which prevents an employee from claiming unfair dismissal once he or she has reached the normal retiring age for his or her job, or, where there is no such age, 65, might discriminate indirectly on grounds of sex against men. It remitted the matter to the employment tribunal to consider whether such discrimination had been established.

See also the Court of Appeal's decision in *Coker and Osamor v Lord Chancellor and the Lord Chancellor's Department* [2002] IRLR 80. The case concerned the decision of the Lord Chancellor to appoint a friend, Garry Hart, to be his special adviser rather than opening up the recruitment process to applications. The claimants argued that this was indirectly discriminatory on grounds of both sex and race, because the proportion of women and black persons in the Lord Chancellor's 'circle of friends and acquaintances' was considerably smaller than that of men and whites. They argued that the Lord Chancellor had applied to them a condition that he should be personally acquainted with the person appointed to the position of his special adviser. The Court of Appeal held that the proportions of women and non-white persons who were otherwise qualified for the position of special adviser to the Lord Chancellor and who were personally known to him were not 'considerably smaller' than the proportions of men and white persons who were so qualified and were personally known to him. The requirement imposed by the Lord Chancellor that he know the person chosen personally would, the Court said, exclude the vast majority within the extended pool, whatever their sex or ethnic origin. This being the case the Court did not accept that the proportions of otherwise qualified women and black persons who knew the Lord Chancellor were 'considerably smaller' than the proportions of men and white persons who did.

Pregnancy. The European Court of Justice has made clear that an employee recruited to undertake a fixed-term six-month contract was unlawfully discriminated against when she was dismissed because her pregnancy prevented her from working for a substantial part of that period (*Tele Danmark A/S v Handels -og Kontorfunktionaerernes Forbund i Danmark (HK)* [2001] ECR I-06993). The contract began on 1 July and the baby was due in early November, the employers dismissing the employee with effect from 30 September. The employer attempted to argue before the Court that the real reason for the dismissal was not the employee's pregnancy but her inability to complete the contract and the fact that she had failed to advise them, on recruitment, of her pregnant state. The Court rejected this argument and ruled that the financial loss to the employer due to the inability to complete the fixed-term contract was irrelevant. Whether the contract was fixed or for an indefinite period was also irrelevant, as was the size of the employer's undertaking. The impact of this decision on small employers is likely to be substantial. **17.19**

The European Court of Justice also held in *Jiminez Melgar v Ayuntamiento de Los Barrios* [2001] ECR I-06915 that Article 10 of the Pregnant Workers' Directive

(92/85/EEC) applies to women who take maternity leave or become pregnant during a fixed-term contract. Non-renewal of a fixed-term contract was held not to be a dismissal as far as Article 10 is concerned but it would, if connected to the pregnancy or maternity leave, amount to sex discrimination.

17.20   **Sexual orientation discrimination.**   n71: The question of whether sexual orientation discrimination is within the scope of the Sex Discrimination Act was further considered in *MacDonald v Ministry of Defence* [2001] IRLR 431 and *Pearce v Governing Body of Mayfield School* [2002] ICR 198. In *Pearce* Hale LJ expressed the view (*obiter*) that the Act, read subject to section 3 of the Human Rights Act so as to make it compatible with Articles 8 and 14 of the European Convention on Human Rights, regulated sexual orientation discrimination. The cases are discussed further at Supplement, para 17.148.

(b) Acts of discrimination

17.24   **Discrimination in employment.**   n95: In *D'Souza v London Borough of Lambeth* [2001] EWCA Civ 794 the Court of Appeal confirmed that the Race Relations Act 1976 did not apply to post-termination discrimination by an employer. The Court rejected the argument that the claimant's inability to pursue a race discrimination claim post-termination breached Article 6 of the Convention. In *Rhys-Harper v Relaxion Group plc* [2001] IRLR 460 the Court of Appeal adopted the same approach to post-employment discrimination under the Sex Discrimination Act 1975, reading the decision of the EAT in *Coote v Granada* [1999] ICR 100 narrowly to apply only to those cases in which victimisation was at issue. The employees' appeals in these cases are awaiting hearing by the House of Lords.

17.34   **General exclusions.**   See Supplement, para 17.66, and the impact of the decision in *Liversidge v Chief Constable of Bedfordshire Police* [2002] IRLR 651.

(3) Equal pay

(b) The right to equal pay

17.42   When considering an equal pay claim the following principles should be applied:

- the fact that the applicant and the comparator have the same job title or are in the same job category is not conclusive in relation to the question of whether it is like work or work of equal value;
- each aspect of the remuneration package should be considered when determining equality or otherwise of pay;
- once the applicant shows there is like work etc and that there is a difference in pay it is for the employer to prove there is no breach of the principle of equal pay; and

- factors which did not apply at the time that the pay differential arose cannot later be used to explain or justify any difference (indeed the case raises the spectre of justification in equal pay cases).

See, further, *Brunnhofer v Bank Der Osterreichischen Postparkasse AG* [2001] ECR I-04961.

(c) Remedies

n202: The House of Lords in *Preston & Others v Wolverhampton Healthcare NHS Trust* [2001] ICR 217 ruled that the six-month limitation period is not in breach of European Community law. **17.47**

(4) European Community Law

(c) Sex discrimination

For a discussion of the implications of the EC Burden of Proof Directive and section 63A of the Sex Discrimination Act 1975, see Supplement, para 17.17A. **17.52**

(5) Racial discrimination

(c) Acts of discrimination

The EC Race Directive (2000/43/EC) has similar provisions to what is now section 63A of the Sex Discrimination Act 1975, which, in effect, places the burden of proof on the employer to disprove race discrimination once the employee presents a *prima facie* case. The Race Directive must be in force by 19 July 2003. It appears from the draft regulations published in October 2002 that the changes required by the Directive will be implemented only in relation to discrimination on grounds of race and ethnic or national origin and not on the grounds of colour and nationality which are also regulated by the Race Relations Act 1976. **17.58**

Discrimination in employment. See the developments discussed at Supplement, para 17.24. **17.59**

General exclusions. The Court of Appeal at [2002] IRLR 651 confirmed the EAT's decision in *Liversidge v Chief Constable of Bedfordshire Police* [2002] IRLR 15 that, on the proper construction of section 16 of the Race Relations Act 1976, a chief constable (or the Commissioner of Police of the Metropolis) cannot be vicariously or constructively liable for the actions of his officers. This decision only applies in relation to acts of discrimination alleged to have occurred prior to the coming into force of the Race Relations (Amendment) Act 2000 on 2 April 2001. **17.66**

A number of cases are pending in the EAT to decide the impact, if any, of the *Liversidge* decision in relation to the equivalent section 17 of the Sex Discrimination Act 1975 which survives the Race Relations (Amendment) Act

2000. Some commentators believe that amendment of section 17 was deemed to be unnecessary given that the provision would be interpreted, in accordance with the Equal Treatment Directive (76/207/EEC), so as to make chief constables vicariously liable for discrimination by their officers.

In *Chief Constable of Cumbria v McGlennon* [2002] ICR 1156 the EAT distinguished *Liversidge* and ruled that chief constables would be liable for discrimination by their officers in cases such as where the officers were acting on behalf of the chief constable in accordance with his power to delegate certain acts under the Police Act 1996. Acts done under this Act include decisions in relation to the promotion and posting of officers.

(6) Disability discrimination

(a) Introduction

17.69 Where the applicant or employee complains of symptoms for which there is no physical cause, and the medical opinion is that the symptoms are caused by the person's mental state, the person will not be regarded as suffering from a disability (*Rugamer v Sony Music Entertainment UK Ltd; McNicol v Balfour Beatty Rail Maintenance Ltd* [2001] IRLR 644, EAT) unless the mental state amounts to a clinically well-recognised mental illness.

In a claim under the Disability Discrimination Act 1995 the crucial question is whether the claimant was disabled within the meaning of the Act at the time of the alleged act of discrimination (*Cruickshank v VAW Motorcast* [2002] IRLR 24, EAT).

The EAT held in *EKPE v Metropolitan Police Commissioner* [2001] IRLR 605 that the question whether an impairment had a 'substantial' effect on an applicant's 'normal day to day' activities depends on looking at the evidence as a whole; and should not be addressed by reaching a specific conclusion on each of the specific aspects which are claimed to be examples of the impairment. A tribunal should focus on whether any of the activities listed in paragraphs 4(a) to (h) of Schedule 1 to the Disability Discrimination Act 1995 have been affected. As a matter of principle, evidence of the applicant's duties at work and the way they are performed, particularly if they include 'normal day to day' activities, is relevant to the assessment the tribunal must make; see *Law Hospital NHS Trust v Rush* [2001] IRLR 611.

(b) The meaning of discrimination

17.71 Justification was considered in *Jones v The Post Office* [2001] IRLR 384 in which the employer removed a disabled employee from driving duties and later allowed him to return only to limited driving duties on the grounds that his disability (insulin-dependent diabetes) posed a risk to health and safety. The employers claimed that their actions were justified because they believed that the claimant's disability might cause him to lose control of the vehicle. The claimant argued that, where the employers sought to rely on their belief as a justification for discrimination, the tribunal was obliged to determine whether that belief was correct, whether in this case his disability in fact caused a real safety risk. The Court of Appeal disagreed and ruled that the tribunal should not have dismissed the employer's justification simply because a more thorough medical or health and safety analysis at the time might have revealed a different story about the impact of the diabetes. The reason given by the employer to justify disability discrimination must be 'material' and 'substantial'. But an employer should only lose on the issue of justification where it undertook no risk assessment, ignored any risk assessment undertaken, acted without any proper medical evidence or otherwise acted outside the range of reasonable responses open to it as an employer.

C. The Law Under the European Convention

(2) The scope of the right

n397a: But see the views of Sedley LJ on this point in *Malekshad v Howard de Walden Estates Ltd* [2001] EWCA Civ 761, discussed at Supplement, para 17.163.   **17.83**

(3) The 'ambit' of a Convention right

n411: See also *Wessels-Bergervoet v The Netherlands* (Judgment of 4 June 2002) and *Prince Hans-Adam II of Liechtenstein v Germany* (2002) 11 BHRC 526.   **17.87**

(4) The meaning of 'discrimination'

The case of *Camp & Bourimi v The Netherlands* (2002) 34 EHRR 59 concerned an application by a mother of a child whose partner died before the parents were married or the child born and without a will having been left by the father. The parents had lived together before the father's death and the mother wished to continue to live in their formerly shared home, a wish opposed by members of the father's family who moved into the couple's home. The Netherlands Supreme Court overturned an injunction granted to the applicant which ordered the father's family to vacate the house. The mother argued in Strasbourg that, had she been married to the father, she would have had the right under Dutch law to reside in the property alone and the injunction would have been granted; further that her son would have the right to inherit. The law therefore discriminated against unmarried parents. She argued that there was a breach of Articles 8 and 14, the latter on the basis of 'birth'. The Court of Human Rights confirmed again that a difference in treatment is only discriminatory if it has no objective and reasonable justification, that is if it   **17.89** does not pursue a legitimate aim or if there is not a reasonable relationship of proportionality between the means employed and the aim sought to be realised. Reference was made to the state's 'margin of appreciation'. The Court accepted that there was a need to protect the rights of other heirs and that this constituted a legitimate aim, but that the means were not proportionate. The other heirs were aware of the unborn child's existence and that in these circumstances the protection was disproportionate.

(5) Establishing a difference of treatment

17.94 In *Eliazer v The Netherlands* (Judgment of 16 October 2001) the Court of Human Rights ruled that there was no breach of Article 14 where a claimant complained that he received a more severe sentence as a consequence of failing to attend his criminal trial than a defendant who was convicted after having attended. The Court held that the claimant could not properly compare himself with someone who attended the trial. See also *Nerva v UK* (2002) 36 EHRR 4.

(8) Discrimination cases before the Court

(b) Discrimination cases

17.111 **Sex discrimination.**   In *Dahlab v Switzerland* (Judgment of 15 February 2001) the Court decided that a ban preventing the applicant wearing a Muslim headscarf while teaching was not imposed on her because she was a woman but to pursue the legitimate aim of ensuring the neutrality of state primary education.

In *Willis v United Kingdom* (2002) 35 EHRR 21 it was held that there was a breach of Article 14 in conjunction with Article 1 of the First Protocol when the male applicant was refused a widow's payment and a widowed mother's allowance on the death of his wife who had been the main breadwinner.

17.118 **Discrimination on the ground of national origin.**   The Court found that there was no breach of Article 14 in the case of *Ozgur Gundem v Turkey* (2001) 31 EHRR 1083 in which a newspaper had alleged that the respondent state had failed to protect it against attacks by protestors and assaults on its staff. Here the Turkish government believed that the newspaper was a propaganda tool for the Kurdistan Workers' Party and that the attacks were made by unknown opponents of their politics. The Court found that the failure by the state to take preventative steps to allow the newspaper to operate effectively was a breach of Article 10 (see Main Work, para 15.183) but that there was no reason to believe that the restrictions on freedom of expression resulted from or could be attributed to a difference in treatment based on nationality or origin or any of the other grounds protected by Article 14.

In *Magee v United Kingdom* (2001) 31 EHRR 822 the Court rejected the argument that a difference in the rules governing the access of terrorist suspects to lawyers between Northern Ireland and the rest of the United Kingdom was discrimination on grounds of national origin or association with a national minority. The difference in treatment depended on the geographical location where the individual was arrested and did not amount to discriminatory treatment within the meaning of Article 14.

Discrimination on other grounds.   In the case of *Sommerfield v Germany* [2002]   **17.122**
1 FLR 119 a father wished to have contact with a child of his born out of wedlock. The Court said that the relevant authorities had to strike a fair balance between the interests of the child and those of the parent. Here the Court held that the civil court should not have accepted the child's refusal to see the parent without seeking and considering expert psychological evidence. The Court went further and said that the state should not treat those born in and out of wedlock differently without very good reason. The Court found that there had been a breach of Article 14. Divorced fathers were generally allowed access to their children whereas fathers who had not been married had to prove their case where there were any objections from the mother or child. The Court said that any concerns the courts may have about the need to protect a child whose father had never been married to the child's mother could be achieved by separate relevant child-protection provisions. Very similar facts produced the same result in *Hoffman v Germany* [2002] 1 FLR 119. Likewise, in *Sahin v Germany* [2002] FLR 119 the Court held that there had been a breach of Article 14 where the civil court had failed to hear evidence from the child (who might have supported the father's application for access) because the appointed expert said she should not be asked questions about her father.

The case of *Chapman v United Kingdom* (2001) 10 BHRC 48 concerned the rights of gypsies to reside in a green-belt site in England. The applicant, Mrs Chapman, her husband and children lived a relatively nomadic life but, for the sake of the education of their children, had decided to apply for permission to reside in their mobile home on a field in a green-belt site on a permanent basis. That application was refused. An application was then made by Mrs Chapman to build a bungalow on the same site. This application was also refused, predominantly because of the environmental effect in terms of its impact on the appearance of the area concerned. The majority of the Court found that there was no breach of Article 8 or 14. The Court took the view that proper regard had been given to the applicant's difficulties, both under the regulatory framework of English planning law and by the relevant planning authorities when exercising their discretion in considering the particular circumstances of her case. There was, then, no breach of Article 8. As for Article 14, the Court held that the interference with the rights of the applicant and her family was proportionate when weighed against the need to preserve the environment, and so there was no breach.

What is perhaps most interesting about this case is the minority decision. Eight of the judges expressed the view that there was an emerging consensus amongst Member States that the special needs of minorities required protection, and that it was vital to preserve cultural diversity within the community. They also commented that there was a significant shortfall of official, lawful sites available for gypsies in the United Kingdom as a whole. They expressed the view that there appeared to be a presumption on the part of the planning officers that gypsy sites were not to be regarded as appropriate in green-belt areas unless special circumstances applied and that, in reality, only token weight was given to the applicant's interests or the associated public interest in maintaining cultural diversity. The minority held that long-term failures at local government level to make effective provision for gypsies amounted to a breach of Article 8, and felt no need to comment on Article 14 as a consequence.

D. The Impact of the Human Rights Act

(3) General impact

(a) Introduction

17.139   See, generally, K Monaghan, 'Limitations and Opportunities: A Review of the Likely Impact of Article 14' [2001] EHRLR 167.

When a court is invited to consider an Article 14 issue it will usually be appropriate for it to approach its task in a structured way. There are four questions to be considered:

- do the facts fall within the ambit of one or more of the substantive Convention provisions (for the relevant Convention rights, see section 1(1) of the Human Rights Act 1998)?
- if so, was there different treatment as respects that right between the complainant on the one hand and other persons put forward for comparison ('the chosen comparators') on the other?
- were the chosen comparators in an analogous situation to the complainant's situation?
- if so, did the difference in treatment have an objective and reasonable justification? In other words, did it pursue a legitimate aim and did the differential treatment bear a reasonable relationship of proportionality to the aim sought to be achieved?

See, further, *Michalak v London Borough of Wandsworth* [2002] 4 All ER 1136, para 20, and see also *Mendoza v Ghaidan* [2002] 4 All ER 1162.

In *Mendoza v Ghaidan* [2002] 4 All ER 1162 the Court of Appeal emphasised that, although deference was due to Parliament in areas of economic and social policy-making, where discrimination against a minority was concerned the courts were entitled to be satisfied that there was a proper and rational justification for the difference in treatment. This was a matter involving rights of high constitutional importance where the courts were equipped to arrive at a judgment. It was a 'classic role of the courts to be concerned with the protection of such minority rights' (para 44).

(c) Sexual orientation discrimination

The Court of Session in the case of *MacDonald v Ministry of Defence* [2001] IRLR **17.148** 431 overturned the decision made below that 'sex' in the Sex Discrimination Act 1975 should, in the light of Articles 8 and 14, be interpreted as including protection from discrimination on the grounds of sexual orientation. The consequences of the decision of the court below were clear—it meant that an action could be brought against a private individual or corporation where Articles 8 or 14 could not be relied upon directly. The Court of Session reviewed the United Kingdom and Strasbourg authorities and concluded that it was not the intention of Parliament that the word 'sex' should bear a meaning any wider than 'gender'.

In *MacDonald* Lord Prosser, dissenting, took the view that section 3 of the Human Rights Act required an interpretation of the Sex Discrimination Act 1975 which regulated discrimination on grounds of sexual orientation. While he agreed with the rest of the court that 'sex' in the context of the Act meant only 'gender', he thought it possible to interpret the Act to cover sexual orientation discrimination by holding that the comparator to be considered was not a heterosexual person of the same sex but a heterosexual person of the opposite sex. In other words, sexuality is *not* a relevant circumstance for the purpose of identifying the comparator of the opposite sex under section 5(3) of the 1975 Act. In *Pearce v The Governing Body of Mayfield School* [2002] ICR 198 Hale LJ formed part of a unanimous Court of Appeal which rejected the claimant's case on the grounds that the matters forming the subject of her complaint took place prior to 2 October 2000 and were therefore outside the scope of the non-retroactive Human Rights Act. But Hale LJ agreed *obiter* with the approach taken by Lord Prosser in *MacDonald* on the possibility of interpreting the Sex Discrimination Act to regulate discrimination on grounds of sexual orientation. By contrast, Judge LJ (at para 80) was unpersuaded by Hale LJ's views and Henry LJ (at para 86) declined to express a view. It is nevertheless submitted that the analysis of Hale LJ should be followed; the powerful rule of construction under section 3 of the Human Rights Act requires the court to give effect to a *possible* interpretation of section 5(3) which gives effect to Articles 8 and 14 (see, generally, Supplement, para 4.28).

In *Mendoza v Ghaidan* [2002] 4 All ER 1162 (as to which see also Supplement, para 17.163A) the Court of Appeal rejected the submission that discrimination on the grounds of sexual orientation is excluded from the protection of Article 14. It was held that

> Sexual orientation is now clearly recognised as an impermissible ground of discrimination, on the same level as the examples, which is all they are, specifically set out in the text of Article 14 (para 32).

See, generally, R Wintemute, 'Lesbian and Gay Inequality Act 2000: The Potential of the Human Rights Act 1998 and the Need for an Equality Act 2001' [2000] EHRLR 603.

(4) Specific areas of impact

(f) Housing law

17.163 In *Malekshad v Howard de Walden Estates Ltd* [2002] QB 364 the Court of Appeal had to consider whether section 2 of the Leasehold Reform Act 1967 breached Article 14 by excluding from its provisions concerning enfranchisement properties which are not structurally detached and of which a material part lies above or below a part of the structure not comprised in the property. The Court of Appeal accepted that the provision did discriminate against tenants of flats or other dwellings which overhang other units of accommodation in the same building, but ruled that the provision was based on a sound policy which was not disproportionate. The case law on enfranchisement had interpreted section 2 to mean that the overlap in the buildings must be of sufficient substance or significance that any enfranchisement would prejudice the enjoyment of others. As such there was no breach of Article 14. Sedley LJ went on to say:

> it is not necessary to decide whether the text of Clayton and Tomlinson *The Law of Human Rights* is correct in para 17.83 . . . to suggest that Article 14 governs the enjoyment not only of Convention rights but of rights which the state voluntarily guarantees. I doubt for my part whether the *Belgium Linguistics Case (No 2)* (1968) 1 EHRR 252 goes further than establishing that Article 14 applies not only to the minimum steps required of the state in the discharge of its positive obligations but to the totality of steps which it decides to take to that end.

Where a tenant in a secure tenancy died and the brother-in-law of his first cousin wished to continue to reside there the Court of Appeal held that the local authority did not breach Articles 8 and 14 by refusing to let him do so. The Court held that the protection against discrimination on the grounds of birth or status did not extend to refusing residence to such a distant relative and the local authority was entitled to grant successor status to closer relatives only (*Michalak v London Borough of Wandsworth* [2002] 4 All ER 1136).

17.163A In *Mendoza v Ghaidan* [2002] 4 All ER 1162 the Court of Appeal held that there was no rational reason for the exclusion of same-sex relationships from the 'succession provisions' of paragraph 2 of Schedule 1 to the Rent Act 1977 and that, as a result, the provision was incompatible with Article 14. However, the Court was able to remove the incompatibility by using section 3 of the Human Rights Act 1998 and construing the words 'as his or her wife or husband' to mean 'as *if they were* his or her wife or husband'. This had the effect of allowing long-term same-sex partners to succeed to a protected tenancy on the same basis as long-term heterosexual partners.

(g) Immigration law

The anti-terrorism provisions, which were passed into law as a consequence of the incidents of 11 September 2001, were considered in *A and Others v Secretary of State for the Home Department* [2002] UKHRR 1141. The applicants, all foreign nationals, were detained without charge under the Anti-Terrorism, Crime and Security Act 2001 because they were suspected of being involved in terrorist activities. The Special Immigration Appeals Commission ('SIAC') accepted that there was a breach of Article 14 in conjunction with Article 5, because there were no grounds for differentiating between foreign nationals and UK nationals. The Court of Appeal reversed SIAC's finding on the grounds that there were objective, justifiable and relevant grounds for selecting only alien terrorists suspects for detention.

17.164

(h) Local government law

n625: See, now, the decision of the Court in *Chapman v UK* (2001) 10 BHRC 48, discussed at Supplement, para 17.122.

17.165

(ha) Planning and environment law

In *George Clarke v Secretary of State for the Environment, Transport and the Regions* [2002] EWCA Civ 819 the court considered the application of a romany gypsy who lived with his family in a caravan and whose application for planning permission to place the caravan on a site owned by him had been turned down by the planning inspectorate. It was held that, although the planning inspector had properly taken into account the offer which had been made to the applicant and his family of alternative modern accommodation, he should have given proper weight to the applicant's assertion that such accommodation would be unsuitable for his and his family's lifestyle. It could be a breach of Articles 8 and 14 to force the applicant to take accommodation which was unsuitable, and the inspector's reasons did not state whether he had taken such a consideration into account before reaching his decision.

17.165A

(i) Police law

In *R (Marper) v Chief Constable of South Yorkshire* [2002] 1 WLR 3223 the claimant argued that a statutory provision which allowed the retention by the police of DNA samples taken from acquitted defendants was a breach of Article 14

17.166

taken with Article 8. It was held that the discrimination relied on was not within the categories of discrimination referred to in Article 14. In any event, the court held it was proper to treat those who had already given a sample differently from those who had not when it came to the question of retention.

(k) Social security law

17.168 The right to housing benefit has been the subject of a challenge under Articles 8 and 14 in a recent case concerning the deprivation of that benefit. In *R (Tucker) v Secretary of State for Social Security* [2001] EWCA Civ 1646 the DSS had, after nine years of providing housing benefit, withdrawn it from the applicant on the grounds that the father of one of her children was the landlord–owner of the property in relation to which her claims had always been made. A specific provision in the Social Security Contributions and Benefits Act 1992 (section 130) and regulation 7(1)(d) of the Housing Benefit (General) Amendment (No 2) Regulations 1998, SI 1998/3257, prevents payments in these circumstances. It was not disputed by either side that Ms Tucker fell foul of these provisions but it was argued on her behalf that the provisions were incompatible with Convention law. It was held that the legislation was proportionate and necessary to eradicate abuse of the benefit system. The fact that the provisions did not allow for an exception such as in the present case or provided a saving to allow for transitional change did not render the regulation disproportionate.

17.169 In *Wilkinson v Inland Revenue Commissioners* [2002] STC 347 Moses J considered the impact of section 262 of the Income and Corporation Taxes Act 1988 in relation to the widow's bereavement allowance which, it was alleged, discriminated against widowers and was incompatible with Article 14. He held that the Inland Revenue was under no duty to issue extra-statutory concessions to correct any difference in treatment and that its refusal to exercise its right to make a concession was within section 6(2)(b) of the Human Rights Act 1998.

The impact of benefits on widowers was also considered in *Hooper v Secretary of State for Works and Pensions* [2002] UKHRR 785. In this case the claimants' wives had died before changes to the discriminatory provision of widows' benefits were brought about by the Welfare Reform and Pensions Act 1999 (which came into force in April 2001 without retrospective effect). The claimants alleged a breach of Articles 8 and 14. Moses J held that the Government was under a duty to monitor statutory measures which may have a discriminatory effect, but that it was entitled to wait until 1998 to produce a consultation paper which ultimately produced the legislation designed to achieve equality. The Government was in a better position to make an overall assessment of how limited resources should be deployed to meet a need to

redress inequality and was best placed to assess when the time had come to remove any advantage afforded to women. This had, after all, been an advantage
in the past given to women because of their historical disadvantage in the
labour market.

In *R (Reynolds) v Secretary of State for Work and Pensions* [2002] EWHC Admin
426 a challenge was made to age-related differences in the level of jobseeker's allowance (Jobseeker's Allowance Regulations 1996, SI 1996/207, reg 79, and section 4 of the Jobseekers Act 1995). Wilson J dismissed the claim and held that
there was no breach of Article 14 (taken in conjunction with Article 1 of the First
Protocol) as the level of payment of jobseeker's allowance at a lower level to applicants under 25 could be justified on the grounds that most people in that age
group lived less independently from their parents and had fewer outgoings.
Further, as they tended to earn less, any benefits replacing lost earnings could jus-
tifiably be at a lower level.

(l) Other areas of impact

Civil procedure rules.   It has been argued that the rules governing the payment | **17.170A**
by a party of a sum representing security for costs could be in breach of Article 14
where the order for payment is made on the grounds of the person's residence
abroad. The Court of Appeal in *Nasser v United Bank of Kuwait* [2001] EWCA
Civ 556 held that CPR 25.13 and 15 did not breach Article 14 if a proper discretion was exercised in making the order on grounds that the party was resident in a
country where enforcement of any judgment would cause extra burden and costs.
Such an order could be objectively justified.

Ecclesiastical law.   In *Aston Cantlow PCC v Wallbank* [2002] Ch 51 it was held | **17.170B**
that the way in which the common law singled out the owners of glebe lands from
other landowners, making them liable for chancel repairs, was unjustifiably discriminatory, and so contrary both to Article 1 of the First Protocol and to Article
14 read with it.

The claimant in *R (Pretty) v DPP* [2002] 1 AC 800 suffered from motor neurone | **17.170C**
disease as a result of which she was paralysed from the neck down. She alleged that
the state's refusal to guarantee her husband immunity from criminal charges in
connection with any assisted suicide on her part breached Article 14 read with a
variety of other Articles of the Convention on the ground that she was being less
favourably treated than those people who were physically capable of committing
suicide themselves. In dismissing her case the House of Lords held that the law
confers no right on a person to commit suicide, but Lord Hope of Craighead
stated that the list of grounds for discrimination as set out in Article 14 was not
closed and that 'other status' could include physical or mental capacity, as the
Canadian Charter recognises.

Appendix 1: The Canadian Charter of Rights

(1) The interpretation of section 15

17.172   For a discussion of the developing and controversial case law, see I Binnie, 'Equality Rights in Canada: Judicial Usurpation or Missed Opportunities', in G Huscroft and Paul Rishworth (eds), *Litigating Rights* (Hart Publishing, 2002).

17.178A   In *Montreal v Quebec* (2000) 8 BHRC 478 the Supreme Court considered the meaning of 'handicap' in section 10 of the Quebec Charter. The applicants had each been refused employment on the basis of conditions which, at the time of refusal, did not result in any functional limitations on their ability to perform the work concerned, but which gave rise to future risks. The Supreme Court adopted a broad interpretation of the word 'handicap' as including 'both an ailment, even one with no resulting functional limitation, as well as the perception of such an ailment' (para 72). It refused to adopt a narrow definition of the word, holding that it could be the result of 'physical limitation, an ailment, a social construct, a perceived limitation or a combination of all these factors' (para 79).

In *Granovsky v Canada* (2001) 10 BHRC 619 the applicant was claiming a disability pension and complained that the failure to take into account previous temporary disability when considering his pension contribution record was discriminatory. The Supreme Court held that, whilst section 15 cannot alleviate or eliminate the functional limitations of disability, it can address the way in which the state responds to the disabled by making three broad inquiries. Firstly, does the impugned law: (a) draw a formal distinction between the claimant and others on the basis of one or more personal characteristics; or (b) fail to take into account the claimant's already disadvantaged position within society resulting in substantively differential treatment between the claimant and others on the basis of one or more personal characteristics? If so, there is differential treatment for the purpose of section 15(1). Secondly, was the claimant subject to differential treatment on the basis of one or more of the enumerated and analogous grounds? Thirdly, does the differential treatment discriminate in a substantive sense in remedying such ills as prejudice, stereotyping, and historical disadvantage (applying *Law v Canada* [1999] 1 SCR 497)? Although the applicant was the victim of differential treatment this did not perpetuate the view that persons with temporary disabilities are less capable or less worthy of recognition or value as human beings or as members as society. In addition, the provision aimed to ameliorate the position of groups within society who have suffered disadvantage by exclusion from mainstream society by affording differential treatment to those with a history of severe and permanent disabilities, rather than by assisting the more fortunate such as the applicant.

A provision which required preference for Canadian citizens in relation to public service employment was discriminatory under section 15 but was clearly designed to enhance and emphasise the value of citizenship and was therefore justified under section 1 (*Lavoie v Canada* (2002) 13 BHRC 60). Similarly, a statute which excluded separated spouses from eligibility for a spouse's allowance was discriminatory but was justified under section 1 (*Collins v Canada* (2002) 112 ACWS (3d) 972).

The statutory definition of 'spouses' as persons who had cohabited continuously for not less than three years was not discriminatory under section 15. The differential treatment suffered by a person who had cohabited for only 18 months was not based on a prohibited ground of discrimination. Although marital status was an analogous ground, the status being a member of a cohabiting relationship for less than three years was not (*Breberic v Niksic* (2002) CRDJ 1437).

(2) Analogous grounds

A complaint that the offence of obscenity discriminated against the gay and les- **17.183**
bian community was rejected in *Little Sisters Book and Art Emporium v Canada (Ministry of Justice)* [2001] 2 LCR 436. In *BC College of Teachers v Trinity Western University* (2001) 10 BHRC 425 a private institution ran teacher training programmes which were designed to reflect its Christian world view. The programme was refused approval because its guidelines embodied discrimination against homosexuals. Although the institution was exempt from the Charter of Rights as a private institution, the regulatory body was nevertheless entitled to look at human rights instruments to determine whether or not the training was in the public interest. However, the Supreme Court observed that neither religious freedom or the guarantee against sexual orientation discrimination was absolute. The proper place to draw the line was between belief and conduct. The freedom to hold beliefs is broader than freedom to act on them; and *absent* any concrete evidence that the programme would foster discrimination in state schools, the freedom of individuals to adhere to certain religious beliefs whilst training should be respected.

In *Halpern v Canada (A-G)* (2002) 215 DLR (4th) 223 the Ontario Superior Court of Justice held that the common law rule which defines marriage as being 'the lawful union of one man and one woman to the exclusion of all others' was inconsistent with constitutional values and offended the equality rights of gays and lesbians under section 15 of the Charter. The denial of equal marriage rights violated section 15 by drawing a distinction on the basis of sex and sexual orientation that withheld the equal benefit of the law in a manner which offended the human dignity of gays and lesbians. Procreation was not a pressing and substantial objective of the rules relating to marriage and no other sufficiently important objective was established such as would override the section 15 rights of gays and lesbians.

The appropriate remedy was for the court to declare the common law definition constitutionally invalid but to suspend the operation of that declaration for 24 months to enable Parliament to create remedial provisions. The majority held that if Parliament did not act the common law rule should be reformulated as 'the lawful union of two persons to the exclusion of all others'.

Appendix 2: The New Zealand Bill of Rights Act

17.201   In *Living Word Distributors v Human Rights Action Group* [2001] 2 LRC 233 the Court of Appeal considered an application by a human rights organisation which objected to the importation of religious videos which stigmatised homosexuals. The Court of Appeal quashed the decision of the Film and Literature Board of Review banning the videos.

Appendix 3: Human Rights Cases in Other Jurisdictions

(2) Australia

17.209   In *McBain v State of Victoria* [2000] FCA 1009 the Federal Court of Australia held that the denial of infertility treatment to single, unmarried women was discrimination on the basis of marital status, contrary to the provisions of sex discrimination legislation.

(4) Hong Kong

17.213A   In *Equal Opportunities Commission v Director of Education* [2001] HKCFI 654 the High Court declared unlawful certain aspects of the public schooling system, whereby girls were treated differently to boys. The offending provisions consisted of:

- a *scaling* mechanism, which scaled the scores of all primary students in their school assessments to ensure that they could be fairly compared with scores given by other primary schools, and which was employed on a gender basis;
- a *banding* mechanism, which banded all students into broad orders of academic merit, which was employed on a gender basis; and
- a form of *gender quota* which was employed to ensure that a fixed ratio of boys and girls were admitted to individual co-educational secondary schools.

(5) India

17.218   In *Harihan v Reserve Bank of India* [2001] 3 LRC 71 the petitioners sought to strike down a statutory provision to the effect that the guardian of a minor was 'the father, and after him, the mother' as being incompatible with Articles 14 and 15 of the Constitution. The Supreme Court upheld the statutory provision on the basis that 'after' meant 'in the absence of' and that it covered any situation in which the father was unsuitable to act as guardian. As a result, the statute did not prevent a mother being the guardian of a minor during the father's lifetime and was compatible with Articles 14 and 15. The Court stressed the importance of the international instruments which direct state parties to take appropriate measures to prevent discrimination against women and the obligation on the domestic courts to give due regard to international conventions and norms.

The case of *Danial Latifi v Union of India* (2002) 3 CHRLD 258 concerned the statutory exemption of Muslim men from financial obligations imposed by India's Criminal Procedure Code in relation to the financial support of ex-wives. The petitioners challenged the constitutional validity of the statutory exemption as discriminatory contrary to Article 14 of the Constitution. The Supreme Court noted that, in a society dominated both economically and socially by males, women devote themselves to the family. If that 'investment' was lost through divorce, women needed to be protected. Hence, regardless of their religion, women needed to have their basic human rights recognised and protected since everyone was entitled to social justice. The Court upheld the statutory exemption, but reinterpreted the legislation so that women were entitled to financial provision from their husbands by virtue of a statutory provision other than the Criminal Procedure Code.

(7A) Namibia

The Supreme Court of Namibia held in *Chairperson of the Immigration Selection Board v Frank* (2001) 3 CHRLD 179 that Article 10 (which prohibited discrimination) did not cover discrimination on the ground of sexual orientation. The Court relied on the absence in Article 10, unlike the comparable provision in the South African Constitution, of any express reference to sexual orientation. The Court also ruled that Article 14 (which protected the family) did not apply to a homosexual relationship. Again, the Court relied on the absence of any express reference to homosexual relationships in that article, and the lack of specific protection for homosexuals in the relevant provisions of the African Charter and the ICCPR.

17.223A

(8) South Africa

In *Hoffmann v South African Airways* [2001] 2 LRC 277 the Constitutional Court found that the refusal by South African Airways to employ the appellant as a cabin attendant because he was HIV-positive impaired his dignity and

17.233A

constituted unfair discrimination. It was unnecessary for the court to consider whether the discrimination was on the ground of 'disability' under section 9(3). The question of justification did not arise because the court was not dealing with a law of general application.

Unfair discrimination was also found in *Satchwell v President of South Africa* (2002) 13 BHRC 108. The Constitutional Court confirmed a High Court order declaring sections 8 and 9 of the Judges' Remuneration and Conditions of Employment Act 88 of 1989 and corresponding regulations unconstitutional to the extent that they afforded benefits to the spouses of judges but not to their same-sex life partners. The court did not consider whether the legislation also offended against heterosexual partners in permanent life-lasting relationships, although that point was conceded by the government.

17.237 The court also declined to make a finding of unfair discrimination in *Ex p Critchfield* 1999 (3) SA 132, holding that it was not unfair discrimination to have regard to maternity as a factor in deciding child custody. The court noted, however, that there would be unfair discrimination if too much weight was placed on that factor.

17.237A The court declined to make a finding of unfair discrimination in *Ex p Critchfield* 1999 (3) SA 132 (which concerned a challenge to the practice of having regard to maternity as a factor in deciding child custody, although the court did accept that there would be unfair discrimination if too much weight was placed on that factor). In *Poswa v MEC for Economic Affairs* 2001 (6) BCLR 545 the Supreme Court of Appeal ruled that, even if a prohibition on spouses of public servants being members of gaming boards was unfair discrimination on the basis of status, such discrimination was justified in order to counter corruption. And in *Minister of Defence v Potsane* 2001 (11) BCLR 1137 it was ruled that no unfair discrimination had occurred when soldiers were subject to disciplinary machinery different to that applicable to civilians.

In *Van der Walt v Metcash Trading Limited* 2002 (5) BCLR 454 the Supreme Court of Appeal had treated two applications for leave to appeal differently on two successive days, even though the applications were based on substantially identical facts. A majority of the Constitutional Court held that this differential treatment did not breach any constitutional right of the applicants, including rights of access to court and equality. Justice Goldstone, writing the judgment with which the majority concurred, held that while it was unfortunate that contrary orders should be issued in substantially identical cases, there was nothing to suggest that either of the orders were arbitrary. The panels were required to exercise discretion in determing the prospects of success on appeal, and in exercising such discretion reasonable minds might well differ. That did not make either order incorrect.

(10) Zimbabwe

The Zimbabwe Supreme Court has upheld the criminalisation of homosexual   **17.244**
acts (see *Banana v State* (2000) 8 BHRC 345). The court stated that the
Constitution did not prohibit discrimination on the basis of sexual orientation,
and commented on the conservative nature of society in Zimbabwe.

18

RIGHT TO ENJOYMENT OF POSSESSIONS

C. The Law Under the European Convention

(1) Introduction

For a useful overview, see Halstead, 'Human Property Rights' [2002] 66 Conv 153. **18.26**

n67: The UK argued strongly against the inclusion of Article 1, in part because it wanted to retain the right to expropriate without compensation; see, generally, A W B Simpson, *Human Rights and the End of Empire: Britain and the Genesis of the European Convention* (Oxford University Press, 2001), ch 15.

(2) Nature and scope of the right

(a) Introduction

In *Jokela v Finland* (Judgment of 21 May 2002) the Court held that the right to peaceful enjoyment of possessions in Article 1 of Protocol 1 included 'the expectation   **18.30**

of a reasonable consistency between interrelated albeit separate decisions concerning the same property' where its value had been assessed at very different levels for expropriation and inheritance tax purposes. See also Supplement, para
6.30.

(c) 'Possessions'

18.34 'Possessions' can be existing possessions or assets, including claims in respect of
which the applicant has at least a 'legitimate expectation' of obtaining effective enjoyment. However, an old property right which it has long been impossible to
enjoy effectively or a conditional claim which has lapsed because the condition
has not been fulfilled are not 'possessions' within the meaning of Article 1; see
Prince Hans-Adam II of Liechtenstein v Germany (2002) 11 BHRC 526, para 83,
and *Malhous v Czech Republic* (Decision of 13 December 2000).

18.36 Claims for benefits due to teachers which had been successful at first instance but
which were the subject of appeals were 'possessions' within the meaning of Article
1 because, in the light of the prevailing domestic law, the applicants had a legitimate expectation that they would be successful (*Smokovitis v Greece*, Judgment of
11 April 2002, para 32). Future income only constitutes a 'possession' if it has
been earned and there is an enforceable claim for its recovery (*Ambruosi v Italy*
(2002) 35 EHRR 125).

The fact that Article 1 of the First Protocol cannot be interpreted as giving an individual a right to a pension in a particular amount has been emphasised in a
number of cases; see *Kuna v Germany* (Decision of 10 April 2001) and *Rajkovic v
Croatia* (Decision of 3 May 2001). However, the effect of Article 14 and Article 1
of the First Protocol taken together in an appropriate case may in practice give rise
to a right to a pension in a particular amount. In *Wessels-Bergervoet v Netherlands*
(Judgment of 4 June 2002) the applicant argued that the reduction of her state
pension under a rule that rendered insurance of a married woman dependent at
any time upon whether her husband was so insured breached Article 1, taken together with Article 14. The Court held that the applicant's right to a pension
under the scheme was a 'possession' under Article 1, and that the reduction by reason of her sex violated Article 14. (Cf *R (Carson) v Secretary of State for Work and
Pensions* [2002] 3 All ER 994.)

The Court of Human Rights held in *Willis v United Kingdom* (2002) 35 EHRR
21 that a right to a widow's payment and widowed mother's allowance under the
Social Security Contributions and Benefits Act 1992 amounted to a 'possession'
under Article 1, in the case of a widower who had failed to qualify for such benefits by reason of his sex. The applicant also argued that entitlement in the future
to a widow's pension was a 'possession' within Article 1. The Court did not, however, address the argument, rejecting that aspect of the applicant's claim on Article
14 grounds alone.

n102a: See also *In the Matter of Lynn Adams (Application for Judicial Review)*, 20 November 2001 (Court of Session).

(3) 'Interference'

(c) 'Control of use'

n137: See also *Palumbo (Edoardo) v Italy* (Judgment of 30 November 2000) **18.46** where the Court held that the applicant's inability to obtain possession of his apartment from a tenant for over seven years amounted to control of use of his property and gave rise to a violation of Article 1 of the First Protocol.

In *Saggio v Italy* (Judgment of 25 October 2001) the Court held that institution by the state of extraordinary liquidation proceedings in relation to a corporate debtor of the applicant constituted 'control of use' of the 'possession' represented by his future income. However, the applicant's argument that the long duration of the liquidation process (proceedings were still pending over five years on) violated Article 1 was rejected. The Court accepted that the process had to provide certain procedural safeguards so as to ensure that the operation of the system and its impact on individuals' property rights were neither arbitrary nor unforeseeable, but held that the main reason for the delay was the debtor's lack of financial resources and the applicant's difficulty in recovering the money owed.

The right of the state to secure the payment of penalties is subject to the rule in the **18.48** first sentence of the first paragraph of Article 1 and there must, therefore, be a reasonable relationship of proportionality between the means employed and the end sought to be realised (see, for example, *Phillips v United Kingdom* (2002) 11 BHRC 280, para 51): in the light of the importance of the fight against drug trafficking the interference constituted by confiscation orders is not disproportionate.

(d) Other interferences

In *Pialopoulos v Greece* (2001) 33 EHRR 39, para 56, the Court held that various **18.52** measures taken by planning authorities in an attempt to expropriate the applicants' property did not amount to either a deprivation of property or a control of the use of the property.

In *Antonetto v Italy* (Judgment of 20 July 2000) the failure of the administrative authorities to demolish an illegally constructed building partially deprived the applicant of light and a view and thereby reduced the value of her property. As a result, there was an interference with the applicant's rights under the first sentence of the first paragraph of Article 1 of the First Protocol. See, further, J-J Paradissis, 'Unlawful Planning Development and the Right to Peaceful Enjoyment of Possessions: The *Antonetto* Case' [2002] JPL 674.

In *Smokovitis v Greece* (Judgment of 11 April 2002) the applicants were temporary teaching staff who brought proceedings against their school for a supplement to their salary, to which they alleged they were entitled under a ministerial
decision. Their action was successful at first instance but legislation was passed
while the appeal was pending declaring the ministerial decision to apply to permanent staff only. The Court held that the legislation extinguishing the applicants' claims was neither an expropriation nor a measure to control the use of
property but fell to be dealt with under the first sentence of the first paragraph of
Article 1.

(4) The right to compensation for interferences with possessions

(b) Compensation for deprivation of property

18.57   In *Gaganus v Turkey* (Judgment of 5 June 2001) the Court made it clear that, in
general, Article 1 of the First Protocol required the payment of compensation in
the case of expropriation in the public interest and that, without the payment of a
sum bearing a reasonable relationship to the value of the property, the deprivation
was unlikely to be justifiable. Turkey was found to be in breach of Article 1 of the
First Protocol as a result of delays in the payment of compensation which were not
compensated by the payment of interest. A fair balance between the protection of
the applicants' right to property and the general interest of the community had
not been struck. The Court found violations of Article 1 of the First Protocol
against Turkey on the same basis in 20 other cases decided on 5 June 2001 and in
a further 20 cases decided on 3 July 2001.

18.58   See also *The Former King of Greece and Others v Greece* (2000) 33 EHRR 21 in
which the Court found that there was no objective justification for depriving the
former King of Greece of his property without the payment of compensation. The
Court held that unrelated tax exemptions and the writing off of taxes owed by the
former royal family were not relevant to the issue of the proportionality of the interference. However, such matters might be taken into account when the Court
comes to consider the applicants' claims for just satisfaction (the determination of
which has been reserved).

(5) Justification

(d) Justification and the 'fair balance test'

18.77   In cases involving control over the ownership or use of property in the interest of
public health or safety the judgment of the national legislature will be respected
unless it is manifestly arbitrary or unreasonable. Thus, a series of applications
under Article 1 relating to the statutory ban on handguns in the United Kingdom
by gun manufacturers (*Danimark v United Kingdom* (2000) 30 EHRR CD 144)

and operators of shooting centres (*CEM Firearms and Bradford Shooting Centre v United Kingdom* (2000) 30 EHRR CD 156) were held to be inadmissible.

In *Jokela v Finland* (Judgment of 21 May 2002) the failure by two public bodies **18.80** to give a 'sufficient explanation' for their very different valuations of the same property for expropriation and inheritance tax purposes precluded the state from justifying that inconsistency in circumstances where, analysed separately, both the expropriation decision and the levy of inheritance tax fell within the state's margin of appreciation; see Supplement, para 18.30. The Court remarked, *obiter*, in *Burdov v Russia* (Judgment of 7 May 2002) that failure by the state to pay compensation to the applicant pursuant to court orders could not be justified by reference to a lack of state funds.

The 'fair balance' test has been held not to have been satisfied in a number of recent cases: **18.81**

- In *Ambruosi v Italy* (2002) 35 EHRR 125 a decree which prevented the recovery of costs from the unsuccessful defendant and which had the practical effect of requiring the applicant lawyer to seek fees directly from impecunious clients was held to impose an excessive burden on the applicant and upset, to her detriment, the fair balance.
- In *Smokovitis v Greece* (Judgment of 11 April 2002) the Court held that the fair balance was upset by the retroactive effect of legislation which gave an unfavourable interpretation to a measure pursuant to which the applicants were bringing a claim for a salary supplement. See, further, Supplement, para 18.52.
- In *SA Dangeville v France* (Judgment of 16 April 2002) it was held that the inability of a company to enforce a debt against the state and the lack of domestic proceedings providing sufficient remedy upset the fair balance between the demands of the general interest and the requirements of the protection of the right to the enjoyment of possessions.

D. The Impact of the Human Rights Act

(2) United Kingdom cases

(a) Introduction

The United Kingdom was held to be in violation of Article 14, in conjunction **18.83** with Article 1 of the First Protocol, in *Willis v United Kingdom* (2002) 35 EHRR 21. See Supplement, para 18.95.

(f) State benefits

In *Willis v United Kingdom* (2002) 35 EHRR 21 the United Kingdom was found **18.95** to have breached Article 1, in conjunction with Article 14. The applicant widower challenged his lack of entitlement under the Social Security Contributions and Benefits Act 1992 to a widow's payment, widowed mother's allowance and (in future) to a widow's pension. The Court held that the absence of entitlement to the first two types of benefit constituted a breach, *inter alia*, of Article 14 in conjunction with Article 1. The claim in respect of the widow's pension was, however, rejected on the grounds that, as the situation then stood, a widow in the applicant's position would not yet be entitled to the benefit, so there could be no discrimination under Article 14. See also Supplement, para 18.39.

The Court of Session has held that the livelihood of a self-employed manager of foxhounds and his tied house are 'possessions' (*Re Adams, Petition for Judicial Review*, 31 July 2002, para 130).

(3) General impact

(aa) Definition of 'possessions'

18.98A   Qualified regulatory approval ('not to be marketed') for a chemical product was held not to amount to a 'possession' covered by Article 1 of the First Protocol in *R (Amvac Chemical UK Limited) v Secretary of State for the Environment, Food and Rural Affairs & Others* [2001] EWHC Admin 1011. In *R (Toovey & Another) v Law Society* [2002] EWHC Admin 391 it was held that the claimants' applications for a discretionary waiver of Solicitors' Indemnity Fund contributions were also not 'possessions' under Article 1.

In *Matthews v Ministry of Defence* [2002] 3 All ER 513 the Court of Appeal accepted that the assertion that a right of action in tort was a 'possession' was supported by the Strasbourg jurisprudence. However, issue of a certificate under section 10 of the Crown Proceedings Act 1947 did not amount to a deprivation of that 'possession', since the right was always subject to the provisions of that section.

(a) Property litigation

18.99   There are *dicta* by the Court of Appeal in *JA Pye (Oxford) Ltd v Graham* [2001] 2 WLR 1293 concerning the application of Article 1 of the First Protocol to section 15 of the Limitation Act 1980 (which provides a 12-year limitation period in respect of actions for the recovery of land). Although the Court of Appeal expressed some doubt as to whether Article 1 'impinges' on section 15, it held that any interference with rights conferred by Article 1 could be justified for several reasons. These included the need to avoid real injustice in the adjudication of stale claims, to ensure certainty of title and to promote 'social stability'. However, in *Family Housing Association v Donellan* (2001) 30 EG 114 (CS) Park J held that a claim that section 15 was contrary to Article 1 of the First Protocol was unarguable. This was because that part of Article 1 was directed against expropriations by the state, for public purposes, and was not directed against matters that were essentially ones of private law. Adverse possession did not involve the type of deprivation of possessions that Article 1 of the First Protocol prohibited. The decision of the Court of Appeal in *Pye* was overruled by the House of Lords at [2002] UKHL 30. However, the application of Article 1 of the First Protocol was not considered.

In *Marcic v Thames Water Utilities Ltd* [2001] 3 All ER 698 (H H J Havery) it was held that a failure by a statutory undertaker to carry out works to bring to an end the repeated flooding of the claimant's property constituted an interference with his rights under Article 1 of the First Protocol. The defendant had interfered with the claimant's enjoyment of his possessions by failing to carry out the work and had not demonstrated that its system of priorities struck a fair balance between the interests of the claimant and those of the defendant's other customers. The decision was upheld by the Court of Appeal at [2002] QB 929 on different grounds (common law of nuisance), but the Court gave its approval to the approach taken by the judge in applying Article 1. See, further, Kimblin, 'Nuisance and Damages under the HRA' (2002) 146 SJ 220. The House of Lords has given leave to appeal in this case at [2002] 1 WLR 2274.

In *Aston Cantlow Parish Church Council v Wallbank* [2002] Ch 51 the Court of Appeal held that the liability of the owner of former rectorial glebe land to pay the cost of chancel repairs was a form of taxation. It went on to say that the broad principles which animate the Convention 'include a requirement that the legitimate aim of taxation in the public interest must be pursued by means which are not completely arbitrary or out of all proportion to their purpose' (para 44).

The liability to pay for chancel repairs was held to be a tax which operates entirely arbitrarily. This was because the land to which it attaches does not differ relevantly from any other freehold land and because the liability might arise at any time and in almost any amount. The Court of Appeal also took into account the fact that this liability was not part of a considered system voted on by a representative legislature but was a residual common law liability. For a critique of the *Wallbank* decision, see S Whale, 'Pawnbrokers and Parishes: The Protection of Property under the Human Rights Act' [2002] EHRLR 67.

In *Fuller v Happy Shopper Markets Ltd* [2001] 1 WLR 1681 Lightman J suggested that the self-help remedy of distress involves a serious interference with the right of the tenant under Article 1 of the First Protocol with the result that

> The human rights implications of levying distress must be in the forefront of the mind of the landlord before he takes this step and he must fully satisfy himself that taking this action is in accordance with the law.

(b) Taxation

See *R (Professional Contractors Group Ltd and Others) v Inland Revenue Commissioners* [2002] STC 165 in which Article 1 of the First Protocol was **18.100** unsuccessfully raised as 'a fall-back argument' against a change in the income tax regime. In *R v Dimsey* [2001] 3 WLR 843 it was argued that it was inconsistent with Article 1 for sums transferred from a UK-resident tax avoider to offshore companies to be treated as those companies' income for tax purposes, where the same sums were deemed by section 739(2) of the Income and Corporation Taxes Act 1988 to be the income of the tax avoider for tax purposes. The House of Lords held that this outcome was 'well within the margin of appreciation allowed to member states in respect of tax legislation', noting that 'the public interest requires that legislation designed to combat tax avoidance should be effective'. That public interest outweighed the claimant's 'mainly theoretical' objections to the regime.

(d) Other areas of impact

18.101A   In *Holder v Law Society* [2002] EWHC 1559 it was held that the intervention by the Law Society in a solicitor's practice under Schedule 1 to the Solicitors Act 1974 is an interference with the peaceful enjoyment of possessions and it is necessary to consider, on the facts of each case, whether a fair balance has been struck. As a result, although the intervention was 'entirely justified' on conventional principles, the judge refused to give summary judgment to the Law Society on the solicitor's claim under the Human Rights Act 1998 for an order that the intervention be withdrawn. However, in *Wright v Law Society*, 9 September 2002, H H J Behrens doubted whether Article 1 of the First Protocol 'alters or affects the position' in this context in the light of the Law Society's obligation to consider the public interest before deciding whether to exercise its intervention powers.

18.101B   In *Re Adams, Petition for Judicial Review*, 31 July 2002, para 130, the Court of Session held that the Protection of Wild Mammals (Scotland) Act 2002, which made it a criminal offence to engage in mounted foxhunting with dogs, was not a breach of Article 1. It was within the discretionary area of judgment of the Scottish Parliament to strike the balance by controlling the use of property, in accordance with the general interest in the prevention of cruelty to animals, without paying compensation. See, generally, R Singh and D Thomas, 'The Human Rights Act Implications on a Ban on Hunting with Dogs' [2002] EHRLR 28.

(4) Specific areas of impact

(a) Commercial law

18.102A   In *Al-Kishtaini v Shanshal* [2001] 2 All ER (Comm) 601 the claimant sought to recover a payment made in contravention of directions issued by the Treasury to implement United Nations sanctions against Iraq. The Court of Appeal held that such payments could not be recovered on the grounds of illegality. Having assumed (without deciding) that the defence of illegality might give rise to a deprivation of possessions for the purpose of Article 1 of the First Protocol, the court held that such a deprivation could be justified under the public interest exception in the second sentence of Article 1. In reaching this decision, the court relied principally upon two matters. First, the directions prohibiting the transfer were made in order to implement resolutions of the UN Security Council. Secondly, the prohibition on payment was not absolute: the claimant could have sought permission from the Bank of England to make the transfer but he failed to do so.

In *Wilson v First County Trust (No 2)* [2002] QB 74 the Court of Appeal held that **18.102B** section 127(3) of the Consumer Credit Act 1974 was incompatible with the rights guaranteed by Article 1 of the First Protocol. The court held that section 127(3) (which creates an absolute bar to the enforcement of a consumer credit agreement in the absence of a document signed by the debtor containing all the prescribed terms) deprived the creditor of its ability to enjoy the benefit of contractual rights arising from the agreement and of rights arising from the delivery of security. Although the court acknowledged that the judicial control of enforcement was a legitimate means of pursuing a legitimate policy objective, it held that the inflexible prohibition on enforcement was disproportionate to that aim (see also *Wilson v First County Trust* [2001] QB 407). For a critique of the *Wilson* decision, see S Whale, 'Pawnbrokers and Parishes: The Protection of Property under the Human Rights Act' [2002] HRLR 67; and see also N Bamforth, 'Human Rights and Consumer Credit' [2002] LQR 203.

(c) Planning and environmental law

In *R (MWH & H Ward Estates Ltd) v Monmouthshire County Council* [2002] **18.105A** EWHC Admin 229 it was held that entry upon the claimant's land by the council to carry out land drainage works under section 64 of the Land Drainage Act 1991 did not contravene Article 1 of the First Protocol. The court cited the obligation to pay compensation under section 14(5) of the 1991 Act as a major ground for its conclusion that the interference was justified.

See, generally, M McMereux, 'Deriving Environmental Rights from the European Convention on Human Rights and Fundamental Freedoms' (2001) 21 OJLS 521.

(d) Social security

The right to contributions-based jobseeker's allowance was held to be a 'posses- **18.109** sion' for the purposes of Article 1 of the First Protocol in *R (Reynolds) v Secretary of State for Work and Pensions* [2002] EWHC Admin 426.

The United Kingdom's social security regime in relation to widows has been the subject of two declarations of incompatibility, through failures to comply with Article 14 in conjunction with Article 1 of the First Protocol. In *Hooper v Secretary of State for Work and Pensions* [2002] UKHRR 785 Moses J held that sections 37 and 38 of the Social Security Contributions and Benefits Act 1992 were incompatible with the two Articles, since widowers were not entitled to either widow's payment or widowed mother's allowance. The provision of a widow's pension to widows only was, however, held to be objectively justified on the grounds that widows had historically been disadvantaged on the labour market to a greater extent than widowers. A similar decision has since been reached by the Strasbourg Court in *Willis v United Kingdom* (2002) 35 EHRR 21, as to which see Supplement, para 18.95. In *Wilkinson v Inland Revenue Commissioners* (2002) STC 347, also a decision of Moses J, a declaration of incompatibility was made in relation to section 262 of the Income and Corporation Taxes Act 1988. Widowers are not entitled to widow's bereavement allowance, but may be granted it at the discretion of the Inland Revenue under section 262 of the 1988 Act. The absence of a duty to issue such a concession, and thereby correct the discrimination, was incompatible with Article 14, taken together with Article 1 of the First Protocol.

(e) Confiscation orders

18.109A In *R v Benjafield; R v Rezvi* [2002] 2 WLR 235 the House of Lords considered the application of Article 1 of the First Protocol to the statutory regimes for the making of confiscation orders laid down in the Drug Trafficking Act 1994 and (in relation to other offences) in the Criminal Justice Act 1988, as amended by the Proceeds of Crime Act 1995. Proceedings under both schemes involve a reversal of the onus of proof which, in effect, requires the defendant to establish that his assets have an innocent source. If he fails to do so, the court will assume that they are the proceeds of drug trafficking or other crime. The House of Lords held that the interference with a defendant's rights under Article 1 was justified, citing in support the identical conclusion of the Court of Human Rights in *Phillips v United Kingdom* (2002) 11 BHRC 280. The legislation was 'a precise, fair and proportionate response to the important need to protect the public' (para 17).

(f) Seizure and forfeiture

18.109B A considerable number of challenges have been brought under Article 1 of the First Protocol to decisions by Customs Officers to seize and/or forfeit vehicles containing excise goods under the Customs and Excise Management Act 1979 and the Excise Duty (Personal Reliefs) Order 1992, SI 1992/3155. In *Lindsay v Customs & Excise Commissioners* [2002] 1 WLR 1766 the Court of Appeal considered the Commissioners' policy of only restoring seized vehicles in exceptional circumstances. The Court held that it 'would not have been prepared to condemn' the policy had it been one that applied to those who were using their cars for commercial smuggling, but held that proportionality required cases of non-commercial smuggling to be considered on their particular facts, including the scale of importation, whether it is a 'first offence', whether there was an attempt at concealment or dissimulation, the value of the vehicle and the degree of hardship that will be caused by forfeiture. See also *R (Hoverspeed Limited) v Commissioners of Customs & Excise* [2002] EWHC Admin 1630.

Section 141(1)(b) of the Customs and Excise Management Act 1979 provides that goods are liable for forfeiture if they are 'mixed, packed or found with' goods which are liable to forfeiture. In *Fox v HM Customs & Excise* [2002] EWHC Admin 1244 the claimant's excise goods were seized together with those of his travelling companion. The travelling companion later failed to contest the liability to forfeiture of his goods, which were accordingly condemned. The claimant alleged that his half of the goods was not liable to forfeiture. Lightman J held that it was 'grossly unjust' to conclude that, by virtue of section 141(b), the companion's failure to contest the liability to forfeiture of his goods had effectively divested the claimant of ownership of his goods. Section 141(b) had to be construed so as to permit the claimant to challenge the conclusion that the companion's goods were liable to forfeiture. In this way breach of the claimant's rights under Article 1 was avoided.

In *International Transport Roth GmbH & Others v Secretary of State for the Home Department* [2002] 3 WLR 344 the Court of Appeal held that the scheme under Part II of the Immigration and Asylum Act 1999, which penalised those who carried clandestine entrants into the United Kingdom, was incompatible with Article 6 of the Convention and Article 1 of the First Protocol. Under the scheme, a carrier entering the UK who was found to have clandestine entrants as stowaways was obliged to pay a fixed fine of £2,000 in respect of each entrant, on pain of detention and forfeiture of the vehicle with which the carrier made his living. The Court held by a majority that the scale and inflexibility of the penalty imposed an excessive burden upon the carriers, disproportionate to the important social goal which the scheme sought to promote.

(g) Leasehold property

In *R v Secretary of State for the Environment, ex p Spath Holme Ltd* [2001] 2 WLR   **18.109C**
15, 24, 25, Lord Bingham rejected the argument that the power conferred on the Secretary of State by section 31 of the Landlord and Tenant Act 1985 to limit the maximum fair rent was so broad that the order made by the Secretary of State pursuant to that section could not be said to be 'provided for by law' as required by the second rule in Article 1 of the First Protocol. His Lordship also expressed the view that it was the order of the Secretary of State itself rather than the empowering provision in the statute which had to satisfy that requirement. In any event, Lord Bingham concluded that any interference with the rights of the landlord pursuant to Article 1 of the First Protocol would be justifiable by reference to the general interests of the community. In *Spath Holme Ltd v United Kingdom* (2002) 35 EHRR

CD 106 the Court of Human Rights rejected an application by the claimant as manifestly ill-founded. This was because states had a wide margin of appreciation in determining the existence of social problems, particularly those of a housing nature, and the ways in which they should be remedied. The effects of the order were not disproportionate to the legitimate aim pursued.

It has been suggested that the common law rule which allows one joint tenant to give notice to quit (the rule in *Hammersmith v Monk* [1992] 1 AC 478), thus terminating the tenancy of the others, may be contrary to Article 1 and/or Article 8; see I Loveland, 'Rethinking the Rule in *Hammersmith v Monk* from a Human Rights Perspective' [2002] EHRLR 327.

Appendix 1: The Canadian Charter of Rights

18.111   In *Authorson v A-G of Canada* (2000) CRDJ 36 (Quebec CA) the plaintiff represented a class of disabled veterans who claimed that they were entitled to interest on pensions and allowances being administered by the Department of Veterans' Affairs. The defendant sought to rely on a statutory defence which barred such claims. The court rejected the argument that this was contrary to section 7 of the Charter on the basis that the section did not include economic rights (relying on *Re Aluminium Co v Queen* (1986) 29 DLR (4th) 583). However, it upheld the plaintiff's argument based on the Canadian Bill of Rights. The section was declared inoperative because

> it offends the Bill of Rights, by infringing the right to enjoyment of property, the right not to be deprived of property except by due process of law and the right to a fair hearing in accordance with the Principles of Fundamental Justice.

Appendix 3: Human Rights Cases in Other Jurisdictions

(2) Australia

18.121   In *Smith v ANL Ltd* (2000) 176 ALR 449 the plaintiff complained that the effect of various statutory provisions was to prevent him from bringing actions in tort and breach of contract against his employer for compensation for personal injury. The High Court of Australia held that the statutory provisions were invalid because they were laws for the acquisition of property but did not provide just terms as required by section 51(xxxi) of the Constitution. This case was followed by the Federal Court in *Australian Capital Territory v Pinter* [2002] FCAFC 186 which held that amendments to the criminal injuries compensation legislation which retrospectively extinguished the statutory right to claim an amount for pain and suffering was an 'acquisition of property' and was not on 'just terms'.

(2A) Dominica

Section 6(1) of the Constitution protects a person from deprivation of property **18.124A**
without payment within a reasonable time of adequate compensation. In *A-G v
Theodore* [2001] 1 LRC 13 the Eastern Caribbean Court of Appeal considered a
provision of the Roads Ordinance which provided for expropriation 'without
compensation'. It was held that this provision was unconstitutional on its face.
However, paragraph 2(1) of the transitional provisions of the Constitution provided that existing laws 'shall be construed with such modifications, adaptations,
qualifications and exceptions' as may be necessary to bring them into conformity
with the Constitution. As a result, the court deleted the words 'without compensation' and replaced them with 'with compensation'.

(4) India

There is no deprivation of property when people are prevented from selling ciga- **18.127**
rettes and bidis on trains and railway platforms (*Shankarbhai H Patel v Union of
India*, AIR 2000, Gujarat High Court). The mere fact that the sale of cigarettes
and bidis had not been objected to in the past did not confer any right on sellers
to continue their trade. Nor did the ban deprive the sellers of earned benefits.

(5) Ireland

The Proceeds of Crime Act 1996, which allows the confiscation of the proceeds of **18.133A**
crime, does not violate the guarantees of private property under the Constitution;
see *Clancy v Ireland* [1988] IR 326, approved by the Supreme Court in *Murphy v
Criminal Assets Bureau* [2001] IESC 63.

(5A) Jamaica

In *Panton v Minister of Finance* [2001] UKPC 33 the Privy Council held that **18.133B**
when the Minister took over the temporary management of a bank under regulatory powers there was no 'taking of the property' of shareholders. The statutory
provisions were of a regulatory and not a confiscatory nature and no obligation for
compensation arose.

(9) South Africa

In *First National Bank of SA Ltd v Commissioner for the South African Revenue* **18.143**
Services 2002 (7) BCLR 702 the Constitutional Court held that certain provisions
of the Customs and Excise Act were constitutionally invalid to the extent that they
provided that goods owned by persons other than the person liable for a customs
debt were subject to detention, lien and sale. The purpose of section 25 was both to
protect existing private property rights and to serve the public interest: its purpose

was to strike a proportionate balance between the two. A deprivation was 'arbitrary' under section 25 if the 'law' authorizing the deprivation did not provide sufficient reason for it or was procedurally unfair. No sufficient reason existed for depriving a person other than the customs debtor of goods and, as a result, the deprivation was 'arbitrary'.

18.143A   Section 26(3) of the Constitution provides that

> No one may be evicted from their home, or have their home demolished, without an order of the court made after considering all the relevant circumstances.

In *Ellis v Viljoen* 2001 (5) BCLR 487 (C) the High Court rejected the argument that this provision did not affect the common law position in relation to actions for possession of land occupied as a home. If the only relevant circumstances placed before the court were that the plaintiff was the owner and the defendant was in possession, the court should make an order. The burden was on the defendant to plead and prove other relevant circumstances. This approach was consistent with section 25(1) of the Constitution (*Ross v South Peninsula Municipality* 2000 (1) SA 589 (C) not followed).

(10) Trinidad and Tobago

18.144   The constitutional rights to the enjoyment of property include the right of possession which vests a possessory title in the possessor. However, a claim for the return of a car held by the police should not be brought by way of constitutional motion (*Jaroo v Attorney-General of Trinidad and Tobago* [2002] 1 WLR 705).

(11) Zimbabwe

18.147   In *Law Society of Zimbabwe v Minister of Finance* [2000] 4 LRC 52 the Supreme Court struck down a withholding tax scheme. The court noted that the combination of withholding tax coupled with a clearance certificate and refunds where necessary was *prima facie* reasonable. However, the scheme provided for no relationship between the money withheld and tax later found to be due. Further, the scheme created an indiscriminate system which failed to determine who was liable, and for what amount.

In *Commercial Farmers Union v Minister of Lands, Agriculture and Resettlement* [2001] 2 LRC 521 it was held that an amendment to the Land Acquisition Act was null and void because it was in conflict with the constitutional requirement that 'reasonable notice' be given of the intention to acquire property (section 16(1)(b) of the Constitution).

19

THE RIGHT TO EDUCATION

B. The Right in English Law

(7) School admissions and parental choice

The essential question for the appeals committee under Schedule 24 to the **19.22**
School Standards and Framework Act 1998 is whether it was perverse in the light
of the admission arrangements to refuse to admit the particular child; see *R
(London Borough of Hounslow) v School Admission Appeals Panel* [2002] EWCA
Civ 900.

(8) Children with special needs

(b) The obligation owed to children with special educational needs

n88: The Special Educational Needs and Disability Act 2001, which is expected   **19.24**
to come into force shortly, introduces a new section 316 into the Education 1996

Act to give a strengthened right to a mainstream education for children with special educational needs. If no section 324 statement is maintained for the child, he must be educated in a mainstream school; if such a statement is maintained, he must be educated in a mainstream school unless that is incompatible with: (a) the wishes of his parent; or (b) the provision of efficient education for other children.

(c) Negligence and special educational needs

19.29 The case of *Phelps v Hillingdon London Borough Council* [2001] 1 AC 619 was distinguished in *H v Isle of Wight Council*, 23 February 2001 (Wright J), where the claimant alleged the school had been negligent in not dealing adequately with her dyslexia. It was held that *Phelps* was a case dealing with professional negligence and not breach of statutory duty, and therefore the usual test in *Bolam v Friern Hospital Management Committee* [1957] 1 WLR 583 applied. See also *Robinson v St Helens MBC* [2002] EWCA Civ 1099.

See, generally, Duncan Fairgrieve, 'Pushing Back the Boundaries of Public Authority Liability: Tort Law Enters the Classroom' [2002] PL 288.

19.29A The House of Lords has considered the issue of negligence again in the context of sexual abuse at a school for boys with emotional and behavioural difficulties (*Lister & Others v Hesley Hall Ltd* [2001] 2 WLR 1311). It was held that the historic test for determining vicarious liability was inappropriate. The proper approach is broadly to assess the nature of the perpetrator's employment and ask whether the torts were so closely connected with his employment that it would be fair to hold the school liable. In this case he had been employed to care for the boys at the school and as such his employer was vicariously liable for those acts. The case of *ST v North Yorkshire County Council* [1999] IRLR 98 was overruled.

n104: *Phelps v Hillingdon London Borough Council* is now reported at [2000] 3 WLR 776.

(9) The right to free school transport

19.30 A local education authority was entitled to refuse to pay for transport when it had determined that a particular school was suitable and it was within walking distance of the child's home. The fact that the parents chose, after the determination of suitability, to send the child to another school outside normal walking distance did not assist them (*R v Vale of Glamorgan County Council, ex p J* [2001] EWCA Civ 593).

In *R (T) v Leeds City Council* [2002] ELR 91 it was accepted that payments in relation to school transport could be challenged under Article 2 of the First Protocol in conjunction with Article 14. The case concerned the legality of a policy which provided discretionary payment for attendance at certain

Christian schools, but not others; the application failed in that case due to the lack of an Orthodox Jewish school at a similar distance as the relevant Christian schools.

(10) Expulsion from schools

Where a graduate student was withdrawn from the register at a university, it was **19.33** held that the Board of Graduate Studies had not acted fairly towards the applicant. Although there was no principle of fairness which required that a person should be entitled to challenge or make representations in relation to a purely academic judgment, each case had to be considered on its facts. The case was not a challenge to an academic judgment but to the process by which it was determined that the applicant should not be reinstated (*R v Cambridge University, ex p Persaud* [2001] ELR 480).

Where a local authority had been involved in the setting up of an independent appeal panel and the panel took action based on guidance by the Secretary of State regarding violent pupils, there was no breach of the common law duty to ensure independence and impartiality. Further, the guidance had not usurped the panel's function (*R (S) v Brent London Borough Council* [2002] ELR 57).

The latter point was then appealed. The Court of Appeal held that paragraphs 17 and 18 of the Secretary of State's Guidance contained in Circular 10/99 did not fetter the discretion of the LEA appeal panel (*S v London Borough of Brent* [2002] EWCA Civ 693). Paragraph 17 stated that where a head teacher had excluded a pupil in accordance with published discipline policy then the appeal panel should not normally direct reinstatement. Paragraph 18 listed a number of circumstances of exclusion which the Secretary of State regarded as inappropriate for reinstatement. It was held that the use of the word 'normally' made it clear to appeal panels that they always had an independent judgment to make.

n128: See also *R (C, A Child) v Sefton Metropolitan Borough Council Independent Appeals Panel* [2001] ELR 393 in which Scott Baker J expressed the view that the headteacher or panel were not obliged to carry out the equivalent of a state trial and were not required to hear oral evidence when determining a dispute of fact involving allegations of violence by one pupil against another.

C. The Law Under the European Convention

(1) Introduction

n140: See, generally, A W B Simpson, *Human Rights and the End of Empire:* **19.35** *Britain and the Genesis of the European Convention* (Oxford University Press, 2001), ch 15.

(2) **The right to education**

(a) *Introduction*

19.41A There is a potential overlap with other provisions of the Convention. For instance, breach of the right to education was argued in several recent cases involving gypsies who had set up homes in caravans in breach of planning laws. In resisting removal the applicants claimed both a breach of their right of respect for private life, home, discrimination as gypsies, right to peaceful enjoyment of their possessions, and also breach of their children's right to education; see *Coster v United Kingdom* (2001) 33 EHRR 479; *Lee v United Kingdom* (2001) 33 EHRR 677; *Smith v United Kingdom* (2001) 33 EHRR 712. The Court found no violation, none of the applicants managing to substantiate their claims.

(b) *The right of access to existing educational institutions*

19.44 In *Cyprus v Turkey* (2002) 11 BHRC 45 the Court found a violation of the right to education of children of Greek Cypriots living in North Cyprus. The Turkish authorities had abolished the Greek language secondary school facilities which had been present before the invasion. Since the right to education does not specify the language in which education must be conducted there was no breach of the primary right to education. However the Court held that the option available to the children to continue their secondary education at Turkish or English medium schools was unrealistic, for the children had already received their education to date in Greek. The actions of the Turkish authorities, therefore, constituted a denial of the substance of the right.

(c) *The right to an effective education*

19.45 In *Eren v Turkey* (Decision of 6 June 2002) a complaint that a decision to annul the applicant's exam results was held to be admissible under Article 2 of the First Protocol.

(3) **Right to educate children in accordance with parental convictions**

(a) *Introduction*

19.53 See, generally, C Evans, *Freedom of Religion Under the European Convention on Human Rights* (Oxford University Press, 2001), 88–96.

(c) *The extent of the obligation*

19.63 In *Alonso and Merino v Spain* (Decision of 25 May 2000) the second applicant complained about sex education lessons for the first applicant, her daughter. The Court held that the content of the school curriculum was in principle a question for the Contracting States to decide but that it was not permissible for states to use teaching to pursue an aim of indoctrination which could be considered incompatible with parents' religious and philosophical convictions. However, the lessons had been aimed at giving pupils objective information about human sexual behaviour and were not a source of indoctrination. In addition, there was a large network of private schools in Spain and it had not been suggested that there was any obstacle to the first applicant attending such an establishment. As the parents had opted for the public education system, the right to respect for their beliefs and ideas as guaranteed by Article 2 of Protocol 1 could not be interpreted so as to confer on them the right to demand different lessons for their daughter in line with their own convictions. As a result, the application was manifestly ill founded.

D. The Impact of the Human Rights Act

(1) Introduction

In *R (O) v St James Roman Catholic Primary School Appeal Panel* [2001] ELR 469 **19.71** it was held that there was no question of incompatibility with Convention rights where the Appeals Panel had dismissed an appeal against the denial of a place on the grounds that the statutory class size limit of 30 would have been exceeded had the pupil been admitted and that it would have prejudiced efficient education or the efficient use of resources.

(3) The impact

(a) Introduction

In *R (Holub) v Secretary of State for the Home Department* [2001] 1 WLR 1359, **19.84** para 25, the Court of Appeal held that the right to education was accurately stated in the following terms:

> The general right to education comprises four separate rights (none of which are absolute):
>   (i)   right to access to such educational establishments as exist;
>   (ii)   right to effective (but not the most effective possible);
>   (iii)   a right to official recognition of academic qualifications . . .
> As regards the right to an effective education, for the right to education to be meaningful the quality of the education must reach a minimum standard.

(b) Education

Access to Education. The refusal by a local authority to provide a grant for a **19.85** full-time vocational dance course to a schoolboy was held not to be a breach of Article 2 of the First Protocol because consideration had to be given to what would be unreasonable public expenditure and there was no duty to provide funding for this kind of education. The local authority was entitled to take into account various considerations in rejecting the application, including that the applicant had not exhausted all avenues of alternative funding and had not demonstrated that he could not achieve his desired aim in an ordinary school (*R v Birmingham City Council, ex p Youngson* [2001] LGR 218).

There is considerable doubt whether Article 2 of the First Protocol entitles an individual to access to a university (*R (Mitchell) v Coventry University* [2001] ELR 594).

19.86   **Discipline and expulsion.**   A broad assertion that exclusions and admission panels are not independent and therefore breach Article 2 of the First Protocol (and/or Article 6) in that the governing body or local education authority appoints and trains the panel members was rejected in *R v Head Teacher of Alperton Community School and Others, ex p B and Others* [2001] ELR 351. It was also confirmed that the combined effect of the Education Act 1996 and the Human Rights Act was not to create a civil right to receive an education suitable to one's needs as the state retains the right to regulate education.

A trade dispute which arose because teachers refused to teach an unruly child prompted a claim by the child under Article 2 of the First Protocol. Here, the child was taken from his usual class and educated by supply teachers in a different room. The Court of Appeal held that the child had no claim against the teachers or its union as he had not been denied an education and, further, the educational needs of the other children were best supported by his removal to another room (*P v National Association of Schoolmasters/Union of Women Teachers* [2001] IRLR 532).

19.87   **Respect for parental convictions.**   Since the coming into force of the Human Rights Act 1998 the religious conviction of a parent is something to which due weight must be given in considering admission to a particular school. In *R (K) v Newham London Borough Council* [2002] EWHC Admin 405 Collins J quashed the decision of the Independent Appeals Panel to refuse admission to the daughter of the claimant, a devout Muslim, to the single-sex school which he had indicated to be his preference. The relevant form did not enable the parent to indicate the reason for their preference; and when a single-sex school was listed as first preference it did not follow that the parent has chosen it because it was a single-sex school. The policy fell down on the failure to identify whether the preference for the single-sex school was based on the fact that it was single-sex as opposed to any other consideration. Collins J stated that respect for parental convictions required some positive action on the part of the state, following *Valsamis v Greece* (1996) 24 EHRR 294, and in the context of an admission decision due weight must be given to such conviction.

A belief that corporal punishment should be imposed could not properly be described as a philosophical or religious conviction (*R (Williamson) v Secretary of State for Education and Employment* [2003] 1 All ER 385). In that case Christian parents argued that they were entitled to send their children to schools which administer corporal punishment as an exercise of their human rights, and that therefore section 548 of the Education Act 1996, as amended by section 131 of the School Standards and Framework Act 1998, should not be construed as completely abolishing the use of corporal punishment in independent schools. The Court of Appeal held that belief in the desirability of corporal punishment, although in accordance with the relevant religious faith, did not embody or define the belief or conviction, and was therefore not a religious conviction in its own right.

The Special Educational Needs Tribunal had no duty to assume parental preferences on any grounds other than those specifically put forward by the parents which were live at the hearing (*S v London Borough of Hackney and Special Educational Needs Tribunal* [2001] EWHC Admin 572). Thus where the preference for a Catholic school was indicated in the grounds of appeal but was never raised as an issue, the tribunal could not be criticised for not having taken it into account.

Special educational needs.   See, generally, J Black-Branch, 'Equality, Non-discrimination and the Right to Special Education: From International Law to the Human Rights Act' [2000] EHRLR 297.   **19.92**

(d) Immigration

An issue which has arisen in cases concerned with the deportation of asylum seekers is the impact of the removal of a child from his education in the United Kingdom. The Court of Appeal has held that ECHR case law establishes that the right to an education is not absolute and so must be balanced against the interest in maintaining a fair immigration policy. The question was whether the Secretary of State's decision was proportionate. A child's right to an education whilst in the United Kingdom did not carry with it by its nature the right to remain. In exercising his discretion when dealing with an application for asylum, and in making a decision to deport, the Secretary of State did have to take into account any educational difficulties caused by the removal (here, back to Poland) as part of the need to determine if there are any compassionate grounds for granting exceptional leave to remain. But he did not have to consider whether the education in the country of origin would be a breach there of Article 2 of the First Protocol. The right to an education meant a right to an effective education of a minimum standard—it is not enough to say that the child would receive a better education in the UK (*R (Holub) v Secretary of State for the Home Department* [2001] 1 WLR 1359).   **19.94A**

Appendix 1: The Canadian Charter of Rights

In *Arsenault-Cameron v Prince Edward Island* (2000) 9 BHRC 90 the Supreme Court held that section 23 had to be interpreted purposively in a manner consistent   **19.97** with the development of official-language communities in Canada. A Minister's decision that a minority language would not be provided in a locally accessible school, but instead in a less accessible school, was quashed. Minority-language parents and their representatives were in the best position to identify local needs. The Minister had failed to give proper weight to the promotion and preservation of minority-language culture.

Appendix 2: Human Rights Cases in Other Jurisdictions

(3) Ireland

19.110   In *Sinnott v Minister for Education* [2001] 2 IR 505 a majority of the Irish Supreme Court held that the state's constitutional obligation to provide free primary education did not oblige the state to provide education to an educationally subnormal person once that person had reached 18 years of age.

(4) South Africa

19.112   In *Christian Education South Africa v Minister of Education* (2001) 9 BHRC 53 the South African Constitutional Court was faced with the problem of whether, in enacting a law prohibiting corporal punishment in schools, Parliament had violated the rights of parents of children in independent schools who, in line with their Christian religious convictions, had consented to its use. The court held that the limitation of rights was reasonable and justified in relation to the purpose, importance and effect of the provision which resulted in the limitation.

20

ELECTORAL RIGHTS

B. The Rights in English Law

(1) Introduction

The Political Parties, Elections and Referendums Act 2000 establishes an **20.04A** Electoral Commission whose function it will be, after each election (whether in UK or Europe) or referendum, to prepare and publish a report on the administration of the election or referendum. The Commission is also empowered to report to the Secretary of State on an interim basis on the registration of political parties and the regulation of their income and expenditure; political advertising; the redistribution of seats at parliamentary elections; and other such matters relating to elections and referendums as the Commission decides. It has to be consulted on changes to electoral law and procedure. Part II of the Act sets out rules for the registration of political parties, which is necessary before a party is able to field a particular candidate in an election. Part IV of the Act contains rules restricting donations to and sponsorship of registered political parties. Part V deals with the control of campaign expenditure.

(2) Voter qualifications

20.05 The statutory provisions relating to the entitlement to vote are now contained in section 1(1) of the Representation of the People Act 2000. For a general discussion of the Act, see H Lardy, 'Democracy by Default: The Representation of the People Act 2000' (2001) 64 MLR 63.

n12: The requirement for a three-month period of residence for registration in the register of parliamentary electors for Northern Ireland is now contained in section 4(2) of the Representation of the People Act 2000.

n13: The provisions of the Representation of the People Act 1985 have been amended by the Representation of People Act 2000.

(3) Candidate qualifications

20.09 The registration of political parties is now provided for by Part II of the Political Parties, Elections and Referendums Act 2000. For a general discussion of the history and effect of the statutory provisions for the registration of political parties, see O Gay, 'What's In a Name? Political Parties, Lists and Candidates in the United Kingdom' [2001] PL 245.

n36: Now section 28(4) of the Political Parties, Elections and Referendums Act 2000, section 29(2) of which applies the same rules to the registration of an emblem representing the political party.

n37: Now section 37 of the Political Parties, Elections and Referendums Act 2000.

(4) Electoral boundaries

20.11 Under Part I of the Political Parties, Elections and Referendums Act 2000, the old Boundary Commissions are to be replaced by four Boundary Committees (for England, Scotland, Northern Ireland and Wales) under the control of the Commission. There is also provision for the transfer of Local Government Boundary Committee functions to the New Boundary Committees or the Commission.

(5) Election campaigns and publicity

20.13 The current provisions relating to campaign finance are to be found in the Political Parties, Elections and Referendums Act 2000.

20.14 The Political Parties, Elections and Referendums Act 2000 lays down strict rules relating to donations to and sponsorship of both registered parties (Part IV, Chapters I and II) and to and of individuals (Chapter V and Schedule 7). In essence a donation cannot be accepted unless it has come from a permissible donor and cannot be accepted if the donee is unable to ascertain the identity of the donor. A permissible donor is defined in section 54 as being:

- an individual registered to vote;
- a company which carried on business in the UK, is registered under the Companies Act 1985 or Companies (Northern Ireland) Order 1986, and is incorporated within the UK or other Member State;
- a trade union in the list kept under the Trade Union and Labour Relations (Consolidation) Act 1992 or the Industrial Relations (Northern Ireland) Order 1992;
- a registered political party;
- a building society;
- a friendly society registered under the Friendly Societies Act 1974;
- a limited liability partnership; or
- an unincorporated association.

n47: See now section 37 of the Political Parties, Elections and Referendums Act 2000.   **20.15**

C. The Law Under the European Convention

(2) The nature of a 'legislature'

Elections to a municipal council (see *Cherepkov v Russia*, Decision of 25 January 2000, and *Salleras Llinares v Spain*, Decision of 12 October 2000); or a regional council (*Malarde v France*, Decision of 5 September 2000) are not within Article 3 of the First Protocol.   **20.22**

(3) The content of the right

(d) *Voter and candidate qualifications*

The case of *Podkolzina v Latvia* (Judgment of 9 April 2002) concerned a complaint by the applicant that he had been removed from a list of candidates because of insufficient competence in the Latvian language. The obligation in domestic law for candidates to the national parliament to have an adequate command of the official language pursued a legitimate aim. However, decisions concerning the compliance by individual candidates with eligibility conditions had to avoid arbitrariness and, in particular, had to be taken by a body offering a minimum number of guarantees of impartiality. In the absence of any objective guarantees, the procedure followed in the applicant's case was incompatible with the Convention's procedural requirements of fairness and legal certainty. As a result,   **20.29** the decision to remove the applicant from the candidate list could not be deemed proportionate to the legitimate aim pursued and there was a violation of Article 3 of the First Protocol.

(e) Election expenses and contributions

20.31   In *Antonopolous v Greece* (Decision of 29 March 2001) the Court considered a complaint by a Greek political party which complained, *inter alia*, that it had only been allocated five minutes of broadcast time, in contrast to the 20 minutes allocated to parties which had obtained at least 0.5 per cent of the vote at the previous European Parliamentary election. The Court held that this difference was not unjustified, disproportionate or discriminatory and held that the complaint was inadmissible.

(f) Rights of elected representatives

20.31A   Article 3 guarantees the right of every individual to stand for election and, once elected, to exercise his or her mandate. The removal of the parliamentary rights of elected members of a political party when that party was dissolved by court order was a breach of Article 3 (*Selim Sadak v Turkey*, Judgment of 11 June 2002).

D.   The Impact of the Human Rights Act

(3)   Impact of the Human Rights Act on electoral law

(b) Voter and candidate qualifications

20.40   In *R (Pearson and Martinez) v Secretary of State for the Home Department* [2001] HRLR 31 the applicants argued that the provision under section 3 of the Representation of People Act 1983 which prevented them, as prison inmates serving discretionary life sentences, from voting, was a breach of Article 3 of the First Protocol. The applicants contended that their position could be distinguished from that of mandatory lifers. The Administrative Court held that this denial was legitimate and proportionate as being part of forfeiture as punishment. Article 14 was also deployed but Kennedy LJ expressed the view that it added nothing more to Article 3. The decision appears to accord with the state's ability to restrict the right, where appropriate. It appears that the same argument would apply to the provisions dealing with those detained under the Mental Health Act 1983, the new section 3A of which (inserted by the Representation of People Act 2000) disenfranchises those detained in mental homes who are offenders. One of the applicants, Mr Hirst, has made an application to Strasbourg which has been communicated to the UK government.

The refusal by an electoral registration officer to accede to an individual's request that his name and address on the electoral register should not be supplied to commercial organisations was held to be unlawful in *R (Robertson) v Wakefield Metropolitan Council and Secretary of State for the Home Department* [2002] 2 WLR 889. One of the reasons for the decision was that it constituted an unjustifiable restriction on the claimant's right to vote. Although the imposition of conditions on the right to vote could be lawful if made in pursuit of a legitimate aim and not disproportionate, and states had a wide margin of appreciation (following *Mathieu-Mohin and Clerfayt v Belgium* (1987) 10 EHRR 1), the absence of an individual right of objection rendered the interference disproportionate.

Appendix 1: The Canadian Charter of Rights

(5) Political parties

It has been held that the provisions of the Canada Elections Act RSC 1985 which provided for the payment of deposits are consistent with section 3 of the Charter. However, it has also been held that a provision that 50 per cent of the deposit was forfeit unless the candidate received 15 per cent of the votes cast infringed section 3 and could not be justified under section 1 (see *Figueroa v A-G of Canada* (1999) 170 DLR (4th) 647). **20.57A**

The 50-candidate threshold for the registration of a political party did not infringe the right of a candidate of a non-registered party to run for election (*Figueroa v A-G of Canada* (2000) 189 DLR (4th) 577, Ontario CA). However, the prohibition against identification of party affiliation on the ballot of candidates from non-registered parties did infringe the right to vote. **20.57B**

Appendix 3: Human Rights Cases in Other Jurisdictions

(1) Introduction

The Supreme Court has struck down laws restricting the number of terms which can be served by members of Congress (*US Terms Limits Inc v Thornton* (1995) 514 US 779) and requiring ballots to indicate if a candidate had opposed such 'term limit' measures (*Cook v Gralike*, 28 February 2001). **20.66**

In what was perhaps the most famous constitutional case of the past year, a bare majority of the Supreme Court overturned a decision of the Supreme Court of Florida ordering recounts in the US Presidential election (*Bush v Gore*, 12 December 2000). It was held that the manual recounts violated the Equal Protection clause. In a powerful dissent, Stevens J suggested that the majority had brought the Supreme Court into disrepute.

(3) Hong Kong

20.73A Electoral arrangements restricting the right to stand for village office, or to vote for such candidates, to indigenous villagers were held to be contrary to the right to take part in the conduct of public affairs (*Chan Wah v Hong Hav Rural Community* [2000] 1 HKLRD 411; *Secretary for Justice v Chan Wah* [2000] 3 HKLRD 641).

(4) Ireland

20.75 In *Breathnach v Government of Ireland* [2000] IEHC 53 it was pointed out that in the absence of any 'disqualifying legislation' all citizens, including those serving prison sentences have a constitutional right to vote. The Government's argument that it was entitled to restrict the exercise of that right by reason of a person's detention in lawful custody was rejected.

20.78A In *Redmond v Minister for the Environment* [2001] IEHC 128 the High Court declared unconstitutional the need for a deposit before a candidate could stand for election. Herbert J's reasoning was as follows:

> 89. I am satisfied, having considered the evidence, and the submissions of Counsel, that the deposits systems . . . are not equal or fair in the manner in which they discriminate between the Plaintiff and other citizens of the State as regards electability to membership of Dáil Eireann and the European Parliament. In my judgment none of the matters advanced by the Defendants as stated to be necessary to prevent abuse of the electoral system are sufficient to justify such discrimination and unfairness.
>
> 90. What might be categorised as a type of 'floodgates' argument, that is, that but for these deposit provisions an excessively large number of citizens would stand for election for membership of Dáil Eireann and the European Parliament and thereby overwhelm the system of election, and in the case of Dáil Eireann elections undermine the democratic nature of the State, is not supported by any evidence other than the opinion of [an expert witness] that this is so.
>
> 91. There was evidence that persons genuinely interested in becoming members of Dáil Eireannn and who, one assumes, had sufficient means themselves or had access to monetary assistance were not deterred by these deposit provisions or by their predecessors and despite the loss of their deposits, often on several occasions, persisted until they had achieved such membership. . . . In my judgment, no connection has been established between the existence of these deposit requirements and the numbers of citizens who have stood for election to Dáil Eireann or the European Parliament over the past 64 years.
>
> 92. It is altogether improbable that the percentage of poor adult citizens likely to offer themselves for election to these Institutions would be any greater than has been the case with respect to their more fortunate fellow citizens in the same period. In my judgment all the arguments which postulate the emergence, but for these deposit requirements, of 'excessively large' numbers of candidates or suggest that but for these requirements there would be, 'major' increases in the numbers of adult citizens wishing to stand for election to Dáil Eireann or the European Parliament appear to be based upon surmise and no evidential link has been shown to exist

between the number of persons in fact standing for election and these requirements. 93. Likewise, I find no evidence to support the proposition that individual voters would be confused or confounded by an increase in the number of candidates on a ballot paper. It was accepted by the Defendants that Irish voters have shown a high degree of sophistication in making political decisions within what some political theorists consider to be a very complex system of voting. I see no reason why I should accept that such an electorate would suddenly become bereft of this capacity of discernment in the face of a larger choice of candidates on a ballot paper. In the absence of some compelling evidence I simply could not accept such an argument.

(7) Zimbabwe

In *Movement for Democratic Change v Chinamasa* [2001] 3 LRC 673 a number of **20.85** unsuccessful election candidates challenged the results of the 2000 Zimbabwe election. After those applications were made, the President issued a Notice under electoral legislation, declaring that any inconsistencies during the elections were deemed not to be in breach of electoral legislation, and therefore valid. The Notice was challenged by the main opposition party, and one of its members, who was an unsuccessful election candidate. The grounds of challenge were that the Notice contravened the constitutional rights to equal protection, and the right to be afforded a hearing within a reasonable time by an independent and impartial court. The Supreme Court of Zimbabwe declared the Notice null and void, holding that the right of full and unimpeded access to the courts is of cardinal importance for the adjudication of justiciable disputes.

21

REMEDIES UNDER THE HUMAN RIGHTS ACT

A. Introduction: Section 8 of the Human Rights Act

(1) The provisions of section 8

21.02 In *Brown v Stott* [2001] 1 WLR 817, 847 Lord Hope suggested that the decision to omit Article 13 (the right to an effective remedy) as one of the Convention rights enacted under section 1 of the Human Rights Act 1998 is that sections 7 to 9 of the Act are intended to lay down an appropriate remedial structure for giving effect to Convention rights. However, recent decisions in the context of section 3 of the Act generate uncertainty in the Act's remedial scope. In the case of *In re S (Care Order: Implementation of Care Plan)* [2002] 2 WLR 720 the House of Lords drew a distinction between a statutory provision that is incompatible with the Convention, and a statute which contains a lacuna so that the legislation fails to provide a mechanism for preventing or remedying breaches of the Convention. The former plainly prevents the court from doing anything other than granting a declaration of incompatibility under section 4: sections 7 to 9 do not bite because section 6(2) saves the relevant act of a public authority from unlawfulness. The latter cannot be the subject of a declaration of incompatibility (*R (H) v Mental Health Review Tribunal* [2002] EWHC Admin 1522), but its implications for sections 7 to 9 are less clear. The Lords in *In re S* rejected an attempt by the Court of Appeal at [2001] 2 FLR 582 to create compatibility by 'reading in' a certain role for the court (see, further, Supplement, para 21.154) on the ground that Parliament had excluded such a role, if not expressly then by necessary implication. This meant that the Court of Appeal had crossed the boundary between interpreting and making legislation. It might, however, be argued that *In re S* does not preclude the possibility of a legislative lacuna essentially as to *remedies* not engaging section 6(2), and therefore remaining capable of being filled—at least partially—by the careful use of powers under section 8(1) without offending the evident or implicit will of Parliament. This area of uncertainty might have been avoided had Article 13 been included among the rights enacted by the Human Rights Act.

21.03 The wide discretion the court exercises under section 8 was illustrated by *A-G's Reference (No 2 of 2001)* [2001] 1 WLR 1869 where the Court of Appeal rejected the argument that a breach of the obligation to determine a charge within a reasonable time under Article 6(1) required the court as a public authority to stay the proceedings. The case is discussed further at Supplement, para 21.119.

(2) The scope of the power to grant a remedy

21.07 The power to grant 'appropriate relief' under section 38 of the Constitution Act 1996 was extensively analysed by the Constitutional Court in *Hoffmann v South African Airways* [2001] 2 LRC 277. It was held at paragraphs 42 to 45 that 'appropriate relief' must be construed purposively and must be fair and just in the circumstances of the particular case. Fairness requires consideration of the interests of all those who might be affected by the order so, for example, in the context of employment, this will require consideration not only of the interests of the prospective employee but also the interests of the employer. The balancing process must be guided by the objective:

- to address the wrong occasioned by the infringement of the constitutional right;
- to deter future violations;
- to make an order that can be complied with; and
- of fairness to all those who might be affected by the relief.

Invariably, the nature of the right infringed and the nature of the infringement will provide guidance as to the appropriate relief in a particular case. Therefore, in determining appropriate relief, it is important to analyse the nature of the constitutional infringement and strike effectively at its source. Ngcobo J went on to find that the infringement in issue was the refusal to employ the applicant solely because he was HIV-positive; and concluded that reinstatement was the appropriate remedy.

B. Damages Under the Human Rights Act

(2) The nature of damages under the Human Rights Act

(b) Public law remedy

The principles in *Simpson v A-G* were considered in two recent New Zealand **21.16** cases. In *Manga v A-G* [2000] 2 NZLR 65 the plaintiff was a serving prisoner who was held in prison longer than he should have been and was entitled to damages for false imprisonment and compensation for arbitrary detention in breach of section 22 of the New Zealand Bill of Rights Act 1990. Hammond J dealt (at 81) with the differences between the two remedies in what has been described as a 'comprehensive judgment' (see *Dunlea v A-G* [2000] 3 NZLR 136, 156, *per* Thomas J, dissenting):

> Cases based upon violations of the Bill of Rights are about vindication of statutory policies which are not 'just' private: they have overarching public dimensions.

Hammond J went on to hold that in the circumstances there was nothing outside the compensatory damages in tort for which an award of compensation under the Bill of Rights Act would be appropriate. However, it was appropriate for the court to make a declaration that the plaintiff was wrongfully imprisoned in breach of his rights under section 22.

A slightly different approach was taken by the majority of the Court of Appeal in *Dunlea v A-G* [2000] 3 NZLR 136. In that case damages were claimed for unreasonable searches under the New Zealand Bill of Rights Act 1990, in addition to compensation for the torts of assault, false imprisonment and trespass to the person and property. The Court of Appeal expressly declined to treat the case as the opportunity to resolve the question of whether a different approach should be adopted towards fixing compensation under the New Zealand Bill of Rights Act 1990 compared to fixing damages for tort arising out of essentially the same facts. Nevertheless, the view was expressed *obiter* that there were strong reasons for not adopting a different approach for three reasons:

• in most cases the plaintiff also had a right to damages in tort;
• an extensive survey conducted by the Law Commission into damages for breach of human rights in the United States, Canada, Ireland, the Caribbean, India, Sri Lanka, the European Union and under the European Convention had concluded that the number of cases where damages is awarded is not high and that the courts draw on tortious principles when calculating damages; and
• the tortious award of damages requires an assessment to be made of the right infringed, both generally and to the individual.

See also *Small v A-G* (2000) 6 HRNZ 218 (compensatory damages of NZ$20,000 (about £6,000) for unreasonable search in breach of section 21 of the New Zealand Bill of Rights Act 1990).

In *Peters v Marksman* [2001] 1 LRC 1 the High Court of St Vincent and the Grenadines awarded damages, including exemplary damages, for degrading and inhuman treatment of a prisoner. After a review of the authorities on damages for breach of constitutional rights, damages of $225,000 (about £52,000) were awarded.

(d) The position under the Human Rights Act

21.21 The Law Commission in its report, *Damages under the Human Rights Act 1998* (Law Com no 266), paras 4.21–4.26, expresses the view that damages for tort are the most obvious analogy to damages under section 8 of the Human Rights Act and suggests that the courts might find it appropriate to treat the rules in tort as the *prima facie* measure to be applied unless the results are inconsistent with Strasbourg case law.

The Commission goes on to point out a number of differences between Convention and tortious principles:

• the Court of Human Rights has never awarded punitive damages;
• the Court of Human Rights awards damages for pure economic loss irrespective of whether the state has acted intentionally or negligently; and

- the Court of Human Rights regularly awards damages to compensate parents whose right of respect for family life has been infringed when state action has led them to lose contact with their children.

However, the Commission suggests that even when Strasbourg jurisprudence provides no answer to the question before the court, care must be taken. For example, under domestic law the remoteness rule varies between intentional and non-intentional torts. Under the Human Rights Act the measure most likely to achieve just satisfaction must be selected.

Damages have been awarded in only two cases under the Human Rights Act. The **21.24** case of *Marcic v Thames Water Utilities Ltd (No 2)* [2001] 4 All ER 326, TCC, provides a tentative example of quantification of section 8 damages by reference to analogous tort principles. H H J Havery had earlier decided at [2001] 3 All ER 698 that the failure of the defendant to carry out works to bring to an end repeated flooding at the claimant's home was a breach of Article 8(1), as well as an interference with peaceful enjoyment of possessions under Article 1 of the First Protocol, which the defendant had failed to justify. He had considered himself bound by authority to dismiss an alternative claim in private nuisance. The judge refused a mandatory injunction compelling the defendant to carry out the works. But by analogy with the principles governing remedies for private nuisance, the judge ruled that damages under section 8 should include an award, in lieu of an injunction, in respect of future losses. He rejected the defendant's contention that an award of damages for future wrongs is contrary to Strasbourg jurisprudence. It is submitted that the judge's approach is consistent with the willingness of the European Court (reflected in its Article 41 judgments in *Smith and Grady (No 2) v United Kingdom* (2001) 31 EHRR 24 and *Lustig-Prean and Beckett (No 2) v United Kingdom* (2001) 31 EHRR 23) to award compensation for the post-judgment consequences of a violation of a Convention right. The effect of the judge's decision was short-lived, however, because the Court of Appeal at [2002] QB 929 subsequently held Thames liable at common law, the resulting award of tort damages displacing any requirement for just satisfaction. The liability issues are currently pending in the House of Lords. The result is that authoritative guidance on the relationship between section 8 damages and tort principles is still awaited.

In *R (Bernard) v London Borough of Enfield, The Times*, 11 November 2002, damages were award under section 8 where the claimants, a severely disabled woman, C, and her husband–carer, B, had been left in unsuitable accommodation for 20 months in breach of their rights under Article 8. Sullivan J took the view that awards should be comparable to tortious awards and there was no justification for a reduction that would reduce awards below the level of tortious damages. The award set should not be minimal because that would diminish respect for the policy underlying the 1998 Act. The local government ombudsman's recommended awards were the best available comparison because this case was, in essence, a case of maladministration. The appropriate award was £10,000 to be divided as £8,000 to C and £2,000 to B.

(3) Jurisdiction to award damages under the Act

21.25 CPR 33.9 deals with claims for damages founded on findings of another court or tribunal. For the matters a claimant is required to include in a statement of case in relation to such a claim, see the Practice Direction to CPR Part 16, para 16.1(2)(e).

n.62: See now CPR 54.3(2).

(4) Damages for judicial acts

21.26 The impact of the Human Rights Act on damages for judicial acts is considered in detail in Appendix A to the Law Commission's report, *Damages Under the Human Rights Act 1998* (Law Com no 266).

21.28 The courts have signalled an unwillingness to allow claimants to circumvent the restrictions in section 9(3) and (4) by pursuing alternative claims for compensation against non-judicial office holders where the claim relates in substance to judicial conduct. In *Director-General of Fair Trading v Proprietary Association of Great Britain and Another* [2002] 1 WLR 269 the Court of Appeal rejected an attempt to recover from the Lord Chancellor the costs thrown away following that court's judgment in *In re Medicaments and Related Classes of Goods (No 2)* [2001] 1 WLR 700. Complex proceedings in the Restrictive Practices Court had to be rerun at considerable expense, the original hearing having been infected by a breach of the independence and impartiality requirement of Article 6(1).

(5) 'Just satisfaction' under the Convention

(b) The Convention principles

21.34 **Compensation is discretionary.**   In *Brumarescu v Romania* (2001) 33 EHRR 36 a Grand Chamber ordered a *restitutionary* remedy instead of damages. The applicant's complaint arose out of the nationalisation of his parents' home. The Court had earlier found that Article 6 had been breached; and that there had been no justification for the deprivation of property under Article 1 of the First Protocol. The Grand Chamber took the view that in the circumstances of the case the return of the property would put the applicant so far as possible in the situation equivalent to the one he would have been if there had been no breach of Article 1. It stated at para 20:

> The Contracting States that are parties to a case are in principle free to choose the means whereby they will comply with a judgment in which the Court has found a

breach. This discretion as to the manner of the execution of a judgment reflects the freedom of choice attaching to the primary obligation of the Contracting State under the Convention to secure the rights and freedoms guaranteed (Article 1). If the nature of the breach allows *restitutio in integrum*, it is for the respondent state to effect it. If, on the other hand, national law does not allow—or allows only partial—reparation to be made for the consequences of the breach, Article 41 empowers the Court to afford the injured party such satisfaction as appears to it to be appropriate . . .

In *Damages Under the Human Rights Act 1998* (Law Com no 266), paras 3.31–3.57, the Law Commission identifies a number of factors which are relevant to the discretion the Court exercises when making an award of damages:

- the other measures taken by the public authority in remedying the breach (for example, where there are breaches of Article 6, the grant of a retrial which complies with Article 6);
- a finding of a breach is sufficient just satisfaction without the need to pay any compensation;
- whether the loss suffered by the applicant is sufficient to render an award of compensation necessary;
- the seriousness of the Convention violation;
- the conduct of the respondent (for example, whether its conduct is offensive or whether it has a record of previous violations); and
- the conduct of the applicant.

There must be a 'causal link' between compensation and breach.   The Law Commission in *Damages Under the Human Rights Act 1998* (Law Com no 266), paras 3.58–3.69, argues that the Court takes two different approaches to causation which are impossible to reconcile. In some cases it applies a strict causation test which bars the claims for damages, particularly for financial loss. In other cases, however, it is willing to speculate upon hypothetical events and make substantial awards.   **21.38**

(c) 'Just satisfaction' in practice

Compensation for financial loss.   In *Z v United Kingdom* (2002) 34 EHRR 3, paras 119–27, the Court adopted a more rigorous approach in assessing financial loss which may be of particular assistance for cases under the Human Rights Act. See similarly, the Article 41 judgments in *Smith and Grady (No 2) v United Kingdom* (2001) 31 EHRR 24 and *Lustig-Prean and Beckett (No 2) v United Kingdom* (2001) 31 EHRR 23, in which the Court carefully assessed loss of future employment benefits by reference to the chances of each applicant having gone on to earn certain remuneration and pension entitlement had he or she not been discharged from the armed services pursuant to a policy which infringed Article 8(1). The Court in effect assimilated its approach to that taken in   **21.39**

Community law where breach of Treaty or Directive provisions on equal treatment brings about a loss of employment (for example, *Ministry of Defence v Cannock* [1994] ICR 918).

In Part VI of *Damages Under the Human Rights Act 1998* (Law Com no 266), the Law Commission undertakes an article-by-article analysis of Court awards of just satisfaction.

n99: For an updated table of the 'Court's Findings of Pecuniary Loss', see J Simor and B Emmerson, *Human Rights Practice* (Sweet & Maxwell, 2000), Appendix A9.

21.41 **Compensation for non-financial loss.** In Part VI of *Damages Under the Human Rights Act 1998* (Law Com no 266), the Law Commission undertakes an article-by-article analysis of Court awards of just satisfaction.

n127: The awards in *Smith and Grady (No 2) v United Kingdom* (2001) 31 EHRR 24 and *Lustig-Prean and Beckett (No 2) v United Kingdom* (2001) 31 EHRR 23 included sums of £19,000 per applicant for injury to feelings. The Court's finding of a violation of Article 8(1) at (1999) 7 BHRC 65 was based on the discriminatory singling out of homosexual members of the armed services for intrusive investigative activity and, ultimately, dismissal.

21.46 **The right to life under Article 2.** For an analysis of relevant cases, see *Damages Under the Human Rights Act 1998* (Law Com no 266), paras 6.3–6.13.

21.47 **Inhuman treatment in breach of Article 3.** For an analysis of relevant cases, see *Damages Under the Human Rights Act 1998* (Law Com no 266), paras 6.15–6.25.

21.48 **Unlawful arrest or detention under Article 5.** For an analysis of relevant cases, see *Damages Under the Human Rights Act 1998* (Law Com no 266), paras 6.26–6.80.

21.49 **Breach of fair trial rights under Article 6.** For an analysis of relevant cases, see *Damages Under the Human Rights Act 1998* (Law Com no 266), paras 6.81–6.146.

21.52 **The right of respect for private and family life, the home and correspondence under Article 8.** For an analysis of relevant cases, see *Damages Under the Human Rights Act 1998* (Law Com no 266), paras 6.152–6.189.

Substantial awards for pecuniary and non-pecuniary loss were made in *Smith and Grady (No 2) v United Kingdom* (2001) 31 EHRR 24 and *Lustig-Prean and Beckett (No 2) v United Kingdom* (2001) 31 EHRR 23 (Article 41 judgments), following the Court's finding at (2001) 31 EHRR 24 that the right to respect for private life had been breached by the Government's policy of discharging homosexual personnel from the armed services.

In *Hatton and Others v United Kingdom* (2002) 34 EHRR 1 the Court made (of **21.54** its own motion) awards for non-pecuniary environmental harm falling significantly short of the rather extreme circumstances of *López Ostra*. Each applicant was awarded £4,000 to compensate for disruption of sleep resulting from the Government's approval of night flights at Heathrow Airport. Those sums are broadly comparable with the present value of the awards in *Guerra v Italy*, cited in the Main Work (equivalent to about £3,500 in 1998). (A review of the Chamber finding of a violation of Article 8(1) in *Hatton* is currently pending before the Grand Chamber.)

Freedom of religion under Article 9.   For an analysis of relevant cases, see   **21.55** *Damages Under the Human Rights Act 1998* (Law Com no 266), paras 6.190–6.192.

Freedom of expression under Article 10.   For an analysis of relevant cases, see   **21.56** *Damages Under the Human Rights Act 1998* (Law Com no 266), paras 6.193–6.203.

Freedom of assembly and association under Article 11.   For an analysis of relevant   **21.56A** cases, see *Damages Under the Human Rights Act 1998* (Law Com no 266), paras 6.204–6.210. In *Wilson v United Kingdom* (2002) 35 EHRR 20 the Court made awards of €7,730 (£4,800) for non-pecuniary loss suffered by each individual applicant following a successful complaint that UK law infringed Article 11 by permitting an employer to penalise trade union members by remunerating them less favourably than those employees who agreed to relinquish union membership and bargaining rights. The Court declined to award pecuniary loss.

The prohibition against discrimination under Article 14.   For an analysis of   **21.57** relevant cases, see *Damages Under the Human Rights Act 1998* (Law Com no 266), paras 6.213–6.222.

The right to quiet enjoyment of property under Article 1 of the First Protocol.   **21.58** For an analysis of relevant cases, see *Damages Under the Human Rights Act 1998* (Law Com no 266), paras 6.223–6.235. See also *Brumarescu v Romania* (Judgment of 23 January 2001) where the Court made a restitutionary order requiring the state to return property it had nationalised without justification. The case is discussed further at Supplement, para 21.34. In *Gaganus v Turkey* (Judgment of 5 June 2001) the Court awarded US$5,392 for pecuniary loss and US$1,000 for non-pecuniary loss, the applicant having suffered delay and undercompensation (corrected only at a later stage of the domestic process) following compulsory acquisition of property.

The right to education under Article 2 of the First Protocol.   For an analysis of   **21.59** relevant cases, see *Damages Under the Human Rights Act 1998* (Law Com no 266), paras 6.236–6.238.

21.59A **The right to free elections under Article 3 of the First Protocol.** For an analysis of relevant cases, see *Damages Under the Human Rights Act 1998* (Law Com no 266), paras 6.239–6.240. For a recent example, see *Selim Sadak and Others v Turkey* (Judgment of 11 June 2002): awards of €50,000 (£30,500) each to Members of Parliament removed from office and banned from political activity following the dissolution of their party.

(6) Damages under the Human Rights Act

(a) Introduction

21.65 Lord Woolf has suggested extrajudicially (see 'The Human Rights Act and Remedies', in M Andenas and D Fairgrieve (eds), *Judicial Review in International Perspective: Liber Amicorum for Lord Slynn of Hadley Volume II* (Kluwer, 2000)) that eight possible principles should be applied when considering an award for damages:

- If there is any other remedy in addition to damages, the other remedy should usually be granted initially and damages should only be granted if necessary in addition.
- The court should not award exemplary or aggravated damages.
- An award should be 'of no greater sum than that necessary to achieve just satisfaction'. If it is necessary for a decision to be retaken, the court should wait and see what the outcome is.
- The amount of damages awarded should be 'moderate' and 'normally on the low side by comparison to tortious awards'.
- The award should be restricted to compensating the victim for what has happened 'so far as the unlawful conduct exceeds what could lawfully happen'.
- Failure by the claimant to take preventative or remedial action will reduce the amount of damages.
- There is no reason to distinguish between pecuniary and non-pecuniary loss. What matters is that the loss should be 'real [and] clearly caused by the conduct contrary to the Act'.
- Domestic rules as to costs will probably cover any costs or expense incurred by the complainant.

However, in *R (Bernard) v London Borough of Enfield*, *The Times*, 11 November 2002, para 59, Sullivan J held that there was no justification for reducing awards under the Human Rights Act below the level of tortious damages.

The award in *Marcic v Thames Water Utilities (No 2)* [2001] 4 All ER 326, TCC, included damages in lieu of an injunction, covering future harm resulting from the defendant's continued failure to carry out flood prevention works. The case is discussed at Supplement, para 21.24.

(b) Aggravated and exemplary damages and the Human Rights Act

The House of Lords in *Kuddus v Chief Constable of Leicestershire* [2001] 2 WLR **21.71**
1789 reversed the Court of Appeal's decision (see *The Times*, 16 March 2000)
which had applied the principles set out in *AB v South West Water Services* [1993]
QB 507. The House of Lords held that the power to award exemplary damages is
not limited to causes of action which were recognised before 1964 as justifying
such an award. There is therefore no longer a bar to a court awarding exemplary
damages under the Human Rights Act. Nevertheless, as is submitted at Main
Work, paras 21.71–21.74, exemplary damages will not be awarded under the Act.

n245: The House of Lords in *Kuddus v Chief Constable of Leicestershire* [2001] 2
WLR 1789 reversed the decision of the Court of Appeal.

In *Dunlea v A-G* [2000] 3 NZLR 136, 148 (Keith J) the New Zealand Court of **21.73**
Appeal left open the question as to whether exemplary damages could be awarded
under the New Zealand Bill of Rights Act 1990. See also Thomas J at 158 and
160, and *PF Sugrue Ltd v A-G* (2000) 6 HRNZ 235, and for awards of exemplary
damages in negligence cases in New Zealand, see *A v Bottrill*, 6 September 2002,
PC.

In *Basu v State of West Bengal* [1997] 2 LRC 1 the Supreme Court of India stated
that, in the assessment of compensation in cases of infringements of fundamental
rights, the emphasis has to be on the compensatory and not on the punitive element. See also *Charles v A-G* [2001] 2 LRC 169.

The decision in *AB v South West Water Services* [1993] QB 507 was reversed by the **21.74**
House of Lords in *Kuddus v Chief Constable of Leicestershire* [2001] 2 WLR 1789
which is discussed further at Supplement, para 21.71.

(7) Misfeasance in public office

(a) The nature of the tort

n257: The House of Lords in *Kuddus v Chief Constable of Leicestershire* [2001] 2 **21.75**
WLR 1789 reversed the decision of the Court of Appeal.

C. Remedies in Judicial Review Proceedings

(1) Introduction

On 2 October 2000 the rules for judicial review under CPR, Sch 1, R 53 were re- **21.84**
placed by CPR, Pt 54. CPR 54.1 defines a 'claim for judicial review' as 'a claim to
review the lawfulness of (i) an enactment; or (ii) a decision, action or failure to act
in relation to the exercise of a public function'. *Certiorari* is now known as a

'quashing order', *mandamus* as a 'mandatory order' and prohibition as a 'prohibiting order'.

A claim for judicial review is now made in the Administrative Court in accordance with the procedure set out in CPR, Part 54 and PD 54.

21.85   *Certiorari* is now known as a 'quashing order', *mandamus* as a 'mandatory order' and prohibition as a 'prohibiting order' and may be sought in judicial review proceedings under Pt 54.2.

   n282: CPR, Sch 1, R 53.1(1)(a) has been replaced by CPR 54.2.

21.86   **n284:** CPR, Sch 1, R 53.1(2) has been replaced by CPR 54.3(1).

   n285: CPR, Sch 1, R 53.7(1)(b) has been replaced by CPR 54.3(2). The new provision expressly reaffirms the rule that damages *alone* may not be claimed in judicial review proceedings.

(2) Interim orders

(b) Interim relief to restrain a breach of Convention rights

21.94   In *Napier v The Scottish Ministers* [2002] UKHRR 308 the Court of Session (Outer House) on a petition for judicial review granted interim relief requiring the transfer of a prisoner where the petition disclosed a *prima facie* case that the existing conditions of confinement infringed Article 3. The Court proceeded on the basis that: (i) each application should be decided on its merits, and to do so would not offend the desirability of treating all prisoners alike; and (ii) the balance of convenience favoured the grant of relief. In *William Sinclair Holdings Ltd v English Nature* [2001] EWHC Admin 408 the Administrative Court granted an interim injunction to a party considered to have a 'strongly arguable' case that the procedure for designation of part of its land as a Site of Special Scientific Interest infringed its rights under Article 6(1), where on the evidence the commercial harm the owner would have suffered if relief were refused outweighed the limited prejudice to English Nature flowing from grant of interim relief pending the substantive hearing.

(3) The nature of prerogative orders

21.95   *Certiorari* is now known as a 'quashing order' and *mandamus* is now known as a 'mandatory order'.

   n313: CPR, Sch 1, R 53.9(4) has been replaced by CPR 54.19(1)(b).

21.97   *Mandamus* is now known as a 'mandatory order'.

   In *Chavunduka v Commissioner of Police* [2001] 2 LRC 77 the Zimbabwe Supreme Court granted an order of *mandamus* requiring the Commissioner of

Police to institute and/or complete comprehensive and diligent investigations into allegations of the illegal detention and torture of two journalists.

In *R (Wright) v Secretary of State for the Home Department* [2002] HRLR 1 Jackson J made a mandatory order requiring the Home Secretary to set up an independent investigation into the circumstances of a prisoner's death in custody.

(4) Declarations and injunctions in judicial review proceedings

See now CPR 54.3(1) and section 31(2) of the Supreme Court Act 1981 (the text of which is substantially the same as the text of the former CPR, Sch 1, R 53.1(2), as reproduced in the Main Work).   **21.98A**

A declaration will be refused where its effect would be to outflank the policy un-   **21.98B**
derlying a statutory restriction on the grant of prerogative remedies against a court; see *R (Shields) v Crown Court at Liverpool and Lord Chancellor's Department* [2001] UKHRR 610. Section 29(3) of the Supreme Court Act 1981 precludes the grant of a quashing order in relation to the jurisdiction of the Crown Court in matters relating to trial on indictment, but does not in terms preclude the making of a declaration. However, the effect of section 29(3) is preserved by section 9(2) of the Human Rights Act and the Divisional Court declined to make a declaration about the fairness of pending criminal proceedings in lieu of a quashing order. See also *R (Regentford Ltd) v Crown Court at Canterbury* [2001] HRLR 18.

(5) Damages in judicial review proceedings

See now CPR 54.3(2), 54.6(1)(c) and paragraph 5.3 of the accompanying   **21.101**
Practice Direction.

Where judicial review proceedings include a claim for section 8 damages, the proper practice is to stand over the claim to a separate hearing after consideration of the substantive public law and Convention issues; see *R (B) v Mental Health Review Tribunal and Secretary of State for the Home Department* [2002] EWHC Admin 1553. That follows the practice in relation to claims for common law damages in judicial review proceedings.

(6) The discretionary nature of remedies in judicial review proceedings

In *R v Falmouth and Truro Port Health Authority, ex p South West Water* [2000] 3   **21.104**
WLR 1464 the Court of Appeal emphasised that where a claimant had a statutory right of appeal, permission for judicial review should only rarely be granted. It was necessary to examine all the relevant circumstances which would include the comparative speed, expense and finality of the alternative processes, the need and scope for fact finding, the desirability of an authoritative ruling on

any point of law arising and the apparent strength of the claimant's substantive challenge.

21.108   The relationship between refusal of permission on the ground of delay, and refusal of relief on that ground following the substantive hearing, has long been problematic. A practical solution was adopted by the Court of Appeal in *R v Lichfield District Council & Williams, ex p Lichfield Securities* [2001] EWCA Civ 304. Where delay has been considered at the permission stage, relief will not be refused on that ground at the substantive stage save in restricted circumstances. The principles governing the effect of alleged delay in bringing proceedings have in turn been expressly influenced by Convention considerations. In *R (Burkett) v London Borough of Hammersmith & Fulham* [2002] 1 WLR 1593 the House of Lords overturned the conventional understanding that a third-party challenge to the grant of planning permission is brought 'promptly' (cf CPR 54.5(1)(a)) only if lodged within six weeks of the local planning authority's resolution. The House questioned whether the ill-defined concept of 'promptness' is itself compatible with Convention principles. Lord Steyn (at paras 49, 53) held: 'The lack of certainty is a recipe for sterile procedural disputes and unjust results. . . . there is at the very least doubt whether the obligation to apply "promptly" is sufficiently certain to comply with European Community law and the Convention for the Protection of Human Rights and Fundamental Freedoms.'

D. Remedies in Criminal Proceedings

(1) Introduction

21.111   In the wake of *Kebilene*, the higher courts have steadfastly refused to sanction the creation of novel or alternative avenues for the resolution of Convention issues in criminal proceedings, in particular proceedings on indictment. The courts have been particularly resistant to the invention of new interim remedies, insisting that in general criminal proceedings (especially proceedings on indictment) should run their course, so that alleged breaches of the Convention during the first instance proceedings may be addressed as part of the ordinary appellate process. See *R (Shields) v Crown Court at Liverpool and Lord Chancellor's Department* [2001] UKHRR 610 (preserving the effect of section 29(3) of the Supreme Court Act 1981 in relation to fairness complaints arising during proceedings on indictment) and *R v Bossino*, 5 October 2000, CA (declining to recognise an interlocutory appellate jurisdiction in the Criminal Division of the Court of Appeal). This restrictive approach has even been applied where there is *no* appellate machinery capable of curing an alleged breach of Convention rights in the trial process; see *R (Regentford Ltd) v Crown Court at Canterbury* [2001] HRLR 18 (unappealable order in relation to costs).

(4) Stay of proceedings

(b) The position under the Human Rights Act

The limited circumstance in which it will be appropriate to grant a stay (as suggested in the Main Work) has been confirmed by the approach taken by the Court of Appeal in *A-G's Reference (No 2 of 2001)* [2001] 1 WLR 1869. The Court of Appeal held that a stay should only be granted if a fair trial is no longer possible or if it could be said that trying the accused would in itself be unfair. Such an approach is open to criticism because of its 'all or nothing' character: the possibility of compensation, in domestic law at any rate, is made somewhat theoretical by the restrictions in section 9 of the Human Rights Act on damages for judicial acts. However, an alternative mechanism for remedying delay, short of granting a stay, was recognised by the Privy Council in *Mills v HM Advocate* [2002] 3 WLR 1597, a decision on a Scottish devolution issue. The Privy Council held that the proper approach to remedying a violation of the reasonable time requirement was first to identify the remedy *prima facie* appropriate in domestic law and then to consider, by reference to Strasbourg jurisprudence, whether that could be regarded as providing adequate just satisfaction. Referring to the Strasbourg judgment in *Beck v Norway* (26 June 2001) the Privy Council held that a reduction in sentence could afford just satisfaction for delay, and upheld the High Court of Justiciary's decision to reduce the original sentence by nine months. In *Mills* the delay occurred at the appellate stage, but the principle is likely to prove attractive to the domestic courts regardless of the stage at which delay arises. **21.119**

(5) Quashing a conviction on appeal

The Human Rights Act cannot, it appears, be used to generate novel appeal routes where extant legislation creates none, in relation to subsidiary orders of the Crown Court such as those relating to costs (*R (Regentford Ltd) v Crown Court at Canterbury* [2001] HRLR 18) or at an interim stage of criminal proceedings falling outside the interlocutory procedures laid down by the Criminal Procedure and Investigations Act 1996 (*R v Bossino*, 5 October 2000, CA (Criminal Division)). **21.124**

(6) Exclusion of evidence

(b) Exclusion of evidence under the US Bill of Rights

n407: In *Dickerson v US* (2000) 8 BHRC 407 the Supreme Court upheld *Miranda* as announcing a constitutional rule which could not be superseded legislatively. **21.126**

It is now clear that the *prima facie* exclusion rule no longer applies in New Zealand. In *R v Shaheed* [2002] 2 NZLR 377 the majority of a seven-judge Court **21.130** of Appeal concluded that, in place of the *prima facie* exclusion rule, admissibility should be determined by conducting a balancing exercise in which, as a starting point, appropriate and significant weight is given to the breach of a right guaranteed by the Bill of Rights Act. The court reviewed the position in relation to the exclusion of evidence in the United States and Canada.

(h) Exclusion of evidence and the Human Rights Act

21.142 In *R v P* [2001] 2 WLR 463 the House of Lords held that the decision of the Court of Human Rights in *Khan v United Kingdom* (2000) 8 BHRC 310 made it clear (at 475B–C) that, in considering questions of the use of evidence obtained in breach of Article 8

> The criterion to be applied is the criterion of fairness in article 6 which is likewise the criterion to be applied by the judge under section 78.

See also *R v Bailey* [2001] EWCA Crim 733.

21.144 The suggested approach in the Main Work concerning the exclusion of evidence obtained in breach of Convention rights is unlikely to be applied as result of the decision of the House of Lords in *R v P* [2001] 2 WLR 463 which is discussed at Supplement, para 21.142. In *A-G's Reference (No 3 of 1999)* [2001] 2 WLR 56 the House of Lords pointed out that there was no principle in Convention law requiring the automatic exclusion of illegally obtained evidence (*per* Lord Steyn at 64G) and, apart from express statutory provisions, 'nowhere in the Commonwealth does there appear any remorseless principle of the exclusion of evidence unlawfully obtained' (Lord Cooke at 66A). See also *R v Mason* [2002] EWCA Crim 385.

E. Remedies in Private Law Proceedings

(2) Injunctions

21.150 It is debatable whether the 'likelihood of success' test under section 12(3) constitutes a significantly higher hurdle than the traditional 'real prospect of success' test for the grant of interim injunctions; see *Imutran Ltd v Uncaged Campaigns Ltd* [2001] 2 All ER 385. Where restraint of publication is supported by a sufficiently potent personal interest—in particular a strong privacy interest underpinned by Article 8—the court may be willing to exercise other discretionary powers in a way that restricts the Article 10 rights of the would-be publisher, for example, the power under CPR 39.2(4) to prevent disclosure of a litigant's identity; see *H (A Healthcare Worker) v N (A Health Authority) and Associated Newspapers Ltd* [2002] EWCA Civ 195 (protection of identify of HIV-positive health worker).

(3) Exclusion of evidence

In the county court case of *Hesketh v Courts plc* (14 May 2001) it was held that sur- **21.151**
reptitious video evidence taken by fraud investigators in a personal injury case
who had obtained an invitation to stay with the claimant at his home for the week-
end should be excluded.

(4) Other remedies

(a) Structural orders

Though there is so far no specific section 8 case law on structural orders, some- **21.154**
thing of the likely attitude of the courts can be gleaned from the case of *In re S
(Care Order: Implementation of Care Plan)*. The House of Lords at [2002] 2 AC
291 reversed a bold attempt by the Court of Appeal at [2001] 2 FLR 582 to
achieve Convention-compatibility by superimposing additional powers and duties (including a novel role for the courts) on the express statutory framework for
local authorities' functions in relation to children following the making of a care
order. The Lords considered that the Court of Appeal had overstepped the constitutional boundary, marked out by section 3 of the Human Rights Act, between
interpreting and making legislation. Parliament had chosen to give the local authority, not the court, responsibility for evaluating facts and merits. The episode
suggests that courts may face constitutional objections to the making of a structural or similar order that seeks actively to involve the court in the post-judgment
decision-making processes of a public authority. The implications of *In re S* for the
Act's remedial provisions in general are considered at Supplement, para 21.02.

(b) Other remedies

In *Peters v Marksman* [2001] 1 LRC 1 the High Court of St Vincent ordered the **21.155**
Attorney-General to proceed forthwith with the institution of disciplinary proceedings against the defendant Superintendent of Prisons who had ordered the
applicant to be flogged with the cat-o'-nine-tails and to be kept in a solitary confinement with foot-leggings and handcuffs.

Just as the criminal courts have begun to explore the relationship between delay
contrary to Article 6(1) and their power to stay proceedings (see Supplement,
para. 21.119) so the courts in civil and administrative jurisdictions have had to
consider the proper approach to redressing breaches of the 'reasonable time' requirement. In *Lafarge Redland Aggregates v The Scottish Ministers* [2001] Env LR
504 the Court of Session (Outer House) found that a delay of nine-and-a-half
years in the Ministerial determination of an application for minerals planning
permission infringed the requirement. The court made an order requiring that the
application be determined (whereupon the Scottish Ministers determined the application by refusal).

However, in *Freshbake Foods Ltd v Wheeler* (14 May 2001) the EAT declined to allow an appeal against an employment tribunal's decision on the ground of delay alone, holding that to do so would be self-defeating since the consequent remission of the case to the tribunal would simply create further delay. It is submitted that such reasoning is at least questionable, since: (i) it is in apparent conflict with recent Strasbourg jurisprudence on the relationship between Articles 6 and 13 (see Supplement, para. 21.160); (ii) the only remaining remedy would lie in separate litigation for compensation, compounding the original delay with the additional problem of multiplication of proceedings; and (iii) where (as will often be the case) the delay is attributable to a judicial act or omission, the effect of section 9 is to bar even that course.

These considerations do not undermine the powers of the court on judicial review to grant appropriate relief, including a declaration, where the gist of the complaint is that a policy or administrative practice produces delay in contravention of a Convention right; see *R (C) v Mental Health Review Tribunal (London South & South West)* [2001] 1 WLR 176 (declaration made that a uniform policy of not listing the hearing of an application by a patient under section 3 of the Mental Health Act 1983 until eight weeks from the date of application was incompatible with Article 5(4)). It is submitted that there is similarly no reason why declaratory relief should not be granted where the complaint of delay arises under Article 6(1), whether on judicial review or in ordinary civil proceedings. Arguably the *Freshbake* case is simply an illustration of: (i) the restriction of remedies to those within a particular court or tribunal's powers (which in the case of a tribunal will rarely include the making of a declaration); and (ii) the breadth of judicial discretion in assessing the justice and appropriateness of a particular remedy.

Appendix: Article 13 of the Convention

(2) The scope of the right

21.160   The Court took a different approach to the interrelationship between Article 6 and Article 13 in *Kudla v Poland* (Judgment of 26 October 2000). Where there is no overlap between the complaint (such as breaching Article 6 by failing to hold a hearing within a reasonable time), the Court will now examine the separate issue of whether there is an effective remedy to complain about the length of the proceedings. More recently, in *Nuvoli v Italy* (Judgment of 16 May 2002) the possibility of making a request to the president of the relevant court, who enjoyed wide discretion and was under no obligation to give reasons, was held not to constitute an effective remedy for a complaint as to the length of pending criminal proceedings. In that case the Court does not appear to have been concerned with possible overlap between the Article 6(1) and 13 complaints, concentrating instead on the proposition that as it had declared both complaints admissible it was entitled to rule on the merits of either or both. This is plainly a developing area of the Court's jurisprudence.

(4) The 'effectiveness' of the remedy

The inability of a prisoner to challenge an award of 28 additional days' imprison- **21.169** ment made under prison disciplinary proceedings was found to be a breach of Article 13 in *Keenan v United Kingdom* (2001) 33 EHRR 913. The Court also decided that the absence of any remedy for the parents arising out of the prisoner's subsequent suicide also violated Article 13. The inability of the parents to prove that the prisoner had suffered 'damage' in the sense recognised by domestic law and the absence of any remedy which would have established where the responsibility lay for his death each constituted a breach of Article 13.

(b) Effective investigations

In the important case of *Z v United Kingdom* (2002) 34 EHRR 3 the Court held **21.171** that the failure to provide an effective investigation into a local authority's inhuman treatment of children in care was a breach of Article 13. The contravention of Article 3 is discussed at Supplement, para 8.28A.

(5) *Wednesbury* review as an 'effective remedy'

The Court held in *Bensaid v United Kingdom* (2001) 33 EHRR 205 that Article **21.177** 13 was satisfied where the domestic courts in judicial review proceedings gave a careful and detailed scrutiny of the claim that deportation would expose the applicant to the risk of inhuman and degrading treatment. The fact that the scrutiny took place against a background that the decision was being assessed against the criteria of rationality and perversity did not deprive the procedure of its effectiveness.

However, in *Hatton v United Kingdom* (2002) 34 EHRR 1 the Court of Human Rights had little choice but to recognise that judicial review, at any rate before commencement of the main provisions of the Human Rights Act, had been an ineffective remedy for the applicant's Article 8 complaints. Much as in *Smith and Grady* (Main Work, para 21.178) where the domestic courts had explicitly held that their jurisdiction was confined to the traditional grounds of review which excluded consideration of the issue central to the Article 8 complaints, namely whether the Government's approval of night operations at Heathrow Airport was a proportionate interference with the rights of the applicants (see *R v Secretary of State for Transport, ex p Richmond upon Thames LBC* [1996] 1 WLR 1460, CA).

This issue is now largely a historical one. As the domestic courts are now obliged to apply the proportionality test on a complaint of incompatibility with a

Convention right, it will be difficult for an applicant to persuade the Court of Human Rights that a remedy sought in judicial review proceedings after 2 October 2000 is, without more, ineffective in terms of Article 13. For the Court's acknowledgment of the effect of the commencement of the Human Rights Act in relation to Article 13, see *Goodwin v United Kingdom* (2002) 35 EHRR 447, para 113.

22

HUMAN RIGHTS ACT PROCEDURE

A. Introduction

(3) Rules of procedure under the Human Rights Act

The following rules have now been made under the Human Rights Act: **22.09**

- Civil Procedure (Amendment No 4) Rules 2000, SI 2000/2092;
- Family Proceedings (Amendment) Rules 2000, SI 2000/2267;
- Criminal Appeals (Amendment) Rules 2000, SI 2000/2036;
- Courts-Martial Appeal (Amendment) Rules 2000, SI 2000/2228;
- Proscribed Organisations Appeal Commission (Human Rights Act Proceedings) Rules 2001, SI 2001/127.

The latest edition of the House of Lords' *Practice Directions and Standing Orders Applicable to Civil Appeals* (dated June 2001) and *Practice Direction and Standing Orders Applicable to Criminal Appeals* (dated June 2001) makes provision for the Act. Relevant provisions are reproduced in the Appendix to this Supplement.

B. Standing Under the Human Rights Act

(2) Who can be a 'victim'?

22.21 n39: See also the decision of the Constitutional Court of South Africa in *Investigating Directorate v Hyundai Motor Distributors* (2000) 10 BCLR 1079 in which it was accepted that a company had standing to assert privacy rights.

22.23 However, in *Re Medicaments (No 4)* [2002] 1 WLR 269 the Court of Appeal took a restrictive view of standing under the Human Rights Act. It was held that the appellant association ('PAGB') was not a 'victim' for the purposes of Article 34 (reliance was placed on *Hodgson v United Kingdom* (1987) 10 EHRR 506 and *Ahmed v United Kingdom* (1995) 20 EHRR CD 72, 77–8). The Court of Appeal said that

> in the present context, the rules [that is, of the Restrictive Practices Court] provided a route by which the individual parties could have been formally represented by PAGB, but they chose not to follow that route. In those circumstances, PAGB cannot properly be regarded as a victim for the purposes of making a claim under section 7(1) of the 1998 Act.

It is difficult to see how this approach can be justified in the context of the Convention case law.

22.26 In *Ayuntamiento de Mula v Spain* (Decision of 1 February 2001) it was held that a town council did not have standing to make an application under the Convention.

In *R (Westminster City Council) v Mayor of London* [2002] EWHC 2440 Maurice Kay J held that a local authority was not a victim and could not make any challenges under the Human Rights Act.

n55: See also *Cha'are Shalom Ve Tsedek v France* (Decision of 28 June 2000).

(3) The meaning of 'victim'

(b) Public interest challenges

22.30 In *Tanrikulu and Others v Turkey* (Decision of 6 November 2001) it was held that applications by readers of a newspaper whose circulation had been banned in their region were manifestly ill-founded on the basis that they had not shown that the prohibition had any direct effect upon them. Applications by journalists on the newspaper were, however, admissible, since the prohibition had real repercussions on the manner in which they exercised their profession.

n91: See also *Burdov v Russia* (Judgment of 7 May 2002).

(d) Shareholders as victims

See also *GJ v Luxembourg* [2000] BPIR 1021 in which the applicant was held to be entitled to bring a complaint under Article 6(1) concerning the liquidation of the limited liability company in which he held 90 per cent of the shares. The complaint was in relation to the activities of the liquidators, consequently it was impossible for the company, as a legal personality, to bring the complaint.   **22.36**

In *Humberclyde Finance Group v Hicks & Others*, 19 November 2001 (Neuberger J), the debtor company's counterclaim was subject to mandatory set-off provisions and was compromised by the Official Receiver pursuant to an order of the Court of Appeal. The first defendant, the only shareholder in the company, attempted to bring a counterclaim in his own name, on the basis that the wrongful actions of his co-defendants had caused a diminution in value of his shareholding, thereby interfering with his rights under Article 1 of the First Protocol. The judge held that the first defendant was barred from pursuing the counterclaim, in the light of both *Johnson v Gore Wood & Co (A Firm)* [2001] 2 WLR 72 and *Agrotexim v Greece* (1995) 21 EHRR 250. The compromise of the company's claim was 'the same as if the Company's claim had been voluntarily compromised during proceedings with the defendants', and could not possibly represent 'the sort of "factual impossibility" which the Human Rights Court had in mind in *Agrotexim*' (para 46). Neuberger J commented that the Court in *Agrotexim* had taken 'the same general view as the House of Lords in *Johnson*'.

(4) Potential, future and indirect victims

(b) Future victims

In *R (Hirst) v Secretary of State for Home Department* [2002] EWHC Admin 1592 Moses J held that a discretionary life prisoner whose sentence was due to be reviewed by a discretionary lifer panel within a few months of the application was not a 'victim' for the purposes of section 7 of the Human Rights Act 1998.   **22.40**

(c) Indirect victims

In *R v Secretary of State for the Home Department, ex p Holub* [2001] 1 WLR 1359, para 14, the Court of Appeal expressed the view *obiter* that the parents of a minor whose Convention rights had been breached had standing to bring proceedings under section 7. In *Scozzari and Giunta v Italy* (2002) 35 EHRR 12 the Court of Human Rights held that a parent who had been deprived of parental rights had standing to bring an application on behalf of the child.   **22.42**

(5) Public interest challenges under the Human Rights Act

22.47 In *R (Pretty) v DPP* [2002] 1 AC 800 Lord Hobhouse said (at para 116):

> In exceptional circumstances it may be proper for a member of the public to bring proceedings against the Crown for a declaration that certain proposed conduct is lawful and name the Attorney General as the formal defendant to the claim. But that is not what occurred here and, even then, the court would have a discretion which it would normally exercise to refuse to rule upon hypothetical facts.

In *R (Rusbridger) v Attorney-General* [2002] EWCA Civ 391 the applicants were a newspaper writer and editor who had, respectively, written and published an article in support of the creation of a republic to replace the monarchy in the United Kingdom. The Attorney-General, when contacted by the newspaper, had refused to guarantee that no prosecution would ensue under section 3 of the Treason and Felony Act 1848. There had, however, been no such prosecution for over 100 years. The applicants sought, *inter alia*, a declaration as to the effect of section 3 or alternatively a declaration of incompatibility. The Administrative Court refused permission to apply for judicial review. In the Court of Appeal it was common ground that the court had jurisdiction to make a declaration as to what construction should be put on section 3 in the light of the Human Rights Act 1998. The court held that, although such jurisdiction would be exercised sparingly, it was arguable that it was in the public interest that any incompatibility be declared so that remedial action might be considered by the Secretary of State for the Home Department. The House of Lords have granted the Attorney-General provisional leave to appeal against this decision.

C. Commencing Proceedings

(1) The appropriate court

(a) The basic principle

22.52 A claim for judicial review is now made in the Administrative Court in accordance with the procedure set out in CPR, Part 54 and PD 54. CPR 54.1 defines a 'claim for judicial review' as 'a claim to review the lawfulness of (i) an enactment; or (ii) a decision, action or failure to act in relation to the exercise of a public function'.

22.53 The approach suggested in the Main Work was not followed in *R (Rusbridger) v Attorney-General* [2001] EWHC Admin 529. In that case the Administrative Court accepted the submission that the procedural distinction between public and private law claims is unaffected by the provisions of section 8 of the Human Rights Act 1998. Silber J said that the definition in CPR, Part 54:

does not expressly exclude applications under the Human Rights Act ('HRA') and I do not believe that there are any reasons why such applications should be impliedly excluded. On the contrary, there is a strong argument for ensuring that all applications falling within Part 54 . . . are covered by that regime, of which one significant feature is the requirement to obtain permission from the court in order to pursue such a claim so as . . . to prevent abuse. I consider that this threshold should be passed by all applications falling within the Part 54 definition, irrespective of whether or not they are made pursuant to the HRA.

The point does not appear to have been fully argued and it is submitted that this decision cannot stand with the flexible approach suggested by cases such as *Clark v University of Lincolnshire* [2000] 1 WLR 1988. When the *Rusbridger* case, discussed at Supplement, para 22.47, was considered by the Court of Appeal at [2002] EWCA Civ 391 the 'procedural exclusivity' aspect was not further discussed.

In *R (Heather) v Leonard Cheshire Foundation* [2002] 2 All ER 936 Lord Woolf CJ, approaching the same issue from the opposite direction (that, is considering whether judicial review ceased to be an appropriate procedure where no 'public function' had been identified), remarked that a more flexible approach prevailed under the CPR regime. He stated (at paras 38 and 39):

> There was . . . an idea that if LCF was not performing a public function, proceedings by way of judicial review were wrong. This is an echo of the old demarcation disputes as to when judicial review was or was not appropriate under RSC Ord 53. CPR Pt 54 is intended to avoid any such disputes which are wholly unproductive . . . We wish to make it clear that the CPR provide a framework which is sufficiently flexible to enable all the issues between the parties to be determined.

See, generally, D Oliver, 'The Human Rights Act and Public Law/Private Law Divides' [2000] EHRLR 343.

(b) Rules of court

22.57 CPR 30.3(2)(g) now provides that when considering whether to transfer proceedings between the county court and the High Court, the court must have regard to whether the prospect of a declaration of incompatibility under section 4 of the Human Rights Act 1998 has arisen or may arise.

22.57A Organisations which are proscribed under section 3 of, and Schedule 2 to, the Terrorism Act 2000 can apply under section 4 of the Act to the Secretary of State for deproscription. Refusal of such an application can be appealed to the Proscribed Organisations Appeal Commission, whose procedures are governed by the Proscribed Organisations Appeal Commission (Procedure) Rules 2001, SI 2001/443. By the Proscribed Organisations Appeal Commission (Human Rights Act Proceedings) Rules 2001, SI 2001/127, the Commission is declared to be the appropriate tribunal to hear any actions against the Secretary of State under section 7(1)(a) of the Human Rights Act which arise from the refusal of such an application.

(2) Time limits

(a) The 12-month rule

22.58   CPR, Sch 1, R 55 has been repealed. PD 52, para 17.3, now provides that the appellant's notice must be filed within 28 days after the date of the decision. Where a statement of reasons is given later, the period is calculated from the date that this statement is received by the appellant (see para 17.4).

(c) Exceptions to the 12-month rule

22.62   CPR, Sch 1, R 53 has been repealed. Claims for judicial review are now governed by CPR, Part 54. CPR 54.5(1) provides that the claim form must be filed promptly and, in any event, not later than three months after the grounds to make the claim first arose. This requirement was recently discussed by the House of Lords in *R (Burkett & Another) v Hammersmith & Fulham LBC* [2002] 1 WLR 1593. It was suggested, *obiter*, that the obligation to apply 'promptly' may not be sufficiently certain to comply with Article 6. CPR 54.5(2) provides that time limits may not be extended by agreement between the parties. However, the court may extend time pursuant to CPR 3.1(2)(a) if there is a good reason for doing so.

22.63   CPR, Sch 1, R 53.4(1) has been repealed and replaced by CPR 54.5(2).

22.65   n183: CPR, Sch 1, R 53.4(1) has been repealed and replaced by CPR 54.5(2).

(d) Time limits and judicial review proceedings

22.66   n183: CPR, Sch 1, R 53 has been repealed; see now CPR 54.5 which is discussed in Supplement, para 22.62.

(3) Parties

(b) Declarations of incompatibility and the Crown

22.73   **Statutory provisions.**   In *Whittaker v Watson (t/a P & M Watson Haulage)* [2002] ICR 1244 the Employment Appeal Tribunal held that it did not have jurisdiction to rule on the compatibility of legislation with the Convention, as it was not a 'court' within section 4(5) of the Act. Lindsay J, giving the judgment of the tribunal, remarked that it was an odd conclusion that the President of the tribunal, or any High Court judge, could hear submissions as to compatibility when sitting alone, but not if sitting with lay members, and questioned whether that result was intended. Lindsay J went on to suggest that, in such cases, it would be helpful for the President simply to deal with the appeal on paper, where appropriate adjourning or dismissing the appeal and giving leave to appeal.

22.77   **Procedure in civil proceedings.**   The position is now governed by CPR 19.4A which provides that the court may not make a declaration of incompatibility unless

21 days' formal notice (or such other period as the court directs) has been given to the Crown. PD 19, para 6.4, provides that the notice must be served on the person named in the list published under section 17 of the Crown Proceedings Act 1947 (the current list is annexed to the Practice Direction). The notice will be in the form directed by the court (PD 19, para 6.4(2)). The court may require the assistance of the parties in its preparation (PD 19, para 6.4(3)). The Minister or the person nominated by him must, if he wishes to be joined in the proceedings, give notice of this intention (CPR 19.4A(2)). Where the Minister has nominated another person to be joined, the notice must be accompanied by the written nomination (which may be signed on behalf of the Minister (see PD 19, para 6.5)). A similar notice procedure must also be followed where a claim is made under sections 7(1)(a) and 9(3) of the Human Rights Act for damages in respect of a judicial act (see PD 19, para 6.6). In addition, the Court of Appeal said in *Poplar Housing and Regeneration Community Association Ltd v Donoghue* [2002] QB 48 that:

- The formal notice which the Human Rights Act 1998 and the Civil Procedure Rules require should always be given by the court. This is because the court will be in the best position to assess whether there is a likelihood of a declaration of incompatibility being made.
- So as to give the Crown as much notice as possible, whenever a party is seeking a declaration of incompatibility or acknowledges that a declaration of incompatibility may be made, it should give as much informal notice to the Crown as practical of the proceedings and the issues that are involved.
- The formal and informal notice to the Crown should be given to a person named in the list published under section 17 of the Crown Proceedings Act 1947.
- At the same time as the party gives notice informally to the Crown, it should send a copy of such notice to the court so that the court is alerted to the fact that it will have to consider whether a formal notice should be given. It should also send a copy of the notice to the other parties.
- The court to which the notice should be sent is the court that will hear the proceedings. That is a trial court, at the level of the High Court or, in the case of appeals, the Court of Appeal in the case of appeals to that court and the High Court in the case of appeals to the High Court.

The county court cannot make a declaration of incompatibility (section 4(5) of the Human Rights Act 1998).

Where proceedings are brought in the county court and the question of making a **22.77A** declaration of incompatibility may arise or has arisen, CPR, Part 33.3(2) states that the High Court (under section 41(1) of the County Courts Act 1984) and the county court (under section 42(2) of the Act) must have regard to transferring the proceedings to the High Court. PD 30, para 7, states that a transfer should only be made if there is a real prospect that a declaration of incompatibility will be made.

22.80   **The procedure in criminal proceedings.**   The Criminal Appeal (Amendment) Rules 2000, SI 2000/2036, have amended the Criminal Appeal Rules 1968, SI 1968/1262, under the powers conferred by section 5 of the Human Rights Act 1998. Those amendments require a notice of the grounds of appeal to include notice of any application for a declaration of incompatibility or of any issue for the decision of the court which may lead to the making of such a declaration (see rule 2(a) of the Criminal Appeal (Amendment) Rules 2000). A declaration of incompatibility shall not be made unless written notice has been given to the Crown (para 2(b)). This rule (which becomes rule 14A of the 1968 Rules) provides that the notice must be given to the person named in the list published under section 17 of the Crown Proceedings Act 1947 (or, in case of doubt, the Treasury Solicitor).

The notice of application must contain an outline of the issues in the case, specify the prosecutor and appellant, provide details of the trial from which the appeal lies and state the provision of primary legislation and the Convention right in question (para 2(b)). Unless the court otherwise directs, if the Minister wishes to be joined or to nominate another person to be joined, he should give written notice to the court and the other parties. The rule also provides that where the Minister has nominated another person, the notice should be accompanied by a written nomination signed by or on behalf of the Minister. The amendments to the Criminal Appeal Rules are set out in detail at Supplement, para 22.130A. The changes made to the Courts-Martial Rules are discussed further at Supplement, para 22.130B.

In *R v A* [2001] 1 WLR 789 the House of Lords expressed the view that the role performed by the DPP on behalf of the Crown is different from the role Ministers perform in the discharge of their executive responsibilities and permitted the Home Secretary to be joined as a party to the challenge to the 'rape shield' case, *R v A (No 2)* [2001] 2 WLR 1546, discussed at Supplement, para 11.352.

(c) Third party interventions

22.83   **Introduction.**   For criticism of third party 'public interest' interventions in public law cases, see C Harlow, 'Public Law and Popular Justice' [2002] MLR 1.

22.84   **The current procedure.**   CPR, Sch 1, R 53 has now been repealed and replaced by CPR, Part 54. The Pre-Action Protocol for Judicial Review (see Supplement, para 22.98A) stipulates (at paras 11 and 17) that 'interested parties' should be named by the claimant in the letter of claim, and that the letter and response should be sent to all interested parties. 'Interested party' is defined in CPR 54.1(1)(f) as any person who is 'directly affected' by the claim.

If proceedings are commenced, the claim form must be served, unless the court otherwise directs, on any person the claimant considers to be an interested party (see CPR 54.7). Such a person must file an acknowledgement of service if he wishes to take part in the judicial review (CPR 54.8). If he fails to do so, he may not take part in the hearing to decide whether permission should be given unless the court specifically permits him to do so (CPR 54.9(1)(a)). However, such a party may still take part in the hearing of the judicial review provided that he complies with the rules and any order of the court regarding the service of evidence and of detailed additional grounds for contesting or supporting the claim (CPR 54.9(1)(b)). In addition, 'any person' may apply for permission to file evidence or make representations at the hearing of the claim for judicial review (CPR 54.17(1)). However, such an application should be made promptly (CPR 54.17(2)).

Under CPR 52.1(3)(e) the 'respondent' to an appeal includes any person permit- **22.85** ted by the appeal court to be a party to the appeal. The House of Lords' *Practice Directions Applicable to Civil Appeals* set out a procedure for applications to intervene. In particular, Practice Direction 36.1 (June 2001 edition) provides that a petition for leave to intervene must state whether leave is sought for written interventions alone or for both written and oral interventions. The petition should be certified with the consent of the parties or, in the event that such consent is refused, with a certificate of service on the parties. Save where the Crown has been joined in proceedings below pursuant to section 5 of the Human Rights Act (see Practice Direction 36.2), participation in the court below does not entitle a person to intervene in the House of Lords.

Whether opposed by the parties or not, the petition for leave will be referred to an Appeal Committee. However, the Practice Direction does not identify the criteria which will be applied by the Appellate Committee when considering the petition.

D. Relying on Convention Rights in Proceedings

(1) The basic principles

Rules and Practice Directions have now been made in order to ensure than no **22.89** party is taken by surprise by a human rights issue (PD 16, para 16.1, discussed further at Supplement, para 22.116) and rule 10 of the Family Proceedings (Amendment) Rules 2000, SI 2000/2267 (discussed further at Supplement, para 22.131).

(2) Incompatible acts prior to 2 October 2000

It is now clear that a defendant convicted of an offence prior to 2 October 2000 **22.92** cannot rely on breaches of Convention rights before that date in support of his appeal (see *R v Lambert* [2001] 3 WLR 206 and, generally, Supplement, para

3.75A). The same reasoning would prevent a party to civil proceedings relying on Convention rights in an appeal where the breaches arose prior to 2 October 2001.

E. Procedural Issues in Judicial Review Proceedings

(1) Introduction

22.96   However, in *R (Alconbury Developments Ltd) v Secretary of State for the Environment, Transport and the Regions* [2001] 2 WLR 1389, para 169, Lord Clyde said:

> The suggestion was advanced that, if the respondents were correct in their contention that the present proceedings are in breach of Article 6(1), the scope of judicial review might somehow be enlarged so as to provide a complete remedy . . . I consider that it might well be difficult to achieve a sufficient enlargement to meet the purpose without jeopardising the constitutional balance between the role of the court and the role of the executive.

See also the remarks of Lord Nolan at para 62.

(3) The Notice of Application

22.98   By CPR 8.2 and 54.6, in a claim for judicial review the claim form must state the relief sought and the grounds on which it is sought. Further, more detailed, requirements are imposed by PD 54, para 5.3, and PD 16, para 15, in the case of a Human Rights Act claim. Where the claimant seeks to rely on any provision of, or right arising under, the Act or seeks a remedy available pursuant to the Act, the claim form must state that fact. In addition, the claim form must state precisely the Convention right alleged to have been infringed and give details of the alleged infringement.

Where the Convention right is a qualified right (see Main Work, paras 6.90ff) although it is not a specific requirement, the claimant would be well advised to set out matters to be relied upon in support of the contention that the interference was not 'justified' under the Convention.

In addition, the claim form must:

i.   state whether the relief sought includes a declaration of incompatibility pursuant to section 4 of the Act and, if so, give precise details of the legislative provision which is alleged to be incompatible and details of the alleged incompatibility;

ii. state whether the relief sought includes damages in respect of a judicial act to which section 9(3) of the Act applies (see Main Work, paras 5.110ff) and, if so, the judicial act complained of and the court or tribunal which is alleged to have made it;

iii. give details of any finding of unlawfulness by another court or tribunal upon which the claim is based.

Under the new procedure, the claim form must now be served on the defendant and interested parties within seven days of the date of issue (CPR 54.7). A person who wishes to take part in the judicial review application must file an acknowledgment of service (CPR 54.8(1)) within 21 days (CPR 54.8(1)). Where the person intends to contest the claim he must set out a summary of his grounds for doing so (CPR 54.8(4)(a)(i)).

The Pre-Action Protocol for Judicial Review came into force on 4 March 2002. **22.98A**
All claims for judicial review must now indicate that the protocol has been complied with, and reasons for non-compliance must be given in the claim form. The protocol provides for a letter of claim (a standard form is annexed to the protocol) to be sent to the defendant, in order to identify the dispute and explore settlement possibilities before action. Defendants are expected to respond (again, a standard form is annexed) within 14 days, enclosing relevant documentation.

(4) The application for permission

When permission is given in a case in which a claim is made under the Human **22.99**
Rights Act 1998 a direction may be made for giving notice to the Crown or joining the Crown as a party (PD 54, para 10).

Guidance on bringing urgent applications for permission is to be found in *Practice Statement (Administrative Courts: Listing and Urgent Cases)* [2002] 1 WLR 810.

(6) Disclosure and further information

PD 54, para 12.1, provides that disclosure is not required unless the court orders **22.102**
otherwise. The defendant is, however, required by para 16(d) of the Pre-Action Protocol to include any relevant documentation requested by the claimant with the letter of response or, failing that, an explanation as to why the documents are not being enclosed. No specific provision covers requests for further information under CPR, Part 18 and, it appears, they can be made.

(7) Evidence and the hearing

(c) Evidence in human rights cases
CPR, Sch 1, R 53.9(5) has been repealed. A similar power to order a claim to con- **22.110**
tinue as if it had not been started under Part 54 is conferred by CPR 54.20.

(d) Costs
In *R v Secretary of State for Transport and the Regions, ex p Challenger* [2000] HRLR **22.113**
630 Harrison J refused to make an order in favour of the respondents in a case involving an Article 6 challenge. The judge took into account the submission that it was desirable to facilitate access to the courts to enable people to seek to vindicate

their human rights under the Human Rights Act 1998 but stressed that each case had to be decided on its merits. See also *R (Smeaton (On Behalf of the Society for the Protection of Unborn Children)) v Schering Health Care Ltd & Others* [2002] EWHC Admin 866 in which the Administrative Court refused to depart from the ordinary principle that costs follow the event where the claim had been almost certainly 'doomed to failure'.

F. Procedural Issues in Other Proceedings

(1) Civil proceedings

(a) Introduction

22.116 PD 16 now sets out the requirements in relation to the contents of a statement of case where a party is seeking to rely on any provision of, or right arising under, the Human Rights Act or seeks a remedy available under the Act (see Supplement, para 22.118).

22.117 The draft PD 30, para 7.1, referred to in the Main Work, was not put into effect. Under CPR, Part 7.11, any claim made under section 7(1) of the Human Rights Act in respect of a judicial act may only be brought in the High Court. The draft CPR 33.9, discussed in the Main Work, was also not put in effect. Where a remedy is sought under section 7 of the Human Rights Act in respect of a judicial act which is alleged to have infringed the claimant's Convention rights under Article 5, and is based on a finding by a court or tribunal that there was an infringement, the court hearing the claim may:

- proceed on the basis of that finding but is not required to do so; and
- may reach its own conclusion in the light of that finding and of the evidence heard by that other court or tribunal.

(b) Statements of case

22.118 Where a party seeks to rely on any provision of, or right arising under, the Human Rights Act or seeks a remedy available under the Act, he must state that fact in his statement of case (PD 16, para 16.1). In addition, the statement of case must:

- give precise details of the Convention right which it is alleged has been infringed and details of the alleged infringement;
- specify the relief sought;
- state whether the relief sought includes a declaration of incompatibility pursuant to section 4 of the Act and, if so, give precise details of the legislative provision which is alleged to be incompatible and details of the alleged incompatibility;

- state whether the relief sought includes damages in respect of a judicial act to which section 9(3) of the Act applies (see Main Work, paras 5.110ff) and, if so, the judicial act complained of and the court or tribunal which is alleged to have made it; and
- give details of any finding of unlawfulness by another court or tribunal upon which the claim is based.

(ba) Transfers to the High Court

Where a transfer of proceedings from the county court to the High Court is con- **22.122A**
sidered by the High Court (under section 41(1) of the County Courts Act 1984)
or by the county court (under section 42(2) of the 1984 Act), the court must,
under CPR, Part 30.3(2)(g), have regard to whether the making of a declaration
of incompatibility under section 4 of the Human Rights Act has arisen or may
arise. PD 30, para 7, states that a transfer should only be made if there is a real
prospect that a declaration of incompatibility will be made.

(d) Appeals to the House of Lords

The House of Lords' *Practice Directions and Standing Orders Applicable to Civil* **22.123A**
Appeals have been revised. Direction 31 of the June 2001 edition states:

- Where a party seeks to challenge an act of a public authority under the Human Rights Act, the intent must be clearly stated in the petition for leave to appeal. A petition for appeal which raises such a point must include the words 'in accordance with the Human Rights Act' at the appropriate part of the prayer of the petition. The details of the Convention rights which it is alleged have been infringed and of the infringement must be set out in the statement of facts and issues and dealt with in a separate paragraph in the cases.
- The Crown is entitled to be joined as a party in any cause where the House is considering whether to declare a provision of primary or subordinate legislation incompatible with a Convention right. In any cause where the House is considering (or is being asked to consider) whether to make, uphold or reverse such a declaration, whether or not the Crown is already a party to the appeal, the Clerk of the Parliaments will notify the appropriate Law Officers.
- Where the issue arises in respect of a judicial act, the Clerk of the Parliament will notify the Crown through the Treasury Solicitors.
- The person notified under the above provisions shall within 21 days (or any period extended by the Principal Clerk) serve on the parties and lodge in the Judicial Office a notice stating whether or not the Crown intends to intervene in the appeal and who will represent the Crown.
- Once joined to the cause, the case for the Crown shall be lodged in accordance with Direction 15.

- The House may order the postponement or adjournment of the hearing of the appeal for the purpose of giving effect to the provisions of this Direction or the requirements of the Act.

(2) Criminal proceedings

(a) Procedural issues

22.125 **n300:** The Criminal Appeal (Amendment) Rules 2000, SI 2000/2036 (which are discussed at Supplement, para 22.80), set out the procedure relating to declarations of incompatibility. However, the scope of these rules is limited to criminal appeals.

(b) Time issues in criminal proceedings

22.130 A criminal defendant cannot rely in an appeal on breaches of the Human Rights Act which took place prior to 2 October 2000 as a result of the decision of the House of Lords in *R v Lambert* [2001] 3 WLR 206.

(c) Appeals to the Court of Appeal

22.130A The Criminal Appeals Rules 1968, SI 1968/1262, have been amended by the Criminal Appeal (Amendment) Rules 2000, SI 2000/2036, to deal with human rights issues. Rule 2(a) has been amended and states:

- A notice of grounds of appeal or application set out in Form 3 shall include notice of any application to be made to the court for a declaration of incompatibility under section 4 of the Human Rights Act.
- The notice or application shall give notice of any issue for the court to decide which may lead it to make such a declaration.
- Where the grounds of appeal or application include such a notice, a copy of it shall be served on the prosecutor by the appellant.

The inserted rule 14A lays down the procedure where a declaration of incompatibility is sought. It states:

- The court shall not consider making a declaration of incompatibility unless it has given written notice to the Crown.
- Where a written notice has been given to the Crown, a Minister or other person entitled under the Human Rights Act to be joined as a party, that person shall be joined on giving written notice to the court.
- A notice must be given to the person identified in the list published under section 17(1) of the Crown Proceedings Act 1947 or, in a case of doubt, to the Treasury Solicitors.
- The notice shall provide an outline of the issues in the case and specify: (i) the prosecutor; (ii) the date, judge and court of the trial which is under appeal; and (iii) the provision of primary legislation and the Convention right in question.

- Any consideration of whether a declaration of incompatibility shall be made shall be adjourned for: (i) 21 days from the date of the notice given above; or (ii) such other period (specified in the notice) as the court will allow in order that the relevant Minister or other person may seek to be joined and prepare his case.
- Unless the court directs otherwise, the Minister or other person entitled to be joined shall, if he is joined, give written notice to the court and every other party.
- Where a Minister has nominated a person to be joined as a party under section 5(2) of the Human Rights Act, the notice given by the Minister shall be accompanied by a written nomination signed by the Minister.

(c) Courts-martial appeals

The Courts-Martial Appeal Rules 1968, SI 1968/1071, have been amended to take account of the Human Rights Act by the Courts-Martial Appeal (Amendment) Rules 2000, SI 2000/2228. Rule 4(1A) of the amended rules states: **22.130B**

- The notice of application for leave to appeal shall specify any application to be made for a declaration of incompatibility under section 4.
- The notice shall specify any issue for the court to decide which may lead to a declaration of incompatibility.
- Where the notice of application includes such an application or issue, a copy of it shall be served by the appellant on the person to whom a petition may be presented under rule 3(1).

Rule 8A lays down the procedure for declarations of incompatibility and states:

- The court shall not consider making a declaration of incompatibility unless it has given written notice to the Crown.
- Where notice has been given to the Crown, a Minister or other person entitled under the Human Rights Act shall be so joined on giving written notice to the court.
- The notice shall be served on the person identified in the list published under section 17(1) of the Crown Proceedings Act 1947 or, in a case of doubt, on the Treasury Solicitors.
- The notice shall provide an outline of the issues in the case and specify: (i) the appellant, (ii) the person to whom his petition was presented under rule 3(1) or to whom it was sent under rule 3(3), (iii) the date on which and place at which the court-martial was held and the provision of primary legislation and the Convention right in question.
- Any consideration of whether a declaration of incompatibility should be made shall be adjourned for 21 days from the date of the notice or such other period specified in the notice as the court will allow in order that the Minister or other person may seek to be joined and prepare his case.

- Unless the court directs otherwise, the Minister or other person entitled under the Human Rights Act to be joined shall, if he is joined, give written notice to the court and to every other party.
- Where a Minister of the Crown has nominated a person to be joined as a party under section 5(2) of the Human Rights Act, the notice shall be accompanied by a written nomination signed by the Minister.

Rule 19A provides that any declaration of incompatibility shall be served on all the parties to the proceeding and, if the Minister has not been joined, on the person served with the notice under rule 8A.

(e) Appeals to the House of Lords

22.130C   The *Practice Directions and Standing Orders Applicable to Criminal Appeals* dated June 2001 now make specific provision for the Human Rights Act. Direction 34 states:

- Where a party seeks to challenge the act of a public authority under the Act, that intention must clearly be stated in the petition for leave to appeal; and must include the words 'in accordance with the Human Rights Act 1998' at the appropriate place in the prayer of the petition. The details of the Convention rights which have allegedly been infringed and the infringement must be set out in the statement of facts and issues and must be dealt with in a separate paragraph of the cases.
- The Crown is entitled to be joined as a party in any cause where the House of Lords is considering whether to declare a provision of primary or subordinate legislation incompatible with a Convention right. In any cause where the House is considering or being asked to consider whether to make, uphold or reverse such a declaration, the Clerk of the Parliament shall notify the appropriate Law Officers.
- Where the issue arises in respect of a judicial act, the Clerk of the Parliament will notify the Crown.
- Anyone notified under the Direction as above shall, within 21 days of receiving the notice (or within the period if it has been extended), serve a notice on the parties (and lodge a notice in the Judicial Office) stating whether or not the Crown intends to intervene in the appeal; and who will represent the Crown.
- Once joined, the case for the Crown is to be lodged in accordance with Direction 16.
- The House of Lords may order the postponement or adjournment of the hearing to give effect to the provisions of Direction 30 or the requirements of the Human Rights Act.

In *R v A* [2001] 1 WLR 789 the Home Secretary was allowed to be joined as a party in the challenge to the 'rape shield' case; see, further, Supplement, para 22.80.

(3) Family proceedings

Rules made in relation to family proceedings are similar to those which have been   **22.131**
made for civil proceedings in general. A party who seeks to rely on any provision
of, or right under, the Human Rights Act or a remedy available under the Act must
state that fact in his originating document or in his answer (see rule 10.26(2)(a) of
the Family Proceedings Rules 1991 (inserted by the Family Proceedings
(Amendment) Rules 2000, SI 2000/2267)). That document must give precise details of the Convention right which is alleged to have been infringed, give details
of the alleged infringement, specify the relief sought and state whether such relief
includes a declaration of incompatibility (rule 10.26(2)(b)). As with other proceedings, a declaration of incompatibility cannot be made unless notice has been
given to the Crown (rule 10.26(4)) and the rules make provision for the Minister
or person nominated by him to be joined in the proceedings (rule 10.26(5)–(17)).
There are additional requirements for a claim or appeal made under section 9(3)
of the Human Rights Act in respect of a judicial act (rule 10.26(18)–(21)). Finally,
a Practice Direction has been made regarding the citation of authority and the judicial allocation of cases which may lead to declarations of incompatibility or
which involve claims relating to judicial acts (*Practice Direction (Family
Proceedings: Human Rights* [2000] 1 WLR 1782).

23

COURT OF HUMAN RIGHTS PROCEDURE

A. Introduction and Background

(2) Background

In 2001 a total of 13,858 applications were registered (compared with 8,396 in   **23.07**
1999 and 10,486 in 2000). The largest number from one state was again Russia
with 2,108 (1,325 in 2000) followed by Poland with 1,763 (775 in 2000) and
France with 1,117 (1,033 in 2000). A total of 474 applications were registered

from the United Kingdom (626 in 2000). A total of 9,728 applications were disposed of in 2001 (compared to 7,624 in 2000). Judgments were given in a total of 888 cases (479 of which related to the complaints of unreasonable delay under Article 6).

However, the backlog of cases continues to rise. On 31 December 2000 there were 16,765 applications pending before the court (compared to 15,858 in 2000 and 12,635 in 1999). In response to concerns about the ability of the Court to deal with its increasing caseload, the Committee of Ministers set up an Evaluation Group, which reported in September 2001. The report recommended preparation of a draft Protocol to the Convention which would empower the Court to decline to examine in detail applications raising no substantial issue under the Convention. The report also recommended 'the creation within the Court of a new and separate division for the preliminary examination of applications', a recommendation which on its face is somewhat surprising, given that the Commission was abolished primarily to increase efficiency (see Main Work, para 23.06). In November 2001 the Committee of Ministers instructed the Ministers' Deputies to pursue urgent consideration of all the recommendations; see, generally, A Mowbray, 'Proposals for Reform of the European Court of Human Rights' [2001] PL 252.

(4) The role of precedent

23.09A n17c: See also *Stafford v United Kingdom* (2002) 35 EHRR 32, discussed at Supplement, para 10.167, and *Goodwin v United Kingdom* (2002) 35 EHRR 18. In the latter case the Court decided that the lack of legal recognition given to a post-operative transsexual breached Article 8, which decision differed from the views taken by the Court in *Cossey v United Kingdom* (1980) 13 EHRR 622, *Rees v United Kingdom* (1986) 9 EHRR 56 and *Sheffield and Horsham v United Kingdom* (1990) 13 EHRR 163.

D. Admissibility

(4) Subject matter of the complaint

23.41 In *Frette v France* (Decision of 12 June 2001) the applicant's complaint that his request for authorisation to adopt had been rejected on the sole ground that he was an unmarried homosexual man was inadmissible *ratione materiae* under Articles 12 and 14 because the Convention does not guarantee the right to adoption (the complaint was admissible under Articles 6, 8 and 14). In *Hill v Spain* (Decision of 4 December 2001) the Court rejected the applicant's assertion that he had a right under the Convention to an effective remedy in domestic law to enforce a decision in his favour of the UN Human Rights Committee.

(5) Jurisdiction as to time

Where a final decision given after the Convention came into force was closely **23.42** bound up with events which took place before it came into force the application was inadmissible as to time (*Jovanović v Croatia*, Decision of 28 February 2002).

(6) Jurisdiction as to place

In *Bankovic & Others v Belgium & Others* (2002) 11 BHRC 435 the applicants **23.43** were citizens of the Federal Republic of Yugoslavia whose families had sustained losses as a result of a NATO air strike upon a radio television station in Belgrade. The Court, having conducted a review of the *travaux préparatoires*, international instruments and its own decisions relevant to the interpretation of Article 1 of the Convention, held the claim to be inadmissible *ratione loci*. The Court took a restrictive view of the concept of 'jurisdiction', holding that it was an 'essentially territorial' notion (paras 60–1). Cases such as *Loizidou v Turkey* (1995) 20 EHRR 745 were explained on the basis that the respondent had, as a result of military action, 'exercised effective control of an area outside its national territory' (para 70). The Court summarised the position as follows (para 71):

> In sum, the case law of the Court demonstrates that its recognition of the exercise of extra-territorial jurisdiction by a Contracting State is exceptional; it has done so when the respondent State, through the effective control of the relevant territory and its inhabitants abroad as a consequence of military occupation or through the consent, invitation or acquiescence of the Government of that territory, exercises all or some of the public powers normally to be exercised by that Government.

The Court emphasised that it had to have regard to the 'special character of the convention as a constitutional instrument of European public order' and the 'essentially regional vocation of the convention system' (para 80). As a result of these considerations, there was no 'jurisdictional link' between the persons who were victims of the act complained of and the respondent states. The impugned action of the respondent states did not engage their Convention responsibility and, as a result, the application was inadmissible.

(7) Exhaustion of domestic remedies

(a) General

The existence of mere doubts as to the prospects of success of a particular remedy **23.44** which does not clearly appear to be futile is not a valid reason for failing to exhaust domestic remedies; see *Milošević v Netherlands* (Decision of 19 March 2002).

For a discussion about the exhaustion of domestic remedies under Article 5(2)(b) of the First Optional Protocol to the International Covenant on Civil and Political Rights, see S Joseph, J Schultz and M Castan, *The International Covenant on Civil and Political Rights: Cases, Materials and Commentary* (Oxford University Press, 2001), ch 6.

(8) Six-month time limit

23.51 If no effective remedies are available, the six-month time limit starts running in principle from the date of the act complained of. However, special considerations can apply in exceptional cases where applicants who availed themselves of a domestic remedy only became aware, or should have become aware, at a later stage of circumstances that made that remedy ineffective. In such instances, the six-month period may be calculated from that time (*Hazan v Turkey*, Decision of 10 January 2002).

For the purposes of computation of the period, months are calendar months, regardless of their actual duration (*Istituto di Vigilanza v Italy* (1993) 18 EHRR 367; *Loveridge v United Kingdom*, Decision of 23 October 2001).

In *Edwards v United Kingdom* (Decision of 7 June 2001) the application related to a death in 1994. The applicants were advised in February 1996 that civil proceedings would not be economic and, in November 1997, they chose not to pursue proceedings. A non-statutory inquiry set up by the Prison Service and Social Services did not report until 15 June 1998. Their application was not introduced until 14 December 1998. The Court said that

> Normally, the six-month period runs from the final decision in the process of exhaustion of domestic remedies. Where it is clear from the outset however that no effective remedy is available to the applicant, the period runs from the date of the acts or measures complained of . . . Where . . . an applicant avails himself of an apparently existing remedy and only subsequently becomes aware of circumstances which render the remedy ineffective, the Court considers that it may be appropriate for the purposes of Article 35(1) to take the start of the six month period from the date when the applicant first became or ought to have become aware of those circumstances.

The Court held that it was not unreasonable for the applicants to await the Inquiry Report. (See also *Akar & Others v Turkey*, Decision of 27 November 2001.)

In *Haralambidis v Greece* (Decision of 29 March 2001) it was held that where the applicant is not entitled to service of a written copy of the final domestic decision, time runs from the date on which the decision was finalised, that being when the parties were definitely able to find out its content. In *Loveridge v United Kingdom* (Decision of 23 October 2001) time was held to run from the date of oral judgment by the Court of Appeal, and not from the date of service of a sealed copy of the judgment.

In *Rezgui v France* (Decision of 7 November 2000) the applicant had brought a criminal complaint and had asked to be joined as civil party. The criminal complaint had been dismissed. The applicant had sought to appeal as a civil party although he had no right to do so under the Code of Criminal Procedure. Such an appeal did not constitute a remedy requiring exhaustion within the meaning of the Convention. As a result, the final domestic decision for the purposes of the six-month time limit was that dismissing the criminal complaint. The application was dismissed as out of time.

In *Paar v Hungary* (Decision of 20 September 2001) the final decision was served on the applicant's lawyer over six months before the introduction of the application, and was forwarded to the applicant's last known address, from which she had moved. As a result, the applicant received the decision considerably later. The Court held the application to be time-barred, as the late receipt of the decision could not be imputed to the state. Having been a party to civil proceedings, the applicant 'could reasonably be expected to have made arrangements so that mail addressed to her was forwarded to a new address, in particular as she was represented by a lawyer'. **23.52**

The running of the six-month time limit is, as a general rule, interrupted by the first letter from the applicant indicating an intention to lodge an application and giving some indication of the nature of the complaints made. As regards complaints not included in the initial application, the running of the six-month time limit is not interrupted until the date when the complaint is first submitted to a Convention organ (see, for example, *Allan v United Kingdom*, Decision of 28 August 2001).

Although, in general, the date of introduction of an application is the date of the first letter setting out the complaints raised, where a significant period lapses before the applicant provides further details, the Court will examine the circumstances in order to determine the 'date of introduction'. Where there was a delay of ten months in returning the application form the date of its return was taken as the date of introduction with the result that the application was out of time (*Gaillard v France*, Decision of 11 June 2000).

Where a company's predecessor in title submitted an introductory letter within the six-month limit, but its successor in title was not mentioned as an applicant until expiry of that time limit, it was held to be artificial to regard the two companies as separate applicants, and the application in the name of the successor in title was held to be admissible (*Credit Bank & Others v Bulgaria*, Decision of 30 April 2002).

E. Interim Procedural Measures

(1) Interim remedies

In *Nivette v France* (Decision of 14 December 2000) the Court considered the expulsion of an American national to the United States where he faced the possibility **23.57** of a full life sentence. The application was communicated under Article 3 and the Court made an order for interim measures. In *Einhorn v France* (Decision of 19 July 2001) the Court lifted interim measures imposed on 12 July 2001 to postpone the extradition of the applicant to the USA. It had been reported that the applicant had tried to commit suicide but, on receipt of a medical report, the Court was satisfied that the applicant was fit to travel under medical and police supervision.

(5) Striking out

23.65   In *Akman v Turkey* (Judgment of 26 June 2001) the Court struck out an application under Article 37(1)(c) after the Turkish government made a unilateral declaration regretting death from the use of excess force as in the circumstances of the applicant's son and offering an *ex gratia* payment of £85,000. Various undertakings were offered by the Turkish government. The applicant asked the Court to proceed with its decision. The Court considered that, in the circumstances, it was no longer justified to continue the examination of the application which was, therefore, struck out of the list. See also *Haran v Turkey* (Decision of 26 March 2002) and *TA v Turkey* (Decision of 9 April 2002). In *SG v France* (Decision of 18 September 2001) the application was struck out after the applicant's death because his heirs had no legitimate pecuniary or non-pecuniary interest in continuing his Article 6 complaints.

APPENDICES—CONTENTS

UNITED KINGDOM MATERIALS

APPENDIX A

Human Rights Act 1998: Amendments and Repeals

Section 14

The following provisions were repealed by the Human Rights Act (Amendment) Order 2001, SI 2001/1216, which came into force on 1 April 2001, to reflect the withdrawal by the UK Government of the derogation from Article 5(3) of the Convention, which was set out in Part I of Schedule 3 to the Act. (The withdrawal of the derogation was effective from 26 February 2001 following the implementation of Schedule 8 to the Terrorism Act 2000.)

- in subsection (1), from '(a)' to '(b)';
- subsection (2); and
- in subsection (4), '(b)'.

Section 16

The following provisions were repealed by the Human Rights Act (Amendment) Order 2001, SI 2001/1216, which came into force on 1 April 2001, to reflect the withdrawal by the UK Government of the derogation from Article 5(3) of the Convention, which was set out in Part I of Schedule 3 to the Act. (The withdrawal of the derogation was effective from 26 February 2001 following the implementation of Schedule 8 to the Terrorism Act 2000.)

- in subsection (1), from '(a)' to 'any other derogation';
- in subsection (2)(a), '(a) or (b)';
- in subsection (3), '(b)'; and
- in subsection (4), '(b)'.

Schedule 2

Paragraph 7 (reproduced below) was added by the Scotland Act 1998 (Consequential Modifications) Order 2000, SI 2000/2040, art 2, Schedule, Pt I, para 21, with effect from 27 July 2000:

'7.—(1) This paragraph applies in relation to—
    (a) any remedial order made, and any draft of such an order proposed to be made—
        (i) by the Scottish Ministers; or
        (ii) within devolved competence (within the meaning of the Scotland Act 1998) by Her Majesty in Council; and
    (b) any document or statement to be laid in connection with such an order (or proposed order).

(2)   This Schedule has effect in relation to any such order (or proposed order), document or statement subject to the following modifications.

(3)   Any reference to Parliament, each House of Parliament or both Houses of Parliament shall be construed as a reference to the Scottish Parliament.

(4)   Paragraph 6 does not apply and instead, in calculating any period for the purposes of this Schedule, no account is to be taken of any time during which the Scottish Parliament is dissolved or is in recess for more than four days.'

Schedule 3, Part I

Part I of Schedule 3 was repealed by the Human Rights Act (Amendment) Order 2001, SI 2001/1216, which came into force on 1 April 2001, to reflect the withdrawal by the UK Government of the derogation from Article 5(3) of the Convention, which was set out here. (The withdrawal of the derogation was effective from 26 February 2001 following the implementation of Schedule 8 to the Terrorism Act 2000.)

APPENDIX C

Rules of Court and Practice Directions under the Human Rights Act 1998

CIVIL PROCEDURE RULES AND PRACTICE DIRECTIONS

Relevant extracts from the Civil Procedure Rules and the supplementary Practice Directions are reproduced below. They take into account the 24th Update from the Lord Chancellor's Department. For the Rules in their entirety and details of the 25th Update, which is scheduled to be published in early December 2001, see further www.lcd.gov.uk.

PART 7
HOW TO START PROCEEDINGS—THE CLAIM FORM

Human Rights

7.11 (1) A claim under section 7(1)(a) of the Human Rights Act 1998 in respect of a judicial act may be brought only in the High Court.

(2) Any other claim under section 7(1)(a) of that Act may be brought in any court.

PRACTICE DIRECTION 16
STATEMENTS OF CASE

Human Rights

15.1 A party who seeks to rely on any provision of or right arising under the Human Rights Act 1998 or seeks a remedy available under that Act—

(1) must state that fact in his statement of case; and

(2) must in his statement of case—
    (a) give precise details of the Convention right which it is alleged has been infringed and details of the alleged infringement;
    (b) specify the relief sought;
    (c) state if the relief sought includes—
        (i) a declaration of incompatibility in accordance with section 4 of that Act, or
        (ii) damages in respect of a judicial act to which section 9(3) of that Act applies;
    (d) where the relief sought includes a declaration of incompatibility in accordance with section 4 of that Act, give precise details of the legislative provision alleged to be incompatible and details of the alleged incompatibility;

(e) where the claim is founded on a finding of unlawfulness by another court or tribunal, give details of the finding; and

(f) where the claim is founded on a judicial act which is alleged to have infringed a Convention right of the party as provided by section 9 of the Human Rights Act 1998, the judicial act complained of and the court or tribunal which is alleged to have made it.

(The practice direction to Part 19 provides for notice to be given and parties joined in the circumstances referred to in (c), (d) and (f).)

15.2 A party who seeks to amend his statement of case to include the matters referred to in paragraph 15.1 must, unless the court orders otherwise, do so as soon as possible.

(Part 17 provides for the amendment of a statement of case.)

PART 19
ADDITION AND SUBSTITUTION OF PARTIES

Human Rights

19.4A *Section 4 of the Human Rights Act 1998*

(1) The court may not make a declaration of incompatibility in accordance with section 4 of the Human Rights Act 1998 unless 21 days' notice, or such other period of notice as the court directs, has been given to the Crown.

(2) Where notice has been given to the Crown a Minister, or other person permitted by that Act, shall be joined as a party on giving notice to the court.

(Only courts specified in section 4 of the Human Rights Act 1998 can make a declaration of incompatibility.)

Section 9 of the Human Rights Act 1998

(3) Where a claim is made under that Act for damages in respect of a judicial act—
(a) that claim must be set out in the statement of case or the appeal notice; and
(b) notice must be given to the Crown.

(4) Where paragraph (3) applies and the appropriate person has not applied to be joined as a party within 21 days, or such other period as the court directs, after the notice is served, the court may join the appropriate person as a party.

(A practice direction makes provision for these notices.)

PRACTICE DIRECTION 19
ADDITION AND SUBSTITUTION OF PARTIES

Human Rights, Joining the Crown

Section 4 of the Human Rights Act 1998

6.1 Where a party has included in his statement of case—

(1) a claim for a declaration of incompatibility in accordance with section 4 of the Human Rights Act 1998, or
(2) an issue for the court to decide which may lead to the court considering making a declaration,

then the court may at any time consider whether notice should be given to the Crown as required by that Act and give directions for the content and service of the notice. The rule allows a period of 21 days before the court will make the declaration but the court may vary this period of time.

6.2 The court will normally consider the issues and give the directions referred to in paragraph 6.1 at the case management conference.

6.3 Where a party amends his statement of case to include any matter referred to in paragraph 6.1, then the court will consider whether notice should be given to the Crown and give directions for the content and service of the notice.

(The practice direction to CPR Part 16 requires a party to include issues under the Human Rights Act 1998 in his statement of case.)

6.4 (1) The notice given under rule 19.4A must be served on the person named in the list published under section 17 of the Crown Proceedings Act 1947.

(The list, made by the Minister for the Civil Service, is annexed to this practice direction.)

(2) The notice will be in the form directed by the court but will normally include the directions given by the court and all the statements of case in the claim. The notice will also be served on all the parties.

(3) The court may require the parties to assist in the preparation of the notice.

(4) In the circumstances described in the National Assembly for Wales (Transfer of Functions) (No 2) Order 2000 the notice must also be served on the National Assembly for Wales.

(Section 5(3) of the Human Rights Act 1998 provides that the Crown may give notice that it intends to become a party at any stage in the proceedings once notice has been given.)

6.5 Unless the court orders otherwise, the Minister or other person permitted by the Human Rights Act 1998 to be joined as a party must, if he wishes to be joined, give notice of his intention to be joined as a party to the court and every other party. Where the Minister has nominated a person to be joined as a party the notice must be accompanied by the written nomination.

(Section 5(2)(a) of the Human Rights Act 1998 permits a person nominated by a Minister of the Crown to be joined as a party. The nomination may be signed on behalf of the Minister.)

Section 9 of the Human Rights Act 1998
6.6 (1) The procedure in paragraphs 6.1 to 6.5 also applies where a claim is made under sections 7(1)(a) and 9(3) of the Human Rights Act 1998 for damages in respect of a judicial act.

(2) Notice must be given to the Lord Chancellor and should be served on the Treasury Solicitor on his behalf, except where the judicial act is of a Court-Martial when the appropriate person is the Secretary of State for Defence and the notice must be served on the Treasury Solicitor on his behalf.

(3) The notice will also give details of the judicial act, which is the subject of the claim for damages, and of the court or tribunal that made it.

(Section 9(4) of the Human Rights Act 1998 provides that no award of damages may be made against the Crown as provided for in section 9(3) unless the appropriate person is joined in the proceedings. The appropriate person is the Minister responsible for the court concerned or a person or department nominated by him (section 9(5) of the Act).)

PART 30

TRANSFER

Transfer between county courts and within the High Court

30.2 (1) A county court may order proceedings before that court, or any part of them (such as a counterclaim or an application made in the proceedings), to be transferred to another county court if it is satisfied that—

403

(a) an order should be made having regard to the criteria in rule 30.3; or

(b) proceedings for—

    (i) the detailed assessment of costs; or

    (ii) the enforcement of a judgment or order,

could be more conveniently or fairly taken in that other county court.

(2) If proceedings have been started in the wrong county court, a judge of the county court may order that the proceedings—

(a) be transferred to the county court in which they ought to have been started;

(b) continue in the county court in which they have been started; or

(c) be struck out.

(3) An application for an order under paragraph (1) or (2) must be made to the county court where the claim is proceeding.

(4) The High Court may, having regard to the criteria in rule 30.3, order proceedings in the Royal Courts of Justice or a district registry, or any part of such proceedings (such as a counterclaim or an application made in the proceedings), to be transferred—

(a) from the Royal Courts of Justice to a district registry; or

(b) from a district registry to the Royal Courts of Justice or to another district registry.

(5) A district registry may order proceedings before it for the detailed assessment of costs to be transferred to another district registry if it is satisfied that the proceedings could be more conveniently or fairly taken in that other district registry.

(6) An application for an order under paragraph (4) or (5) must, if the claim is proceeding in a district registry, be made to that registry.

(7) Where some enactment, other than these Rules, requires proceedings to be started in a particular county court, neither paragraphs (1) nor (2) give the court power to order proceedings to be transferred to a county court which is not the court in which they should have been started or to order them to continue in the wrong court.

(8) Probate proceedings may only be transferred under paragraph (4) to the Chancery Division at the Royal Courts of Justice or to one of the Chancery district registries.

Criteria for a transfer order

30.3 (1) Paragraph (2) sets out the matters to which the court must have regard when considering whether to make an order under—

(a) section 40(2), 41(1) or 42(2) of the County Courts Act 1984 (transfer between the High Court and a county court);

(b) rule 30.2(1) (transfer between county courts); or

(c) rule 30.2(4) (transfer between the Royal Courts of Justice and the district registries).

(2) The matters to which the court must have regard include—

(a) the financial value of the claim and the amount in dispute, if different;

(b) whether it would be more convenient or fair for hearings (including the trial) to be held in some other court;

(c) the availability of a judge specialising in the type of claim in question;

(d) whether the facts, legal issues, remedies or procedures involved are simple or complex;

(e) the importance of the outcome of the claim to the public in general;

(f) the facilities available at the court where the claim is being dealt with and whether they may be inadequate because of any disabilities of a party or potential witness;

(g)   whether the making of a declaration of incompatibility under section 4 of the Human Rights Act 1998 has arisen or may arise.

PRACTICE DIRECTION 30
TRANSFER

Transfer on the criterion in rule 30.3(2)(g)

7   A transfer should only be made on the basis of the criterion in rule 30.3(2)(g) where there is a real prospect that a declaration of incompatibility will be made.

PART 33
MISCELLANEOUS RULES ABOUT EVIDENCE

Human Rights

33.9 (1)   This rule applies where a claim is—
   (a)   for a remedy under section 7 of the Human Rights Act 1998 in respect of a judicial act which is alleged to have infringed the claimant's Article 5 Convention rights; and
   (b)   based on a finding by a court or tribunal that the claimant's Convention rights have been infringed.

   (2)   The court hearing the claim—
   (a)   may proceed on the basis of the finding of that other court or tribunal that there has been an infringement but it is not required to do so, and
   (b)   may reach its own conclusion in the light of that finding and of the evidence heard by that other court or tribunal.

PRACTICE DIRECTION 39
MISCELLANEOUS PROVISIONS RELATING TO HEARINGS

Citation of authorities Human Rights

8.1   If it is necessary for a party to give evidence at a hearing of an authority referred to in section 2 of the Human Rights Act 1998—

   (1)   the authority to be cited should be an authoritative and complete report; and

   (2)   the party must give to the court and any other party a list of the authorities he intends to cite and copies of the reports not less than three days before the hearing.

(Section 2(1) of the Human Rights Act 1998 requires the court to take into account the authorities listed there.)

   (3)   Copies of the complete original texts issued by the European Court and Commission either paper based or from the Court's judgment database (HUDOC), which is available on the Internet, may be used.

PRACTICE DIRECTION 54
JUDICIAL REVIEW

Human rights

5.3 Where the claimant is seeking to raise any issue under the Human Rights Act 1998, or seeks a remedy available under that Act, the claim form must include the information required by paragraph 16 of the practice direction supplementing Part 16.

HOUSE OF LORDS' PRACTICE DIRECTIONS AND STANDING ORDERS APPLICABLE TO CIVIL APPEALS

The latest edition of the House of Lords' *Practice Directions and Standing Orders Applicable to Civil Appeals* ('the Blue Book'), dated June 2001, includes Direction 31 on the European Convention of Human Rights reproduced below. (For the full text of the Blue Book, see www.the-stationery-office.co.uk/pa/ld.)

European Convention on Human Rights

31.1 Where a party seeks to challenge an act of a public authority under the Human Rights Act 1998, that intent must be clearly stated in a petition for leave to appeal as one of the reasons. A petition of appeal which raises such a point must include the words 'in accordance with the Human Rights Act 1998' at the appropriate place in the prayer of the petition; and the point must be drawn to the attention of the Judicial Office in accordance with Direction 9.6. The details of the Convention right which it is alleged has been infringed and of the infringement must be set out in the statement of facts and issues and dealt with in a separate paragraph of the cases.

31.2 The Crown is entitled to be joined as a party in any cause where the House is considering whether to declare that a provision of primary or subordinate legislation is incompatible with a Convention right. In any cause where the House is considering, or is being asked to consider, whether to make, uphold or reverse such a declaration, whether or not the Crown is already a party to the appeal, the Clerk of the Parliaments will notify the appropriate Law Officer(s).

31.3 Where such an issue is raised in respect of a judicial act, the Clerk of the Parliaments will notify the Crown through the Treasury Solicitor as agent for the Lord Chancellor.

31.4 The person notified under Direction 31.2 or 31.3 should, within 21 days of receiving such notice or such extended period as the Principal Clerk may allow, serve on the parties and lodge in the Judicial Office a notice stating whether or not the Crown intends to intervene in the appeal; and the identity of the Minister or other person who is to be joined as a party to the appeal.

31.5 Once joined to the cause, the case for the Minister or other person is to be lodged in accordance with Direction 15.

31.6 The House may order the postponement or adjournment of the hearing of the appeal for the purpose of giving effect to the provisions of this Direction or the requirements of the Act.

FAMILY PROCEEDINGS RULES AND PRACTICE DIRECTIONS

FAMILY PROCEEDINGS RULES 1991, SI 1991/1247

40 Rule 10 of the Family Proceedings (Amendment) Rules 2000, SI 2000/2267, amended the Family Proceedings Rules 1991, SI 1991/1247, by inserting a new rule 10.26 (reproduced below), to provide a procedural code for cases concerning the Human Rights Act 1998. (For the full text of the statutory instruments, see www.hmso.gov.uk.)

Human Rights Act 1998

10.26.—(1)   In this rule:—

"originating document" means a petition, application, originating application, originating summons or other originating process;

"answer" means an answer or other document filed or served by a party in reply to an originating document (but not an acknowledgement of service);

"Convention right" has the same meaning as in the Human Rights Act 1998;

"declaration of incompatibility" means a declaration of incompatibility under section 4 of the Human Rights Act 1998.

(2)   A party who seeks to rely on any provision of or right arising under the Human Rights Act 1998 or seeks a remedy available under that Act—
  (a)   shall state that fact in his originating document or (as the case may be) answer; and
  (b)   shall in his originating document or (as the case may be) answer:—
      (i)   give precise details of the Convention right which it is alleged has been infringed and details of the alleged infringement;
      (ii)   specify the relief sought;
      (iii) state if the relief sought includes a declaration of incompatibility.

(3)   A party who seeks to amend his originating document or (as the case may be) answer to include the matters referred to in paragraph (2) shall, unless the court orders otherwise, do so as soon as possible and in any event not less than 28 days before the hearing.

(4)   The court shall not make a declaration of incompatibility unless 21 days' notice, or such other period of notice as the court directs, has been given to the Crown.

(5)   Where notice has been given to the Crown a Minister, or other person permitted by the Human Rights Act 1998, shall be joined as a party on giving notice to the court.

(6)   Where a party has included in his originating document or (as the case may be) answer:
  (a)   a claim for a declaration of incompatibility, or
  (b)   an issue for the court to decide which may lead to the court considering making a declaration of incompatibility,

then the court may at any time consider whether notice should be given to the Crown as required by the Human Rights Act 1998 and give directions for the content and service of the notice.

(7)   In the case of an appeal for which permission to appeal is required, the court shall, unless it decides that it is appropriate to do so at another stage in the proceedings, consider the issues and give the directions referred to in paragraph (6) when deciding whether to give such permission.

(8)   If paragraph (7) does not apply, and a hearing for directions would, but for this rule, be held, the court shall, unless it decides that it is appropriate to do so at another stage in the proceedings, consider the issues and give the directions referred to in paragraph (6) at the hearing for directions.

(9)   If neither paragraph (7) nor paragraph (8) applies, the court shall consider the issues and give the directions referred to in paragraph (6) when it considers it appropriate to do so, and may fix a hearing for this purpose.

(10) Where a party amends his originating document or (as the case may be) answer to include any matter referred to in paragraph (6)(a), then the court will consider whether notice should be given to the Crown and give directions for the content and service of the notice.

(11) In paragraphs (12) to (16), "notice" means the notice given under paragraph (4).

(12) The notice shall be served on the person named in the list published under section 17 of the Crown Proceedings Act 1947.

(13) The notice shall be in the form directed by the court.

(14) Unless the court orders otherwise, the notice shall be accompanied by the directions given by the court and the originating document and any answers in the proceedings.

(15) Copies of the notice shall be served on all the parties.

(16) The court may require the parties to assist in the preparation of the notice.

(17) Unless the court orders otherwise, the Minister or other person permitted by the Human Rights Act 1998 to be joined as a party shall, if he wishes to be joined, give notice of his intention to be joined as a party to the court and every other party, and where the Minister has nominated a person to be joined as a party the notice must be accompanied by the written nomination.

(18) Where a claim is made under section 9(3) of the Human Rights Act 1998 in respect of a judicial act the procedure in paragraphs (6) to (17) shall also apply, but the notice to be given to the Crown:

    (a) shall be given to the Lord Chancellor and shall be served on the Treasury Solicitor on his behalf; and

    (b) shall also give details of the judicial act which is the subject of the claim and of the court that made it.

(19) Where in any appeal a claim is made in respect of a judicial act to which sections 9(3) and (4) of that Act applies—

    (a) that claim must be set out in the notice of appeal; and

    (b) notice must be given to the Crown in accordance with paragraph (18).

(20) The appellant must in a notice of appeal to which paragraph (19)(a) applies—

    (a) state that a claim is being made under section 9(3) of the Human Rights Act 1998; and

    (b) give details of—

        (i)   the Convention right which it is alleged has been infringed;

        (ii) the infringement;

        (iii) the judicial act complained of; and

        (iv) the court which made it.

(21) Where paragraph (19) applies and the appropriate person (as defined in section 9(5) of the Human Rights Act 1998) has not applied within 21 days, or such other period as the court directs, after the notice is served to be joined as a party, the court may join the appropriate person as a party.

(22) On any application or appeal concerning—

    (a) a committal order;

    (b) a refusal to grant habeas corpus; or

    (c) a secure accommodation order made under section 25 of the Act of 1989,

if the court ordering the release of the person concludes that his Convention rights have been infringed by the making of the order to which the application or appeal relates, the judgment or order should so state, but if the court does not do so, that failure will not prevent another court from deciding the matter.

PRACTICE DIRECTION (FAMILY DIVISION: CITATION OF AUTHORITIES)

1. It is directed that the following practice shall apply as from 2 October 2000 in all family proceedings.

Citation of authorities

2. When an authority referred to in s 2 of the Human Rights Act 1998 is to be cited at a hearing:

    (a) the authority to be cited shall be an authoritative and complete report;

    (b) the court must be provided with a list of authorities it is intended to cite and copies of the reports:—

        (i) in cases to which the President's Direction (Court Bundles) dated 10 March 2000 applies, as part of the bundle;

        (ii) otherwise, not less than two clear days before the hearing, and

    (c) copies of the complete original texts issued by the European Court and Commission, either paper based or from the court's judgment database (HUDOC) which is available on the Internet, may be used.

Allocation to judges

3. (1) The hearing and determination of the following will be confined to a High Court judge:

    (a) a claim for a declaration of incompatibility under s 4 of the Act; or

    (b) an issue which may lead to the court considering making such a declaration.

    (2) The hearing and determination of a claim made under the Act in respect of a judicial act shall be confined in the High Court to a High Court judge and in county courts to a circuit judge.

Issued with the concurrence and approval of the Lord Chancellor.

DAME ELIZABETH BUTLER-SLOSS P.

24 July 2000

CRIMINAL PROCEDURE RULES AND PRACTICE DIRECTIONS

CRIMINAL APPEAL RULES 1968, SI 1968/1262

The Criminal Appeal (Amendment) Rules 2000, SI 2000/2036, which came into force on 2 October 2000, inserted rules 2(2)(aa), (ab), 14A, 15(1)(e) (reproduced below), in the Criminal Appeal Rules 1968, SI 1968/1262, to provide the Crown with notice of issues relating to the Human Rights compatibility of primary legislation. (For the full text of the statutory instruments, see www.hmso.gov.uk.)

Rule 2

    (aa) A notice of the grounds of appeal or application set out in Form 3 shall include notice—

        (i) of any application to be made to the court for a declaration of incompatibility under section 4 of the Human Rights Act 1998; or

        (ii) of any issue for the court to decide which may lead to the court making such a declaration.

    (ab) Where the grounds of appeal or application include notice in accordance with paragraph (aa) above, a copy of the notice shall be served on the prosecutor by the appellant.

Rule 14A

    (1) The court shall not consider making a declaration of incompatibility under section 4 of the Human Rights Act 1998 unless it has given written notice to the Crown.

(2)   Where notice has been given to the Crown, a Minister, or other person entitled under the Human Rights Act 1998 to be joined as a party, shall be so joined on giving written notice to the court.

(3)   A notice given under paragraph (1) above shall be given to—

(a) the person named in the list published under section 17(1) of the Crown Proceedings Act 1947; or

(b) in the case of doubt as to whether any and if so which of those departments is appropriate, the Treasury Solicitor.

(4)   A notice given under paragraph (1) above shall provide an outline of the issues in the case and specify—

(a) the prosecutor and appellant;

(b) the date, judge and court of the trial in the proceedings from which the appeal lies;

(c) the provision of primary legislation and the Convention right under question.

(5)   Any consideration of whether a declaration of incompatibility should be made shall be adjourned for—

(a) 21 days from the date of the notice given under paragraph (1) above; or

(b) such other period (specified in the notice), as the court shall allow in order that the relevant Minister or other person may seek to be joined and prepare his case.

(6)   Unless the court otherwise directs, the Minister or other person entitled under the Human Rights Act 1998 to be joined as a party shall, if he is to be joined, give written notice to the court and every other party.

(7)   Where a Minister of the Crown has nominated a person to be joined as a party by virtue of section 5(2)(a) of the Human Rights Act 1998, a notice under paragraph (6) above shall be accompanied by a written nomination signed by or on behalf of the Minister.

Rule 15

(e) in the case of a declaration of incompatibility under section 4 of the Human Rights Act 1998, the declaration shall be served on—

(i) all of the parties to the proceedings; and

(ii) where a Minister of the Crown has not been joined as a party, the Crown (in accordance with rule 14A(3) above).

COURTS-MARTIAL (APPEAL) RULES 1968, SI 1968/1071

Rules 3, 5 and 16 of the Courts-Martial Appeal (Amendment) Rules 2000, SI 2000/2228, which came into force on 2 October 2000, amended the Courts-Martial (Appeal) Rules 1968, SI 1968/1071, by inserting rules 4(1A), (1B), 8A and 19(1A) (reproduced below) to provide the procedure for the making of a declaration of incompatibility, and in particular for the service of notice on the Crown as required by section 5 of the Human Rights Act 1998. (For the full text of the statutory instruments, see www.hmso.gov.uk.)

Rule 4(1A)

(1A) A notice of application for leave to appeal shall specify—

(a)   any application to be made to the court for a declaration of incompatibility under section 4 of the Human Rights Act 1998; or

(b)   any issue for the court to decide which may lead to the court making such a declaration.

(1B) Where the notice of application for leave to appeal includes an application or issue in accordance with paragraph (1A), a copy of the notice shall be served by the appellant on the person to whom a petition may be presented under rule 3(1), whichever is appropriate in the circumstances.

Rule 8A

(1)   The court shall not consider making a declaration of incompatibility under section 4 of the Human Rights Act 1998 unless it has given written notice to the Crown.

(2)   Where notice has been given to the Crown, a Minister or other person entitled under the Human Rights Act 1998 shall be so joined on giving written notice to the court.

(3)   A notice given under paragraph (1) shall be served on—
    (a)   the person named in the list published under section 17(1) of the Crown Proceedings Act 1947; or
    (b)   in case of doubt as to whether any and if so which of those departments is appropriate, on the Treasury Solicitor.

(4)   A notice given under paragraph (1) shall provide an outline of the issues in the case and specify—
    (a)   the appellant;
    (b)   the person to whom his petition was presented under rule 3(1), or to whom it was sent under rule 3(3);
    (c)   the date on which and place at which the court-martial was held; and
    (d)   the provision of primary legislation and the Convention right in question.

(5)   Any consideration of whether a declaration of incompatibility should be made shall be adjourned for—
    (a)   21 days from the date of the notice given under paragraph (1); or
    (b)   such other period specified in the notice as the court shall allow, in order that the relevant Minister or other person may seek to be joined and to prepare his case.

(6)   Unless the court otherwise directs, the Minister or other person entitled under the Human Rights Act 1998 to be joined as a party shall, if he is to be joined, give written notice to the court and to every other party.

(7)   Where a Minister of the Crown has nominated a person to be joined as a party by virtue of section 5(2)(a) of the Human Rights Act 1998, a notice under paragraph (6) shall be accompanied by a written nomination signed by or on behalf of the Minister.

Rule 19(1A)

(1A) In the case of a declaration of incompatibility under section 4 of the Human Rights Act 1998, the declaration shall be served on—
    (a)   all the parties to the proceedings; and
    (b)   where a Minister of the Crown has not been joined as a party, the person on whom notice has been served under rule 8A(3).

HOUSE OF LORDS' PRACTICE DIRECTIONS AND STANDING ORDERS APPLICABLE TO CRIMINAL APPEALS

The latest edition of the House of Lords' *Practice Directions and Standing Orders Applicable to Criminal Appeals* ('the Red Book'), dated June 2001, includes Direction 30 on the European Convention of Human Rights reproduced below. (For the full text of the Red Book, see www.the-stationery-office.co.uk/pa/ld.)

30.1 Where a party seeks to challenge an act of a public authority under the Human Rights Act 1998, that intent must be clearly stated in a petition for leave to appeal as one of the reasons. A petition of appeal which raises such a point must include the words 'in accordance with the Human Rights Act 1998' at the appropriate place in the prayer of the petition; and the point must be drawn to the attention of the Judicial Office in accordance with Direction 10.7. The details of the Convention right which it is alleged has been infringed and of the infringement must be set out in the statement of facts and issues and dealt with in a separate paragraph of the cases.

30.2 The Crown is entitled to be joined as a party in any cause where the House is considering whether to declare that a provision of primary or subordinate legislation is incompatible with a Convention right. In any cause where the House is considering, or is being asked to consider, whether to make, uphold or reverse such a declaration, whether or not the Crown is already a party to the appeal, the Clerk of the Parliaments will notify the appropriate Law Officer(s).

30.3 Where such an issue is raised in respect of a judicial act, the Clerk of the Parliaments will notify the Crown through the Treasury Solicitor as agent for the Lord Chancellor.

30.4 The person notified under Direction 30.2 or 30.3 should, within 21 days of receiving such notice or such extended period as the Principal Clerk may allow, serve on the parties and lodge in the Judicial Office a notice stating whether or not the Crown intends to intervene in the appeal; and the identity of the Minister or other person who is to be joined as a party to the appeal.

30.5 Once joined to the cause, the case for the Minister or other person is to be lodged in accordance with Direction 16.

30.6 The House may order the postponement or adjournment of the hearing of the appeal for the purpose of giving effect to the provisions of this Direction or the requirements of the Act.

Charter of Fundamental Rights of the European Union (2000/c 364/01)

PREAMBLE

The peoples of Europe, in creating an ever closer union among them, are resolved to share a peaceful future based on common values. Conscious of its spiritual and moral heritage, the Union is founded on the indivisible, universal values of human dignity, freedom, equality and solidarity; it is based on the principles of democracy and the rule of law. It places the individual at the heart of its activities, by establishing the citizenship of the Union and by creating an area of freedom, security and justice. The Union contributes to the preservation and to the development of these common values while respecting the diversity of the cultures and traditions of the peoples of Europe as well as the national identities of the Member States and the organisation of their public authorities at national,regional and local levels; it seeks to promote balanced and sustainable development and ensures free movement of persons, goods, services and capital, and the freedom of establishment. To this end, it is necessary to strengthen the protection of fundamental rights in the light of changes in society, social progress and scientific and technological developments by making those rights more visible in a Charter. This Charter reaffirms, with due regard for the powers and tasks of the Community and the Union and the principle of subsidiarity, the rights as they result, in particular, from the constitutional traditions and international obligations common to the Member States, the Treaty on European Union, the Community Treaties, the European Convention for the Protection of Human Rights and Fundamental Freedoms, the Social Charters adopted by the Community and by the Council of Europe and the case-law of the Court of Justice of the European Communities and of the European Court of Human Rights. Enjoyment of these rights entails responsibilities and duties with regard to other persons, to the human community and to future generations. The Union therefore recognises the rights, freedoms and principles set out hereafter.

Chapter I—Dignity

Article 1

Human dignity

Human dignity is inviolable. It must be respected and protected.

Article 2

Right to life

1. Everyone has the right to life.
2. No one shall be condemned to the death penalty, or executed.

Article 3

Right to the integrity of the person

1. Everyone has the right to respect for his or her physical and mental integrity.

2. In the fields of medicine and biology, the following must be respected in particular:

- the free and informed consent of the person concerned, according to the procedures laid down by law,
- the prohibition of eugenic practices, in particular those aiming at the selection of persons,
- the prohibition on making the human body and its parts as such a source of financial gain,
- the prohibition of the reproductive cloning of human beings.

Article 4

Prohibition of torture and inhuman or degrading treatment or punishment

No one shall be subjected to torture or to inhuman or degrading treatment or punishment.

Article 5

Prohibition of slavery and forced labour

1. No one shall be held in slavery or servitude.

2. No one shall be required to perform forced or compulsory labour.

3. Trafficking in human beings is prohibited.

Chapter II—Freedoms

Article 6

Right to liberty and security

Everyone has the right to liberty and security of person.

Article 7

Respect for private and family life

Everyone has the right to respect for his or her private and family life, home and communications.

Article 8

Protection of personal data

1. Everyone has the right to the protection of personal data concerning him or her.

2. Such data must be processed fairly for specified purposes and on the basis of the consent of the person concerned or some other legitimate basis laid down by law. Everyone has the right of access to data which has been collected concerning him or her, and the right to have it rectified.

3. Compliance with these rules shall be subject to control by an independent authority.

Article 9

Right to marry and right to found a family

The right to marry and the right to found a family shall be guaranteed in accordance with the national laws governing the exercise of these rights.

Article 10

Freedom of thought, conscience and religion

1. Everyone has the right to freedom of thought, conscience and religion. This right includes freedom to change religion or belief and freedom, either alone or in community with others and

in public or in private, to manifest religion or belief, in worship, teaching, practice and observance.

2. The right to conscientious objection is recognised, in accordance with the national laws governing the exercise of this right.

Article 11

Freedom of expression and information

1. Everyone has the right to freedom of expression. This right shall include freedom to hold opinions and to receive and impart information and ideas without interference by public authority and regardless of frontiers.

2. The freedom and pluralism of the media shall be respected.

Article 12

Freedom of assembly and of association

1. Everyone has the right to freedom of peaceful assembly and to freedom of association at all levels, in particular in political, trade union and civic matters, which implies the right of everyone to form and to join trade unions for the protection of his or her interests.

2. Political parties at Union level contribute to expressing the political will of the citizens of the Union.

Article 13

Freedom of the arts and sciences

The arts and scientific research shall be free of constraint. Academic freedom shall be respected.

Article 14

Right to education

1. Everyone has the right to education and to have access to vocational and continuing training.

2. This right includes the possibility to receive free compulsory education.

3. The freedom to found educational establishments with due respect for democratic principles and the right of parents to ensure the education and teaching of their children in conformity with their religious, philosophical and pedagogical convictions shall be respected, in accordance with the national laws governing the exercise of such freedom and right.

Article 15

Freedom to choose an occupation and right to engage in work

1. Everyone has the right to engage in work and to pursue a freely chosen or accepted occupation.

2. Every citizen of the Union has the freedom to seek employment, to work, to exercise the right of establishment and to provide services in any Member State.

3. Nationals of third countries who are authorised to work in the territories of the Member States are entitled to working conditions equivalent to those of citizens of the Union.

Article 16

Freedom to conduct a business

The freedom to conduct a business in accordance with Community law and national laws and practices is recognised.

Article 17

Right to property

1. Everyone has the right to own, use, dispose of and bequeath his or her lawfully acquired possessions. No one may be deprived of his or her possessions, except in the public interest and in the cases and under the conditions provided for by law, subject to fair compensation being paid in good time for their loss. The use of property may be regulated by law insofar as is necessary for the general interest.

2. Intellectual property shall be protected.

Article 18

Right to asylum

The right to asylum shall be guaranteed with due respect for the rules of the Geneva Convention of 28 July 1951 and the Protocol of 31 January 1967 relating to the status of refugees and in accordance with the Treaty establishing the European Community.

Article 19

Protection in the event of removal, expulsion or extradition

1. Collective expulsions are prohibited.

2. No one may be removed, expelled or extradited to a State where there is a serious risk that he or she would be subjected to the death penalty, torture or other inhuman or degrading treatment or punishment.

CHAPTER III—EQUALITY

Article 20

Equality before the law

Everyone is equal before the law.

Article 21

Non-discrimination

1. Any discrimination based on any ground such as sex, race, colour, ethnic or social origin, genetic features, language, religion or belief, political or any other opinion, membership of a national minority, property, birth, disability, age or sexual orientation shall be prohibited.

2. Within the scope of application of the Treaty establishing the European Community and of the Treaty on European Union, and without prejudice to the special provisions of those Treaties, any discrimination on grounds of nationality shall be prohibited.

Article 22

Cultural, religious and linguistic diversity

The Union shall respect cultural, religious and linguistic diversity.

Article 23

Equality between men and women

Equality between men and women must be ensured in all areas, including employment, work and pay.

The principle of equality shall not prevent the maintenance or adoption of measures providing for specific advantages in favour of the under-represented sex.

Article 24

The rights of the child

1. Children shall have the right to such protection and care as is necessary for their well-being. They may express their views freely. Such views shall be taken into consideration on matters which concern them in accordance with their age and maturity.

2. In all actions relating to children, whether taken by public authorities or private institutions, the child's best interests must be a primary consideration.

3. Every child shall have the right to maintain on a regular basis a personal relationship and direct contact with both his or her parents, unless that is contrary to his or her interests.

Article 25

The rights of the elderly

The Union recognises and respects the rights of the elderly to lead a life of dignity and independence and to participate in social and cultural life.

Article 26

Integration of persons with disabilities

The Union recognises and respects the right of persons with disabilities to benefit from measures designed to ensure their independence, social and occupational integration and participation in the life of the community.

CHAPTER IV—SOLIDARITY

Article 27

Workers' right to information and consultation within the undertaking

Workers or their representatives must, at the appropriate levels, be guaranteed information and consultation in good time in the cases and under the conditions provided for by Community law and national laws and practices.

Article 28

Right of collective bargaining and action

Workers and employers, or their respective organisations, have, in accordance with Community law and national laws and practices, the right to negotiate and conclude collective agreements at the appropriate levels and, in cases of conflicts of interest, to take collective action to defend their interests, including strike action.

Article 29

Right of access to placement services

Everyone has the right of access to a free placement service.

Article 30

Protection in the event of unjustified dismissal

Every worker has the right to protection against unjustified dismissal, in accordance with Community law and national laws and practices.

Article 31

Fair and just working conditions

1. Every worker has the right to working conditions which respect his or her health, safety and dignity.

2. Every worker has the right to limitation of maximum working hours, to daily and weekly rest periods and to an annual period of paid leave.

Article 32

Prohibition of child labour and protection of young people at work

The employment of children is prohibited. The minimum age of admission to employment may not be lower than the minimum school-leaving age, without prejudice to such rules as may be more favourable to young people and except for limited derogations.

Young people admitted to work must have working conditions appropriate to their age and be protected against economic exploitation and any work likely to harm their safety, health or physical, mental, moral or social development or to interfere with their education.

Article 33

Family and professional life

1. The family shall enjoy legal, economic and social protection.

2. To reconcile family and professional life, everyone shall have the right to protection from dismissal for a reason connected with maternity and the right to paid maternity leave and to parental leave following the birth or adoption of a child.

Article 34

Social security and social assistance

1. The Union recognises and respects the entitlement to social security benefits and social services providing protection in cases such as maternity, illness, industrial accidents, dependency or old age, and in the case of loss of employment, in accordance with the procedures laid down by Community law and national laws and practices.

2. Everyone residing and moving legally within the European Union is entitled to social security benefits and social advantages in accordance with Community law and national laws and practices.

3. In order to combat social exclusion and poverty, the Union recognises and respects the right to social and housing assistance so as to ensure a decent existence for all those who lack sufficient resources, in accordance with the procedures laid down by Community law and national laws and practices.

Article 35

Health care

Everyone has the right of access to preventive health care and the right to benefit from medical treatment under the conditions established by national laws and practices. A high level of human health protection shall be ensured in the definition and implementation of all Union policies and activities.

Article 36

Access to services of general economic interest

The Union recognises and respects access to services of general economic interest as provided for in national laws and practices, in accordance with the Treaty establishing the European Community, in order to promote the social and territorial cohesion of the Union.

Article 37

Environmental protection

A high level of environmental protection and the improvement of the quality of the environment must be integrated into the policies of the Union and ensured in accordance with the principle of sustainable development.

Article 38

Consumer protection

Union policies shall ensure a high level of consumer protection.

CHAPTER V—CITIZEN'S RIGHTS

Article 39

Right to vote and to stand as a candidate at elections to the European Parliament

1. Every citizen of the Union has the right to vote and to stand as a candidate at elections to the European Parliament in the Member State in which he or she resides, under the same conditions as nationals of that State.

2. Members of the European Parliament shall be elected by direct universal suffrage in a free and secret ballot.

Article 40

Right to vote and to stand as a candidate at municipal elections

Every citizen of the Union has the right to vote and to stand as a candidate at municipal elections in the Member State in which he or she resides under the same conditions as nationals of that State.

Article 41

Right to good administration

1. Every person has the right to have his or her affairs handled impartially, fairly and within a reasonable time by the institutions and bodies of the Union.

2. This right includes:

- the right of every person to be heard, before any individual measure which would affect him or her adversely is taken;
- the right of every person to have access to his or her file, while respecting the legitimate interests of confidentiality and of professional and business secrecy;
- the obligation of the administration to give reasons for its decisions.

3. Every person has the right to have the Community make good any damage caused by its institutions or by its servants in the performance of their duties, in accordance with the general principles common to the laws of the Member States.

4. Every person may write to the institutions of the Union in one of the languages of the Treaties and must have an answer in the same language.

Article 42

Right of access to documents

Any citizen of the Union, and any natural or legal person residing or having its registered office in a Member State, has a right of access to European Parliament, Council and Commission documents.

Article 43

Ombudsman

Any citizen of the Union and any natural or legal person residing or having its registered office in a Member State has the right to refer to the Ombudsman of the Union cases of maladministration in the activities of the Community institutions or bodies, with the exception of the Court of Justice and the Court of First Instance acting in their judicial role.

Article 44

Right to petition

Any citizen of the Union and any natural or legal person residing or having its registered office in a Member State has the right to petition the European Parliament.

Article 45

Freedom of movement and of residence

1. Every citizen of the Union has the right to move and reside freely within the territory of the Member States.

2. Freedom of movement and residence may be granted, in accordance with the Treaty establishing the European Community, to nationals of third countries legally resident in the territory of a Member State.

Article 46

Diplomatic and consular protection

Every citizen of the Union shall, in the territory of a third country in which the Member State of which he or she is a national is not represented, be entitled to protection by the diplomatic or consular authorities of any Member State, on the same conditions as the nationals of that Member State.

CHAPTER VI—JUSTICE

Article 47

Right to an effective remedy and to a fair trial

Everyone whose rights and freedoms guaranteed by the law of the Union are violated has the right to an effective remedy before a tribunal in compliance with the conditions laid down in this Article.

Everyone is entitled to a fair and public hearing within a reasonable time by an independent and impartial tribunal previously established by law. Everyone shall have the possibility of being advised, defended and represented.

Legal aid shall be made available to those who lack sufficient resources insofar as such aid is necessary to ensure effective access to justice.

Article 48

Presumption of innocence and right of defence

1. Everyone who has been charged shall be presumed innocent until proved guilty according to law.

2. Respect for the rights of the defence of anyone who has been charged shall be guaranteed.

Article 49

Principles of legality and proportionality of criminal offences and penalties

1. No one shall be held guilty of any criminal offence on account of any act or omission which did not constitute a criminal offence under national law or international law at the time when it was committed. Nor shall a heavier penalty be imposed than that which was applicable at the time the criminal offence was committed. If, subsequent to the commission of a criminal offence, the law provides for a lighter penalty, that penalty shall be applicable.

2. This Article shall not prejudice the trial and punishment of any person for any act or omission which, at the time when it was committed, was criminal according to the general principles recognised by the community of nations.

3. The severity of penalties must not be disproportionate to the criminal offence.

Article 50

Right not to be tried or punished twice in criminal proceedings for the same criminal offence

No one shall be liable to be tried or punished again in criminal proceedings for an offence for which he or she has already been finally acquitted or convicted within the Union in accordance with the law.

Chapter VII—General Provisions

Article 51

Scope

1. The provisions of this Charter are addressed to the institutions and bodies of the Union with due regard for the principle of subsidiarity and to the Member States only when they are implementing Union law. They shall therefore respect the rights, observe the principles and promote the application thereof in accordance with their respective powers.

2. This Charter does not establish any new power or task for the Community or the Union, or modify powers and tasks defined by the Treaties.

Article 52

Scope of guaranteed rights

1. Any limitation on the exercise of the rights and freedoms recognised by this Charter must be provided for by law and respect the essence of those rights and freedoms. Subject to the principle of proportionality, limitations may be made only if they are necessary and genuinely meet objectives of general interest recognised by the Union or the need to protect the rights and freedoms of others.

2. Rights recognised by this Charter which are based on the Community Treaties or the Treaty on European Union shall be exercised under the conditions and within the limits defined by those Treaties.

3. In so far as this Charter contains rights which correspond to rights guaranteed by the Convention for the Protection of Human Rights and Fundamental Freedoms, the meaning and scope of those rights shall be the same as those laid down by the said Convention. This provision shall not prevent Union law providing more extensive protection.

Article 53

Level of protection

Nothing in this Charter shall be interpreted as restricting or adversely affecting human rights and fundamental freedoms as recognised, in their respective fields of application, by Union law and international law and by international agreements to which the Union, the Community or all the Member States are party, including the European Convention for the Protection of Human Rights and Fundamental Freedoms, and by the Member States' constitutions.

Article 54

Prohibition of abuse of rights

Nothing in this Charter shall be interpreted as implying any right to engage in any activity or to perform any act aimed at the destruction of any of the rights and freedoms recognised in this Charter or at their limitation to a greater extent than is provided for herein.

INDEX